FATHER OF
AITH MISSIONS

The Life and Times of Anthony Norris Groves

ROBERT BERNARD DANN

D1513332

The author welcomes comments and enquiries sent care of
Tamarisk Publications or John Ritchie Ltd.

First edition 2004
Second edition 2021

© Robert Bernard Dann 2004, 2021

ISBN: 978-0-9538565-5-8

Published by: Tamarisk Publications, Chester, United Kingdom
Email: tamariskbooks@yahoo.co.uk

UK distributor:
John Ritchie Ltd, 40 Beansburn, Kilmarnock, Ayrshire KA3 1RL, United
Kingdom
Phone: 00 44 1563 536394
Email: sales@johnritchie.co.uk
Web: https://www.ritchiechristianmedia.co.uk/

USA distributor:
Lewis & Roth Publishers, 307 Delaware Dr, Colorado Springs, CO 80909
Phone: (719) 494-1800
Fax: (719) 494-1802
Toll Free (800) 477-3239
Web: https://www.lewisandroth.com/

Printed in Scotland by Bell and Bain Ltd, Glasgow

FATHER OF
FAITH MISSIONS

The Life and Times of Anthony Norris Groves

ROBERT BERNARD DANN

Norris and Mary Groves with Henry, Frank and Little Mary,
Illustration by Miss P Carter from "Family Adventure" by W. T. Stunt (c.1957).

Contents

Appendices

Maps

Introduction

W hen I was first asked to write a biography of Anthony Norris Groves, I wondered why no one else, during the century and a half since his death, had felt led to do so – especially as the name of Groves is revered in certain circles almost as that of a founding father. Only one volume has ever been written about him, and its author, G H Lang, did little more than take the main incidents of his life as convenient pegs on which to hang his own perception of the Brethren movement. He made little or no attempt to understand the man himself.

Then as my research progressed, I began to suspect the reason why all sensible authors had shunned the task. Extraordinarily difficult it would be to compose an inspiring and uplifting biography – the kind of book that people will actually want to read – about a man who was convinced he had led a "worse than useless life", who considered himself no more than a "poor and wretched cumberer of the ground". Clearly this was going to be no hagiography – no tale of great and heroic achievements, no accolade to a champion overcoming obstacles, resolving doubts and triumphing over all opposition with success and glory shining on his noble brow. My research raised, in fact, more questions than it answered, and left me wondering what was to be accomplished by a book about an idealist who never felt his ideals were fulfilled.

Or was that the wrong way to look at it? Stories of missionary success fill our bookshelves, but the real world is more complex than many writers care to admit. The real world is a place where hopes are frustrated, unpleasant things happen to good people and plans go wrong. Our fondest dreams remain unfulfilled. And we ask, Where is God in all this? Can our evangelical theology account for the facts of a life like that of Norris Groves, or are there insights we have yet to grasp, hard questions we have yet to face, clues we have yet to identify – pieces still missing (if the metaphor be not too ambitious) from the jigsaw puzzle of life? Groves himself struggled to make sense of many things, and to express the sense he made of them in the pages of his journal. As I came to know him better, I was intrigued to observe a man like ourselves (though far more devoted to Christ) wrestling with the questions we face day by day in this astonishing and often perplexing world – and to see him, in the thick of the battle, coming up with some radical and inspiring answers. The further I travelled with him, the more convinced I became that this book must be written, for it covers ground rarely traversed by evangelical writers.

My job is made more difficult by the fact that the bulk of Groves's personal letters and hand-written journals appear to have vanished without trace. Shortly after his death, his second wife Harriet sifted through his personal effects in the process of compiling her monumental *Memoir*, and although its 652 pages contain a vast reservoir of information, it leaves many gaps in the story and many questions unanswered. Modesty allowed Harriet Groves to make almost no reference to her own work as a missionary wife, and she was naturally inclined to omit anything that might reflect badly on her husband. To her credit, she took heed of the advice sent by his eldest son, Henry, asking her to portray his father exactly as he was: to let the facts, however awkward, speak for themselves. "Biography," said Henry, "is the history of what *God* has done, and its *faithfulness* is its profit."[1]

Henry's words have encouraged me to complete my task and – probably more foolhardy than brave – to do it "faithfully". It is *a history of what God has done*, and in considering that history my ambition is simply, as Norris Groves would have put it, "to know the mind of the Lord." In the end, this is not a book about a wonderful man, but about a wholehearted, modest, emotional, likeable man who aspired to serve a wonderful God. And it is a book about the God he served.

Throughout his life, Norris Groves was a man who struck sparks. Many who met him found their hearts strangely warmed. In some a flame was kindled. A few caught fire. His significance lies not in what he personally accomplished, which we might think relatively little, but in the impact of his character and ideas on others who went on to accomplish a great deal. We must follow his trail, and also the paths of those who met him, knew him, learned from him and were inspired by him. This will take us round some odd corners and down some unlikely alleys, and these may prove as intriguing and as stimulating as anything on the main highway.

Whatever his faults, Norris Groves was deeply loved. Wherever he went he made friends, and my hope is that this book may win for him friends in a new generation to whom he yet remains a stranger. If (perhaps as a result of this volume) other Groves papers come to light, they may help to make sense of some puzzles that remain, or show us facets of a character so far hidden from us. That is a pleasant prospect.

---

[1]   M514

Preface

In her *Memoir of A N Groves*, Harriet Groves felt free to edit her husband's journals and letters, and to "improve" their grammar, syntax, and at times their vocabulary. I have chosen to quote directly from Norris Groves's original journals, rather than from the *Memoir*, except in a few cases where his original phraseology actually obscures his meaning. Where this is so, the footnote gives the *Memoir* reference first, followed by the *Journal* reference in brackets.

Punctuation and spelling in quotations from nineteenth-century sources have been simplified and standardised in accordance with modern fashion, but archaic place names have often been retained, and standardised for the sake of consistency, with a note of their current form where necessary.

Biblical quotations are taken from the New International Version except where otherwise noted.

In this second edition I have taken the opportunity to make a few minor corrections to the text, to update some source references, and to add some additional reminiscences from contemporaries who met and knew Norris Groves.

Primary sources are indicated in footnotes using the following abbreviations accompanied by the appropriate page number(s):

D	Christian Devotedness (2nd edn.)
J	Journal of a Journey to Baghdad
M	Memoir of Anthony Norris Groves (3rd edn.)
R	Journal of a Residence at Baghdad

The following abbreviations are used for particular missionary agencies:

ABCFM	American Board of Commissioners for Foreign Missions
BMS	Baptist Missionary Society
CIM	China Inland Mission
CMS	Church Missionary Society
LMS	London Missionary Society
LSPCJ	London Society for Promoting Christianity amongst the Jews
SPCK	Society for Promoting Christian Knowledge
SPG	Society for the Propagation of the Gospel

English translations of the Bible are identified as follows:

AV	Authorised Version (King James Version)

GNB	Good News Bible
NIV	New International Version
NRSV	New Revised Standard Version
RSV	Revised Standard Version

Acknowledgements

L ike every biographer I have gathered facts and ideas from the extensive research of other people. Their names are mentioned in my footnotes and bibliography. I am especially indebted in this respect to Dr Timothy C F Stunt, who generously provided me with information gleaned from the widely scattered library archives.

The engraving of Northernhay House (1853) by G Townsend is from Henry Beasley, *Views in Devonshire* (c.1853-75) and is reproduced with the kind permission of Devon Archives and Local Studies Service.

The line drawing of Norris and Mary Groves with Henry, Frank and little Mary is by Miss P Carter, from *Family Adventure* by W T Stunt (first published in the children's magazine "From Other Lands", Oct 1956 to Dec 1957, then as a book by Echoes of Service, c.1957).

The engraving of the bridge of boats in Baghdad (1882) is from *Royal Geographical Readers no. 5* (London, T Nelson & Sons, 1883) and is reproduced by courtesy of Alamy Ltd, Abingdon.

The photograph of Hermann Gundert is from *Hermann Gundert, Quellen zu seinem Leben und Werk* by A. Frenz, page 242, and was kindly sent to me by Gertraud Frenz of Hermann Gundert Gesellschaft, Stuttgart.

The first edition of this book brought the unexpected pleasure of personal contact with several relatives and descendants of Anthony Norris Groves. In particular I would like to thank Heather Magee, Ros Fletcher, Anne Wolstencroft and Dr John Owen for sharing with me their own extensive explorations in their genealogy and history. I hope this book will continue to be a blessing to the family.

"Two masters I cannot serve,
and therefore I simply choose the Lord."

Norris Groves [1]

1

The Gates of Baghdad

Ten years before David Livingstone first took ship for Africa, a thirty-four-year-old Englishman, with his wife and two boys, climbed off his weary horse at the gates of Baghdad. They had trekked more than two thousand miles over desert, rocks and mountains to bring the good news of Jesus Christ to the ancient capital of the Arabian Nights, the "city of a hundred mosques".[2]

Anthony Norris Groves was not quite the first evangelical missionary to the Muslim world. He had been just a boy of eleven when Henry Martyn landed at Calcutta in 1806.[3] He was twenty when the Church Missionary Society set up its printing press on the island of Malta.[4] He was twenty-seven when the Basel Mission sent its earliest pioneers to the Caucasus,[5] twenty-eight when the American Presbyterians established a tentative foothold in Beirut.[6] And Karl Pfander in the foothills of Armenia was already hard at work on the first draft of his *Mizan ul-Haqq* when the Groves family finally set off for the East in 1829.[7] But whilst others had nibbled at the edges of the Islamic world, Norris Groves planned to set up home at its very heart, in a place known to his generation as "the headquarters of Islamism"[8] – the formidable Muslim stronghold of Baghdad. Here he would establish what was to become the first Protestant mission to Arabic-speaking Muslims.

Groves went to Baghdad for a very simple reason: he believed God had sent him. He was not appointed by a mission board with wealthy directors to guarantee secure communications and a regular salary. He did not command the respect given to a man ordained to the ministry of a prominent church denomination. He did not have a team of experienced colleagues to advise in matters of language and culture. He did not have anyone to offer support in time of sickness or political unrest. He did not even have a Bible in the language spoken by the people around him. But he did have the promises of God (which he believed) and a heart taught to love everyone he met (whatever their background), and he had a vision to take those promises and that love personally to millions who knew nothing of it.

In fact Anthony Norris Groves was a pioneer among pioneers. The previous century had produced some brave initiatives in gospel work overseas. Some of the earliest missionary societies had already been labouring for thirty years. "But their activities were hampered, and the natural growth of churches hindered, by the fact that they worked on the plan of Western organisation, and transplanted the organised church systems of the West instead of planting churches of the apostolic type shown in the New Testament."[9] When Groves packed his bags and set off for Baghdad, he was determined to leave behind him everything he had known of British Christianity, to forget the accumulated customs of eighteen hundred years. He took with him his Bible and a determination to teach exactly what he found in its pages to the people of the East.

ENDNOTES

[1] *On the Liberty of Ministry*, 78

[2] Eadie, 198

[3] Richter, 93; Vander Werff, 31; Neill, *History*, 266

[4] Richter, 95; Vander Werff, 154

[5] Richter, 98-100; Vander Werff, 100

[6] Fisk, Parsons, Smith and their ABCFM colleagues, believing evangelism among Muslims to be inadvisable, directed their attention to Jews and members of the Eastern churches (Richter, 186-189; Vander Werff, 103-108, 118-119; Harris, 50-51; Neill, *History*, 303).

[7] Stock II, 152. The *Mizan ul-Haqq* is discussed in Chapter 25 of this book.

[8] Eadie, 191; Stern, 34, 40

[9] Lang, *Groves*, 18

"The true servant of God knows better than any man
the real value of money,
the value of time,
the value of talents."

Norris Groves [1]

2

Every Earthly Thing

Born on 1st February 1795 in the small village of Newton Valence, Hampshire (in the south of England), Anthony Norris Groves was one of six children. He was always known as Norris. Being the only boy in the family he no doubt enjoyed the attention – and suffered the good-natured teasing – of his five sisters, two older and three younger than himself.[2]

Their home was by all accounts a happy and affectionate one, though by no means free from misfortune. His father had "a very generous disposition" and was "fond of giving liberally to others."[3] Always ready to support a good cause, Mr Groves senior evidently found it difficult at times to distinguish a good cause from a rash venture. Or perhaps he was just unlucky. Owner of a prosperous salt-refining business in Lymington, he was persuaded to invest his savings in a large ship, the *Royal George*; all was lost when the ship caught fire and sank.[4] Thousands of pounds were then given to draining and reclaiming some land near the sea – until the outbreak of war forced a cheap sale whilst the fields were still too wet for cultivation. Finally, his own business was undermined by an employee who revealed the chemical secret of salt refining to a rival company. All this meant that Norris Groves grew up in a household familiar with great schemes, with financial crises, and with an awareness that security lay in the affection of a happy family rather than the buffer of a large bank account. His father's determination that money should be *used* rather than accumulated was his greatest legacy to young Norris.

His mother is described as "a most remarkable woman". Intelligent and energetic, bearing cheerfully every reverse of fortune, and refusing to find fault in others – least of all in her husband – she had a wonderful ability to make the best of every circumstance. "Her character left a deep impression on the hearts of all her children."[5]

Young Norris was enrolled at the most highly approved of the small local schools, for Mr Groves believed money invested in education was money well spent. Then at the age of about eleven, having outgrown the educational possibilities of Lymington, the boy was spruced up and packed off to secondary school in Fulham, at that time a fashionable town six miles to the west of

London.[6] Here he could live as a lodger with his aunt and her husband, Mr James Thompson, a prosperous dentist with a practice in Hanover Square.[7]

Little has been preserved from this time. We do know, however, that the school required its boys to attend the local parish church, and Norris Groves, aged thirteen or fourteen, acquired the habit of hiding a small novel inside his Prayer Book to help relieve the tedium of the services. Though he was a serious boy with some religious feelings, he admits at this period to no understanding of the gospel. But it was here that he heard a sermon preached by John Owen which turned his thoughts in a fresh and exhilarating direction: "When I was a schoolboy, attending Mr Owen's preaching at Fulham, *India* (I know not how or why) occupied my wishes, for I knew not Christ."[8] It would be such a noble thing – indeed "it would be a worthy object to die for, to go to India to win but one idolater from hopeless death to life and peace. Little did I then think that I was ten times worse than he, as great a sinner and with none of his excuses."[9] These exalted feelings soon wore off, but as the months and years passed, the idea of overseas missionary service came back to him again and again. In fact it never really left him.

Eventually the time came to leave school. After a short period studying chemistry with the firm of Savory and Moore in London, Norris was ready to commence professional training as a dentist under the watchful eye of his uncle. At the same time he "walked the hospitals" with one of Mr Thompson's sons, gaining practical experience of symptoms, surgery and medicinal remedies.

The great metropolis hummed around him and like many a teenage boy he was attracted to the pleasures and ambitions of the world. But stronger still was his attachment to his cousin Mary Thompson. For her sake as much as his own he shunned all that might be considered coarse or vulgar. Mary was a sensitive girl with an interest in religion. As they walked to church, or round the garden of the beautiful house at Fulham, their conversation often turned to spiritual things, and one of the first presents Norris ever gave his young love was a Bible.

Their friendship continued for three years but it was beset by anxiety. Mary's mother had no objection to their attachment but Mary's father saw things in quite a different light. Though he had always treated Norris with kindness, the lad was, to him, a poor relation upon whom they had taken pity. The apprentice, moreover, despite his conscientious work and blameless behaviour, had shown no sign of any exceptional ability or any likelihood that he could keep Mary in the affluence to which she was accustomed. Indeed, Mr Thompson knew all about his brother-in-law's financial indiscretions; he had lent a thousand pounds to Norris's father and there was no sign it would ever be returned.

Eventually the apprenticeship was completed. Norris Groves was now eighteen years old and he knew enough of dentistry to put up a brass plaque with his own name on it. "My hopes were young," he reflected, "and my prospects bright, and with a sad yet hoping heart I left London."[10]

Finding a suitable place in the town of Plymouth (on the south-west coast of England), he was soon sought out by an ever-increasing clientele. Perhaps a steady income and a secure future would incline Mr Thompson to view him more favourably, so he wrote to Mary asking leave to speak to her father. She decided to ask him herself. His brusque reply left no room for doubt or hope. He absolutely refused to consider the possibility of their marrying, and having received such an answer Norris felt obliged to offer his respects and promise never to contact Mary again without her father's consent. Knowing Mr Thompson to be a man who having made up his mind rarely changed it, they were both thrown into despair – especially as his main objection lay in the fact that they were first cousins, a circumstance they could do nothing to change.

Norris Groves pitched himself into his work. He filled his spare time by attending scientific lectures and demonstrations. He joined the Athenaeum, a literary society, where he could develop his ability to speak persuasively on various subjects and where he made a number of evangelical Christian friends. Days went by; then hearing in a roundabout way that Mary was unwell he became "supremely miserable". Attending the parish church his grieving heart found comfort and consolation through the ministry of two evangelical clergymen, Joseph Richards and Thomas Hitchins. Gradually, through their influence, Groves was drawn to personal faith in Christ. The year was 1816, and the editor of his *Memoir* observes, "This was evidently the great turning point in his spiritual history."[11] Now, in all sincerity, "he was able to profess himself a disciple of Christ."[12]

Even so, his heart was filled with doubts. He was uncertain about his future, about Mary, even about his acceptance with God. Richards and Hitchins endeavoured to reassure him. "They did all they could for me," he later recalled, "yet my soul had much and deep sorrow to go through before it knew either the peace or the power of Jesus' blood."[13]

At this time the Church Missionary Society regularly sent representatives to speak about its work wherever evangelical clergy would make them welcome. Despairing of human happiness Groves resolved to offer himself "to the Lord and missionary work." He wrote to the secretary of the CMS, and received a kind and encouraging reply.[14] His thoughts, though, were still directed to what he could do for God rather than what God had done for him, and as he pondered his course he was torn between his exalted spiritual aspirations and the more down-to-earth ambition he still cherished of impressing Mary's parents with his success as a man of the world. Torn two ways, he struggled with the guilty feeling that he was not as devoted to the cause of God as he ought to be.

Two hundred miles separated the young lovers, but the vow of silence made it feel much more. Neither of them could know how the other was feeling. While Norris was absorbing the stimulating ideas and ideals of the wider world, Mary remained tied to her home duties within the circle of her immediate family. Her sister had fallen seriously ill, and it was given to Mary to care for her. Disappointment and tedium weakened what little remained of her childhood faith. Day after day, the strain took its toll on her physical health, and when her sister eventually died, Mr Thompson, having lost one daughter, feared losing another. No longer could he refuse his consent to her happiness. All of a sudden, Norris tells us, "he became as willing that we should be married as he had before been anxious that we should not."[15] The wedding in October 1816 quite restored Mary to her former health!

The fears and doubts that had beset their courtship made their marriage a special joy to Norris and Mary Groves. Still no more than twenty-one years old, the young dentist decided to move from Plymouth to Exeter, a substantial city some forty miles to the east which might offer better prospects for his career. He bought the leasehold on a large property called Northernhay House and here established his dental surgery.[16]

The next five years passed rapidly. Still perhaps concerned to shake off the stigma of the poor relation, he welcomed the opportunity to mix in fashionable society. At the same time, he reminded himself, he would make no secret of his adherence to the established Church of England, and he determined, after the fashion of Jane Austen's heroes, to develop a style of conversation both worldly-wise and witty "in order to gain influence over those I came in contact with."[17] With this in mind, he devoted his spare time to studying literature and science. Before long, however, he began to wonder whether this was right. Certainly it was not the way Christ and the apostles had set about their work for the gospel. They influenced others not by humorous banter and encyclopedic knowledge, but by compassion for the needy and a plain statement of serious truth.

It was at this time that Norris Groves met Bessie and Charlotte Paget. They were sisters, a pair very much like the biblical Martha and Mary – one forever bustling about the Lord's business, the other quietly meditating on his word.[18] Bessie spoke openly to him about his need to accept and believe God's love for him. The sisters' unashamed devotion to Jesus made Norris feel awkward, especially as they were not members of the Church of England; indeed, they bore the stigma of Dissent.[19] But the better he came to know Bessie Paget, the more he was impressed with "her holy unselfish soul" and her loving concern for people such as himself. "She kept instructing me," he said, "as my obstinacy and self-will would allow, yet always bore most gently and lovingly with me."[20] The scriptures she showed him finally brought the young dentist into assurance of salvation. Abandoning all hope of making himself worthy of God's love, he put his trust completely in Christ as Saviour. Immediately, his missionary longings revived – no longer as a means of finding favour with

God, but now as a natural desire to share with others the assurance he had obtained. But what would Mary make of all this?

He confessed, "In the joy of possessing one who had so truly loved me, and after five years of trial, I for a moment quite forgot all my promises to the Lord and his work abroad."[21] Such things, however, could not now be kept secret; he had to tell Mary of his long-felt desire to become a missionary. She was by no means pleased. "After we were married and the first joy of surmounted difficulties had passed away, our religious judgments could not long remain uncontrasted, and I soon powerfully felt they were awfully different, either from her having gone back through sorrow, or from my having got forward, or partly perhaps from both. But it now became the *settled bent of her life* to root out my desire to go out as a missionary and to reduce me to the same state of religious feelings as herself."[22] Not surprisingly, their home life became somewhat strained. She did not like Norris's keen evangelical friends, and he did not take to the more conventional company she preferred. It was simplest to keep to themselves, rarely inviting anyone home and rarely visiting anyone.

Two little boys and a baby girl came to brighten their home, and one might think the young couple had all they could possibly wish for.[23] Indeed, many might envy a man like Norris Groves with an attractive affectionate wife, a growing family and a flourishing career, little suspecting the spiritual trials within. "We were greatly prospering in the world," he said. "Her family were delighted and happy, and these things embraced all she ever knew or thought of happiness; but it was not so with me; *I had given myself to the Lord* and to a work I had not fulfilled… By six years' opposition her mind had settled down into a fixed resistance… Often did I, with every earthly thing that a man could desire, feel most miserable. I had a wife who loved me, dear little children, and a most lucrative profession, yet I had not the Lord's presence as in days past, and therefore I was miserable."[24]

He looked for comfort in the Bible. Convinced that its message was true, he felt he must discover exactly what it said, and as he pored over its pages he resolved to put into practice whatever he might find there. But the more he read, the more perplexed he became. For in this book – indeed, in the words of Christ himself – were instructions, directions and commands that appeared crystal clear, but which no one seemed to have noticed before. Certainly no one seemed to be following them. Groves began to put down his thoughts on paper. In 1825 a small booklet was printed. Its title was *Christian Devotedness*, and it bore the subtitle "The Consideration of our Saviour's Precept: Lay not up for yourselves treasures upon earth." Though only twenty-eight pages in length, and published privately by a layman with no theological training, it made an astonishing impact.

Throughout the ages, preachers both famous and obscure had encouraged the wealthy to assist those less privileged than themselves. By charitable works and wisely placed patronage, a Christian born into a prosperous family would do his bit to encourage "the deserving poor"; whilst one born into a humble family, through diligence, truthfulness and thrift, might aspire to earn an honest living and provide for his dependants. Providence required both "the rich man in his castle" and "the poor man at his gate" to play their part in maintaining a stable society. In our day, the custom at Harvest Festival of sending food to the needy still lingers as a remnant from those benevolent times. But living in a land where every town possessed slums in which hundreds of families lacked essential food, clothing and medicine, and faced by a world still entirely ignorant of Christ, should the rich Christian be doing more? To the time-honoured system of sporadic and seasonal benevolence, Norris Groves suggested a radical alternative. He proposed that the wealthy Christian actually become poor. The disciple of Christ will place in his Lord's hands all he possesses, to be used from then on for the benefit of others. And Groves determined not merely to quote the teaching of Jesus on this subject, but to obey it.[25]

How would Mary take to such ideas? As the wife of a professional man she had certain standards to maintain. She might well be expected to feel like one assistant surgeon's wife in 1859 who confided, "I must not do our household work, or carry my baby out: or I should lose caste. We must keep a servant."[26] But more to the point was her anxiety that the children might be left destitute if their parents improvidently failed to store up a sum for possible future needs. The history of Norris's own father lent weight to her fears.

But Groves tells us, "As I was walking round the garden at Northernhay one day, underneath that great elm tree near the gate, I said to Mary, 'My love, I think we ought to lay by something regularly for the Lord, for you recollect when we commenced our career we often said, if we ever possessed a thousand a year, it would be the height of our wishes. Now we have much more than this; therefore let us begin to give some.'" To that extent Mary was willing to be generous, and she readily agreed that a tenth of their income could be given away.

Day by day, while her husband attended to the teeth of Exeter, Mary looked for ways to distribute the tenth. She walked down to the poorer parts of town to visit homes where there might be families in need. This was a courageous undertaking for a young woman whose upbringing had been very sheltered. Until then her interests had extended no further than her children, her husband and "the cultivation of a few flowers, and painting from nature".[27] Now she was exposed to squalor, vice and perhaps danger, from which a sensitive soul would shrink. But it was to prove the making of her. Her new contact with the wider world, and personal experience of difficulties faced by the poor and the aged, shifted her thoughts from herself to others.

One of those she met at this time was a woman called Mary Walker who "had a bad husband, great poverty and a most agonising, slow mortification of the feet and hands." Yet despite her troubles poor Mary Walker had something her visitor lacked, for Mary Groves could see that whatever problems she faced, "faith and love and praise mounted over all." This poor woman enjoyed a living relationship with God that Mary, however hard she tried, could not seem to attain. A bitter struggle began in her heart – a longing for real faith, yet a fear that such faith would lead once again to the question of missionary work overseas. Confused and apprehensive, she told Norris nothing of her heart-searching. Instead, he later recalled, "She took to her bed, told me she felt she was dying, and gave me directions what to do in the event of her death." Groves was "almost distracted". It took some weeks before she recovered sufficiently to resume her visits and even then, "feeling that hell was yawning for her, she felt she was keeping me back."[28]

One day, visiting the local prison, Mary attended the chapel attached to the institution, as she often did. The chaplain was speaking on a passage from the first letter to the Corinthians, chapter one: "God has chosen the weak things of the world…" How utterly weak she felt, how far from God, how incapable of supporting her husband in all he wished to do! Yet if God had chosen the weak, might he not find some small use even for her, "the most worthless of his creatures"? But feeling quite incapable of becoming a missionary, she "buried all these thoughts". The following week Norris and Mary were invited to the home of a friend. Here they found the same chaplain, who expounded the same passage, and "the Holy Ghost seemed to say to her 'That's for you, poor troubled soul: take it and go in peace.'" She was overwhelmed by the realisation that "God has chosen the weak things," and when they returned home, she told her husband everything. "From that day," Norris recalled, "the Lord began to let light shine into our dwelling."[29]

The Paget sisters continued to pray for Mary, and so did her husband's other evangelical friends. She still seemed to think that she must make herself a Christian by serving Christ. "They often talked to me," she said, "and I often read, of the happiness of religion, but I can truly say I never knew what misery was till I was concerned about religion and endeavoured to frame my life according to its rules. The manifest powerless inadequacy of my efforts to attain my standard left me always further removed from hope and peace than when I never knew or thought of the likeness of Christ as a thing to be aimed after." But the turning point was not far away. A faith previously confined to "the abstract sense of what is right" and the "fear of punishment" was suddenly transformed by the realisation of God's love for her. It changed everything. She later recalled, "It was not till the Holy Ghost was pleased of his infinite mercy to reveal *the love of my Heavenly Father in Christ*, as existing in himself before all ages, contemplating me with pity and purposing to save me by his grace, and to conform me to the image of him whom my soul loves, that I really had peace or confidence or strength."[30] Norris was thrilled to see the change in her – depending no longer on what she must do for her Saviour but on what he had done for her. And all at once, "the days became too short to tell of the Lord's goodness and think of our happiness." In the past Mary had been shy, tense and prone to worry, but now, complete in Christ and filled with his Spirit, she became, in her husband's words, "active, decided, and with a strong independent judgment."[31]

Every Saturday afternoon Norris Groves closed his practice and set off for Hampshire to visit his mother who was far from well. Arriving in the middle of the night he took his turn watching over the old lady, returning early on the Monday morning to see the first clients of the day.[32] At this time the big house at Northernhay was also home to a young man, John Groves, a distant cousin who had come to learn the art of dentistry, and his infant sister Emma.[33] Before long the family circle would be augmented by a most unlikely stranger. He went by the name of John Kitto, and his story will require a chapter of its own.

Others came to visit. One was Solomon Alexander, the young Jewish rabbi from the synagogue in Plymouth. Alexander was a cultured man, about twenty-five years old and recently married. He had long been searching for the truth, and after discussions with Groves and other friends, told them he had read the entire New Testament with an open mind and with much interest. Eventually he announced his resignation from the synagogue, for he had put his faith in Christ. The Jewish community of Plymouth was appalled; they came continually to Alexander's house, remonstrating and urging him to change his mind. With his future uncertain, he was baptised at St Andrew's Church in Plymouth in June 1825. He and his young wife then travelled directly to Exeter where Norris and Mary Groves had offered them refuge and the opportunity for fellowship and prayer. Mrs Alexander was baptised shortly afterwards. She, in particular, had a strong concern to make the gospel of Christ known to those who had never heard, and there was much conversation round the fireside on the subject of missions.[34] After five weeks at Northernhay, the Jewish couple found lodgings of their own and remained in Exeter for a year, during which time Alexander taught Groves the basics of the Hebrew language. Alexander's conversion had impressed two other young men from the local Jewish community, Belsom and Abrahams, who in turn came to Exeter to find out more. Both were men of high moral principles, and Belsom, in particular, had many questions. Drawn to faith in Christ, they were baptised on Christmas Day 1825. Again, it was to the Groves household they went after the ceremony.[35]

Meanwhile, the booklet *Christian Devotedness* was doing its quiet work. In fact one of its earliest achievements was to lose the family the services of their private tutor. Whilst attending university in Scotland, Robert Nesbit had belonged to a group of students with keen missionary interests, though he was determined to suppress all thought of himself becoming a missionary. On his arrival in Exeter, Groves urged him to reconsider the question, and showed him the booklet. Nesbit's months of "sore spiritual depression" were over.[36] He immediately sent a copy of *Christian Devotedness* to his fellow-students at St Andrews University and shortly afterwards offered himself to the Scottish Missionary Society for service in India.[37]

Some weeks passed and a new tutor was engaged to help Groves in his study of classical Greek and Latin, and to educate the boys Henry and Frank, now aged eight and six. He was a serious young man, twenty-one years of age, also a graduate of St Andrews, by the name of Henry Craik. Settling in at Northernhay, in August 1826, he recorded his first impressions of his new employer, his admiration tinged with a measure of native Scots caution: "He is a most interesting, a most noble character. The chief features of his mind are generosity, heavenly-mindedness, great talent, persuasive eloquence, gentleness, humility, learning. I know not what faults I may yet discover, but as yet I have reason to believe there scarcely does exist a more noble character."[38]

Hidden faults there may have been but Craik's host was certainly a character engaged in noble causes. In March 1826, at a public meeting held to organise a petition against slavery for presentation to the House of Lords, one of the main speakers was A N Groves. The following year he was joint secretary of the Devon and Exeter Society for the Abolition of Slavery throughout the British Dominions.[39] Fresh news from the mission field again revived his interest in work overseas, and again, he tells us, it was southern India where "my heart was first set". The subject of missions was still not one he could raise with Mary, but he did feel free to speak to her on another matter. "Dearest Mary," he said, "since the Lord has so graciously received our little dedication of a tenth, and made it the means of so blessing us, perhaps he would graciously also receive more at our hands." "Well," she agreed, "it shall be so. We have now three little children: let it stand as one, and be a fourth." Mary disposed of some clothes she did not need, along with various household ornaments. They now had more to give away, and "in visiting the poor no weather hindered her." "The more we gave," testified Norris, "the more we were blessed."[40]

Despite this, Groves admitted, "with respect to property we had only yet gone a certain way; some may think it far enough, others too far; but my heart, which had been so blessed that it could not contain its blessing, felt that, so long as anything was kept back from so gracious a Lord who had dealt so bountifully by us, it was as though nothing were given." And this, he tells us, "led me to propose one day to my dearest Mary that as the Lord had blessed us more and more, in all that we had given up for him, perhaps he would accept *all* from our loving grateful hearts." Tears came to her eyes. "My dear," she said, "I think it would be most wicked; consider the dear little children." Norris did not press the point: "I saw the time was not come."[41]

But knowing he had set his heart on it, Mary suggested that they ask their lodger, John Kitto, to "search out the mind of the Lord from the New Testament and say what he thought." Kitto, profoundly impressed by the sincerity of Groves's commitment to Christ, considered the matter and gave his opinion that they were "more than free" to give everything away; it would be a wonderful testimony of their "sense of the value of the true riches". Then "after the deepest thought and most earnest prayer Mary without reserve gave it all up," and never, we are told, regretted the step. Husband and wife felt free at last of a "great burden". "We had no object now in life," he confided, "but living to the Lord and the Church."[42] And this, they believed, would be far better for the children than leaving them a large inheritance.

Still, however, the subject of overseas mission had not been raised. Just at this time, a visitor arrived in Exeter, a certain Bishop Chase from Ohio. The American frontier, he said, offered a wide open door for Christian work. At that time, barely twenty years had passed since the creation of the state of Ohio, and from there many migrants set out for the west. This made it a strategic centre, with a continual influx of settlers, rapidly growing towns and a constant flow of traffic in every direction.[43] Though Indians and buffalo still roamed the western plains, the Erie canal was under construction, and steamboats had just appeared on the Ohio river and the Great Lakes. But what interested Norris Groves was the fact that Chase "had *given up all* for the Lord's cause in Ohio," and he gladly accepted an invitation to spend Sunday with the bishop in the home of a mutual friend. Here Chase asked him to consider taking his family to America. The old missionary vision revived. Groves began to think that the challenge of Ohio, where most people spoke English and enjoyed the benefits of Western technology, might be a challenge that Mary could respond to more easily than the alien cultures of southern India. The next day Chase came for lunch with the Groves family, and seated at table their visitor turned to the boys Henry and Frank. "Well, my little men," he said, "will you go to Ohio? There are plenty of peaches in Ohio." Norris Groves turned to poor Mary and asked, "Well dear, will you go?" She burst into tears. Comforting her as best he could in the presence of their guest, he promised not to urge her further. Four months went by, then one day she came to him. "You may write," she said, "to Bishop Chase, and say we will come." Groves wrote, and they waited for a reply. Days and weeks passed; no answer came. It seemed that Ohio was not, after all, the place for them. "Well Norris," said Mary, "you had better write again to the Church Missionary Society and say we are ready to go *anywhere*."[44]

So it was that in July 1825 Edward Bickersteth, Secretary of the CMS, arrived from London to talk with them. Ten years had passed since Norris Groves first offered himself to the Society for work overseas. Few educated men were willing to go to the mission field, and this young dentist with linguistic interests seemed to Bickersteth distinctly promising. They explained everything to him; they told how they had pledged themselves to "the cause of missions". But one question remained: should they stay at home and support missionaries by means of their professional income, or should they go as missionaries themselves? The question was made more pertinent by the fact that Mary stood to inherit ten or twelve thousand pounds on the death of her father, and her father would certainly find someone else to whom he could leave the money if he discovered their intention to give it away and disappear to the far ends of the earth. Bickersteth's answer was plain: "If you are called of the Lord to the work, *money cannot* be set against it. It is men whom the Lord sends, and he stands in need of men more than money."[45]

This was all they needed to hear, and the decision was made. The CMS committee suggested that they might be most useful in the Mediterranean area, based initially on the island of Malta where a team was already writing and printing tracts for widespread distribution.[46] Groves, of course, must train for ordination in the Anglican Church. He would enrol as a part-time student at Trinity College, Dublin, whilst maintaining his practice in Exeter. This would qualify him to sit the quarterly examinations that would lead in the course of three years to ordination. Bickersteth himself had given up his profession as an attorney, bringing in a thousand pounds or more a year, preferring to serve with the CMS for only three or four hundred. "And he assures me," Groves remarked, "that he has never once regretted it. On the contrary, he looks on it with peculiar thankfulness."[47] Here was a man after their own heart, and his advice exactly matched their own inclinations.

A year and a half sped by as Groves pursued his studies. Then in March 1827 another letter arrived from the CMS. The committee had received a visit from a travelling evangelist by the name of Joseph Wolff, who spoke of a vast unreached area in the Middle East, stretching through Turkey, Syria and Persia, where Christian scriptures might be received and read with interest if only someone could be found to distribute them. These were the heartlands of the Muslim world, and up to that point no Protestant mission had felt able to establish a base there. Would Norris and Mary Groves be willing to go to Persia? This was a prospect more difficult than southern India or Malta, and far more difficult than Ohio. It was a question requiring more time and much prayer.[48]

ENDNOTES

[1] D16

[2] The register of baptisms for the parish of Newton Valence contains the following entry: "Anthony, son of Mr Anthony Groves of Lymington and Lydia his wife, was privately baptised 5 Feb. 1795." The boy's father, grandfather and great-grandfather were all called Anthony Groves, which may have led to some confusion. The name Norris was presumably adopted later, being the family name of his paternal grandmother (see Appendix v. Genealogy).

[3] M1. The Hampshire Directory of 1828 describes Anthony Groves of Lymington as a grocer and tea dealer.

[4] M1. The merchant vessel HCS Royal George was built in 1820 for the East India Company. On Christmas Eve 1825, having just loaded a cargo of tea at Whampoa in southern China, she was found to be on fire and quickly sank. No life was lost, but the ship and cargo were both totally destroyed (Tuck, 113).

[5] M2

[6] Norris attended Burlington House Academy, a prestigious private school, run at this time by Dr Robert Roy (*Memoir* first edn,14; Timothy Stunt, private communication).

[7] The exact address was 22 George Street. A little later, around 1820, it was James Thompson (or his son, also called James) who requested a London jeweller, Claudius Ash, to construct a set of false teeth with plates, springs and swivels of gold, which launched the famous dental manufacturing company of that name.

[8] M242. John Owen was a founder-member and secretary of the British and Foreign Bible Society. He should not be confused with the celebrated seventeenth century Puritan of the same name.

[9] M24

[10] M24

[11] M25

[12] M3. Richards and Hitchins belonged to a circle of evangelical clergy with Arminian convictions. Associated with them was Samuel Whitlock Gandy, and also Robert Lampen who was later known in Plymouth as a strong opponent of Calvinism (Stunt, *Awakening*, 119). Gandy wrote a hymn about the Paschal Lamb greatly appreciated by Groves throughout his life (M3, 504).

[13] M25

[14] The CMS was founded in 1799 as the "Society for Missions to Africa and the East". It still exists as a major missionary agency of the Church of England.

[15] M26. The wedding was reported in the *Exeter Flying Post*, 7th Nov. 1816, p.4.

[16] Northernhay House was located within Northernhay Park just outside the city walls of Exeter. It commanded extensive views across this spacious public parkland to the Longbrook Valley and the high woods of Duryard. The property stood in its own large walled garden, with a coach house and stabling for two horses. It comprised two parlours, a kitchen, pantry, servants' hall, six bedrooms, laundry room, cellar and brew house. (As untreated water was not fit to drink, many large houses at this time brewed small beer for daily consumption.) When first built and furnished, a ninety-nine year lease on the property was offered for sale in the Sherborne Mercury

newspaper in July 1789. Twenty-seven years later, in July 1816, the house was again advertised, and the leasehold bought soon afterwards by Norris Groves. The seller was the Rev. Edward Back, curate of St David's Church, who was a teacher at the Exeter Free Grammar School and then went to work in Nova Scotia (Cornforth, "Exeter Memories"). It was probably Mary's dowry that enabled her husband to make this substantial investment.

[17] M27

[18] M565n. Groves, according to his editor, spelt her name as Bessie in one letter (M205) and Bessy in another (M38), although her formal name was Elizabeth.

[19] The term Dissenter or Nonconformist was applied to any member of a Protestant denomination outside of the Established Church (the Church of England).

[20] M40, M558, and M25 where Bessie is simply called "a dear friend in Exeter". In later life Groves often referred to her as his "mother in God".

[21] M26

[22] M27

[23] Henry was born in 1818, Frank (Francis Anthony) in 1820, and little Mary in 1822. Henry and Frank were christened in the church of St David, Exeter on 18 June 1819 and 17 March 1820 respectively, although Henry was actually born several months earlier, in November 1818, according to Pickering, *Chief Men*, 98.

[24] M27. Groves was now earning £1500 a year (Müller, *Narrative*, I, 44). A middle-class tradesman or clerk at this time would expect an annual income of about £100 to £300 (Harrison, 131).

[25] The message of *Christian Devotedness* is discussed in Chapter 6 of this book.

[26] Kerr-Jarrett, 45

[27] M27

[28] M28

[29] M29. The chaplain was John Marriott from the village of Broad Clyst, about five miles from Exeter. He wrote the well-known hymn, "Thou Whose Almighty Word". Marriott was influential, along with Bessie Paget, in Groves's shift towards a more Calvinistic theology around 1824. His nephew, William Caldecott, became a close friend of Groves.

[30] R175-176

[31] M29

[32] M4. Mrs Groves died, after six months' illness, on 24th July 1823 (M2).

[33] M4. John and Emma Groves were third cousins of Norris Groves, sharing with him the same great-great-grandparents. Their father was an innkeeper on the Isle of Wight (Gundert, 32; UK Census 1851).

[34] In 1841 Michael Solomon Alexander became the first Anglican Bishop of Jerusalem.

[35] Groves encouraged these Jewish converts to learn a trade, and in due course Belsom became a saddler and Abrahams a tailor. Belsom spoke fluent English and was active almost immediately as a missionary among the Jews. For a period Abrahams's income provided for both himself and his friend, and in later years Groves often referred to this arrangement as an example of practical partnership in missionary service. In the course of time Abrahams too became "a teacher of the gospel" in

London, and Groves was delighted to hear him preach there in 1836 (M527-528, 460).

[36] Mitchell, 28

[37] Groves to Bickersteth, 14 Mar. 1826. One of these students was Alexander Duff, who later, like Nesbit, became a missionary educator in India (Mitchell, 13).

St Andrews was a small town on the east coast. Its university was the first to be established in Scotland. The St Andrews students belonged to a circle influenced by Thomas Chalmers, Professor of Moral Philosophy, who was a fervent and idealistic evangelical. In protest at the subordination of the Church of Scotland to state control, he subsequently, in 1843, took a leading part in the defection of nearly half its membership to form the Free Church of Scotland (Brown, 168; Stunt, *Awakening*, 224).

[38] Coad, 19; Rowdon, *Origins*, 112

[39] Stunt, *Awakening*, 121

[40] M29-30

[41] M30

[42] M31

[43] Chicago at this time (1830) had barely 100 inhabitants. Within forty years, the population of the city would increase to 306,000, and by 1890 to 1.1 million (Kerr-Jarrett, 64).

[44] M32

[45] M32

[46] CMS Minutes, 9 Aug. 1825; Groves to Bickersteth, 15 Sep. 1825

[47] M13

[48] CMS Minutes, 20 Feb. 1827; M19. At that time the name Persia denoted a rather large and ill-defined geographical area lying between Turkey and India. In addition to the political entity of the largely mountainous Persian Empire (modern Iran), it included the wide fertile valley of the Tigris and Euphrates rivers (modern Iraq), belonging not to the Persian but to the Ottoman Empire.

"There is no one so low but that he may rise."

John Kitto [1]

3

A Workhouse Boy

In 1803 two young Cornishmen came to Plymouth. The Kitto brothers looked for lodgings and then for work, willing to build walls, barns, houses or anything else that a stonemason could set his hand to. In the same street lived a widow by the name of Mrs Picken with her two daughters. After a short courtship, John Kitto married Elizabeth; his brother married Mary.

John was only nineteen or twenty years old, his wife two years younger. The following year, on the fourth of December 1804, their first child was born. Small and frail, Johnny junior was not expected to live more than a few hours, but his refusal to die presaged a stubbornness somewhat out of the ordinary. Life was not easy: most of the father's earnings went on alcohol, and more than one night he spent in the local jail. A baby sister came along, and the young family sank towards destitution. From five in the morning till ten at night Elizabeth Kitto toiled as a cleaner in a big house, earning what she could for her children's food and clothing. But it was hardly sufficient.

With no one at home to look after him, Johnny, aged three, was sent "to his grandmother's poor garret". He never forgot the kindness and affection of the old lady, "more than a mother to me". With little thought for her own poverty and the hardships of a life beset with difficulties, Mrs Picken devoted herself to her odd dwarf-like grandson. She taught him to sew and make simple things with his hands, and she took him out almost every day to gather nuts and berries for their table from the fields and lanes around Plymouth. In the evenings she told him stories of ghosts, hobgoblins, fairies and witches.

Next door lived a shoemaker, a "merry cordwainer". Awl and leather in hand, he would sometimes entertain little Johnny with tales of Bluebeard, Cinderella, Jack the Giant-killer, and Beauty and the Beast. Then came the breathtaking moment when the boy discovered that these stories were not the shoemaker's own invention but could be found in printed books adorned with pictures for the price of a few pence. Indeed, they were displayed for sale at that very time in the shop window of Mrs Barnicle at the head of Market Street. Before long he discovered a second-hand bookstall in a local market where a halfpenny could be invested even more advantageously than with Mrs Barnicle. On his grandmother's shelves he found *Pilgrim's Progress* and *Gulliver's Travels*, and he honoured these heirlooms by decorating the engravings with blue indigo using a feather for a brush.[2] Old Mrs Picken encouraged his reading; sitting quietly, turning over the pages, he was no trouble at all. She borrowed books from her neighbours, and soon the strange little boy had read every volume in the street.

At the age of eight Johnny was enrolled in a local school. He was not there long. Try as she might, his grandmother could not afford the fees, a penny a day, and his father offered little help. Failing to produce his penny he was sent home. The same happened at a second school, then a third and a fourth. "When the fees could be saved from the ale cup, the boy attended school, and when not he stayed at home."[3] Recurring headaches made his attendance even more erratic during these brief three years that served for his formal education.

When his grandmother, half paralysed with increasing age, could no longer provide for him, Johnny Kitto returned to his parents' house. He occupied an attic in the roof, seven feet by four, "ventilated by an aperture that admitted the wind and could not exclude the rain, and was furnished with a rickety table, framed originally to stand on three feet but now sustaining itself with difficulty on two."[4] His chief pleasure was to take a small book to some shady spot in the fields nearby, but as his mother was out most of the day he was left in charge of the younger children and did most of his reading at night by the light of some small burning sticks gathered from here and there.

Time passed and Johnny must do something to earn his keep: he was sent to work for a barber. "Old Wigmore" had practised his trade on board a ship-of-war; he had a fund of improbable seaman's tales and a sour face "all over red by drinking spirituous liquors".[5] The boy arrived to open the shop one morning, with a bundle of his master's best razors under his arm. Waiting for him was a woman, who begged him to run and fetch the barber immediately. Leaving the razors in her care he hastened to do her bidding, and returned to find her and the bundle gone. All the suspicion fell on him as an accomplice in the theft, and so ended his first attempt to make his innocent way in the adult world.

As occasional building jobs came his father's way, Johnny, now aged twelve, was called upon to assist with fetching and carrying stones and bricks. After work the boy would sit outside the alehouse door, then help him stagger home. One February afternoon, father and son were repairing the roof of a house in Plymouth. As the weary lad, in his ragged smock, stepped with a load of slates from the ladder to the rooftop, he slipped and fell some thirty-five feet to the ground. He lay unconscious, bleeding profusely from mouth and nose. Regaining his senses briefly as they picked him up, he could not imagine why he was lying on the ground or why so many people were staring at him. Unconscious for more than a week, he then lay in bed for a further four months. A physician did his best for the boy, with "leeches applied to my temples and under my ears" and "plenty of nauseous physic [i.e. medicine]" but nothing could be done to change or disguise the fact that the accident had left little Johnny Kitto totally deaf. He could hear nothing at all. When he eventually tried to walk, he found he had lost his sense of balance, and the fracture to his skull severely aggravated the headaches that had already incapacitated so many of his schooldays.

To earn a few pence Johnny Kitto now took to scavenging the Plymouth shoreline for "rope, iron and other nautical fragments", until one day he trod heavily on a broken bottle and his foot was severely cut. He then tried his hand at painting, and with far more ambition than artistic ability managed to sell some crude watercolours of "human heads, houses, flowers, birds and trees". As he hawked his work from door to door, he saw handwritten notices in the house windows, such as "Logins for singel men" and "Rooms to leet enquair withing". He prepared correctly spelt signs with coloured capitals, shyly offering them for a few coppers. But he could not hear what his prospective customers were saying, and though some showed their sympathy others did not bother to hide their impatience.

All the halfpennies he earned he spent on old books – literature, history and knowledge of any sort – and he was often to be seen poring over the tiny print with his back to a tree or amongst the crags above the breaking surf. Each little volume became a well-loved friend, every page bringing the stimulus of fresh ideas and impressions, providing for the deaf boy the interest and companionship that those who hear may take so easily for granted. "I was a diligent collector of all the odds and ends of knowledge that fell in my way," he later recalled. "I read all the bills that were posted on dead walls and empty houses. I studied all the title pages and open leaves that appeared in the windows of booksellers' shops." Once a fortnight he visited a bookstall in Devonport. "I could tell at a glance," he said, "what books had been sold and what additions had been made since my last visit." Sometimes he would contrive to read half a book before the stallholder moved him on; he would return the following week to complete it, only to find it gone. He reckoned booksellers the most fortunate of men for "if they sell the books they are happy in the money they get, but if they do not sell them they are happy in the books they retain."[6]

He went to great pains to compile indexes for the volumes in his own small collection, but as most were borrowed he trained himself to remember the points of greatest interest and wrote extensive notes and summaries for future reference. In later years he was moved to "look back on that poor and deaf boy, in his utter loneliness, devoting himself to objects in which none around him could sympathize, and to pursuits which none could even understand." People thought him distinctly odd. Lack of encouragement and sympathy he later counted "among the sorest trials of that day", for he was too shy and too deaf to find any friends who might share his interests. Left alone for days on end to please himself and wander where he willed, he grew up locked into his own little world. After the accident, recalled Kitto, "I never was a *lad*... While other lads were employed with trifles, I thought as a man, felt as a man and acted as a man... While my compeers found amusement in their balls, their tops or their kites, I occupied myself with a book, a pen or a pencil."[7]

Times were hard, and grew harder as Kitto senior, no longer sober enough for work of any kind, failed to provide for his pinched and ragged family. Responsibility for them was taken up by the local authorities, and shortly before his fifteenth birthday, in November 1819, young John was sent to the Plymouth workhouse. Here he was surrounded by strangers, expected to know what was going on and understand the instructions given to him. The other boys soon found ways of amusing themselves at his expense. His attempts at speech were so embarrassing they were soon abandoned; he had to improvise a rudimentary means of communication by signs.

The parish workhouse, still in its earliest form at this time, was intended as a compassionate provision at public expense for the destitute and disabled. It provided those in need with simple food and adequate clothing, a warm dry bed if they required it, and guaranteed work. John Kitto was free to come and go, and to sleep at home if he wished, but in the workhouse itself the rules were strict, the uniform demeaning, and freedom limited. The rooms and corridors were stark and cheerless, and probably smelt none too fresh. Here, in the Hospital of the Poor's Portion, he was taught to make list-slippers, a type of soft felt shoe worn by seamen carrying gunpowder in the wooden ships of the day. For this work he received a penny a week.

He was grateful for the kindness of Mr Burnard, the master of the workhouse, and for the teacher who protected him from the rougher boys and encouraged him to write for the benefit of the other inmates. He began to put down his thoughts in a journal, dedicating it "to the memory of Cecilia Picken, my Grandmother and the dearest friend I ever had." He recorded his height as 4ft 8ins, described his "laboured asthmatic breathing", and observed that a somewhat precocious growth of fuzz on his upper lip exposed him to the stares of passers-by. He was very self-conscious, acutely aware of both his uncommon intellectual interests and his conspicuous physical oddity. He found it hard to look anyone in the eye and later admitted, "My manners are awkward and clownish. I am short in stature, stoop much in walking, and walk as though I feared I should fall at every step, with my hands almost always, when I walk, in my pockets."[8] His sense of balance had been so badly affected by his fall that he confessed, "After dark I stagger like a drunken man." To those who saw him, he seemed "not far removed from idiotcy."[9] Or so he thought.

Writing a journal was a common enough pastime in those days, and like many others he jotted down his thoughts on current events such as the death of Napoleon Bonaparte and the acquittal of Queen Caroline.[10] He tried to copy the stately style he had seen in the published journals of famous men – rather ponderous and pompous, no doubt, to the mind of our more hurried age. At times his thoughts turned to religion, especially to the mysterious ways of Providence, but then he confessed, "I fear I am deplorably ignorant in religious matters."[11] On the sad death of his beloved grandmother he recorded his heartfelt hope that "in the presence of our God we may meet again – meet again never to part – never again to be subject to the frail laws of mortality." And then, "Accursed be the atheist who seeks to deprive man of his noblest privilege – of his hopes of immortality."[12] He applied, at this time, for confirmation in the Church of England. When the day came, at the cathedral, he got lost in the crowd. Though he had memorized his catechism perfectly, he could not hear what was happening or follow the order of service. No one offered to help him, and he came home no more confirmed than when he went.[13]

In 1821, aged seventeen, the workhouse authorities arranged for him to be apprenticed to a shoemaker by the name of Bowden. This was good news indeed. It meant he would be free from the jostling and the taunting of the workhouse boys. He would be trained in a craft, able to earn his living, equipped to be a man. He wrote triumphantly in his journal, "I am no longer a workhouse boy – I am an apprentice."[14] The terms of the apprenticeship gave his master almost unlimited powers over him, and Kitto now entered on two months of unremitting anguish. Bowden beat him mercilessly about the ears and head whenever he failed to understand what was required of him. He was frequently overcome by tears of anger and humiliation; the bruises on his face told their own story. Labouring sixteen, sometimes eighteen hours a day left no time or energy for the reading that made life worth living. Morbid ideas filled his mind and he began to think of suicide. With painstaking care, he composed a written appeal to the magistrates describing his woes and his aspirations. Eventually his case was heard, and the document binding him to his apprenticeship "with its formidable appendage of seals and signatures" was annulled.

John Kitto, back once more on his three-legged stool in the workhouse, had seen for himself that the pen could achieve great things, and the ambition grew in his heart to present to the world a work in poetry or prose that would immortalize his name. What a great thing, "to be esteemed by the wise, the learned and the good"! He studied his previous writings with a critical eye and began to experiment with words, seeing how the rhythm of a sentence, its emotional intensity and its power to persuade, could be changed by the choice of one word or another, or by rearranging its various clauses. Encouraged by Mr Burnard, he sent off an essay to a local newspaper, the *Plymouth Weekly Journal*, which to his great delight was accepted for publication. He had free time too, when his day's work was done, for the solitary walks that helped to lift dark and gloomy thoughts from his over-sensitive nature. The invigorating views of the sea, the waves breaking on the rocks, the bustling activity of the ships in the harbour and the shady woods of Mount Edgecumbe all soothed his spirit, refreshed his mind and inspired him with hopes that he could become a writer. Soon some more of his essays appeared in the newspaper, describing his thoughts, especially on childhood and suffering, and bearing titles such as *Home* and *Contemplation*.

A certain Mr Harvey, a "mathematician and man of science", happened to be in a bookshop one day, when he saw a curious thing – a stunted youth with an awkward demeanour and a "poor-house uniform" lovingly turning over the pages of an expensively bound book. Harvey asked about him and shortly afterwards, with the help of some literary friends, arranged for Kitto to become an assistant in the local library. There he could write some more essays which they would find means to publish. So it was that John Kitto, aged eighteen, finally left the workhouse.

The library was a paradise to him. He browsed happily along its shelves of literature, history and especially metaphysics, a subject which embraced psychology, sociology and aspects of theology and philosophy – anything in fact which touched on the mind, nature and behaviour of man. About this time a Quaker gentleman by the name of Prideaux invited the young librarian to his home. Kitto returned "laden with books" and, more importantly, with counsels "which I then thought and now think the most valuable and quickening which I ever received." With relish Kitto noted Mr Prideaux's "grand point... that it was the duty of every rational creature to devote whatever talents God had given him to useful purposes... and that so far as I did this... so far might I expect his blessing."[15] From this time on, the task of "improving" his God-given talent became the great motivation of John Kitto's life.

Kitto's literary benefactors encouraged him to attend the local parish church. He was reluctant. He could not hear the prayers or the music or sermon, so what was the point of going? Reading the Bible and theological works at home seemed an altogether more useful way of cultivating "religious impressions", and he embarked on a scheme to read two chapters of the Bible every morning, and two every evening, with prayer. A commentary on the Epistles, he said, if they could find him one, would help in understanding what he read. But his study of the Bible depressed him. The commandments were plain to see, but they brought only a sense of failure and guilt. The atoning work of Christ on the cross was clearly stated, but "I do not feel myself sufficiently grateful to him." Kitto's attempts at prayer were frustrated by wandering thoughts: "I rise from my knees more guilty than when I began to kneel."[16] And finally he confessed, "I am afraid that mine is a cold theoretic belief, rather than an effectual and saving faith."[17] The religious ideal was there before him, and yet beyond his reach. "I have always regarded with reverence those illustrious men who, fired with apostolic zeal and unappalled by the probabilities of difficulty and danger, have left their friends and their country in order to promulgate the gospel of mercy and truth in far distant countries, in lands pervaded by religious darkness and sunk into intellectual degradation. What glory, what dignity, equals that attached to the character of an ambassador of God! What triumph can be so noble and so pure as that of him who is enabled to exclaim, 'I have awakened a sinner to repentance, I have turned an idolater to the true God, I have been instrumental in saving a soul from death.' To me there appears to be something exceedingly grand and impressive in the very name of *Missionary*... it is still nearly identified with my *beau ideal* of human perfection."[18] But he himself fell far short of such distinction.

Discovering that deafness would be no disqualification, he wondered if he might aspire to become a clergyman, perhaps "in some retired and obscure curacy" of the Church of England, "where I should have no other business than the delightful one of instructing others in their duty to God and their fellow-men, and in which I should have sufficient leisure to read, to study and to write."[19] Yet Kitto felt far from confident of his standing even as a Christian: "This *theoretical* faith I feel to be utterly insufficient, unattended by practical results, and these practical results I do not experience."[20] Looking back on this period he confessed to complete ignorance of "the instructing influences of the Holy Spirit". "The Bible, although I read it, was long a sealed book to me," he said. "I was inclined rather to erect myself into a judge over the sacred volume than to suffer it to pass judgment upon me."[21]

The eventual publication of the *Essays and Letters of John Kitto* in 1825, after many hindrances and delays, actually brought Kitto little satisfaction. The morbid reaction which afflicts many an author once his best efforts have been displayed before the public gaze was compounded by the fact that Kitto's views on some subjects had changed since handing over his manuscript. And it was, he feared, on account of his physical disabilities rather than his intellectual qualities that his benefactors had been moved to finance the project. He resolved that if ever he went into print again it must be on a more worthy subject, and written anonymously, for him to be sure it stood on its merits alone. In fact ten years were to pass before his next published work, years in which he would undergo a discipline of toil and sorrow, wounded affections, loneliness, rejection, mortal dangers by land and sea, and all the horrors of plague, flood, famine and war.

In 1824 a letter sent by Kitto to the editor of a local newspaper came to the attention of a certain Mr Groves, a dentist practising in Exeter. Enquiring about its writer, Norris Groves heard about his disabilities and misfortunes, and his spiritual aspirations. He offered the young man accommodation, a modest income, and instruction in dentistry, in return for his services five hours a day constructing artificial teeth from "the tusks of certain foreign animals".[22] Kitto found his new employer "a gentleman of retired and literary habits, living in a pleasant situation with a large garden surrounding his residence." But it was not the career prospects that attracted Kitto, nor the pleasant situation and large garden; it was the character of Groves himself. Never had poor John Kitto met a man who could so joyfully entrust the smallest details of his daily life to the care of a loving heavenly Father. "The example of Mr Groves quite electrified him," commented Kitto's biographer, "and every fibre of his heart vibrated under the living impression. A vital and decided change passed over him."[23] For the first time in his life he felt he had seen real faith in action, and it convinced him that he had never till then been a real Christian at all. His prayers for a genuine heartfelt faith were now, at last, about to be answered.

Living and eating with Norris, Mary and the children, John Kitto became one of the family. It was a real Christian family, where everything was said with love, where the youngsters were courteous and helpful, and where the presence of Christ sanctified the simplest of daily chores. The deafness of their lodger was no impediment to the interest and affection they all expressed towards him. He experienced, in his own words, "an alteration most deeply felt in the heart, and entering into every feeling, every passion of the mind, insomuch that I should now be disgusted with much in which I once delighted, and many things are now most pleasant and delightful which once were indifferent to me."[24] John Kitto had known kind benefactors before, but never one like Groves. "The other gentlemen," he observed, "are more anxious for my fame than for my happiness; that is, they would rather see me celebrated than obscurely happy; whereas, on the other hand, Mr Groves does not care a fig about fame or distinction or anything of that sort."[25] The vision opening up before Kitto was the noblest of all visions: to "promote the happiness" of all who believed in Jesus, and to find ways of "extending the Kingdom" to those still beyond its reach. And how was he, in his deafness, to do this? With his pen, of course.

His letters to friends in Plymouth testify to the reality of his new-found relationship with the living Christ, "making me perpetually to act and think from the simple motive of love to our Divine Master."[26] In his free time, he began to accompany Groves on expeditions to the poorer parts of town, where they distributed tracts and Groves talked with the people about the way of salvation. Kitto admitted to being shocked by the "scenes of licentiousness and demoralization" and "scenes of brutal violence". He encouraged the slum children to write to him, and he wrote back "earnest, faithful and beautiful replies".[27] He later said of these forays into the dirtier parts of Exeter, "There are few, if any, accessible rooms or houses in which I have not been twice, or once at least."[28] He started to attend worship with Groves, and he describes a particular day, "one of the most pleasant in my life," in which "I have for the first time, partaken of the Communion."[29] John Kitto, at last, had found what he was looking for.

ENDNOTES

[1] Eadie, 434

[2] Indigo: a dye commonly added to water for washing clothes in order to whiten the linen, which tended to turn yellow with age.

[3] Eadie, 16

[4] Eadie, 23-24

[5] Eadie, 22

[6] Eadie, 280-281

[7] Ryland, 40, 93

[8] Eadie, 40

[9] Ryland, 122

[10] In 1820 Caroline, wife of George IV, was suspected of unfaithfulness and threatened with divorce.

[11] Eadie, 54

[12] Eadie, 47

[13] Eadie, 59

[14] Eadie, 64

[15] Ryland, 84

[16] Eadie, 90

[17] Eadie, 91

[18] Ryland, 125

[19] Ryland, 135-136; Eadie, 91

[20] Ryland, 136

[21] Ryland, 160

[22] Ryland, 148. A large part of the dentist's work at this time consisted of extractions, the treatment of gum abscesses, and the fitting of plates of false teeth held in place with springs. The rich preferred teeth made of silver, gold, mother of pearl or agate, filed to shape. The poor made do with Waterloo Teeth (removed from corpses after the battle), which were prone to rot and discolour. False teeth were set in cast metal or soft natural rubber (until the introduction of hard rubber around 1850), and considerable discomfort often resulted from loose and ill-fitting dentures. By this period, dentists were experimenting with mechanical drills of various sorts, and cavities were filled with lead or a thin layer of gold foil. Oil of cloves and cinnamon were prescribed for temporary relief of toothache but anaesthetics were not used at all in dental surgery until the 1840s.

[23] Eadie, 93

[24] Ryland, 168; Eadie, 98

[25] M5

[26] Eadie, 98

[27] Eadie, 99, 417

[28] Ryland, 191

[29] Eadie, 97-98

"I long to unite with the constraining love of Jesus
wherever I see it lodged
in a true heart
with a tender conscience."

Norris Groves [1]

4

All Hands Together

It was autumn 1826 when Norris Groves crossed the Irish Sea to sit his first examinations at Trinity College in Dublin. Here he was invited to a drawing room meeting for informal prayer and Bible study with other evangelical members of the Church of England. It was a pleasure to see their desire for more wholehearted devotedness to Christ, but Groves was surprised to find that Nonconformists were also welcomed to these meetings. Separation from the Established Church was, to his mind, a grave matter, contributing to an unhealthy sense of rivalry, and it allowed the unconverted to mock at the failure of Christians to agree among themselves. Indeed, Groves tells us, "I was so high a churchman that I never went to a dissenting place of worship, nor intimately knew a Dissenter except Bessie and Charlotte."[2]

For the time being he held his peace, but as his studies required him to come to Dublin every three months, he gradually became accustomed to the idea of praying with Dissenters; and as far as he could tell, they seemed to be genuine and devoted Christians with the same love for Christ that he had seen in his other Nonconformist friends, the Paget sisters and Henry Craik, the newly appointed tutor for his boys.[3] "From my first going to Dublin," he tells us, "many of my deep-rooted prejudices gave way. I saw those strongly marked distinctions that exist in England little regarded. The prevalence of the common enemy, Popery, joined all hands together."[4]

Although Ireland today comprises only eight per cent of the total population of the British Isles, it was the home, throughout the first half of the nineteenth century, of almost a third.[5] Since 1801 Ireland had formed part of the United Kingdom, and there was much traffic between London and Dublin, with a steady inflow of English settlers. The mass of people were Roman Catholics – poor farming families in the villages of the countryside and manual labourers in the crowded quarters of the larger towns. Richer families occupied substantial homes in the better parts of Dublin – government officials, commercial and professional men, academics and some landowning aristocracy. These were Protestant immigrants, drawn from both Anglican and Nonconformist traditions. Then between the years 1825 and 1827 there was a remarkable movement, sometimes called the "Irish Reformation", when Protestant preachers went out among the rural Catholics. Some of the evangelists were clergymen of the Establishment, but others were commissioned by agencies such as the British and Foreign Bible Society and the Scripture Readers Society, which included among their patrons both Churchmen and Dissenters.[6] Opening up the word of God by cottage firesides, they had seen many conversions. In fact, so vast was the field of labour that Establishment and Nonconformist evangelists could find ample scope for their energies without treading on one another's toes, and a degree of fellow-feeling sprang up among them that enabled them to pray together, share their experiences and encourage one another. By April 1827 Groves could report, "What a wonderful state of things appears to be arising in Ireland!"[7] Here indeed were Christians united as in the days of the apostles, without any of the denominational requirements or prejudices that elsewhere divided brother from brother.

The group which first welcomed Norris Groves to Dublin was one of three which later joined forces and eventually provided him with some of his closest friends and co-workers. One of its leaders was a newly qualified lawyer with private means by the name of John Gifford Bellett. He was a young Englishman, from a family settled in Ireland, with a pleasant open face and a gentle courteous manner. Born in the same year, he and Groves had much in common. Bellett had attended school in Exeter, and then enjoyed four years at Trinity College, Dublin, where Groves himself was now studying. A periodic visitor to their circle during the years 1827-8 was a young curate of the Church of Ireland by the name of John Nelson Darby. He was an old university friend of Bellett's, now working as an itinerant evangelist in the Wicklow mountains to the south. We shall hear more of him.

In the spring of 1827, Groves was accompanied to Dublin by Bessie Paget. Introduced to the drawing room meeting, she was pleased to find believers from various traditions gathered together, as in the days of the early church, for the study of the apostles' teaching, for fellowship and for prayer – though not yet, she noticed, for the *breaking of bread*.[8] Groves found his mind preoccupied with this very question. As they all held a common faith in Christ, why should they not remember him in bread and wine too, as he had commanded?[9] Afterwards John Bellett confided to Miss Paget something that must have delighted her: "Groves has just been telling me that it appeared to him from scripture that believers, meeting together as disciples of Christ, were free to break bread together as their Lord had admonished them; and that in as far as the practice of the apostles could be a guide, every Lord's Day should be set apart for thus remembering the Lord's death and obeying his parting command."[10]

This, as yet, was a step further than Bellett was willing to go. To his mind, Bible study and prayer could be enjoyed by Christians from any background meeting together wherever convenient, and Nonconformist friends such as Miss Paget were welcome to join them, but the Communion was a different matter – it was a sacrament to be administered by a priest in a consecrated church building. Groves did not press the point. He still considered himself a committed Anglican in any case and disapproved in general of Nonconformists. His convictions, however, were soon to be put to a most searching test.

On their return to England (in the early summer of 1827), Bessie Paget asked him if he would be willing to lead some Sunday evening meetings in the Devonshire village of Poltimore. She had procured a cottage where poor people could gather for instruction in the scriptures. But it was undoubtedly a meeting of Dissenters, and as a matter of principle he had "never yet gone near a dissenting place of worship."[11] What is more, he knew there was in Poltimore a parish church and a clergyman in charge. If he became a teacher of Nonconformists, in direct competition with the Church of England, the ensuing complaints would jeopardise his plans for ordination as an Anglican minister. But in his own words, "It worked on my mind till I could not but go; and I went… Yet I only allowed this going to Poltimore as a particular exception, in consequence of the notorious inadequacy of the clergyman there." It was only a cottage, after all, with just a handful of poor people, and he would do no more than explain a few verses from the word of God.

The time was drawing near for his next visit to Dublin when Norris Groves met a missionary recently returned from Calcutta, a Congregationalist by the name of Henry Townley. "Why are you wasting your time in going through college," asked Townley, "if you intend going to the East?" Ordination, Groves replied, would provide a degree of security. If forced to return from overseas sick or disabled, he could obtain a living as a clergyman somewhere in England. But in the back of his mind arose a nagging doubt. The kind of security to be found in ordination and a clerical appointment rode uncomfortably on the back of a call to forsake all and go to the uttermost parts, as though faith in God's faithfulness would not be sufficient. Groves was troubled: "As we walked home, Mary said, 'Don't you think there is great force in Mr Townley's question?'" Yes, there was great force in it, but not sufficient, he thought, to abandon his imminent trip. He had prepared thoroughly for the examination; the cost of the ferry to Dublin was already provided, the money put aside in a safe place. If he gave up his studies now, his previous year's work would be wasted, people would say he was fickle, and Mary's family would have further cause to doubt his sense and his character. The trip to Dublin must go ahead, and then nine months would pass before the next examination – ample time to review the matter. Mary was not convinced; these seemed worldly reasons rather than spiritual ones. But Norris dismissed her doubts: on Monday he would go.[12]

In the early hours of Sunday morning, they were wakened by a loud crash. Groves raced downstairs. In the dining room he found papers scattered about the floor, the little drawers of his writing desk broken open, the money gone.

Investigating more carefully, he discovered that the £40 reserved for his trip to Dublin had been taken; the £16 in a different drawer, set aside for taxes, remained untouched. Then, he tells us, "As I was returning up stairs, I met dearest Mary in the hall and said, 'Well, my love, the thieves have been here and taken all the money.' 'And now,' she said, 'you won't go to Dublin.' 'No,' I replied, 'that I won't.' And we spent one of the happiest Sundays I ever recollect, in thinking on the Lord's goodness in so caring for us as to stop our way up when he does not wish us to go. Some thought it right; others thought it foolish; it mattered not to us – we had not a doubt it was of the Lord."[13]

Groves received a visit at this time from a schoolmaster, William Hake, who was faced by "certain difficulties which involved leaving his wife and children penniless, so far as he knew, or following a course that his conscience disapproved."[14] Groves advised him to do what his conscience told him. Hake took his advice and a short time later called again, asking Groves rather pointedly if he believed war to be inherently wrong. Groves agreed that fighting was not something a Christian should do. In that case, asked Hake, how could Groves seek ordination as an Anglican clergyman? How could he sign his name to the Thirty-nine Articles of the Church of England when one of them stated: "It is lawful for Christian men, at the commandment of the Magistrate, to wear weapons and serve in the wars"? Groves was taken aback: "It had, till that moment, never occurred to me. I read it, and replied, 'I never would sign it.'"[15] So, in the summer of 1827, at the age of thirty-two, Norris Groves finally withdrew from Trinity College and abandoned his plans to become an Anglican clergyman.

He still, however, considered himself an Anglican, and he still had his heart set on missionary service. He went up to London to ask the committee of the CMS if they might allow him to go overseas as a layman. They replied that he certainly could do so but would not be permitted to celebrate the Lord's Supper without the presence of an ordained minister. This, to his mind, was a formidable stumbling block. Where in Persia would he find a clergyman to officiate at Communion? If the Church of England could offer no more than this, perhaps he should think of becoming a Nonconformist minister. In his own words, "I... felt some ordination to be necessary, but hated the thought of being made a sectarian." Then suddenly, "the thought was brought to my mind that ordination of any kind to preach the gospel is no requirement of scripture. To me it was the removal of a mountain." He hastened to find his wife: "I told dearest Mary my discovery and my joy." To her, it was already quite obvious; she could not think what all the fuss was about: "Indeed, she had received the truth in such power that she seemed only to desire to *know* the mind of God that she might fulfil it." From then on, without the authorisation or support of any denomination, he would preach wherever the Lord led him, and take the Lord's Supper with any who loved Christ.[16]

Returning for a farewell visit to Dublin towards the end of 1828, Groves found Bellett still hesitant to do anything that would offend his friends and relations in the Church of Ireland. Christians of every denomination, thought Bellett, might pray and study the scriptures together, but surely an ordained minister was required to shepherd the flock and minister the sacraments. Yet there was a certain logic to Groves's argument, and an evident blessing when Groves himself preached by invitation in some of the Nonconformist chapels of the city. Then, as they walked together down Lower Pembroke Street, Groves turned to his friend and said, "This, I doubt not, is the mind of God concerning us, that we should come together in all simplicity as disciples, not waiting on any pulpit or minister, but trusting that the Lord would edify us together, by ministering as he pleased and saw good from the midst of ourselves." This was a turning point for Bellett: "At the moment he spoke these words, I was assured my soul had got the right idea, and that moment – I remember it as if it were yesterday, and could point you out the place – it was the birth place of my mind... as a Brother."[17] They would meet simply as a company of disciples, to share together in the apostles' teaching, fellowship, prayer and breaking of bread, without ministers, sacraments or rules of any kind.

Shortly after this, Bellett's group combined with two others in Dublin. One had gathered around an obstinate young man with side whiskers and spectacles by the name of Edward Cronin. Recently converted from Roman Catholicism, Cronin "had not been deterred from following his convictions, even though an episcopal fist had promptly knocked him down on the spot upon being found reading a Protestant version of the scriptures."[18] On account of his health he had come several times to Dublin from the south of Ireland, and when visiting the city had attended several Congregationalist churches, all of which made him welcome at Communion. Eventually he started a course of study as a medical student, and hearing that he was now permanently resident in Dublin they advised him to apply for membership in one or other of the churches. Seeing his reluctance, they informed him he would not be allowed to partake of Communion until he did so. This troubled him, for obtaining membership in any one of the churches would mean disclaiming membership in each of the others. By devoting himself exclusively to one group of Christians, he must withdraw from others to whom he felt equally attached. The upshot was that he refused to apply for membership in any of them, stating his view that "the Church of God was one, and that all who believed were members of that one Body."[19] At the same time he had what he called "a growing feeling of opposition to one-man ministry", and ceasing to attend any place of worship he "spent many a Lord's Day morning under a tree or haystack during the time of their service." But he was not entirely alone. There were others in the Congregationalist churches who had much sympathy with Cronin's position – among them Edward Wilson, Assistant Secretary of the Bible Society in

Dublin. Before long a small group had started to meet with him "for breaking of bread and prayer" in the back parlour of Cronin's house. By November 1829, Bellett, Cronin, Darby and another friend, Francis Hutchinson, had started meeting regularly to "break bread" at Hutchinson's rather larger dwelling in Fitzwilliam Square.[20]

The third group involved three friends who enjoyed close fellowship in Christian work during the week but went their separate ways on Sundays. Two were Anglicans, the other a Baptist. Neither in the Anglican nor in the Baptist church could they remember their Lord together in bread and wine, despite their common faith and happy fellowship in Christian service. Eventually they decided, in token of their unity in Christ, to meet in one of their homes and celebrate the Lord's Supper together.[21] So blessed was this hour of worship that they began to meet regularly and before long others, both men and women, were added to their number. Their meetings were deliberately informal, like those described in the New Testament: "When you meet for worship, one person has a hymn, another a teaching, another a revelation from God... Everything must be of help to the church... All of you may proclaim God's message, one by one, so that everyone will learn and be encouraged."[22] Indeed they found, as in the days of the apostles, that "the Spirit's presence is shown in some way in each person for the good of all... But it is one and the same Spirit who does all this; as he wishes, he gives a different gift to each person."[23]

One of the three friends was John Vesey Parnell, son and heir of the first Baron Congleton. Born in Baker Street, London, almost a hundred years before Conan Doyle installed Sherlock Holmes in number 221B, John Parnell had no evangelical upbringing, although his aristocratic mother taught him to say his prayers morning and evening, and his uncle had earnest Christian friends both Anglican and Nonconformist.[24] As an undergraduate at Edinburgh University, dissatisfied by the endless round of balls and parties, Parnell had felt a longing to know God. A friend advised him that if he wished to know God he should study Paul's Letter to the Romans, for that was the subject of the Letter. In order to grasp exactly what the text said, Parnell decided to copy out the whole of it by hand. At the eighth verse of the eighth chapter he came to the words, "So they that are in the flesh *cannot please God.*" That is exactly my problem, he thought, and what is the solution? Then came the realisation, "I cannot please God, *but Jesus can.*" And this was followed by the assurance, "God receives sinners *for Jesus' sake*, and he will receive *me.*"[25]

The baron was greatly displeased to hear that his son had become an evangelical Christian, and immediately procured for him an army commission, no doubt hoping that the excitements of military life would displace his religious interests. John replied that, though he wished to obey his father in all personal matters, he could obey only God when it came to the things of God. His father realised that obeying God would make it difficult for a young man to achieve distinction as a military officer, and to John's great relief he annulled the commission and granted him a small allowance with freedom to make his own way in life. The Honourable John Parnell, heir to the baronetcy of Congleton, then began to preach to passers-by in the open air like any common labouring man, cheerfully accepting ribald comment and buckets of water over his head and his Bible. Shortly afterwards, inheriting a substantial property from an uncle, he found he could live quite comfortably from the rents received from his tenants. Into his hands at this time there came a small booklet with the title *Christian Devotedness*. So sound and convincing was its message that he there and then dedicated all he had to the work of God. His income he now called "the Lord's money". He saw it as "a trust committed to him, and to be used only as he who gave it might indicate."[26]

It was John Parnell, still aged only twenty-five, who eventually drew the three Dublin fellowships together. Up to this point their gatherings had attracted intellectuals – university men, medics, lawyers and clergy – to beautifully furnished homes in the nicer parts of town. But in May 1830 Parnell rented a large auction room in Aungier Street. This, they hoped, would be less intimidating for the poorer people of the city, and here they started to meet every Lord's Day.[27]

So it was that leaders of outstanding intellectual and spiritual calibre were drawn together in one city at one time – wealthy, fashionable, educated, and sufficiently confident to challenge traditional religious assumptions. These were the tentative beginnings of "a movement that looked to the Bible, and the Bible alone, for the solution of the ecclesiastical and religious problems of the day."[28] There was an air of excitement about the new venture. The watercolour artist William Collingwood later described what John Parnell told him about the earliest days: "The chief aim was to exhibit, in a scriptural way, *the common brotherhood of all believers*. They recognised no special membership. That they belonged to Christ was the only term of communion; that they loved one another was the power of their fellowship. In principle, it embraced all whose faith and walk showed that they had spiritual life; in practice, all such of these as would avail themselves of it. This ideal could be attained only by a return to the absolute simplicity of the apostolic model as found in the New Testament. To bring in anything of a contentious character would defeat it. There must be nothing that human tradition had introduced to divide God's people. None must be stumbled or grieved by the presence of what was not clearly and strictly scriptural."[29]

Looking back on those days, Edward Cronin fondly recalled, "Oh the blessed seasons to my soul, with John Parnell, William Stokes and others, while moving the furniture aside and laying the simple table with its bread and wine on Saturday evenings – seasons of joy never to be forgotten – for surely we had the Master's smile and sanction in the beginning of such a movement as this was!"[30]

ENDNOTES

[1] M288

[2] M38

[3] In his youth Craik had been a Presbyterian associated with the "established" Church of Scotland. Early in 1826, attending the General Assembly of the Church of Scotland, he had become disillusioned and his sympathies shifted towards Baptist nonconformity. Whilst acting as tutor at Northernhay his spare time was given to detailed linguistic analysis of the Greek New Testament and to advanced study of biblical Hebrew. He preached regularly in a schoolroom at Heavitree, and at Bessie Paget's cottage meeting in Poltimore (Rowdon, *Origins*, 111-113).

[4] M38

[5] Harrison, 24, 28. It was not until 1921 that Ireland would be divided politically into "independent" Eire (the Irish Republic) and "loyal" Ulster (Northern Ireland, remaining an integral part of the United Kingdom). At the period we are studying, the Church of Ireland was the "established" church, equivalent to the Church of England; it had its own bishops subject to the authority of the British parliament. But the almost universal loyalty of the populace to Roman Catholicism meant that the Irish had never considered themselves members of the Established Church in the way that was customary to the people of mainland Britain. The problem came to a head in the late 1820s when the Irish bishops required converts from Roman Catholicism to swear allegiance to the British Crown, recognising the King of England as "Supreme Governor of the Church". At a stroke this made conversion to Christ a political act. Many, such as John Nelson Darby, who at that time was still an Establishment clergyman, were appalled at the stifling effect this would have on their preaching of the gospel among the Irish Catholics (Stunt, *Awakening*, 171, 277).

[6] The British and Foreign Bible Society (BFBS) was often simply called "the Bible Society". In 1827 the Assistant Secretary of the Scripture Readers Society in Dublin was Edward Cronin (Stunt, *Awakening*, 178).

[7] M20

[8] Acts 2:42

[9] Lk 22:19; 1 Cor 11:23-26

[10] M39. See Acts 20:7.

[11] M40

[12] M41. A chronology of events, reconstructed from the *Memoir* and from extant letters and minutes, appears in Appendix iv of this book.

[13] M41-42. This took place on Sunday 21st October 1827 and was reported in a local newspaper: "The house of Mr Groves, dentist, at Northernhay was entered by thieves, between the hours of 3 and 4 o'clock on Sunday morning, and robbed of bank notes and cash to the amount of between 50*l*. and 60*l*. This daring act was effected by scaling the outer wall, and entering the house by the parlour window; two candles on the table were lit by the thieves, and the *Secretaire* broken open. A paper containing cash to the amount of 7*l*. put aside for a particular use escaped the search of the depredators, who deliberately selected from a small box the silver it contained, leaving the copper as unworthy of their notice. In proceeding into the

interior of the house, they knocked down a hat-horse, and this (as they appear to have suspected) alarmed the inmates, who on coming down stairs found the robbers had decamped." (*Exeter Flying Post*, 24th Oct. 1827 p.4. See also *Salisbury and Winchester Journal*, 29th Oct. 1827.)

Seventeen months later a local newspaper reported the arrest and trial of a tailor by the name of Thomas Salter, on a charge of theft. He was a married man with several young children. "The officer declared that on going to his house to apprehend him they had never seen such a scene of wretchedness... whilst nothing worthy of the name of a bed or furniture was in the house." As the magistrates questioned the accused, "Mr Groves, dentist, on whom he had committed the theft, declared he would not proceed against a fellow creature in such distress, and instantly tendered him pecuniary aid, the Magistrates and others present doing the same" (*Exeter Flying Post*, 19 Mar 1829 p.3). Hanging was the statutory penalty for burglary and theft from a dwelling house, and would remain so until 1837. I am grateful to Timothy Stunt for this marvellous illustration of Norris Groves's character and also of his personal influence on others.

[14] M41. Hake's scruples about dishonest practices had earlier led to his withdrawal from his employment with an Exeter draper (Groves E K, *Successors*, 370).

[15] M41

[16] M42

[17] That is to say, as one identified with the Brethren (Bellett, *Interesting Reminiscences*, 4-5).

[18] Bromley, 40

[19] *Interesting Reminiscences*, 15-16. If experience elsewhere can be a guide, it might also involve a promise not to partake of Communion with friends from other denominations. In many places, the whole system of formal membership had been corrupted by the tendency of Nonconformist deacons to accept wealthy men as "members" without any token of their conversion to Christ (Groves E K, *Successors*, 184).

[20] *Interesting Reminiscences*, 16-17. Hutchinson, who had preferred a fixed order of service, died in 1833.

[21] Collingwood, 5-6

[22] 1 Cor 14:26, 31 GNB

[23] 1 Cor 12:7, 11 GNB

[24] John Parnell was nephew to the evangelist Thomas Parnell (often called "Tract Parnell") and cousin to the Irish nationalist Charles Stewart Parnell.

[25] Groves H, *Congleton*, 10

[26] *Congleton*, 24

[27] *Interesting Reminiscences*, 6

[28] Rowdon, *Origins*, 37

[29] Collingwood, 9. William Collingwood was the father of the more famous artist W G Collingwood.

[30] *Interesting Reminiscences*, 17

"We are ready to go anywhere."

Mary Groves [1]

5

A Strange Dilemma

As the prospect of Persia opened up before Norris and Mary Groves, the time had come to share their plans with their wider family, and especially with Mary's parents. So far, the sacrifices had been all their own. Now they would be asking others to sacrifice – to let their children and grandchildren sail into the unknown without any sure prospect of seeing them again. Mr and Mrs Thompson were distraught at the news. Their "wounded affections and disappointed hopes" were hard for their daughter and her husband to bear. But harsher means were then tried; relations became quite strained. Mr Thompson declared that Mary would inherit nothing from him. He then wrote alluding to the thousand pounds still owed him by Norris's father. This hurt Norris deeply. It was not his debt, but he wrote back saying he would never leave England until he had personally paid every penny.[2]

This put them in a serious predicament. Having given away so much, they did not have a thousand pounds to send. Indeed, it could take several years to accumulate that amount, especially as they were committed to supporting a number of poor people on their present income. And that income itself was dwindling, for people had heard the dentist was leaving and so turned elsewhere for dental care. Mary was forced to make further economies in the housekeeping simply to meet their expenses.

Where was God in all this? Long years had already passed since the first call to missionary service, and faced by yet another unforeseen frustration Norris lost all appetite for food. It "set me almost as far as ever from the hope of leaving," he said, "except..." – and this made all the difference – "except that dear Mary was on my side. And by so much as she had hindered me in the first years of our marriage, by so much the more did she now encourage me, and kept up my heart which was almost bowed down." Indeed, so determined was Mary, that her parents said she was even worse than her husband. Groves commented, "Indeed, she was just so much the *better* as she appeared to the natural eye worse."[3]

Time passed, and with hard work and frugal expenditure, the first hundred of the thousand pounds were scraped together and sent to Mr Thompson. A few weeks after this, however, news came to the Groves household which suddenly changed the whole picture: Mary's father had died quite unexpectedly. It was April 1827. She left immediately to join the rest of her family in Fulham. Norris, all too aware of the tensions that had come between them, felt he would be unwelcome at such a time, and stayed in Exeter. On Mary's arrival, however, word was sent, asking him to come immediately. When he reached them, he learned that Mr Thompson had drawn up a new will two or three days before his death. Mary was to receive her share of the inheritance after all, amounting probably to more than £10,000,[4] and the thousand pounds was signed over to Norris as a gift. Even the hundred pounds he had sent was returned to him. There was now no financial constraint, nothing to hold them back: they could go to Persia! Yet, just as this dawned on them, the family began to assail them with every argument, "offering all that love could offer" to make them change their mind. "The Lord gave us strength," said Norris, "and we overcame this last trial, simply saying that if there had been a human being living to whom we could have yielded when the Lord said 'Go!' it would have been him [i.e. Mr Thompson] who was gone. They felt its force and kindly desisted. We then felt that the Lord had indeed not only rolled difficulties out of our way, but had turned those very difficulties into the means of enabling us to go more happily."[5]

It was time to loosen their last remaining home ties. In January 1828 Norris sold his leasehold on Northernhay House and gave the dental practice to his young relative, John Groves, accepting nothing in return.[6] The family went to live with Bessie and Charlotte Paget. Their troubles, however, were far from over. It was little Mary, now five years old, who worried them. "She was a very lively child, and though the youngest in the family, quite took a lead with her brothers."[7] But her health had never been robust, and at this very time it seemed her strength was failing. The decision was made to spend some days in the nearby village of Exmouth, where the sea breezes might prove more healthy. But little Mary came back from the seaside no better at all. Could they take her to the East in such a delicate state? Plans must be shelved until she was well enough to travel. But then, Groves tells us, "The Lord decided this also. He ripened her, as the first ripe fruit, and took her to 'wait in hope of a better resurrection.'"[8]

For just over a year, Norris and Mary Groves, with young Henry and Frank, stayed in the Exeter home of the Paget sisters. Here Groves had much time to pray and read the Bible and prepare himself for work overseas. Every morning he shared his thoughts from the scriptures with the household and with seven Christian families who lived in small cottages belonging to Bessie and Charlotte. It was a time of great blessing, and to both Norris and Mary "the loss of their only daughter was used of God as a means by which they became yet more separate from earth, and while it made their path clear, it strengthened them to devote themselves to God." The fragile loves and fleeting hopes of a fallen world seemed bathed in the light of eternity. A friend present at that time tells us that, "could she have obtained the consent of her only remaining parent, she would gladly have formed one of their missionary party – so precious and glorious a thing did it seem to forsake all for Jesus."[9]

Poring over the pages of his Bible, Groves grew increasingly convinced that the key to all blessing lay simply in discerning the will of God and following it. And the will of God was shown, as clear as day, in the pages of scripture, where holy men had been led by his Spirit to record for posterity the principles they received from him. The New Testament showed exactly how the apostles of Christ had been led by the Spirit of God, and it showed how wonderfully they had been blessed. From this time onwards it became the settled pattern of his life, to "search out the mind of the Lord" from the scriptures, to rediscover "the faith that was once for all entrusted to the saints," to know the mystery "revealed by the Spirit to God's holy apostles and prophets."[10] It meant setting aside human customs, traditions and expectations – as though eighteen hundred years of Christian history had never happened – in order to do exactly what the disciples of Jesus had done.

In the New Testament Groves saw adult believers baptised by immersion as an expression of their personal faith in Christ. And so the realisation came that he must, as an adult believer, be baptised by immersion. This was a radical step for a public figure who had already been "baptised" as an infant; it was reported in the local newspaper and became a topic of widespread comment. He told how a Baptist minister, the following day, crossed the street to greet him as a brother Baptist. A brother he agreed to be, but not a Baptist. Another friend enquired, "Of course, you must be a Baptist now you are baptised." Not at all! he replied. "I desire to follow *all* in those things in which they follow Christ, but I would not, by joining one party, cut myself off from others." His baptism, he insisted, was not into a denomination or into a church, but into Christ. "Then taking up the ring on which his keys hung, he said, 'If these keys were to hold by one another, all would go if one fell. But as each of them is attached to this strong ring, so should we each take hold of Christ, not of any of the systems of men, and then we shall be safe and united. We should keep together, not because of any human system, but because Jesus is *one*.'"[11]

His friends were perplexed. He was no longer an Anglican, and he refused to be considered a Baptist; what denomination, then, did he belong to? He was content, as he was throughout his life, to be known simply as a Christian: "My full persuasion is that, inasmuch as any one glories either in being of the Church of England, Scotland, Baptist, Independent, Wesleyan etc., his glory is his shame... For as the apostle said, were any of them crucified for you? The only legitimate ground for glorying is that we are among the ransomed of the Lord by his grace."[12]

One of his closest friends, a young curate named William Caldecott, reproached him for leaving the Established Church and thus causing further division in the body of Christ. "You say I quitted *your* communion," replied Groves. "If you mean, by that, that I do not now break bread with the Church of England, this is not true. But if you mean that I do not *exclusively* join you, it is quite true, feeling this spirit of exclusiveness to be of the very essence of schism, which the apostle so strongly reproves in the Corinthians."[13] Although a Christian does not *belong* to Paul or Apollos or Cephas, he can surely enjoy fellowship with each of them: "I therefore know no distinction, but am ready to break the bread and drink the cup of holy joy with all who love the Lord and will not lightly speak evil of his name. I feel every saint to be a holy person because Christ dwells in him and manifests himself where he worships, and though his faults be as many as the hairs of his head, my duty still is, with my Lord, to join him as a member of the mystical body and to hold communion and fellowship with him in any work of the Lord in which he may be engaged."[14]

But how could someone aspire to be a missionary, asked Caldecott, without belonging to any denomination? How could he preach if not ordained or authorised by any church? Was it not presumptuous to appoint himself, on his own authority, a teacher of God's word? "I trust not," replied Groves, "for if I am, the work will come to nought. I trust I exercise it on the nomination of my Lord by his Spirit… If you can point out any other nomination as necessary, or that there are any persons excluded until they are appointed by man, I hope I am willing to weigh the evidence you bring."[15]

Groves had searched the scriptures on this very point. He could see no separation there between clergy and laity, no trace of a system whereby one man would be the "minister" and the others pay for his services. The practice of "ordination" at the hands of a bishop seemed both unscriptural and unhealthy, a distortion of God's original design. It perpetuated the notion that the incumbent received his authority from men rather than from the Holy Spirit, that he would be bound by the requirements of a human institution rather than of God, that he represented and served a denomination rather than the whole Church of Christ. And the entire scheme had been discredited in Groves's eyes by the common experience of ordained men who knew less of faith and godliness than their most illiterate parishioners.[16]

Yet Norris Groves did not enjoy conflict. He did not like upsetting people. Just as it was painful, in certain respects, for him to publish his booklet on *Christian Devotedness*, knowing that some would dislike him for it, he found it equally difficult when friends turned from him on account of his views concerning Christian ministry. He tried to speak kindly and patiently to any who questioned and confronted him, but like the apostle in similar circumstances, he believed his ultimate aim must be to please God, not man.[17] And he was willing to pay the price. "For the mystical body of Christ, my prayer is that I may very gladly spend and be spent," he said, "even though the more abundantly I love, the less I be loved."[18]

Despite his resignation from the CMS, despite the financial setbacks, the personal loss, the family opposition, the alienation of friends, Norris Groves had not wavered in his missionary purpose. Nor had he lost interest in Persia, a place still waiting to hear the true gospel of Christ, a place for which, Mr Bickersteth told him, "they had for years endeavoured, but without success, to obtain a missionary."[19] It was all part of God's training for a man called to do what had never been done before. Looking back over months gone by, Groves could give thanks for everything. He was glad they had not gone to America – a door which had closed, like that of Bithynia to the apostle Paul, no doubt to redirect them to a place of greater need. "There are so many secular advantages in Ohio that many may be expected to go there," he said, "whereas few, very few, will feel themselves able to go to Persia."[20]

Persia was a challenge which appealed to the romantic in Groves. The home of Turks, Jews, Armenians and Arabs as well as Persians, the hardest place and the place of greatest need: certainly a heroic choice, but was it *the Lord's* choice? Mary's was the quieter faith of one not naturally brave or heroic. But her husband knew the secret of her strength: "I never heard a soul breathe a more simple, firm and unostentatious faith in God. She never had a doubt but that it was for the Lord she left all that was naturally dear to her, to expose herself to dangers from which, with a constitutional timidity, she shrunk [*sic*]."[21] Seeking the mind of the Lord, doing his perfect will, they could trust him for his blessing and protection. Without ordination, denomination, salary or human security, they would go to Persia – husband, wife and two little boys. Faith in God: that was all they would need.

ENDNOTES

[1] M32

[2] M2. His father was still alive, and would remain so for a further eight years. We know nothing more about the personal circumstances of Mr Anthony Groves senior, beyond the fact that he died in Bristol on 22nd June 1835 (Müller, *Narrative*, I, 137).

[3] M33-34

[4] M32

[5] M34

[6] John Groves relocated the dental practice to Bedford Circus, nearer the city centre. From July 1828 until 1834, Northernhay House was home to William Hake's preparatory boarding school. During the 125 years of its existence, the property was occupied by two Mayors, three wine merchants, a Member of Parliament, a

brewer, a dentist, a doctor and two schools. After becoming very dilapidated it was finally demolished in 1914 (Cornforth, "Exeter Memories").

[7] M529

[8] M34. In a letter he wrote, "Our dear sweet little Mary is gone to glory; a little fragrant apple from the Beloved's garden below, taken to shed its fragrance above" (M49).

[9] M35. The "friend" was Harriet Baynes who recalled the incident thirty years later.

[10] Jude 3; Eph 3:5

[11] M36. The exact location of Groves's baptism as an adult is not known.

[12] M49

[13] 1 Cor 1:10-13; 3:1-9

[14] M48

[15] M48-49

[16] The social and religious condition of England at this period is discussed in Appendix i of this book.

[17] 1 Thess 2:4

[18] M49

[19] M50

[20] M20

[21] R170

"I think it
not only a great loss of present comfort
but a great sin
not to trust God's promises."

Norris Groves [1]

6

A New Way of Living

The booklet *Christian Devotedness* lacks all the literary graces. Norris Groves was not a great writer, and this was his first serious attempt to put his thoughts publicly into print. Yet unlike many a more talented author, he had something to say that was both fresh and practical. So radical, indeed, and so persuasive, were the ideas presented in these twenty-eight small pages that their publication would mark a turning point in the history of Christian missions.

It was in a rare moment of leisure that Groves picked up his goose-feather pen and plied it as a man with a burden to impart: "The writer of the following pages has been deeply affected by the consideration of the strange and melancholy fact – that Christianity has made little or no progress for fifteen successive centuries." Why, he asks, is the gospel not winning souls from heathen darkness and gathering men and women out of every tribe, nation and tongue as in the days of the apostles and their successors? What is the difference between then and now? The difference is not hard to discern. The early Christians loved their Saviour and loved each other, and their love is shown in all they said and did. They gave themselves, their time, their property, their talents to Christ their Lord, and they laid down their very lives for their brothers. And if we were to love as they did, suggested Groves, perhaps we would see in our day what they saw in theirs.

The early church knew poverty first hand. It was not wealthy; it had no ample resources to finance the advance of the gospel throughout the world. Jesus himself grew up as a poor boy in a poor family in a poor country: "For you know the grace of our Lord Jesus Christ, that though he was rich, yet for your sakes *he became poor*."[2] His followers, too, were poor men who had given up their jobs – literally forsaken all – and had learnt to pray each day for their daily bread. One might think poverty a hardship, but neither Jesus nor his disciples saw it that way. "Blessed are you who are poor," said Christ, "for yours is the kingdom of God."[3] The poor are compelled by their circumstances to pray, to trust, to depend on God, and this is surely the happiest of all conditions to be in.

The rich man, in contrast, has all he needs. Well able to provide for himself, he has no need to depend on a Heavenly Father. "How hard it is for the rich to enter the kingdom of God," said Jesus, for "no one can serve two masters... You cannot serve both God and Money."⁴ Many are those, indeed, who lose their soul as they fill their barns. "Be on your guard," said Jesus, "against all kinds of greed; a man's life does not consist in the abundance of his possessions."⁵ The earning of money, the borrowing of money, the spending of money, the investment of money: all this business with money, and so much of it concerned for future security! "O you of little faith!"⁶ "I tell you, do not worry about your life, what you will eat or drink; or about your body, what you will wear. Is not life more important than food, and the body more important than clothes?... So do not worry, saying, 'What shall we eat?' or 'What shall we drink?' or 'What shall we wear?' For the pagans run after all these things, and your heavenly Father knows that you need them. But seek first his kingdom and his righteousness, and all these things will be given to you as well."⁷ And then Jesus gives the simplest and gentlest of instructions. "Sell your possessions and give to the poor. Provide purses for yourselves that will not wear out, a treasure in heaven that will not be exhausted, where no thief comes near and no moth destroys. For where your treasure is, there your heart will be also."⁸

This was not guaranteed to be a popular message. Few would dare to preach it from any modern pulpit, and its very novelty inclines the hearer to suspect it. Sell your possessions indeed! A critic might allege that the words of Jesus are not to be taken literally; they were, perhaps, deliberately exaggerated in order to produce an effect. So then, says Groves, let us see how our Lord and his disciples understood what he said. Did they take his words literally or not?

When a young man came enquiring what good thing he must do to inherit eternal life, Jesus mentioned several duties that he had already fulfilled, then added, "You still lack one thing. Sell everything you have and give to the poor, and you will have treasure in heaven. Then come, follow me."⁹ Did the young man take this to be an exaggerated sentiment, an ideal with no practical application? No, he took it literally and "went away sad, because he had great wealth."¹⁰ And now, said Groves, we learn the true lesson of this encounter – not that riches were a snare merely to this particular man, as some might think, but a snare to any one of us. For Jesus immediately says, "It is easier for a camel to go through the eye of a needle than for a rich man to enter the kingdom of God." Peter, hearing this, had no doubt about his meaning, for he confessed, "We have left all we had to follow you." In fact he and his fellow fishermen had forsaken their home, work, family, possessions, comforts, leisure and privacy. They had taken their Master's words literally and given up all they had in order to serve him.¹¹

But surely, someone will object, only the Twelve were called to do this. In reply, Groves points to the poor widow who put into the temple treasury "two very small copper coins... She, out of her poverty, put in everything – *all she had to live on.*"[12] How foolish! the critic would think. And Groves agrees: "In the world's estimation nothing could be more improvident or more improper than her conduct, and I fear that few of us would have the heart to commend one who should go and do likewise. But how does our blessed Lord judge, who judges not according to appearance but righteous judgment? Observing that she acts quite according to his precept of giving up all, he does not call his disciples round him to warn them by her example not to take his words literally... but on the contrary, points out carefully the peculiarity and unequalled greatness of her sacrifice, and holds her up to admiration on account of it."[13]

But might we not say that this principle of "forsaking all" was just a temporary arrangement, suited to three short years of itinerant ministry in Galilee and Judea, then afterwards abandoned? Groves thought not. After the ascension of Christ, we observe the disciples in Jerusalem. "Selling their possessions and goods, they gave to anyone as he had need... All the believers were one in heart and mind. No one claimed that any of his possessions was his own, but they shared everything they had... There were no needy persons among them. For from time to time those who owned lands or houses sold them, brought the money from the sales and put it at the apostles' feet, and it was distributed to anyone as he had need."[14] And yet, we might wonder, was this not merely an experiment attempted by the Jerusalem church, found impracticable and later discontinued? Why so? asks Groves. "By what arguments can it be shown that such a 'union of heart and soul' as is here described is not just as important to us now as it was to the primitive Christians? If this community of hearts and possessions was according to the mind of the Spirit then, why not now?"[15]

The pattern is consistent. We have our Lord's teaching; we have his example; we have his instructions to the young man; we have his commendation of the widow; we have the example of his disciples; and now we have that of the whole Christian community in Jerusalem. Do they not speak with one voice that we should sell what we have, give to those in greater need and trust God for our daily bread? And all this before we have yet considered the great missionary apostle who could describe himself as "poor yet making many rich; having nothing and yet possessing everything."[16] All, from beginning to end, offer the same testimony, set the same example; and all saw the same wonderful results. "Their overflowing joy and their extreme poverty welled up in rich generosity."[17]

Having taught this, Jesus gave further guidance to his disciples. He said, "Go into all the world and preach the good news to all creation."[18] This, Groves observed, was "the parting command of our blessed Saviour", and because the apostles took it literally we in Britain have heard the gospel, though living so far from the place of its birth. "Had there been the same doubt of the meaning and obligation of this precept in the infancy of Christianity which these last ages have exhibited, it would scarcely have extended its influence beyond the confines of Judea."[19] In fact the apostles believed the gospel to be "the power of God for the salvation of everyone who believes"; they considered all things rubbish in comparison with the call to know Christ and make him known.[20]

Why then, asked Groves, "Why has this spirit for so many centuries been slumbering? Because men have been seeking every one his own things and not the things of Christ… Those who are surrounded by the cares and comforts of this world have so many earthly claims and relations to adjust that the general result will be that of standing still, and the enquiry 'Who will go for us?' will sound unwelcome to the ear, will chill, not animate, the noblest sympathies of the heart, and set the seal of silence on the lips."[21] Why are there still millions who have never heard there is a God who loves them, that there is a Saviour who died for them, that there is life beyond the grave? They have never heard because no one has gone to tell them. And why has no one gone? Because few are willing to give up their wealth, their pleasure, their comfort, and their human security. "Oh! If every one who believed himself ransomed by the precious blood of Christ felt himself so entirely the purchased possession of him who thus so dearly bought him, as to determine henceforth to know nothing save Jesus Christ and him crucified, not to labour for anything but that the unspeakably glad tidings of salvation through him might be spread throughout the world…, how soon would the wants of the whole habitable earth be answered by thousands crying out 'Here am I, send me', while those sheep to whom the glad tidings would be borne would discern the Shepherd's voice, receive with thankfulness such messengers of peace, seeing by their fruits 'that God was in them of a truth.'"[22]

This, then, is the message of *Christian Devotedness*. The remainder of the booklet is given to answering the objections that Groves knew would be raised against it. Does someone protest, for example, saying: That was a special time with special circumstances; those were special men with a special calling? Perhaps indeed that was a special time, admitted Groves, but is not *this* also a special time? Indeed, is not every age a special time? "Is there in the holy scriptures any limitation as to the *time* when the love which distinguished the primitive church was to be in exercise?"[23] Are the days gone when disciples of Christ might gladly take up their cross and follow him?

But if we cast aside our financial security in order to live "by faith" – if we give all we have to the work of God, or if we go ourselves as missionaries of the gospel – how can we be sure our future needs will be met? In reply Groves points to all the promises of God. Our Father has said, "I will never fail you or forsake you," so we can respond with confidence, declaring, "The Lord is my helper; I will not be afraid."[24] And then, "Which of you, if his son asks for bread, will give him a stone? Or if he asks for a fish, will give him a snake? If you, then, though you are evil, know how to give good gifts to your children, how much more will your Father in Heaven give good gifts to those who ask him!"[25] How did Jesus himself provide for his widowed mother? He left her poor, and in the care of a poor man – a man who could say, like his companion, "Silver and gold have I none"[26] – but he left her knowing that there is one in heaven who "sustains the fatherless and the widow."[27] Whatever our condition we may safely entrust ourselves to the care of him who loved us and gave himself for us. "So intensely am I convinced of this truth," said Groves, "that I can with my whole heart pray for myself and all who are nearest and dearest to me that we be so circumstanced in life as to be compelled to live by faith on the divine promises day by day."[28]

But what about the future needs of our children? Norris Groves, of course, lived in an age of incurable diseases and many business failures; there was no health service or social security to support the unfortunate. It was considered part of a father's responsibility that he should lay up sufficient in savings and property to guarantee a home and a small income for his dependants in the event of his death. Many, however, would not rest until they had amassed a large fortune for their heirs. "All our misconceptions on this subject," said Groves, "seem to arise from one deeply-rooted opinion, learnt of Satan and the world over which he presides: that riches and comforts are better for our children than poverty and dependence. The whole tenor of the New Testament, however, pronounces the opinion to be false."[29]

What, then, will be best for our children? Christian parents will wish, above all, for their children to become followers of Christ. And how may they help them to do so? Surely by following Christ themselves – by showing that his word can be trusted, that the dedication of time, abilities and resources to his service brings happiness beyond any to be found in the luxurious pleasures of the world. Can we expect *them* to trust in God when *our own* trust is in extensive property and industrial investments? Can we expect *them* to believe "there is no other name under heaven given to men by which we must be saved" if *we* live as though the world had no need to hear that name? Can we expect *them* to believe in the love of God when *our own* selfish hearts are hardened against our neighbours? The widow's two coins placed in the treasury would have left her family in no doubt that her faith in God was a real faith.

But what if our children should find themselves in need? Surely, replied Groves, God who provides for us will provide for them. If his "good and acceptable and perfect will" includes times when they have little, he will make that a means of blessing to them; indeed, it was a course he chose for his own beloved Son.[30] In time of need, walking by faith, our children will grow in patience, in wisdom and in love; they will seek all the more to please God, to trust his promises; they will pray and see answers to prayer. And if other Christians are led of necessity to care for the fatherless in their affliction it will be no more than is required by the word of God.[31] But even if we could leave our children great riches, we could not guarantee their comfort in a world where thieves break in, where moth and rust destroy, where fortunes may be lost overnight, where sickness and death sweep away the rich as easily as the poor. True security is found not in the promise of a large inheritance but in the assurance of a Father's love. This is what we are called to pass on to our children.

These scriptural principles, said Groves, are so clear that they hardly need explanation. The problem is not in understanding what Jesus said or what the early Christians did. The problem lies in our fallen human nature which hates and fears these ideas, and will do all it can to suppress them. How blind, indeed, is a man who prefers bondage to freedom! "Surely it is a most unspeakable privilege to be allowed to cast all our cares upon God, and to feel that we are thereby delivered from the slavery of earthly expectations." No longer worried lest a benefactor or church or business take offence and cut us off, we can speak the truth in love without fear of man. No longer tempted, when seeking spiritual guidance, by financial considerations; no longer concerned that accident or sickness or commercial failure will leave us destitute. "What is the 'glorious liberty of the children of God' but to be dependent only upon one 'who giveth liberally and upbraideth not', who says 'Ask and ye shall receive'?"[32] Living by faith sets us free to walk with God.

Resolving, then, to be "good stewards of God's varied grace", we have the joy of passing on God's perfect gifts to others.[33] "May I not appeal," said Groves, "to any who have experienced the joy of knowing the unspeakable gift of God, and ask: Would you exchange this knowledge, with all the comforts and blessings it has been the means of imparting, for a hundred worlds, were they offered? Let us not then withhold the means by which others may obtain this sanctifying knowledge and heavenly consolation."[34] Loving our neighbours as ourselves, we see them supplied with the necessities of life for this world and eternity. And if some of us are called to sacrificial labour as evangelists or missionaries, others are called to sacrificial labour for their support. A Christian of limited means is not denied the privilege of giving what he can, and a Christian blessed with abundance may provide for whole cities and nations to hear the word of God. Not content to give a token or a tenth, each is privileged to dedicate all he has to Christ. "Whatever the bounty of God may bestow upon us, above a sufficiency for our present necessities, is to be esteemed a *blessing* in proportion as it is distributed to relieve the temporal and spiritual wants of others."[35] It is of money that the apostle speaks when he says, "Whoever sows sparingly will also reap sparingly, and whoever sows generously will also reap generously. Each man should give what he has decided in his heart to give, not reluctantly or under compulsion, for God loves a cheerful giver. And God is able to make all grace abound to you, so that in all things at all times, having all that you need, you will abound in every good work." And why does God allow some to be rich? "You will be made rich in every way," said the apostle, "so that you can be *generous on every occasion*."[36]

But the willingness of a Christian to part with money does not mean he is careless in its use. "The true servant of God," said Groves, "knows better than any man the real value of money, the value of time, the value of talents." He is diligent at work, and never wastes a moment; he develops his God-given abilities, putting his best energies into all he does. "When his heavenly Father sends him prosperity beyond what is sufficient for his immediate wants, he does not ask himself: May not I possibly need this superabundance at some future period? Or... may not my wife or children or relatives?" "He knows," says Groves, "that the best security for all spiritual blessings and all temporal mercies, both to himself and his friends, lies in doing the will and trusting unreservedly in the promises of that God who hath said, 'Can a mother forget her sucking child, that she should not have compassion on the fruit of her womb? Yea, she may forget; yet will not I forget thee.' What therefore he has freely received, he freely gives; and trusts for the future the promises of his heavenly Father."[37] So Groves concludes, "The Christian motto should be – Labour hard, consume little, give much, and all to Christ."[38]

What an impact the Church might have on the world if every Christian lived this way! In the early centuries, pagan crowds watched the apostles and martyrs cheerfully exchanging the comforts of this world for the greater comforts of the next. "How differently would the heathen look on our endeavours, if the hardy and suffering spirit of primitive times were to descend again on the silken age into which we are fallen, and if they perceived in us that love which led them to endure all things for the elect's sake, that they may also obtain the salvation which is in Christ Jesus with eternal glory." How powerful our testimony would be if those around us could see us making real personal sacrifices for our beliefs. "If we call on those, who know nothing of the savour of that Name which is as ointment poured forth, to give up all for Christ (and this you literally do to every Hindu and Mohammedan), let us who thus call, and who profess to know much of the power of his name, do so likewise; that they may catch a kindred spirit from a living exhibition. Let us evidence, in very deed, that we love not the world, neither the things of the world, but that the love of the Father is in us."[39]

"In this world's history," Groves concluded, "great things are not accomplished but by great sacrifices."[40] If love led Christ to lay down his *life* for us, will love not lead us to lay down our *superfluities* for others? "If anyone has material possessions and sees his brother in need but has no pity on him, how can the love of God be in him? Dear children, let us not love with words or tongue but with actions and in truth."[41] The Christian at home and the evangelist on the mission field will share the bread earned by the one and the souls won by the other. Each will make sacrifices and each will have a part in the reward. The world may consider this foolish, but we shall say with the apostle, "If we are out of our mind, it is for the sake of God; if we are in our right mind, it is for you. For Christ's love compels us, because we are convinced that one died for all, and therefore all died. And he died for all, that those who live *should no longer live for themselves* but for him who died for them and was raised again."[42]

Groves draws his work to a close by recapitulating "the reasons why it appears to me that our Saviour spoke literal truth... when he used such expressions as these: 'Lay not up for yourselves treasures upon earth' and 'Sell all that thou hast'":

1. because he commanded the young man to do so;
2. because he commended the poor widow for doing so;
3. because the apostles, and all who believed at Jerusalem, did so;
4. because without this it is impossible to "love your neighbour as yourself";
5. because it provides for the gospel to be taken into all the world;
6. because it enables the giver to be useful, happy and full of faith.[43]

This, then, was the theme of *Christian Devotedness*. It was no great work of literature. Its sentences unwieldy and its content quite plain, it was hardly more than a series of Bible verses with exhortations to believe and act. But many who read it were cut to the heart.

It was written, of course, in an age when sickness and death were common – a generation without antiseptics and penicillin, with no access to state benefits – where children frequently *were* left as orphans with no visible means of support. Giving money away was no more sensible to Groves's contemporaries than to ours, and if his argument seems audacious now, it will have seemed all the more challenging then. Strange to say, it met with a far warmer response in 1825 than it is likely to receive from us – perhaps because eternal realities were more real in those days, and worldly comforts less comfortable.

And yet, even then, many considered Groves's views extreme and impracticable. For the second edition in 1829 he wrote a preface, answering as far as he could the further objections raised against him. To reject the ideals he proposes, and in one's own mind to justify their rejection, is not difficult; but criticism of Groves himself has a hollow ring. He did not simply tell others what the Bible taught, or what they should do about it. Having declared his convictions, he acted on them. As the second edition of *Christian Devotedness* rolled off the press, Norris Groves was already making plans for Persia. He had sold his house and furniture, given away his dental practice, donated all he possessed to the poor and to the work of the gospel. Never has a man more completely practised what he preached.

ENDNOTES

[1] M17
[2] 2 Cor 8:9
[3] Lk 6:20, 24
[4] Mk 10:23; Mt 6:24
[5] Lk 12:15
[6] Mt 6:30b
[7] Mt 6:25, 31-33
[8] Lk 12:33-34
[9] Lk 18:22
[10] Mk 10:22
[11] D4
[12] Mk 12:41-44
[13] D7
[14] Acts 2:45; 4:32-35
[15] D7. In the case of the Jerusalem church, Groves believed that the essential point was not the common *possession* of property, but the generous *use* of property. He pointed to the same principle taught by Paul to the church in Corinth: "Our desire is not that others might be relieved while you are hard pressed, but that there might be equality. At the present time your plenty will supply what they need, so that in turn their plenty will supply what you need. Then there will be equality" (2 Cor 8:13-15). A Christian who has more than he requires will always be looking for ways to assist any brother or sister in need. And if he in turn should find himself in need, there will always be a brother or sister somewhere able and willing to help.
[16] 2 Cor 6:10
[17] 2 Cor 8:2
[18] Mk 16:15
[19] D10
[20] Rom 1:16. See Phil 3:8.
[21] D10-11
[22] D14. Groves later remarked, "Whole-hearted apostles caught whole-hearted men, and we have sunk, sunk, till, instead of whole hearts we catch divided hearts – instead of their whole selves, but a few gleanings of their superfluities" (*Christian Influence*, 43).
[23] D8
[24] Heb 13:5-6
[25] Mt 7:9-11
[26] Acts 3:6 AV
[27] Ps 146:9. See Ps 68:5.
[28] D22
[29] D12

[30] See Heb 2:10; 5:8. Critics alleged that there was one scripture which controverted Groves's ideas: "If anyone does not provide for his relatives, and especially for his immediate family, he has denied the faith and is worse than an unbeliever" (1 Tim 5:8). This verse, replied Groves, far from undermining our principle, actually illustrates it, for the apostle is urging his readers to generosity in meeting the actual present needs of widows, making no reference at all to the possible future wants of children.

[31] Jas 1:27 AV

[32] D13 (Rom 8:21; Jas 1:5; Jn 16:24 AV)

[33] 1 Pet 4:10 RSV. See Jas 1:17.

[34] D11

[35] In India Groves met a certain Mr Pearce who owned "a large printing establishment, the whole profits of which he bestows on the promotion of God's cause." Pearce and his wife "seem very devoted and very happy" (M319).

[36] 2 Cor 9:6-11

[37] D18-19 (referring to Is 49:15 AV)

[38] D16

[39] D14-15 (referring to 1 Jn 2:15 AV)

[40] D25

[41] 1 Jn 3:17-19

[42] 2 Cor 5:13-16

[43] D23

"The great point is to get each man to stand
in his individual conscience
before God."

Norris Groves [1]

7

Two Thin Men

F rank Newman was a schoolboy with straight black hair, a thin face and a large beak of a nose. He had bright blue eyes, a rather solemn manner, and a very precise way of speaking. Despite his shyness he was known to be a committed Christian, and many times suffered the consequences: "I soon underwent various persecution [*sic*] from my schoolfellows on account of it: the worst kind consisted in their deliberate attempts to corrupt me."[2]

He was an intelligent boy, and one particular day he brought a question to the evangelical clergyman who taught his class. How was it possible, he wondered, to reconcile a belief in divine justice with the idea that God had predestined some individuals to heaven and some to hell? Not that he would doubt the doctrine, of course, if it were taught in the word of God – simply that it did not seem, at that moment, very reasonable. The clergyman encouraged this humble spirit and Newman tells us, "Such was the beginning and foundation of my faith – an unhesitating unconditional acceptance of whatever was found in the Bible." He thought perhaps he might one day become a clergyman himself, or even a missionary to the heathen.

At the age of sixteen Frank Newman was "confirmed" and about a year later registered in all sincerity his acceptance of the Thirty-nine Articles of the Church of England, a requirement for entry to Oxford University. It was a "pleasure," he said, for "I well knew and loved the Articles." Arriving at Oxford, however, he had a surprise. "Very few academicians could be said to believe them. Of the young men, not one in five seemed to have any religious convictions at all." And this, despite the fact that they too had signed the Articles. Here were the elite of his generation, scorning the time-honoured principles of the Church. He asked them why. There were many reasons, they replied, but to take just one, the Article which asserts that Christ carried "his flesh and bones" with him into heaven. Did that not conflict with the text, "Flesh and blood shall not inherit the kingdom of God"?

Further surprises were in store. The Christians he had known as a boy all abstained from worldly activities on the Lord's Day, but to his bewilderment he now found at least one university clergyman who "rejoiced in seeing his parishioners play at cricket on Sunday", maintaining that "Sunday had nothing to do with the Sabbath, nor the Sabbath with us."[3]

The young freshman began to search the scriptures in earnest to see if what he had been taught as a child was right. One of the first things to impress him was an evident contrast between the morality of the Old Testament and that of the New: "The systematic use of the Old Testament by the Puritans, as if it were the rule of life to Christians, I saw to be a glaring mistake."[4] His thoughts turned to clergymen he had known, and bishops in particular, remembering "how little favourably I was impressed, when a boy, by the lawn sleeves, wig, artificial voice and manner of the Bishop of London."[5] He began to wonder why a Lord Bishop must be addressed by the title "Right Reverend Father in God" when Christ had said, "Call no man Father on earth, for one is your Father, who is in heaven." And many a bishop he knew to be "an unspiritual, and it may be a wicked, man," yet endowed with the right "by his authoritative voice absolutely to bestow on the candidate for Priesthood the power to forgive or retain sins."[6] His mind turned to the custom of baptising babies, and he looked in vain for any such thing in the pages of the New Testament. He found his elder brother John not merely approving this practice but supporting the idea that infants, through their baptism, became Christians. This was not what the apostles had taught: "It was as clear as daylight to me that they held a totally different doctrine."[7]

Frank was troubled. He looked around for a mentor to help him in his perplexity, but found no one. His brother John, with whom he shared lodgings, had no sympathy at all with his concern to question the traditions of the Church. John Henry Newman was already set on a path that would take him beyond his present High-Church Anglicanism to the scarlet cloak of a Roman Catholic cardinal. "Nor was there any elder resident at Oxford, accessible to me, who united all the qualities I wanted in an advisor. Nothing was left for me but to cast myself on him who is named the Father of Lights and resolve to follow the light which he might give, however opposed to my own prejudices and however I might be condemned by men."[8] When the time came for Frank to sit his exams, he had to sign once again, according to the rules of the University, the Thirty-nine Articles. He suppressed his qualms, especially concerning infant baptism, and signed, "unable to conceal from myself that I did not believe this sentence."[9] The alternative was to leave without his degree.

Frank Newman was a young man who could not help thinking. His problem was that few could match his mental stamina and none could, or would, make time to discuss his questions with him. As he studied the Bible, he followed with interest the logical arguments of the apostle Paul, but he struggled to make sense of the more enigmatic teachings of Jesus. The Gospels contained too many paradoxes, too many obscurities, for the intellect to be able to grasp their true meaning or their significance for the present day. But Newman was humble enough to feel himself a learner and to regard difficulties in understanding as proof of inadequacy in himself rather than in the scriptures. Indeed, his reading of the early Church Fathers and the great Ecumenical Councils only confirmed his conviction that the Bible, rather than Church articles, edicts or traditions, must stand as the divine authority for the people of God. A longing to experience the simplicity of Christian fellowship as it had been in the days of the apostles now took hold of young Frank Newman. He had read a number of missionary biographies which greatly impressed him, and though unable on conscientious grounds to enter the ministry of the Church of England, his thoughts turned to the possibilities of missionary service overseas without any such connection.

Having taken his degree in 1826 with highest honours (a double first in classics and mathematics), he was asked to teach and supervise the work of undergraduates. The following year he accepted a post as private tutor to the family of a leading barrister in Ireland by the name of Edward Pennefather. Newman liked what he saw of the evangelical Christians in Ireland – so active and wholehearted in comparison with the formal religiosity of Oxford. "I have glimpses of what a Christian ought to be... There is a simple and unhesitating belief of the Word, joy in believing, and a consequent life in Christ; life as a citizen no longer of this world but of heaven."[10]

It was in the home of Pennefather that Newman met a man who seemed well qualified to be the mentor he had long hoped for. "There was a young relative of his, a most remarkable man, who rapidly gained an immense sway over me." This was the brother-in-law of his employer, and his name was John Nelson Darby. Even before the age of thirty, Darby had the appearance of an Old Testament prophet: "a fallen cheek, a bloodshot eye... a seldom shaven beard, a shabby suit of clothes and a generally neglected person."[11] Darby had taken high honours at Dublin University, but then abandoned his plans for a career in Law for ethical reasons; his conscience would not allow him to take a brief lest he should be selling his talents to defeat justice. And so, Newman tells us, he "took Holy Orders and became an indefatigable curate in the mountains of Wicklow. Every evening he sallied forth to teach in the cabins, and roving far and wide over mountain and amid bogs was seldom home before midnight." His emaciated frame, his ascetic disregard for personal comfort and his warm sympathies led the poor country people to regard him as a "genuine saint of the ancient breed".[12]

On first acquaintance, the fastidious Newman had been repelled by Darby's preference for coarse, perhaps even ragged, clothing and his indifference to food and rest. Yet so effective was "the Irish clergyman" in winning the trust of the poor Catholic families that Newman was soon convinced that "a dozen such men would have done more to convert all Ireland to Protestantism than the whole apparatus of the Church Establishment."[13] Here, at last, was a real Christian of the apostolic mould, and Frank Newman, Fellow of Balliol College, Oxford, willingly accompanied his new friend into the humble Irish cottages, "visiting and reading to the people who cannot read."[14] "For the first time in my life," he declared, "I saw a man earnestly turning into reality the principles which others confessed with their lips only."[15]

Five years older than himself, John Darby was a man Newman could look on as an intellectual equal and as a spiritual superior: "With keen logical powers, he had warm sympathies, solid judgment of character, thoughtful tenderness and total self-abandonment." Issues that to Newman had been a cause of distressing doubt were to Darby matters of confident assurance, and he could always give good reasons for his certainty. Darby, at this time, read nothing but the Bible. Every word of scripture he held to be inspired by God and profitable. But surely, asked Newman, some scriptures refer to past events and no longer apply today. What would we have lost, for example, if our Bibles contained no record of Paul's request, "Bring the cloak that I left with Carpus at Troas, and my scrolls, especially the parchments"? "I should certainly have lost," replied Darby without hesitation, "for that is exactly the verse which alone saved me from selling my little library. No! every word, depend upon it, is from the Spirit and is for eternal service."[16]

The questions of infant baptism and episcopal authority were no doubt raised, and though Darby (as an ordained Anglican clergyman) failed to persuade his new disciple to approve the official line, this does not seem to have troubled Newman unduly. "For the first time in my life," he confessed, "I found myself under the dominion of a superior... Indeed, but for a few weaknesses which warned me that he might err, I could have accepted him as an apostle commissioned to reveal the mind of God."[17]

Darby encouraged him, in view of the imminent return of Christ, to abandon all thoughts of an academic career. The work of mathematicians, artists and historians, he said, would all be burned to ashes. The only thing worth doing was preaching the simple gospel to peasant and scholar alike. Newman's missionary zeal was rekindled. Ordination in the Church of England was out of the question, and his limited experience of Nonconformity had not impressed him, so the question arose in his mind, "Was I at liberty to preach to the heathen without ordination?" Was it possible to be a missionary without being a clergyman? "To teach a church, of course, needs the sanction of the church," but to teach the heathen was a "natural right". More than that, it was an obligation. The failure, after eighteen hundred years, to have taught the gospel of Christ to the whole world was, thought Newman, "a scandalous reproach on Christendom." And why had the Church failed in its missionary task? "Is it not, perhaps, because those who are in Church office cannot go, and the mass of the laity think it no business of theirs?... The laity leave all to the clergy, and the clergy have more than enough to do."[18]

It was at this juncture that Frank Newman came across a small booklet entitled *Christian Devotedness* by a certain Mr Groves of Exeter who was "going to Persia as a teacher of Christianity." "I read his tract, and was inflamed with the greatest admiration, judging immediately that this was the man whom I should rejoice to aid or serve."[19]

Frank Newman returned to England full of enthusiasm. Finding brother John at home, he recounted his Irish experiences. It troubled him to find John "so well spoken of in all quarters". He wondered how his older brother "was going on spiritually", for popularity was not something to be desired in a true disciple of Christ.[20] Frank had seen, in his own words, "glimpses of what a Christian ought to be"; he had felt the power in "a simple and unhesitating belief of the Word"; he had tasted the joy of "life as a citizen no longer of this world but of heaven."[21] But John had little sympathy with all this.

Returning to Oxford, Newman invited John Nelson Darby to visit his university friends. They plied their guest with questions, and Newman was delighted to see how his mentor immediately became a sort of evangelical father-confessor to a number of the university men. Perhaps some of them would catch the vision for real apostolic Christianity. Perhaps some, through reading *Christian Devotedness*, would feel called, like him, to the mission field. "As Groves was a magnet to draw me, so I might draw others."[22] Such was his hope.

The intellectual challenge of presenting the gospel to other cultures now engaged the mind of Frank Newman. The "Evidences" which he had studied at Oxford, and which served to persuade the Westerner of the truth of Christianity, would be all but useless, he reckoned, in other parts of the world where people were accustomed to view Christians as "great conquerors, powerful avengers, sharp traders – often lax in morals and apparently without religion." "The fine theories of a Christian teacher," he thought, "would be as vain to convert a Mohammedan or Hindoo to Christianity as the soundness of Seneca's moral treatises to convert me to Roman paganism." How then could the peoples of the world be persuaded to accept the gospel of Christ? "I could see no other way to this but by an entire church being formed of new elements on a heathen soil... I imagined a little colony so animated by primitive faith, love and disinterestedness [i.e. unselfishness] that the collective moral influence of all might interpret and enforce the words of the few who preached."[23] The strategy was very simple. A missionary team would settle in a Muslim or Hindu city and start meeting together as a church. It would be a spiritual church, not a state church, and as the local people saw the reality of their faith some would turn to Christ and join them. Hearing of this progress, other workers would be encouraged to come out and strengthen the team. Then as the church grew, some of its members would move further into unreached areas and plant similar churches throughout the East until the gospel had spread everywhere.

Such was the missionary vision of Frank Newman. He hoped, as soon possible, to set out with "some Irish friends" and join Norris Groves in Persia: "What I might do there I knew not. I did not go as a minister of religion... But I thought I knew many ways in which I might be of service, and I was prepared to act according to circumstances." But there was one thing which held him back. He had proposed marriage to Maria Giberne, a young lady of great charm, character and intelligence, two years older than himself. And she had not yet replied.

ENDNOTES

[1] M448

[2] Newman, *Phases of Faith*, 1. His full name was Francis William Newman.

[3] *Phases*, 4

[4] *Phases*, 4-5

[5] *Phases*, 11-12. Lawn: a fine linen or cotton fabric, originally from *Laon*, a town in France where linen was made.

[6] *Phases*, 14

[7] *Phases*, 10

[8] *Phases*, 8

[9] The twenty-seventh of the Articles states that baptism is "a sign of Regeneration or New Birth whereby, as by an instrument, they that receive baptism rightly are grafted into the church." Through this baptism, "the promises of forgiveness of sin and of our adoption to be the sons of God by the Holy Ghost are visibly signed and sealed". The Article then declares the baptism of "young children" to be "most agreeable with the institution of Christ". The order of service for "Public Baptism of Infants" in the Book of Common Prayer commences with a petition that the infant, through baptism "may receive remission of his sins by spiritual regeneration... that he may be born again and be made an heir of everlasting salvation." The service closes by assuring those present that, having been baptised, "this Child is regenerate, and grafted into the body of Christ's Church." As almost everyone in Britain was baptised in this way, Britain was considered a Christian country and everyone in it a Christian.

[10] Letter to J H Newman, quoted by Stunt, *Awakening*, 206.

[11] *Phases*, 17

[12] *Phases*, 17

[13] *Phases*, 18

[14] Letter quoted by Stunt, *Awakening*, 207.

[15] *Phases*, 18

[16] *Phases*, 19

[17] *Phases*, 20-21

[18] *Phases*, 24

[19] *Phases*, 24

[20] Letter quoted by Stunt, *Awakening*, 216.

[21] Letter to J H Newman, quoted by Stunt, *Awakening*, 206.
[22] *Phases*, 28
[23] *Phases*, 27-28

"I do not desire to bring you over to any church,
but to the simple truth of God's word."

Norris Groves [1]

8

To Remember the Lord

I t was June 1828 and Norris Groves was winding up his affairs in England. Once the family had gone, of course, their tutor Henry Craik would be out of a job. Groves recommended him to John Synge, a friend with two young sons in the nearby town of Teignmouth.[2] Settling there, Craik began to preach regularly at a Baptist chapel in the nearby village of Shaldon. But his thoughts, too, were beginning to turn to service overseas.

By midsummer the following year Craik was writing to the Baptist Missionary Society about work in India when he chanced to meet a rather unconventional young man of his own age by the name of George Müller. They were both twenty-three years old. Müller was a German, recently converted and enrolled at a missionary training college in Bethnal Green near London. Here he was preparing for missionary service with the London Society for Promoting Christianity amongst the Jews. He had come to Devonshire for a short break, which he hoped would improve his health. It certainly did.

In London George Müller had heard about a prosperous Exeter dentist, a man who had given up his £1500-a-year practice in order to go as a missionary to Persia. "This made such an impression on me," Müller declared, "and delighted me so, that I not only marked it down in my journal, but also wrote about it to my German friends."[3] Henry Craik, in Devonshire, would be able to tell him more about this unusual dentist.

Müller and Craik liked one another straightaway. What especially pleased Müller in his new friend was "his warmth of heart towards the Lord",[4] and this, Craik told him, along with many other things, was a blessing that had come to him during his two years with the Groves family at Northernhay. "It was not at St Andrews," he said, "it was not at Plymouth; it was at Exeter that the Lord taught me those lessons of dependence on himself and of catholic fellowship which I have sought to carry out."[5]

About this time a small booklet with the unusual title of *Christian Devotedness* came into Müller's hands, and what he read moved him deeply. In fact it changed the course of his life. He experienced something, he said, "like a second conversion".[6] He later described it as "an entire and full surrender of heart. I gave myself fully to the Lord. Honour, pleasure, money, my physical powers, my mental powers, all was laid down at the feet of Jesus, and I became a great lover of the word of God."[7] Müller was impressed especially by the thought that God does not lie, that Christ does not deceive, and that therefore the words spoken in the Bible are the literal truth; a Christian can trust and obey, with the assurance that God will never fail him. Returning to London much refreshed, he invited his fellow students to join him every morning from six to eight for a time of prayer and Bible study at which each would share what God had shown him from the portion they had read. Then, unwilling to wait for his missionary diploma, he went out among the Jews of London, distributing tracts and explaining the gospel to passers-by. Although the London Society required its workers to give their time to Jews, Müller was soon talking about Christ with anyone the Lord brought to him. He began to chafe under the authority of a committee that required him to look to them for authorisation, finance, and direction. It seemed more biblical to look simply to the Lord.

A few months later, in December 1829, Müller had a couple of weeks' vacation. He decided to pay a second visit to Devonshire. Despite his broken English and guttural German accent, there were opportunities to preach in a number of small Nonconformist chapels, including one in Teignmouth, just across the river from Henry Craik's in Shaldon. To Müller's surprise he was invited to become its pastor. He accepted, on one condition: that he would be free to preach elsewhere as the Spirit might lead. Resigning from the Society, he set himself to study the New Testament in earnest, to discover exactly how a church should be led. He asked for baptism by immersion, and he resolved to trust God for the supply of his personal needs through prayer – without a stated salary, or debts, or appeals to other people. Proposing that the congregation "break bread" on the first day of every week, he encouraged free participation in meetings for worship and study of the scriptures.[8]

Once a week George Müller preached in a small chapel in Exeter. On such occasions he needed somewhere to stay overnight, and Bessie Paget recommended a room in the boarding school now occupying the big house at Northernhay.[9] The young housekeeper who worked there turned out to be the sister of the remarkable dentist, its previous owner. Musical, artistic and intelligent, Mary Groves shared her brother's devotion to Christ and his willingness to trust the Lord implicitly in all things, and she quickly earned the admiration and affection of the young German. On 7th October 1830 they were married in the local parish church, and from then on the names of Groves and Müller were united by family as well as spiritual ties.

In the spring of 1832, Henry Craik and the Müllers felt they should all move to Bristol, where they shortly afterwards established Bethesda Chapel. This was the beginning of a partnership in Christian service that would last thirty-six years.

About sixty miles to the north of Exeter lay the town of Barnstaple. In 1831 a fashionable young solicitor by the name of Robert Cleaver Chapman was invited by a relative, a local lawyer, to visit Barnstaple and assist an independent church in its work among the poor.[10] Turning his back on a promising career, and giving away "his private fortune", he accepted the invitation to become the pastor of this little congregation – on condition that he be quite free to teach all he found written in the word of God. As he did so, the church began to develop along lines that would be familiar to Müller, Craik and the circle of friends in Dublin. At first Chapman had taken lodgings in a worker's cottage, and later occupied a tiny house in the most squalid part of town. He never considered himself a gifted preacher but he was a man of great kindness, and numbers soon rose to four hundred around the Lord's Table every Sunday. It was here in later years that Bessie Paget found her spiritual home.[11]

The group meeting at Aungier Street in Dublin is sometimes considered the earliest of the Brethren assemblies.[12] It was certainly one of the earliest, and the subsequent activities and writings of those involved have made it one of the best known. But the contribution of Chapman, Müller and Craik to the next phase of the movement was of equal, if not greater, importance. These three wise, balanced, spiritual men each had something special to offer. Robert Chapman, without any denominational background, was a man of outstanding pastoral ability. Müller introduced a large dose of practical German pietism, and Craik added an element of reputable Nonconformist scholarship. Together they brought a measure of stability, and a far greater breadth of experience, to a movement hitherto drawn largely from Anglican sources.

Although Dublin and Devonshire were focal points at this period, there were similar developments in many other parts of the British Isles – as there were in Europe and in America – and some of them at a considerably earlier date. A popular movement that meets a universal need will often spring up simultaneously in places far apart. In fact there was at this time a general feeling of restlessness. The early years of the nineteenth century, with their greater population mobility and increasing educational opportunities, were marked by a general questioning of traditional beliefs and practices. No longer were Christians content for their parish priests to be worldly men with more interest in politics or blood-sports than the spiritual welfare of their flock. No longer were worshippers satisfied to take Communion alongside unconverted and, in some cases, notoriously wicked fellow parishioners. No longer would they accept without question the Articles of Religion and the Book of Common Prayer along with the accumulated traditions of past generations. Nowhere in scripture could they find that a Christian must pay a weekly rent for his pew, nor any reference to an ordained priest appointed to administer sacraments, nor any requirement for a man to possess a licence before he could preach, nor that he should preach only on consecrated ground. Some turned to the Nonconformist churches of the day, but found their services dry, academic and joyless, dominated by ministers in black robes – narrow-minded men, puritanical, critical and pompously authoritarian, shielding their flock from the contamination of contact with other Christians. Even the Methodists, after the death of John Wesley in 1791, had become a confused, politically compromised and sadly divided body: they still practised infant baptism, rarely took Communion, and languished under the control of ordained ministers and national councils considerably less gifted than their founder.[13]

There was, of course, much in the older churches that was good, and many still faithfully preached the gospel. Abundant corruptions and superstitions had been purged by the English Reformation of the sixteenth and seventeenth centuries. Yet the question remained, *Had the Reformation gone far enough?* The distinction between clergy and laity persisted. The congregation still "went to church" in order to "hear divine service", and much time and money were devoted to buildings. The services themselves were structured and formal, with procedures of standing, sitting and kneeling, and in many cases with prayers and confessions read out of a book. Proceedings were conducted by a minister with specially qualified assistants, and the entire content of the service, including the hymns, had been planned in advance. All this was quite different from the informal meetings described in the New Testament, where "to each is given the manifestation of the Spirit for the common good," and where, "when you come together, each one has a hymn, a lesson, a revelation... for you can all prophesy one by one so that all may learn and all be encouraged."[14]

As the nineteenth century progressed, intelligent men and women became increasingly frustrated with the passive role allotted to them in church and chapel, yet so set in their ways were the institutions of both Establishment and Dissent that hope of improvement seemed to have long since faded. Many people felt the time had come for a fresh start – to discover how the Holy Spirit had led the apostles and their converts, and then follow the apostolic example as closely as possible. Norris Groves was by no means alone in his desire for a recovery of genuine New Testament Christianity. In many parts of the British Isles, Europe, America and further afield, others were moving in the same direction. In 1834 Groves could say, "Sometimes my heart overflows with the thought of visiting the little churches."[15] It is to these "little churches" that our attention now must turn.

As early as 1807 we have a record of events at Camowen Green, near Omagh in the north of Ireland. A Presbyterian church had for many months languished without a minister, when a member of the church by the name of James Buchanan received a visit from two itinerant evangelists, Robert and James Haldane. Their vision for gospel outreach and their resolve to ignore denominational distinctions inspired a number of young men, who started to meet for prayer in Buchanan's home. Buchanan felt that, though there was no minister among them, these men were preaching like apostles and should therefore be able, like the apostles, to take bread and wine in remembrance of their Lord.[16] Before long they were meeting together "as a Church of the living God at Camowen Green". Their resolution was "that we should not attend to any act of worship unless we saw it clearly ordered and practised by the first churches in the New Testament." On the first day of each week the men took turns to lead the meeting, and they encouraged one another to participate in praise and prayer according to their varied spiritual gifts.[17]

In 1815 Buchanan left Ireland to become British consul in New York. Here he found a number of immigrants like himself, who told him of similar groups they had known in other parts of the British Isles. The result was a letter sent to all those they were aware of, and in due course a response from twenty-two in Ireland, Scotland, England and America, describing their views and practices. These replies were published in 1820, accompanied by a preface noting the remarkable similarity to be seen in these scattered fellowships, springing up spontaneously and independently in places far apart. The reason evidently lay in the fact that their sole authority was the Bible, believed and obeyed in all simplicity. They met on the first day of each week to remember Christ with bread and wine; they taught and exhorted one another from the scriptures, with prayers, praises, thanksgiving and a collection for the poor. They had their own recognised elders and deacons, or else were waiting for them to emerge from among their number, but they refused to regard their leaders as clergy. On the contrary, "they consider the existence of such an order among disciples as utterly incompatible with the holy scriptures and with the character and interests of the churches of God." The twenty-two who responded were by no means the only groups of this type. In fact the reply received from Dalkeith asserted that most towns of any size had a fellowship like this, and the letter from Paisley affirmed that there were between thirty and forty in Scotland alone. As for Ireland, the reply from Monaghan stated that there were "a good number of similarly minded people in both North and South."[18]

Across the Atlantic similar things were happening. In British Guiana (Guyana) there was an Anglican rector by the name of Leonard Strong. As a young midshipman in the West Indies, he had been converted after a close brush with death when a boat capsized, and he later felt the call of God to return and preach the gospel to the slaves on the plantations, doing whatever he could to relieve their many sufferings. This did not make him popular with the plantation owners, who threatened to shoot him. Undaunted, Strong continued preaching until forcibly removed to Georgetown. Here, in 1837, he resigned from the Church of England, gave up his comfortable manse and stipend, and after careful study of the New Testament, decided to meet for "breaking of bread" with those who had come to Christ through his ministry. At the first meeting, nearly two thousand West Indians crowded into a large shed used for drying coffee, and from that remarkable beginning other independent worshipping groups were formed in various parts of the Caribbean. In 1849 Strong himself returned to Britain and joined the young assembly, or fellowship of believers, in Torquay.[19]

A group in Canada traced its origins to the initiative of a Belfast architect, Thomas McCall, who had emigrated to work on the Canadian Pacific railway. He was at breakfast with his wife one bright Sunday morning in a lonely place many miles from the nearest church when she declared she would like to remember the Lord with bread and wine. Her husband, a Baptist by conviction, objected, "You cannot do that, dear, as we have no clergyman here." "There is no need for a clergyman," she replied. "Our Lord has said, 'Where two or three are gathered together in my name there am I in the midst of them.'" Finding no answer to this, he asked what she would do for wine. She picked up a bunch of grapes, squeezed the juice into a cup and placed a loaf of bread on the table. "You and I are two, Tom, so let us now claim his promise." From these simple beginnings grew a substantial fellowship in Montreal.[20]

In Geneva an assembly had been formed in 1817 by a group of Christians disenchanted with the Company of Pastors who held authority over the church established by Calvin. The priesthood of all believers was a principle dear to them – as in theory to all Protestants – but they claimed to see little sign of it in practice until they began to meet together at Bourg-de-Four. Here they established a plural leadership and started to share in the Lord's Supper every Sunday, encouraging the spontaneous participation of "gifted brothers". During the 1820s a number of similar assemblies appeared in the Swiss cantons of Vaud and Berne.[21]

In August 1843 George Müller, with his wife, paid a visit to his Prussian homeland. At that time the large majority of believers in Germany were connected with the Lutheran state church. There were few Nonconformists. The Baptists, indeed, were a small and embattled minority, and held what Müller considered "most exclusive separatist views".[22] Müller was invited to address a series of meetings arranged for him by a Baptist church in Stuttgart, but knowing his willingness to take Communion with Lutherans, baptised only as infants, some of the church leaders refused to accept him at the Lord's Table. Nothing would persuade them to change their mind, and eventually seventeen members, to his regret, withdrew from the church, preferring to "break bread" with him in his room. Müller's visit extended over six months, and during this time the company meeting with him grew to twenty-five. He taught them how to conduct a meeting by waiting on the Holy Spirit for guidance, each contributing whatever the Lord might give. He encouraged them to pray spontaneously, following the theme on which the Spirit was leading them, choosing appropriate hymns, scriptures and subjects of exhortation. From this small beginning, several similar groups were established in other parts of Germany. Müller, by his own account, sought to widen the sympathies of those associated with him so they might enjoy fellowship with true Christians from any denominational background whilst continuing to maintain their own simple meetings with free participation according to the New Testament pattern.[23]

In Scotland, in the early 1840s, an earnest Congregationalist minister from Hamilton preached with great effect in the nearby town of Wishaw. A number believed and "full of the joy of salvation" began to meet together to read the scriptures and encourage one another. The minister himself was quite an enterprising man but found his converts even more so when they resolved to leave the Congregationalist Church. Gathering in a workshop in 1847, they set down their principles. "In much weakness, but in good earnest, we commenced study of the word of God for our mutual instruction, and soon learned that the Church, in her primitive state, was 'one body' with Christ the Head, and was known only by his name. This led us to acknowledge no other name but Christ, and to make our only tests of membership union with Christ and peace with God by faith in Christ. And wherever we found a saved sinner, there did we find a fellow-disciple and members of one body [*sic*], and therefore resolved to hold fellowship with all such who would hold it with us; and that nothing in the world would separate us from any individual member but the discovery of a want of Christianity in that individual. We also saw that it was the duty of every gifted brother to teach in the church what he believed God had taught him, though he might differ in opinion in some things. This principle obtaining amongst us, we could never think of differing in affection, and in this did we see the beautiful adaptation of the New Testament church order to restore and keep the Church in its primitive unity and purity." The following year, in the face of "severe criticism and persecution", four were baptised in the River Calder, and shortly afterwards a large crowd witnessed the baptism in the same place of twenty more.[24]

Many such initiatives were taken by people in quite humble circumstances, but there were stirrings of the same sort in more privileged circles. On the 6th February 1831, Henry Bulteel, curate of St Ebbe's in Oxford, was appointed to preach, after the customary procession through the streets of the city, to the assembled staff and students of Oxford University. Few sermons have ever made such an impression. Bulteel condemned the failure of the Church of England to adhere to the Calvinism of its own Thirty-nine Articles, he questioned the validity of its subjection to the state, and he threatened divine judgment on its tolerance of unworthy ministers. The rector of Exeter College was one profoundly affected. He afterwards remarked, "Well I must say I quailed, for indeed it is true. You all know that we do have young men brought to be qualified for ordination, and we have to sign the papers declaring that they are called by the Holy Ghost, some of them ungodly young men."[25]

Another impressed by the sermon was Benjamin Wills Newton, a Fellow of Exeter College. The previous year, as we have seen, John Nelson Darby had visited Oxford at the invitation of Frank Newman, who introduced him to Newton and to another Oxford student, George Vicesimus Wigram. Thoroughly unsettled by Bulteel's sermon and by his discussions with Newman and Darby, Newton abandoned his plans for ordination in the Church of England. In 1832 he resigned from the University and returned to his home in Plymouth. Here he had already met several times with Wigram and others for informal fellowship "where each was free to read, to speak, to pray, or to give out a hymn."[26] When Wigram proposed that they take bread and wine together in remembrance of their Lord, Newton readily agreed. Men of intellect, influence and spiritual gift were added to this group, including a sea captain, Percy Francis Hall, who had sold his possessions and resigned his naval commission on conscientious grounds, and Samuel Prideaux Tregelles, who later became a significant New Testament scholar. As for Benjamin Newton, he was to become one of the most influential writers among the early Brethren, especially on prophetic and Christological themes. Visiting them, John Darby was impressed with what he saw, and he became a regular visitor to these earliest "Plymouth Brethren". They spent much of their spare time together, enjoying communal meals and informal fellowship, and a number went out every Sunday on horseback to preach in neighbouring towns and villages. Before long, their efforts had led to the establishment of similar groups in a number of places nearby. In Plymouth itself the assembly grew rapidly and within a few years numbered several hundred.[27]

About this time, in the midlands of England, a new vicar was appointed to a parish church at Hereford. Though known to be a good and philanthropic man, it seemed to his parishioners that he did not preach the gospel as clearly as his predecessor. In his congregation were a number of gifted and educated men, well taught in the scriptures and frustrated by the fact that, not being ordained, they had no opportunity to participate in the regular services of the church. It happened that one of their wives came to Plymouth, where she heard Percy Hall. His thoughtful expositions of scripture were far more inspiring than the sermons she was accustomed to, and the upshot was an invitation for Hall to visit Hereford. In 1837 he and his family left Plymouth and settled there. Three or four hundred, from varied backgrounds, began to meet regularly for the Lord's Supper, including many who came in from the country round about.[28]

Although most of these early initiatives occurred in provincial towns and villages, London was not neglected. In 1838 a fellowship in Tottenham was established by the influential Howard family after withdrawing from the Society of Friends, and in the same year (or perhaps earlier) George Wigram, encouraged by John Darby, came from Plymouth to launch a similar group in Camden Town. During the 1840s a number of other London assemblies came into being, notably that in Hackney whose members regularly visited the poor with practical and medical help.[29]

Many of these new fellowships, especially in the west of England, were linked by an awareness of one another, and could trace their origin back to Groves, Parnell and their friends in Dublin. But others had started with no knowledge of events elsewhere. In Shaftesbury, Dorset, for example, there were two men who "had left the state church". They arranged cottage meetings "for the study of the scriptures", and then gospel meetings, which led to several conversions. In 1842, as numbers increased, they moved to a schoolroom, as they described it, "for the purpose of breaking bread without any reference to sectarian practices, and wishing to assume no other name than that of brethren and sisters in the Lord Jesus Christ in whose name it was their desire to meet to commemorate his dying love."[30]

In nearby Blandford, Christians from several Nonconformist congregations had organised a charity school. They met week by week to pray for the work and to encourage one another from the scriptures. On one occasion, the discussion turned to the question of how and why the earliest Christians had met for the "breaking of bread". The Bible showed that this was a normal part of the regular meetings of the early church.[31] Unlike the "sacrament" offered at rare intervals by their own ministers, they found that "on the first day of the week" the early Christians "came together to break bread."[32] They decided to do the same, at an hour when no service was being held elsewhere. Hearing of this, the Nonconformist ministers denounced them and annulled their church membership. Shunned by their former friends, they started to preach the gospel publicly in Blandford itself and the surrounding villages. Soon there were conversions. A young evangelist from Exeter visited them, bringing news of similar fellowships in many places, and they were drawn into contact with the wider movement.[33]

As time went by, these scattered groups, throughout the United Kingdom and further afield, became aware of one another. By 1840 Norris Groves himself knew of almost two hundred in England and Ireland.[34] The majority of their leaders were young in years and progressive in thought; and gifted preachers and teachers were soon travelling widely to encourage and foster informal links of fellowship between them. The Brethren movement was under way. To outside observers it was a mysterious, enigmatic phenomenon, perhaps even a little odd. It had no ordained ministers, no acknowledged leader, no address, no headquarters or organisation, no official list of members, no monetary subscription, no statement of belief or purpose. In fact it did not seem likely to survive very long. Despite this it proved to be a movement of extraordinary spiritual vigour. And it was this movement, with its spreading network of independent fellowships, that came to regard Norris Groves as one of its earliest and greatest pioneers, and drew much strength and inspiration from his personal devotion to the call of Christ.

Appendix ii of this book describes the subsequent growth of the Brethren movement, looks in more detail at its original principles, and briefly considers its significance in the present day.

ENDNOTES

[1] M69 (J95-96)

[2] Synge was a wealthy landowner whose permanent home was Glanmore Castle near Dublin. He had been one of the earliest group meeting with Bellett and his friends. He subsequently chaired the Powerscourt conference of 1833, but chose to remain within the Established Church.

[3] Müller, *Narrative*, I, 44. Born in 1805, George Müller was ten years younger than Norris Groves.

[4] Tayler, xi-xii, quoted by Coad, 37.

[5] Groves H, *Darbyism*, 25

[6] Müller, *Narrative*, I, 48

[7] Müller, letter to J G Logan dated 17th July 1895 (referring to July 1829), reproduced in Lang, *Groves*, 39.

[8] Edward K Groves observes that "Mr Müller and Mr Craik, at Teignmouth, had commenced the weekly breaking of bread, connected with an open ministry, more than three months before anything of the kind was known in Plymouth, and while Mr Darby... was preaching in the pulpits of the Church of England" (*Conversations*, 141). In view of 1 Tim 2:11-14 and 1 Cor 14:34-38 the open ministry was generally restricted to men.

[9] Groves E K, *Successors*, 394. The headmaster was William Hake. At this time his wife was a permanent invalid.

[10] Chapman had recently come to personal faith in Christ at an independent Baptist chapel in London whose pastor, James Harrington Evans, was a man of academic distinction and ecumenical principles. Converted after his ordination, Evans had resigned his curacy in the Church of England on scriptural grounds (Coad, 70-71).

[11] Beattie, 52-54. Spurgeon called Chapman "the saintliest man I ever knew". John Nelson Darby said, "We talk of the heavenlies, but Robert Chapman lives in them." Chapman remained, throughout his life, a close friend of Norris Groves, of George Müller and of Hudson Taylor. It was from his church that Bowden and Beer were sent to India, and he became a "referee" of the China Inland Mission.

[12] The Brethren, often called Christian Brethren, were sometimes labelled Plymouth Brethren by those outside the movement who believed Plymouth to be their place of origin or centre of influence – perhaps because the first Brethren periodical, *The Christian Witness*, was published there from 1834 until its demise in 1841. In the New Testament the word "brethren", designating a company of Christians, appears

almost two hundred times. The general acceptance of this term no doubt reflects the egalitarian ethos of the movement from its earliest days: "Be not ye called Rabbi: for one is your Master, even Christ, and all ye are brethren" (Matt 23:8 AV).

[13] This is, of course, a historical study relating to churches of the early nineteenth century. It should not be taken to imply any criticism of the modern representatives of these denominations. The social and religious condition of England at this period is discussed further in Appendix i of this book.

[14] 1 Cor 12:7; 14:26 & 31 RSV

[15] M333. Our knowledge of the early Brethren, outside the literary circles of Dublin, Plymouth and Bristol, depends almost entirely on the verbal reminiscences of those who were present at the time. Inevitably, much information has been lost, and some may have been misremembered, but what remains probably provides a fair representation of what actually happened, especially when supported by circumstantial detail.

[16] Lk 22:19; 1 Cor 11:23-26

[17] Rowdon, *Origins*, 23-24; Coad, 82

[18] Rowdon, *Origins*, 23-25. In 1833 John Darby wrote, "I hear the north [of Ireland] is dotted with little bodies meeting as you do" (Letter dated 30 April 1833, quoted by Coad, 82; Rowdon, *Origins*, 25).

[19] Beattie, 65-67. In 1853 Groves visited Torquay and "heard a nice gospel sermon from dear Mr Strong with whom I have a most extended unity of judgment" (M486).

[20] Beattie, 40-41

[21] The early development of these Swiss groups is described in detail by Stunt, *Awakening*, 25-89.

[22] Neatby, 96

[23] Müller, *Narrative*, I, 517-530, 558; Neatby, 96-100

[24] Beattie, 202-203

[25] Rowdon, *Origins*, 67

[26] Letter from Darby to Tholuck, reproduced in Bellett, *Early Days*, 35; Rowdon, 76.

[27] Rowdon, *Origins*, 76-77; Coad, 63-68

[28] Beattie, 35-38

[29] Beattie, 77; Rowdon, *Origins*, 161-163; Stunt, *Early Brethren*, 20-21. John Eliot Howard, aged about thirty at this time, was an expert in the uses of the drug quinine (a recent discovery which helped to reduce fever and relieve symptoms of malaria). He was elected a Fellow of the Royal Society in 1874.

[30] Beattie, 72

[31] Acts 2:42

[32] Acts 20:7

[33] This was Henry Dyer, who became one of the founding editors of *The Missionary Echo*, later renamed *Echoes of Service* (Beattie, 73-75).

[34] Groves, *Remarks on a Pamphlet*, 133

"By keeping a man at home
who ought to be seeking his Lord's glory abroad,
you as much weaken the Church at home,
as by sending abroad one who ought to stay."

Norris Groves [1]

9

Whom He has Chosen

A s his own plans were taking shape, Norris Groves wondered what would become of "poor Kitto". Where might this peculiar young man find a place to be useful in the service of God? Enquiring with his friend Edward Bickersteth, Groves discovered that the Church Missionary Society was in need of workers for its printing operations. Making books! Could there be a more ideal task for Kitto the bookworm? And amid the continuous clatter of the printshop press, his total deafness would be, for once, an actual advantage.

So it was that in July 1825 John Kitto moved into the student residence of the new CMS training college in Islington, and this onetime barber, builder, artist, cobbler, librarian and dental assistant began to learn, under the eye of Mr Watts the printer, the rudiments of typesetting. Financial support came from Groves himself and from Kitto's wider circle of benevolent friends. The other inhabitants of the college were eighteen trainee missionaries, some English, some German, and as he got to know them better Kitto was impressed by their keen Christian character and enthusiasm for the work of the gospel. He set himself a disciplined programme of personal Bible study and prayer, and on Wednesdays he fasted. His training involved setting Greek types, and he also experimented with the Persian fonts used for Henry Martyn's New Testament. He still carried something to read wherever he went, in his pocket or in the crown of his hat, and was often to be seen with his eyes glued to a book or magazine as he ambled to and from his work. In his hours of leisure he explored the bookstalls of London, which were far better stocked than those of Devon.[2] When the weather was fine he walked out with pockets full of gospel tracts to enjoy the fields, woods and hedgerows around Islington, and also, he tells us, to bring a word from their Creator to anyone he might chance to meet along the way.[3]

One day John Kitto found himself in church without a hymnbook. Seeing his predicament, the young lady next to him kindly offered to share hers. He knew nothing about her, neither her name nor her family. Some days later he happened to go into a shop, where the kind shopkeeper invited him into the parlour to see the prize-books her six children had won at Sunday school. He asked to see the children, to compliment them on their success, but they were all at school – except, that is, for the eldest daughter. When summoned to meet the visitor, she turned out to be the girl whose hymnbook he had shared. Her name was Hannah. John Kitto found good reason to visit the shop again, and then more frequently, and eventually there were plans for marriage. Norris Groves, having earlier advised him against a similar attachment, did not, this time, try to dissuade him.[4]

As the days passed, Kitto found much of his work placing lead characters in print frames tedious. It happened that the printshop sometimes ran out of Persian fonts, so finding nothing to do there he went home. Some days, knowing there was no work in hand, he did not turn up at all. Kitto had seen his arrival in Islington as a step towards his ambition to be a missionary and an author, and it was on terms of equality that he enjoyed fellowship with the missionary trainees in the college. Why should he spend his time, he wondered, doing work that "a mere printer might perform much better and more efficiently than myself"?[5] His deafness had prevented any very detailed discussion between him and the CMS about the work expected of him, and the mission evidently held a less grandiose view of his future career. In Mr Watts' eyes he was simply a printshop worker, a novice, and a severely handicapped one at that. Mr Watts did not like him reading on the job and did not take kindly to his absences. He was warned to mend his ways if he wished for a printshop post abroad. Kitto promptly resigned from the CMS.

Deprived by his disability of the social interaction that most of us take for granted, John Kitto's well-being, perhaps even his sanity, depended on the mental and spiritual stimulation of his reading. Few of his contemporaries would understand this. He belonged, moreover, to a social class that had begun to regard the principles of "self-help" with almost religious veneration. Magazines such as *Family Friend* encouraged their readers to redeem the time that might otherwise be "wasted on trifles or indolence".[6] The famous manual *Self-Help* by Samuel Smiles, published in 1859, contained cheering examples of "mutual improvement societies" established during the preceding decades, along with true stories of labouring men and women who had acquired by their own efforts the ability to write and speak with authority on political, scientific, literary and religious topics. The "improvement" of innate capabilities through "industry" was seen as the key to "character" and to "success in life". Habits of "orderliness", "prudence" and "thrift" could make any working man "respectable" and "independent", enabling him to provide for a secure, healthy and happy family. All this was meat and drink to John Kitto. He was determined to "improve" himself, to develop his full potential, to equip himself for "usefulness". In practice it meant that every second was precious. "I cannot accuse myself," he said in 1824, "of having wasted or misemployed a moment of my time since I left the workhouse."[7] He even begrudged six hours a night for sleep. And like all self-motivators, he worked best on his own, floundering restlessly at work required of him by someone else but taking endless pains in pursuit of a project suggested by his own imagination.

His benefactors were by no means pleased to hear of his resignation; they wrote with rebukes, exhortations and threats. The students at the missionary college were more sympathetic, and in prospect of leaving them Kitto began to regret his rather hasty and petulant decision. Norris Groves, supported by a Plymouth clergyman, interceded with the CMS, and in due course he was reinstated, after giving a somewhat rash promise to "abandon literary pursuits". Kitto was intensely grateful to his friend and wrote appreciatively of Groves: "He did not say, like others, 'Lie in the bed of your own making;' but though himself the most aggrieved, has come forth repeatedly to my help."[8]

Rather than return him to Mr Watts, plans were made for Kitto to go overseas immediately – directly to the printshop in Malta. On 20th June 1827, he boarded the ship *Wilberforce* and embarked for the Mediterranean. He looked forward keenly to Hannah following a few months later, and to the prospect of marriage.

For some months Kitto had grown increasingly reluctant to speak, preferring to write every communication on a slate. During his six-week voyage, however, his two Christian companions on board were a German doctor and a converted Polish Jew. With the utmost kindness, they urged him not to lose the ability to pronounce words. Eventually, Kitto tells us, "they entered into a conspiracy, in which the captain of the ship joined, not to understand a word I said otherwise than orally, throughout the voyage."[9] Never having been at sea before, Kitto was particularly interested in the workings of a sailing ship: "As I had much to ask… I made very great progress with my tongue." Soon he was able to talk freely again, to strangers and even to foreigners, resorting to the slate only when completely unable to make himself understood.

From out at sea Kitto looked back on the familiar hills of Devon, sensitive both to a "feeling of desolateness" and to a consciousness of God's presence with him. One advantage of his head-injury and resulting lack of balance was that he suffered not the slightest discomfort from seasickness, an ability that greatly impressed the ship's captain. He chose to sleep on deck in order to enjoy the sunrise and sunset, and to miss nothing of the scenery – the mountains of Portugal, the straits of Gibraltar, then the distant coasts of Africa and southern Europe divided by the blue expanse of the Mediterranean Sea. On the evening of 30th July the ship entered the harbour of La Valetta, and next morning Kitto and his companions disembarked in Malta.

On arrival, he was shown round the three presses and introduced to the six other workers and native translators. Kitto liked what he saw of his new colleagues, and especially his capable supervisor, the scholarly William Jowett: "Of all the men I know, Mr Jowett is second to none in any valuable or useful quality or endowment; or if second to any, only to Mr Groves."[10] The CMS workers had a busy programme of preaching and teaching as well as writing, translating and printing gospel tracts and books in Greek, Arabic, Maltese and Italian. In Malta itself, distribution of tracts was forbidden by authority of the Roman Catholic Church, but quantities of literature were sent to neighbouring countries. As Kitto's responsibilities were explained to him, he felt he could at last call himself a missionary, or at least an assistant to missionaries. He started to learn the principles of written Arabic, as this was to be his speciality. Until then, no one in the printshop, apart from Jowett himself, knew how to work the Arabic type.

For several weeks, while accommodation was being arranged for him, Kitto slept on the floor in a room bare of furniture. But with the prospect of marriage and of usefulness before him, he was perfectly happy. Sacrifices and difficulties he could willingly accept for the sake of such a high and noble calling; few in secular employment, and few in the homeland, could feel their lives so well spent as the team of workers at the printing press. "I love Malta," he confided. "As a Missionary and a Christian I feel that the place in which I am is the best place for me, for I am now really aware of no other in which I could hope to be equally useful."[11]

But time passed, and Kitto became anxious. For eight months he had received no word from his fiancée. Regularly he had written to her, care of the CMS committee in London, but he began to wonder, had his letters been forwarded? And had her letters to him been sent on by the committee?[12] When word finally came, it was to confirm his worst fears: "She who was dearer to me than all other things my heart ever knew" had abandoned him and married someone else. He went to his room, shut the door, and did not come out for two days. It was later discovered that Kitto's letters never reached the young lady. Her mother, disapproving of him, encouraged her to think he had forgotten her.

Kitto sank rapidly towards the morbid state of his earlier years. The faith with which he had tried to comfort others now brought little consolation. Providence had sent him blow upon blow: his stunted birth, the poverty of his home... followed by the fall, his deafness and recurrent pain; then mocked, misunderstood, beaten around the head and ears, twice wounded by a committee with power to command his time, his happiness and all his hopes; and now betrayed by his dearest love. All his feelings told him he was "one marked out for pain, trouble and bitterness, to whom expectation is delusive and all hope vain."[13] He tried to sleep, but sleep would not come; he read late into the night, but reading brought no relief. "I became dangerously ill," he observed, "and we all thought that my cares and my afflictions, my miscalculations and my errors would now be terminated."[14]

His missionary colleagues were sympathetic. They took him riding in the countryside and showed him round the historic parts of La Valetta, but nothing seemed to help. Never much good on his feet, Kitto no longer had the strength to stand ten hours a day at the press. And though no fault was found with his typesetting, or with his hours of work, his employers suspected it was nocturnal reading that had sapped his energy; he had broken his promise to relinquish "literary pursuits". A labouring man, they told him, should take exercise and build up his physique, not skulk indoors. And if he would not pull himself together, there was only one solution.

His eighteen months in Malta, having started so brightly, ended with a crushing sense of failure. He had proved himself quite unworthy to be a missionary. What would Mr Groves and his other benefactors say? They had borne with all his ups and downs so far, but their patience must be sorely tried. He packed his few belongings and climbed on board ship for home. It was January 1829. During his voyage out, he had gazed enraptured at the mountains of Granada. Now "his heart was too hard and cold to care two pins for all the snowy mountains in the universe."[15]

Arriving in London, Kitto found Norris Groves caught up with enthusiasm for his mission to the East. The dentist, it seemed, had not lost faith in his former apprentice and even invited Kitto to join the party to Persia. Kitto, however, had no heart for such a brave endeavour; he returned to the familiar streets of Plymouth. Here his former benefactors said there was no more they could do for him. His "repeated breaches with the Missionary Committee" were proof enough of a proud and obstinate spirit. He had squandered every opportunity offered for advancement and usefulness. Profoundly hurt, Kitto wrapped himself in a dignified reserve that alienated the few friends still remaining to him.

The CMS had granted him, on his dismissal from Malta, a quarter's salary and a gift of £30. With this he decided to set up "a stationer's shop or circulating library" in a village near Plymouth. His funds were soon exhausted, however, and he was forced to pawn his watch and other articles. At this point Norris Groves stepped in once more. As a man with some business experience, he warned Kitto that chances of financial success for his shop were small. How would he like to work instead as a printer's assistant with John Synge and Henry Craik in Teignmouth? Kitto agreed. As the time drew near for Groves's departure, Kitto went up to London to bid farewell to his kindest and most understanding friend. Whilst there, he heard news of the young woman who had jilted him. To his shock and surprise, she had died that very week, seemingly full of remorse for her treatment of him. He resolved to go and "look on her corpse" where it lay in Islington. This experience profoundly affected him, and along with his recent rifts in Plymouth, completed his disenchantment with the land of his birth.

It was a time of profound spiritual upheaval for John Kitto, and not without its value, for he later wrote, "I doubt if my heart were ever truly converted to

God till after I was at Plymouth the last time."[16] When Groves again asked him to come to Persia, he immediately agreed. He should consider carefully, advised Groves, before giving up the prospect of a respectable job with a guaranteed income in favour of a missionary calling that offered hardship and danger with nothing more than the supply of his daily needs in answer to prayer. But his mind was made up. He would serve as tutor to the Groves boys, Henry and Frank, aged ten and nine.

In fact Kitto's accumulation of general knowledge, acquired through his years of avid reading, equipped him reasonably well for such a task, although his total deafness and slurred speech, and his lack of any cultured upbringing and formal education might make him an unusual teacher. He could certainly not ensure that the boys' conversation was gracious and grammatically correct. But whatever others might think of John Kitto at the age of twenty-four, Groves had not lost faith in him – neither his intellectual ability, nor his Christian beliefs, nor his commitment to hard work. Nevertheless, he left Kitto in no doubt that he was going to Persia as a tutor, not as a missionary. This was something Kitto did not quite understand, but he was not inclined to argue. The boys were lively and intelligent, and had already learnt to communicate with him quite fluently on their fingers, spelling each word letter by letter.

Norris Groves himself was in his element, visiting friends and speaking about the call of Christ to take the gospel into all the world. There was enthusiasm everywhere. The prospect of being Christ's personal representative in Persia, what a wonderful privilege – to be "a watchman at the outports [*sic*] of his kingdom."[17] "Ah! my dear friend," he wrote to Caldecott, "it is a glorious cause, and one much at variance with the snares, temptations and allurements of this world. It has, doubtless, its own peculiar trials, but they are spiritual. I know no state where such close communion with God is necessarily kept up, as where you are almost placed, like the ravens, to be fed day by day from your Father's hands."[18] But Norris Groves was far too mature a Christian, and far too humble a man, to play the hero for long. No one was more aware than he of the frailties of human nature – the reality of bearing spiritual treasure in jars of clay. It was not the prospect of a man doing something for God that fired the imagination of so many in Devon and Ireland and London; it was the expectation of *what God would do* through the simplest of men, in response to prayer and faith.

Settled in temporary accommodation in London, the air of excitement in the Groves household showed no sign of abating as people came and went and letters arrived from friends further afield. "Many have offered to accompany us," Mary wrote, "and we have sometimes felt we should have a large party: a few days afterwards we have found ourselves standing alone. But our God has been very good in enabling us to feel that in the end we shall have those whom he himself had chosen for us."[19] It was a cosmopolitan circle. The Scot

Henry Craik received a strong invitation to join them, but declined for family reasons. Others interested were the Devonshire army officer George Wigram, the Irish doctor Edward Cronin, the Jewish craftsmen Abrahams and Belsom, the London-Irish aristocrat John Parnell and the Oxford scholar Frank Newman of French Huguenot descent. George Müller, the German, was not yet on the scene. The Cornishman John Kitto was quite moved by it all: "When I first became acquainted with Mr Groves's design, words can but poorly describe the feelings it inspired. The step was so opposed to the selfish calculations of human policy and interest, and indicated so warm and intense an appreciation of the supreme importance of unseen realities; there was so much to relinquish, so much opposition and injurious treatment to encounter, and so heavy a cross to be borne, that I contemplated it as the most exalted exhibition of devotedness to the cause of a crucified Saviour that… can possibly be made. It manifested a martyr's energy, and fortitude and zeal."[20]

One thing, however, was not yet decided. Where exactly were they aiming for? In which of the countless cities of the Middle East should they set up their base? Perhaps Bushehr on the eastern shore of the Persian Gulf, perhaps Basra at the head of the Gulf, both easily accessible by sea; or maybe somewhere in the Persian highlands.[21] How could they decide? As the time for departure drew near, Groves was invited to call upon a wealthy lady. She was an Armenian from Persia, "a native of the country", and she wished to travel with her negro servant and other attendants in the safety of their company to join her husband, Major Robert Taylor, recently appointed as British Resident in Baghdad.[22] At first her request seemed to Groves "a great charge", and yet, coming at that very moment, perhaps providential. He accepted the responsibility cheerfully, "hoping that the Lord has set up his candle in her heart."[23] The party eventually comprised Norris and Mary Groves with their two boys, Henry and Frank, Groves's sister Lydia, Mr Bathie (a young Scotsman recruited in Ireland), a young lady by the name of Charlotte Taylor,[24] and John Kitto, in addition to Mrs Taylor and her four servants. Others were hoping to form a second party to follow them a few weeks later.

Groves laid plans for the first stage of their journey. Whilst making enquiries with a London shipping company, he was invited to breakfast with a friend, and found at the table none other than John Parnell, whom he had known in Dublin. Parnell had just made one of those fortunate mistakes which in the purposes of God turn out to be a blessing in disguise. That morning he was actually supposed to be in Portsmouth to meet a wealthy Christian friend by the name of Puget, but he had mistaken the day. Puget was about to sell a large ocean-going yacht. Impressed by the turn of events, Parnell set off for Portsmouth immediately, where he found his friend quite willing to change his plans and undertake a final cruise before parting with the boat. There and then, a passage to St Petersburg was offered to the missionary party free of charge. In the Russian capital they would meet up with Mrs Taylor and her entourage for the next stage overland.

ENDNOTES

1 M225

2 Kitto whimsically described the advantages of bookstall browsing: it is a form of recreation that costs nothing, provides healthy outdoor exercise and gives training in the social skills required to pacify booksellers. In addition, it helps develop the memory, for what is read must be remembered until such time as it can be written down. And as the browser has the freedom of every bookstall, Kitto remarked, "Few would be able to boast a larger library than myself" (Eadie, 117-118).

3 Eadie, 128-130

4 Eadie, 119, 100

5 Eadie, 133

6 Harrison, 170

7 Eadie, 123

8 Eadie, 137

9 Eadie, 142

10 Ryland, 263; M7

11 Ryland, 266

12 At this time there was no Royal Mail. Letters were entrusted to local carriers, some of whom were more reliable than others. Not till 1840 was the Penny Post introduced for letters within the British Isles, and even then overseas mail continued to be sent by special arrangement with trading companies, military posts and banks.

13 Eadie, 157

14 Eadie, 151

15 Eadie, 154

16 Eadie, 208

17 Letter to Caldecott, April 1827 (M19).

18 Letter dated June 1825 (M12), referring to Lk 12:24.

19 M50

20 Written in 1826 (M30-31, citing Ryland, 203).

21 At this time Bushehr (generally spelt Bushire) and Basra (Bussora) are mentioned as possible destinations in a letter from Groves to Henry Drummond (?April 1829). Basra is mentioned in another, from Groves to Dr Robert Pinkerton (23 May 1829).

22 The British Resident was a diplomatic official appointed by the East India Company and supported by the British government. He would deal with local authorities for the protection of British commerce and the promotion of British influence.

23 Letter from Mary Groves to Caldecott, 15 May 1829 (M51).

24 Miss Taylor's Christian name, though not mentioned by Groves or Kitto, is evident from a letter in the Basel Mission archives (Pfander to Blumhardt, 1 Nov. 1829). She was almost certainly no relation to Major Taylor.

Two Routes to Baghdad, 1829 and 1830–32

"These are deeply interesting countries
to those who can be happy in bestowing all their strength
in planting under the prospect
that others will reap the fruits."

Norris Groves [1]

10

Actually On My Way

On 12th June 1829 the party set sail from Gravesend with Puget and Parnell in the yacht *Osprey*.² A small group stood on the shore to wave them off, including Bessie Paget who had come all the way from Devonshire to see them prayerfully on their way. The wind was at first against them, but though they could make little progress there was plenty to be done. The missionary team assembled on deck with the yacht's crew for worship every morning and evening. They met at other times on their own for Bible study and prayer, and they composed lengthy letters to friends and family. Henry and Frank (aged ten and nine) enjoyed exploring the boat and climbing the rigging. Groves himself wrote triumphantly to Caldecott: "After many years of reflection about the work of a missionary, I am now actually on my way." He was looking forward to the fresh challenge: "The hand of the Lord is strong upon us all, enabling us to hope in his mercy and believe in his promises... May the Lord, of his great mercy, keep among us the spirit of love and brotherly union; this is a very earnest prayer of mine, for it is so lovely to see brethren dwell together in unity."³

They braved a heavy storm in the Kattegat;⁴ all the passengers had to stay below and most were seasick. Groves was pleased to see John Kitto happy and getting on well with the boys. This "leads us to feel assured that he is really sent us by the Lord."⁵ Kitto himself had a dream in which the helm of the ship was held in the limp hand of the lover he had lost, whereupon a thick mist came down upon them. When it cleared, the helm was "in the hand of the Master himself. There was nothing terrible in the appearance. He was as in the days of his sojourning among men – meek, lowly and kind. Yet I trembled. But he said to me, 'Fear not, for I am with thee'... This was the Pilot who never yet made shipwreck of aught that he ever guided; and our safety now was assured."⁶ After a brief halt for repairs in Copenhagen, they sailed through the Baltic and eventually reached St Petersburg.

The arrival of the yacht with its unusual party of travellers caused quite a stir. Introduced to the Christian community in St Petersburg, Groves spoke about the life of faith and the call to preach Christ to the ends of the earth: "I cannot but rejoice in the sensation which the coming of this little yacht on such an errand has excited in the minds of many! It has stirred them up to desires and, I trust, actions of which they had not thought before… I think it may prove a stimulus to many others who hitherto have been satisfied in contributing a yearly guinea to the cause of God among the heathen."[7] The minister of a Congregationalist church visited them that evening. "He is really a true person," Groves remarked. "His congregation love him and each other, and there seems a sweet harmony among them, unaffected, I think I may say, by those lesser differences of opinion which so much try the Church of God in England."[8]

With his transparent sincerity Norris Groves had the ability to draw out from new acquaintances the warmth of devotion to Christ he felt himself; it mattered not to what denomination they belonged. His heart was drawn to a couple connected with the Bible Society, and to a military man "devoted to the cause of God and willing to help in every good work." A third was "a simple affectionate Christian", who "dwelt very strongly on the importance of being indifferent to what men think and on the importance of what Christ thinks; also on the expediency of not pouring out faster than we take in." They were introduced to an evangelical Quaker lady, Miss Sarah Kilham, who had opened a school for girls, "half of whom were slaves". She taught reading, writing, numeracy, and useful domestic skills such as sewing, "and, above all, their duty to God and man, which is done in a way beautifully simple and impressive." Miss Kilham was one of the first unmarried women to serve as an overseas missionary. Without the advantage of natural good looks, she had the "unfading beauty of a gentle and quiet spirit, which is of great worth in God's sight."[9] Evidently in John Kitto's too, for he wrote, "I count it among the best fruits of my travel, to have formed so inestimable a friendship."[10]

Lydia Groves, Norris's younger sister, had not been well during the sea voyage. The next stage of the journey would be far more arduous – an overland trek likely to tax the endurance of the strongest. As the company prepared to move on she was advised by a local physician to return to England.[11] The depleted party (Norris and Mary Groves, Henry and Frank, John Kitto and Charlotte Taylor) were now joined by Bathie and Mrs Taylor with her entourage, who had preceded them to St Petersburg. After three weeks they finally set off in two large horse-drawn carriages, their baggage in a cart, fortified with many prayers and laden with offerings – a bag of biscuits, sugar, coffee, cakes and a quantity of lemons. The cost of their accommodation and their onward transport had all been paid by the friends they had made in St Petersburg, and Groves reflected, "I trust this will make us doubly careful to spend all for his glory and as little as possible for ourselves."[12] They were in good spirits, handing out Russian and Armenian scriptures as they went. Sunday they enjoyed as a day of rest, and took the opportunity to "give a Russian Testament to a little girl, who read it very well."[13]

So focused was Groves on the spiritual destitution of the places they passed through, and so preoccupied with horse dealers, baggage carriers and innkeepers, that he quite neglected to follow the nineteenth-century convention of recording the traveller's impressions of rivers and mountains, buildings, farming techniques, and the clothing and customs of the people. Kitto was a little more observant, although he could hear nothing of what was said by the guide who travelled with them. Despite its outward manners of courtesy and politeness, he was not impressed by Tsarist Russia: its "air of military despotism – the strut of office which meets you at every turn," its toleration of negro slavery, its scanty bookshops, its superstitious Orthodoxy with black-robed priests conspicuous in the streets, and worshippers bowing and crossing themselves before the pictures and statues displayed in the public places. Here indeed was the feudal system in its most rigid form.[14] Moscow was a city which pleased Kitto more, although they could find little Christian fellowship there. Beyond Moscow their carriage wheel broke several times, and once the axle caught fire, but providentially the accidents always happened "where help was immediately at hand".[15]

Along the road they came upon a gypsy encampment, and Kitto wondered why so little thought had been given to sharing the gospel with the gypsies who regularly sold their wares from door to door in England and throughout Europe. With their love of the itinerant life, what wonderful missionaries they would make in the Islamic East![16] In the churchyard at Ekinnouskoy, Kitto came upon a newly dug grave, and kneeling beside it a very old woman and a younger woman "with her lips to the consecrated earth" and three children – all weeping for one who was a son, a husband and a father. Here in this foreign land, a poor family were brought face to face with death and felt just as any English family would feel. "Death, thought I, is a terrible thing, after all that philosophers have said and written and acted – terrible to the dead, terrible to the living. It was intended to be terrible... Is it not terrible to close the eye for ever on the happy vales and ancient mountains? Is it not terrible to hear no more the voices which have been our music?... Oh! it is terrible, very terrible to die." And yet, mused Kitto, it is the anguish of death that makes us long all the more eagerly for the world to come, for the resurrection of the body and the joy of reunion with our loved ones: "I believe the Bible, without doubt or reservation... And with these bright prospects before us, there may even be moments in which, feeling the dissolution of these elements a necessary preliminary to full enjoyment, we may eagerly look forward to that hour when this material shall have vanished like a cloud."[17]

In many places along the way people asked for medical help, hoping or perhaps assuming that a European party would include a doctor. Groves was happy to do what he could, and his medicines were eagerly received.[18] The further east they travelled, the rougher became the roads, and the dirtier the inns. Still some way short of the river Volga, the back spring of their carriage broke and they had to go in search of a blacksmith. A little further on, after a particularly arduous stage, two of the horses collapsed and died. The days were too hot for comfort, and the nights near to freezing. Five nights in succession they slept without changing their clothes.

At Sarepta, near Volgograd, they rested for a couple of days at a substantial farm settlement of four hundred people, established by Moravian missionaries from Germany some sixty-three years earlier. Groves learned something of their history from its leader John Martin Niluhmoun and commented, "he is a pleasing man and speaks French freely".[19] Itinerant outreach among the nomadic tribes of pagan Calmucs had won them a number of converts, but the government had recently compelled these to join the Russian Orthodox Church, and forbidden the Moravians to preach or teach any more among the native people of the region. Groves was saddened to see the settlement continuing as it was, "no longer a missionary station but simply a colony of artificers [i.e. craftsmen]."[20] Experience of such Christian communities also led him to wonder if their commitment to "external order and regularity" actually hindered warm personal affection towards Christ and an eager desire to please him. He was reminded of the liturgical cathedral services of the Church of England, beautifully performed by choristers and congregation whose minds were engaged throughout with other matters.[21] Following the course of the Volga down to its great delta at the northern end of the Caspian Sea, the party eventually reached the town of Astrakhan, fourteen hundred miles from St Petersburg. Somewhat to their surprise, they were "very little fatigued and even in better health than when they set out".[22]

In Astrakhan they found a Scottish Presbyterian by the name of William Glen hard at work translating the Bible into Persian (Farsi); he had reached the book of Ezekiel. Kitto was impressed with the self-discipline of their host. "At his appointed hour he withdrew and was seen no more until the labour of his day was ended." Then in the evening he was free to offer "the most cordial hospitality... and consideration for his visitors." Here was one who could quietly resist the temptation felt by many missionaries to drop what they are doing and accompany well-meaning visitors on trips to see the local sights. He did find time, however, to introduce Groves to a number of men from the Armenian Church, including some priests, who were "very easy of access and kind but still given up to the world and having an external religion in which they had no heart."[23] Fellowship with Glen and his wife was stimulating and (if one can read between the lines of his journal) typical of Groves in its remarkable blend of spirited doctrinal disputation and sweet brotherly affection. A week later when Groves left, he did so, "deeply impressed with all the kindness and Christian love which had been manifested to us by the dear Glens, and with the hope that we may meet again, if it be the Lord's will, to renew many of those communications we had together, when experience will have either confirmed or corrected them."[24]

To this point they had been guided by a courier from St Petersburg, and now an Armenian merchant offered to accompany them on the next stage of their journey. South of Astrakhan was sandy desert. As the country grew wilder they were glad to join a caravan with a military escort. The inns became shabbier and the rocks steeper as they entered the wooded gorges of the Caucasian mountains. Forced by the threat of bandits to travel in a large convoy, they found the accommodation in each place they reached woefully inadequate for the number of travellers. At one point their carriages were stuck in the mud for five hours, and lacking sufficient horses the party was forced to split up. Further on they were accompanied through rough country by an escort of "three hundred Tartar carts".[25] During the night in Catherinegrad a fire broke out, and they watched as the adjoining wooden buildings were pulled down to prevent the flames spreading. The blaze was finally checked a short distance from the house where they were lodged.

Progress was slow, and sometimes they had to wait three or four days for horses. The animals laboured heavily as their attendants flogged and cursed them up the winding rocky tracks. Descending a steep hill in the Caucasus mountains, part of the brake on Mrs Taylor's heavy carriage came away, and "the carriage and horses flew like lightning down the hill," overturning with a crash at the bottom. Mrs Taylor was fortunate to escape serious injury, and the Groves family even more fortunate that a damaged wheel on their carriage, unnoticed for many miles, had not cast them over the precipice into the river Kur. Groves was prompted again to review in detail all the providential circumstances of their journey. Thirteen days and nights without a change of clothes finally brought them down at sunset into the town of Teflis, "a very disagreeable place," where they searched the narrow streets for lodgings.[26]

Groves sold the carriages, and for the next stage hired three covered "German waggons", tougher than the carriages but with no springs at all. He gave some thought to their eventual destination. It was by no means clear in his mind where they should go. Further on, in Shushi, he hoped to find friends who could help them learn one or more of the languages. Perhaps they should stop there for a while. If so, he must leave the family whilst continuing himself with Mrs Taylor and her party to join her husband at his present post in Basra. Perhaps Major Taylor would be kind enough to help him find a house in Basra to serve as a base for their mission. On the other hand, Bushehr might be a more strategic location, with roads extending from the coast into the Persian highlands as far as the great cities of Shiraz and Isfahan. Perhaps he should travel on alone, take a look at each of these places, including Shiraz and

Isfahan, and assess all the possibilities before coming to a decision. As he confided these thoughts to his journal, a visitor arrived with news that Major Taylor was now in Baghdad.[27]

In Teflis itself Groves was pleased to find the pastor of a German colony, a man whose "bodily health was weak but his soul was near his Lord". Though burdened by the care of a "divided little body" of evangelical believers, "he had still a missionary spirit" and longed to be away preaching the gospel to the Nestorian or Chaldean Christians, whose priests had evidently left them in ignorance of it.[28] The German waggons proved to be real bone-shakers, and the ladies in particular suffered bumps and bruises all the way to Shushi. But they were thankful that the weather had so far been good. Their journey would have taken far longer if rain had turned the unpaved roads to mud.

Shushi was a small town perched on a hill, with a high wall for ease of defence. Most of the houses were made of dried clay on a wattle frame. The party received a "most affectionate and brotherly welcome" from five Swiss and German missionaries. These were Lutherans, trained at the Basel Mission Institute, who had opened a school and were translating books and selections of scripture into the dialects spoken by the local Armenian and Muslim populations.[29] Norris Groves found them men after his own heart: "In all my acquaintance with missionaries, I never met five such at one time."[30] Looking back on the fellowship they enjoyed together, he later recalled, "Never had I enjoyed more brotherly affection and counsel than with this dear missionary family. Never did I feel more in the spirit of that precept of the apostle, to exhort one another, than with them."[31] Like Groves, the Basel missionaries had realised "the importance of laying aside everything of this world's greatness, and descending to the level of the people." Although their house might seem primitive and very sparsely furnished from a European perspective, it was still "the best house in Shushi". This they had found to be a stumbling block to the people of the town, who could not see they had sacrificed anything at all for the sake of the gospel. The only solution would be to move to a smaller house.

Groves discussed his options with his new friends. They agreed that, rather than dividing the family and spending time in Shushi, there was much to be said for continuing immediately to Baghdad.[32] In fact for some months their own thoughts had been fixed on the needs and opportunities for a permanent mission in that area. Delighted with the dedicated spirit of these German workers, Groves was privately praying that one or other might even be led to join him. That evening after tea, two of them walked across town with him to help negotiate places for his party in a caravan to Tabriz, and on the way he told them of his prayer. To his surprise, this "created a great emotion in both their minds." In fact news of his plans had reached them before he did, and they had sensed God's leading to send one of their own group with him. The one they had in mind was Karl Gottlieb Pfander. Having already written the first draft of an evangelistic book for Muslims, Pfander wished to study Persian and Arabic for a couple of years in a location where these languages were spoken. Groves was overwhelmed. "Thus the Lord has most graciously answered my prayer and given me a dear brother who has the same views and the same objects with myself and who also understands Turkish, one who will be a great comfort and a medium of communication with the people around us."[33]

Karl Pfander was a stocky young man, genial and good-natured with a round face and dark hair. Born in Würtemburg in southern Germany in 1803, he was eight years younger than Groves. One of nine children, the son of a village baker, he had a record of success at the local school and then at grammar school in Stuttgart. At the age of sixteen he had already decided to be a missionary and in due course was accepted at the newly established evangelical Institute at Basel in Switzerland. His studies here had included the Arabic language and the Qur'an, and after arriving at Shushi he had quickly learned Armenian, Persian and the Tartar dialect of Turkish. His background lay in the Pietist wing of the Lutheran state church with its strong tradition of disciplined Christian living heartily enjoyed by evangelical craftsmen, tradesmen and shopkeepers. All this, along with his cheerful optimism and his outstanding evangelistic abilities, made him an ideal fellow-worker for the team in Baghdad. He was at this time a widower, his wife having died in Shushi a year after their marriage.

Pfander was convinced that the entire Islamic world had reached a turning point in its history and was, indeed, ripe for conversion to Christ. Islam, he believed, was a divine scourge sent for a time to chastise the apostate churches of the East. Returning to the true faith, they would see Islam collapse before their united evangelical testimony and the vigorous preaching of the gospel. The disintegration of the Ottoman Empire,[34] the advent of Western technology, the extension of superior European moral, social and political systems, the renascent missionary vision of the Protestant churches, the recent translation of the scriptures into native tongues – all these remarkable signs of change heralded the imminent conversion of the Islamic world. The old complacencies of the East would give way to disillusionment, followed by a willing acceptance of the new order. Social and political leaders must adopt Western innovations or face extinction, and therefore missionary effort should be focused on the conversion of educated, forward-thinking men who would usher their own people into a new age of universal Christian civilisation. This was the theory that filled Karl Pfander with cheerful optimism even as he jolted from town to town preaching and distributing literature in the mountains round Shushi, an object of rumour and suspicion, cursed, stoned and spat upon, and often in fear for his life. Groves and Pfander would have much to talk about as they travelled.[35]

The next stage of their journey took them on horseback through the mountains of Georgia and Armenia to Tabriz. With them went six large boxes of

Bibles, New Testaments and other scriptures from Shushi for use in Baghdad. The ladies, riding side-saddle, suffered "much fatigue". Kitto was thrown four times, once landing on his head. Having lost his cap he was fortunate at that moment to be wearing a thick turban. One of the Muslims in the caravan came to see how he was after his fall, and kindly brought him a piece of cake. It was a good thing, he told Kitto, that the flimsy cap had been lost, as replacing it with the turban had saved his head. "It was not only a good thing but a providential thing," replied Kitto, adding for his own encouragement, "God has not done with me yet; I have more yet to do in this world, and more to suffer!"[36]

Horses were twice stolen from their encampment before they finally crossed into Persian territory. To celebrate, they "had a little evening service together and offered up a hymn of praise where perhaps it had never been heard before." Then followed seven arduous days as their twenty remaining horses carried them, their belongings and their escort "over almost impassable roads", fortunately without tipping any of them into "the yawning abyss", and so to Tabriz.[37]

Here Charlotte Taylor left them to marry a certain Mr Nisbet of the East India Company, prompting Kitto to express his disapproval of single missionary ladies going out to the East.[38] Their devotion to the cause of mission, he suspected, was prone to crumble as soon as they met one of the many eligible bachelors who at that time occupied British diplomatic or commercial posts. Groves gained a handsome contribution from Nisbet, but lost a promising worker. He calculated that the money they had brought with them from England would not have provided for all the expenses of their journey, yet the unforeseen provision made for them repeatedly along the way had covered all their needs. "I cannot help being overwhelmed with the Lord's goodness in this respect. Instead of being in want, we have always had more than enough."[39]

Whilst in Tabriz, Kitto was introduced to a kindly government official called John McNeill, who proved to be a fund of information about the customs of Bible lands, and who took the trouble with paper and pen to answer the questions put to him. An interest was awakened which would have far-reaching consequences for the young visitor.[40]

A few days later the party joined up with another mixed company of travellers, and the caravan moved on through the mountains of Kurdistan. There followed a nightmare period of torrential rain, frightful roads, robbers, agitation, fierce dogs, and "daggers being drawn on the slightest provocation". One particular evening a quarrel arose between the Kurds and the Persians concerning the accommodation of the travellers; there were so many in the caravan that local Kurdish families must be turned out of their homes to accommodate them. Their host for the night was a Kurd of the Sunnite sect who had recently heard of Kurdish villages burned by the Persian authorities, leaving Kurdish families helpless and homeless in the mountains. He was not best pleased to discover, among the company, some Persians of the opposing, Shiite sect who were carrying some corpses for burial in a holy place. To make matters worse, the Armenian agents going ahead to arrange accommodation had allegedly "used violence" in attempting to take a fresh horse. All this "so roused the indignation of the master of the house... that he, assisted by his companions, drove them from his house and beat their horses out of the yard. An old woman, from a vantage point on the wall, set the dogs at them, and one of the Kurds was about to run his dagger into a fine horse belonging to Mrs Taylor's servant." At this point Pfander stepped in and succeeded in calming the protagonists. The party was eventually taken into the poor home of a Kurd in the next town. His wife dried their clothes, and here they were safe if not exactly comfortable. The experience served as an impressive introduction to the racial and religious complexities of the East.[41]

On the next section they met an army detachment. One of the officers turned out to be an Englishman. Surprised to find them unarmed and defenceless on such a road, he advised the party to turn back immediately on account of "the unsettled state of the country". He declared that he himself would hardly feel safe accompanied by "two battalions of soldiers". "We told him our confidence was from a higher power than such weapons," said Groves. Others also advised against travelling on, but both Pfander and Groves thought it best to continue "in firm reliance on our Lord and therefore with perfect happiness."[42] At one stopping place knives were again drawn in a dispute over a horse, and one member of the convoy was beaten by the Kurdish inhabitants. Their horses, in fact, were "very much fatigued", lacking proper food and shelter at night in these ruined and deserted villages. Ahead of them now were the armed partisans of two brothers fighting for the title of Pasha (provincial governor) of Suleimaniya. The younger was said to have paid 10,000 *toumans* for the position, whereupon the elder paid 12,000 and assembled a body of men to depose him.

In Suleimaniya Groves was pleased to give a New Testament and other books to some Nestorian Christians. He learned from their priest that they held a service every day but read the scriptures in a language·which was not understood.[43] Karl Pfander, like the first martyr Stephen, was discovering that opponents unable to "stand up against his wisdom and the Spirit by whom he spoke" would soon find more than words to hurl at him. Groves reported, "Mr Pfander had some conversation with one of the Kurds on the subject of religion. He became very angry, and showed much of his natural ferocity, though he did not appear to be an ill-disposed man. This awakened a thought in our hearts that, should we labour among them, our lives must be little valued in our sight, for this man during the conversation laid his hand on his dagger and reiterating a curse said, 'Stop, say not another word, for I must become an infidel if I listen to what you say.'"[44]

Just one mountain pass now remained between them and their destination, an area reputed to be infested with bandits. As the caravan of horses, baggage mules and drivers prepared for the climb, Groves tells us, "One of them, on seeing my belt without a dagger, at the foot of the mountain defile, seemed pressing on me the necessity of supplying myself with one; but I pointed to heaven as the source of my safety, which he seemed to understand." Halfway up they heard the cry, "Robbers!" In the mêlée a bandit was captured. So ragged was he that Groves suspected that the very clothes a missionary wore could tempt a man to attack and strip him. The peasants along the track were dressed little better. One member of the caravan was disturbed that night by thieves, and another lost three horses and some baggage. The missionary party, however, remained unscathed, and a month after leaving Tabriz, they finally entered the gates of Baghdad. "We can now say," Groves wrote, "having finished our long and perilous journey, that from St Petersburg to Baghdad we have not lost from a thread to a shoe-latchet, but have all, with all our goods, been brought hither in safety."[45] It was the sixth of December 1829. Six months had passed since they sailed from Gravesend; they had travelled almost five thousand miles, half of that on unmade tracks through sand, rocks and mud.

The hand of God upon them for good seemed all the more evident when news reached them of other travellers. A British doctor had been attacked and robbed of everything on his way to Basra, not by bandits but by the Pasha's own officers and customs men, and this while he was in a British boat belonging to the Resident, guarded by twenty-five armed *sepoys* and bearing the British flag.[46] At about the same time, a German archaeologist had been murdered in the very mountains through which they had passed. His fate particularly impressed Groves: "This unfortunate traveller was running these risks and exposing himself to these dangers for a reputation, which perhaps will now remain only in the memory of a few who knew him; probably most of his papers perished with him... And though his reputation were to spread as widely as the confines of the world, where is he gone who should enjoy it?... Oh! if they do this for a 'name', if they labour thus to collect that which is of little or no use when it is collected, what ought we not to venture in serving our Lord?"[47]

John Kitto, too, saw the hand of God in every detail of the journey, indeed in every detail of his life so far: "I do most truly believe in the doctrine of a *particular* providence... It is a doctrine from which I have, in the course of my life, derived much consolation and support, and I would not, for a great deal, relinquish the satisfaction it is so capable of affording."[48] With his physical awkwardness, his antipathy to exercise, and his "ten thousand fireside attachments", John Kitto was not a natural traveller. His total deafness meant he would not find it easy to adapt to new languages and cultures, and his meagre education would make him an improbable choice as a tutor for two intelligent young boys. His earliest literary ambitions, his hopes of marriage and his first plans for missionary service had all failed, yet here he was – perhaps the most unlikely person to be placed by God as a pioneer in the heart of the Muslim world. "So true it is," he observed, "that 'a man's heart deviseth his way, but the Lord directeth his steps.' None have had cause to feel this more strongly than myself; and with my past experience I am almost tired of devising anything at all, but am inclined to sit down quietly and take whatever it pleases God to send me, whether it appear to me good or evil, pleasant or painful."[49] Along with this went a profound sense of gratitude to the man who had given him a second chance, who had shown "unexampled and persevering and untired kindness to me."[50] Through sorrow and humiliation, Kitto had matured. He had learned to count his blessings rather than his disappointments, and he could face life with a quieter trust, a happier sense of genuine thankfulness, and a calm acceptance of whatever tomorrow might bring.

At midnight the little company set out on the final stage of their journey.

ENDNOTES

[1] R202

[2] Gravesend: an anchorage in the Thames estuary about twenty miles east of London.

[3] M53

[4] Kattegat: the sea between Denmark and Sweden.

[5] J12

[6] Ryland, 302; Eadie, 168. Kitto had this dream after landing at St Petersburg.

[7] M55. Guinea: a British gold coin taken out of circulation in 1813, worth one pound and one shilling. As a unit of currency, the guinea was still used after this date in certain transactions such as fees charged for professional services.

[8] M54 (J19)

[9] 1 Pet 3:4

[10] Eadie, 170. For the life and work of Sarah Kilham see Rosslyn & Tosi, 219, 231-5.

[11] Prior to Kitto's recruitment, Lydia was intending to serve as teacher for the Groves children (CMS Minutes, 9 Aug. 1825). Her administrative skills might have been a great asset to the work, especially in India. They were later put to good use in Müller's orphanage (Groves E K, *Successors*, 11).

[12] J28; M55

[13] J34; M56

[14] Serfdom would not be abolished in Russia until 1861, and slavery in America not till the defeat of the southern states in 1865.

[15] J37; M56

[16] Eadie, 172

[17] Eadie, 173-176

[18] The medicines used at this period were generally bought from drug wholesalers and mixed by the physician or pharmacist himself. The ingredients included various plant extracts such as emetine, quinine, myrrh, ipecac and cinchonine, some of which had only recently been discovered in the New World. Mercury (used especially in calomel) was the mainstay of remedies for skin complaints and syphilis. Arsenic was an ingredient in many tonics. Cod-liver oil and malt extract were prescribed "to fortify the system". Morphine was offered as a sedative and anaesthetic. The individual practitioner would employ his own judgment in deciding the proportions of ingredients, the amount and frequency of the dose, the occasions for bloodletting, and the diet most suitable for the patient – all of which tended to make his profession more of an art than a science. The danger of contagion was common knowledge, but the role of polluted water (cholera, typhoid) and insect vectors, such as fleas (plague) and mosquitoes (malaria), had not yet been realised (Bynum, 119, 121, 164-165).

[19] J47. Groves had learned to read and write French at school but admitted to "some difficulty in conversation".

[20] J47-49 (M59); Zwick, 14-28

[21] J52 (M60-61)

[22] M62

[23] The Armenian Church was a monophysite body founded in the early fourth century as the national church of the first officially Christian nation, Armenia. It severed its connection with the Greek Orthodox Church in AD 552, and its patriarch resides in the holy city of Etschmiezin (Edschmiadsin) in the foothills of Mount Ararat. The traditional Armenian Bible contains some books found in no other Bible. In the fifteenth century many Armenians joined the Roman Catholic Church and became known as Armenian Catholics.

[24] J67; M62. Dr William Glen of the Edinburgh Society might be considered the first Protestant missionary to establish an ongoing evangelistic outreach to Muslims. His Persian Old Testament was used for many years in conjunction with Henry Martyn's New Testament (Vander Werff, 100; Richter, 403).

[25] Tartars (or Tatars): a people of Mongolian origin settled in many parts of the Russian and Persian empires and speaking their own language of a Turkic type – a residue of invasions under Genghis Khan in the thirteenth century. In the mid-nineteenth century most were nominal Muslims, converted from Buddhism, still adhering to ancient shamanistic and animistic practices.

[26] M65. Teflis, sometimes spelt Tiflis, is the modern town of Tbilisi in Georgia.

[27] J72-73, 77, 94

[28] J76; M65. Nestorian Christians: a body led since the fifth century by its own patriarch, who after AD 762 resided for several centuries in Baghdad. Of Assyrian descent and preferring the title "Assyrian Christians", they traditionally maintained that Christ possessed two natures, and that the divine *Logos* clothed itself with humanity but did not truly become man. Renowned for scholarship and for the founding of schools and hospitals, the Nestorian Church flourished for several centuries and spread with great missionary zeal from Persia to India, Arabia, and even to China and Tartary. They generally speak a form of Aramaic (Syriac) or Arabic. A Nestorian community, known as the Mar Thoma Church, still survives

in south-western India. The Chaldean Church comprises a body of Nestorians who from the sixteenth century onwards accepted the authority of the Pope in Rome whilst retaining their own Patriarch.

[29] J79; M66. The Shushi mission commenced around 1825 under the leadership of Felician Martin von Zaremba (J81-83; Richter, 97-100). Possession of the modern town of Shushi (or Shusha) is disputed between Armenia and Azerbaijan.

[30] Letter from Groves to Pearson, 14 Oct. 1829.

[31] J89; M67

[32] J84-85. The fact that Major Taylor was now settled in Baghdad figured largely in Groves's decision to make his initial base there rather than Basra (Groves to Pearson, 14 Oct. 1829). In 1824 Joseph Wolff had spent a month in Baghdad, "preaching to the Jews and circulating hundreds of Bibles". It was a place with obvious potential for evangelistic outreach (Wolff, I, 327-328; J114).

[33] J80; M67; letter from Pfander dated 20 Oct. 1829 in *Gazette des Missions Evangéliques*.

[34] Ottoman Empire: a powerful Muslim state with its capital in Constantinople (Istanbul) controlling territories in eastern Europe, North Africa and Asia from the late thirteenth century until the end of the First World War.

[35] Alexander Duff in India had a similar optimistic view of the potential for mass conversion of Hindus through the introduction of a British educational system. Christian educators in China and Japan expressed the same hopes in their own spheres. Groves himself was not convinced there would be a golden age *before* the second coming of Christ. (See Chapter 29 of this book.)

[36] Ryland, 369-370

[37] J89-90; M68

[38] Eadie, 187. Alexander Nisbet was a committed Christian. He hoped to start a small school in Tabriz and to offer hospitality to any missionaries who might pass through (J94, 97; Eadie, 254).

[39] J98; M69

[40] Eadie, 188

[41] J101-102; M69-70

[42] J104-105; M71

[43] J109; M73. This would be ancient Syriac, a liturgical form of Aramaic.

[44] J108; M73

[45] J111; M74

[46] Sepoys: Indian soldiers trained in European fashion

[47] M81

[48] Ryland, 374; Eadie, 189

[49] Eadie, 199 (Prov 16:9 AV)

[50] Eadie, 199

"In this world's history,
great things are not accomplished
but by great sacrifices."

Norris Groves [1]

11

The Headquarters of Islamism

The weary travellers were welcomed to "the city of a hundred mosques"[2] by the British representative of the East India Company, known officially as "the Resident". Major Robert Taylor met them at daybreak, twenty miles outside town, and led them through its winding streets to his substantial home. Delighted to see his wife in good health after such an arduous journey, he offered a house adjacent to his own for the use of the missionary team, and a teacher who could help them with the Arabic language. To Kitto's delight he also allowed them free access to his library.[3] Relieved that all had gone so well, Groves made copious notes in his journal, concluding, "God has put into our hands all we could desire at this point of our mission."[4] His idea was to make Baghdad a base for outreach to the surrounding region and for longer expeditions into the mountains of Kurdistan and Persia. Kitto's expectations were somewhat more sedentary: "I have no locomotive talents and shall probably be a fixture here, writing books and tracts, and bringing up the little boys."[5]

Baghdad was a city with a glorious past, now sadly in decay. The once glittering capital of Harun Ar-Rashid, scene of the wild and racy adventures of the *Arabian Nights*, could no longer boast a palace as sumptuous as any depicted in those merry pages. Between the years 750 and 1258, Baghdad had been the political capital of the "House of Islam", its rulers recognised as the *Caliphs* or "Successors" of the Prophet Muhammad. But after the sacking of the city by the Mongols in 1258, power had shifted to Constantinople (Istanbul), the seat of the Ottoman Empire, and for more than two hundred years Baghdad had languished in subjection to Turkish rule.[6]

The Turks had inherited and developed the Islamic *dhimmi* system, regulating the rights and obligations of subject peoples refusing to convert to Islam. In reality, every generation of Christians and Jews under Muslim authority had been harassed and exploited with impunity, especially in the territories to the east of the capital.[7] *Dhimmi* status required a contractual relationship, with accredited representatives of each racial and religious group guaranteeing political submission in return for governmental protection. Members of all the Orthodox churches were represented to the government by the Greek Orthodox patriarch in Constantinople, despite the fact that many had no contact with him and, indeed, looked to patriarchs of their own in Antioch, Jerusalem or Alexandria. Adherents of the various monophysite sects,[8] such as the Syrian Jacobites and the Egyptian Copts, were similarly lumped together for administrative purposes and identified as "Armenians", represented by the Armenian patriarch. The channelling of all matters through these two patriarchs naturally raised the political stakes in the appointment of these men and of their administrative staffs. Conspiracy and strife abounded, and bribes were offered and received to secure the rise or fall of particular Christian factions. Throughout the eighteenth century the Greek Orthodox patriarchate changed hands thirty-one times. The previous century had seen sixty-one such changes. A system like this could lead only to corruption and demoralization within the Christian communities, and no doubt the mullahs and imams enjoyed the spectacle.

Located on the wide plain of the river Tigris, the city of Baghdad lay just six hours' march from the equally famous Euphrates, about fifty miles north of the site occupied by ancient Babylon. Although the Industrial Revolution had hardly as yet (in 1829) touched the region, the trade-routes to the East had long been exploited by European merchants seeking spices, silks and other luxury goods for the markets of the West.[9] Some had received official charters from the Ottoman administration, with exemption from customs dues and from certain Islamic criminal procedures, along with rights to recruit local agents, translators and facilitators for commercial purposes. Members of the Eastern churches had often been engaged for such activities and enjoyed, in consequence, a degree of protection under the wing of their foreign masters.[10]

Through the efforts of Jesuit and Franciscan missionaries from the sixteenth century onwards, there had been many defections both of laity and clergy, and especially of the commercial classes, to Roman Catholicism. The result was the formation of the so-called "Uniate" communions – Greek Catholic, Coptic Catholic, Syrian Catholic, Chaldean Catholic and Armenian Catholic, and in Lebanon the Maronite Church – which retained their own liturgies under the authority of Rome.[11] This all added to a sense of confusion, mistrust and rivalry among those who maintained a Christian identity in the Middle East, and reinforced the conviction of the Muslim majority that theirs was a vastly superior religion. It was into this complex situation that Norris Groves and his friends were called to bring a simple gospel of salvation through faith in Christ.

Groves's first impression of Baghdad was somewhat overwhelming: a sense of "chilling opposition to all one's natural and spiritual feelings... an impenetrable brazen wall."[12] The city was governed by a pasha, who received his authority from Constantinople. Baghdad itself contained 70,000 Muslims, some 9000 Jews, and about 2000 identified as Christians, including 700 Armenians, a few Aramaic-speaking Syrians, the rest Roman Catholics.[13]

Among the Muslim populace, superficial courtesy veiled a general hatred of both Christians and Jews, inculcated in the children from their earliest years. Kitto felt he had come to "a place where a man's head can hardly be considered as safe as his hat in England."[14] The foreigner was resented and suspected, both as an unbelieving infidel and as a probable spy in the pay of a nation with expansionist ambitions. Nothing could be guaranteed beyond the loving purposes of God. "I have no care for my life," said Pfander. "It will be preserved as long as it is needed for the service of the Almighty."[15] "Sometimes," wrote Groves, "a boy may call us 'dog' and manifest his ill-will by some such expressions, but this is not often, nor does it proceed further."[16] There was no guarantee, however, that it would never "proceed further", and the concern to avoid the impression that they were agents of a foreign power was one of the reasons prompting Groves to move away from the house of the British Resident as soon as possible.[17]

One of the first questions they must decide was which language to learn. Their enquiries ascertained that colloquial Arabic was spoken as a first or second language by more than eighty per cent of the population of Baghdad, and throughout the surrounding region too. This, Groves concluded, was the language that he and the boys must tackle first.[18] Mary, for work amongst the women and children, would learn Armenian.[19] Pfander was already making great strides in his Arabic studies with a moolah from the local mosque.[20]

Groves made extensive enquiries about the beliefs of the various Christian sects. He was surprised to find that the Muslim tribes of Arabs in the region were mostly Shiites, followers of Ali, rather than Sunnites, followers of Omar.[21] He heard about the Druses, who had split from orthodox Islam,[22] and the Yazidis, who were said to worship the devil.[23] The first Eastern Christians he met, Armenians and Arabic-speaking Roman Catholics, seemed strongly attached to their traditions by long-standing racial and family ties, and showed little understanding of the gospel or of a personal relationship with God. Groves suggested a writing project to Kitto: he could compile a handbook describing all the sects, cults and religions of the Middle East, commenting on everything of interest to Christian missionaries seeking to work among them.

Every Sunday morning they came together, as they had in England, for Bible reading, fellowship, breaking of bread and prayer. Friday evenings were devoted to fasting and prayer for the outpouring of the Holy Spirit. Then as the first wave of culture shock started to wear off, they began to discuss what they might do to introduce to the diverse religious groups, with their age-old rites and observances, the reality of a living Saviour. Groves expressed his view that "the two great objects of the church in the latter days seem to me to be (independent of growing up herself into the stature of the fulness of Christ) the publication of the testimony of Jesus in all lands, and the calling out of the sheep of Christ that may be imprisoned in all the Babylonish systems that are in the world."[24] This meant both talking directly with Muslims about Christ and striving at the same time to awaken the apostate Eastern churches from their slumbers. There were many thousands of nominal Christians throughout the Middle East. If only they could be truly converted and sent out to preach the gospel, what wonderful results might be seen! Pfander had heard of one or two Eastern Christians elsewhere who had been genuinely born again. "To the Mohammedans also," wrote Groves optimistically, "these converts from among the fallen churches become invaluable preachers, from their facility in the vernacular language and from their being continually exposed to the question why they do not [observe Islamic customs]; whereas in our case [being foreigners] they are satisfied with simply making up their minds that their religion is best for them and ours best for us."[25] But it would not be easy. "We cannot help feeling," he said, "that the difficulties among the Mohammedans and apostate Christian churches are great beyond anything that can be imagined previous to experience. The difficulties of absolute falsehood are as nothing to those of perverted truth... In everything it is the same – prayer, praise, love – all is perverted, and yet the name retained."[26]

To help with cleaning, cooking and general chores they engaged an Armenian man, and with more difficulty, a Syrian widow, a Roman Catholic with a four-year-old boy. The Armenian, Groves noted, "seems really interested about knowing in what real Christianity consists. He feels that the Armenian system of fasts and festivals, fasting from meat and butter but getting drunk on arrack and wine, cannot be that which the Lord delights in. He seems very anxious to learn to read."[27] The Roman Catholics in general were marked by "a sort of sullen suspicion which seems almost an inseparable part of their system".[28] Perhaps this was partly because their bishop "had given out that we were worse than either the Mohammedans or Jews."[29] The Jews seemed even less promising. One, who had spent some time in India, was quite rich but dressed almost in rags so that no one might think to steal or defraud him of what he had. "Nothing," remarked Groves, "can exceed the degraded state of the Jews, who seem utterly destitute of every moral principle... It is the constant practice here among the Jews, when they hear our blessed Lord's name mentioned, or mention it themselves, to curse him."[30] As for the Muslims, Groves heard the reply of their Arabic teacher to Pfander's question, Why don't you wish to read Christian books? "If I did so," he said, "my head would be turned and I should become an infidel."[31] "How often," Groves commented, "is fanaticism the child of doubt and fear!" How could the kingdom of God ever come to such a place? "Mohammedans will not hear, and the Christians do not care for any of these things; but if the Lord prosper our labour, we shall see what the end will be when the almighty word of God is understood."[32]

Passing through Baghdad at this time was a certain Dr Montefiore on his way to Bombay. He described how he had opened a free clinic for the poor in

India. On the first day twelve patients had come; the next day seventy-two. On the third day, "the street in which he lived was filled, and he was obliged to give it up."[33] The kindly doctor had simply been overwhelmed with patients. Nonetheless, there might be some potential in this idea for Baghdad. Groves, of course, was a dentist rather than a doctor, yet his early training had given him a wide general knowledge of medical matters. Perhaps he could avoid exhausting his time, his energy and the small supply of medicines he had brought from England, by restricting himself to a single branch of medicine, such as ophthalmics, since diseases of the eye seemed particularly troublesome in that hot dry climate. Would this, he wondered, be a way of winning the trust and respect of the people and introducing them to the Saviour?[34]

As word went round, neighbours started to come to the house for treatment, and some stayed to talk with Pfander about spiritual concerns. One of these was a Muslim who dared not make public his personal belief in the gospel, hoping some day to go to India and change his religion there in safety. This prompted Groves to write, "There is this one value in medical practice which I never so fully felt before – that it affords to Mohammedans an unsuspected excuse for coming to us."[35] He was brave enough to operate on a number of cataracts, and several people who had been blind for many years regained their sight. Groves's medical knowledge and Pfander's evangelistic skills were enabling them to work together, and to achieve more than they could have expected separately.[36]

A packet of letters brought news from friends in Britain and cheered them all with assurances of love and prayer. Among the letters was one from Groves's sister Mary, who had recently met an interesting young German by the name of George Müller, but there was no news yet of a second party setting out to join them. The original team had been depleted by the return of Lydia Groves and the marriage of Charlotte Taylor, and also, on his arrival in Baghdad, by the departure of Bathie to join Major Taylor in the service of the East India Company. The addition of Karl Pfander had been an unexpected blessing, but he might not be with them long. The need for reinforcements was urgent.

They had been in Baghdad only two months when the idea of starting a school was suggested; perhaps this would enable them to become accepted in the community. They found the Armenians quite responsive to the proposal, the Roman Catholics much less so. Mission schools had not figured in Groves's thoughts when he left England, and during their journey through Russia he had expressed his view that educating the labouring classes tended merely to "pride, rebellion, infidelity and discontent".[37] But he had seen Miss Kilham's school for girls in St Petersburg, he had seen the school run by the Basel missionaries in Shushi, and now he was surrounded by thousands who claimed to be Christians but had never been able to read the Christian scriptures in their own language. Perhaps, if they were taught to read the Bible, they would understand the way of salvation and become preachers of the gospel among their own people and among the Muslims too. Groves's mind now seized on the vision for a school, where boys and girls might learn how to "translate God's word with understanding". The others agreed. "On consultation, both my dearest Mary, myself, and Mr Pfander thought that the Lord's children and saints must take the work the Lord gives, particularly as there appeared no immediate prospect of other work."[38]

Three months after their arrival in Baghdad they found a good house in the Armenian quarter of the city. It would be large enough for them all, and it had a substantial area on the ground floor that could serve as a schoolroom. There was also a central courtyard where they could keep a few animals. But there was a problem with the house. For generations, the law in Arab lands had decreed that the properties of Jews and Christians should not rise higher than those of Muslims. It happened that the best room in this house, "the most airy one", was upstairs, above the street where Muslims had to walk. To avoid all cause of offence, they decided to leave this room unused.[39] An impoverished Armenian *wartabiet*, or priest, was then signed on as temporary schoolmaster. Though steeped in his own religious tradition, he was a humble man, keen to extend his knowledge and willing for the scriptures to be taught to the Armenian children.

From the rooftop they could discreetly watch men passing in the street below. All except the poorer Jews had some kind of headgear. The Turks were easy to identify, with black moustaches, clad in a sort of loose suit, and on their heads a simple red fez. The Christians (Armenians and Roman Catholics) mostly sported a moustache, though some preferred a beard, and wound a small cloth round their heads. The Arab Muslims wore loose flowing garments and were generally bearded, with a full turban. Sometimes the Muslims shaved their heads, leaving a large tuft of hair on top, and some had their tuft or beard dyed red.[40] Kitto admired the elegance of Arab dress, and especially the turban. "After having seen almost every variety of masculine head-dress," he remarked, "I venture to pronounce that none are more graceful, imposing or useful, perhaps, in a hot country."[41] Kitto was also impressed with the elegant form of much architecture in Baghdad, especially the brick-built arches and courtyards in the larger houses, and the towers and blue-tiled tapering minarets that graced the skyline. The tall date palms and the groves of orange trees and orchards brought a welcome splash of green to parts of the city. But there were many cripples, many blind people, many disabled and deformed children, and many beggars chanting and calling out for alms in the filthy narrow streets.[42]

The school opened on 19th April, and on the first day forty-three boys and two girls came.[43] In addition to the "general table of good and bad behaviour" and the register "of absence and of attendance", Groves and Pfander had thought carefully about the lessons to be taught. Until then, children in the schools run by the Armenian churches had been instructed in the archaic written form of the Armenian language, which "neither they nor their teachers understand". The traditional teaching method was simply for each boy to chant his appointed text at the top of his voice amidst a cacophony of other boys chanting theirs. Surely it would be better to teach them in an orderly fashion how to read quietly the language they actually spoke. Then another possibility came into view, something quite unexpected. There were families asking for English lessons, seeing this as an entrance into the commercial and political sphere of British influence in the East. Could the English language be used as a medium for the gospel? Perhaps it could, thought Groves, "for people will bear opposition to their own views more easily in another language than in their own... and thus truth may slide gently in."[44]

In the end they decided to start by teaching the children to read colloquial Arabic. This was understood by almost everyone (both Arabs and Armenians) and it was the language that both Groves and Pfander were currently learning.[45] But Groves would also prepare lessons in English. He developed his own method, one that would benefit himself as much as the children: "They bring me Arabic phrases, and as far as my knowledge extends, I give them the meaning in English; and when that fails I write it down for enquiry from the moolah next day. And then by asking words in Arabic every day for the boys to give me the English, I at last get the expressions so impressed on my memory that when I want them they arise almost without thought."[46] But would the Islamic authorities allow such a school to continue? It seemed that the Roman Catholics had tried to start something similar, but ancient laws forbade the erection of new churches in lands conquered by Islam, and "as the Mohammedans could not clearly distinguish between schools and churches, they would not permit the undertaking to be carried into effect."[47] It must be made a matter for special prayer.

Their house was probably similar to most others, sharing a wall with its neighbours on either side and opening on to a common courtyard that connected with the street. It would have a flat roof of dried clay about a metre thick, built up on a matting base supported by thick wooden beams. The busy street was loud with the cries of peddlars and beggars. The houses opposite, plain and crumbling on the outside, would be sumptuously furnished within, their bare facades sporting the occasional lattice but no windows. Hiding in the cracks and crevices would be the usual assemblage of rats, mice, cockroaches and scorpions, and perhaps the occasional snake emerging after dark. Outside the front door, the first rain would turn the dusty ground to mud and deposit rubbish and sewage everywhere, but fortunately it rarely rained in Baghdad, and only in the winter. The family acquired four or five hens and a couple of goats, and the boys looked after some tame pigeons. Their meals consisted mainly of bread, dates and fruit, the sustenance of the poor, although rice could also be bought, and occasionally mutton or chicken. More rarely, the local market or a generous friend might provide the meat of a camel, a wild gazelle, or even a wild boar (forbidden to Muslims) caught among the reeds by the river. Water was carried to their door by men who filled their goatskins at a nearby well. On social occasions, the richer residents of Baghdad drank thick coffee, without milk or sugar, in a minute cup of delicate china set in a silver holder, each cup holding about a tablespoonful. Very stimulating, Kitto observed, it was more like a drug than a beverage.[48]

Two weeks after the opening of the school, the numbers had risen to fifty-eight boys and nine girls. They expanded into a second room. Other girls were turned away for want of a female teacher; the schoolmaster's wife was willing enough to help, but she "knows very little of anything."[49] Then, to the delight of the whole household, a parcel arrived containing copies of the Sermon on the Mount in the colloquial Armenian of Shushi. This was the spoken language rather than the ancient liturgical form, though produced in an area far to the north. They decided immediately that all the pupils with a sufficient knowledge of the alphabet should start to learn one verse each day. Groves reckoned that some, at least, of the parents "were much pleased with the children learning the scriptures in the vulgar dialect", especially as "they were unable to understand the ancient language still read in their churches."[50] There was much to encourage. In addition to progress with the school, there had been several requests for scriptures, a number of friends kept coming back for discussion, and every day they were making more progress with the languages. Typically, Groves gave all the praise to God and all the credit to Pfander. "I cannot sufficiently thank God for sending my dear brother Pfander with me, for had it not been for him I could not have attempted anything, so that all that has now been done must rather be considered his than mine."[51]

He was also grateful to the scattered missionaries hard at work translating the Bible in various places, and especially to the printshop in Malta where William Jowett and his colleagues were "silently spending their strength for the use of others" – typesetting, proofreading, printing, binding and sending out the finished scriptures and schoolbooks in the many diverse dialects of the Middle East.[52] But using the spoken form of a language raised its own difficulties. Vocabulary and syntax varied so greatly from one region to another that almost every city needed its individual translation. Before long Groves was encouraging their Armenian schoolmaster to make his own version of the New Testament using local words and phrases. This man and his father enjoyed ongoing discussions with Pfander about the origins of Christian faith and practice: "They said they had heard from their books that in the time of the apostles men were without form of prayer, and were enabled to pray from their hearts, but that it was not so now." They had questions too about the Lord's Supper and seemed "anxious to know more".[53] Two Jews came to buy

Hebrew New Testaments, two more came for conversation with Pfander, and even the Muslim moolah who taught them Arabic was now reading the New Testament with another moolah.[54]

Mary was pregnant, the baby due in October. Learning to communicate in Armenian with her Syrian housemaid, she seemed to be adapting well. Norris was pleased to see how well she had responded to the discomforts and to the frustrations of trying to make a home and raise a family in a city lacking almost everything she was accustomed to. Many are the stresses of life during the first days in a foreign land, especially when the language is barely understood. The need to buy unfamiliar food with strange coins in a local market, the continuous battle against vermin, the unpleasant smells, the flies and mosquitoes, the physical weariness brought on by stomach troubles, the unremitting heat of summer, the constant street noise, the Call to Prayer from the mosque waking the whole family every night, the fretfulness of children cramped within the confines of a small house shared by colleagues, employees and visitors: all this can create tensions within the best of marriages. But Norris and Mary grew, throughout this time, in their devotion to one another. "My sorrows, my hopes, my fears, she shared and bore them all,"[55] said Groves. Mary was "daily growing in the simple assurance of her Lord's love and desiring under heaven neither to know nor serve any other than him."[56] And as she began to understand the language, God was evidently preparing her for great usefulness among the women of Baghdad.

A seasonal infestation of fleas tormented the whole family for about six weeks in early summer. Polite company did not normally admit to a personal acquaintance with fleas, but "during that season," Kitto remarked, "even English ladies are not ashamed to complain of them."[57] As summer advanced, Groves was pleased to find that, even teaching six hours a day, he could bear the heat reasonably well. During the daytime the coolest place was in the basement, and at night they slept on the roof where the breeze brought some relief. By mid-August, the temperatures had reached 118°F (48°C) in the shade and 158°F (almost 71°C) in the sun. "This is the time when the dates ripen," he observed, "and the most oppressive in the year, but by the Lord's great mercy we are all in health and strength... I can truly say it is far more tolerable than I expected, and yet there are few places on the face of the earth hotter."[58]

They were all pleased with the progress of the school. Having established a method that would "bring God's word before them in a form intelligible and clear," Groves and Pfander found that the young boys were now able to read, write and translate their spoken Armenian better than their elder brothers who had studied only the literary form of the language. "The boys are making double the progress they did under the old system. This is all of the Lord; and in fact, when I think of the doubts expressed, before we commenced, of our being allowed to work at all, and consider the quietness and peace the Lord has permitted us to enjoy in the prosecution of our work, I desire more entirely to cast my whole soul, with all its purposes and plans, on the Lord, and not to move but as he guides."[59] There was no serious opposition, although some of the parents grumbled about their children memorising the Armenian New Testament rather than the traditional *Shammakirke* prayers. Some asked, "Who are these people? Are they wiser than our bishops and ancient fathers?" But "the schoolmaster is truly on our side," Groves thought, as indeed were "the hearts of many of the children."[60]

The interest shown by the little Armenian girls in some simple stories written in the colloquial language confirmed his conviction that the spoken idiom reached the heart, and that books and tracts in this form could revolutionize the reading habits of a people too long cowed by a literary and ecclesiastical elite. "I believe I have many times mentioned the deep-rooted opposition which exists among the clergy and literary men in the East to having anything translated into the vulgar dialects. They are worse than the literati of Europe used to be with their Latin, many among whom but lately came to see that it was no disgrace to communicate their ideas in a vernacular dress. As the common sense of mankind has triumphed over the literary pride of the learned [in Europe], so we shall find that babes will one day overthrow the literary pride of these Orientals."[61]

As everything seemed so positive they began to think and pray about the possibility of extending the school to admit children from Muslim homes. For this they would need an Arabic-speaking schoolmaster in addition to the Armenian. Here they met an impasse, for no Muslim teacher would consent to his pupils reading the Christian scriptures. "For two months," Groves wrote in mid-July, "we have been trying without success to obtain one, so great is their prejudice against teaching Christians at all, but especially themselves to read the New Testament."[62] Eventually their prayers were answered, even beyond their expectations, for the Muslim teacher, settling in, showed himself remarkably open-minded: "Our new moolah has expressed his surprise at the contents of the New Testament, and wonders how Mohammedans can speak against it as they do."[63] The newcomer arranged to meet each Sunday with the Armenian teacher to read the Bible together. It was a case of the blind leading the blind, thought Groves, but the Holy Spirit could enlighten them both.

The missionary team continued to wear Western clothes. The trousers and jackets of the men were to some extent familiar to the people of Baghdad, and not far different from the garments of the Turks, who had long frequented the city. In traditional Muslim society the different races and religious groups had been required by custom and by law to identify themselves with distinctive clothing,[64] and to break this taboo might do more harm than good. There were signs of change, however, and not just in the matter of clothing. The recent decision of the Pasha to clad a regiment of his soldiers in Western-style uniform was symbolic of a growing awareness of European culture and technology, as Pfander had foreseen, arousing the interest of some and the resentment of others. "Things cannot remain as they are," Groves judged, "whether they continue to advance as they are now doing, or whether bigotry be allowed to make a last vain effort to regain her ancient position; still some decided change must be the final result of the present state of things."[65]

He was intrigued, especially, by the Pasha's interest in a proposal from the Bristol Steam Company to investigate the possibilities of steam navigation on the river Euphrates, opening up a route to India that would reduce the journey from London to Bombay by ten days.[66] If the Euphrates route proved feasible, Mesopotamia would become a major thoroughfare for British trade to the East.[67] Arabs, Armenians and Turks would find themselves introduced willy-nilly to Western customs, ideas and knowledge. And not only would the country be opened to wider horizons, but missionary workers, passing through on their way to India, would bring encouragement, prayer and teaching to the churches that Groves hoped to see spring up along the banks of the Tigris and Euphrates. "I feel the Lord is preparing great changes in the heart of this nation," he remarked.[68] "However, we are in the Lord's hands, and he will bring to pass what concerns his own honour, and we will wait and see. A much greater opening has taken place since we came here than we could have hoped for, and much more will yet open upon us than we can now foresee."[69]

ENDNOTES

[1] D25

[2] This was Kitto's description (Eadie, 198).

[3] Major Taylor's library would be well stocked: "He knew sixteen languages, which he spoke with great fluency; and he was a great Arabic and Persian scholar, and could read the most difficult Arabic manuscripts with the greatest ease" (Wolff, I, 328-329). In 1830 Major Taylor acquired from the ruins of Nineveh a hexagonal clay tablet covered in cuneiform writing. It contains Sennacherib's account of his invasion of Judah in 701 BC and is known as the Taylor Prism.

[4] J111; M75

[5] Ryland, 374; Eadie, 190. Kitto taught the boys Hebrew, scripture, theology, history, geography, writing, arithmetic and English composition (Eadie, 161).

[6] Stern, 35-45. The ruling dynasty in Baghdad bore the title 'Abbasids, claiming descent from 'Abbas, uncle of the Prophet. Before the 'Abbasid supremacy, Damascus had been the religious capital of the Islamic world. In 1258 power shifted firstly to Cairo (under the rule of the Mamelukes) and then Istanbul (from 1517 until 1924 when military defeat destroyed the Ottoman Empire and led to the creation of modern Turkey). There has been no further caliphal city to take over from Istanbul as the seat of Sunnite Islam.

[7] Richter, 59-62. Certain concessions were granted in the western Ottoman territories, where Greek, Slav, Bulgar and other non-Muslim races were liable to be in league with European powers. For detailed documentation see Bat Ye'or, *The Dhimmi*.

[8] Monophysites: Christian sects teaching that there is only one nature in the person of Christ, primarily divine but with human attributes.

[9] European manufactured goods did not penetrate Mesopotamia until the following decade. In fact the worldwide quest for raw materials launched by British manufacturers did not really take off until the 1880s, when in twenty years one fifth of the world's land surface was added to the empire of Queen Victoria. The Baghdad mission predated all this by half a century.

[10] The Muslims tended to look down on trade as unbefitting the dignity of a cultured people, and they disdained, in any case, all unnecessary contact with foreign infidels. This left an uncontested commercial niche for families with a Christian or Jewish identity. Belonging, as they generally did, to minority ethnic groups, the nominal Christians had the advantage of being more familiar with foreign languages, or at least more motivated to acquire them. Business relations with foreigners promised them some respite from their inferior status under Islam and perhaps a certain amount of political security. Individuals in the employ of a foreign enterprise might well find themselves under the protection of a foreign power, and there were French and Italian dukedoms and kingdoms, in cahoots with the politically ambitious Papal State, which had regularly interfered in Eastern affairs since the time of the Crusades (Cragg, 121-128).

[11] Maronite Christians: a monophysite body, deriving its name from St. Maron, who founded a monastery in Syria in AD 400. They speak Arabic but use ancient Syriac as a liturgical language. Whilst submitting to the authority of the Pope in Rome, they maintain their own patriarch on Mount Lebanon. They are traditional enemies of the Druses.

[12] J131; M77

[13] J131, 134; M77. Aramaic: the ancient language of the Aramaeans, a semi-nomadic Semitic people who settled in many parts of the Middle East, adopted as the common or trade language with the expansion of the Persian Empire from the sixth century BC. It was largely, but not entirely, replaced by Arabic from the thirteenth century onwards.

[14] Eadie, 191

[15] Zwemer, *Pfander*, 221

[16] J135; M80

[17] Major Taylor certainly put no pressure on them to do so, saying he would gladly do anything he could for the party, urging them never to let the work stand still for want of funds: he would happily supply whatever they might need.

[18] J116-117; M76. His original intention had been to start with Turkish and then move on to Persian (J84, 112).

[19] R169; M111

[20] Moolah (also Moulah or Mollah, now more commonly spelt Mullah): a Muslim scholar, teacher or religious leader, especially in Persia, Mesopotamia and Turkey.

Rarely did missionaries of that generation possess even a rudimentary dictionary or primer in the spoken form of their chosen language. Cassette tapes, of course, lay almost a century and a half in the future. It was necessary to find a patient informant who would repeat words over and over again, and painstakingly correct the pronunciation and syntax of the student. A good informant was hard to find: even if well paid, few had the necessary patience. Mastery of colloquial speech was made more difficult by the European educational emphasis on reading and writing foreign languages rather than correctly pronouncing them. Many nineteenth-century missionaries could speak fluently but with an accent so atrocious that only those accustomed to it could understand what they said. It was possible to get by in the streets and markets with a basic vocabulary and grammar... but to explain moral principles, to detect the fallacies in other religious systems, and to explain the gospel in such a way that it made sense and was seen to be good news – this required many years of concentrated effort. Pfander, with his remarkable linguistic talent, would have encouraged Groves to set himself high standards.

[21] R31

[22] Druses (or Druzes): a group founded in the eleventh century AD, named after their founder Ad-Darazi.

[23] Yazidis: a sect based in the area round Mosul (Nineveh), combining elements of Islam and Christianity and incorporating a belief in the devil as an agent of God. (Yazid is the local name for the devil.) Groves found the Yazidis to be "declared enemies of the Mohammedans whom they hate; but on the whole... they are not unfriendly towards Christians" (M101).

[24] R56; M91. By "Babylonish systems" Groves means apostate churches, i.e. churches taken into "captivity" just as the nation of Israel had been taken into captivity in Babylon. In 1520 Luther had published a treatise entitled *The Babylonian Captivity of the Church*.

[25] M117 (R93)

[26] R19; M88

[27] J135; M77. Arrack: a coarse colourless spirit distilled from grain, rice, sugar etc., milky white when mixed with water (from Arabic *'araq* = "sweat, perspiration").

[28] J131; M77

[29] R277

[30] J133; R21; M78

[31] J132; M77

[32] R21

[33] J112, 117; M76

[34] It is not clear why Groves chose ophthalmics rather than dentistry – perhaps because the people of Baghdad, when suffering from a sore tooth, went to a native practitioner who simply pulled it out. There would be no demand for fillings or dentures.

[35] M82

[36] Commencing in April 1830, this might be considered the first evangelical mission to Muslims in the Arab world. The American Presbyterians, located in Beirut intermittently from 1823 onwards, spoke Arabic but confined their ministry to

nominal Christians and Jews. Elsewhere, the attention of men such as Henry Martyn, William Glen and Pfander's colleagues of the Basel Mission had been directed to Muslims who spoke languages other than Arabic, although Martyn himself attempted a preliminary draft for an Arabic translation of the New Testament (Richter, 93-100, 186-189; Vander Werff, 31-32, 100-108, 118-119).

[37] M59

[38] R169

[39] M80. Some of these property rules are detailed in Bat Ye'or, *The Dhimmi*, 193, 341.

[40] Eadie, 196

[41] Eadie, 221

[42] Stern, 35-36

[43] M83

[44] M85 (R5)

[45] The colloquial Arabic of Baghdad included many words of Turkish and Persian origin, with verbal contractions that would sound quite barbarous to any scholar instructed in the classical language of the Qur'an. But Groves believed that a missionary must at all costs learn the language spoken by the people. Indeed, "it is the very instrument of his labour. And let such a missionary feel infinitely happier to hear it said he speaks very low Arabic but that everybody understands him than very pure but which is unintelligible except to the Mollahs [*sic*]" (R214).

[46] M86

[47] J138; M80; Bat Ye'or, *The Dhimmi*, 195

[48] Eadie, 194; Stern, 36

[49] M85

[50] M87

[51] R2; M85

[52] J134; M87. For more about Jowett, see Stunt, *Awakening*, 140-141. Before leaving England Groves had sent off a small lithographic press along with some other baggage for delivery to Basra via Bombay. The press, if it eventually arrived, would now be useful, he thought, in producing materials for the school (J134).

[53] R18; M88

[54] R16-18. Groves and Pfander had found it preferable to sell the scriptures whenever possible. Experience had shown that copies given away would be considered of small value and often burnt.

[55] R163; M160

[56] R151; M151

[57] Eadie, 193

[58] R26-27; M89

[59] M91 (R55)

[60] R65-66

[61] R98; M119; also R211. Groves observed that the Armenian clergy "obstinately resist the scriptures being translated into the modern languages, because, say they, the ancient language was spoken in Paradise and will be the language of heaven, and that therefore translating the sacred book into that which is modern is a desecration. How wonderfully does Satan blind men, and how by one contrivance or another

does he endeavour to keep God's word from them as a real intelligible book which the Spirit of God makes plain even to the most unlettered. But the more we discover him endeavouring to pervert God's word from becoming intelligible, the more we should strive to let every soul have the testimony of God concerning his life in Christ in a language he understands. In this point of view I look to the schools with comfort" (R28-29).

[62] R20; M88

[63] R30

[64] Bat Ye'or, *The Dhimmi*, 66 etc.

[65] R12

[66] R9; M102; also M290. Commencing from the Mediterranean coast with a caravan overland to the headwaters of the Euphrates, the route would then follow the course of the river as far as the Persian Gulf (with provision of local fruit and vegetables along the way), from where a sea passage to Bombay would be quick and comfortable. This would compare very favourably with the other options facing travellers from Europe to India at that time – either the long overland route through Constantinople (Istanbul) or else a five-day trek through the Egyptian desert followed by the stormy passage of the Red Sea.

[67] Mesopotamia: the wide plain occupied by the Tigris and Euphrates rivers, leading down to the Persian Gulf (from the Greek, meaning "between rivers").

[68] R4

[69] R12

"Faith rests in God for the present,
and
waits on God for the future."

Henry Groves [1]

12

Our Little Stock

W hen Norris Groves left England, his intention was to blaze a trail for others to follow. Once a base had been established in Baghdad, workers would itinerate throughout the region and then settle further afield in other promising centres. With this in mind he continued to question travellers who arrived from distant parts, and wrote careful notes in his journal about the possibilities of Christian work in each place and with each religious faction. He was particularly impressed with the potential for gospel work amongst the Jacobites: "It is impossible to consider such an immense Christian population as that in Diarbekr without feeling a wish to pour in upon it the fountains of living waters which we are so abundantly blessed with. Oh that someone would come out and settle down in such a place as Diarbekr – what an abundant field of labour!"[2]

Two Armenian priests from outlying regions came to see Pfander; they wished to discuss the possibility of opening schools in their area. A positive invitation also came from some leading men in Mosul, a city on the upper Tigris opposite the ruins of ancient Nineveh. With nine or ten thousand Jews in Baghdad, a Jewish school here might also be a possibility, offering instruction in the local Arabic and Persian dialects as well as the ancient Hebrew of their own scriptures.[3]

The Jewish community seemed, in principle, well disposed towards the British. In fact Groves observed among all the minority groups "a wish that the English power might prevail here." The abuse they suffered, along with the general corruption of commerce and politics, allied to a widespread belief that "our government in India is mild and equitable", meant that "most of them would gladly exchange their present condition and be subject to the British government."[4] Yet Groves was careful to express no opinion on political matters. "I feel my path is to live in subjection to the powers that be... We have to show them by this that our kingdom is not of this world and that these are not things about which we contend."[5]

The political situation was far from stable. Under the nominal authority of the Sultan, the real government of the Ottoman Empire lay in the hands of a cabinet of ministers in Constantinople. They were known collectively as the Sublime Porte, a garbled French rendering of their official Turkish designation, *Babi Ali*, meaning the Supreme Gate. At this time it was widely believed that Daoud Pasha, the governor of Baghdad, wished to throw off the Ottoman yoke and establish an independent territory in Mesopotamia. His four predecessors had all been murdered (the last of them on Daoud's own orders), but since then he had managed, through various stratagems, to keep his head and his power intact for thirteen years.[6] Several messengers had been sent from Constantinople to arrest or assassinate him, but none had ever returned to report success.

August came, and in the heat of the summer the inhabitants of Baghdad observed with growing apprehension twenty or thirty thousand Arabs with weapons assembling outside the city. Daoud Pasha negotiated to buy them off, and the crisis seemed to have passed, then suddenly there were signs of renewed activity outside the walls – guns moved into position, preparations to blockade and bombard the city. "Things here seem most unsettled," Groves wrote calmly on 19th August (1830), "and require us to live in very simple faith as to what a day may bring forth."[7]

Rumours were now heard of fighting in the hills between rival Arab factions. Outbreaks of cholera in the surrounding regions, followed by plague, were described by travellers arriving in Baghdad. It was difficult to know how seriously to take such reports, but it was certain that travel out of the city was no longer safe. Caravans heading for Baghdad had been plundered by Arab tribes, and a party of five Englishmen had recently been attacked on their way to Constantinople; three were murdered, along with a Maltese servant, and the others only escaped with the loss of their baggage and papers. In addition to the twenty or thirty thousand encamped around the city walls, other and larger armies were said to be assembling at a greater distance. On 21st October Groves wrote, "It appears that the Sultan is determined to act at once, and decidedly, against this pasha. We are now therefore to expect a siege and a state of anxiety and fear in this city for some months; but the Lord who sitteth in the heavens is ordering all for his own glory, and for our safety, and he will provide for us."[8]

Somewhere along the way a second bundle of letters from England had been lost – hardly surprising in the circumstances, but a sad blow for those who, without newspapers, radio or telephone, longed for news and encouragement from home and perhaps some word concerning possible reinforcements. A money order sent in such letters was the only way for financial support to reach them. "I have no other hope of letters than what my most gracious Lord's proved love gives me," said Groves. "All which he really desires me to have I shall receive, and more I would desire not to wish for."[9]

In September (1830), definite news came of a severe outbreak of cholera in Tabriz in the Persian highlands, 330 miles to the north. Soon cholera fatalities were also reported from Kerkuk, only 140 miles away. "The Pasha seems perplexed to know, in the event of its reaching Baghdad where he shall go with his family for safety," reported Groves. "It is certainly an awful thing to look at Tabriz where, they say, eight or nine thousand have died out of 60,000." But there was no cause for anxiety: "Blessed be the Lord's holy name. Our charter runs, that in the pestilence, 'though ten thousand fall at thy right hand it shall not come nigh thee.' On this therefore we repose our hearts."[10] The Lord's faithfulness is sure: "We have in our dwellings a light in these days that they know nothing of, who know not our God either in his power or his love, so that the heart is enabled to cast all, even the dearest to it, on the exceeding abundance of his mercy."[11]

Six days later messengers brought news not only of cholera at Tabriz, but also the plague! Cholera was fearsome enough, but "plague" was a word that struck terror into all who heard it. The intense pain of the smooth red oval swellings in the groin, armpits and neck would be followed inexorably by delirium and death. By all accounts, Tabriz was in a terrible state. Many, it was said, just died of fear. They "collected themselves together in large bodies, crying and beseeching God to turn away his judgments from them. This they did bareheaded and without shoes, humbling themselves, they said, because they knew they were great sinners."[12] According to letters received, 23,000 of the inhabitants of Tabriz had perished, and the villages round about were deserted. "The corn has never been reaped, and the cattle were wandering about without owners."[13] Famine seemed a most likely consequence. Groves took the precaution of laying in supplies of wheat, rice, soap and candles. Baghdad itself was filled with dread: "Although they are almost frightened out of their reason at the prospect of the plague and cholera, they have actually allowed the whole caravan from Tabriz to come into the city without quarantine or any kind of precaution."[14] "Our moolah is dreadfully depressed today at the prospect of the cholera and plague coming here, and he said to me he thought the end of the world must be near because of these wars, pestilences and plagues."[15]

Groves was inclined to agree: "Surely these are among the signs of the times, but the Lord's command to us is 'Let not your hearts be troubled.'" The servants of God were called to proclaim the gospel and leave all other concerns to him. Yet it was by no means clear they would be allowed to continue with that proclamation. "We have just heard," he wrote, "that an order has been given out in one of the mosques that the Mohammedans shall receive no printed books. Whether this watchfulness is the result of Mr Pfander having employed a man, a Jew, to sell Bibles, Testaments and Psalters, or whether at the suggestion from the Roman Catholic bishop, I know not."[16]

To their own Muslim moolah it made no difference at all. He was still reading the New Testament with the Armenian teacher, "who seems very sanguine that he will become a Christian."[17] At all events, thought Groves, he can now accept or reject the true gospel rather than the perversion of it he had been taught to despise. Early in October Groves quietly observed a wonderful scene in the schoolroom: the Muslim moolah sitting at one window reading the Arabic New Testament while the Armenian schoolteacher sat at a table explaining the New Testament to the son of the local Armenian priest (a young man currently preparing for the priesthood himself).[18] Although Groves might feel his own knowledge of the languages inadequate, and though circumstances were far from auspicious, there could be no doubt that gospel seeds were being sown.

In the midst of all this, on 10th October (1830), Groves opened his journal to record the safe delivery of their baby. "The Lord has blessed us with a little girl, and every thing has been ordered by him most happily so that we have wanted nothing that the luxury or wealth of England could supply."[19] During her pregnancy Mary had followed with great interest the progress of the school, especially of the girls, though not able to give much help herself. After the baby's birth, however, "as soon as she got about, she undertook it heartily, and the dear little children were so attached to their employments that they used to come on their holidays." She had made sufficient progress with colloquial Armenian that she could write out for them in large characters the simple stories, each one with a gospel message, translated into the local dialect. And "the dear little children were so interested by them that they exceedingly desired to take them home and read them to their mothers."[20]

Norris Groves himself had visited all their immediate neighbours, offering help to any who were ill and providing free medicines for the poor. Many gathered outside his door at certain times of the day. A female servant from their neighbour's house begged him to come and see her brother. She was a young Chaldean woman, aged about nineteen and her name was Harnie.[21] They had recently arrived as refugees from Mosul where their family fortune had been lost through injustice and extortion. Groves found the brother severely affected by tuberculosis, his wife and his children already dead. Groves continued to visit the sufferer, week after week, month after month, offering all the medical care and spiritual comfort he could with his very limited Arabic. When her brother finally died, Harnie could not forget the kindness of her neighbours and begged the Groves family to take her as a servant simply in return for food and lodging. Nobody then knew she would remain with them on these terms for twenty-five years.[22]

Meanwhile, Karl Pfander was looking for an opportunity to discuss the gospel openly with the Islamic scholars of Baghdad. For generations the harassed Christians of the Eastern churches had maintained an uneasy truce with their Muslim masters, grateful for a measure of peace but never thinking to engage them in debate or attempt their conversion to Christianity. The Muslims of Baghdad had never met anyone like Pfander, and he in turn was feeling his way, refining his arguments, seeking fresh illustrations, and looking for the kind of decisive evidence that would prove unanswerable. The uninstructed might suppose there was little difference between Islam and Christianity. After all, both proclaimed an all-seeing, all-knowing, all-powerful Creator, and both warned of a devil who endeavoured to lead mankind astray. They each looked to a divinely inspired book and followed a divinely appointed messenger. They had many of the same prophets, angels, and forms of prayer. Yet, closer familiarity with the scriptures of the two religions would reveal irreconcilable differences. As the nineteenth century progressed, the translation and circulation of the Bible and the Qur'an would bring home more clearly to both sides the impossibility of compromise.[23] But Pfander was ahead of all this, carrying the debate to his opponents in a way that was quite new to them.

Records survive of several discussions during the Middle Ages between Muslim and Christian scholars, conducted in a gentlemanly fashion as a form of court entertainment. In Baghdad itself, during the reign of the Caliph al-Mahdi (AD 775-85) and his successor al-Ma'mun (AD 813-33), there had been a flowering of scholarly interest in the Greek heritage of scientific and logical thought. At this time, the Nestorian patriarch Timothy I enjoyed frequent audiences with the Caliph, which gave him occasion to demonstrate and justify his beliefs.[24] Shortly afterwards, around 830, a series of letters were exchanged between a Christian called al-Kindi and a Muslim called al-Hashimi, both officials at the court of the Caliph al-Ma'mun; these were copied and distributed by the Christians.[25] Five hundred years later Raymund Lull had developed a carefully reasoned apologetic whilst preaching to the Muslims of Tunis, eventually suffering martyrdom at their hands in AD 1315.[26] Then two centuries passed before Jesuit missionaries engaged in religious debate with Muslim scholars in the sixteenth-century court of the Mughal emperor Akbar in northern India.[27] None of these contacts had yielded any notable results, and Pfander had only such rather distant and inconsequential examples to follow.

He was frustrated by the uncooperative character of the Muslim moolah he had paid to teach him Persian (Farsi); the man refused to help him translate anything into his own language. "The difficulty of getting teachers here is very great," Groves commented, "so great is their contempt of Christians." Although these mosque teachers would read or converse with a foreigner in Persian, they would do nothing to facilitate the introduction of foreign books, either religious or secular, to their people. During his nine months in Baghdad, Pfander had achieved his goals in Arabic, and now announced that he really needed to spend a period of time in the mountains of Persia, where he could make better progress with Farsi, before returning to Shushi. Early next year, he said, he would have to leave them.[28]

Norris Groves had hoped that additional workers would soon join him in Baghdad. The imminent loss of Pfander, and the failure of any letters to arrive, left him torn between hope and doubt. Must he and Mary and "poor Kitto" continue on their own with no help or counsel from godly friends? "Sometimes when faith was in full exercise, I felt assured that the Lord was doing all things well; at others I hardly knew what to think." But then, "suddenly there came in three Tartars bringing us three packets so full of Christian love and sympathy, and with such good tidings that it almost overcame our hearts, weak from long abstinence."[29]

Best of all was the news that a group was on its way to them. Some had dropped out; others had joined up. One of those coming was the generous easy-going John Parnell; another was Edward Cronin, resolute and wholehearted. Cronin's determination had not wavered even with the death of his wife just before their departure. Accompanying them were Cronin's elderly mother, his infant daughter Minny, and his sister Nancy who was engaged to Parnell. A late addition was Frank Newman, who left England in some disarray, having suffered a rebuff from the young lady to whom he had proposed marriage. The party was completed by an Irish schoolmaster by the name of John Hamilton, a friend of Parnell's.[30] Groves reproached himself for his earlier doubts. "Whilst not at all more than what I ought to have expected, it was more than I had faith to expect."[31] In fact they were already well on their way. Having opted for the route through France, they would sail up the Mediterranean as far as the coast of Syria, then overland to Aleppo (Halab), from where they could take boats down the Euphrates as far as Baghdad.

A second Armenian schoolmaster was also on his way to join them: he would teach the older boys. He came with good recommendations, having been trained in European methods at Calcutta, but Groves's recent experiences tempered his enthusiasm: "Those whom we think promise everything often occasion us nothing but anxiety; and those from whom we expect the least, we have reason abundantly to bless God for having sent us. So wisely, so graciously, and yet in so sovereign a way does the Lord bring to pass his purposes and bless his servants that every thought of confidence in any creature may be destroyed, and that the soul by a thousand disappointments when it has reposed elsewhere may at last be compelled to learn only to repose on the bosom of its Father where love and faithfulness eternally dwell, and may be convinced of the vanity of its past expectations from any other source."[32]

From mid-November, almost three months go by without an entry in Groves's journal. December marked the passing of a year since their arrival in Baghdad, and a very full and busy year it had been. Then comes Groves's first entry for 1831. On 14th February, "I have this day settled all my accounts and find after everything is paid... that our little stock will last us with the Lord's blessing two months longer, and then we know not whence we are to be supplied, but the Lord does not allow us to be anxious. He has so wonderfully provided for us hitherto that it would be most ungrateful to have an anxious thought."[33] For almost six months they had received no letters or gifts. When some boxes arrived from Bombay containing medicines, scriptures and a small printing press, there was just enough in hand to pay the cost demanded for transport.

News came of further outbreaks of plague to the north, and of political manoeuvrings and fresh armed forces threatening to attack the city and depose the Pasha. Two days later, "I was much struck by a remark of our moolah yesterday when speaking of the horror he felt at the prospect of the plague coming here. He said, the sword he did not mind but the plague he did, for one was the work of man, the other of God. I replied that, feeling the God who directs the plague to be my Father who loved me, I knew he would not suffer it to come nigh me unless he had no longer any thing for me to do, and then it would come as a summons from a scene of labour and many trials to one of endless joy. He said, 'Yes! It is very well for you not to fear death who believe in Christ as having atoned for you, but I fear to die.'"[34] Visitors continued to come – Jews, Syrians, Roman Catholics and an Armenian priest; all asked questions and requested Bibles.

A month later the situation was unchanged: no further news of reinforcements, no letters or money – just rumours of wars and uprisings, reports of plague and cholera. "But I have been much struck of late with the peculiar dealings of God towards his chosen," wrote Groves. How pertinent was the pillar of cloud and fire that "brought darkness to the one side and light to the other" in the days of Moses. "As of old, the pillar that was all darkness to the enemy was light to the 'church in the wilderness', so now this dark cloud, the darkness of which may be felt, which is spreading from one end of the Christian and Mohammedan world to the other, has towards the church in her pilgrimage its full steady bright light surmounted by 'Behold he cometh!'"[35]

On 28th February the last remaining cash was within a month of running out when a bundle arrived containing twenty-six letters "from most of our dearest friends in England". Their kindness meant that "the Lord had provided us with supplies for at least four months to come." The family met together that evening "to bless the Lord for the past and supplicate his continued blessing for the future – that he would accomplish what he had begun and that our hearts may never cease to praise and bless him."[36] Fully justified now was their determination to give all they had to the Lord and, in their poverty, trust him to provide: "O how hard it is to persuade the rebellious will and proud heart that to depend on our Father's love for our constant support is more for the soul's health than to be clothed in purple and fare sumptuously every day from what we call our own resources; and yet how plain it is to spiritual vision." But best of all was the news that their friends had actually arrived in Aleppo, just five hundred miles away, "only waiting for the termination of disturbances to join us." "This," wrote Groves, "overwhelmed us with joy and praise, and this welcome news reaches us just as our dear brother Pfander is on the point of leaving us alone."[37]

That same day they received an interesting visitor. "A Mohammedan *effendi*[38] was with us today, a very amiable young man who sees many evil things in the customs of his people arising out of the Mohammedan laws. He said he came to borrow an Arabic Bible for a poor schoolmaster, which I gladly lent; whether it be really for a schoolmaster or for himself I do not know."[39] Like many Christian workers among Muslims, Groves was puzzled to see how severely they will condemn the morals of their own people whilst urging the foreigner to join them. Despite their belief "that all Christians will become Mohammedans, no people can have a worse opinion of the state of the professors of their religion than the Mohammedans have."[40]

On 13th March Karl Pfander finally set off for Isfahan: "It was a great rending to us all, and has left a vacuum we cannot easily hope to have filled up in all its parts."[41] As a farewell gift they made their German friend some dried Chaldean sausages called *pastourma*. Some of these he took with him, most he left behind; they would prove valuable in the days ahead. Visitors continued to come to the house, and Groves, feeling the want of Pfander's linguistic skills, did his best to help them spiritually. A Jew came to borrow an Arabic Bible; another to read and discuss a portion with him. A Syrian invited Groves to visit his home in the northern highlands, and plans were made for a Syriac Bible to be sent to his bishop.[42] A Roman Catholic priest came and read some passages from the Psalms. An Armenian priest requested four or five Armenian Bibles for some villages on the far side of the Persian mountains. A letter arrived declaring that the Armenian Bishop of Tabriz had read one of their tracts. Indeed, "He said he would read it in his church to his flock" and would like them to open a school in Tabriz if a suitable teacher could be found.[43] The family prayed together for all these people.

Mary, no doubt, was looking forward to the coming of Nancy and Mrs Cronin. So far, with her "simple truth of purpose and unaffected love and confidence in her Lord", she was coping well.[44] "My dearest, dearest wife," Groves calls her, "the joy, the help, and companion of all in which I was engaged."[45] They discussed every aspect of the work and committed it to the Lord: "On any essential point, for some years, we have never had divided judgment... In every work of faith or labour of love her desire was to animate, not to hinder... She has been to me in the relation of Christian wife and Missionary wife just what I felt I so much, so very much needed."[46] The home she made for them, despite the difficulties, was a happy place.

The baby was well and seemed quite content. John Kitto continued his lessons with young Henry and Frank, who gave him every respect despite his disability. The boys were rapidly picking up colloquial Arabic from the moolah and from two Armenian boys now living with them. When some other boys quizzed the Armenian pair about failing to keep the fifty-day fast observed by their church, they went to look for a New Testament. Helped by Henry and Frank, they found the answer, "We are no worse if we do not eat, and no better if we do,"[47] and showed it to their friends. Groves, of course, was delighted to hear about this. He confided to his journal, "There is a growing tendency in the minds of the children to feel that God's word is the one rule by which all that is imposed on them must be justified, and thence the necessity of understanding it; and this principle upsets at once the whole system of ignorant mummery which is now called, or thought to be, the religion of Jesus here."[48]

Outside their home, however, things were looking grim. The city was surrounded now by not just one army but two. On the night of 19th March the family was kept awake by the sound of shouting and gunfire. The following day, "Two tribes of Arabs whom the Pasha has brought up to help him in the approaching contest, in consequence of some feud between them came to blows, and all last night and this morning were firing at one another in that quarter of the city which is on the other side of the river where they are stationed. It caused much alarm and may be but a precursor to general confusion and greater trials; but the Lord Jehovah who sitteth on the everlasting hills is our shield and defence. The firing has since ceased and one of the tribes has been driven out of Baghdad."[49] Apprehensive of further unrest, Major Taylor kindly offered them the safety of the Residency with its thick walls and stout gates, its servants and its armed guard of thirty *sepoys*. Groves was grateful for the offer, but declined. He would not have it known that his faith lay in armed men. It was safe, he believed, to trust in God alone.[50]

ENDNOTES

[1] *Congleton*, 23

[2] R24-25. Jacobites: a Christian faction named after Jacob (a mid-sixth century monk) which formed a separate monophysite church in AD 451. Their patriarch has his official seat in Antioch but normally resides in a monastery at Diarbekr (now usually spelt Diyarbakir) in eastern Turkey. Jacobite monks were noted for their rigorous asceticism and extravagant superstition. Although the Jacobites and Nestorians both held heretical views concerning the deity and humanity of Christ, the editor of Groves's *Memoir* considered that, by separating at an early date from the Roman Catholic Church, they had "escaped many of its corruptions, and in purity of doctrine on other points, as well as in manners, they have usually risen above it" (M101).

[3] R21

[4] R15; M98. The people of the Middle East felt a certain ambivalence towards the foreigners in their midst. There was envy and admiration for a race that controlled India and much of the rest of the world with a technology bordering on the

miraculous, but also a suspicion that their presence implied a desire to spy out the land and in course of time to take possession of it and change its time-honoured customs and religion.

[5] R16; M99

[6] R247

[7] R29

[8] R64; M100

[9] R29; M98. Money orders could be taken to Jewish or Armenian agents in the city and exchanged for cash. Major Taylor had already offered to lend money should they need it, but Groves, on scriptural grounds, was averse to borrowing (Rom 13:8).

[10] R41; M106 (referring to Ps 91:7 AV)

[11] R41; M106

[12] R47; M108

[13] R71-72

[14] M108 (R49)

[15] R48-49

[16] R43

[17] R54

[18] R56

[19] R58; M92

[20] R169-170

[21] Chaldean: a term used at this period to refer to people of Assyrian descent who belonged to the Chaldean Church. They generally spoke Arabic or Aramaic.

[22] Groves H, *Faithful Hanie*, 17, 23-26; M532. Her name was variously spelt Hannai, Hanai, or Hanie (once as Haney), occasionally anglicised as Hannah, but Edward Groves tells us that the family always called her Harnie (the *ar* being pronounced as a long *a*, as in "father") (Groves E K, *Successors*, 37). She appears in the UK census of 1861 as Harnie Thomas.

[23] Muslim scholars would come to regard Christianity as a polytheistic confusion built upon the irrational foundation of corrupted scriptures. Christian scholars would see Islam as a perversion of revealed truth denying the deity and the atonement of Christ. In fact there was disagreement not merely about matters of faith but also matters of historical fact (the preservation of uncorrupted scriptures and the actual death of Christ) on which the matters of faith depended.

[24] Powell, 6ff

[25] Christological questions preoccupied debate in the Caliph's court, perhaps because the Christian community itself was so divided on this issue; it had been divided long before the coming of Islam.

[26] See Zwemer, *Raymund Lull*.

[27] Powell, 18. Mughal (or Mogul) Empire: a powerful Muslim state established in northern India by peoples of Mongolian origin in the sixteenth and early seventeenth centuries.

[28] R35; M36. Before settling in Baghdad, Groves had hoped to accompany Pfander on his exploratory trip into the Persian highlands (J84, 92). With responsibility for a wife and young family in addition to the school, he now evidently felt unable to do so.

[29] M103 (R35-36)

[30] R301

[31] M105 (R38)

[32] M111 (R73)

[33] M112-113 (R74)

[34] M113 (R76)

[35] R86; M115-116 (referring to Exodus 14)

[36] The letters were dated September 1830, carried to Aleppo by Parnell's party and forwarded from there. They reached Groves six months after they were written and evidently contained money orders that could be exchanged for cash.

[37] R78-79 (M114). The party reached Aleppo on 11th January 1831.

[38] Effendi: a scholar or man of social standing in the Ottoman Empire.

[39] M115 (R79-80)

[40] R101; M121

[41] R80. Pfander's story continues in Chapter 25 of this book.

[42] Syriac: a dialect of Aramaic spoken in the Middle East until about the thirteenth century AD, and still in use as a formal liturgical language in some Eastern churches. The term Syriac is also used of the modern colloquial Aramaic spoken by people with a Christian identity in certain areas.

[43] R84

[44] R144

[45] R150

[46] R143-144

[47] 1 Cor 8:8

[48] M116 (R92-93)

[49] R94; M117

[50] Eadie, 202

"As the great object of our lives is
to illustrate his love to us,
we believe that in the midst of
these awful circumstances
he will fill our tongues with praise,
as he now fills our hearts with peace."

Norris Groves [1]

13

This Unhappy City

"The plague has now, we believe, absolutely entered this unhappy city." So reads the entry in Norris Groves's journal for 28th March 1831. "Major Taylor and all those connected with the Residency are preparing to leave for the mountains of Kurdistan. They have most kindly invited us to go with them and form part of their family. This is most truly kind, and there are many things to recommend it – the opportunities it would afford Mary for learning Armenian, and me Arabic, and for observation on the country and people, besides our being delivered from all apparent danger, either from the sword which threatens us from without or the pestilence within."[2]

As most of the leading Armenian and Roman Catholic families were planning to leave in the same caravan as the Taylors, Groves and his own family would find themselves friendless and defenceless, if they remained in Baghdad, amidst a turbulent and riotous populace. "But there are considerations that outweigh these. In the first place, we feel that while we have the Lord's work on our hands we ought not to fly and leave it. Again, if we go it is likely that for many months we cannot return to our work, whereas the plague may cease in a month. Opportunities of usefulness may arise during the plague which a more unembarrassed time may not present. And our dear friends from Aleppo may come and find no asylum [i.e. refuge]. The Lord gives us great peace and quietness of mind in resting under his most gracious and loving care, and as the great object of our lives is to illustrate his love to us, we believe that in the midst of these awful circumstances he will fill our tongues with praise, as he now fills our hearts with peace."[3]

Kitto was not quite so sure. "You will wish to know," he wrote to a friend in England, "how we are personally affected in the prospect of plague and siege. I am sure Mr Groves feels no personal anxiety on this subject. While he laments the misery which the people have in prospect, he is fully persuaded (and I endeavour to get the same feeling, and do *in limine*[4] concur with him) that we shall be safe; or if we are visited by the pestilence or the sword it will be for some wise and useful purpose. He thinks it would be a very poor return for the protection we received from Almighty Providence during our long and perilous journey, particularly in the mountains of Kurdistan, were we, in the prospect of new dangers, to distrust that care by which we have hitherto been preserved." Persuaded that Groves was right, Kitto still wondered whether some practical steps to increase their safety might not be wise. "Now, for myself, I am afraid that I think more precaution [to be] consistent with reliance on the providence of God than he does. However I am ashamed to feel any anxiety, which no one about me feels, and in fact I do not feel much; but what I may feel when the crisis arrives I do not calculate upon."[5]

Visiting the homes of the afflicted, Norris Groves saw for himself the first victims of the plague. There could be no doubt about it. "There are about twenty cases, and the number is increasing. Thus then, this long expected scourge has visited this city and our Father only knows when the awful visitation may cease. We can only cast ourselves into his holy and loving hands for safety and peace, and there we do cast ourselves with all that is dearest to us in this world... Dear Mary is much staid on her God and feels that, as he has been so he will be to us, a hiding-place in every storm."[6] One difficult decision still had to be made. "We have been forced to take the most painful step of breaking up our school, for it would have been quite impossible to collect eighty children together from different parts of the city without exposing all to danger."[7] But the main practical concern of the household was how to obtain water, dependent as they were on the water-carriers who brought it from door to door. "And they say," Groves remarked, "that when the plague becomes intense all the water-carriers cease to ply. But the Lord hath said, in the time of famine ye shall be satisfied. On this promise we rest in peace."[8]

They looked carefully together through the promises of God recorded in scripture: "How blessed the 91st Psalm feels at such moments as these, in looking round on one's little family, to know that every arrow that flies, winged with death, is no random shot, but that the Lord who is your life and by whom your life is hid in God, directs them all. Call upon me, says the Lord, in the day of trouble, and I will deliver *thee*, and thou shalt *glorify me*. Blessed Lord, when thou hast (as thou most assuredly wilt do) delivered us, may we never forget to glorify and bless thee. Oh! What a blessed feeling it is to know that you are not under the general but the especial and particular government of Jehovah – that he has redeemed you, and you are his – that he has engraven you on the palms of his hands, and that day and night he is watching to preserve you."[9]

So far, deaths from the plague were confined to the Muslim and Jewish areas of the city. But in those quarters, five hundred a day were being carried out for burial, on some days a thousand or more. Caravans of travellers were hastily assembling. An "immense crowd of poor Jews", along with many Armenians and Roman Catholics, were willing to risk violence and robbery along the road in order to escape from the city. Shouting and gunfire on the other side of the river wakened the family one night. It seemed louder and more violent than previous disturbances, and indicated perhaps that the besieging forces were breaking into the city. "After an hour's suspense we heard it was a concourse of Arabs met to supplicate from God the removal of the plague... We trust it may be the Lord's gracious purpose to take off the heaviness of his judgment and spare yet a little longer this sinful city."[10]

But the pestilence continued. During these first two weeks, from a total population of some 75,000, seven thousand perished.[11] In the midst of these horrifying scenes, ominous news of impending war in Europe only added to the apocalyptic sense of earthly convulsion – the prospect of a final conflagration and the return of Christ: "Oh how joyful a thought it is that the Lord is at hand and our pilgrimage nearly ending."[12]

In the cool of the evening Norris and Mary would walk together on the flat roof of their house, reminiscing about old times and their friends in England, thankful that so many devoted Christians were praying for them.[13] Mary, in particular, thought much about the coming of the Lord, and as her husband later recalled, "this spread a gilded halo round every trial." "Often she would say to me, 'I never enjoyed such spiritual peace as since I have been in Baghdad – such an unvarying sense of nearness to Christ and assurance of his love and care. We came out trusting only under his wing, and he will never forsake us.'"[14] Surely he had brought them to that very place at that very time, and he knew for what good purposes. "Sometimes, on looking round on our dear little circle," said Groves, "the old heavy faithless flesh would seek its quiet sheltered retreat under the lofty elms at Exeter, but the Lord never allows the spirit for one moment to desire otherwise than to wait and see the salvation of our God, who will for his name's sake do wonderfully for us, that our hearts may rejoice in him." Then in the next breath, "We hear the enemy is within three days of the city."[15]

Outside their door the streets were almost deserted. "The poor inhabitants know not what to do. If they remain in the city they die of the plague; if they leave it they fall into the hands of the Arabs who strip them."[16] As if this were not enough, the water level of the Tigris was steadily rising. In places the river had overflowed its banks, and reports said two thousand houses had been flooded. Two days passed in suspense: "Stillness continues to prevail over the city like the calm which precedes a convulsion. Our neighbours are preparing for defence by getting armed men into their houses, but we sit down under the shadow of the Almighty's wings, fully assured that in his name we shall boast ourselves."[17]

Word came from Major Taylor; he was still in Baghdad, having found the road to the mountains cut off. Four of his servants had contracted the plague, and one of his Indian *sepoys* had died of it already. He was now hoping to take his family, servants and officials by boat down the Tigris to the relative safety of Basra. Again he offered Groves and his household a passage. Should they go? The school was closed; it was unsafe to go out visiting or distributing literature;

there seemed nothing useful for them do in Baghdad. The pestilence was advancing street by street through the inner quarters of the city. Should they not gratefully accept the offer? "Having no immediate occupation here at present," wrote Groves, "I feel quite free to accept it, but there are considerations that prevent us. Hitherto the Lord has kept us safe, and no symptom of plague has appeared in our dwelling, though it is all around us."[18] The place of danger, he thought, was exactly the place where they should be, as a testimony to the church and to the world that faith in the care of a Heavenly Father was not a vain or foolish thing. And God, they believed, would honour such faith by providing complete protection: "We feel indeed that we owe it to our Lord's love to be careful for nothing, neither to run or make haste as others, but to stand still and see the salvation of our God."[19]

This seemed to be providentially confirmed by something overheard in the street: "There was a curious conversation going on last night among some Mohammedans outside our window relative to the plague, which they said was an especial judgment on them and the Jews but from which Christ would deliver the Nazarenes; and in all these calamities it is remarkable how doubly heavy they fall on these two classes... From these visitations *as judgments*, we have an especial promise of protection, and we trust in the midst of them some good may spring up. At all events we feel that we shall have quite met our dear Lord's mind in giving this people a last opportunity of hearing, ere their house is left to them desolate."[20]

But other reasons also carried weight. Travelling in a crowded boat would be by no means the best way to avoid contagion. The plague might well reach Basra, in any case, before they did; many had already fled from infected areas to take refuge there. Also in their minds was the consideration that travel and lodging in a crowded city would be expensive, and finding themselves three hundred miles from Baghdad through the kindness of Major Taylor, they might not then have the means to return. The only advantage in leaving would be to escape the armies seeking to depose the Pasha. "On the whole," concluded Groves, "we feel we may hold on with the Lord's blessing, but if we were once to leave our present post it might be very difficult to regain it."[21]

An offer then came from "some very kind Armenians": places in a caravan to Damascus. From Damascus they might even be able to travel on and meet their friends in Aleppo. The Armenian schoolmaster, with his young nephew Serkies, decided to join the caravan, but Groves confided, "Still we do not see clearly our permission to go, and the Lord has given us all such perfect peace in staying, and such perfect health, that we are even unwilling to go."[22] In point of fact, it was already too late; they later heard that almost all the crew and passengers of Major Taylor's boat perished. And the caravan to Damascus, after suffering "the most complicated misery both from the flood and the plague," eventually turned back having failed to reach its destination. Mary's mind was as firmly set against leaving Baghdad as her husband's. "The Lord has given me no desire nor sense of the desirableness of moving," she said, "which I feel assured he would have done had he seen it best."[23]

The day after the Taylors' departure Groves wrote, "The plague has just entered our neighbour's dwelling, where they have collected together nearly thirty persons, not simply their own family. It seems as if a spirit of infatuation had seized them, for instead of making their numbers as small as possible they seem to congregate as many as they can."[24] Fifteen hundred were now dying every day within Baghdad alone. Parties were out burying the dead; otherwise the city was deserted. Their Arabic teacher came in, having just bought a burial sheet for himself and for his brother and mother. "The Mohammedans look on those who die of the plague as martyrs," observed Groves, "and no wailing is made for them, so amidst all these desolations there is a stillness which, when one knows the cause, is very frightful."[25]

On 16th April, "The son of Gaspar Khan, our next neighbour is dead. Two have been carried out from a little passage opposite our house today... The population of Baghdad cannot exceed 80,000 and of this number more than half have fled, so that the mortality of two thousand a day is going on among considerably less than 40,000 people. But the Lord tells us, when we hear or see these things not to have our hearts troubled for our redemption draweth nigh... Surely every principle of dissolution is operating in the midst of the Ottoman and Persian empires. Plagues, earthquakes and civil wars all mark that the days of the Lord's coming are at hand, and this is our hope."[26]

Orphaned children were wandering the streets, not knowing where to go. "A little girl of about twelve years old was seen carrying an infant in her arms, and being asked whose it was she said she did not know but had found it in the road having heard that both its parents were dead." The following day (24th April), "A poor Armenian woman has just been here to beg a little sugar for a little infant she picked up in the street this morning, and she says another neighbour of hers has picked up two more. They have just been digging graves beside our house... Oh when will the Lord come to put an end to these scenes...! In one short month not less than 30,000 souls have passed from time to eternity in this city, and yet even now, no diminution apparently of deaths. Surely the judgment of the Lord is on this land?"[27]

The river continued to rise. By now the plains surrounding Baghdad were completely under water. The barley harvest was totally destroyed, and many people trying to escape found themselves trapped. "The caravan which left for Damascus yesterday can neither advance or return on account of the water." The level of the Tigris was now only a few inches lower than the main streets of the city itself. Groves answered a knock at the door. Major Taylor's servant stood there, but his attention was taken up with a woman lying in the doorway, obviously dying of the plague and already unconscious. The servant had a message. A wall of the Residency had fallen, undermined by the rising water. Groves felt obliged to go out and help them rescue Major Taylor's personal belongings. While he was there, news was brought to the servant that his aunt was dead: the eighth near relation he had lost.[28]

Groves described the scenes in his journal: "All you see passing have a little bunch of herbs or a rose or an onion to smell to."[29] But the plague, of course, was caused by bacteria from fleas carried by rats. As the water rose, the rats were driven out of drains and gutters into the houses. The medicines then available were of little use. It was possible to "reduce the fever", and to "support the constitution", but this did nothing for the painful carbuncles and large glandular swellings, and could not relieve the physical exhaustion, the "oppression on the brain", then the delirium and seizures, followed by unconsciousness and death.[30]

Every day they watched the bodies carried out from the houses along the little alleyway on the other side of the street. On 25th April Groves noted, "The man who sold cotton for burying the dead, the price of which he raised from 45 to 95 *piastres*, and who lived only two doors from us, died yesterday… I have been enabled by the Lord's goodness to get all our water jars filled, though at twenty times the usual price."[31] "Some of the Mohammedans, our neighbours, were sitting under our windows last evening and were observing that while two or three had been taken from every house, we only had remained free. And this is of the Lord's marvellous love. We consist of thirteen, including the schoolmaster's family, and the Lord has given his destroying angel charge to pass over our door."[32] A little later, "The poor women who have taken charge of the two poor little infants have sent to us for food for them… It may be to be instrumental in saving some of these poor little infants, and in helping the orphans that remain, that the Lord has allowed us to stay here. They are all Mohammedan children… Very respectable persons are coming to the door to beg a little bread, or a little butter, or some other simple necessity of life."[33]

The food stored in the house had to suffice, for there was nothing in the markets or shops, and it must be eaten cold and raw, as there was no wood for a fire. Water for drinking could not be obtained at any price; the ritual ablutions of the Muslims took priority. "Every waterman you stop answers he is carrying it to wash the bodies of the dead." So clothes must remain dirty and the bathtub unused. Soon they would have to go out and find a well, or else draw water from the polluted river. "For ourselves personally, the Lord has allowed us great peace and assured confidence in his loving care and in the truth of his promise that our bread and our water shall be sure; but certainly nothing but the service of such a Lord as he is would keep me in the scenes which these countries do exhibit, and I feel assured will, till the Lord has finished his judgments on them for the contempt of the name, nature and offices of the Son of God. Yet I linger in the hope he has a remnant even among them, for whose return these convulsions are preparing the way."[34] Mary viewed all these things calmly. "I never in England enjoyed that sweet sense of my Lord's loving care that I have enjoyed in Baghdad," she said.[35] Henry and Frank played quietly on the flat roof and looked after their pigeons and other livestock in the courtyard. The baby still seemed well. Kitto was happy with a pile of books; he remained indoors, calmly absorbing the contents of Major Taylor's library.

Having lost half his soldiers, and all but four of his hundred-strong personal bodyguard, Daoud Pasha was evidently about to run the gauntlet of the hostile tribes outside the walls in an attempt to reach safety further down the river. The city would then be at the mercy of any force desiring to occupy it. Yet even he, desperate to leave (with his palace in ruins, his stud horses running round the streets and his corn supplies plundered, much to the relief of the poor), could not collect forty men to man his yacht, "for all fear of him is now past, and love for him they have none."[36] Every other boat had long since gone.

On 26th April Norris Groves confided, "Our anxieties have been greatly increased by the illness of our dear little baby."[37] The child was very fretful, and "by night Mary had hardly any rest."[38] Although providence could be seen in every incident, and Mary herself marvelled at "the peace she enjoyed in the Lord", it is not difficult to read between the brave lines and see that the increasing heat of summer, the overcrowded conditions, the awful scenes they had witnessed, and the personal danger they were in, had built up feelings of intense weariness. "Missionaries in these countries have need of a very simple faith," Groves confessed, "which can glory in God's will being done though all their plans come to nothing… Yet it requires great confidence in God's love, and much experience of it, for the soul to remain in peace, stayed on him."[39]

On the night of 27th April the river Tigris rose again, to a level far higher than ever before in living memory. "Today all thoughts are turned from the plague to the inundation, which from the falling of a portion of the city wall on the north-west side last night, let the water in full stream into the city. The Jews' quarter is inundated, and two hundred houses fell there last night. We are hourly expecting to hear that every part of the city is overflowed… Such is the structure of the houses that if the water remains near the foundations long the city must become a mass of ruins. The mortar they use in building is very like plaster of Paris which sets very hard and does very well when all is dry, but as soon as ever water is applied, it all crumbles to powder."[40] The poorer quarters were in an even worse state: "the houses of the poor are nothing but mud."[41]

The following day they heard that seven thousand houses had collapsed, "from one end of the city to the other, burying the sick, the dying and the dead, with many of those in health, in one common grave." Fifteen thousand people perished beneath the falling masonry. "Hosts of fugitives" trying to escape from the plague were cut off along the road and trapped in buildings or on rising ground above the floodwaters where they were slowly starving to death.

And yet, "the Lord has stopped the water just at the top of our street," reported Groves, "by a little ledge of high ground so that as yet we are dry."[42] "We have taken one poor little Mohammedan baby, about three or four years old, from the streets and are supplying a poor Armenian woman with pap [i.e. bread and milk] for another." It was a heart-rending sight to watch "little children from a month or six weeks to two to four years crying for a home, hungry and naked and wretched and knowing not what to do nor where to go."[43]

It was 29th April when tidings of the Damascus caravan came in. Norris and Mary's decision not to join it was now fully justified, for plague had carried off nine of the party, four had drowned, and the remainder, attempting to retrace their steps to Baghdad, had been trapped by rising floodwaters. One of the dead was their Armenian schoolmaster. Another caravan, attempting to escape to Persia, had been forced back by Arab raiders, then by floods and lack of food.

In Baghdad itself the water seemed no higher and, if anything, appeared to be receding, although their own basement was completely flooded. The next day things looked a little better. "Today, blessed be God's holy name, the waters have sunk more than a yard." But this brought its own problems. "There seems now every prospect that the moment the waters decrease, the surrounding Arabs will come in and plunder the city. Yet even this is in the Lord's hands. Our wisdom has ever been to sit still and see the salvation of our God."[44]

A week later reports confirmed that more than half the city had collapsed into the floodwaters. There was floating rubbish everywhere and a stench of rotting flesh and sewage. People were crowded together wherever they might find shelter; twenty or thirty were occupying the house next door. Every day the summer heat grew stronger and the risk of infection increased with the submergence of so many drains, graves and rubbish dumps. "The wonder, physically speaking, seems to be not that five out of seven have died but that the remaining two escaped," commented Kitto.[45] "In these countries," he added, "people have no other resource than to run away when the plague appears. In the present case, however, this common resource was precluded by the inundation, as if the Agent of Destruction acted with design... in unbinding the rivers, that the waters might confine his victims, as in a prison, awaiting execution."[46]

The sufferings of modern Babylon seemed to surpass even those of Nebuchadnezzar's proud capital two and a half thousand years earlier. As God had destroyed the one, he seemed intent on destroying the other. "Babylon has fallen, has fallen!" the scriptures thundered. "All the images of her gods lie shattered on the ground."[47] "She has sinned against the Lord... She surrenders, her towers fall, her walls are torn down."[48] And as judgment was decreed for ancient Babylon, judgment was foretold for the Babylon of this present age. "Woe! Woe! O great city, O Babylon, city of power! In one hour your doom has come!"[49] "So shall her plagues come in a single day, pestilence and mourning and famine, and she shall be burned with fire; for mighty is the Lord God who judges her."[50]

"Oh how does the glory of the Caliphate lie in ashes!" Groves remarked.[51] Surely it could be no coincidence. At the very moment when God's servants come to show the way of salvation, the old order is swept away – such a destruction as would prepare the way of the Lord. "Amidst all these trials to the servants of God," said Groves, "my heart does not despair for the work of the Lord, for no ordinary judgments seem necessary to break the pride and hatred of this most proud and contemptuous people."[52] He thought of the Papacy, so recently stripped of its political power, and now the "House of Islam" thrown down. Surely as "the wrath of God is pouring out… the two antichrists are beginning to draw near their end."[53]

Nights and days passed with no sign of relief: nowhere for the children to go out and play, nowhere for them to walk amidst green fields or breathe fresh air. "I can only look forward for comfort to that day," sighed Groves, "when the Lord himself will come to put an end to this dispensation of desolation and introduce his own peace. Yea, come Lord Jesus, come quickly."[54] Mary's heart "has been so set on her Lord's coming of late that it seemed quite to absorb her thoughts."[55]

On 1st May, "Today as I passed along the street I saw numbers of dead bodies lying unburied, and the dogs eating with avidity the loathsome food." Their Arabic teacher was dead; his son reported that in the quarter where they lived not one human being was left alive. The dead now so greatly outnumbered the living that burial was hardly possible; bodies were just thrown in the river: "Yet amidst all this the Lord suffers not the destroying angel to enter our dwelling, but we feel the Lord has commanded the man with the inkhorn to write us down to be spared, as this is one of the vials of God's wrath on his enemies."[56] Many entire families had been wiped out, and in many others only one or two remained. "But I hear of none save our own," wrote Groves, "where death has not entered."[57]

Ten days went by without sight of a water carrier. Eventually, on 3rd May, "we had our water jars filled again today." "Your water shall be sure,"[58] Groves quoted, and "we who are alone and without a friend within hundreds of miles in any direction have been supplied by our Lord's gracious ordering. Thus he puts a new song into our mouths, even a song of thanksgiving." "Today all are well," he added optimistically. "Even our dear little baby is quite recovered."[59]

Throughout that week the floodwater continued to go down. When Groves ventured out again there were "many recovering from the plague, walking about, leaning on sticks and sitting by the wayside." But many more were still dying, and thieves were starting to loot the deserted houses. Some rice had found its way into the city and also some wood. Mary, worn out with caring for the sick baby, was clearly feeling the effects of their long ordeal. Norris himself was struggling with weakness and discouragement. On 7ᵗʰ May, "This is an anxious evening. Dear Mary is taken ill – nothing that would at any other time alarm me, but now a very little creates anxiety. Yet her heart is reposing on her Lord with perfect peace and waiting his will."[60]

The following day, "The Lord has this day manifested that the attack of my dear, dear wife is the plague, and of a very dangerous and malignant kind, so that our hearts are prostrate in the Lord's hand. As I think the infection can only have come through me, I have little hope of escaping, unless by the Lord's special intervention. It is indeed an awful moment, the prospect of leaving a little family in such a country at such a time. Yet my dearest wife's faith triumphs over these circumstances."[61] "I marvel at the Lord's dealings," said Mary herself, "but not more than at my own peace in such circumstances."[62] With a severe headache and difficulty opening her eyes, she did her best to comfort her husband. Death is something that comes to all, she reminded him: "The difference between a child of God and the worldling is not in death, but in the *hope* the one has in Jesus while the other is without hope and without God in the world." A little later Groves wrote, "She is now continually sleeping, and when roused feels it difficult to keep her dear mind fixed on any subject for a minute."[63]

Next day, "My dearest, dearest wife still alive, and not apparently worse than yesterday. Oh! if it were the Lord's holy blessed will to spare her, it would indeed rejoice my poor foolish heart, but the Lord has enabled me to cast my wife, myself and my dear, dear children on his holy love, and to await the issue. Oh! what wrath there must be against these lands, if not only the inhabitants are swept away, but the Lord transplants also his own, who would teach them, to his own garden of peace. My soul has just been refreshed by these two verses of Psalm 116: 'Return unto thy rest, O my soul, for the Lord hath dealt bountifully with thee.' He has taken one of thy olive branches to glory and is now perhaps about to take another, for 'precious in the sight of the Lord is the death of his saints,' for he only takes them from the evil to come… Our heavenly Father's love we have too often proved to doubt it now. But poor nature is bowed very, very low when I look at my dear boys and little babe, and see only poor little Kitto to be left for their care for hundreds of miles around… but the Lord has said 'Leave your fatherless children unto me' and to him we desire to leave them. We did feel assured that the Lord would spare our dear little united happy family, but his ways are not our ways, nor his thoughts our thoughts."[64] "Doubtless he will reveal in his own good time the reason why he has acted so contrary, not only to mine, but especially my dear wife's strongest convictions which were that he would preserve us all safe through this calamity."[65]

Night and day he attended to Mary's needs, allowing no one else near, in the hope that the rest of the family might avoid infection.[66] For a while she seemed to rally, and her mind cleared sufficiently that she asked to see the baby. But hopes of her recovery faded again as delirium took over. "How hard," he reflected, "for the soul to see the object of its longest and best grounded earthly affections suffering, without the power of affording relief, knowing too that a heavenly Father who has sent it *can* relieve it and yet seems to turn a deaf ear to one's cries... The Lord has shown me in the 22nd Psalm a more wonderful cry *apparently* unheeded, and the Holy Ghost has... enabled me to acquiesce in my Father's will though I now see not the end [i.e. purpose] of his holy and blessed ways. Dear, dear spirit! She will soon wing her way to where her heart has long been, and if I am spared I shall perhaps have reason to bless God for having removed her thus early."[67]

He continued to sit beside her, keeping the flies from her face through times of deep sleep and incoherent wakefulness. If Groves himself were not already carrying the infection, he would surely have it now. "My last night's attendance on my dear wife leaves me little hope of escaping the plague," he admitted, "unless it be our Father's special will to preserve me, for in her delirium she required so many times to be lifted from place to place, and to have all her clothes changed, that I can now only cry to the Lord to preserve me, if it may be, a little while, for the dear children's sake."[68]

Two other members of the household, the schoolmaster's wife and the woman who did the cooking, were now showing symptoms of the plague. Kitto, Harnie and the boys were quarantined with the baby in a separate room. They took turns looking after her, though she was "rather cross from want of amusement, and from her teeth."[69] Every day Groves went over to read and pray with them through the open window on the other side of the courtyard. The baby held out her hands and called to him; she could not understand why he refused to pick her up.

At this moment came a remarkable answer to prayer in the form of a local woman called Mariam. As a servant of Mrs Taylor she had been with them on their long overland journey from St Petersburg, and during that time had become "much attached to dear Mary". Though surrounded by the sick and dying, Mariam had not caught the plague herself and seemed blessed with some immunity. She could speak English after a fashion, and she proved to be a wonderful nurse: "a ray of light," Groves said, "arising in the midst of my darkness." "Surely the Lord heard my cry in the day of my deep distress, for such a person could not be got again within a thousand miles." Mariam took over the task of nursing Mary, washing her and changing her clothes, and solemnly declared she would not leave the family until they were all either well or dead.[70]

So far, Groves himself had no sign of swellings or other symptoms of the plague. Nevertheless, he took the precaution of passing his accounts over to Kitto, along with the scanty funds still remaining as provision for the children, although "poor Kitto is so little able to provide even for himself, much less for the little boys."[71] Mariam promised to remain with them if necessary, until the Taylors could make arrangements for the children, and Harnie was proving to be a capable cook. Surely, in all this, the Lord was with them.

ENDNOTES

[1] M120 (R97)
[2] R96-97; M119
[3] M119-120 (R97)
[4] *In limine*: at the outset, to start with (Latin).
[5] Eadie, 201-202
[6] M120 (R99)
[7] M120 (R99)
[8] R100; M121 paraphrasing Ps 37:19
[9] R101-102; M121-122
[10] M122 (R106)
[11] Eadie, 203
[12] M122 (R107)
[13] R167
[14] R170-171
[15] M123 (R107)
[16] R110
[17] R107-108
[18] R109; M124
[19] R110; M125
[20] R110-111; M125. Nazarenes: a Qur'anic term commonly used by Muslims in referring to Westerners, with the assumption that all are followers of Jesus of Nazareth.
[21] R109; M124
[22] R111-112
[23] R142; M145
[24] M126 (R112)
[25] M125 (R110)
[26] R114-115; M127-128
[27] R118-119; M130
[28] R122
[29] R114
[30] R138
[31] R120; M131-132

[32] R120; M131
[33] R121, 126
[34] R125-126
[35] R143
[36] R127
[37] R124
[38] R140
[39] R128
[40] R124
[41] R125
[42] R126
[43] R127-128
[44] R132, 130
[45] Eadie, 213
[46] Eadie, 212
[47] Is 21:9
[48] Jer 50:14-15
[49] Rev 18:10
[50] Rev 18:8 RSV
[51] R128. Caliphate: the spiritual and temporal authority governing the Islamic faithful, inherited in line of succession from Muhammad himself and assumed at this period by the Sultan of the Ottoman Empire with the personal title of "Caliph".
[52] R127
[53] R122
[54] R134
[55] R147. It was common for Christians at that period to study the "signs of the times" in the light of biblical prophecy. In a sermon on the Apocalypse in 1799 the Baptist Andrew Fuller had declared, "The last branch of the last of the four beasts is now in its dying agonies. No sooner will it be proclaimed 'Babylon is fallen' than the marriage of the Lamb will come" (George, 183 n.11; see Rev 18 and 19).
[56] Inkhorn: a small pot containing ink, usually made of horn (Ezek 9:2, 3, 11 AV).
[57] R133
[58] Referring to Is 33:16.
[59] R134
[60] M144 (R140)
[61] R140-141
[62] R141
[63] R141. Morphine had been used as a sedative in Britain since the beginning of the nineteenth century, but its poisonous and addictive qualities made most physicians reluctant to offer it. During the overland journey to Baghdad, Groves tells us that, although "a little anxious on the subject", he had found relief in "opium" from the "attacks" brought on by cold every two or three weeks (J47). He almost certainly used morphine when conducting cataract operations, and probably administered it to his wife at this time.
[64] R142-143

[65] R150-151

[66] Groves presumably thought the plague was transmitted by personal contact, unaware of the role of rats and fleas. Thirty years would pass before Louis Pasteur discovered in 1861 that infectious diseases were caused by living "germs" (microscopic bacteria, viruses, protozoa etc). Prior to this, sickness was generally attributed to miasma (bad air), foul water or dirt, and the remedy would be fumigation (to purify the air), purgatives (to rid the body of corruption) and bleeding (to reduce tension in the arteries).

[67] R146-147. Questions relating to suffering, providence, and the significance of Old Testament promises, are considered in Chapter 30 of this book.

[68] R148

[69] R155

[70] R148-149; M149-150. We actually know very little about Mariam (also called Marian or Miriam). Groves's journal entry for 21st May 1831 comments, "Miriam is most kind to my sweet little helpless babe" (R163). The editor of the *Memoir* later changes this to "Hannai is most kind…" (M160), which might lead us to suppose that Mariam and Harnie were the same person. In fact, Mariam was "an old servant" of Mrs Rich, the wife of the previous Resident in Baghdad. She had spent some time with Mrs Taylor in England, attended her on the journey to Baghdad, and was expecting to return eventually to her duties with the Taylor household (R149-150). In contrast, Harnie was a young refugee from Mosul who happened to work next door to the Groves family, "and became his devoted servant from the day that her brother, whom he attended medically, fell a victim to consumption" (Groves E K, *Successors*, 37; see also Groves H, *Faithful Hanie*, 28).

[71] R149

"Truly, whatever makes Jesus precious,
and eternity a reality,
is most blessed,
though it cuts up all earthly things by the roots."

Norris Groves [1]

14

Blessed be the Hand

It was barely seven days after the appearance of the first symptoms that Mary Groves passed away quietly, "without a sigh and without a groan". That very day, 14th May 1831, the shops reopened and vegetables were seen on the streets. The price of drinking water came down to its normal level. The plague was past. "To think that so near the end we should have been thus visited, how mysterious!" pondered Groves.[2] Her body, wrapped in a sheet, was laid on a hurdle of palm branches tied with cords on the back of a horse and taken away for burial by two strangers. "No one followed her beloved remains to the grave," said Kitto, "and no funeral rites were performed there. Indeed, we know not the spot of her interment."[3] To do otherwise would have exposed her grieving family to further risk of infection.

Norris Groves sat for hours, absorbed in his own thoughts; there was nothing else to do. Kitto, having suffered so much himself, always felt duty bound to offer a word of comfort to others in time of sorrow. But for once he had nothing to say to a man who always seemed to live on a higher spiritual plane than himself, and for almost two days he could say nothing about it at all: "I have sat for hours watching him with an anxiety which I cannot describe and which unfitted me for reading or study of any kind."[4] No doubt a prayerful and sympathetic silence can be of greater comfort to one whose loss is so utterly beyond words, and Kitto may have been wise to wait for the older man to speak. But Groves himself was now far from well, admitting to "symptoms similar to those with which my dearest Mary's illness commenced – pains in the head and heaviness, pains in the back, and shooting pains through the [neck] glands and the arms."[5] In a high fever he closed his journal on the night of 16th May with final exhortations to whoever might read it, not knowing if he would ever take up his pen again.

Norris Groves was by no means confident he would live. "I certainly never expected again to have written in this journal," he confided the following day.[6] Yet the fever seemed to have lifted. Looking back on his recovery, "It was most gracious of the Lord, when he let the plague reach me, and laid me on my couch, to give me the sweetest comfort from a full assurance of his favour and forgiveness when there was, as I thought, but a step between me and death."[7]

All anxiety for the children had melted away. "So abundantly did the Lord allow his love to pass before me, so fully did he assure me of his loving care, that I felt no doubt for them. And for myself, the prospect of soon joining him was specially exhilarating... I never felt more the preciousness of such a salvation as the gospel of Jesus provides for the sinner than when I was, as I thought, just entering eternity."[8]

While Groves continued weakly to live, the schoolmaster's wife died, and also the cook, leaving her seven-year-old son an orphan in their care.[9] Kitto himself faced the prospect of death calmly, expressed as always with a literary flourish: "Life has not been altogether so pleasant a thing to me to give an interest of much intensity to a question which at most involves no more than its possible loss."[10] He hoped for better things beyond the grave, and wrote a farewell note to his mother and the rest of his family: "In the case of my death, you will, my dear mother, perhaps feel it as a little trial. If so, may that and every other trial be blessed to you in bringing you nearer to Jesus Christ who became himself a man of sorrows and acquainted with grief for our sake. That will be a blessed thing, whatever it be, which brings us nearer to him and carries you more frequently to your Bible."[11]

On the evening of 20th May the household faced a fresh hazard. For a day or two past, Groves had noticed a trickle of dust falling through a crack in the wall of his bedroom. Knowing the basement was full of water, he called the boys and Harnie to help move everything out – all his personal belongings and clothes, and Mary's too – while Kitto held the baby. Barely ten minutes after the final items had been shifted, the arch beneath the floor gave way, and the whole room collapsed into the flooded basement. "Blessed be the Hand," declared Kitto, "that supported the arch till such precious lives were withdrawn from the danger."[12] But that was not all. A few days later, "I was sitting in my room," said Kitto, "when I felt the house shake and was almost suffocated by a cloud of dust, and rushing out found, as soon as the dust had settled a little, that the wall of the same room... had collapsed, and with it a great portion of the roof or terrace of the house." Once again, Harnie "with the baby in her arms" had escaped the fall by only a few minutes. Groves, struggling with physical weakness and personal grief, was comforted to see his "dear and loving Father" protecting them from further harm. "This has been a day of mercies at the hand of the Most High," he wrote bravely. He regretted he was such a "poor wayward scholar", learning so slowly and painfully "to kiss the hand that wounds, to bless the hand that pours out sorrow, and to submit with all my soul though I see not a ray of light."[13] "I feel Christ my Lord has in store for me in himself some great and special good in exchange for all this, but my poor weak faithless heart does not yet see the way of his going forth."[14]

That night thieves attempted three times to force the outer door. Eventually they gave up and went away. A new pasha at the head of a fresh army had entered Baghdad, without evident bloodshed, but no one knew what he would do once established in the city whilst his predecessor remained there too, recovering slowly from infection. Henry complained of a swelling in his neck, an enlarged gland, undoubtedly the plague. The following day he seemed somewhat better, but Kitto was unwell. The next day Kitto was better but "the dear baby is very unwell." The days, wrote Groves, "move heavily on", with "short intervals of sweet peace" and then fresh anxieties that "plunge me into the depths of sorrow and astonishment." "I remain in absolute darkness as to the meaning of my Lord and Father."[15] "Yet I know the Lord will heal; he will bind up what he has broken... Oh my heart longs for Christian communion, someone to whom I can talk of Jesus and his ways, and with whom I may take counsel."[16] He hoped his friends in England were praying for him. Never had he felt so much in need of prayer as at this time when his own heavy heart found prayer so difficult. A packet of letters arrived, but rather than cheering they depressed him with their blithe confidence in the Lord's protection and hopes for the work he and Mary would be doing together. Some clothes came in a small package for the baby, but would she live to wear them? There was no news from Aleppo.

At last, on 7th June, a messenger came from Major Taylor in Basra. A few miles outside Baghdad the messenger had been "stripped to his shirt" and all his letters taken, but he could tell them that the Taylors were well, though most of their party had died, including the Arab seamen who were found to have hidden an infected corpse in the boat for several days. But Basra was now itself a battle ground. The governor had been driven out of the city by a band of Arabs and was about to attempt its recapture. A little satisfaction came to Groves from knowing that if they had attempted to seek refuge there with the Taylors they would hardly have been safer than in Baghdad.

With two pashas now in Baghdad, a third was advancing on the city with troops of his own. Proclamations and counter-proclamations, and the sound of cannons and mortars, added to the general confusion. With an advancing army barely six miles away, "the whole city is in a state of commotion... everyone armed with swords, pistols and guns." As there was now no recognised or effective authority in Baghdad, robbers began to plunder the occupied as well as the deserted houses of the city. Refusing to keep any weapons with them, Groves noted, "The only men besides myself are Kitto who is deaf and the schoolmaster's father who is blind, but the Lord is our hope and our exceeding great reward."[17] Sounds of shouting and gunfire came from the palace, and Kitto saw Daoud Pasha, under a strong guard, carried past their door to stand trial before the sole surviving member of the family he had supplanted and slaughtered.

There seemed little prospect of progress for the gospel in the foreseeable future. Groves reflected, "When all the difficulties of these countries follow upon one another as rapidly as they have of late done here, it seems very difficult to see how the word of life is to go forth as a testimony. Yet it will, for the Lord hath said it; therefore let not our hearts fail or our hands hang down, for the Lord of all circumstances, who governs the most disastrous as well as the most prosperous, is our own Lord... Wherever the blasting influence of Mohammedanism extends, how iron-bound all appears against the truth, yet even this the Lord will soften by his love or break by his power."[18] Brave words, yet reports from Syria showed that workers there "scarcely know of an individual to whom their message has been peace."[19] Who could blame him for wistful thoughts of more productive fields elsewhere! "No one can imagine the disheartening feelings," he said, "that often try the missionary's heart in the countries where Mohammedanism is professed and dominant, and where your mouth is sealed. Among heathens, and especially in India, you can publish your testimony, and this is a great comfort to the heart that knows what a testimony it is and what promises are connected with its publication."[20]

Much of his time was now devoted to caring for the baby. Some days well, some days fretful, she was the focus of all his affection, and attending to her needs helped to distract him from darker thoughts. One night thieves shot through the door, demanding gunpowder and weapons; they went away only after Groves had reasoned with them and given them a little money. Turning next day to his journal he wrote, "Oh my dear Mary, what a contrast to your kingdom of peace and love! Lord Jesus come quickly! For this I can now truly bless God that she is freed from this season of trouble and anxiety. The dear children bear it better than I could have hoped... It has been a great comfort to me today to think on Noah's case, that God did not forget him amidst a condemned world."[21] A few days later the thieves came back, demanding arrack, but left quietly when none could be found: "The Lord thus graciously takes care of us. They look on me as a sort of *dervish* because I do not drink arrack, nor use weapons of war, nor take men to guard my house."[22]

Fighting broke out again; this time between those who wished to kill Daoud Pasha and those who favoured sparing his life. Some people said that the forces outside the gate were not those of a third pasha but simply a deception plotted by one of the first two. Barricades had been erected in the streets, musket balls flew above the roof of the house, and the nearby palace was on fire. Screams were heard from the far end of the street in the Jewish quarter, where houses and shops were being plundered. The Pasha of Mosul, who had usurped Daoud's position, was now himself held captive; some said he had been killed. The crier once again proclaimed Daoud as pasha, but an army was certainly at the city walls and seemed set to commence a siege. Such was the disorder that no person or property was safe, and food was hard to obtain anywhere.

It was difficult for Groves to know what was going on, especially as his knowledge of the local languages was still rudimentary. This was an added frustration. He had been in Baghdad a bare eighteen months, and for much of that time the demands of the school and the needs of his family had made serious study very difficult. Then the onset of the plague and the death of his Arabic language teacher had brought progress to a complete halt. He had engaged a man educated in Bombay to compile an Armenian-English dictionary of twenty thousand words, containing both colloquial and literary forms with explanations and examples. Halfway through this monumental task the man had died, and the likelihood of finding someone to complete it seemed remote. Baghdad was not, in any case, the easiest place to learn a language. Its size and reputation had attracted generations of immigrants from every part of the Middle East. Its streets and markets echoed with the sound of Arabic, Armenian, Persian, Turkish, Kurdish, Aramaic and Hebrew, and most of these had both a spoken and a written form that differed in many particulars. Shopkeepers, stallholders, government officials, religious leaders, neighbours, water-sellers, servants, schoolmasters and schoolchildren – all these had to be dealt with every day, and it was hard to remain sufficiently focused on any one of the languages to learn it thoroughly. Groves pondered the problem. "I shall never feel a missionary till I can deliver my message clearly and intelligibly," he said. "Till then I endeavour to drop a word, as it may be offered, and to instill a principle, as an occasion may occur…, but the Lord daily comforts me, amidst the delays and trials of faith, by the clearest conviction of the large sphere of usefulness there is when once this is attained."[23]

No one had ever said it would be easy. "Notwithstanding, however, all difficulties and all discouragements… my soul was never more assured of the value of missionary labours among any people, it matters not whom, than now."[24] The elderly father of their late schoolmaster had understood much of the Bible and declared his conviction that believing God's word mattered more than belonging to a particular church. Groves was encouraged: "I think this aged man understands and feels there is but one Church in the world." What is more, in conversation with Harnie the old man had spoken about "the importance of having a translation that every woman and child can understand."[25] Here, at least, was some small yield from seed sown in such strange conditions, and this despite the fact that Groves spoke Arabic, and the old man, who was very deaf, understood only Armenian and Turkish. "It is almost impossible for a missionary (even of the humblest pretensions, and in the lowest degree qualified for his calling, which I can I think with unaffected truth say I feel to be my own case) to live among these people and not to lead them to some most important principles."[26] Norris Groves was not going to give up.

The baby meanwhile was suffering from "purulent ophthalmia", for three or four days quite unable to open her eyes. Then on 2nd July, "In the evening, as I was looking out, I saw the man come into the courtyard who brings and collects letters for Aleppo, and in his hand a letter for me. With what eagerness did I seize it." And with what disappointment to discover that the friends in Aleppo had made no further plans to join him! On the contrary, they proposed that he leave Baghdad to assist them in Aleppo. "I… receive this last trying providence at my loving Father's hands… The Lord allows me to feel assured he will yet do something for me." Groves had no thought of leaving Baghdad: "I feel daily more and more that my place in the church is very low, and it matters very little where I am for any good that is in me. Yet by remaining I keep the way open for those who are more able." Having already invested so much, and at such a cost, it could surely not be right to abandon the attempt as a total loss. In the Lord's will, there must come a harvest in Baghdad, to be reaped in joy, though sown in tears: "Until the Lord, therefore, raises his fiery cloudy pillar and bids me forth, I shall pursue my plan of endeavouring to converse in Arabic till the Lord is pleased to open my mouth by degrees, or as he please, to publish his whole truth."[27] If the others declined to join him, he would continue alone. Yet "to the dear boys it has been a great disappointment, for it was the constant theme of their conversation, and a cheering expectation, to see friends from England."[28]

It was now mid-July, and summer was once again at its full heat. The family could not seek refuge, as they had the previous year, in the cooler basement rooms; these were still three feet deep in water. Mosquitoes had bred profusely on the flooded plains and now filled the house, biting continuously day and night. For several weeks it was almost impossible to sleep. In the streets of the city, self-styled prophets and astrologers predicted further desolations. The Sunday worship circle was much reduced, and the blockading factions outside the walls prevented any mail from England bringing help or comfort. Groves struggled with loneliness and discouragement, burdened with the management of the household, the constant need for food and water, and all the tasks previously undertaken by Mary. If only the friends from Aleppo had come, he would have been spared these additional burdens. The boys were fretting, wanting to leave Baghdad, and the baby remained very frail. Kitto continued to read and write, largely oblivious of outside activity, undisturbed in his deafness by the continuous din of gunfire, drums and shouting.

Norris Groves at this time sank into periods of profound introspection, depressed at his inability to rejoice in the Lord. He thought how easy it had been to appear an outstanding Christian when blessed with a loving wife, a comfortable home, a rewarding profession and a stimulating circle of godly friends; and how hard to maintain any Christian spirit at all when stripped bare and exposed to a thousand weaknesses. "My heart," he confessed, "is very sad to think how profitless a servant I have been."[29] Mercifully, the black moods were interspersed with more hopeful thoughts: "The sense of my Father's love and Saviour's sympathy has never been taken from me amidst all my trials.

Nay, I do feel that the Lord is fitting me, by suffering and separation, for the work to which he has called me."[30]

With the passing of the plague, people were once more active in the streets, and Groves had conversations about spiritual things with those he met – some Roman Catholics recently arrived from Syria, a group of Armenians and a Jacobite – and he was encouraged by the thought that he was "getting on a little in the colloquial language of the country."[31] People knocked periodically on the door, seeking medical treatment, and he did what he could for them. One Muslim, at least, was drawn to Christ – an officer of the Pasha's household who came for attention to his leg where a plague sore had become infected. "In Islam," the officer declared, "there is no mercy, no pity." Then, turning to Groves, "Did you ever see me before I came about my leg?" "No." "Yet you had mercy upon me, and cured me and my daughter (who also had had the plague), and why? It was from your heart – there was mercy there."[32] Some Eastern Christians, too, were willing to hear about the meaning of true faith. A discussion with two Roman Catholic merchants confirmed Groves in thinking that the best way to help such people was to make them think carefully about what they already professed to believe. "In these countries, where religious expressions are in everyone's mouth, a missionary has most valuable employment, as he is able to bring their minds back to their own expressions, to their own import and power."[33] Yes, there was much to be done in Baghdad.

While Groves struggled to pick up the pieces, his long-awaited friends were settling down to life on the far side of the Syrian desert. The party had left Dublin by steamer the previous September (1830), carrying a considerable quantity of luggage: several trunks of books, "a large medicine chest" belonging to Dr Cronin, and "a lithographic press in two very heavy boxes" requested by Groves. The medicine chest had been left behind in the confusion at Dublin docks; it caught them up further down the river. After a stormy voyage they landed in Bordeaux on the west coast of France.

Here John Parnell and Nancy Cronin had hoped to arrange their wedding. As Nancy's father was an Irish Roman Catholic, her mother a Protestant, and John's parents agnostics of the English aristocracy, the young couple had intended to avoid the peril of religious discord, the expense of high society celebrations and the obligation to visit widely scattered relatives, by having a quiet ceremony with just a few friends in some out-of-the-way spot. On enquiry in Bordeaux, however, they discovered that French law required several months' residence before they could apply for marriage. The party decided to press on by road and canal to Marseille. Further storms and heavy seas followed in the Mediterranean, and it was late December before they finally landed on the Syrian coast at Latakia (al-Ladhiqiyah). In addition to

John Parnell and Nancy, the company comprised her brother Edward Cronin, his infant daughter Minny and their mother, along with the two men, Hamilton and Newman. Parnell's biographer pictures how they all "slept that night on the shores of Asia... on a spot that had been frequented by apostles and martyrs."[34] It seemed a strange turn of events that the gospel of Christ, carried in apostolic times from Syria to Europe, should be making the return journey to a land that now hardly knew it.

Frank Newman was enjoying the company of his "Irish friends". Unlike John Nelson Darby, they did not demand his agreement with their every opinion: "The dear companions of my travels no more aimed to guide my thoughts than I theirs. Neither ambition nor suspicion found their place in our hearts, and my mind was thus able again without disturbance to develop its own tendencies."[35] Their desire, like his, was to recover the beliefs and methods of the apostolic age, setting aside the accumulated religious traditions of eighteen centuries: "Hence arose in me a conscious and continuous effort to read the New Testament with fresh eyes and without bias, and so to take up the real doctrines of the heavenly and everlasting gospel."[36] His study, as they travelled, led him to suspect that contemporary churches, in trying to explain the idea of the Holy Trinity, verged on Tri-theism. To the uninstructed, "three Persons" could only mean "three people" and thus three gods, and any attempt to preach three gods in a Muslim country would be doomed to failure. Did not the New Testament, in any case, teach that the Father was the "only true God",[37] and that both Christ and the Holy Spirit had come *from* the Father – not as separate beings but rather as aspects of, or emanations from, the Father? Newman observed that the apostles were never charged by the Jews with polytheism – no doubt because they never at any time proclaimed "three Persons" – and if we follow their example, he suggested, our hearers will have no cause to suspect us of it. He shared his thoughts with his companions and was pleased to find that, whether or not they were fully convinced, their friendship remained just as warm as before. By nature, Parnell and Cronin were practical men, little concerned with the kind of theological contentions that, to John Darby, would have been a red rag to a bull.

So far the party had met with no success in their attempts to recruit an Arab guide and interpreter who might accompany them to Baghdad. Parnell's money had failed to do the trick in Bordeaux, in Marseille, and now in Latakia, so they faced the first stage of their overland trek of 120 miles, from the coast inland to Aleppo, without any means of communicating with the muleteers or with anyone who might sell them food along the way. Nothing daunted, they set off in heavy rain. Hazards abounded as they forded swollen rivers, enquired after victuals and endured bitter cold, sheltering in open country at night beneath their piles of baggage. On such rocky paths the women could not safely ride side-saddle; they would more than likely slide off the animal's back. There was nothing for it but to sit astride. Nancy proved quite adaptable but old Mrs Cronin, obliged to hitch up her heavy Irish skirts, exclaimed to her son, "Ach Edward, I expected they would persecute and murdher us, but I never thought to ride across a mule! [*sic*]"[38] Three times her mule came down, depositing the poor lady in the mud. Cronin himself was carrying the little girl. At one point they rode for eleven hours without stopping or eating. Other times there were delays when the roads were blocked by armed men engaged in civil war. Still no opportunity had been found for John and Nancy to marry; there was no authorised minister or government official in Latakia. "But we trust in you O Lord," they said. "Our times are in your hands."[39]

On 10th January (1831) the company finally reached Aleppo. Planning the next stage to Baghdad, however, they met an immovable obstacle. All the pack animals – camels, horses and mules – had been commandeered by the Ottoman authorities, and the Sultan would not allow a single caravan to start for Baghdad. There was no alternative but to find temporary lodgings in Aleppo and make use of the time by starting to learn Arabic. While Cronin introduced himself as a doctor, offering free medical care, Parnell went in search of someone who could licence marriages. The British Consul was not sure if he could – no one had asked him before – and there was a long delay while a despatch was sent overland through 750 miles of mountains to the British Ambassador in Constantinople.

Locked up in a certain house in Aleppo was a large quantity of Bibles and New Testaments. They had been sent some time previously by the Jewish evangelist Joseph Wolff on behalf of the Bible Society in London. Parnell received permission to retrieve these and carry them on to Baghdad. Eventually he found the house, obtained the key, and went in. Strewn about the floor were scriptures in Arabic, Turkish, Syriac and Armenian, many of them damp and mouldy. Those that were still usable they picked up and packed for the journey. Permission finally came for John and Nancy to be married by the Consul, and life settled down to a regular pattern.

Meanwhile in Baghdad the fighting continued throughout July, as did the intense, almost suffocating heat of summer. Musket balls, cannon balls and shells continued to fly above the rooftop where Groves and the rest of the family slept at night. The night air offered some relief from the heat trapped in the building during the day, although three members of an Arab family sleeping on a neighbouring rooftop were killed outright when a shell fell on them. A musket ball hit the wall beside Groves, and another just missed him as he ducked his head. People were regularly murdered in the streets, and a Muslim friend told of his own great anxiety for his property, his life and the safety of his womenfolk, should the besieging army storm the city. "What a relief to know that my dear Mary is with her Lord," reflected Groves.[40] Three months had now passed since her death.

Famine was a real danger. The poor could not afford food at six times its usual price, and dysentery was spreading, as many were eating things unfit for consumption. Henry and Frank had not been outside the house for five months. "I cannot but feel it is a great mercy of the Lord that they are so happy and contented," confided Groves. "I have never heard, during all this time, one word of complaint from them."[41] Sunday, he remarked, is "a day that always dawns with sweet peace on my soul."[42] His thoughts would turn to times of happy fellowship in days gone by – the company of saints in Dublin, or Exeter, or even of their own little group in Baghdad before its decimation. The baby was still very ill; for most of the time his mind was preoccupied with her needs.

At the beginning of August some neighbouring families asked for a contribution to the cost of enlisting forty armed men to guard the neighbourhood. "This I saw my way clear in declining," Groves noted, "believing that for Christ's servants the sword is not a lawful defence."[43] Though no longer confident, as he had been, that danger and death must pass them by, he would still choose to suffer whatever the Lord might send rather than shirk his command to love his enemies, turn the other cheek and give to any who asked of him. A sheep among wolves he felt himself to be, yet having forsaken all to follow Christ, he had few possessions left to interest thieves, which made it easier to deal with them pacifically.[44] "This is the time of our faith," he remarked. "The time of our knowledge is, as St Paul says, to come – for at best now we see through a glass darkly."[45] Reading a biography of Henry Martyn, he was moved again "to seek a fuller and more abiding union with Jesus" and to "make the most of my talent, that I be not numbered among the slothful servants at my dear Lord's most glorious and blessed appearing."[46] The baby was undoubtedly dying and clung constantly to her father.

The siege continued through August, and so scarce was food within the walls that "numbers of poor people are crying at the gates to be let out, that they may not be starved in the city."[47] Eventually five thousand of the most desperate were allowed to leave, despite the knowledge that others who had escaped were stripped by the besieging forces and sent back. Once the defenders sallied out, killing a hundred of the enemy and capturing a further hundred and fifty, whose heads were then cut off in cold blood. Someone who came for medical treatment told Groves that individuals who previously had only small cash to their name were now "seen riding about on fine horses and trappings, covered with gold and pearls etc. and… many who before were in very good circumstances are, by the robbery of those who should protect them, reduced to beggary."[48] While the household was asleep one night, thieves, in search of wheat or rice, broke into the ground floor and took some clothes and furnishings before they were disturbed. Fortunately, the more essential things were safely hidden and remained untouched.

On 24th August the baby died. Again Groves was thankful that Mary had not lived to see those toilsome anxious days and nights or suffer the final grief and loss. "The Lord took her [Mary] from the evil to come, and has now taken the dear little object of her love to her – to join her little sainted sister and dear little brother. Four of us are gone, and three are left."[49]

Without the baby to care for, Norris Groves was now free to think about the future. Four days after her death, he could write almost cheerfully, "Today I feel the Lord has given me a victory by turning my thoughts off my miserable self and temporary circumstances to the contemplation of the happiness of those who are gone before me, and by enabling me to feel set off on my journey to meet them and drawing every day one day's journey nearer."[50] With a fresh perspective, a degree of physical health and fewer home duties, he now had sufficient strength to plan ahead. "I therefore now purpose, the Lord enabling me, after nearly six months interruption, to return to the studies preparatory to my future duties as an itinerating missionary. To this service I ever thought the Lord had called me." There was nothing to tie him to any one place. The boys, under the care of their tutor, "will soon be of an age to move about with me," or perhaps, if they preferred, to go to a boarding school in England.[51] For widespread itineration Groves reckoned three languages were essential: Arabic, Turkish and Persian. "This, I feel, unless the Lord very especially helps me, will be *to me* no ordinary labour." Indeed, to a mature man of thirty-six, without any conspicuous linguistic ability, it would be a daunting task, yet one he could willingly attempt for the sake of his Master. Many men of the world had been able to learn these languages for purposes of commerce, so "I trust the Lord will not allow me to faint or be discouraged till, for his own service, I have attained them."[52]

But outside their own four walls, as though to mock all plans for Christian outreach, the situation remained as grim as ever. "This wretched city has suffered to an almost unparalleled extent the judgments of God within the last six months. The plague swept away more than two-thirds of its inhabitants, the flood has thrown down nearly two-thirds of its houses… and we are now suffering under daily increasing famine, and we have yet hanging over our heads the revengeful sword of resisted authority and the unprincipled plunder of a lawless soldiery to complete the devastation."[53] The region lay in Ottoman territory, but now the hostile forces of the Persian Empire were massing on the border barely four hundred miles to the east; invasion seemed imminent. Meanwhile, in the city itself, a band of mercenary soldiers, "who employ their time in making and drinking arrack," were happily "knocking down the walls of the palace wherever they yield a hollow sound, in search of the hidden treasures of the Pasha."[54] Elsewhere men were pulling down the roofs of the bazaars to sell the wood for fuel, destroying all the shops and filling the remaining alleys with rubble. "It seems as if the angel of destruction was resting on this city as on Babylon, to sweep it from the earth... every element at work seems wickedness."[55] Armed bands, continuously drunk, were shooting without provocation at anyone passing in the street. Daoud Pasha sent for Groves to attend him at the palace; a carbuncle had lost him one joint on his toe and looked likely to destroy another. Groves noted that, in payment for his services, the Pasha "made me a present of three small cucumbers... And this may convey some idea to what extent the privations of the poor have gone, when the Pasha can hardly command a cucumber."[56] Then, "as I returned from the Pasha a man levelled a gun at me" – probably a demonstration of bravado rather than a serious attempt at murder, but unsettling none the less. Groves was comforted by a renewed conviction that God was in control: "without his permission not one hair of our heads shall fall."[57]

ENDNOTES

[1] M445
[2] R153-154
[3] Eadie, 204
[4] Eadie, 206
[5] R155
[6] R156
[7] R303
[8] R157
[9] M157
[10] Eadie, 202
[11] Eadie, 208
[12] Eadie, 211-212
[13] R160-161
[14] R163
[15] R170
[16] R165-166
[17] R179-180
[18] R178-179
[19] He had received a letter from the American Presbyterian William Goodell of the ABCFM (R179).
[20] R179
[21] R181-182
[22] R203. Dervish: a Muslim ascetic, often a member of a fraternity known for particular rites and trance-like states.
[23] R202
[24] R183

[25] R211
[26] R210
[27] R200; M178
[28] R201
[29] R230
[30] R223
[31] R214
[32] R215
[33] R216
[34] Groves H, *Congleton*, 27
[35] *Phases*, 28-29
[36] *Phases*, 29
[37] Jn 17:3
[38] Newman, *Personal Narrative*, 12 (Sieveking, 35)
[39] *Congleton*, 29 (referring to Ps 31:14-15)
[40] R224
[41] R242
[42] R222
[43] R226
[44] Obedience to one precept, Groves observed, made obedience to others all the easier: "How beautifully all our blessed Lord's precepts hang together, and fit the one the other. If you consent to follow him in his poverty as he has commanded, you have little to fear in following his other commands of non-resistance" (R226).
[45] M205
[46] R228-229
[47] R234
[48] R236
[49] R238. Details of the birth and death of the "little brother" are not recorded in Groves's *Memoir* or journals.
[50] R239-240
[51] R240
[52] R241
[53] R236
[54] R244
[55] R244-245
[56] R243-244
[57] R243

"Amidst these tempests
I sometimes think 'tis hard to live.
Yet, my dear friend,
it is sweet to live hardly for Jesus."

Norris Groves [1]

15

News from Aleppo

September came without any resolution to Baghdad's many woes, and for the first time Norris Groves's determination to remain at his post seems to have wavered. "Weak in body and mind," he confessed, "I could sometimes almost impatiently wish for a change… For myself, I know not if my mind preys on my body, or my body on my mind… yet I feel on the whole thus much, that if it appeared the Lord's most gracious pleasure to direct my steps away from this place for a season, I should be thankful. Nevertheless, I desire to say from my heart, not my will, O Lord, but thine be done. In Arabic I think I make daily progress, and I feel fully assured, should the Lord spare my life for this blessed work, that I shall one day be able to preach the unsearchable riches of Christ intelligibly, perhaps even fluently."[2]

Opportunities for private conversation with individuals and small groups could occupy him from dawn till dusk, and there was an urgent need for someone to translate simple gospel literature into the local dialects. "As to tracts," he said, "at present we have none. The Turkish Armenian tracts printed at Malta are not clearly understood here."[3] No more comprehensible were the existing Arabic materials from Syria or the Turkish literature produced in Constantinople. Thoughts of leaving might have a great attraction, but there was plenty to be done by one who would stay.

Wheat and rice stored up before the plague had kept them adequately, though frugally, fed for a year. The *pastourma* sausages, though "somewhat dry and hard as wood," had provided welcome variety, along with two or three eggs a day from the hens, a little meat from the pigeons, and milk for the baby from the two goats. One of the goats had already been slaughtered and its meat shared with the poor. The other was now taken and "potted in its fat" to provide a continuing supply for the weeks ahead. The wheat and rice, soap and candles were only just running out. The Taylors, before they left, had instructed Groves to help himself from stocks at the Residency, and he was grateful now to take advantage of their kindness. Fetching what he needed day by day ensured a regular supply without offering thieves the temptation of large stores in their own home. "Thus the Lord has provided for us till now, and if we have not had abundance, we have never suffered from want."[4] Of the whole population of Baghdad, in fact, none had been better supplied than the Groves household. On 15th September he wrote, "Today we killed two fowls to have a little fresh meat. Thus the Lord has kept us through all this time of trial, and we have enough remaining for five or six days, blessed be his holy name."[5]

That same day Daoud Pasha broke out of the city and escaped, leaving Ali Pasha to take possession. The besieging army entered without resistance, the thieves fled, and wheat and vegetables were fetched in from the countryside. A packet of letters was brought from the palace, including one from Major Taylor offering to make arrangements for Henry and Frank to return to England if they wished.[6] At the end of September, news came that a consignment of scriptures from the Bible Society had reached Basra; another consignment was on its way from Constantinople. With the prospect of restarting scripture distribution, and despite the fact that a hostile Persian army had reached Suleimaniya barely 160 miles away, Groves felt encouraged once again to remain where he was.

Then typhus fever took him. For a month he was prostrate. "I had lost all appetite, strength and ability to sleep, accompanied by that strange overwhelming depression of mind that inclines one to weep, one knows not why."[7] And these were merely the early stages of a disease that typically produced body pains, rash and high fever, with a weakened heartbeat, total exhaustion and often delirium. Once again John Kitto and Harnie were responsible for the household. For five months Kitto had not ventured outside. When at last he did, on 1st October, in order to get "a book or two from Major Taylor's library", he found the streets unrecognisable, familiar faces gone, the lavish interiors of fallen houses displayed amidst the rubble for all to see.[8]

A man came with news of Karl Pfander. Shortly after leaving Baghdad, the German evangelist had been forced to flee for his life after a frank discussion with some Muslims in the caravan. Eventually reaching Isfahan, Pfander trekked north through the mountains to Tabriz, arriving there just between two outbreaks of plague. Knowing the character of the man and of the country, it is likely that every waking moment was spent in religious debate and distribution of controversial literature. He was treated with great respect in some places, great hatred in others. From Kermanshah (Bakhtaran) his own letters report that the *'ulama*, the local Islamic teachers, "did all they could to incite the people against me and my books. They preached against me this morning in their chief mosque and told the people that it is their obligation and duty to destroy my books… that every house in which such a book is kept will have no luck in the future, that the leather binding is made of pigskin and so on, and that I deserve to be put to death."[9]

As Norris Groves slowly convalesced, some of the older boys returned, asking if the school was likely to reopen. "I certainly never felt teaching in a school to be my proper work, and now much less than ever," he admitted, "yet they need instruction and desire it…May the Lord give me a wise and

understanding heart, that I may rightly see the service he requires of me."
If the school were to restart, thought Groves, "I should not be surprised if
many Roman Catholics came, for they all acknowledge that our boys learned
more in three months than theirs in two years."[10] Again he was longing to
discuss the possibilities with his friends in Aleppo. There was still no sign
of them. In fact their letters reported that Mrs Cronin was "daily getting
weaker and weaker".[11] Nancy Parnell was pregnant, shortly to be confined,
and reinforcements expected from Britain would need to be met in Aleppo
itself. So there seemed no chance of them travelling just yet. Despite his
disappointment, Groves knew there was, in any case, no secure way through
the desolate countryside, foul with the stench of rotting matter and despoiled
by armed partisans and bandits. One encouragement was the group's agreement
on the subject of baptism; those already christened in infancy had now been
baptised as adult believers. "Thus the last little difference that I know between
us is closed. How gracious the Lord is!"[12]

Frank Newman's first and notably unsuccessful attempts to explain the
gospel to a Muslim carpenter in Aleppo, and to an Englishman "of rather low
tastes", had dampened his enthusiasm for the missionary task, though not his
interest in things Oriental.[13] Previously averse to smoking, he now resolved
to identify with the people, and bought himself an enormously long Turkish
pipe with an amber mouthpiece. In fact he bought two, one for himself and the
other for any guest who might chance to call. He wrote again to Maria Giberne,
begging her to come out, marry him in Aleppo, and join the missionary team;
a second time she refused. He took to wearing a Syrian gown and heelless
slippers, but finding he had to waddle in order to keep the slippers on his feet,
began to wonder a little anxiously if dressing and acting like a Turk might in
the course of time change his habits, his physique and even his personality.
That autumn Newman went down with a "fever". Cronin leeched his temples
and bled his right arm, then tried calomel, all without effect.[14] As his weakness
increased and his pulse grew more rapid, they became seriously alarmed. Days
passed and his condition worsened; there seemed nothing more they could do
for him, and eventually they gave up all hope of his recovery. John Parnell
suggested anointing him with oil, according to James 5:14, and praying over
him. This they did, then for seventeen days Newman hovered between life
and death. Eventually he began to rally, and slowly regained strength. Parnell
went to the market and bought him a horse, "for he who grudged anything to
himself never grudged it to another."[15] Fresh air and exercise, Parnell hoped,
would aid his friend's convalescence.

Aleppo was then shaken by a small earthquake, perhaps a warning that a
major quake was imminent. Locusts devoured the surrounding countryside,
and the populace was agitated by fears of a fresh outbreak of plague. Hearing
a British doctor was stationed there, the Pasha of Baghdad sent to Edward

Cronin offering a substantial sum if he would come immediately and enter his service in Baghdad. But the Pasha could not accept responsibility for the safety of the ladies and would not allow them to accompany him. Cronin politely refused. Hamilton, who had been ill for much of the time, and felt himself incapable of learning a foreign language, decided it was time to go home. John and Nancy Parnell, though both far from well, determined to see him comfortably on board ship for France. They set off with him back to the coast. The travelling was rough, and Nancy, heavily pregnant, fell from her donkey. There was no doctor; she was badly hurt, and though she struggled on to Latakia, she died there a few days later.[16]

Meanwhile in Baghdad Groves received visits from some of the principal Roman Catholic merchants. Repaying the courtesy a few days later, he found they welcomed him "with the greatest kindness", and he took the opportunity to show them what the scriptures say about a truly Christian lifestyle. "It seems perfectly new to them to have the sentiments or conduct of themselves or others measured by this holy and blessed book. Such a use they never in their lives saw made of it, so that it strikes them exceedingly... I feel that the door for my particular line of usefulness is opening, and as I advance in the practical use of the language, I have confidence the Lord will yet show me greater things than these."[17] The recent death of the bishop meant that there was now no official opposition; thirty of the Roman Catholic boys were ready to start school as soon as he could find a teacher for them. The visit of some Jews (among them a rabbi who, "disbelieving Judaism", was reading the New Testament) prompted another prayer for increased ability with language: "If there is any gift my soul longs for, it is to be able to speak to every one in his own tongue, wherein he was born, the wonderful works of God... as for instance with these Jews, they know little Arabic and I do not know German and thus we stand incapable of any such conversation as is likely to search the heart."[18]

By late October (1831), eight months had passed since Norris Groves received a letter or any financial support from England. With all the difficulties he had faced – no news and no converts – he wondered if his supporters had lost confidence in him. "I often think my dear friends in England will be sadly discouraged at the Lord's dealings with our mission... However, should their faith and hope fail, the Lord will either raise up others or find me some little occupation by which I may live." In fact Groves had a remarkable testimony to God's provision: "He has supplied me, I know not how, in the midst of famine, pestilence and war. And though I have heard from none in England for more than a year, especially from those that supply my wants, the Lord has not suffered me to want, or to be in debt. And though the necessities of life have amounted to almost twenty times their value during our late trials, he has not suffered me personally to be much affected by it. His loving-kindness and care have been wonderful."[19]

Then at last the letters came, forwarded from Bombay and, among them, gifts for the support of the school. This meant he could now look for an Armenian teacher in addition to recommencing his own English classes: "Altogether it seems to me the Lord's will I should try again, and in due time when I am fit for other service he may raise up help that will take this out of my hands. I desire to be ready to do any work, however humble and contrary to my nature, that I think the Lord appoints for me."[20] As the populace trickled back to Baghdad, the number of visitors increased and quantities of scriptures were once more going out. By Christmas he had sold all his Hebrew Bibles and sent two parcels of Persian New Testaments for use in the mountains.

Despite these renewed opportunities, his friends in Aleppo still showed no inclination to join him. So if they would not come, perhaps he should go, taking the boys with him, to see them there – at least for a few days' consultation and prayer. He began to make preparation for travel. But when he added up the probable expenses of the journey, the total came to more than he possessed. He was about to give up the idea when a letter arrived from England containing a gift sufficient to cover the cost. He wrote immediately to the donor, "Since I left England, this is the first purpose I really thought desirable that the want of sufficient money has put a stop to – and this you see but for a moment. Not but that I can get money at any time, but I am determined not to borrow money till my affairs come to the utmost straits, and then only for the simplest necessities."[21]

Then once again his hopes were dashed. At the last minute he "heard a very bad account" of the Arab sheikh leading the caravan he had planned to join. The trip to Aleppo was abandoned and he thanked God he had discovered the man's true character before it was too late, "before I was alone involved with him in the desert, where indeed you are fearfully at their mercy." Perhaps there would be another caravan heading in that direction soon.

But the Baghdad journal closes here with the melancholy words, "Jan.16th 1832 – My dear little boy, Frank, is just laid down in a fever, so I cannot now go to Aleppo. Thus the Lord frustrates all our plans and purposes."[22] It looked like typhoid, and for some days Frank's life was in the balance. His brother Henry later wrote about their father's anxieties at this time: "They were days of darkness, and wave on wave seemed to roll over him. His spirit, naturally buoyant, seemed to be crushed to the earth, and often have I wept alone to see the sadness of his aching heart."[23] In fact, if Groves had gone to Aleppo at this point of time, he would have arrived to find his friends gone. Looking back on this later, it was possible to see the hand of Providence working through the unhappy turn of events. Looking further back, if Parnell, Cronin and their party had continued directly to Baghdad on arriving in Aleppo, they would have arrived there exactly the same time as the plague. Again, the delay would seem providential.

Early in 1832 the first foreigner to reach Baghdad, after its long months of suffering, arrived outside the city. Dr John McNeill describes the scene before him. "When we entered Baghdad we passed from the gate to the British Residency, a distance of perhaps half a mile, over heaps of ruins in which the lines of the narrow streets could no longer be traced. Out of a dilapidated building near the Residency emerged Mr Groves, one of his boys and Kitto coming to see us... They were all emaciated, wan and depressed with suffering, with insufficient nourishment and long confinement, but indeed, although the worst was already passed, it was wonderful to find them so cheerful after all they had endured."[24] McNeill thought Frank should have a change of air, and not just Frank – they would all benefit from a change. A trip down the Tigris was arranged, and Henry later recalled, "I almost think I feel now the relief it was, for a little, to turn our back upon a city that seemed to have been under the special curse of God. The heavens seemed brighter, all around more peaceful, and the heart seemed free, in the absence of those things which recalled to the mind so much of sorrows and sufferings."[25]

Once away from the city, Norris Groves found himself reluctant to return, especially as fresh outbreaks of plague were reported from Baghdad. He was strongly tempted to continue down the Tigris with the boys and head for home.[26] Kitto was delighted to spend some time with McNeill and to develop the idea they had already discussed at Tabriz, of illuminating the obscure cultural allusions in the Bible by reference to Oriental customs still to be observed in the nineteenth century.[27] Henry and Frank acted as interpreters, spelling out on their fingers what McNeill and Kitto wished to say to each other.

Then, a few days after returning to Baghdad, they had a great surprise. At last, as Henry recalled, "the unspeakable pleasure of welcoming those whose coming had been looked forward to for so many months with such longing anxiety."[28] In April (1832) the depleted party had finally set out from Aleppo, riding camels at dead of night on the first stage of their five-hundred-mile journey across the desert. It had been an eventful trip.

At a place called Aintab (Gaziantep), they had given a Turkish New Testament to a man who asked for one, then gave away a few more. Rumours ran through the town. A moolah complained to the governor, who summoned Parnell and Cronin and ordered them to leave the next morning. The following day a crowd had gathered and followed them out of town, increasing in number and excitement along the way. Insults gave place to small stones, then larger ones, and in the uproar a large portion of their luggage was lost or stolen. Cronin was knocked down by the mob, and indeed, left for dead. His friends turned back and found him lying, bloody and barely conscious, at the roadside. "One of my companions was caught by the mob," wrote Newman, "and beaten (as they probably thought) to death. But he recovered very similarly to Paul, in Acts 14:20, after long lying senseless."[29] That evening Cronin was sufficiently recovered to continue the journey. Travelling east through a wilderness of crumbling chalk they crossed the Euphrates and paused at Urfah (ancient Ur). From here, like Abraham, they set out in faith – having extricated themselves from the clutches of an unscrupulous governor, who attempted to intimidate and extort money from them. Parnell was suffering from "the fever", and at one point, faced by a large body of "wandering Arabs bent on plunder", they could do nothing but dismount and kneel in prayer. To their relief the band rode off without harming them. One night, three of their four horses were stolen by robbers, which forced all but Mrs Cronin to continue the journey on foot. Thankful eventually to reach Mosul without any more serious injury, they stayed only long enough for the construction of rafts supported by inflated goatskins. On these they piled what remained of their luggage and floated two hundred and fifty miles down the Tigris – deep, rapid, smooth, white with clay held in suspension, and painfully cold – as far as Baghdad.[30]

For Norris Groves, the presence of his friends was medicine to a wounded soul. Hours passed in conversation and prayer, and in long discussions as they read the scriptures together. His spirits began to revive. Henry was old enough to appreciate what it all meant: "I look back upon that period of quiet and of peace after the trials of the plague, the inundation, the famine and the sword as perhaps the most memorable of my life." It was a time when godly men, drawn together by sympathy and love, and by sorrows shared, experienced much "close, holy and earnest walking before God and of direct dealing with God."[31] Earnestly they sought to understand and obey the words of Christ and his apostles, and there was much "recommending of truth to the conscience". Groves drew comfort from the confidence they had in the love of God and before long he felt able to write, "My faith sometimes feels a little strong, from the strength of their faith."[32]

They possessed all things in common, meeting for prayer every morning, and on Fridays for extended prayer with fasting. As Henry recalled, these prayer times were "rendered fragrant with the presence of Jesus… It was felt that every word was heard, and that every word brought its answer."[33] The power of the Holy Spirit was a living reality, and their Bible study was intensely practical. "In nothing was this period more marked than for the earnest study of the Word. It was regarded truly as 'the light unto the feet and the lamp unto the path' of the child of God; obedience to it in everything being the one thing needful to those who would love the Lord."[34] And as for the many difficulties they faced, these just inspired in them a bolder and more audacious faith. "The very impenetrability of the cloud that appeared to hang over those benighted and desolated countries seemed to strengthen that faith that could say 'nothing is impossible to him that believeth.'"[35]

Unlike Parnell and Cronin, Frank Newman had never previously met Norris Groves. Shortly after their arrival he wrote down his first impressions: "Groves has not at all disappointed me... He is what I expected from his book, and a great deal more. He has a practical, organising, directing energy which fits him to be the centre of many persons, especially since it is combined with entire unselfishness and a total absence of personal ambition."[36] Newman was interested that "several (chiefly Persians) have come privately and begged New Testaments to send to their friends in Persia." Yet he wondered how far Groves could communicate anything significant to these enquirers. It would take many years of concentrated effort before a missionary would be able to speak the language fluently, and even then it seemed highly improbable that any Muslim could be persuaded to abandon the beliefs and customs of his people. Was not the attempt bound, sooner or later, to lead to conflict or even violence? "I am apt to be sadly faithless," Newman admitted, "and to see nothing but difficulties." But whatever others might think of Newman's tendency to ask awkward questions, Groves spoke warmly of his young recruit: "I love him as my soul, for the faithfulness and truth which the God of grace has given him."[37]

Living with them now was an Armenian boy, Serkies Davids, who had been one of the students in the school. He was the nephew of their old schoolmaster. Attempting to escape from Baghdad at the time of the plague, they had been trapped by the floodwaters. Surrounded for several weeks by harrowing scenes of misery and starvation, Serkies had watched his uncle die before returning to the city. Knowing his family were all dead, Groves had offered him a home, and Serkies soon became a firm friend of Henry's. Profoundly affected by his recent experiences and by the love he found in the Groves household, he was pleased when Henry suggested reading the Bible and praying together. Before long, to the great joy of everyone, they were both moved to declare a personal faith in Christ.[38]

As soon as he could, John Parnell purchased a larger house in the heart of the city, one of the few that had not been washed away by the floods, and they started to repair and clean it up. After much prayer, the team decided to set up a dispensary for medicine, and an eye clinic, as well as a small hospital where the doctor Edward Cronin could treat some of the more serious cases.[39] Serkies and Henry made themselves useful, bandaging sores and ulcers, and giving food to the poor who called every afternoon. Hundreds came for medical attention, and many heard the gospel. "There was much that was pleasant in the grateful feelings of some," wrote Henry, but one at least "seemed to feel that he had conferred an honour in allowing himself to be nursed by Christian infidels." This particular man had been found frost-bitten, lying at a street corner in "a loathsome condition", unable to move hand or foot. He was nursed night and day for many weeks, and when finally healed, walked out of the door cursing both the Christians and their religion.[40]

Newman was perplexed by the difficulty of conveying an inward faith to a people accustomed to an outward display of piety. Muslims who observed the missionary team would think them good people, but obviously irreligious – for they did not pray at street corners, nor did they include the name of God in every sentence they spoke. How then, wondered Newman, could a Christian *demonstrate*, in a simple visible way, the reality of his faith so that the Muslims around him would be led to enquire about his beliefs? This question continued to puzzle him.

Early contacts with members of the Eastern churches seemed more encouraging, and Newman was impressed with the opportunities Groves had found among the Armenians and Roman Catholics. "At present I conceive he has nearly the whole Christian population here in his hands." Largely ignorant of the faith they claimed to believe, some were responding with interest to simple teaching from the Bible and seemed quite willing to read it for themselves. The team agreed that their time and effort might be most usefully spent with these nominal Christians, and they commenced a regular plan of daily door-to-door visitation in the Armenian and Roman Catholic quarters. During the hours when Cronin and Groves were occupied in the clinic, John Parnell studied Turkish and Persian, and searched the scriptures for words of encouragement that might help the others. Frank Newman was teaching English and geography to the older boys in the school and in his spare time compiling an Arabic dictionary.

Cronin's mother had been unwell throughout the long journey from England, and her condition had not improved in Aleppo. In fact she was "worn out by fatigue and anxiety".[41] The rigours of the Syrian desert finally proved too much for her, and shortly after reaching Baghdad she died. Cronin had now lost wife, sister and mother in the space of three years. With the exception of little Minny and the servant Harnie, it was an all-male household, and this made it difficult for them to do much for the many women with medical or spiritual needs, or for the families of the men who came to see them. Major Taylor's Armenian wife had a sister whose husband had died in Baghdad during the plague. Introduced to the missionary team, she professed personal faith in Christ. The arrival of an unmarried Christian lady in their midst was a momentous event for the three widowers (Groves, Cronin and Parnell) and the two bachelors (Kitto and Newman). The story has been told that they drew lots for her. The reality is that they prayed concerning her, and John Parnell felt led to propose. Some would look askance at a British aristocrat tying himself to a Middle Eastern widow, a few years older than himself, the mother of two children. We cannot know the inner reasons for his decision: genuine affection? loneliness? or simply a desire to forward the work of the gospel among the women of Baghdad? Henry Groves, in his biography of Parnell, hints at the latter, but we are safest simply to regard it as an answer to prayer.[42]

By midsummer, Kitto's thoughts were turning to England. Newman and Parnell had taken over the task of educating Henry and Frank, so their former tutor now found himself at a loose end. With his deafness, there was little he could usefully do. "I confess I see not," he said, "how any one free from the obligations of detaining duties could prefer to live in this miserable land."[43] Frank Newman probably shared this point of view. He had not, he said, enjoyed a day of real health since arriving in the East. Newman's heart was in England in any case. Before leaving, and again from Aleppo, he had proposed to Maria Giberne. He must see her again for one last attempt. In September (1832), Kitto and Newman left for England; they were charged with recruiting new workers for the Baghdad mission. Kitto packed up his precious library and sent it on board ship for London via India. We do not know what happened to it: he never saw it again.[44]

But the trials of the Baghdad mission were not yet over. In January (1833), Henry contracted rheumatic fever. With his lungs severely affected, he seemed to be sinking fast. Little could be done with the medicines then available, and such cases had small chance of survival. Norris promised his son that, whatever the cost, he would carry him to the Mediterranean and, if necessary, to England. Poor Henry longed to see England again "and if to die, to die there". But in his weakness Henry wondered, was this sickness not just Satan's device to break up the mission and bring all its plans to nothing?

It was a question they had discussed at length: how far the devil could interfere with the sovereign work of God, and how actively he should be resisted. Before the arrival of his friends, Groves had accepted everything from his Father's hand, without giving thought to the powers of darkness, but the vigorous minds of his companions seemed to shed fresh light on the question. He wrote now to William Caldecott, sharing their more recent thoughts: "Christians generally have little other notion of Satan than of evil personified, instead of his being an intelligent and active foe, ever on the watch to wound and enfeeble the church. I believe the real power of the Enemy will be increased in proportion to the careless security of his opponent. We have felt again and again his effort to drive us away from our work."[45] They all prayed, and prayed again, but Henry had no assurance that he and his father should leave. On the contrary, he became more certain that the Enemy was intent on using his illness to disrupt the work of God. He determined to remain, for life or for death, so the work could go on. A day was set apart for prayer that Henry would be healed. As night fell there was no sign of improvement. He later recalled the scene. "It was late in the evening of a suffering day that all assembled round my bed. We felt [we were] in the presence of the Lord and confident that he would send an answer of peace. There are times when prayer is seen to ascend with much incense before the throne – not doubtful uncertain breathings but living prayers, living words to a living Lord – and such did those prayers offered up in my sick chamber on that evening appear to be. The Lord heard; I slept as I had not done for weeks, and from that day I rapidly recovered."[46]

The company were also praying for Harnie. She cooked their meals, cared lovingly for Minny, nursed anyone who was sick and anticipated all the needs of the household. She recited her Chaldean creed twice a day. Slow she might be at learning to read, but with her wonderful qualities of shrewdness, determination, courage and loyalty, along with her knowledge of the local conditions, culture and language, she contributed what no one else could to the comfort of the household. Still they were not sure if she had really understood the difference between religious duties and personal faith in Christ.

Groves wrote to George Müller and Henry Craik in Bristol, asking them again to consider joining the Baghdad mission: he even sent the cost of their passage out. Müller recorded his willingness to go, and made a methodical list of pros and cons, but confessed to no assurance that it was the right thing. He and Craik had just launched the Bethesda assembly in Bristol and were fully occupied there.[47]

It was the end of April when two men arrived from Damascus. One was a Jewish Christian, Erasmus Calman, the other a Colonel of the British army by the name of Arthur Cotton. Calman was a godly man and an evangelist, and to their great pleasure he decided there and then to join the Baghdad team; he would befriend the Jews and explain the gospel to any who showed interest.[48] Cotton, too, was a thoroughly committed Christian, a military engineer whose job required him to travel widely and who took great interest in the work of the gospel wherever he happened to be. Some time previously the booklet *Christian Devotedness* had come into his hands and, ever since, he had wished to meet its author. Hearing from Groves how the work in Baghdad was hindered by the hardened resistance of the Muslim majority, he wondered whether India might not offer better prospects. A revised charter, he said, had been granted to the East India Company in 1813, which allowed unrestricted missionary work in the areas under its control. Here was a matter for much thought and prayer, and three weeks later, on 21st May (1833), the day of Parnell's marriage, Groves set off with Cotton to see for himself.

Norris Groves was clearly in need of a complete break. There is no doubt that India had long held a special interest for him: his earliest missionary thoughts had been directed to India rather than to Persia. Yet this was no selfish flight from the path of duty. He had every intention of returning to help develop the opportunities for evangelistic work in the Tigris-Euphrates valley and the surrounding highlands. It was at least partly for the sake of Baghdad that he was going in any case. Having suffered an appalling sense of isolation throughout his time there, he was determined that future workers would have friends somewhat nearer than England, friends able to offer fellowship and support in time of need. He was perfectly happy to leave the boys in the care of Cronin and the Parnells. Harnie too was completely dependable. "You must not be anxious about your sons," she told him, "Henry is my right eye, and Frank is my left; and as a man cares for his eyes, so I care for them."[49]

ENDNOTES

[1] R300; M208

[2] R245-246

[3] R253

[4] R251

[5] R258

[6] The death of their mother meant that Henry and Frank stood to receive an inheritance from her family (Ryland, 460).

[7] R274

[8] Eadie, 220

[9] Pfander's journal (1832), quoted by Powell, 153

[10] R276-277

[11] R302; M210

[12] R301. In fact Newman's baptism as an adult was delayed until 1836, probably because of his illness at this time (Sieveking, 61; Rowdon, *Origins*, 195).

[13] *Phases*, 33

[14] R302. Calomel: a colourless tasteless powder consisting chiefly of mercurous chloride (Hg_2Cl_2), used especially as a purgative.

[15] The words of Henry Groves (*Congleton*, 33).

[16] John Parnell's feelings at this time can be easily imagined. Hamilton returned to Ireland, where he became an agent or estate manager for the Parnell property and continued as an active and committed Christian for the rest of his life (Groves H, *Congleton*, 123-124).

[17] R287-288

[18] R281-282; M203

[19] M207 (R298-9). Letters had last reached him in February (1831). As they were written the previous September (1830), Groves had no news of his friends for more than a year, and no indication of any continued financial support.

[20] R277

[21] R305. This attitude contrasts strikingly with that of William Carey, who habitually asked for money and borrowed money whenever he was in need (George, 74, 98, 116 etc).

[22] R306

[23] M215

[24] M215

[25] M215

[26] M223. Dr John McNeill, with his heavily pregnant wife and two armed guards, was on his way to take up the position of Resident in Bushire. Accompanying him

downriver in several sailing boats, they met Major Taylor on his way up, who informed McNeill that his appointment was cancelled on account of plague at Bushire. They all returned to Baghdad. In fact, if they had continued to Bushire as intended, they would have missed the arrival of their missionary colleagues in Baghdad (Ryland, 461-3; Wright, 21).

[27] Eadie, 223

[28] M216

[29] Newman, *Phases*, 134n

[30] Groves H, *Congleton*, 37-38

[31] M216

[32] M223

[33] M218

[34] M218

[35] M216

[36] Newman, *Personal Narrative*, 103

[37] Letter to Kitto dated 23 Sep. 1832 (Eadie, 239-240).

[38] M214

[39] Having studied at the Meath Hospital in Dublin, Edward Cronin was an early pioneer of homeopathic remedies.

[40] M217

[41] *Congleton*, 41

[42] *Congleton*, 43; Smith G, *Duff*, I, 266. The sisters, Rosa and Khatuin, had an adventurous past. When young they had narrowly escaped incarceration in the harem of the Prince of Shiraz. Hidden in a basket they were smuggled away to Bushehr, where in due course they were "respectably educated". Some years later Mrs Taylor and a female servant had been captured on their way to join her husband in India. "Both were made slaves by the Arab pirates of the desert around Muscat," until, "in the darkness of the night," they "made their escape in a boat of the Arabs and drifted out to sea, where they were found very soon by an English ship and were taken in safety to Bombay" (Wolff, I, 336).

[43] Eadie, 233

[44] Newman's story continues in Chapter 23, and Kitto's in Chapter 24 of this book.

[45] M223

[46] M219

[47] Müller, *Narrative*, I, 99-100

[48] Like Groves and his friends, Erasmus Scott Calman had chosen to "live by faith" without salary or promised support. Having arrived in England as a refugee from the persecution of Jews in Russian Latvia, he met A J (Sandy) Scott, and was baptised as a Christian in January 1831. Ten months later he moved to Woolwich, near London, where he became one of Scott's students, living with his family and attending his church. His close connection with Scott at this time means that Calman must have read Groves's first *Journal* (edited by Scott) and *Christian Devotedness*. Parnell tells us that when Calman subsequently left Baghdad, "he went to Jerusalem, refusing to take any money with him beyond what was necessary for the journey, saying that when he arrived at Jerusalem the Lord would provide" (M531-532; Newell,

179-180). Two who met him there observed, "Mr Calman's sweetness of temper and kindly manner gained upon the Jews exceedingly" (Bonar & McCheyne, 226). Seven years later Calman published a remarkable book based on his varied experiences, *Some of the Errors of Modern Judaism Contrasted with the Word of God* (B Wertheim, London, 1840).
[49] M532

Journey of A. N. Groves in India, 1833–34

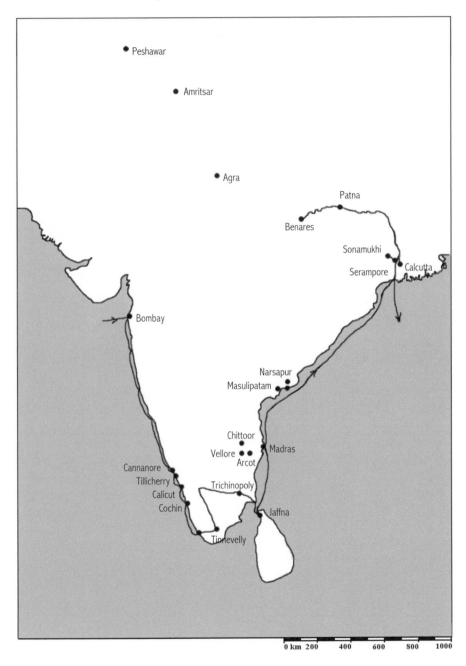

"Labour hard, consume little, give much,
and all to Christ."

Norris Groves [1]

16

A Fresh Vision

To the British of the mid-nineteenth century, all roads led to India. In his second volume of *The History of the Church Missionary Society*, covering the period 1849-1872, Eugene Stock devotes a full 232 pages to the work of the gospel in India and Ceylon, and the remaining 217 pages to all the other countries of the world. Just as Jesus was advised by his brothers to show himself in Jerusalem, so almost any Englishman who aspired to fame, power or wealth would be counselled to spend a term or two in India. Norris Groves was not concerned with fame, power or wealth, but he was profoundly interested in what could be accomplished for the gospel in this vast area under British control. First of all he must discover what was already being done, and then see what other opportunities there might be.

So it was that in May 1833 Groves left Baghdad, boarding a boat down the Tigris with Colonel Cotton. Accompanying them was a young Lebanese friend of Cotton's called Mokayel Trad, an Arabic-speaking member of the Greek Orthodox church who was learning English and growing in his understanding of the gospel. During his few days in Baghdad, Cotton himself had picked up a fever, and as they travelled his condition worsened. Boarding a British man-of-war at Basra, they sailed down the Persian Gulf as far as Bushehr. The heat here was oppressive and Cotton became so seriously ill with an "internal complaint" that his coffin was constructed and all arrangements made for his funeral. Groves, despite the offer of an onward passage to Bombay, refused to leave his new friend, and for two months he and Mokayel nursed the invalid, fanning and sprinkling him with water night and day. Cotton later observed, "There can be no doubt that, under God, I owed my life to the incessant loving care and attention of my two companions."[2] It was July before they finally reached Bombay and, coming ashore, went their separate ways.

Norris Groves, always happy to disciple a young Christian, and keen to make progress with the Arabic language, took Mokayel with him. During the next fourteen months he would travel in India almost three thousand miles – from Bombay (Mumbai) down the west coast almost to the southern tip of the subcontinent, then inland to Tinnevelly (Tirunelveli), then further inland to Trichinopoly (Tiruchchirappalli) and across to the south-east coast; then a brief visit to Ceylon (Sri Lanka), up the east coast to Madras (Chennai) and on towards the Ganges Delta, then inland to Benares (Varanasi) and neighbouring towns before finally reaching the great eastern capital of Calcutta.[3]

On landing in Bombay, however, the first thing to do was introduce himself to the British community. They were mostly civil servants and business and military men with their families, all belonging to the Church of England. They proved most hospitable, and for three months Groves stayed in their homes and enjoyed "sweet communion" with them. This did not mean, however, that he was permitted to preach in their church or address their meetings. There was much he would like to say about Christian unity, about the fatherly care of God, about the second coming of Christ and about forsaking all and following him, but for the time being he could only share it informally: "In Bombay I generally met with kindness, but there was evidently a fear that prevented their wishing me to minister." He was asked to speak instead about the work in Baghdad and about the colleagues he had left there. "I had no heart for either," he confessed. "All I could say of ourselves was that we *desired* to follow Christ; and of our work that it was waiting the Lord's pleasure."[4]

Some encouraging mail arrived from Baghdad: "They give most hopeful accounts of dear Harnie for whom we have all prayed so much."[5] Her religious feelings seemed to have blossomed into a personal faith in Christ. Henry, Frank and Serkies were actively serving the Lord, and all were well. Thinking of his friends, it was John Parnell who gave greatest encouragement, with his selfless devotion and his willingness to live humbly and sacrificially for the sake of Christ: "He has done things simply and solely because he thought it the Lord's pleasure."[6] If anything, Parnell seemed to be taking Christian devotedness even further than Groves himself.

The expatriate community in Bombay spoke of problems at a mission in the far south. A disagreement had arisen between the local committee of the Church Missionary Society and one of their own German missionaries, Karl Rhenius, which threatened to bring to a halt a remarkable work of God in the area of Tinnevelly. At the "earnest solicitations" of his new friends, and after much prayer, Groves decided he should go and see if he, as an impartial outsider, could do anything to help.[7]

Finding places in a traditional *Pattamar* boat, Groves and Mokayel sailed by night down the west coast of India: it was cooler after dark and left the daylight hours free for more useful activity. There were no encumbrances and Groves was happy: "The little carpet I sit on by day serves as my bed by night, and a cloak covers me. I cannot tell you how comfortable it is to be independent of everything but the sunshine of the Lord's countenance."[8] The countryside was refreshingly green – palm trees, temples, ornamental pools of water, thatched villages, and cows and oxen everywhere – though, of course, the language was completely incomprehensible.

Norris Groves was always a keen reader, especially of Christian biography, and particularly when travelling by sea: it helped to put things in perspective. "I have been much delighted with some passages in Tyndale's Life," he remarked. "They seem to have lived in great power of the Holy Ghost in such things as they saw in that day. It made me ashamed of the little troubles which affect me."[9] Further letters from Baghdad showed that the team were all learning Persian, and making good progress with the help, no doubt, of the new Mrs Parnell. "This, I think, more absolutely determines me to go on with Arabic," reflected Groves. Indeed, both languages would be useful for work in the Middle East, and even now, with Mokayel as a companion, "I talk nothing but Arabic from morning to night."[10] Perhaps, on the next stage of the journey, he could find somewhere quiet to stay in Ceylon, and with Mokayel's help write some Arabic tracts for Baghdad.[11]

Moving slowly down the coast, coming ashore in each place, Groves prayed that every conversation would be helpful to the people he met and would provide what was needed for their growth in the things of God.[12] Here and there he found Christians occupying military and administrative positions. He encouraged them to see their service in India not as an opportunity to make money or gain promotion, but rather to give what they could to the people of India for the sake of Christ. Everywhere there was an urgent need for Christian workers. In Cannanore district he found more than a million Indians "and not a soul to teach them – surely the Lord will have pity on their destitution and move the hearts of some to come and help."[13] Fifteen miles further on, in Tillicherry, there were "forty converts without any shepherd".[14] In Nayoor, almost four thousand had recently turned to Christ, but they needed missionaries to settle in their villages and instruct them in the basics of the Christian faith. "O that there were willing helpers!" lamented Groves. "Never did I feel so deep an interest in missions; never did I see a place where twenty such as those I know might labour and reap richly."[15] In Coimbatore a missionary had been present for three years and was already teaching thirty converts. His district contained 800,000 souls and "his labours extend about thirty miles round, but how little can *one* man do! Oh that the Lord may provide more!"[16] Moved by all the possibilities before him, Groves resolved to look for workers with "willing hearts and true" to teach the Indians the word of God and help them become teachers for their own people.

Most of his time in Cannanore was spent talking with members of the British garrison bemused by a recent visit from that boisterous and extrovert missionary to the Jews, Joseph Wolff. Wolff's gospel preaching was sound enough, but his dramatic portrayal of the imminent and cataclysmic second coming of Christ had set a rather wild cat among the sleepy Establishment pigeons. Until then they had been taught to regard the Second Coming as a polite euphemism for death. The apocalyptic excitement aroused by Wolff had led to the conversion of some but the estrangement of others, and a "very harsh sermon" had been preached against him. For a time Groves the peacemaker despaired of any reconciliation. "I am sure everything of strife is of Satan," he observed sadly. Yet forty-eight hours later, "after a day of incessant occupation and rather a long lecture," the conflicting parties sat down to a meal together and fellowship was restored. One of the officers later wrote warmly of Groves's intervention, saying, "He found all in confusion and left all in peace."[17]

During his week in Cannanore, Norris Groves had the opportunity to preach every night at "the soldiers' chapel", discoursing on various themes including "death to the world and life in God", on Christ as Saviour from Satan's works and ways, and on the second coming of the Lord. He talked at length with a young man who asked "how he might be a helper to the truth", and he was pleased to discover "another dear Christian family here who live on as little as they can and give the remainder to the poor."[18]

Groves and Mokayel continued southwards in short stages, pausing to stay with Christian families along the coast. In each place, he shared his thoughts informally about "the liberty and love of the church".[19] Eventually, finding horses to ride, they struck inland towards Tinnevelly.

What made this part of India so unusual was the large number of Indians who already considered themselves Christians. Since the mid-sixteenth century there had been Roman Catholic missionaries in the south of the country. Their method had been to draw families into the Catholic fold and then instruct the children in the doctrines and practices of the Church. The result was a sizeable population that considered itself Roman Catholic without possessing much understanding of the gospel or aspiring to any high degree of Christian holiness. Indian Catholicism tolerated the traditional Hindu caste system and was essentially syncretistic, typified by the use of large religious paintings, especially of the Madonna and Child, which often made it hard to distinguish at first sight between a Catholic chapel and a Hindu temple. The Roman Catholics themselves had built upon a foundation laid by the traditional Mar Thoma Church, established, according to common belief, by the apostle Thomas in the first century. It was among these Indian Roman Catholics that Protestant preaching of the gospel had met with its greatest response.

Arriving in Tinnevelly at the town of Palamcottah (Palayankottai), Groves introduced himself to the senior missionary. Karl Rhenius was a remarkable man, a natural linguist and an outstanding Christian leader. Trained at the Missionary Seminary in Berlin, he was working under the auspices of the CMS who, owing to a shortage of English recruits, were glad to enlist trained Lutheran and Reformed (Calvinist) ministers – Germans, Swiss and Danes – despite the fact that these followed their own Protestant traditions taking no account of the Thirty-nine Articles or the Book of Common Prayer of the Church of England. This was a cause of periodic difficulties between the missionaries and the local

CMS committees appointed to oversee them. Based initially in Madras, Rhenius had expressed to the committee his opinion that the Anglican Prayer Book was unsuited to Indian meetings, that English bishops should not expect to exercise authority over Indian churches, that Indian evangelists should not be obliged to travel hundreds of miles to receive ordination and that no restriction should prevent fellowship with Dissenters in public acts of worship.[20] The result was his relocation to this remote region in the south, with Palamcottah as its centre, where no doubt the committee hoped he would cause less embarrassment. From 1820 onwards he preached here to Roman Catholics and Hindus, and many had responded. In 1828 he commenced a work in Dohnavur, later to become famous as the home of Amy Carmichael.[21]

Rhenius was a fluent Tamil speaker and in addition to translating the New Testament he had compiled a valuable grammar. Alongside the intense and animated character of Norris Groves, he would appear a stable and unemotional man. But he was an excellent organiser – cheerful, tough, intelligent, transparently pure of heart, immovable on questions of principle and, like Groves, entirely consecrated to the service of Christ. Rhenius's strategy was to send out trained Indian catechists to preach and distribute literature.[22] In each village where there was a significant response a small elementary school would be established. As the schools prospered, conversions followed, and the converts were gathered into local fellowships allowing much informal participation. Simple meeting places were freely and willingly constructed by the Indians themselves, "being principally mud with palmyra leaf roofs", and many were large enough for two hundred people.[23]

Norris Groves was hugely impressed with the opportunities for outreach and with the Christian groups he saw under the care of Rhenius: "The other evening, when we had a little meeting at a village, eight families of the *Maravers* or thief caste came desiring Christian instruction, and in the village which sent for a teacher there were twenty-five families ready to submit to Christian instruction. In fact, in every direction, they are anxious to hear."[24] His subsequent travels only confirmed his conviction that Tinnevelly was "a field of usefulness nowhere to be equalled in India."[25] He visited a number of the congregations in various villages and found the meetings to be lively and interesting, with extempore prayer, discussion of Bible passages and the opportunity for all "to give an answer or to say what they feel."[26] "My heart was truly delighted at the sweet simplicity which prevailed in their religious exercises. Daily my desire is strengthening to see the Church free in the use of God's word and in his modes of ministry, every one being free to exercise the gift the Spirit has given."[27] Rhenius might be working as the agent of an Anglican society, but it would be hard to identify these as Anglican churches.

Rhenius and his Lutheran colleagues had long enjoyed the privilege of ordaining catechists to assist in this ministry, but shortly before Groves's arrival in India, a bishop had been appointed in Calcutta. The CMS informed Rhenius that henceforth ordinations would be the bishop's prerogative and that if he wished to dispute this he should go to consult a higher authority in England. Norris Groves listened to the story with interest and a degree of indignation. On no account should he go to England, Groves advised, lest his converts be led astray in his absence, and lest by doing so he lent credence to the idea that Indian churches must be subject to English authority. "There is a deeply interesting work going on here," he confided to his journal, "one that I would strain my last nerve to prevent falling to the ground."[28] Why not write a paper, he suggested to Rhenius, stating the position from his point of view so that supporters of the CMS might understand the facts of the matter. Eventually Rhenius wrote two, "which I think," said Groves, "are calculated to do much good. They are written in a nice spirit, exposing many objectionable things in the Church of England... I feel he is appointed of the Lord for the propagation and upholding of the truth and liberty of the Church of Christ."[29] Encouraged by Groves, Rhenius, for the time being, stayed at his post.

The CMS, however, was adamant that if Rhenius would not submit, he and his three colleagues must go. Under intense pressure he yielded to the authority of the committee, placing everything under the control of the bishop. His Indian converts and co-workers were dismayed. They begged him to change his mind. Seeing their desire expressed so strongly, Rhenius and his three German colleagues then resigned from the CMS, gave up their salary and resumed their work, depending on the Lord alone to provide. They were not left to starve. Gifts came in from friends in Bombay and from Germany, and a few weeks later Groves declared, "God has hitherto wonderfully supported them. And now the Lord will decide where and with whom his blessing shall abide." In Karl Rhenius and his colleagues, Groves had found men after his own heart: "I trust they will show that Societies are not needed to carry on very extensive missionary work any more than to begin it."[30]

From Tinnevelly, Norris Groves travelled north, accompanied by Rhenius and his wife and baby, along with Mokayel and a promising young Indian Christian named John Arulappan who had grown up in one of the schools associated with Rhenius. Along the road they talked with bystanders, preached whenever a crowd gathered, and gave out tracts. Travelling through the Nilgherry Hills, they spent Christmas in Ootacamund. From here Groves and Mokayel moved across country to Trichinopoly, and eventually reached the eastern coast in mid-January 1834. In almost every town along the way they visited expatriate Christians and saw how willing the Indians were to hear the gospel of Christ.

Arriving in Ceylon the following month, Groves hoped to stay with Daniel Poor, an American missionary who a few years earlier had read and commended his booklet *Christian Devotedness*. It was Poor who had passed a copy to Colonel Cotton, and it was through Cotton's desire to meet the author in Baghdad that Groves had been brought to India. "On surveying the way in which the Lord has led me," he mused, "I am often struck with the apparently trivial events on which the most important events in our history hang."[31]

"With very deep regret," Groves left Mokayel in Ceylon with the American missionary team on the Jaffna peninsula, but no doubt it was for the best: "I think it important that he should thoroughly learn English, that he may be useful to his own people."[32] Groves, indeed, had some long-term plans that included Mokayel. If, as seemed likely, steam navigation came to the Euphrates, the trip from Bombay to Baghdad would take only fifteen days, and a work could be envisaged with a dual focus in Mesopotamia and southern India.[33] Groves himself looked forward keenly to an evangelistic trek in the not-too-distant future, accompanied by Mokayel, through all the Arab lands of the eastern Mediterranean, then across the desert to his friends in Baghdad before returning by boat to India. "I yet look forward to having him for a travelling companion," he said, "over many a weary mile in Egypt, Syria, Arabia and Mesopotamia." The young Lebanese, with his natural charm and friendliness, showed promise of being a most useful co-worker: "He preaches the gospel very fearlessly and all his remaining prejudices are fast wearing away."[34] Baghdad would be a good place for Mokayel. But to Norris Groves himself, the thought of Baghdad brought back so many unhappy memories, he did not know if he could face it just yet.

By early February he was once more on the Indian mainland. He had enjoyed the company and the kindness of workers from several denominations in Ceylon, and especially the American Dr John Scudder, "a simple-hearted devoted man," although there had been no opportunity to write any Arabic tracts.[35] Groves had shared his thoughts, as always, about true discipleship (devotion to Christ, simple living and sharing the gospel at every opportunity) and about the second coming of the Lord. Though they pressed him to stay, he felt it best to leave the seeds he had sown and press on, encouraged to hear that some of the missionaries were considering a move to the major unreached cities on the mainland. Failing to find any means of transport, he was forced to wait in a village near Tanjore. "How good the Lord is in ordering my affairs for me!" he reflected, "I am quietly set down here for two days... Thus I have a little season of refreshing solitude and time to look into the secret recesses of the heart and see how things stand after the excitement of the last fortnight."[36]

Reaching Madras, Groves met only a few of the expatriate community but was pleased with their response to what he said. One couple, "while I was with them, began to alter their expensive style of living, and a dear Independent minister and his wife parted with their superfluities in a very sweet spirit."[37] In Madras he tried to put some of his thoughts on paper for "a little tract on Christian liberty".[38] But Norris Groves was tired. For nine months he had been continually on the move, accompanied night and day by Mokayel and by other companions, constantly meeting new people, sensitive to their needs, and trying to encourage them in the path of discipleship and the work of the gospel. In fact Groves was a man whose emotional make-up required a certain amount of space and time to himself. His journal makes occasional reference to "a quiet room" or "a quiet bungalow in the midst of the jungle" or to a degree of privacy whilst being carried in a "palanquin".[39] But it was all too rarely that he could enjoy such a luxury. "You do not know how sweet the rest is to one harassed by being continually in public, or I rather should say, with others," he confided.[40] It was sailing up the coast from Madras in "a little French brig" that he was, for the first time since coming to India, almost completely on his own.[41] He could read, pray, write and let his mind just wander.

Among other things, he looked over a letter he had received from John Nelson Darby. It contained bitter criticism of a mutual friend.[42] It "left on my mind the impression of a Jehu-like zeal which neither pitied nor spared... Surely it does become us, surrounded and eaten up with errors as we are, to touch those of our brother gently." He took the opportunity to compose for Darby's benefit a careful summary of his own views on Christian unity.[43]

He also had time to reflect on the open door he had found in India, especially for preaching the gospel in the rural areas of the south. The Indian Christians he had met were still wonderfully free from the prejudices that divided churches in Europe and America, and yet he saw ominous signs of change: "Never was there a more important moment than the present for India. Up to this time everything in the Church has been as free as our hearts could wish. Persons have been converted, either by reading God's word or through one another, and have drank [*sic*] the living waters, wherever they could find them, full and clear. But now the Church of England is seeking to extend its power, and the Independents and Methodists are seeking to enclose their little flocks."[44] How vital and how urgent was the call to help Christian workers see the importance of establishing biblical Indian churches instead of imposing foreign denominations where they had no right to be! Had God brought him to India at such a time, and for such a purpose? "My object in India," he concluded, "is two-fold: to try to check the operation of these exclusive systems by showing in the Christian Church they are not necessary for all that is *holy* and *moral*; and to try and impress upon every member of Christ's body that he has some ministry given him for the body's edification – and instead of depressing, encouraging each one to come forward and serve the Lord. I have it much at heart, should the Lord spare me, to form a church on these principles; and my earnest desire is to re-model the whole plan of missionary operations so as to bring them to the simple standard of God's word."[45] A worthy vision perhaps, but was it realistic?

ENDNOTES

[1] D16

[2] M530-531

[3] We are fortunate to have edited extracts from Groves's Indian journals, along with passages from personal letters, reproduced in his *Memoir*; they were never published in their entirety. His writing is simple, sensitive and spontaneous, and charmingly careless of the occasional grammatical slip that would find no place, for example, in Kitto's more studied prose. He tells us where he has been, what he has done, whom he has met and what has happened. He records what he has found in scripture, what others have said, what information he has obtained, what thoughts have come to him, and all this without ever striving for effect. He always looks for something positive to commend in the people he meets, and never fails to thank God for everything.

[4] M230. William Carey and his Baptist colleagues were similarly forbidden to preach to British soldiers because they were "not episcopally ordained" (Smith G, *Carey*, 161).

[5] M228

[6] M238. Whilst in Bombay, Groves arranged for a booklet to be printed, with the title *On the Nature of Christian Influence*, in which he developed the thought that a Christian will have more influence for good through "being like Christ" than by acquiring or maintaining an honoured position in the world (M229-230).

[7] M228

[8] M238

[9] M231

[10] M237

[11] M234

[12] Col 4:5-6; Eph 4:29.

[13] M239

[14] M239

[15] M253

[16] M263

[17] M240

[18] M241

[19] M243

[20] Rhenius, 193; Strachan, 36. Rhenius strongly objected to the Prayer Book doctrine of baptismal regeneration and to the indiscriminate baptising of infants, but he believed that the real reason for his dismissal from Madras was "solely because we had too catholic a spirit and desired to embrace all as Christian brethren who hold the Head" (Rhenius to Jowett, 18 July 1835, in Groves, *Tinnevelly Mission*, 36).

[21] Rhenius, 312. His full name was Karl Gottlieb (or Charles Theophilus) Ewald Rhenius. Joseph Wolff, who visited him in 1833, considered Rhenius to be "the greatest missionary that has ever appeared in the Protestant Church" and calculated that "the number of Hindoos to whose conversion he has been instrumental amounts to 12,000" (Wolff, II, 207). Rhenius had established 111 local schools, in which 2553 boys and 146 girls received Christian instruction (Wolff, II, 211).

Protestant work in Tinnevelly had been launched by a gifted and godly Lutheran, working under the auspices of the SPCK, named Christian Schwartz. He served in India for forty-eight years without a break and gained such respect in Tranquebar, Trichinopoly and Tanjore that the churches, numbering thousands of believers, were left in considerable disarray on his death in 1798. The achievement of Rhenius owes much to the earlier labours of Schwartz and his Indian disciple Sathianathan (Satyanathan) (Neill, *History*, 233-235, 272).

[22] The catechists made use of a series of written questions and answers, known as a catechism, covering the basic doctrines of the Christian faith with appropriate Bible references. As early as 1818 Rhenius had written his own Tamil catechism. Preaching and teaching for both adults and children thus took the form of questions asked publicly by the catechist and answers given by those present, with free discussion of matters raised (Rhenius, 135-136).

[23] Groves, *The Present State of the Tinnevelly Mission*, 11. See also Rhenius, 458-460.

[24] M256

[25] M362

[26] *Tinnevelly Mission*, 25

[27] M256. No serious attempt was made to impose western forms of worship on these Indian believers. Groves remarked, "I do not believe that one Tamil Common Prayer Book will be found *in use* among them all" (*Tinnevelly Mission*, 25).

[28] M254

[29] M331

[30] M363. At this time Groves wrote, in defence of Rhenius, *A Brief Account of the Present Circumstances of the Tinnevelly Mission*. In response to a critique of this work by J M Strachan, a second and somewhat expanded edition, with Rhenius's second letter appended, appeared in 1836 under the title, *The Present State of the Tinnevelly Mission*. For a detailed account of "the Rhenius Controversy", see Dann, *Primitivist Missiology*, 52-65.

[31] M273. Poor was a Congregationalist who had served for twenty years with the ABCFM. Groves found him to be "a simple, affectionate and good man", and noted "we have had much conversation on the subject of coming down to the level of the natives" (M273-274).

[32] M279

[33] A small steamboat was actually launched on the Euphrates in 1835, connecting with larger steamers running from the Gulf to Bombay (Groves to Spittler, 24 Dec. 1835). In the event, plans for this Euphrates route were shelved due to political unrest and were finally dropped in 1875 when Disraeli bought controlling shares in the Suez Canal.

[34] M290. On Mokayel Trad's background see Railton, 146-148, 183 and M234, 529. He later became an effective personal evangelist in his homeland of Lebanon and Syria (M531).

[35] M274. Scudder was from the Dutch Reformed Church, working in conjunction with the Congregationalist ABCFM. At a later date the Scudders were associated with the American Methodists.

[36] M279

[37] M285. They were Mr and Mrs John Smith, and in the course of fifteen years their church in Madras sent out at least eight European missionaries to other parts of India (Bromley, 26).

[38] M289. This was printed in Madras in 1834 as *The Liberty of the Christian Ministry*, then reprinted in England the following year with the title *On the Liberty of Ministry in the Church of Christ*.

[39] Palanquin: a cheap form of transport – a reclining chair carried by four men, six feet long, two and a half feet wide and two and a half feet high, and enclosed with curtains.

[40] M261

[41] M284. Even then he had with him an Indian companion, a poor Roman Catholic who was learning to read and who eventually declared to Groves his wish to change his religion: "for who that can read cannot see that yours is the truth?"

[42] Almost certainly Frank Newman (M287).

[43] Dated April 1834, reproduced in full in M533-535 and discussed in Chapter 21 of this book.

[44] M285. Independents: also known as Congregationalists.

[45] M285

"A succession of holy moments
constitutes a holy life."

Norris Groves [1]

17

An Angel's Visit

L ooking back over the past months, Norris Groves could not help comparing the barrenness of Baghdad with the openness of India: "The encouragement the Lord has given me is great beyond all I could have hoped. I cannot tell you how lovingly I have been received, not by one party only, but by all. I cannot *but* believe I am called to service in this country. I have encouraged others to remain faithful to the Lord in their work, and shall I run away? I have wished them to live on little, and shall I retire from the scene and not share their burden with them and show them how? I have desired the dear Church in India to love each other, and to know no distinctions, and shall I not dwell here and practise what I preach?"[2] It was in India, he now believed, that the substantial firstfruits of the gospel among the heathen would be gathered in.

The editor of his journal comments, "His favourite idea at this time was to select a band of devoted men, ready not only to preach Christ fully, but to follow him in a self-sacrificing course, and if need be to labour with their hands for their own support. And the sphere of service which he had in view was an immense district on the eastern coast, then entirely without a missionary."[3] A few such "devoted men" he had already found in India, especially in the army, who might willingly preach and teach, and trust God for their daily needs. The team still in Baghdad, if led to join him in India, would also be a great asset. And surely there would be others in England and Ireland ready to help. A recent letter brought news of "many dear German missionaries waiting to come out, willing to do the humblest work with their hands." These were Lutherans from the same disciplined Pietist circles as Karl Pfander; they might make excellent self-supporting evangelists in the East. Some of these German craftsmen could be useful in Baghdad too, Groves thought: "They might get more access to the people than we could."[4]

In mid-April he reached Calcutta, where he was warmly welcomed by the expatriate community. On the evening of his arrival he heard one of the army chaplains "preach a simple and true sermon" and was afterwards invited to his home. He was delighted to meet the elderly Archdeacon Daniel Corrie, a contemporary and friend of the late Henry Martyn. Corrie proved to be "a dear,

dear old man, a lovely Christian; and his fine and interesting face beams with the love that yet glows in his aged heart."[5] Groves's new friends in Calcutta took him to visit the bishop, who received him "most kindly", and the evening was spent at Corrie's, where he saw Henry Martyn's Bible with all its jottings and hand-written comments.

Taking a boat upriver to Serampore, Norris Groves paid a happy visit to the pioneering Baptist missionaries and met the aged William Carey, "sinking into the grave after more than forty years' service, leaving the world as poor, as to temporal things, as when he entered it. He leaves his widow and children, without a shilling, to the loving care of their brethren." On his travels Groves had heard criticisms levelled at the Baptists – unjust and untrue, he realised, now he had seen their work for himself. "Not perhaps that they have done all things well, but they are certainly in every respect as far above those who censure them as the blue vault of heaven is above the clouds."[6] Of Baptist workers elsewhere, he found most of them open to fellowship with other Christians, and in general he liked what he saw of them: "The Baptist missionaries seem to be good men, particularly when they are not sectarian about communion."[7] One Baptist couple he found "very devoted, living most simply and returning not a little of their salary to the Society."[8] He spent a day with a Baptist missionary, in a town near Calcutta, who preached in the bazaar to a crowd numbering more than a hundred. Another was "a simple humble man" who had been in India thirty years: "I found him quite open to the truth of the Lord's advent, and on numberless other points our hearts so entirely agreed that it was a very happy day."[9]

From here Groves travelled up the River Ganges to Patna, hoping to make contact with a self-supporting missionary by the name of William Start, who had recently come out from England.[10] Groves wondered if Start might accompany him to Burma (Myanmar) and visit a promising Baptist mission there;[11] perhaps they could even find a way to work together. But Start was too busy to travel anywhere – preaching in the bazaar, studying the languages, supervising several small schools in the province of Bihar and investigating possibilities for work "among the independent sheikhs in the neighbourhood of Agra and Delhi." Groves was impressed and a little surprised: "Dear Start is very different from what I had expected. He has a keen clear active mind and a deep acquaintance with heart religion. He is very argumentative and disposed to *prove* things before he receives them. We are quite of one heart and mind in all things connected with the Kingdom." Start was not always an easy companion; his keen insight into human nature "searches a little into the corners of my heart." But Groves was greatly refreshed to find a friend so frank, so wholehearted and so uncomplicated: "I cannot describe to you the comfort I feel in having such a brother as dear Start in India; one in whose integrity and simplicity and devotedness I can so entirely confide. Yet while I am learning from him, he treats me as though he were learning from me... My heart is touched with the Lord's goodness in bringing us together." In Patna itself there were "perhaps 250,000 souls, and all mad upon their idols".[12] The intrepid Start badly needed reinforcements.

In some of the towns inland of Calcutta, Groves found workers discouraged; they had seen few, if any, conversions, and they bewailed the lack of real commitment in those who professed to believe. He spoke once or twice to small missionary gatherings – about the second coming of Jesus and the resurrection of the dead, touching, of course, on spiritual unity and sacrificial discipleship – hoping his words would stir up his hearers to a fresh love for Christ and zeal in his service. At Sonamukhi, near Burdwan, he visited a German couple by the name of Weitbrecht who were running a school.[13] They were very concerned about the plight of little girls sold into a life of ritual prostitution, wondering if they should establish an orphanage, and he made this a matter for special prayer. He met kindness everywhere, and if there was a little prejudice against him from time to time, he found ways to disarm it; no one could doubt his love for all who loved the Lord.

It was now midsummer 1834 and Norris Groves seemed considerably refreshed. Constantly travelling, exploring fresh opportunities, meeting new people, had served to banish from his mind the most painful recollections: "I am beginning again to feel a little revived under the Lord's loving mercies. For many months before I left Baghdad, I was like a tree in winter. I then thought I should never revive, but I now see and feel the Lord has not forgotten to be gracious, and having begun, I know not what he may not do."[14] From time to time he set aside a day for prayer and fasting, remembering by name all he had known in Baghdad and in India – it made a long list. Further letters brought some encouragement, especially the most recent news of Harnie. She had been God's answer to his most desperate prayers three years ago – a wonderful help in all the practical arrangements of the household and especially in caring for the children. As far as human nature went, Groves recalled, "I never saw anything more lovely than her character." And now, "she really has embraced the truth, to the great joy and comfort of them all."[15] But other matters caused concern. Despite the help of Calman among the Jews, the work of the gospel in Baghdad was not getting any easier. Neither Cronin nor Parnell had yet attained competence in a local language; they were struggling with the culture and climate, and with sickness and political unrest; but, above all, they found the people increasingly indifferent to the little they could convey of the gospel and increasingly hardened against it. Would they be able to keep the Baghdad mission going long enough for reinforcements to join them? Norris Groves longed to return and encourage his friends. But the prospect of going back to a place of such heartache – he could not contemplate it just yet, especially when things were going so well in India.

Returning to his temporary base in Calcutta, his pleasure evaporated. Some of the expatriates were unhappy that he had preached and encouraged others to preach who had no ordination or authorisation from the Church of England. Groves, they declared, was promoting schism and disorder, especially in his support of Rhenius against the CMS. It came as a shock when the chaplain took him to task: "I was told I was the greatest enemy the Church of England ever had in India, because no one could help loving my spirit and thus the evil sank tenfold deeper." "But indeed," he protested, "I do not wish to injure but to help her by taking from her all her false confidences."[16] Upset but not intimidated, Groves received the criticism "in love and meekness", and a few days later was invited for a meal. "The chaplain is most kind in many respects. He says they cannot have too much of my spirit or too little of my judgment."[17] But "I do so feel what David means when he says 'when I speak of peace they make ready for war'; every day I have something or other to try me... I have so few like-minded, yet wherever I go, by God's great grace, there have been some one or two who stand."[18] Later news from Baghdad was also disturbing – a fresh outbreak of plague in the city, and armies converging once more on its helpless inhabitants. Perhaps God would have him cut short his Indian visit and head for Bombay as quickly as possible, "that I may be ready the first moment to set sail for the Gulf."[19]

Two weeks later he was still in Calcutta, visiting a school of three hundred boys established by a young Church of Scotland minister, Dr Alexander Duff. After inspecting the lower classes, Groves had the opportunity to examine the older boys on their knowledge of the Bible and the evidences for the Christian faith. It was a moving experience. Norris Groves, with "his earnest beaming countenance" and tears in his eyes, "pouring out his soul on the great theme of salvation," told how the truth of Christianity was proved by the fact that, better than any other religion, it brought glory to God and happiness to man. Many of the boys expressed their agreement. They in turn "with countenances *beaming* with intelligence, and some with deep feeling, pointed out the absence of all these marks in their *own* systems."[20] Turning to Duff, he exclaimed, "This is what I have been in quest of ever since I left old England... I feel that every word is finding its way within. I could empty the whole of my own soul into theirs."[21] Duff answered by opening the door into a large hall where the infants' class was learning the English alphabet. It was here, he said, that the work of conversion began.

The interest that Groves showed in the school was a great encouragement to Duff. The same afternoon, however, his host felt the first symptoms of a "terrible attack of Bengal dysentery which," said Duff, "brought me soon to the very edge of the grave." So severe was the dehydration in such cases that if not checked it could quickly prove fatal. Medical opinion advised an immediate return to the healthier climate of Europe.

Now Norris Groves was forced to make a decision. It was difficult to know exactly how things stood in Baghdad; letters often took eight months to arrive. Reports confirmed that "everything is in the last stage of political disorganisation," and as far as he could tell, his friends were inclined to evacuate and follow him to India. This meant there was no urgent need for him in Baghdad. His recent travels had introduced him to almost all the Christian missions in India and had shown how great the need was for more workers everywhere. By far the most useful thing he could do would be to recruit missionaries for the unreached provinces, and for Baghdad, and to summon help for the lonely pioneers he had met in various places. Duff's illness convinced him that now was the time to go, "hoping by the Lord's gracious help to get a body of men like-minded to work with me."[22]

Enquiring with shipping agents, he looked for "the earliest and cheapest" vessel leaving in the general direction of England. The next few days were frantically busy. "He had many friends to see," Duff tells us, "many enquiries to institute, many preparations to make for his own homeward voyage; and yet, though wearied and worn out in his incessant labours during the day, he insisted on having his couch laid beside mine during the night, that like a true brother he might have it in his power to minister alike to my spiritual and physical necessity. Thus with untiring kindness for about three weeks did he render unto me services which were beyond all price, services which have left indelible impressions on my heart."[23]

Eventually a suitable ship was located, and in July 1834 Groves's fourteen-month survey of Christian missions in India came to an end. The morning before they sailed, Mrs Duff gave birth to a baby boy. Her husband, at death's door, lay "shattered and helpless and all but insensible"; mother, father and baby all had to be carried on board. Groves insisted on Duff occupying his cabin, which meant he had little privacy of his own. Prayer and Bible study occupied most of the time he was not at the bedside of his friend. It happened that the adjoining cabin was occupied by a young woman with a small child; she had recently lost her husband. About eight or nine days out of Calcutta she too was taken ill, and shortly afterwards she died. Groves took the orphan boy under his care, noting in his journal that in less than two months the child was bereft of both father and mother, and he commented, "O that the heart would learn wisdom from these things!"[24] Also with them was a young Hindu hoping to study in England. His name was Anundoo. Every day Groves read two or three chapters with him from the English Bible, praying with him and discussing the gospel for hours on end.[25]

From Calcutta they sailed down the eastern coast of India, then westward with the Trade Winds to the Cape of Good Hope. The journal records little apart from a brief reference to a waterspout, "a few sharks, turtle, dolphin and flying fish," and later "a whale and a few albatrosses". It was a time of relaxation after weeks of bustle: "I cannot help feeling how much better a sea voyage is for the soul than a land journey – at least than those journeys to which I have been accustomed. The constant struggles with a faithless and lying people, the bodily fatigue, the personal danger, the anticipations of renewed difficulties or delays at every stage, all tend to keep the mind unsettled if not ruffled."[26] Three times a day he turned to the Lord in prayer, "bearing before him those who are engraved on my heart."[27] He arranged a meeting on deck every Sunday for the passengers and crew, preaching the gospel to all who would attend. Most did.

Meanwhile in Baghdad things were not going well. Twice more the area was afflicted with plague before the remaining members of the missionary team decided to abandon the work, at least for the time being, and set out to join Groves in India. Cronin was the first to go, with little Minny, and Harnie to care for her, accompanied by Serkies, leaving the Parnell family to follow with Henry and Frank. Calman moved on, to pioneer fresh fields in Syria, and by the end of 1834 nothing remained of the Baghdad mission.[28]

During the voyage Norris Groves wrote notes in his Bible, in spaces not already filled by the comments and annotations painstakingly gathered during past years. Day by day he collected subjects and references for future study and for booklets he wished to compose on various topics. He had "just finished all the precepts of the New Testament" and he "had all the prophecies marked and divided." Apart from his little carpet, his old Bible was all he possessed: "It was indeed almost the only treasure I desired to call my own, and it had been my companion and comfort in many dark and dreary days." He brought the Bible up on deck to read with Anundoo and the orphan boy. The sails clattered, the ship lurched, Groves grabbed the boy to stop him falling, and the Bible was knocked out of his hand. "Yet I know the Lord is good, even in this, and would have me dig and dig again, for more and still richer treasures than I have yet found... It is so strange: I dreamed about a fortnight ago that I dropped my Bible from the very place where I lost it today... Well, it is gone and I think I never shall forget the feeling I had when it fell and I saw it floating away rapidly behind us."[29] Exactly a week later he was asleep on the deck at night when a heavy piece of wood with a long nail fell from the mizzen topsail yard "and the nail stuck through all the clothes I had over me and into my hip. How near we often are to death. Had it fallen on my head, it might have been the last blow I could receive... The Lord alone can make us to sleep in safety."[30] Violent storms followed, with a severe shortage of food, before the ship finally reached shelter at the South African Cape. But the Duffs had felt the benefit of their days at sea and showed signs of a good recovery.

Alexander Duff was an Edinburgh man, trained as a Presbyterian minister in the Church of Scotland. Arriving in India in 1830, he had been disturbed to see how little headway the gospel was making; only the poor villagers of the lowest castes had shown any response. Surely, he thought, in order to transform the country as a whole, the Indian elite must be reached, and the way to reach them would be to offer something they desire – a British education. This education would naturally include the principles of Christianity, the religion of Britain. The idea came at the right time. The expanding influence of British trade was stirring an intellectual interest in the outside world, whilst traditional Hinduism faced growing discontent through its failure to meet the appalling social and spiritual needs of the country. The East India Company had introduced remarkable scientific and technological advances (roads, medicine and steam power), and the developing markets of the Empire had conferred new and unexpected prosperity on the producers of Indian tea, cotton, and jute (for making sacks). Along with this, the British military posts and colonial service had brought to the country a substantial measure of law and order, with efficient administration and genuine justice in the law courts. The boys who came to Duff's school were boys whose parents had seen many benefits in British civilisation.

In 1830 Duff stood before his first class and read out slowly and solemnly the Lord's Prayer in Bengali. He then invited some of the boys themselves to read from the Christian scriptures. Standing beside him throughout the opening ceremony was a brilliant Brahman[31] by the name of Raja Rammohun Roy who, though still a Hindu, had published a book ten years earlier with the remarkable title *The Precepts of Jesus the Guide to Peace and Happiness*.[32] Before long Duff had two hundred intelligent boys of the highest castes making rapid progress in their knowledge of the English language and the Christian religion. Two years later, four of the older boys professed faith in Christ and were baptised. This produced a great furore. Pupils were withdrawn by their parents, and for a time the whole work was threatened with closure. But such was the excellence of Duff's school that ambitious Indian families could not do without it. The number of conversions – a total of about thirty-six in all the years of Duff's service in India – though not great, was immensely significant, for almost all became men of distinction and laid the foundations for some of India's great Christian families. Others, without professing conversion, gained a respect for Christian values and beliefs that made them sympathetic friends to the gospel throughout their future careers. Since that time Christian education has had a major impact on India, and the proportion of educated people among Christians is far higher than that in the population as a whole. Duff, in this sphere, was breaking new ground and breaking it well.

The Scottish minister had heard about Norris Groves before his arrival in Calcutta. Indeed, they had exchanged some friendly letters, and Duff frankly confessed that his "first glow of devotedness" was inspired by a small booklet written by a certain dentist in Exeter.[33] That little tract seemed to find its way everywhere! But Duff had heard rumours that its author held somewhat unconventional views on other matters too; he was not at all sure they would see eye to eye. "Well did I know beforehand," he confessed, "that there were different points connected with the principles of Establishments, church government and such-like, respecting which his opinions differed somewhat widely from mine. But I knew he was a proved man of God who had jeoparded his worldly interest, and even his life, in seeking to promote the cause of the Redeemer in the world." In the event, Duff felt reassured from the moment he first shook hands with his visitor: "No sooner did I meet with him than I felt drawn towards him with the cords of love. He was so warm, so earnest, so wrapt up in his Master's cause, so inflamed with zeal for the salvation of perishing souls, I regarded it as no ordinary privilege that he agreed to take up his abode in my house during his sojourn in Calcutta. I looked for incalculable benefit to my own soul from near and intimate and familiar contact with so fervent and glowing a spirit."[34]

At the Cape of Good Hope the baby was christened Alexander Groves Duff. We are not told how Groves felt about the honour bestowed on him. No doubt the question of adult or infant baptism had been one of the subjects in the daily discussions he enjoyed with the convalescent Duff as his strength returned. They naturally agreed on some things, and agreed to differ on others, but Duff remarked that "all such discussions were carried on, not in the belligerent spirit of ordinary controversialists but in the pacific spirit of earnest truth-seekers... The Bible was our sole standard of reference, and the grand object was to discover the mind of the Lord in fervent prayer for the guidance of his Holy Spirit, who alone is able to lead into all spiritual truth."[35]

They continued up the western coast of Africa, past Spain and then France. Finally on Christmas Eve (1834), England was sighted, and a week later they came ashore in Scotland. "What, humanly speaking, could we have done," reflected Duff many years later, "without the promptly, cheerfully, spontaneously rendered services of such a loving, able and skilful brother in the Lord? Truly his visit to us was like an angel's visit, a visit of surpassing kindness and brotherly love."[36]

Whilst still at sea Norris Groves had looked forward with keen anticipation to seeing his friends in England. "Sometimes my heart overflows with the thought of visiting the little churches," he confided.[37] But now, travelling south by coach from Scotland, he was not so sure what reception he would receive: a warm welcome, no doubt, from Müller and Craik, and from Robert Chapman in Barnstaple; a hostile one, in all likelihood, from Darby and his supporters in Plymouth and London. The prospect of renewing old friendships was a "thrilling delight", but one mixed with "some cloud of doubt". "A thousand times my heart has said 'What awaits thee?' and the answer is 'Cast the burden of the future on the Lord.'"[38]

ENDNOTES

[1] M315

[2] M286

[3] M284

[4] M285

[5] M294

[6] M295. We might wish that all armchair critics would take the trouble, as Groves did, to visit the missionaries and see for themselves!

[7] M301. Despite the protests of his colleague William Ward, Carey would not allow believers to participate in the Lord's Supper at Serampore if baptised only in infancy (George, 164).

[8] M297

[9] M300

[10] Start had formerly been a clergyman of the Church of England and was said to possess "considerable private property" (Coates to Blumhardt, 17 Feb. 1835).

[11] This was Adoniram Judson's mission. Groves had heard good things of the "simplicity, adaptation to the natives and devotion of the Baptist missionaries there," adding, "I long to see some one mission carried on in unison with the principles I feel to be right." He hoped this would prove to be such a one (M274).

[12] M304-305

[13] John Weitbrecht was a cousin of Karl Pfander. It was Pfander, indeed, "who had been partly instrumental, by his example and influence, in first leading his own mind to the contemplation of missionary work" (Weitbrecht, 193, 497). This connection was probably the reason for Groves's visit.

[14] M297

[15] M288

[16] M314

[17] M320

[18] M318

[19] M314

[20] M323

[21] Smith G, *Duff*, I, 267-268

[22] M279

[23] M536

[24] M327

[25] This high caste Bengali had been rejected by his family and baptised in 1832. Groves had promised to settle his substantial debts. In 1841 Anundoo married an English Christian lady in Bristol, and later returned to India as an LMS evangelist. Viewing himself as "an English gentleman", he proved unsuited to evangelism and incapable of earning a living or keeping out of debt (Jackson E M, in Lewis, ed., 26). Harriet Groves judged that "he turned out very unsatisfactorily" (M332).

[26] M343

[27] M351

[28] Groves wrote several times to the Basel Mission urging them to send workers to Baghdad, but without success (Groves to Büchelen, 30 Nov. 1835, 22 Mar. 1836; Groves to Spittler, 7 Apr. 1835, 24 Dec. 1835). Between 1844 and 1852 Henry A Stern of the LSPCJ made Baghdad his base for several lengthy itinerations among the Jews of Mesopotamia and Persia (Stern, *Dawnings*, 34-55, 72, 203, 232). The city was then neglected until the establishment of a CMS base in 1882, which survived bravely but with little encouragement until the First World War (Richter, 330). In 1924 a combination of American churches formed the United Mission in Iraq, which continued until the withdrawal of all Western missionaries in 1969. More recently, Arab workers from Egypt and elsewhere have had some success in planting churches and house groups in Baghdad and the other cities of Iraq, with significant growth following a period of severe persecution in the 1960s and '70s. Their members are mostly of Assyrian and Armenian origin, converts from the eastern Orthodox and Roman Catholic churches.

[29] M342

[30] M345

[31] Brahman (or Brahmin): a member of the highest or priestly caste of Hinduism in India.

[32] Six months prior to the inauguration of Duff's school, Roy had opened a place of worship in Calcutta, establishing his own sect of syncretistic Unitarianism which he called the Hindu Theistic Church. His purpose was to purify Hinduism from within and to provide a spiritual home for Hindus attracted by Christianity who still hesitated to break with their old traditions. Roy had already engaged in a rather unfortunate controversial debate with the Baptist missionaries at Serampore. In 1822 Marshman had published *A Defence of the Deity and Atonement of Jesus Christ, in reply to Rammohun Roy of Calcutta*, no doubt intending to discourage waverers from joining Roy. Further pamphleteering ensued. Roy had frankly recommended Jesus as the greatest of all moral teachers, but the confrontational intellectual style of his missionary opponent, instead of encouraging Roy to take seriously what Jesus said about his person and mission, and perhaps embrace Christianity himself, tended merely to widen the gulf between them (Neill, *India and Pakistan*, 118-119).

[33] M295

[34] M536

[35] M537

[36] M537. Duff later wrote, "It was my delight to know that Mr Groves was struck with the work in which I happened to be engaged when he visited Calcutta. It afforded me not a little consolation and comfort at the time... In a little work of mine, *Missions, the Chief End of the Church*, I have specially noted this visit of Mr Groves" (M323-324). On a subsequent furlough Duff toured the British Isles and then the United States where he preached to Congress and had a private interview with the President. He was a remarkable orator and through his influence hundreds were led to volunteer for foreign missionary service. His pioneering concept of Christian schools as a means of bringing the gospel to the most influential classes proved to be highly significant in the history of Christian mission (Tucker, 136; Vander Werff, 62-66).

[37] M333

[38] M354. Chapter 21 of this book looks in more detail at the widening divergence of view between Groves and Darby. The assembly in Plymouth had recently printed an extract from one of Groves's letters in their magazine *The Christian Witness* but the editor had inserted a disclaimer dissociating himself from Groves's hope for "glory to be restored to the church" (*The Christian Witness*, April 1834).

"I do not know what errors Mr Groves may hold,
but this I know:
that those who never looked into their Bibles
before he came
have learnt, by his coming, to study them."

A British Judge in India [1]

18

Garden of Eden

Refreshed by his restful weeks at sea, Norris Groves set about his recruiting campaign with typical energy. He needed teachers for schools, supervisors for orphanages, agriculturalists and craftsmen for commercial projects, evangelists for street preaching, and once again he needed a tutor for his own sons. Enlisting the help of his German brother-in-law, he set off for Germany and Switzerland.

Acting as both translator and preacher, this was George Müller's first European tour, to be followed in coming years by several more. The Lutheran state church in Germany was said to be as dry as dust, and the Dissenters very subdued. Müller had often been asked why he did not make use of his reputation as a philanthropist to preach the gospel and teach the deeper things of the Christian life in his homeland. As for Groves, he made no secret of his continued hope that his sister and her husband would be led to join him in India. Together they consulted the leaders of the Mission Institute in Basel. Then while Müller spent some time in Germany, Groves went to speak to the Bourg-de-Four assembly in Geneva. Despite some "evil surmisings made and circulated in Germany and Switzerland, both as to the truth of my undertaking and my capability of accomplishing it," the tour was quite productive.[2] Two Swiss workers, Rodolphe de Rodt and Ferdinand Gros, felt led to help with the school and orphanage in Sonamukhi, and as they were ready to go, they left for India immediately. A German tailor named Louis Kälberer offered to help William Start in Patna. A young theology graduate from Tübingen by the name of Hermann Gundert was willing to serve as tutor for the Groves family, and perhaps to do something for the encouragement of Rhenius.[3]

Returning from the continent, Groves saw John Kitto several times in London and was pleased to find him happily married and usefully employed, though perhaps not quite so "devoted" as he had been when under Groves's direct influence. As expected, his visits to Bristol and Barnstaple were a delight; that to Plymouth distinctly uncomfortable. Then in April (1835) Norris Groves remarried.

He had met Harriet Baynes during his days of preparation for Baghdad. She had been one of those caught up with enthusiasm for the mission and brought to a new level of Christian commitment through the words and example of its leader. In his loneliness he had written tentatively in 1833, two years after Mary's death, and received a refusal. Now a further two years later, "hearing that she had been grievously injured and disfigured by a waggon which crushed her face in a narrow Devonshire lane," he again asked, and this time she was willing.[4] Harriet was a highly intelligent woman, "a most interesting companion," and well able to discuss matters of the weightiest theology; she would make an excellent missionary.[5] As for the wedding itself, Groves made it a matter of special prayer. Harriet later recalled that "the hand of the Lord was very apparent in overcoming, in answer to his prayer, many obstacles, and ordering circumstances so as to bring about this union in a very remarkable manner."[6] What she meant by this we do not know.

Norris and Harriet Groves were joined by Gundert and Kälberer in Devon, and soon they were in touch with others who showed interest. Visiting Barnstaple, Groves was introduced by Robert Chapman to some young members of his Ebenezer Chapel. They were William Bowden, a stonemason, and George Beer, a shoemaker, and their wives (both named Elizabeth). All in their early twenties, these were sturdy country people, not well educated but more than willing to respond to the vision Groves had shared for the vast unreached Godavari Delta on the south-east coast of India.[7] Another Devonshire man, a schoolteacher by the name of Nathaniel Brice, was keen to work with William Start in Patna. Shortly afterwards they welcomed two young ladies from French-speaking Switzerland – Marie Monnard, "a teacher of sweet disposition" but somewhat frail health, and Julie Dubois, capable and hard-working, "a farmer's daughter of rigid Calvinistic stock".[8] Also with them was Norris's young cousin Emma, who had been part of the family at Northernhay, and her brother John with his wife Sarah. John Groves is described as "a jovial fox-hunting man whose debts Mr Groves had paid and was now taking out to help in odd ways as he might be able." He had never clearly professed faith in Christ, a cause of concern to his wife and, of course, to the rest of the party. They were praying for him. The group was completed by Harriet's younger brother George Baynes, a devotee of gaiety, merriment and champagne who was "going out to join the army". George had also found his new brother-in-law "useful in discharging debts". So we see it was rather an odd assortment, offering plenty of scope for personal work on the voyage out.[9]

Now with some promising recruits and a new wife, it was time to book their passage to India. The party assembled in Bristol, where a large farewell meeting was hosted by Henry Craik and George Müller (just preparing to open his first orphanage), with a closing prayer from Percy Hall of Plymouth.

Bessie Paget was again among the friends who accompanied the party to their point of departure, this time Milford Haven on the western tip of Wales. When they enquired at the dock, however, there was no sign of the large sailing vessel on which their berths were booked; it had been held up in its passage from Scotland by contrary winds. A month later it had still not arrived, but no doubt the Lord had a purpose in the delay. Some of the party stayed with friends, others in a hotel, and they occupied the time with open-air preaching. Hermann Gundert was surprised by the "simple eloquence and earnestness" of Bowden and Beer, "carrying conviction to the hearts and consciences of their hearers – in painful contrast with the laboured and ineffective sermons he and his fellow theological students had been taught to compose in the seminary." He was also surprised to find "how thoroughly well-grounded they and their wives were in the scriptures, as they diligently sought to enlighten him upon believers' baptism and other cherished truths."[10]

Gundert, though still only twenty-two years of age, had already spent some time studying Indian languages in London and Bristol, and he now started teaching the rudiments of Telugu (spoken in the Godavari Delta) to the couples from Barnstaple. He also introduced Harriet, Emma and the Swiss girls to Bengali, which would be useful in the region round Calcutta, whilst Norris and the two men intending to join Start concentrated on Hindustani.[11] Groves also had time to compose another carefully worded letter to Darby on the subject of Christian unity, which with hindsight appears both wise and prophetic, and all the more impressive when we consider the other matters that must have been occupying his mind at the time. Perhaps, indeed, this was the chief purpose behind the delay.[12]

Eventually the East Indiaman, the *Perfect*, arrived – complete with forty rams, twenty pigs, cows, goats and geese in pens on the main deck, all sent on board by a kind Christian friend who had gone to Scotland for that purpose. The final costs of the journey had been met by a complete stranger from India who called and presented Groves with £200 "in the name of the Lord". Finally "the longed-for north wind was granted them, and the *Perfect* weighed anchor and drew out, leaving behind a snow-bound countryside." It was March 1836. Gospel meetings were held regularly on board for the Scottish sailors, as well as daily prayer meetings and Bible studies for their own party, in which "Groves skilfully drew out the two diffident German brethren."[13] When not affected by seasickness, they worked away at the Indian languages, and Harriet (now obviously pregnant) was helping the Swiss girls learn English.

The ship's captain had served with Nelson at Trafalgar and he regaled them with anecdotes about distant parts of the globe. Friendly at first, he allowed the missionary party to do as they wished. Before long, however, "the offence of the cross estranged him" and "some of the passengers showed open hostility." Forbidden to hold gospel meetings, Groves and his friends went down to the lower decks, where "one young sailor, a great blasphemer though the son of godly parents, was pierced to the soul and converted." Then, to their pleasure, "at this very time, they were greatly cheered by seeing John Groves come out openly for Christ and take his stand before the scoffers." Three months later, in July 1836, they landed at Madras, carried by a small boat "with all their goods through the redoubtable surf". Brice and Kälberer stayed on board to continue up the east coast as far as Calcutta.[14]

Initially the entire party may have intended to disembark in Calcutta. Groves had been greatly encouraged on his previous visit there, and his first thought seems to have been that the whole team should settle there in Bengal. This was certainly Gundert's expectation, and as we have seen, Harriet and Emma had already started to learn Bengali.[15] It is not clear why they came ashore at Madras – perhaps because the southern Indians seemed more responsive to the gospel, perhaps because a base there would allow closer contact with Rhenius, perhaps because the Bowdens and Beers would need help settling in the Godavari Delta, or perhaps simply because Groves had heard that his Baghdad friends and his sons were in Bombay and he wished to see them before disappearing to the far end of the subcontinent.[16]

Finding somewhere to stay in Madras, they were soon delighted to welcome the Parnell family, and Edward Cronin with little Minny, and Serkies... and Harnie too, who had left her homeland to continue caring for the family. And best of all, Henry and Frank, "in good health and greatly grown", now aged seventeen and fifteen. Groves looked round happily at the circle of friends; almost the entire Baghdad team was reunited. Then in August the household was gladdened by the birth of another son, Edward, and faithful Harnie became "a watchful guardian to the dear little boy."[17]

Norris Groves was now forty-one years of age, in good health and still in the prime of life. The idea was for him to act as leader of the mission, to build up a dental practice capable of supporting the group financially, and to minister to foreign and Indian communities in English. One of the Swiss girls would earn a small income offering French tuition a few hours a day, and the others would busy themselves, for the time being, with study of the local languages.

Groves expected to renew the warm friendships established with the expatriate community two years previously. Word, however, had gone round in his absence, condemning him for his support of Rhenius against the CMS. A difficult year followed. He admitted to being "deeply wounded" by the hostility of almost the entire British community in Madras. They had begun to realise that far-reaching consequences could follow from his custom of ignoring church tradition and episcopal authority, and encouraging unauthorised laymen to act like ordained clergymen. Before long his "free, unclerical meetings" were being mocked in the drawing rooms and condemned from the pulpits.[18] After all, the twenty-third of the Church of England's Thirty-nine Articles stated in the baldest fashion, "It is not lawful for any man to take upon him the office of publick preaching, or ministering of the Sacraments in the Congregation, before he be lawfully called and sent to execute the same."

Parnell and Cronin, already inclined, each for his own reasons, to be a little unhappy with his leadership, had their confidence in Groves further shaken by this unexpected opprobrium. They had set out for India expecting to find him there on arrival. Coming ashore at Bombay they discovered he had left for England without making any arrangements for them or for his sons. Had he abandoned them completely? Was he planning to come back? If so, when? And where should they go in the meantime? They did not know what to make of it. In truth, the slowness of the mails from Baghdad had prevented Groves from knowing when they would arrive, as indeed it had prevented them from knowing he had left. But to Parnell, at least, it was a great disappointment. As for Cronin, he was an old friend of John Darby, and Darby at this juncture would have little good to say of Groves. The team seemed to be falling apart. Even before they left Baghdad, Newman's questioning mind and pedantic lack of humour had made him a somewhat uncomfortable companion, and Kitto's unhappiness with Groves's latter tendency to ignore him had cast something of a shadow on their parting. Groves himself must have been saddened by the decision of his friends to abandon the work in Baghdad. It would have brought the feeling that his best efforts and his bitterest sorrows had all been fruitless – four lives lost in three traumatic years without establishing the smallest foothold for ongoing gospel work.

The leadership of the mission was evidently under severe strain. For all that, John Parnell seemed willing enough, though struggling with personal difficulties he could not share. Always loving, always patient, cheerfully accepting every adverse circumstance as the Lord's good and perfect will, Parnell gave his energies to teaching Henry and Frank along with his wife's elder son, and began to visit friends of his family living in India. Groves hoped his own visits attending to the dental needs of British residents would break down barriers and prove his desire to be useful and helpful in contrast to the reputation he seemed to have acquired as a troublemaker. "If they merely charged you with what was true," he lamented, "you would bear it, though they made a crime of what you felt honourable; but there is an eagerness to circulate the most unfounded calumnies, and no willingness to contradict them in those who *know* them to be false. They seem to think, at all events, if it does nothing else, it will tend to sink me."[19] Though never expecting everyone to agree with him, he was surprised by the degree of hostility, and like many another sensitive spirit he began to long wistfully for some earthly Garden of Eden far from the strife of men: "My soul at times feels that if we were lodged in some vast wilderness, only seeking nearness to God, we could be so happy. It seems so hard to be conscious of desiring only the blessing of others and their liberty in Christ and yet to be esteemed a disturber of their peace."[20]

In May John Parnell decided to move with his family to Pulicat, a small coastal town to the north of Madras, a comfortable distance from all unpleasantness. Here he spent much time in prayer, looking earnestly for the way ahead. He saw no evidence that schools and medical practices could produce local churches of keen and active disciples like those described in the New Testament. Much labour and great sacrifice had evidently failed to achieve in Baghdad and in the cities of India what the apostles had accomplished so dramatically in Jerusalem, Antioch and Thessalonica. Frustrated by small results, he longed for the miraculous. Whenever Groves himself was away, Parnell came down to help in leading the small English meeting in Madras where about a dozen gathered every week round the Lord's Table – but surely the Lord wanted more for India than this.

By mid-August (1836) the Bowdens and Beers were ready to open their base in the Godavari Delta, five hundred miles to the north. Parnell offered to go with them and look for a suitable house in the main town of Masulipatam (Machilipatnam). His family background opened doors for him. Introducing his companions to the English officials there, he received a large gift for their support from the Judge and the promise of free medical care from the military doctor. For a month he was the guest of an army major and his wife, during which time they studied the Acts of the Apostles. On Sundays they remembered the Lord in the Breaking of Bread, with open worship and an extempore sermon from Parnell. These meetings continued after he left, having seen the Bowdens and Beers comfortably installed, as he travelled north to investigate the possibilities for work in Bengal.[21]

The intelligent Gundert had already set off to visit Karl Rhenius in Tinnevelly. As a fellow-German, familiar with the Lutheran and Reformed traditions, he was the ideal person to encourage and advise; he was still there more than a month later. The two who had gone to join Start in Patna, and the pair at the school and orphanage in Sonamukhi, all seemed to be adjusting happily to their new work. Serkies, converted in their home in Baghdad, had taken the gospel to every Armenian house in Madras, and to Groves's delight, "*ceased not to visit them* till he was actually turned out. May the Lord abundantly bless the lad. This one fruit of the Baghdad mission at all events is most comforting. He is now living by selling medicines and preaching."[22] In September the Swiss women and Emma opened a small boarding school for girls in Madras.[23] Edward Cronin felt the time had come to move on. In the small town of Calicut on the south-west coast, three hundred and fifty miles away, he would develop the friendships made by Groves during his first visit, and minister in English to the expatriate community. The team was obviously scattering, yet Groves was encouraged to see them gaining experience and putting down roots.

But all was not well. Barely a year later, Cronin announced he was returning to Britain with Minny. John Parnell too, with his wife and her children, was planning to leave. One writer suggests they were "disillusioned by the difficulties and discouragements".[24] Perhaps they were, but it is not certain how much they blamed Groves for this. "Dearest John Parnell...," wrote Groves, "There has not been an unkind word between us, and we part perfectly happy."[25] Less is said of Cronin. With them, in June 1837, went Serkies Davids, who hoped to study medicine in Glasgow. One of the young Swiss women was also going home on account of ill health, and the restive Gundert was talking of striking out on his own.

Bereft of the friends he had so longed for in Baghdad, and actively opposed by the Christians of Madras, Groves now had to make fresh plans for the future. Bowden and Beer were settling well in Godavari, evidently making good progress with Telugu, but nine months had passed since they received any mail from home, or any financial help. When a letter finally came it was from their main supporter to inform them of his conversion to the view that the Church is not called to preach to the heathen, for this will be the task of the Jews in the coming dispensation; he must in consequence withdraw his offer of a yearly donation.[26] Groves too had gone several months without a communication from England: "no home letter, no renewal of supplies, no tangible tokens of sympathy and prayerful interest."[27] Had all the Brethren come to the same conclusion? Had they all decided that preaching to the heathen was not the will of God?

It was a dark moment, and it was then that God "who comforts the downcast" brought them a visitor. It was George Baynes, Harriet's brother, recently "awakened to the truth".[28] He attended their family worship and went to hear Groves preach at a military camp. Feeling that the army "was not the place of the Christian's greatest usefulness", George soon resolved to resign his commission and join them. Here was the first military recruit; more were to follow. The effort Groves had put into preaching in the army chapels was evidently not in vain; soon he was approached by three other young British soldiers with a good knowledge of Indian languages. One of them, named MacCarthy, would give up a position providing him with "thirty-five rupees a month, a horse and a house, that he may do the work of God."[29] Other encouragements followed. Colonel Cotton sent news that Mokayel was on his way to Syria and Lebanon "to preach the gospel in his own country." There was word too of a friend of Serkies travelling to Persia "to preach the gospel there to his own people."[30]

But the Anglican community in Madras still refused to accept Groves and his colleagues; ministry to the expatriate circle had become quite impossible. About a hundred miles away was a town called Chittoor with no resident evangelical missionary. The team prayed for guidance and (if it be the Lord's will) for a suitable house in Chittoor. In July (1837), a month after the coronation of Queen Victoria, they found a large sprawling bungalow for sale on reasonable terms and entered into what they hoped would be a more settled period of missionary service. In September they planted several coffee trees with rows of cotton plants and began to grow their own vegetables in their own "happy valley".[31]

Chittoor was located on the border between areas speaking Telugu to the north and Tamil to the south; it would be possible there to learn both languages. The team now comprised Norris and Harriet with the boys (Henry, Frank and Edward), Hermann Gundert, George Baynes, the Swiss Julie Dubois, Emma Groves, Harnie and "seven little native children". Hearing that Groves was establishing a base in Chittoor, John Arulappan, now aged twenty-seven, asked Rhenius and his colleagues if they might let him go and help. With him came another Indian Christian called Andrew.

There followed a year of blessing. It was a long time since Norris Groves had possessed a home of his own. The fertile fields and shady trees, the surrounding hills, the quietness and the pleasant climate – it all seemed like the imaginary Garden of Eden he had longed for. Boarding schools for boys and girls were soon established, with teaching in English. Concerned also for the village children, Groves built a small room beside the bungalow beneath the shade of some tall mango trees, and before long a day-school was started with lessons in Telugu. Julie was proving to be a most reliable and devoted teacher. Gundert began to itinerate through the surrounding countryside in a bullock cart, with Andrew and another Indian Christian, distributing literature and explaining the gospel. They found many places where the local people would welcome the establishment of a primary school.[32]

In December 1840 Harriet gave birth to a second son, George (generally known as Norris). She had already started to read the Bible with a group of Indian women, and as their numbers increased some had come to a clear faith in Christ.[33] Harriet was, in her own right, a gifted Bible teacher. She was very short-sighted and relied on a monocle for reading. But though she had a great knowledge of scripture and a sound grasp of doctrine, she had no great interest in organising her household. It was Harnie who kept things going at home, looking after the two younger boys whilst Harriet spent her time preparing lessons for the school and for the Indian women.[34]

The schoolroom doubled as a chapel, and here meetings were regularly held for the small foreign community. Soon there were greater numbers joining them at the Lord's Table than there had been in Madras. A nurse attending the wife of a leading member of the English judiciary confided that "a mighty change has taken place in the family. *Then* nothing was thought of but balls and parties; *now* her only thought is how soon she may be able to go out again to attend the ministry of the Word."[35] The local circuit judges invited Groves to preach in the provincial courthouse. He also went regularly, accompanied by Henry, to address expatriate groups in the neighbouring towns of Arcot and Vellore. In these places, despite some rumbling of opposition, his visits stimulated "great searching of the scriptures," "many minds in deep exercise," and "one person I trust is truly converted to God."[36]

Norris Groves was delighted to be working closely with the young Indians Arulappan and Andrew. There was much for them to do, and Groves threw responsibility on them. They taught in the schoolroom, and once a month they set off together on a mission tour – Groves preaching with their interpretation – sleeping in tents and visiting small groups of Indian Christians further afield. In places he left them to meet with Indian believers on their own. "Until we came," he remarked, "no one but an *ordained* native was allowed to celebrate the Lord's Supper or to baptise; and when our Christian brethren Arulappan and Andrew partook of the Lord's Supper with the native Christians it caused more stir and enquiry than you can imagine. The constant reference to God's word has brought, and is bringing, the questions connected with ministry and church government into a perfectly new position in the minds of many."[37] And here, Groves believed, were the first steps towards a truly indigenous Indian church – a church free from foreign control, led by Indians, accountable to Indians.

Arulappan soaked up all the teaching and encouragement that Groves could give him. He received, at this time, a modest salary as a schoolteacher and translator of tracts and other Christian literature. But one day, while Groves was addressing the crowd and he was interpreting, a Brahman in the audience flung out the taunt that if the Englishman did not pay him he would not be preaching Christianity. Arulappan told Groves about this and then made a startling declaration: from that moment he would serve the Lord without wages of any kind. This was a turning point for Arulappan. He resolved to be known as a servant of God, and not of any man; he would not even accept a monthly gift in recognition of his translation work. This was a radical step for an Indian to take, and Groves saw it as a further stage towards a genuinely Indian church.

For a year the little farm flourished in the hands of George Baynes and Hermann Gundert, and contributed to the clothing and feeding of the hundred children now living with them. In 1838 Groves himself travelled eight or nine hundred miles during a period of three months. He visited scattered groups of English-speaking Christians, many of whom hardly ever saw a chaplain except at christenings and funerals. He was encouraged when a number started to minister to one another informally and to break bread as Jesus had commanded, even if no ordained clergyman were present.[38] From time to time word came of lies and exaggerations circulated in the foreign community. He was an extremist, people said, because he considered "Christ's life and words our only rule of life."[39] And he was disruptive, because he encouraged people to follow the Bible rather than the custom of the church. "I have had all manner of evil said against me," Groves admitted, yet "my heart has perfect repose in the thought of being rejected. I only trust I shall always be able to bear it in meekness... accepting all simply as that path in which we are to have fellowship with Jesus, who was so misunderstood and whose principles were so little appreciated even by his apostles and brethren."[40]

Of course, in the spiritual sphere, as in the worldly, it is possible to view all publicity as good publicity. A few weeks later he commented, "The strife is still going on here, some saying 'he is a good man,' others, 'nay, but he deceiveth the people.' But the Lord's work, I trust, is prospering, and religious subjects are now the common topics even in worldly society; some are very angry, others deeply interested."[41] In Chittoor itself, the leading Judge and his wife now regularly came to hear the gospel. "I do not know what errors Mr Groves may hold," said the Judge, "but this I know: that those who never looked into their Bibles before he came have learnt, by his coming, to study them."[42]

ENDNOTES

[1] M388

[2] M360. After this visit, letters from Groves appeared regularly in the printed missionary bulletins produced by the Bourg-de-Four assembly (Stunt, *Awakening*, 302).

[3] Hermann Gundert was born into a Lutheran family with strong Pietist leanings. Ironically it was whilst attending the "faith-shattering lectures" of David Friedrich Strauss at Tübingen that he came to faith in Christ in 1833 (Bromley, 15; Brecht, 136). He was greatly impressed with George Müller, who visited him in Tübingen a year later: "He puts me to the test, admonishes me, fills me with enthusiasm, and is yet another of the voices which convey to me God's compassion" (*Calwer Tagebuch*, 34, quoted by Brecht, 137). See also Gundert, ix; Müller, *Narrative*, I, 124, 127.

[4] Stunt, *Awakening*, 287n. Harriet Baynes had been left with "a deep scar down her left cheek" (Groves E K, *Successors*, 36). Harriet's great-great-grandmother, whose name is unknown, was the slave mistress of a white planter in Jamaica named John Augier (d.1722) (Livesay, Daniel, *Children of Uncertain Fortune*, Univ. N. Carolina Press, 2018). The offspring of such unions were often freed and rose to high standing in the community.

Groves's journal from Baghdad had been read with interest by the whole Baynes household. They were a socially prominent and relatively wealthy family, occupying at that time the large house at Sidmouth in which the Duke of Kent had spent his final days and in which his daughter, the future Queen Victoria, had been a small baby at the time of her father's illness and death (*Successors*, 18).

[5] *Successors*, 97. Many years later her son recalled that when worsted in theological controversy she would say, "Truly this is a grief, and I must bear it" (quoting Jer 10:19 AV; *Successors*, 268).

[6] M356

[7] At the time of his conversion, George Beer "could not probably read, at all events not write [*sic*]" (*The Missionary Reporter*, no. 8, Feb. 1854, 103). Twenty years later he was composing lengthy reports for publication.

[8] Bromley, 14-15

[9] Harriet Groves in her *Memoir* makes no reference to her brother George or to John and Sarah Groves being members of this party (M357). The reason may be that, although they travelled together, these three were not considered to be missionaries. After reaching India they seem to have gone their separate ways. A private letter dated 1840 refers to John Groves making a set of false teeth for an Indian nawab, so he evidently continued to practise dentistry, and this profession is again noted thirty-four years later in his Indian death certificate. The dental practice in Exeter had been passed on to his younger brother Edwin. George was subsequently converted and joined the mission team. After two broken engagements, Emma at the age of sixteen, married Johan Christopher Lehner, one of the pioneers of the Basel Mission in India (Gundert, 17, 32; Bromley, 15).

[10] Bromley, 17-18

[11] Bromley, 19. Hindustani: a dialect of Hindi indigenous to Delhi, spoken by most Indian Muslims and used as a common tongue by the army and by travellers throughout India.

[12] The letter is reproduced in M583ff, Coad, 291ff, Lang, *Groves*, 172ff, and Groves E K, *Conversations*, 188ff.

[13] Bromley, 20

[14] Bromley, 20-21. Brice became a self-supporting Baptist missionary and subsequently compiled *A Romanised Hindustani and English Dictionary*. Kälberer "proved a very worthy brother, eventually becoming an honoured member of the Baptist Missionary Society" (Bromley, 15).

[15] Gundert, ix; Bromley, 25.

[16] In June 1834 Calcutta had impressed Groves as an ideal base for widespread evangelism and for the promotion of practical Christian unity (M321), and this was the destination to which he invited George Müller in January of the following year (Müller, *Narrative*, I, 121). By November his current idea was to launch a mission in the Telugu-speaking area south of Masulipatam and another in the Western Ghats between Cannanore, Mangalore and Mysore (Groves to Büchelen, 30 Nov. 1835). The following March, on the point of departure from England, Calcutta was once more the place to which his mail should be addressed (Groves to Büchelen, 22 Mar. 1836). In the event, he settled in Madras. These fluid plans were typical of Groves and reminiscent of his earlier spontaneous decision, on arrival at Shushi, to make his initial base not as expected in Basra, Bushehr or Shushi itself, but in Baghdad.

[17] M365. Edward was greatly attached to his nurse, who considered Harriet quite unsuited to the task of child-raising (Groves E K, *Successors*, 38-39).

[18] Groves H, *Congleton*, 49

[19] M363

[20] M364

[21] In Bengal Parnell met Start, who returned with him to Madras. Start stayed with the team for almost two months before leaving for a brief furlough in England

(*Congleton*, 54). The subsequent work of the Bowdens and Beers is described in Chapter 27 of this book.

[22] M360

[23] The provision of education for girls was an almost unprecedented innovation. Indeed, India had seen little change since 1821 when Carey's associate William Ward wrote, "To the Hindoo female all education is denied... Not a single school for girls, therefore, all over the country!" Perhaps an even greater burden on womanhood was the custom of betrothing a girl in her infancy, especially when the boy to whom she was promised died, leaving her an infant widow: "As the law prohibits the marriage of widows, she is doomed to remain in this state as long as she lives" (Smith G, *Carey*, 73).

[24] Rowdon, *Origins*, 198. Henry Groves gave two reasons for Parnell's departure: opposition from the European community and the desire for a recovery of miraculous powers (*Congleton*, 56).

[25] M368. The subsequent careers of John Parnell and Edward Cronin are described in Chapter 22.

[26] To do him justice, it should be said that this disciple of Darby enclosed a generous sum for their passage home, or for other purposes. They used it for other purposes (Bromley, 41).

[27] Bromley, 42

[28] M359

[29] M392. It was, perhaps, ironic that a man who had left the Church of England over the issue of pacifism should subsequently spend so much time ministering to soldiers connected with the Anglican chaplaincies. Groves himself observed, "Not particular precepts only but the general spirit of the New Testament I felt to be irreconcilable with a *soldier's* duty and the whole system of warfare" (Groves, *The New Testament in the Blood of Jesus*, 11, quoted by A Minister, *The Perpetuity of the Moral Law*, 11). Although the use of violence was not an issue that Groves would raise "when first consulted by a soldier just awakened to the importance of Jesus", his expectation was that as the soldier grew in faith, "these things would all fall from him as leaves in autumn" (Groves, *Remarks on a Pamphlet*, 34).

[30] M359-360

[31] M390

[32] Gundert, 3ff. Groves had hoped to help and encourage a young and very overworked missionary, John Bilderbeck of the LMS, who had built chapels in various places including Chittoor. It was a disappointment to find Bilderbeck extremely unwelcoming. For a full account of this see Dann, *Primitivist Missiology*, 65-72.

[33] M405

[34] She printed at least one textbook in India, *Questions and Answers on Genesis* (Groves E K, *Successors*, 36, 61).

[35] M379

[36] M379. A message at this time on Ezekiel 33:30-33 produced a particularly dramatic response. He often spoke from the Old Testament: Malachi, Joshua 8, Judges 1 and 2, Numbers 11:4-9, and on the letter to the Laodicean church in Revelation 3,

showing the great difference between complacent worldly religion and "true loyalty to Christ" (M389).

[37] M393. Groves bore patiently with weaknesses evident in some of the Indian workers – selfish greed and malicious complaints in the case of one young man; caste prejudice, thieving and lying in one or two of the women. There was considerable trouble with Andrew's wife, who seemed for a time not truly converted (Gundert, 8, 9, 12, 17 etc).

[38] M393-394. For the command of Jesus see Lk 22:19; 1 Cor 11:23-26.

[39] M378

[40] M376-377. In the spring or summer of 1837 Groves had published a booklet in Madras with the title *The New Testament in the Blood of Jesus, the Sole Rule of Morals and Discipline to the Christian Church*. It met with much criticism, especially for its suggestion that the Ten Commandments are no longer binding on Christians under the new covenant and that the Lord's Day is not to be observed as the Sabbath (Gundert, 9, 10, 23). Harriet in her *Memoir* discreetly avoids all reference to this work, and no copy seems to have survived. We do possess, however, a pamphlet written against it, quoting various portions, along with Groves's reply to this pamphlet (A Minister: *The Perpetuity of the Moral Law*, and Groves, *Remarks on a Pamphlet*).

[41] M380

[42] M388

"He is reduced to a fortnight's provision of bread
but has in hand a good stock
of faith and trust."

Norris Groves (speaking of Karl Rhenius) [1]

19

How Happy I Shall Be

I n May 1838 news came from Tinnevelly: "We heard from dear Rhenius last night. He is reduced to a fortnight's provision of bread but has in hand a good stock of faith and trust." Groves commented, "I am daily more and more resolved to share my last crust with the brethren at Tinnevelly."[2] As many as 11,000 Indian Christians were now under the care of Rhenius and his colleagues. Norris Groves had played no small part in strengthening the German missionary's hand at a crucial time, and the CMS historian states quite baldly that his "breach with the Church was due to Mr Groves's influence."[3] "I do feel great thankfulness," said Groves, "for having been the instrument of keeping Rhenius in his work."[4] It came as a great shock when Rhenius, exhausted by the stresses of the past months, died later that year at the age of only forty-seven. He left Christian groups in nearly three hundred villages over an area of about two thousand square miles.[5]

Word came periodically from other workers. The Bowdens and Beers, though forced to live very economically, had recently preached and distributed tracts at an idol festival, "which shows at least," said Groves, "they have made much progress in the language."[6]

MacCarthy had settled in a Hindu village to the west. He "has marvellous strength. He is inured to the climate and can walk forty miles a day without fatigue... He goes through the Tamil and Telugu country in a little cart filled with books, tracts and things for sale, preaching the gospel to the natives in their own tongues as he passes on, and in English to all the soldiers in the military stations."[7] MacCarthy had seen two Indians converted already, and both were now active in sharing their faith.

Another recruit from the army was "a dear and devoted Christian man" by the name of Walhouse. Frank Groves, now aged twenty and an active missionary in his own right, was keen to start a coffee plantation as a basis for a self-supporting work. In July 1840 Walhouse and Arulappan went with Frank to buy a hundred acres of terraced land at Salem in the Coily Hills, about a hundred and thirty miles to the south of Chittoor. Whilst there, the two Englishmen contracted malaria. Though Frank eventually recovered, the faithful Walhouse did not.[8]

For almost a year Gundert continued to itinerate with Andrew and other Indian workers, and to teach in a school he had established in a village about two miles away. In July 1838 he and Julie Dubois married and left Chittoor to pioneer an unreached area on the south-west coast in connection with the Basel Mission.[9] This was not unexpected, but Groves found it a trial once again to face the prospect of friends and co-workers leaving. Harriet judged that "he cheerfully gave up his most valued fellow-labourers if they felt the Lord had led them to another sphere of service... He liked all with him to feel themselves the *Lord's servants*" – accountable to the Lord, not to him.[10] But it left gaps in the work at Chittoor; the school would certainly miss Julie, and George would find it hard to manage the farm on his own.[11]

Arulappan was preaching and visiting Christian groups over a wide area, and finding that Indians responded best to the gospel when they heard it from Indians – when there was no foreigner present at all. In 1840 he married a girl converted from a Hindu family in Chittoor,[12] and felt the Lord leading them to settle in the Madurai district, south of Trichinopoly (Tiruchchirappalli). Here he would start a purely Indian work. Though sorry, as always, to lose a well-loved helper, Groves did everything he could to encourage Arulappan in this step. He saw indigenous initiatives of this sort as the key to reaching India with the gospel. Two years later the young Indian had succeeded in establishing a Christian village with its own meetings for worship and its own agricultural projects enabling it to be largely self-supporting. It went by the name of Christianpettah, meaning "Christian village".[13]

Whilst still in Madras, planning their move to Chittoor, one issue had weighed particularly heavily with Groves and his colleagues. Experience had shown how difficult life became for Hindus converted to Christ. Disowned by their family and driven out of their village, in a subsistence economy where jobs with wages were scarce, they often had no means of earning their living, no chance of making a home, no prospect of marriage. The greatest need of such converts was for a house and for work. Settling in a rural area, the missionary team had hoped they might establish a farm colony where Indian Christians could live with them in peace.[14]

Norris Groves, with Arulappan's help, now prayerfully considered the options. The climate of Chittoor seemed suitable for mulberry trees, and in 1841 he decided to rent some land from the government, plant the trees and rear silkworms. The experiment was a great success. The Indian schoolboys were taught to pick the leaves and feed the larvae, the girls to spin the silk from the cocoons once they had pupated. A year later their silk had won first prize in Madras. Retired Christians began to come from other parts of India to enjoy the pleasant climate and the spiritual fellowship, and to help oversee the cottage industry. It was a happy time, with every prospect, as the farm developed, of providing work for many Indian Christians.

The time seemed right, indeed, to expand the area under mulberry trees. Out of the blue there came the offer of a loan of 30,000 rupees from a military man who had been converted through the ministry of Groves and wished to express his affectionate appreciation. To borrow money was against the principles Groves had held since his earliest days as a Christian.[15] But Harriet does not shrink from telling us that Norris, George and herself together saw this "as an indication of the mind of God in this matter; and on the strength of present appearances, as of old with regard to the Gibeonites, an agreement was entered upon. And neither party had a misgiving as to its being the *very step needed* to put the whole undertaking at Chittoor on a remunerative footing for carrying out the work of God."[16] So in 1842, with fresh funds available, the area of land was greatly increased. Groves was filled with optimistic anticipation. He obtained a large water tank on a thirty-year lease from the government, and for two months was occupied with supervising the construction of a channel two miles in length to connect the tank to the river.

It was not long, Harriet tells us, before "disease of every kind began among the worms." They tried everything they could to reduce the temperature of the buildings, but to no avail. Then other things started to go wrong. Henry arrived, after a visit to England, accompanied by a young bride. Within a few months she had succumbed to a fever and died; Henry himself, seriously ill, was fortunate to survive. George Baynes left for a brief visit to his relations in England; he never returned.[17] A talented young Brahman asked for baptism; Frank and Norris himself spent hours teaching him mathematics, history, and of course the Bible, but when his mother threatened to drown herself the youth moved to Madras. Here he rose to become interpreter to the Supreme Court – a professed atheist and one well enough instructed in the doctrines of Christianity to vilify them. Harriet wrote, "It was ever a *deep grief* to Mr Groves when he visited him in Madras to find the labour he had bestowed upon him used in the Enemy's service. These are wounds which none but a missionary's heart can fully understand."[18] Fresh efforts were made to restock the farm with silkworms, but disease struck each time. After four years, the attempts were finally abandoned.

As always, Norris Groves blamed himself, and perhaps on this occasion he was right to do so. Afterwards he attributed it, Harriet tells us, to "having been too much engrossed with the external affairs of the mission, which had hindered his enjoying his usual hours of retirement and communion with God." He confessed, "Often we are beguiled into worldly things with an idea that we can make them *subservient* to God's glory; but the things we thought would bend as a bow to shoot arrows against the enemies of God become the means of piercing us through with many sorrows and leading us away from God. Nothing requires more spiritual discernment than to *detect* the snares of the Enemy; they are often so covered over as to appear the leadings of God."

The words of Hosea seemed most apt: "You must return to your God... and wait for your God *always*."[19] Groves put his finger on the point where he felt he had gone wrong: "The prophet says, 'Wait on thy God *continually*,' and the beginning of departure is found in only waiting on God *occasionally*."[20]

Norris Groves was an excellent dentist, a skilled optical surgeon, a brilliant speaker and a wonderful friend to anyone in need, but he was not by nature, and never would be, a business man. The rate of interest he agreed to pay on the loan is not recorded, but it seems to have been unusually high.[21] How easy it is to fail at our strongest point, whether it be meekness as in the case of Moses who petulantly struck the rock, or generosity as in David who stole another man's wife, or courage as in Peter who denied his Lord. Faith, we might think, was Norris Groves's strongest point, but it was at this point he failed. "This first departure from the way of faith," said Harriet, "was, in the providence of God, followed by most bitter consequences."[22]

Groves now set to work in earnest to pay off what he owed. Rice fields and extensive coconut plantations took the place of the mulberry trees, but he no longer cultivated the land himself. He sub-let it to local farmers, Christian and Hindu. Young Edward had been sent to boarding school in England, which meant that the capable Harnie was free to take on the responsibilities of estate manager, supervising the planting of the coconut palms and dealing with the rents.[23] Then in 1846 a consignment of locally produced raw sugar was offered for sale, and Groves, sensing an opportunity to make a quick profit and thus pay off his debts at a stroke, instructed Harnie to buy it. The idea was to ship the sugar to Europe for sale, and then spend some time together as a family in England. All seemed well, and in February 1847 Harriet set off for England via the Cape with young Norris, then aged seven, expecting her husband to follow by the overland route as soon as "certain business" had been completed.[24] The sugar had just been shipped when news broke of a sudden glut in the world sugar market. Its value crashed, and instead of a quick profit the sugar made a serious loss. Groves was devastated.

The first shock gave way to the dull ache of sorrow. "I have no power to see things as I once did," he confided to Henry, "but I know, if the Lord lifts up the light of his countenance upon me, all will be well, and the brightness of eternity will extinguish the darkness of time."[25] It took him a further year in India to pick up what pieces he could. "When I think," he wrote, "on the spiritual sorrows of many past months, nay years, I feel for a moment as one awakened from a dream, to see Jesus, as I have been wont to do, walking in his *own* temple and the heart's doors are thrown *open* to him... It is like a ray from heaven, illuminating and reviving me again... There is a preciousness in Jesus that satisfies when all else fails... He and he only can fill a desolate heart."[26]

His spirits were lifted through reading the *Narrative of some of the Lord's Dealings with George Müller*, recently published by his brother-in-law, describing the creation of the orphanage in Bristol: "It is altogether a wonderful work, and God's favour seems abundantly to rest on it. I should greatly like to see it, but it will be yet more blessed to be present and share in the joy when they are crowned hereafter, if so poor and wretched a cumberer of the ground as I have been may yet share the glories of that happy day."[27] By the grace of God, Müller had achieved so much; and he, it seemed, so little.

Henry, by now a fluent Telugu speaker, was left in charge of affairs in Chittoor while his father visited the English-speaking fellowships in Madras and other towns nearby. Groves took special interest in the expatriate groups at Vellore and Arcot, and hoped to establish an ongoing outreach to the Indians there too.[28] But his mind was far away, in England. Sorely missing the comfort of his wife, and perplexed by news of strange things in the assemblies at Bristol and Plymouth, he found it difficult to sleep: "I sometimes feel sadly depressed, and truly I have reason to be so, looking back on a worse than useless life, and though I know that grace abounds, my heart is often quite devoid of joy."[29] He did his best to comfort an elderly friend: "Dear C is often very low, and I try to keep him up, but God only knows how much I myself want what I try to give him. I know how to point him to the well-springs, and he can often drink and be refreshed, when I seem to live merely to benefit others."[30]

At the age of fifty-two Norris Groves looked back on years that the locust had eaten – so much time and energy expended on commercial matters, on things that he now felt had distracted him from the higher call to care for souls. "It is much my desire," he said, "to give the rest of my short space to an uninterrupted ministry some where or in some form."[31] But what did the future hold? "I feel it hard to believe I can be of use anywhere, but I know it all hangs on the Spirit's enabling my soul to live in God... There are moments when I feel his power slumbering and ready to be awakened, so that I could preach the truth with comfort to myself and blessing to others; then again, I feel like a withered stick, like a man in a famine who is appointed to carry the bread he is never destined to taste."[32]

He visited some Christians in the hills, and one of them wrote to Harriet in England, "The first day he came up, he was so wretchedly out of spirits at not having received your letters etc. and doubtless many other things pressed on him. It was Sunday and his speaking was with *such power*! quite that of *former years* when I first heard him at Chittoor; quite strengthening and refreshing; it spoke to the *hearts* of all, and all were edified. Since he has come up, he is in better spirits, and great grace is upon him. He has had many trials and is a bruised reed. I never saw such humility in anyone. Really, to hear him speak, you would think he was quite useless in the Church, whereas no one is so beloved by all. Even the world can bring no reproach against him: so kind, tender, considerate to all, except when the truth of his Master is concerned and then he is *bold* and *earnest* in commending it."[33]

Shortly after this, Frank arrived from England, newly married and full of fresh ideas. He wanted to set up a sugar production plant near Mysore, about two hundred miles to the west. He and Henry were always intensely loyal to their father. Comforted by their sympathy and their assurance that the Lord would work everything together for good, his spirits showed some signs of reviving: "I feel so thankful for all the experiences through which the Lord has led us, and do trust we may really be the wiser and happier for it. It is such a blessing to have sons who can fully appreciate God's *principles* of acting, so that nothing appears to them in vain."[34]

But Norris Groves now had only younger men around him. Rarely can deep feelings, doubts and needs be shared with one's children or with junior colleagues, and although acquaintances of his own age might be found in the expatriate community, these were but newly awakened to the truth, and none had suffered to the extent he had. Only in England were there friends with the spiritual strength to lift him. A further reading of Müller's *Narrative* refreshed his flagging faith. How wonderful that God was providing for the orphans' needs in answer to prayer! How richly his blessing seemed to rest on the Bethesda assembly, with souls saved and drawn together in Christ! "The love of the dear ones in Bristol," confided Groves, "truly at such a time it is most consoling."[35] A longing filled his heart – to be in Bristol, to see the proof of God's faithfulness with his own eyes. But it was quite impossible to leave the business in Chittoor as it was.

Opportunity came to visit friends in various places and to preach again in the army camps. By January 1848 most of the administrative problems had been resolved, and Groves thankfully booked a passage for England. Just before leaving he enjoyed "a very happy visit" with his sons in Mysore, "delighted to be able to leave them all without a care. They seem so very happy, and everything, as far as we can see, is so promising that not a cloud appears to hang over their prospects."[36] Some of the officers from the army base in Madras gave him a loving send-off, which quite warmed his heart: "I cannot tell you the feeling of thankfulness I have, in parting with them, that we have never had a jar among us for so many years." In the back of his mind was some apprehension about issues he might face in England. Yet so many difficulties had been removed in Chittoor that he could write to Harriet, "I have every prospect of meeting you with a measure of freedom from anxiety that I have not known for years."[37]

It was an uneventful journey, in a steamer described as "a complete Noah's ark, crowded with living creatures". His spirits rose the nearer he came to the coast of England. Landing at Southampton in March (1848), he made his way to Bristol where his wife and friends were waiting for him. Happy fellowship there and at Barnstaple was followed by a trip to London to arrange some business matters. In the capital he was welcomed by a number of old friends including John Parnell (who had now succeeded to the title Lord Congleton), and he spoke in at least one of the assemblies, Orchard Street in Marylebone.

He went to see John Kitto, and found him "in altered circumstances," evidently short of money and out of favour. Wondering how best to help, Groves asked him to write a full account of his most recent misfortunes. Hearing his old Jewish friend Abrahams preach "an excellent sermon", he invited him for breakfast the following day.[38]

Groves then travelled on to other parts of southern England, and to Glasgow where he enquired about Serkies Davids. The young Armenian had completed his medical studies and to Groves's great pleasure had "left a sweet savour of Christ behind him."[39] Serkies went on to practise as a doctor in Manchester until his early death a few years later.[40]

Despite the rigours of travel, the break had done Norris Groves much good; he was sleeping better and his mind was "more tranquil". But then, returning to Bristol he found fresh controversy in the Bethesda assembly. It seemed that Benjamin Newton had propounded certain ideas in Plymouth, concerning the exact nature of the humanity and deity of Christ, to which John Darby took vehement exception. And now Müller and Craik had to endure harsh criticism for failing to support Darby's position. Groves was present during six anxious weeks while the church discussed accusations made against its leaders and against Groves himself. He was saddened by the conflict: "I always feel the very attempt to subject the one adorable Christ of God to a process of mental analysis is, in its very operation, desecrating."[41] The real need was not for a better understanding of the nature of Christ but a deeper love for him and devotion to his service. The assemblies under Darby's influence seemed to be going off at another tangent too – chopping up the Bible into teachings for the Jews and other teachings for the Gentiles, and plotting out detailed schemes for events before and after the Second Coming. "I feel we want a more practical searching ministry," commented Groves, "leaving in a subordinate place dispensational teaching, and antecedent and succeeding circumstances of our Lord's return – especially if mixed with theories that, as they are taught, may be true or false. What we want is spirituality of mind, subduedness of spirit, an ability to look on another's things [i.e. interests] rather than on our own, and power to manifest our spiritual strength by our ability to bear with weakness in others rather than by our skill in finding out faults and failings alike in persons as in systems."[42]

The year of the California gold rush and the European revolutions (1848) marked the final split in the Brethren movement between those who would follow Darby and those who would not. Shortly afterwards, Bessie Paget wrote to Norris and Harriet from Barnstaple, "I have been so broken and cast down by all that has happened to the church of late, that though my confidence in God is unshaken and my thankfulness to him for all his discipline is greater than ever, yet my heart is sick and sore… If I could see you both I would soon convince you my love is unchanged towards you, as it is to all saints, however badly they may have behaved, for they are still my Father's children and members of the same body with myself."[43]

There was little Norris Groves could do for the assemblies in Britain that others such as Müller, Parnell and Chapman were not doing, and so his thoughts turned once more to the East. It would be a relief to get away from the strife and contention. "How happy shall I be," he said, "when all our business is completed and we are on our way to India!"[44] The situation in Chittoor demanded his presence, and he had some new information that would be useful for Henry and Frank in developing their sugar works. So after just fourteen months at home, he set out once again for India, in June 1849, accompanied by Harriet and Mary Leslie, a young girl they had adopted.[45] John Parnell and other friends came to the docks to see them off. Once at sea, they arranged "daily scripture readings", through which two of the soldiers on board "were brought to the saving knowledge of Jesus."[46]

The news was all good when they eventually reached Chittoor. Almost all the administrative complications had been straightened out, and the government had finally, after a long delay, granted a new lease on the farm. Word from both Henry and Frank was encouraging. The work in Arcot had been taken up by American missionary friends and was flourishing.[47]

In February (1850) Harriet presented her husband with a baby girl, "a source of great joy to him". Childbirth was dangerous, and especially so in a hot climate with poor hygiene and many endemic diseases. In the light of past experiences, Groves had taken nothing for granted. "You know the intense relief of having all your anxieties removed," he wrote to his sister-in-law, "and all your wishes and prayers answered."[48] The little girl was given the name Agnes.

Everything continued to go well, with much interest shown in the Christian fellowship at Chittoor itself and further afield, and Groves was inspired with fresh optimism: "Indeed, when I contemplate the mountains of difficulty that, on leaving England, seemed to beset my path, and how, one by one, so many of them have passed away as a mist from the mountain, I can only wait and expect that all which remain will, in his good time, take their flight also."[49]

A special encouragement was the baptism of two Brahmans and their wives in Madras. Other Indians were coming to faith in the groups started by Bowden and Beer in the Godavari area. And further south Arulappan reported 12,000 recent conversions, making a total of 30,000 Indian Christians in his district. This was something of real significance.[50]

With Norris Groves back in harness, the English school was reopened and he resumed his teaching. One of the schoolboys, about thirteen years of age, had told his family he wanted to become a Christian. Hearing this, his parents locked him up for nearly three months, after which he took his place once more in the school. And he was not alone. Others too showed signs of "improved moral judgment" and "intelligence in the things of God". These might seem small results for the effort expended day after day in the schoolroom, but they represented, Groves believed, considerable progress among a people who had previously known nothing of the Gospel, and all the more so in view of the many hindrances – the few workers, the difficult language and the deeply engrained caste system.

Groves continued to minister to the English-speaking community in Chittoor, including a number of high-caste Indians who had learnt English and were asking questions about the Christian faith. Many of them appreciated his weekly lectures on the book of Acts, highlighting the principles followed in the earliest Christian communities. Altogether it was a time of encouragement, especially as Groves could see his sons' sugar industries near Mysore prospering so well.

It all came to an end with the death of one of his closest friends, the chief Judge.[51] A number of new British residents did not like his informal ministry; they preferred to read some prayers and a printed sermon. A new civil authority was appointed; fresh arrangements were made for the Anglican community of Chittoor. Though Harriet was still happy enough teaching in the school, Norris began to feel his work there was drawing to a close. He had spent the past eighteen years in India, apart from two brief trips to England. "My own heart has often turned towards home," he confessed, "and I wait the Lord's leisure to show me the way and the when."[52]

ENDNOTES

[1] M389

[2] Lang, *Aroolappen*, 20; M389

[3] Stock I, 283. In fact Groves made some attempt to reconcile Rhenius with the CMS at a time when Gundert was encouraging him to act independently (Brecht, 139-140).

[4] M331

[5] M389. For two years the future of the churches remained uncertain but all were ultimately taken over by the CMS. The Anglican Church eventually paid Rhenius a generous but rather paradoxical tribute: "To him we owe the practice that in 700 villages in the Tirunelveli diocese the bell rings every evening to call the Christians together for Evensong" (Neill, *India and Pakistan*, 70). The bell might possibly be credited to Rhenius, but not the Evensong.

[6] M383

[7] M392

[8] M543-548

[9] M372, 378. After a short time in Tillicherry, where Groves had earlier found "forty converts without any shepherd", the Gunderts settled in Cannanore, where there were more than a million souls with "a most willing ear... and not a soul to teach them" (M239). In the course of twenty-three years, Dr Gundert subsequently translated a Malayalam Bible, edited a Malayalam periodical, wrote several theological works and various tracts in Malayalam and Tamil, and became known as an expert in the language, culture and history of Kerala province. A grandson of the Gunderts was the poet and novelist Hermann Hesse, Nobel Prize winner for literature in 1946, who expressed great admiration for his grandfather: "the old, the venerable, the mighty, white-bearded, omniscient... I loved, admired and feared him. I expected everything of him, I believed him capable of everything. I never stopped learning from him" (Hermann Hesse, *Kindheit des Zauberers*, Frankfurt/M, 1974, 99f).

[10] M371

[11] It is clear from Gundert's diaries that there had been considerable friction from the start between himself and Harriet. No doubt their cultural backgrounds had much to do with this. She was from a socially prominent English family, brought up to be gracious, courteous and discreet, avoiding unpleasantness at all costs. Gundert's Germanic tendency to speak bluntly and directly (*geradezu*) would seem to her grossly offensive. Even worse would be his willingness to attribute dubious motives and bad character to other Christians. He may have had some justification in considering Harriet dictatorial and possessive in her relations with Indian believers and other missionaries, but any young tutor in England sufficiently ill-mannered to tell the lady of the house such a thing to her face should expect to find his employment terminated forthwith, and in fact Gundert was very quickly deprived of his role as tutor.

Groves did his utmost to ease the tensions and to act as a mediator but it is evident that Gundert's initial respect for him was tinged after two years together by feelings of considerable frustration. The two men were of widely differing temperaments. Where Groves was gentle, thoughtful, sensitive, slow to make decisions and prone to change his plans, Gundert was decisive, efficient and extremely forthright. He found it hard to understand why Groves should be so often and so deeply hurt by his frank speaking. Gundert, aged twenty-four in 1838, was an undoubted genius when it came to foreign languages, whereas Groves, who never found languages easy, had reached a time of life, at the age of forty-three, when the acquisition of new languages becomes increasingly difficult. He had made a start in Hindustani but then thought he should switch to Telugu, then to Tamil, and finally found himself so occupied with ministry in English that Indian languages ceased to figure among his personal priorities. Gundert found this hard to understand. Nevertheless, the two men parted on good terms and kept in periodic contact. After leaving Chittoor, Gundert followed Groves's example in attempting to form Indian churches independent of episcopal and governmental control, and he followed the progress of the Brethren movement with interest. In later life he was appointed head of a Pietist publishing house in Germany. His son David was described in 1869 as being "Plymouth Brethren minded" (Gundert, 24, 33; M378; Brecht, 139-140, 148).

[12] Rajamani, 140

[13] Arulappan's story continues in Chapter 27. Groves's mature reflections on the appointment and support of missionaries were published at this time as "A Letter on Missions to the Heathen" in *The Christian Witness*, April 1840. His ideas are discussed in Chapter 31.

[14] The caste system probably made conversion to Christianity more difficult for the majority of Indians than for any other people in the world. All social relationships were determined by the caste one was born into. To renounce Hinduism would mean becoming an "outcaste", no longer able to relate on terms of equality even to one's own parents and siblings. "No Christian could continue to live in a Hindu village; his wife, if she consented to remain with him, would not be allowed to draw water from the village well, and he and his family would have no part in the communal enterprises of the village" (Neill, *India and Pakistan*, 80). In a strongly communal society younger family members would not be authorized to think for themselves or to claim freedom to worship in a different fashion from the rest of the family. If necessary, they would be compelled to conform – by a severe beating from father or brothers, by the threat of a mother to kill herself, or by being drugged, kidnapped and taken away to a distant part of the country. A solitary outcaste trying to settle in another village would be suspected as a probable criminal on the run; some dire reason must account for his having no family, no friends, no roots. Missionaries often sheltered new converts for their own safety, taking them into their own homes; those not sheltered in this way frequently disappeared. The difficulties faced by Indian Christian converts trying to earn their living are well described by Clark, 259-263.

[15] See for example R305.

[16] M397; Groves E K, *Successors*, 228. George Baynes had frequently borrowed money in the past (Bromley, 15). For the Gibeonites see Joshua 9. The custom of contracted loans had been introduced and long practised by the East India Company. Company agents would advance money to contractors, who then invested in local production of cotton, indigo, silk and opium. The contractor would promise an agreed return to the Company and bear all the risk should the crop fail (Smith G, *Carey*, 91-92).

[17] Like the rest of the Baynes family, George joined the Exclusive Brethren after the split of 1848 (Groves E K, *Successors*, 19).

[18] M399

[19] Hos 12:6

[20] M403-404

[21] On this subject William Carey's biographer remarks, "There is one evil which Carey never ceased to point out… 'the borrowing system of the natives'. While 12% is the so called legal rate of interest, it is never below 36%, and frequently rises to 72%." Carey's solution was to encourage the practice of saving, and he was a prime mover in the introduction of savings banks to India (Smith G, *Carey*, 323-324). The failure of the Indian banks in 1830-33 was largely due to "the rottenness of the system of credit on which commerce and banking were at that time conducted" (Smith G, *Carey*, 412).

[22] M397

[23] Harnie was a remarkable woman and made it her business to see that Groves was not cheated. Once during the siege of Baghdad she had crept into a robber's house at night to retrieve a stolen rug, and here in Chittoor, hearing a thief on the flat roof at midnight, quietly went upstairs, made the man come down with his basket of stolen grain, then tied him to a tree with the basket in front of him till morning (Groves H, *Faithful Hanie*, 30-31; Groves E K, *Successors*, 38).

[24] M412

[25] M413

[26] M414-415

[27] M442

[28] M519

[29] M448

[30] M449

[31] M421

[32] M440

[33] M437

[34] M458

[35] M449

[36] M454

[37] M457

[38] M460

[39] M461

[40] Harriet mentions this in the first edition of her *Memoir* (Sentinel, 255). Henry Groves recalled the conversion of Serkies in Baghdad: "It is truly refreshing to look back on these desolating scenes and to feel that in the bringing to God of that one beloved disciple of the Lord, even if no other end was attained, there was a 'needs be' that my father's steps should have been directed to Baghdad, as when it is said of our blessed Master that 'he must needs go through Samaria' where he was to meet the poor woman at the well of Sychar who found in him the well-springs of eternal life" (M214).

[41] M464

[42] M460-461

[43] M563

[44] M461

[45] Mary Leslie was the illegitimate daughter of a British officer by a Burmese mother. In 1842, at the age of eight, she had been entrusted to their care by her father on his deathbed. She became a devoted Christian worker at Chittoor and an affectionate daughter to Harriet and Norris Groves. She wrote him a long devotional poem for his comfort during his final illness, and another after his death entitled "A Tribute to the Memory of a beloved Father by his adopted Child". In 1865 she married an Anglican clergyman and went to live in Australia (D12; M400, 472, 521; Groves E K, *Successors*, 39).

[46] M465

[47] Harriet recalled, "It was a source of great comfort to him, when he returned to India for the last time, to find that Arcot had been effectually taken up by Dr Henry Scudder, the eldest son of his much esteemed friend, the late Dr Scudder" (M519).

[48] M465

[49] M466

[50] M467

[51] Mr Lovell, the session judge at Chittoor, died on 1st September 1851 (M471).

[52] M468

"Missionaries in these countries
have need of a very simple faith,
which can glory in God's will being done
though all their plans come to nothing."

Norris Groves [1]

20

He Knows What Is Right

Towards the end of 1851 Norris Groves visited Madras and while there was taken ill. "He had the most distressing pains after any exertion, or frequently after taking food." This was the first time his health had suffered a major breakdown during all his years in India – certainly the first occasion it had stopped him preaching and teaching. Harriet tells us that "a severe domestic affliction at this time greatly aggravated his illness, and he became *very* thin."[2] We do not know what this "domestic affliction" was.

A period of rest with his sons in Mysore brought no relief, and after "very severe attacks of pain" throughout January 1852, a return to England was recommended as the only hope for a full recovery. It was midsummer before his affairs were finally wound up amidst increasing weakness, and after much prayer with his family, and many tears from his Indian friends, he bumped down the stony track from Chittoor for the last time. Leaving Harriet to look after the school, he headed for the coast at Madras, accompanied by Frank's young wife whose health also required a change of air. On 14th August 1852 they boarded a steamer for England.

Six weeks later the ship docked at Southampton. It was the year after the Great Exhibition in London, where a fantastic array of exhibits from every part of the British Empire had been displayed in the Crystal Palace before the gaze of a wondering public, none more affected than Queen Victoria herself.

Once on shore, Groves caught a coach to Bristol. He was strong enough to speak several times at Bethesda and other places nearby. In fact his health seemed somewhat improved. Delighted to see his younger sons, he took Edward (now aged sixteen) to London, where plans were made for him to finish his education. After settling some business matters, Groves was welcomed to dinner by his old friend John Parnell (Lord Congleton) and enjoyed fellowship with the Orchard Street assembly in Marylebone. Though eating very little, he kept quite busy, and seemed at times considerably stronger despite the pain that came after any exertion. A middle-aged couple wished to see him. They had previously met in Bengal during his earliest travels in India, and now told him they had been "brought to the knowledge of the truth" through his teaching at that time. Groves confided, "There was something very refreshing in finding that seed sown so many years ago had still continued germinating."[3] He heard of others, blessed through his ministry in India, now actively involved in local assemblies in many parts of Britain.

In the Brook Street assembly at Tottenham an opportunity arose for him to speak about a matter that had long troubled him. Workers such as the Bowdens and Beers were not being adequately supported by their home church – in fact they were almost starving – and national evangelists like Arulappan were labouring with inadequate resources, all unknown to Christians in Britain who might wish to help. The assemblies everywhere seemed taken up with work at home to the detriment of work abroad. The call of the Great Commission, so inspiring to the earliest groups in Dublin and in Devonshire, seemed to have fallen by the wayside. Indeed, during the past fifteen years hardly any missionaries had been sent out by the assemblies, and with the honourable exception of the level-headed George Müller, no one seemed to have any systematic plan to support workers who might feel called to go.[4]

The failure could be attributed partly to a preoccupation with doctrinal matters, partly to a general prejudice against all forms of organisation, partly to the idea promulgated by Darby that the Great Commission would be fulfilled by the Jews in a coming dispensation, and partly in some cases to an extreme Calvinism that left the conversion of the heathen entirely in the hands of God.[5] But the concern raised by Groves struck a chord with the saints at Tottenham. As they prayed they became convinced that the time had come to establish more effective ways of supporting workers overseas and of encouraging others to follow the apostolic example. Groves was delighted to see such a positive response. He confided, in a letter to Harriet, "I went to Tottenham and… endeavoured to interest them about missions, spoke of Bowden, Beer and Arulappan, and in the evening brought the subject before the church, and they hope, in union with believers in Hackney, Orchard Street, and other places to form an effectual committee to care for these things. This has been a great comfort to me. I live in hope that the Lord will yet let his goodness shine upon us and round about us and deliver us from every trial… I feel thankful I came home; many things have been accomplished by it… I am not well, but I have none of that *violent* pain I had for months in India; it hardly now amounts to more than being *very* uncomfortable."[6] Whilst in London, he was advised by two medical men to adopt a "milk diet", which they hoped would ease the discomfort in his stomach.

Returning to Bristol, he was thrilled to observe all the activity in the orphan house, and to see the Müller family – always busy, always prayerful, always caring for the needs of the little ones – "the untiring devotion to it of dear George and Mary, and Lydia, walking there and back every day, and working there all day long. They seem so to love the children."[7] But his digestion was no better: "I cannot eat anything, and if I do, I suffer hours of uneasiness after it."[8]

On 1st February he celebrated his fifty-eighth birthday, and a week later attended the funeral of Harriet's mother in Sidmouth. The old lady had suffered many years of ill health, but now, gazing on her face, "all spoke of peace, perfect everlasting peace."[9] How they would miss "the charm of her sweet harmonising manner".[10] It was a sad loss. Yet for Norris and Harriet the death of Mrs Baynes marked a turning point, for she left a considerable sum of money to her daughter. And it paid off all the remaining debts.[11]

Towards the end of April, free from pain, he wrote cheerfully to Harriet, still in India and still teaching at the school in Chittoor, "The Lord fills my heart with holy joy and confidence. I do not feel an anxiety about the future; all seems bright and full of promise."[12] His health, if anything, seemed to be improving, and he hoped he might soon be well enough to rejoin her. Gone was the deep depression, gone the burdened sense of failure, the struggle with anxiety. Norris Groves had entered the final phase of his life: three months of increasing physical weakness but of exalted and untarnished spiritual joy. "The Lord be praised," he said, "I can truly say he lets me see brightness on every side from his love. I look through the cracks in my clay tabernacle up towards the everlasting hills and have now just concluded all those little earthly cares that must be attended to; I only think on my precious ones and glory."[13] The physicians declared him a dying man. This troubled him not at all, though he sent word to Harriet and money sufficient for her ticket to England.

He went to stay with friends in Malvern, a young couple who had been helped through his ministry in Chittoor. His hostess later wrote to Harriet, "It made my heart ache to see him eating so little – and so patient, always rejoicing in the Lord, some little song of praise for ever on his lips that so much had been smoothed for him. I used to love to hear him speak of the Lord's dealings with him since his marriage and residence in India."[14] Morphine brought considerable relief from the chest spasms that came every few hours, but he was reluctant to take it and for a while refused it altogether. "Precious Harriet," he said. "If it were his will, I should like to meet her again, but he knows what is right."[15]

His thoughts turned once more to Bristol, and his final journey was to the home of George and Mary Müller – *his* home he called it, and the only home he possessed in England.[16] "Such a beautiful day," he said, pleased to be sitting once more in the familiar armchair surrounded by those he loved. Henry Craik happened to call at that moment, and hearing his voice Groves asked to see him. "Then they spoke a few minutes to each other, both their countenances beaming with heavenly peace." Groves suggested that they pray together, and George Müller "offered a short prayer of earnest supplication and heartfelt thankfulness that we had been permitted to meet once more."[17]

Next day Müller helped him arrange his legal affairs while his three sisters and his niece Lydia did all they could for his comfort, "one fanning, another bathing his temples with iced water" and a third bringing a little water or tea to wash out his mouth. "Of every little service rendered to him, he spoke with so much gratitude."[18] He could drink nothing, and at times coughed up quantities of bloody matter. So severe were the spasms of pain that they fully expected him to pass away at any moment. Yet periods of quiet sleep seemed to bring relief and fresh strength. "How precious it is," he said, "to feel that all these human ills are, to the redeemed of the Lord, what the chariots of fire were to Elijah – alarming to look at, but the Father's way of bringing his own home."[19]

For ten days he remained weak but lucid, and relatively free from discomfort, asking to see some members of the Bethesda assembly. George Müller later wrote to comfort Harriet, "He was during those ten days in a most blessed frame of mind. It was truly refreshing to be with him... He was able to cast every burden on God."[20]

Three days before his death he had several visitors. "I went to speak to him," one of them said, "but I stayed to listen to him. I went to give, but I stayed to receive. I went to cheer him, but I stayed to gather comfort and encouragement... It was blessed indeed to hear him speak of Jesus. His emaciated frame, his bodily weakness, his consciousness of the nearness of eternity made more real the power of redemption."[21]

With his voice now reduced to a whisper, he gave Edward a parting blessing. He spoke kindly to young Norris, and affectionately mentioned his other children and Harriet, glad she had been spared the sorrow of these distressing scenes. "My precious wife," he said. "She has been truly a gift of God to me." There was a "sweet smile on his dear face and a beaming heavenly expression."[22] Gone were the doubts, the worries, the regrets, the weight of worldly responsibilities, the pain of discord among brothers, all swept away in the joy of the Lord. "It is a wonderful thing," he said, "to come nigh to God – *a wonderful thing.*"[23] Then, "Pray that the face of my precious Jesus may shine brightly on me at the closing scene; that when my eyes no longer see your dear faces, they may see that bright face which is dearer still, and hear him say, 'Well done' – wonderful! – 'Well done,' and *to me* who never did anything well."[24] A little later, "My sweet sisters, you are watching and waiting to see me depart. I shall be watching and waiting, not to see you depart, but to welcome you into the presence of Jesus."[25]

With his weakness increasing, George Müller stayed at his bedside when not called away by the needs of the orphans. Promises from the word of God brought comfort, as did lines from some well-loved hymns. Müller prayed that the Lord would quickly release the sufferer. Exhausted and emaciated, his heart continued to beat. Half an hour before midnight Müller had just left the room to snatch some sleep when Groves whispered, "Precious Jesus," and then, in Lydia Müller's words, "Leaning his head on his hand, he sweetly fell asleep in Jesus."[26]

ENDNOTES

[1] R128

[2] M471

[3] M480

[4] As early as 1834 Müller had set up his Scriptural Knowledge Institution for Home and Abroad, which had as one of its objectives "to aid missionary efforts". Initially Müller had little to send, but four years later he was receiving substantial sums to be forwarded at his discretion to workers overseas (Rowdon, *Origins*, 202).

[5] Darby's ideas are discussed in Chapter 21 of this book. On contemporary Calvinistic views of mission see Appendix i.

[6] M481

[7] M482. Mary Müller was, of course, his younger sister. Her nephew later remarked of her, "It is hardly possible to describe the intensity of affection with which she was regarded by matrons, teachers and children. In character she formed the exact complement of her husband and supplied the gentleness and sympathy which he did not possess" (Groves E K, *Successors*, 30).

[8] M484

[9] M485

[10] M483

[11] The £4000 still outstanding at his death would be cleared by the sale of the Chittoor property shortly afterwards (*Successors*, 18; M519).

[12] M487

[13] M489

[14] M488

[15] M488

[16] Müller's home at 21 Paul Street, Kingsdown, was an end of terrace house, "solid but not beautiful". Nine steps led up to the front door and there were four storeys in all. At the back of the house was a small garden. The neighbourhood had been fashionable during the previous century but had since become "a little scruffy" (Steer, 53).

[17] M496

[18] M497. The sisters were Mary (b.1800), Eliza (b.1803) and Lydia (b.1805). The description is from the pen of his niece Lydia Müller, daughter of Mary.

[19] M489

[20] M492

[21] M507

[22] M497-498

[23] M503

[24] M504

[25] M505

[26] M501. He died, aged 58 years, from cancer of the stomach on 20th May 1853. Harriet, Harnie, Agnes (aged 3) and their adopted daughter Mary Leslie (aged 19) reached England three months later, not knowing, until they landed, that he was gone (M513).

Harnie, who had refused to wear mourning so long as her master lived, refused to wear anything else after his death. In his will Groves gratefully recorded that "for more than twenty five years she has served me with her whole heart without hire or reward." Harnie herself passed away in 1865 and lies buried with her adopted family in Arno's Vale, Bristol (Groves E K, *Successors*, 39).

"Seeing thou wert here to save and sanctify,
I felt it safe to be with thee."

Norris Groves [1]

21

A Ruffler of Feathers

Norris Groves was gone, but in England and Ireland the ripples continued to spread. His ideas had taken on a life of their own. As early as 1827 he had proposed in Dublin "that believers, meeting together as disciples of Christ, were free to break bread together as their Lord had admonished them; and that in as far as the practice of the apostles could be a guide, every Lord's Day should be set apart for thus remembering the Lord's death and obeying his parting command."[2] Twenty-five years later, small groups meeting for this very purpose were found scattered throughout many parts of the British Isles. As they became aware of one another, gifted teachers began to travel from one to another, and informal links developed between them. The Brethren movement was under way.

These groups were determined to get back to first principles. In the New Testament they saw how the apostles of Christ had been led by the Spirit of God, and they noted the wonderful results that followed. The vision before them was simply to follow the apostolic example as closely as they could. Some members of these groups wrote about their early experiences. One, converted as a boy in Plymouth in 1843, recalled, "I was soon afterwards brought into fellowship with those who, I learnt, assembled upon principles taught in the word of God, where no sectarian wall of division was acknowledged and where there was the liberty of the Spirit of God to minister the truths of scripture by those who were gifted by him for that purpose... The meetings of the assembly were calm, peaceful and hallowed; their singing was soft, slow and thoughtful; their worship evinced the nearness of their communion with the Lord; their prayers were earnest for an increased knowledge of God and for the spread of his truth. Their teaching showed their deep searching of the scriptures under the guidance of the Holy Spirit, while the exercise of the varied ministry, under the power of the Spirit, testified to the blessedness of the teaching of God's word on each important subject... Those were delightful times, so sweet for their simplicity." It was "holy loving fellowship" and everything was "happiness and peace". Yet destined not to last: "It was too fair a scene for Satan to contemplate, and he must by some means mar its beauties and devastate its loveliness."[3]

The man who did most to draw these scattered groups together, and who then contrived to shatter them in pieces, was John Nelson Darby. For fifty years he wrote, travelled, preached and organised indefatigably. His personal energy, his earnest sincerity, his charismatic power and his administrative genius compare with none but John Wesley's. He was a wonderful pastor and counsellor, and an inspiring speaker. He was a man of one Book, and every word of it was the truth, every word to be believed, every word obeyed. Whatever the question, he seemed to have an answer that came straight from heaven. The young Frank Newman, for one, was awestruck: "For the first time in my life, I found myself under the dominion of a superior... I began to ask, 'What will *he* say to this and that?' In *his* reply I always expected to find a higher portion of God's Spirit than in any I could frame for myself. In order to learn divine truth it became to me a surer process to consult him than to search for myself and wait upon God."[4]

Darby was five years older than Newman, and five years younger than Norris Groves. In the early days he had been an occasional visitor to the group meeting with Bellett and his friends in Dublin – a keen young Anglican curate with an interest in prophecy – but he soon became a leading participant in a series of conferences arranged by Lady Powerscourt in the years 1831-3.[5] It was not until 1834 that he finally seceded from the Church of England. As time passed, Darby's brilliant mind began to develop theories that carried him in a direction of his own, and his assertive personality demanded that he carry others with him.

In its final form, his conception of Christian unity was the complete opposite to that proposed from the beginning by Groves. Darby could no longer conceive of a "mystical body" comprising Christians from diverse denominations. The Church, he argued, as seen in the New Testament, was a united, organised, visible society under the authority of the apostles. But where can such a Church be found today? As an Anglican he had initially equated "the Church" with the Church of England and Ireland, but wider experience had shown him that real Christians were found among the Dissenters too. Where then was the true Church, the Church founded by the apostles? Confusions, corruptions and discord had, he believed, destroyed the apostolic Church. It no longer existed. In its place had arisen a Roman Catholic Church, an Anglican Church and many Nonconformist churches. This represented a condition of hopeless apostasy: the Church is fallen, corrupt, ruined. And if the Church is apostate, it stands under the judgment of God. To attempt to build up and repair what God has seen fit to condemn and destroy would be both presumptuous and futile. Therefore, concluded Darby, all who are true Christians must "come out and be separate", and prepare themselves as a holy remnant for the Lord's imminent return. The assemblies that followed Darby were not churches; they were "testimonies", railing *against* the Church and against those who remained in it. And because they were not churches, they should not appoint elders or deacons; they should not prepare any ministry of the Word; they should not send out missionaries; they should simply wait on the Lord for the fulfilment of the Bible prophecies relating to the End Times.[6]

On his early visits to Dublin, Norris Groves had met Darby several times and had found him a kindred spirit – self-denying, an ardent student of the scriptures, preaching the gospel among the poor. But what he had heard of Darby since then troubled him. Groves could not agree with his negative view of the Church. Even in New Testament times there had been faults and failings, divisions and separations among the people of God, but nowhere did the apostles speak of the church as "fallen" or "ruined" or "apostate". In Corinth some preferred Paul, some Cephas, some Apollos, and party-spirit of this nature was rebuked, but its presence did not mean that the judgment of God lay irrevocably on the whole Church throughout the whole world. Was Darby demanding more than the apostles themselves? "If, in the early ages of the church (allowed by all to be the purest) it was so defiled, what ground have *we* to expect greater power and greater purity?" asked Groves.[7]

In 1834 Norris Groves was in India when he received a letter from Darby expounding his views. In reply he felt it right to share his own thoughts "on the principles of union and communion in the Church of Christ."[8] Our life on earth, he observed, is a temporary state preparing us for the perfection of heaven. "Does it not then appear clear that the nearer the principles of the communion of the church on earth assimilate [i.e. become similar] to those which must finally prevail in the kingdom of heaven, the more perfect they must be?" Here is the key, Groves thought, to Christian unity. "Then what are these principles of heavenly communion?" Unity in heaven will not be a result of intellectual agreement on matters of doctrine or church practice; it will be a unity of love embracing all who belong to Christ. And if this is the basis of unity in heaven, should it not be the basis of unity on earth? "*Loving all whom Christ loves* because they bear his impress; let this same rule then decide the question as to the subjects of our communion here on earth: all whom Christ loves, who bear his impress, or whom we ourselves acknowledge as Christians." We may be aware of errors in the doctrine or practice of other believers, but Christ himself is aware of those errors and has never made that a reason for denying them his love. "So long as we judge Christ to be dwelling with a man, that is our warrant for receiving him… and as to his errors, though we bear them weeping, still we must bear them."

But how does this relate to personal involvement in a local church? Although we love all, we cannot worship at any one time with all. Every Christian, then, must find a company with whom to meet regularly. "The first duty to ourselves is in selecting the congregation with whom we should stately worship. It should be where the form is most scriptural, in our persuasion, and the ministrations most spiritual; where there is the sweetest savour of Christ; where our own souls are most edified; where the Lord is most manifestly present with those who minister and those who hear. This is what we owe the Lord, the Church of God, and our own souls." But our commitment to one group of Christians will never separate us from others or require us to shun them. "If my Lord should say to me in any congregation of the almost unnumbered sections of the Church, 'What dost thou here?' I would reply, 'Seeing thou wert here to save and sanctify, I felt it safe to be with thee.' If he again said, as perhaps he may among most of us, 'Didst thou not see abominations here, an admixture of that which was unscriptural, and the absence of that which was scriptural, and in some points error, at least in your judgment?' my answer would be, 'Yea, Lord, but I dared not call that place unholy where thou wert present to bless, nor by refusing communion in worship reject those as unholy whom thou hadst by thy saving power evidently sanctified and set apart for thine own.'"[9]

Visiting England the following year (1835-6), Norris Groves found Darby's views prevailing in many places, and among some of his own closest friends. Waiting at Milford Haven for a ship to India, he had time to consider the matter further. It was a providential moment, an opportunity to gather his thoughts in a second letter that remains a classic of tact and persuasion.[10] He starts by emphasizing the principles they had in common at the beginning and gently reproaches Darby with forsaking those principles, "returning to the city from whence you departed." In the early days they had shared a vision for free, informal, spiritual fellowship, uniting true disciples of Christ from any church or denomination, demonstrating the oneness of his Body that transcended the boundaries of human institutions: "I ever understood our principle of communion to be the possession of the common life or common blood of the family of God (for the life is in the blood); these were our early thoughts, and are my most matured ones. The transition your little bodies have undergone, in no longer standing forth the witnesses for the glorious and simple *truth*, so much as standing forth witnesses against all that they judge error, have lowered them in my apprehension from heaven to earth." Darby and his followers had slipped, all too evidently, from love to animosity, from tolerance to condemnation; and their relations with other Christians were marked no longer by a desire to draw them further into the light but rather to consign them more decidedly into darkness. The result of this, Groves feared, would be that "every individual or society of individuals first comes before the mind as those who might need witnessing against, and all their conduct and principles have first to be examined and approved before they can be received. And the position which this occupying the seat of judgment will place you in will be this: the most narrow-minded and bigoted will rule, because his conscience cannot and will not give way… It is into this position, dear Darby, I feel some little flocks are fast tending, if they have not already attained it."

This was plain speaking, and Groves's advice, if followed, might have saved many "little flocks" much pain.

And yet there were undoubted difficulties faced by an individual trying to co-operate with churches that showed no desire to follow the pattern of scripture. Does not our own walk with the Lord require our separation from all we know to be wrong? Not so, argued Groves. Separation would be justified only "so far as they required us to do what our consciences would not allow, or restrained us from doing what our consciences required." If Christians around us do not do exactly as we might wish, we should be content to "follow the apostolic rule of *not judging other men's consciences*", remembering that it is written, "The man who eats everything must not look down on him who does not, and the man who does not eat everything must not condemn the man who does, for God has accepted him."[11] And however misguided a church may be, if there are true disciples of Christ in it, then they are our brothers and sisters, and "I would infinitely rather bear with all their evils than separate from their good."[12]

But would not simple souls, seeing us in a place where error is upheld, be liable to stumble, assuming we approved all that was taught and practised there? And for this reason should we not avoid such places? Groves thought not: "I feel no one ever expects me, when an acknowledged *visitor* in the house of another, to be answerable for the ordering of that house, or as thereby *approving* it. They would naturally come to the house in which *I* had control, and where the acts were looked upon as *mine*, to form such a judgment. And even in such a case, if I was but *one* among many in the government, no honest mind would make *me* responsible for faults, against which in my place and according to my power I protested, because I submitted to those acts in others rather than forgo a *greater* good or incur a greater evil... Some will not have me hold communion with the Scotts because their views are not satisfactory about the Lord's Supper;[13] others with you because of your views about baptism;[14] others with the Church of England because of her thoughts about ministry. On my principles I receive them all... I make use of my fellowship in the Spirit to enjoy the common life together." Indeed, much good may come from this fellowship: opportunities will no doubt arise to speak the truth in love concerning matters that others may never have considered in the full light of God's word. And Groves concludes, "I naturally unite fixedly with those in whom I see and feel most of the life and power of God. But I am as free to visit other churches, where I see much of disorder, as to visit the houses of my friends, though they govern them not as I could wish. And as I have said, I should feel it equally unreasonable and unkind for any brother to judge me for it."

There is no record of Darby's response to this plea, or of any reply sent by him to India, and there is no indication that he modified his views as a result of it. His principles matched his character, as indeed did Groves's, and though Darby carried many with him at the time, the verdict of history maintains that Groves had the right of it. A growing stream of non-denominational and inter-denominational conferences, colleges, societies and missions, from the mid-nineteenth century to the present day, provides ample proof of that.[15]

Darby had already ruffled feathers in Ireland and stirred up the nest in Plymouth when he set off for Switzerland in 1837. He visited the assemblies which had earlier provided Groves with missionary recruits, including that at Bourg-de-Four in Geneva. He then succeeded in drawing a circle of Methodist churches under his wing with dazzling expositions of prophetic scriptures and damning critiques of their Arminian and holiness doctrines. Subsequent visits provided him with opportunities to make known his distinctive views on the apostasy and ruin of the Church, and in 1842 he was the cause of a major division in the Swiss assemblies.[16]

Revisiting Plymouth in 1845, Darby's jealousy of Benjamin Newton's influence came to a head. Finding fault with his prophetic and Christological interpretations, he condemned Newton and all associated with him, and left with a number of his supporters to start a separate Plymouth assembly of his own. Shortly afterwards he heard that three who remained loyal to Newton had visited Bethesda, the church in Bristol led by Müller and Craik, and had been received at the Lord's Table. Darby was furious. His friend George Wigram travelled personally to Bristol, and tried to accomplish there what Darby had achieved in Plymouth. He failed. Darby himself went twice, with the same result. It was August 1848. Darby and Wigram now declared they would have no further fellowship with Craik or Müller or anyone else associated with Bethesda. The Tottenham assembly was repudiated on the same grounds, because of the welcome it had given Groves.

About this time Wigram published in London what Groves calls "the most false and slanderous charges against our brother Craik".[17] The scholarly Scot was accused of saying something heretical about the nature of Christ to a lady member of his own church. Groves was then present for the "six weeks anxious enquiry" which ensued, during which it was found that the lady could not remember exactly what had been said. But the rift was irreparable. Darby's pronouncements had fragmented that group of friends who first met twenty years previously around the Table of the Lord in Dublin. John Parnell (Lord Congleton) rebuked Darby for his divisive interventions, and eventually broke off relations with him.[18] Edward Cronin supported Darby, ending his friendship with Parnell and with Groves. Percy Hall at first backed Darby, then later changed his mind. John Bellett, still in Dublin, followed Darby but with profound misgivings.[19] The gifted Newton himself, after repeated attempts to restore unity, went his own way and had no further connection with the Brethren.

Not satisfied with this, Darby continued to rage against his former friends. In 1864 he wrote, "The evil at Bethesda is the most unprincipled admission of blasphemers against Christ, the coldest contempt for him I ever came across."[20] This was an astonishing assertion. An early historian of the movement comments, "Now this statement was not merely an incalculable exaggeration; it was absolutely false, root and branch, and an excellent instance of smoke without fire... But statements of this kind were taken on trust by persons who only knew that Darby had been the most potent force in their spiritual development, and saw him in the ordinary course of his life a humane and excellent man; and the results were deplorable."[21] It was the tragic fulfilment of Groves's worst apprehensions expressed in a letter to a friend almost twenty years earlier: "Instead of this being a day in which love *'thinketh no evil'* it seems to me a day in which man glories in paradoxes... to think nothing good but everything evil of a brother; to diminish nought but exaggerate everything; to call nothing by a gentle name, but to designate the most ordinary acts by the most vituperative appellations; and that 'separation' is God's principle of *unity*. I am sure, as man now uses it, it is the devil's main spring of confusion."[22] Frank Newman looked back on Darby's tyranny with distaste: "He only wanted men 'to submit their understandings to God,' that is, to the Bible – that is, to his interpretation!" And the consequences were appalling, "dwarfing men's understandings, contracting their hearts, crushing their moral sensibilities and setting those at variance who ought to love."[23]

There is no doubt that Darby was a great man, by far the most naturally gifted of the early Brethren. Quite apart from his classical and theological scholarship, he could write and speak in several languages, and he eventually translated the whole Bible into French and German as well as English. In total, he founded and guided some fifteen hundred assemblies in Britain, Europe and further afield.[24] His writings fill over forty volumes and include commentaries on most books of the Bible. He was a skilful hymn writer and a superb devotional teacher, able to express himself far more simply when he spoke than when he wrote. To his inferiors he was kindly and sympathetic; he had a wonderful care for children and would help with the most menial of household tasks. He was supported by men of wealth, intellectual ability and social standing, and by a number who had been leaders in the Brethren movement from its earliest days.

The assemblies of French-speaking Switzerland were already eating out of his hand. The following years saw his influence extend to the south of France, where moribund dissenting chapels, having invited him to speak, called upon him to preside and then supported his pamphlet warfare against Swiss and French church leaders. Travelling extensively he added Italy, the United States, Australia and New Zealand to his personal sphere of influence.

From 1848 onwards Darby's lieutenants vigilantly policed the assemblies throughout Britain and beyond, identifying any who might be suspected of holding views or maintaining fellowship with churches or individuals disapproved by him. Groups as far north as Inverness were affected: "Inspired by the subtle and assiduous authority of Brethren hundreds of miles distant, who probably had never heard of this little assembly in the north of Scotland, the Enemy of the Church came in."[25] Every individual fellowship was required to "judge the question" – that is, the wickedness of Bethesda.[26] Almost thirty years later, in the mining town of Larkhall near Motherwell, "a few left the assembly" in 1874 to start a Darbyite group. One who knew them wrote, "It is sad to think that lifelong friends in happy church fellowship should be cut asunder from each other, in some cases for life, because of diversity of opinion and strife arising between two or three persons some hundred miles away. The progress of the assembly was greatly hindered by those seceding from it. It caused much grief and sorrow."[27]

A young friend heard Norris Groves speak at Exmouth on Christmas Eve, six months before his death. "He spoke to the refreshment and delight of all," she recalled. "One told me she felt it was as the voice of God to her soul… I felt so thankful that on the evening of the tea meeting he was led to trace a little the history of Brethrenism, and the downfall of *collective* blessing from the moment that 'separation from evil, God's principle of unity' became their standard of communion. I went along with every word he said, and the language of my heart was 'let me live and die with such as occupy themselves with beholding the beauty of the Lord rather than with detecting and judging evil in their brethren.'"[28] To behold the beauty of the Lord: this was always the deepest desire of Norris Groves. It is the beauty of the Lord that draws us to Christ, and through him to one another.

ENDNOTES

[1] M535
[2] M39
[3] Beattie, 19-21
[4] Newman, *Phases*, 20-21. Darby gives a brief account of his developing thought at this time in a letter reproduced in Bellett, *Early Days*, 27-41.
[5] In 1826 the widowed Theodosia Lady Powerscourt had heard Edward Irving preach in London and had become intensely interested in the study of biblical prophecy in the light of current events. In 1830 Irving visited her home in Ireland and gave a series of lectures in Dublin on "The Second Advent and the Everlasting Kingdom of our Lord". From this time onwards she hosted a monthly meeting for discussion of biblical prophecy. The first annual conference at Powerscourt House, near Bray,

County Wicklow, was held in 1831. It lasted several days and was attended by 35 clergy, 15 laymen and 20 ladies. Groves at this time was in Baghdad. The second conference, in 1832, focused especially on the issue of supernatural gifts, but ended with some acrimony between Darby and the evangelical rector of Powerscourt on the subject of the Church, much to the distress of their hostess. In 1833, among others present were Darby, Bellett, Newton, Hall, Müller and Craik, but proceedings were dominated by Darby, to the great displeasure of Newton who disputed his idea of a "Secret Rapture" and his developing dispensationalism. Groves was still overseas, now on his first tour of India. The following two years Lady Powerscourt hosted smaller, more private gatherings, and she met regularly with the Brethren at Aungier Street. A godly and well-meaning woman with a strong mystical bent, and perhaps more good nature than doctrinal discernment, she died in 1836 at the age of only thirty-six. Groves probably met her, certainly knew of her, and undoubtedly read reports and letters relating to the conferences. It is possible that he visited Powerscourt at some point during the period 1826-9, but he did not attend any of the three major conferences (Neatby, 38-39; Rowdon, *Origins*, 1-2, 86-97; Coad, 110).

[6] Darby presents his arguments in *The Apostasy of the Successive Dispensations* and *Evidence from Scripture of the Passing Away of the Present Dispensation*. To be fair to him, it should be noted that Darby himself was an active evangelist.

[7] M244 (also M421-422)

[8] Groves drew a distinction between "union" (personal fellowship with other individuals) and "communion" (participation in a recognised group).

[9] Letter written in March or early April 1834 (M287; reproduced in M533-535).

[10] Letter dated 10th March 1836 (reproduced in M538ff, Coad, 291ff, Lang, *Groves*, 172ff, and Groves E K, *Conversations*, 188ff). Lang comments, "This letter is of quite unusual importance. Historically, because it is the most authoritative statement of what were the original principles of fellowship of the Brethren, given by him who first suggested them. Next, because it indicates the points upon which departure from those principles first arose, and who led the way in that surrender... It is also interesting as a revelation of the writer, all the more valuable by having been made unconsciously. It reveals penetrating insight, clear judgment upon the issues, incisive statement, and withal that grace of spirit which suffused him even in controversy" (Lang, *Groves*, 172).

[11] Rom 14:3

[12] Groves later pointed out that, despite the errors and the hypocrisy of the Jewish scribes and Pharisees, Jesus willingly taught in their synagogues. This did not mean that Jesus condoned all they did: "He was emphatically 'separate from sinners', not from their persons nor assemblies, but separate from their sins" (M374).

[13] The "Scotts" were A J (Sandy) Scott and his household (Newell, 157).

[14] Darby was an advocate of infant baptism.

[15] These developments are discussed in Chapter 33.

[16] Stunt, *Awakening*, 308

[17] Groves, *The Tottenham Case*, 3; Groves E K, *Conversations*, 153-155. Edward Groves commented, "Mr Craik was a man of so tender a spirit that the very sight of

suffering often brought tears to his eyes, so you can imagine what he had to endure in those days" (*Conversations*, 156).

[18] Coad, 146

[19] John Gifford Bellett eventually wrote more than fifty commentaries, books and tracts on devotional and Christological themes, which were appreciated by Darby's opponents as well as his supporters. Bellett's booklet *A Short Meditation on the Moral Glory of the Lord Jesus Christ* was a formative influence on the Chinese Christian leader Watchman Nee, who translated it into Chinese. It has also been widely distributed in India.

[20] Letter to "a Brother in Sheffield", quoted by Neatby, 190. See also Darby's tract, *The Bethesda Circular*.

[21] Neatby, 190

[22] Letter to Mr G Walker of Teignmouth (M409-410)

[23] Newman, *Phases*, 21

[24] Coad, 107

[25] Beattie, 270

[26] Groves E K, *Conversations*, 162

[27] Beattie, 209

[28] M483

"Though we have had our share of trials,
we have had more than our share of blessing."

Bessie Paget [1]

22

Around that Table

Leaving India in 1837 the doctor Edward Cronin had settled in London and married again. He was still "a warm-hearted man and a fervent Christian",[2] but one who listened too much, we might think, to his old confidant John Nelson Darby, and one who often seemed more sure of what he condemned than what he approved. When Darby denounced Craik and Müller, Cronin felt bound to follow suit. Norris Groves, seeing no reason to break with his sister and her husband, was instantly tarred with the same brush. In 1849 Groves received a letter from Edward Cronin advising his old friend he had become "a partaker of other men's sins" and had therefore "become obnoxious to the prohibition of 2 John 10." For this reason he would no longer be welcome in Cronin's house. It came completely out of the blue and was a great shock to Groves. He and Cronin had shared a medical ministry and a home in Mesopotamia and in India; they had sacrificed much for their work together, spending many hours in fellowship and prayer, through times of both sorrow and joy, in Dublin, Baghdad and Madras. "Not one line or one word preceded this communication, either of warning or enquiry," Groves noted, and then most poignantly, "This letter of rejection concludes an unbroken intimacy and fellowship of twenty-five years."[3]

Cronin was not a particularly sensitive man, and the dominant character of John Darby squashed any finer feelings he might have known towards a friend who had suffered much and who had always shown him the utmost kindness and respect. But loyalty to Darby required it. Groves accepted the rebuff with sorrow, then left it with the Lord. Indeed, that was the safest place to leave it, for the Lord was not yet done with Edward Cronin.

In 1879 the doctor, now seventy-eight years old, visited the town of Ryde on the Isle of Wight, and shared in the Lord's Supper with a group of Christians. It so happened that this group had earned the displeasure of John Darby. The result was a public letter from Darby declaring, "The course of Dr Cronin has been clandestine, untruthful, dishonest and profane."[4] Though this was palpable nonsense it caused many to suspect Cronin of some wickedness whose details were not known to them. It ended a friendship between Cronin and Darby extending over more than fifty years, and it resulted in the excommunication of Cronin by his own assembly at Kennington, London.

Cronin was profoundly affected by this sad turn of events, but his wife even more so. When he died three years later, in 1882, his son wrote of "the great and sore trouble which had broken our beloved mother's heart, hastened her death, and crushed him! I refer to his having been cast out by that body whom he had so loved and laboured for, nearly half a century."[5] The measure given was all too evidently the measure received. Shortly before Cronin's death Edward Groves visited him in London and found his feelings for his old colleague of Baghdad and Madras greatly altered: "He wept like a child as he recalled his early association with my father."[6] Perhaps it is some consolation to know that Cronin died in a state of contentedness, "constantly repeating the names of our Lord."[7]

John Darby, however, still had his own measure to receive. The rejection of Cronin was the catalyst for a serious challenge to his authority by one of his most gifted lieutenants, William Kelly.[8] Darby's final years were embittered by jealousy of his younger rival, and shortly before his death, at the age of eighty-one, he had seen half his followers abandon his camp for the other. It was a devastating realisation. "He had survived precisely to the tragic moment – just long enough to see his work go to pieces in his hands by his own act."[9]

Very different was the story of John Parnell. Of all the men who worked with Norris Groves, Parnell was the one who most took to heart his vision for Christian devotedness. Aristocratic son of a wealthy family, he had more to lose than any in resolving to forsake all and follow Christ, yet from the time of his conversion as a student at Edinburgh University, Parnell's greatest desire was to see a full restoration of the spirit and the blessing of the apostolic age.

When the young William Carey, at a meeting for Baptist ministers in 1786, suggested that Christians might have a responsibility to preach the gospel to the heathen, the aged chairman had retorted, "You are a miserable enthusiast for asking such a question. Certainly nothing can be done before another Pentecost, when an effusion of miraculous gifts including the gift of tongues will give effect to the commission of Christ as at first."[10] Carey himself was willing to go immediately – with or without such an "effusion" – but John Parnell thought the missionary might achieve far more among the heathen if blessed with the spiritual power of the apostles.

This was in his mind as he welcomed the Groves family on board the yacht *Osprey* for the first stage of their journey to St Petersburg. Here, he believed, was a mission after the New Testament pattern, led by a man who took the words of Jesus literally, a man who would heed what the Holy Spirit was saying to the churches, a man who would be bold enough to declare, "Oh! my brother, let us not put the experience of 1500 years against the word of God. If we believe, we shall have what we ask for."[11] With such dedication to apostolic methods, surely Norris Groves and his friends would see apostolic power and apostolic results. Yet belief struggled with unbelief; the possibilities with the realities. Was God going to pour out his Spirit afresh on their generation, or was that for some future time? Indeed, there were moments when Groves himself seemed rather modest in his ambitions. As the *Osprey* battled through stormy seas, he looked back on their months of preparation. "I never had very strong expectations of what we were to do being *manifestly* very great," he said. "But that we shall answer a purpose in God's plans I have no doubt."[12]

On one point they were agreed. The greatest practical obstacle to the missionary task of the Church was the multiplicity of languages in the world and the difficulty of communication with every nation, tribe and tongue. But as they parted – Parnell sailing home in the *Osprey*, Groves and his friends continuing east – there came news of exciting developments in Britain. A family in Scotland by the name of Macdonald, longing to experience the power of the Holy Spirit, had arranged prayer meetings in their home. Their daughter Margaret and another young woman, Mary Campbell, were both chronically ill and permanently bedridden. A visitor came to see them, a young man by the name of Sandy Scott, assistant to the dynamic Edward Irving, pastor of the Scottish Presbyterian church in London. Scott shared Irving's aspiration for a return to the heady ideals of the apostolic age, and he suggested that the family seek a fresh baptism of the Holy Spirit, asking in faith for an outpouring of power from on high. A few months later, in March 1830, Mary Campbell began to speak in unknown tongues, followed shortly afterwards by others; then both the young women found they could get out of bed and resume a healthy active life.[13]

News of these events reached Oxford. A youthful Frank Newman, among others, was impressed. As Benjamin Newton recalls, "In came Newman, excited, into my room, threw down a letter. 'There, that'll convince your incredulity!' It was a letter written from Scotland from the Campbells' house. Newman was quite taken with it."[14] A few months later the popular university preacher Henry Bulteel declared his conviction that gifts of healing and speaking in foreign languages could be experienced by the Church today, and indeed would be instrumental in convincing many unbelievers of the truth. Returning to London, Scott encouraged Irving and his church to pray for a fresh outpouring of the Holy Spirit. Soon there were tongues, prophesyings and healings in London. Two invalids were restored to health through the fervent prayers of Henry Bulteel.

Percy Hall in Plymouth was greatly drawn to these London manifestations, praying that such gifts might also be seen in Plymouth. He was by no means alone among the early Brethren: those attending the Powerscourt conference of 1832 prayed earnestly for a restoration of pentecostal gifts. The man chosen to prepare Norris Groves's earliest journals for publication was Sandy Scott himself, and in his preface to the first volume Scott expressed a hope for Groves "that in the name of Jesus Christ he may cast out devils, speak with new tongues, take up serpents, drink deadly things without hurt, lay hands on the sick and they recover, be filled with the Holy Ghost and wisdom."[15]

In reality, Groves, jolting painfully through eastern Europe, was frustrated by the difficulty of communication with horse-dealers and innkeepers. Reaching Baghdad in December 1829, bemused by the complex medley of Arabic, Armenian, Persian, Turkish, Kurdish, Syriac and Hebrew, he envied the apostles effortlessly addressing a cosmopolitan crowd in which "each one heard them speaking in his own language."[16] He admitted, "I feel the languages to be a great barrier. Whether the Lord will pour down this among the other gifts of the latter days I do not know, but at present it is a great exercise of the missionary's patience."[17] "If there is any gift my soul longs for," he said, "it is to be able to speak to every one in his own tongue, wherein he was born, the wonderful works of God."[18] Long hours spent in hard study of grammar and vocabulary appeared to bring but small progress: "The Lord doubtless sees in this reasons of immense weight, or he would again bestow upon us the gifts of the Spirit as before."[19]

The dearly-held principle of following apostolic practice certainly inclined both Groves and Parnell toward the thought that whatever the apostles did, we could aspire to do – with the same faith and the same holy boldness in our day that they exercised in theirs. "Distinguishing between apostolic times and present times," said Groves, "is to my mind so dangerous a principle, and puts into the hands of anyone so disposed a sword that seems to me to reach the very vitals of the gospel."[20] Some months later John Parnell, travelling east with reinforcements for the Baghdad mission, made this a matter of faith. "If he felt unwell, he took no medicine, but in prayer and fasting looked only to the Lord."[21] Delayed in Aleppo, Frank Newman had fallen seriously ill and indeed, despite the best efforts of the doctor Edward Cronin, seemed on the point of death. Parnell proposed prayer and anointing with oil according to the instruction of James 5:14-16. Newman's recovery confirmed his conviction that divine healing should be asked for and expected. Groves heard about this with interest, suppressing the prejudice he had felt against the chicanery of alleged miraculous cures in contemporary Roman Catholicism: "With regard to miracles, my mind is not at present prepared to accept them fully. But this I do feel – that the apostle Paul, in Corinthians 12 and 14, when speaking of supernatural gifts for the edifying of the Church and doing the work of God, points them out as things to be desired and prayed for then. And if they were desired to be prayed for then, why not now?"[22]

When the party from Aleppo eventually reached Groves in Baghdad, Parnell felt the time had come for them all to pray in earnest for a restoration of those miraculous gifts which had characterised the earliest days of the church and which, he believed, had been withheld on account of unbelief and worldliness. Without the manifest power of the Spirit there seemed little likelihood that preaching and distributing literature would achieve very much in a place such as Baghdad. Feeding the poor, healing the sick, opening schools: it all "seemed utterly ineffectual to the breaking down of the barrier that Mohammedanism raised to the spread of the gospel."[23] The previous year Groves had confided to his journal, "I have had some conversation with Pfander on the cessation of miracles and find our views very similar. He thinks with me that the promise of miraculous interference is now as open to the faith of the church as ever, but that she ceases to exercise faith on the promises which relate to such help. As miracles were designed for unbelievers and not for the church, we must expect to see them arise among missionaries to the heathen."[24] The problem was that few missionaries were to be found anywhere among the heathen, and those few were not expecting anything miraculous. But if evangelists would go out like the apostles, "full of faith and of the Holy Spirit," then surely we might expect signs and wonders at their hands, as at the hands of the apostles.[25]

Four years later Norris Groves was in India, facing a fresh assortment of languages, and he was moved again to enquire wistfully, "Do you think that the full measure of that outpouring of the Spirit promised in Joel will be sent down to prepare the harvest of the Lord before the sounding of the seventh trumpet?"[26] There were letters from England pointing out how little he had achieved in the weakness of the flesh, urging him to return immediately and seek a baptism of the Spirit. "None should go to the heathen," declared one magazine, "till they be baptised with power from on high."[27] But was it necessary to go to England in order to get "power from on high"? And how long should the heathen wait while missionaries were seeking this power? Had he not, with his own eyes, seen "heathen" in Europe and Asia soundly converted through the preaching of missionaries who had simply obeyed the command of Christ to preach, never dreaming they lacked his power or his presence to save those who heard? It was true that the apostles were instructed to wait in Jerusalem to receive the Holy Spirit before setting out to fulfil the Great Commission, but where in the pages of scripture do we find them insisting on their converts doing the same? The gospel message itself is declared to be "the *power* of God unto salvation", and "as it is the power of God unto salvation to the unconverted in England I see not why it should not be as effectual to the unconverted anywhere."[28]

Maybe so, but John Parnell, rejoining Groves in Madras, longed to see such power with his own eyes. In Britain a movement was evidently afoot, blessed with supernatural gifts of the Spirit, that might at last equip the Church for the missionary task. Parnell resolved to go and find out more. Reaching London in June 1837 he enquired about recent developments. Closer experience of Irving and his associates had cooled the interest of many, and led the majority of Parnell's friends to conclude that the manifestations – the tongues, the prophesyings and healings – were for the most part spurious. And the tongues were evidently of no missionary value, as no foreigner could actually understand them.[29]

Even those who had witnessed the first healings in Scotland had begun to doubt what they had seen. Sandy Scott himself "thought almost from the start that the movement was partly a delusion and partly 'a spiritual work *not* of God' (i.e. the work of evil spirits)."[30] By May 1833 Bulteel had also become disillusioned, and Percy Hall's enthusiasm had evaporated when Irving rebuked him for giving up his career as a naval officer. In due course Irving fell out with his own church and ended his short career in obscurity. He died in 1834 of tuberculosis at the age of forty-two, still regretting he had never himself been able to speak in tongues or prophesy, and still believing he would be healed.[31] Frank Newman later wrote, "The Irvingite exposition of the Pauline phenomena appeared to me so correct that I was vehemently predisposed to believe the miraculous tongues."[32] Darby, always jealous of activity outside his control, remained sceptical; he had gone to see for himself. "None of the sounds, vowels or consonants were foreign," he remarked. The tongues comprised the sounds of normal English without the clicks or whirrs to be expected from a foreign language, and the word endings were "moulded after the Latin grammar".[33] The movement had been discredited, for other people, by its failure to convert unbelievers to Christ, by its neglect of the scriptural requirement to interpret the tongues, and by the bondage resulting from strict obedience to the more inane pronouncements of its "prophets". By 1840 little interest remained in the subject of pentecostal manifestations.[34]

John Parnell, with his Armenian wife and her son and daughter, decided to settle in Teignmouth, near Exeter on the south Devon coast. Their house was described as "somewhat primitive," its rent costing just £12 a year (to a man possessing an income of £1200 a year). With a plain wooden table and chairs, steel forks, pewter teaspoons, and no carpets on the floor, it spoke clearly enough of his determination to continue living sacrificially.[35] But whatever its inadequacies, it was a place of warm fellowship. A friend reminisces, "Around that table I often sat with others, thick as bees, while he drew us out in the study of the scriptures which he happily and usefully unfolded... He had a happy faculty of setting every one at ease, fostering any little remark, encouraging and rectifying it."[36] Once, in the home of a Christian couple, Parnell was asked to address a group of their friends. "Better make it a meeting for a Bible Reading," he replied. "Let's take God's word in our hands and see what he will give us."[37] The outcome was a regular gathering where all were free to share thoughts and questions that came to them from the passages read. Many years later he wrote a booklet, *The Open Meeting*, describing how the Holy Spirit will lead participants in an informal gathering, with mutual exhortation and encouragement. He himself "had the happy art at a Bible Reading of drawing out the thoughts of others, so that in his hands the reading never degenerated into an address where all but one were listeners." His wish was "that all might get the benefit of what each had to contribute."[38]

Parnell was always happiest talking with individuals or small groups; he never felt himself a skilled preacher. When he did speak publicly his style was simple and direct, without artifice or embellishment, and his subject always came round sooner or later to the Way of Salvation: "His theme was ever man's ruin and God's remedy." On Sundays he often walked to neighbouring towns to preach the gospel – the morning in Teignmouth, afternoon in Torquay, evening in Newton Abbot – "always oblivious to questions of comfort and health if only souls might be helped by his ministry."[39] His experience abroad had prepared him to suffer hardship and abuse for the sake of Christ; it had also taught him to view the people of Devon, like those of Aleppo and Baghdad, with the eyes of a missionary. His companion on at least one of these early itinerations was his old friend from Dublin, John Nelson Darby.[40]

After about four years in Devonshire, John Parnell had sold almost all his property. "Principal and interest had all gone in the service of his Master."[41] He began to think of getting a job, or starting a business – perhaps as a paper manufacturer. His father was sceptical, thinking him "quite unsuited to undertake secular work of that kind." Perhaps the baron was right. In the event, his father's death shortly afterwards meant that John inherited the family fortune – and the family title with it.

So it was that in 1842 he went to live in London, from now on to be known as Lord Congleton and entitled to sit in the House of Lords. Though choosing not to join either of the political parties, he could vote on matters of national importance. He joined a newly started assembly in Islington where John Darby was a frequent visitor. Every Sunday, during the pause between Prayer at 7 a.m. and Breaking of Bread at 10.30, the company took breakfast together in the meeting room, and many had a hearty appetite, having walked a considerable distance. With the help of some others, Parnell bought an area of vacant land to use as a burial ground. This was a great benefit to the poorer members of the fellowship, who would be excluded as Nonconformists from the parish churchyard but could never afford to buy a plot of their own.

As an aristocrat with a private income, "he never departed from the rule that he made for himself, of devoting one half of all that he received to the Lord's service."[42] The half was set aside regularly, and so long as anything remained in the "charity purse", it was available for helping any deserving case. Throughout his life Parnell objected to the common practice of borrowing money for a good cause and then appealing for help to clear off the debt. He would quote the scripture, "Owe no man any thing,"[43] and point to George Müller as proof that this practical advice could be taken and followed literally. "If the Lord intends you to do the work," said Parnell, "he will send the means to carry it out." Henry Groves agreed with him. Whilst working on his biography of Parnell, Henry thought of the times he had seen a work undertaken with borrowed money and watched that work fail. How much better, observed Henry, to be assured of God's blessing, through his provision, *before* rushing into a course that might take one far from God's will. "How many bitter disappointments would be avoided by thus waiting patiently on him who sees the end as well as the beginning."[44]

From 1845 onwards John Parnell was drawn against his wishes into bitter controversies. His gentle phlegmatic nature made him slow to speak, slow to judge, and reluctant to think the worse of anyone. He would not condemn those he believed to be men of God simply because John Nelson Darby required him to. Darby broke off relations with him, and his old missionary partner Edward Cronin followed suit. Distressed by friction in London, Parnell moved to Brighton. From there he attended many meetings, attempting to heal divisions and restore unity, and many times he went home from such meetings "sorrowful and saddened". With a strong sense of what was honourable and just, Parnell found it hard to accept meanness of spirit in anyone. A young friend remarked, "He is the most utterly truthful man I ever met."[45] His opinion was often asked, and sometimes scorned, but "I never saw a particle of bitterness in our dear friend... I do not remember ever to have heard an unkind word from him, and when unkind words were spoken to him he never appeared to be ruffled by them... There would not have been so many sad divisions among the people of God, had the character of most or all of them resembled his."[46]

Returning to London in 1849 Parnell threw in his lot with the Orchard Street assembly in Marylebone at a time when many of its members were leaving to follow Darby. This came as a great encouragement to those who remained, and one later recalled, "It seemed as if as an angel from God he had come and taken his place among us."[47] In middle life Parnell was in every way a pastor, always ready to bring comfort and practical help to the poor and sick, keeping watch over the souls of any with spiritual needs. But he became increasingly reluctant to preach. He admitted to a friend, "I once tried preaching in a room half emptied by the one before me, and I quite emptied it."[48] To Groves himself he confessed he wished he could do more for the church, then added a charming line, "Still it is no use setting one's self up as a preacher if one is not one."[49] Perhaps so, but there were those who came to faith in Christ through his preaching.

In later years, if he chanced to meet a Christian friend in a public place, Parnell would often take out his Bible, read a verse and engage his companion in discussion without feeling any need to lower his voice. One recalled how he came into a café, and rather than interrupt his young friend's meal, courteously drew up a chair and "sat down by my side, speaking kind words of truth and grace for the benefit of myself and of others who were within hearing of his voice."[50] On another occasion he recognised a Christian coachman on a steamer from Plymouth to Southampton, shook hands with him and said, "We must show our colours at once, or we shall not do it at all." Opening his Bible, "he began unostentatiously to read and comment on the word to the coachman. Soon a few gathered round them and one was heard to say, 'That is one of the Brethren. They are more bold in speaking than others.'"[51]

In 1865 John Parnell's Armenian wife died, shortly after the death of her daughter. Some months later her son also passed away. Then at the age of sixty-two Parnell married again, and the following year his only child, a daughter, was born. Towards the end of his life, he heard again from Edward Cronin who "was humbled, softened, and sought a renewal of former fellowship." Parnell, of course, "received him with all the cordiality of a loving brother's heart"; he "never entertained the smallest animosity."[52]

As for Bessie Paget, she spent the last thirty-five years of her long life in Barnstaple, enjoying happy fellowship with the assembly led by Robert Chapman. Harriet Groves recalls that her home "was open to all the people of God. The poor from the villages shared her hospitality and were sure of a ready welcome when either the market day or business brought them to Barnstaple."[53] Like Harriet and her husband, Bessie Paget "never lost her sense of oneness with *all* she felt *belonged to Jesus*."[54] And she knew well the meaning of Christian devotedness: "Her income was not large but her faith in God unbounded."[55] She believed God was at work in every detail of her daily life. Indeed, "a striking feature in her latter days was the way her own will seemed lost and absorbed in the will of God, so that nothing appeared a disappointment, for she was inwardly persuaded that *all* God did was right."[56] And she firmly believed he was working all things together for good, which meant she could always be thankful. "Though we have had our share of trials," she said, "we have had more than our share of blessing."[57]

A week before her death in March 1863, aged and infirm, her memory sadly weakened, Bessie Paget was able to attend a group meeting for fellowship in her home, and then, "on leaving the room, looked lovingly on all around as her children, saying how she loved to see them happy together."[58] If Norris Groves has been a spiritual father to many, Bessie Paget herself was a spiritual mother to Groves. For her prayer and her willingness to speak about Christ to a young dentist in Exeter, both he and we have much cause to be thankful.

ENDNOTES

[1] M565
[2] Neatby, 190

[3] Groves, *The Tottenham Case*, 7; Neatby, 189-190

[4] Neatby, 288

[5] Neatby, 307

[6] Groves E K, *Successors*, 112

[7] Neatby, 307

[8] William Kelly should not be confused with Thomas Kelly the hymn-writer and leader of the Kellyite churches in Ireland, similar to the Brethren in certain respects.

[9] Neatby, 308

[10] Smith G, *Carey*, 31-32

[11] M224 (in a letter from Groves in Baghdad to Caldecott, Feb. 1833).

[12] M53

[13] Drummond, 139-148; Stunt, *Awakening*, 234. The visitor's full name was Alexander John Scott. These events took place more than seventy years before the earliest phases of the modern Pentecostal movement which gave rise to the Assemblies of God and the various divisions of the Church of God in America and to the Elim Pentecostal churches of the United Kingdom.

[14] Sieveking, 86-87; Stunt, *Awakening*, 252

[15] Jx

[16] Acts 2:6

[17] R69; M109

[18] R281-282

[19] R85

[20] R302-303

[21] Groves H, *Congleton*, 53

[22] R302

[23] *Congleton*, 44. Parnell had already published a small pamphlet on this subject, which seems not to have survived.

[24] J101

[25] In 1833 Groves compared the success of the apostles with the frustration felt by missionaries in his own day: "True they had miracles: and why have not we?... Perhaps because his Church is too little devoted to him to be thus publicly acknowledged by him; or too strong, as we have before observed, in this world's greatness... Or perhaps so schismatical that what the Lord designed to be the glory of the *Church*, if given, would only tend to the exaltation of a *sect*" (*Christian Influence*, 66). The spiritual impoverishment of the Church means that the missionary must now painstakingly study to acquire a knowledge of foreign languages: "Our present need of this knowledge arises from a departure from a simple trust in the power of the Spirit to carry on his own work; for in the primitive times a miraculous knowledge of tongues was given to the Church, that in all things she might look to her Lord alone for power, and that, being set free from the necessity of acquiring them through human intellect, 'no flesh might glory in his presence'" (*Christian Influence*, 33n). Groves went on to suggest that a renewal of devotion, humility and unity *in the entire Church* might lead to a recovery of these miraculous powers.

[26] M291 (Rev 10:7)

[27] M270. The magazine was the *Morning Watch*, issued by the circle associated with Irving, Drummond and the "Albury apostles".

[28] M313-314, 272 (Rom 1:16 AV)

[29] The same hopes that "tongues" would prove to be foreign languages, and thus a key to missionary outreach, were similarly disappointed at a later date in the USA: "By 1906, the year of the Azusa Street revival, the first Pentecostals almost universally believed that when they spoke in tongues, they had spoken in known languages (*xenolalia*) by which they would preach the gospel 'abroad' to the ends of the earth in the last days... Early pentecostal publications were filled with these missionary expectations." The first few issues of the Azusa Street periodical *The Apostolic Faith* brought reports of American Christians, baptised in the Spirit in meetings at Azusa Street, speaking fluent Chinese, Russian, Italian, Arabic, Turkish and so on. Before long, missionaries were on their way to Liberia, Calcutta and Hawaii, confident they would be able to preach the gospel to the heathen without the long labour of language study. Finding they could not do so, most returned home in a state of considerable disillusionment, and by 1908 few with any personal experience of them still believed the tongues experienced at Azusa Street to be real foreign languages (Anderson, Allan, 193-210).

[30] Stunt, *Awakening*, 270

[31] Irving had predicted the second coming of Christ for 1864; it mattered little when eventually the year 1864 came and went, for hardly anyone by then remembered the prediction.

[32] Newman, *Phases*, 119

[33] *Phases*, 119

[34] Towards the end of his life, Groves expressed his view that "the season of supernatural gifts was that of the *infancy* of the Church, and that their withdrawal took place when the Testament was complete and the Church left under the guardianship of the indwelling Spirit – in the period, in short, of her manhood. That this is the doctrine of scripture, I have no doubt. And so far from the absence of those things... being a sign of decay, they mark the period of the Church's progress from infancy to manhood" (M443-444). Parnell, on the other hand, was still inclined to attribute the absence of genuine supernatural gifts to divine displeasure: "We have to remember how shorn of gifts is the Church in our day, how few gifts remain, and this through her self-conceit and self-will and worldliness" (*The Open Meeting*, 6; *Congleton*, 107).

[35] *Congleton*, 62; Lang, *Groves*, 231. Carpets seem to have been regarded with particular disfavour by the early Brethren. Benjamin Newton, also a man of means, lived in a substantial house, without carpets. In fact, a strong egalitarian ethos among the Brethren affected all social relations. Sir Alexander Campbell, for example, insisted on his servants sitting with him at table. One day, arriving late for dinner, he found his servants had already made some progress with the meal. They explained that, as he was so late, they thought it best to begin without him (Neatby, 41-42).

[36] Beattie, 60-61

[37] *Congleton*, 117-118

[38] *Congleton*, 109-110. In 1845 Parnell wrote a popular booklet entitled *Resurrection Life*, which was reprinted at least a dozen times. Fifteen years later he issued a metrical version of the Psalms. Booklets on other topics appeared from time to time.

[39] Bromley, 33

[40] Beattie, 60

[41] *Congleton*, 68

[42] *Congleton*, 115

[43] Rom 13:8 AV

[44] *Congleton*, 116

[45] Bromley, 33; Neatby, 147

[46] *Congleton*, 73-74. This testimony was from the missionary William Start of Patna, who had known Parnell in India and England.

[47] *Congleton*, 82

[48] *Congleton*, 67

[49] Letter written in 1853 (*Congleton*, 88).

[50] *Congleton*, 89

[51] *Congleton*, 68

[52] *Congleton*, 120

[53] M558

[54] M559

[55] M558

[56] M561

[57] M565

[58] M559

"I have very little confidence in man.
My great desire has been to cast myself
on the word of God,
that every judgment of my soul concerning all things
may be right, by being, in all,
the mind of God."

Norris Groves [1]

23

An Eccentric Professor

Travelling back to Britain with John Kitto in 1833, Frank Newman looked forward to seeing his university friends once more – and to recruiting some of them, if they were willing, for the team in Baghdad. Perhaps his old mentor John Darby would come up to Oxford and speak again about the cause of Christ and the Great Commission. But even before Newman came ashore at Gravesend, a shock awaited him: "On my return, and while yet in quarantine on the coast of England, I received an uncomfortable letter from a most intimate spiritual friend, to the effect that painful reports had been every where spread abroad against my soundness in the faith... but my friend expressed a firm hope that when I had explained myself it would all prove to be nothing."[2]

More was to follow. Rumours had reached his brother John to the effect that Frank had preached at "some small meetings of religious people". This was a gross impertinence, declared John Henry Newman, "an assuming of the Priest's office," and what right had he, a mere layman, to act as a priest? Frank could not conceal the hurt as his brother, in a fit of self-righteousness, "separated himself entirely from my private friendship and acquaintance."[3] Frank then hopefully proposed marriage a third time to Maria Giberne, and a third time was rejected.[4] The horizon was closing in.

But Frank Newman was young and fairly resilient, and a few months later his outlook brightened – at least for a while – when he met another Maria, spoke to her of marriage and was accepted. The daughter of a baronet, she was an attractive affectionate girl with a deep and earnest faith, active in her Devonshire assembly, and she was swept off her feet by the attentions of a young man known to her as a brilliant scholar who had forsaken all for the sake of the gospel.[5] A year after their marriage, no doubt to her great pleasure, Frank Newman was baptised as a believer "at a chapel in Bristol".[6]

Though Newman's evangelical faith was, by his own account, sincere and orthodox, there were still unresolved frustrations and doubts in his mind, and no one willing or able to discuss them with him. In September 1833 an Oxford clergyman confided to his diary, "Mr Lambert and Mr Frank Newman called and spent two hours with me this morning. Time chiefly occupied by Newman inveighing against Church of England and all existing churches in the country."[7] Newman's contempt for the naïve triumphalism of religious dignitaries dressed in robes and declaiming in musical tones from the safety of palaces and pulpits had been reinforced by the evident impotence of the evangelical gospel to make any impression on the massive edifices of Islam and Eastern Orthodoxy. His aversion to the pompous pretence of clerics living in luxury was nothing new, but what of the alternative? The brave ideal of a suffering church, so appealing to the young visionary, had now been put to the most rigorous test. And the sordid reality of violence, sickness and death – with few converts to show for years of sacrificial toil – had taken the shine off the romantic notion.

Further letters showed he was now cut off, not just from John, but also from "other members of my family who were living in his house." Then followed more pain. Friends asked him about rumours they had heard – rumours which suggested he was questioning the accepted doctrine of the Holy Trinity. Not so, he replied, for he held as firmly as anyone to the Nicene Creed, which was surely the truest test of orthodoxy. Those who had doubted him seemed reassured, "yet when I was gone away, one after another was turned against me by somebody else whom I had not yet met or did not know: for in every theological conclave which deliberates on joint action, the most bigoted seems always to prevail."[8]

At this point he was stunned to receive from John Darby "a very desultory letter of grave alarm and inquiry, stating that he had heard that I was endeavouring to sound the divine nature by the miserable plummet of human philosophy." The whole church, declared Darby, was against him. Newman was moved to reply in what he thought was "the frankest, most cordial and trusting tone... lovingly, humbly and imploringly." Darby wrote back requiring him to accept definitions and statements concerning the Trinity that, as far as Newman could see, were based on no scripture at all. There followed two more letters from Darby. Their import, Newman tells us, was to "threaten some new acquaintances who were kind to me... that if they did not desist from sheltering me and break off [fellowship] they should, as far as his influence went, themselves everywhere be cut off from Christian communion and recognition." Messages then came thick and fast from individuals and assemblies that would have nothing to do with him: "I found myself separated from persons whom I had trustingly admired and on whom I had most counted for union, with whom I fondly believed myself bound up for eternity."

Gone were his relatives and his closest friends, and with them the circle of Christians he had most admired, for whom "I would have performed menial offices and thought myself honoured, whom I loved solely because I thought them to love God, and of whom I asked nothing but that they would admit me as the meanest and most frail of disciples. My heart was ready to break."[9] His hopeful plans to return to the East with a fresh band of volunteers were killed stone dead, along with his fading vision of a "spiritual church". For no doubt his friends Groves, Parnell and Cronin would receive word of the controversy and reject him, he supposed, as certainly as everyone else. So ended the missionary career of Frank Newman.

Still a believer, still a lover of Christ, he sought some place to worship: "I desired to creep into some obscure congregation and there wait till my mind had ripened as to the right path in circumstances so perplexing."[10] He found one such, and records grateful thanks for their "good will and simple kindness".

From this point on, Frank Newman wrote in great detail about his spiritual pilgrimage, and eventually published his account under the title *Phases of Faith*. The Bible had always been his authority, unquestioned and beyond criticism. Every moral problem had been explained by the doctrine of Development,[11] every textual discrepancy by the ignorance of modern man concerning past events, every paradox by the inability of the human intellect to fully comprehend the eternal God. His mind, however, had long been troubled by the severe Calvinism held by most of his evangelical friends. It seemed unjust that man should be created so weak he was bound to sin, and then consigned to eternal torment for a failing he could not possibly avoid. And to argue that man had free will whilst subject to God's irresistible decrees seemed to make no sense at all. He struggled to accept that all Adam's descendants had been corrupted and made deserving of hell in consequence of what he (not they) had done. And another troublesome doctrine was the idea of a Limited Atonement, the belief that God has so planned it that the majority of individuals are predestined to wrath and cannot possibly find salvation through Christ, for Christ died only for a limited number of chosen individuals and the majority of mankind are not, and never can be, among that number.

Believing that his friends must have some good grounds for holding these doctrines, he had been reluctant to dispute their convictions, hoping that time would clarify matters in his own mind. But now, hurt and rejected, the old doubts came flooding back. To support a doctrinal position, he saw orthodox men misreading and manipulating the words of scripture, evidently to their own satisfaction but not, he must now admit, to his. Cherished theories, thought Newman, were too often buttressed by dishonest scholarship: "The height of orthodoxy is to contradict oneself, and protest that one does not."[12] "On several occasions I had distinctly perceived how serious alarm I gave [*sic*] by resolutely refusing to admit any shiftings and shufflings of language. I felt convinced that if I would but have contradicted myself two or three times and then have added, 'That is the mystery of it,' I could have passed as orthodox with many."[13]

But perhaps it went even deeper than this. Perhaps the very scriptures they misused were unreliable. The difficulties he had faced as a schoolboy in trying to compile a harmony of the Gospels came back to haunt him afresh:

there were details that differed from one Gospel to another and which seemed to conflict. Perhaps the whole thing was a delusion. He began to doubt not just the doctrines but the scriptures that lay behind the doctrines. Never had he heard a convincing explanation of the peculiar discrepancies between the genealogies of Christ recorded in Matthew's Gospel and in Luke's, especially when compared with those in the Old Testament. Again and again he read the passages, and turned them over and over in his mind, and came to a conclusion from which he shrank but could not escape: there is historical error in Matthew's genealogy. Perhaps the chapter in question was spurious, added by a later and uninspired hand, and should therefore be omitted from the Bible. If so, was this the only spurious chapter? Were there more? And if there were, how could we identify them? Other problems came into view. In Stephen's speech the land which Jacob bought from the sons of Hamor seems to be confused with that bought by Abraham from Ephron the Hittite. Jesus himself spoke of Zechariah son of Barachiah as the last of the Old Testament martyrs, but was this not the person who died within the Temple courts, according to Josephus, about forty years after Jesus himself?

The whole question of moral difficulties in the Bible opened up afresh. The murder of Sisera by Jael, the command for Abraham to slay his son; how could God approve, or even demand, such things? Searching for answers, he tried to share his intellectual struggles with an evangelical friend and his wife. The wife, at least, seemed sympathetic, but for some time after their discussion he heard nothing more from them. Then having sent "three affectionate letters", he at last received a letter from his friend, a reply "of vehement accusation". Long afterwards he retained the memory of "the deep wounds he planted in me".[14] Again Newman's mind turned to contemporary teaching concerning the Fall: the idea that the sin of Adam corrupted not just himself but also his descendants to every generation. But is that what the Bible really teaches? Adam's frailty and his disposition to sin actually preceded the Fall, and the consequence of his eating the fruit was not a change in his moral or spiritual nature but rather a change in his physical nature – for Adam began, from that moment, to die. So, what of the descendants of Adam? We sin, not because of what Adam did, but rather because we are of the same fallible nature as Adam before he sinned. We are judged and condemned not because of Adam's sin but because of our own.[15] Step by step, Newman was groping, in his own way, towards a doctrinal position which now has wide support but which was then considered dangerously heretical. And on the question of a limited atonement, so strong was the grip of Calvinism on the evangelical circle of his acquaintance that to doubt Calvinism was to doubt Christianity. And yet, wrote Newman, "I was conscious that in dropping Calvinism I had lost nothing *evangelical*: on the contrary, the gospel which I retained was as spiritual and deep-hearted as before, only more merciful."[16]

About this time he met a Unitarian, a man whose "boldness of thought" along with "much sweetness of mind, largeness of charity, and a timid devoutness" made a pleasing contrast to the rigid and aggressive dogmatism of his other acquaintances.[17] Here was one considered "heretical" or even "unbelieving" by orthodox Evangelicals – one whose thought might be wrong on certain points but was at least honest, charitable and unfettered by bitter prejudice. And wherever his mind might lead him, Newman's heart remained fixed in his devotion to Christ: "I held fast an unabated reverence for the moral and spiritual teaching of the New Testament and had not the most remote conception that anything could ever shatter my belief in its great miracles." As for speculation about the Trinity, the Atonement, Eternal Punishment, "how little had any of these to do with the inward exercises of my soul toward God! He was still the same, immutably glorious. Not one feature of his countenance had altered to my gaze, or could alter." The longing even revived to return to the mission field: "In fact, during this period, I many times yearned to proceed to India, whither my friend Groves had transferred his labours and his hopes."[18] But the fear of rejection by a man he had admired above all others was a thing he could not face.

It was at this point that Frank Newman met Dr Thomas Arnold, headmaster of the famous school at Rugby. Arnold had some rather more radical suggestions. The whole book of Genesis, Arnold believed, could be dismissed as fiction; Noah's deluge was "mythical"; the history of Joseph "a beautiful poem". "I was staggered at this," confessed Newman, and with good reason: "If all were not descended from Adam, what became of St Paul's parallel between the first and second Adam, and the doctrine of Headship and Atonement founded on it?" But so "deeply imbued with Christian devoutness" was Arnold's "vigorous mind" that Newman felt reassured that free enquiry into such matters ran no danger of bringing in its train any "moral mischiefs". Indeed, "free enquiry" became, more than ever, a duty laid upon him.[19]

Further investigation ascertained that geologists now believed "death went on in the animal creation many ages before the existence of man." The conclusion from science seemed clear: "To refer the death of animals to the sin of Adam and Eve is evidently impossible." And yet, "St Paul rests most important conclusions on the fact that one man, by personal sin, brought death upon all his posterity. If this was a fundamental error, religious doctrine also is shaken."[20] Advances in medicine had brought to the modern world a greater understanding of epilepsy and mental disease. Did not the belief of the gospel writers, and of Jesus himself, in demons and evil spirits show them mere children of their time in the primitive naïvety of a mistaken faith? All the miracles, signs and wonders began to seem like the fanciful exaggerations to be expected from a people steeped in religious superstition. With the New Testament in tatters, he began once more to read through the Old Testament, noting every point of difficulty. A further discussion with Arnold and the perusal of "a German volume" (probably by Michaelis) finally destroyed his last remaining confidence in the biblical writings. A simple choice lay before him. He could continue to believe in the divine inspiration, factual accuracy and doctrinal infallibility of the Bible (over against all the findings of intellectual enquiry, moral sensibility and current scientific and historical knowledge); or else he could view it as the imperfect work of primitive men – a collection of pious myths which, though not inspired, might still arouse some noble aspirations. The latter, thought Newman, was the more honest course to take.[21]

Now without an authoritative Bible, was he no longer a Christian? This he would by no means concede. God remained all-mighty, all-knowing and all-righteous – attributes requiring, he believed, no special revelation or written authority. Christ was still "a Saviour from sin, a Teacher and Lord sent from heaven."[22] Regretting that he could no longer discuss matters with Evangelicals without becoming either "cold and defensive" or else "warm and disputatious", he still held to "the supernatural character and works of Jesus", and he believed in the truth of "Peter's testimony to the resurrection". The "conversion of Paul" and "the spread of Christianity" also found a place among his reasons for clinging to an orthodox though increasingly vague faith. And even when the factual foundations were gone, the moral ideals of Christianity still held him. He attempted to hang those ideals on humanistic pegs such as the "improvement" of mankind and the progress of "civilisation".

Months went by and he could still read the Bible with pleasure, although it was the pleasure of "religious sentiment", requiring neither belief nor obedience. Gradually Jesus faded from his worship of God, and he began to see himself as a theist, with no creed beyond "the heart's belief in the sympathy of God with individual man."[23] His relationship with the divine, he claimed, seemed not one whit changed from what he had enjoyed in his evangelical phase. If anything, it was more serene, for his faith was now untroubled by matters of science, archaeology and textual analysis; it had become a religion with no factual content at all.

To this point, we can probably feel a degree of sympathy for a man from whom we have reluctantly parted company. But the darkest of Newman's ever-darkening "phases" lies yet ahead, and we cannot give a fair account of his life without recording his ultimate convictions. As he reaches the final "phase of faith", the detached and generally relaxed style of his previous chapters gives place to a tense, touchy, defensive complaint addressed to an offended reviewer before he finally grasps the ghastly nettle and asserts his considered opinion that the character of Jesus was marred by "vain conceit... blundering self-sufficiency... error and arrogance." The Gospels, he says, describe a man who is "pretentious... unintelligible...claiming to act a part for which he is imperfectly prepared." And finally, "So far from being the picture of perfection, it sometimes seems to me the picture of a conscious and wilful impostor... a vain and vacillating pretender."[24] The final portion of *Phases of Faith* is almost pathologically defensive. In 1860 he added thirty-six pages to the sixth edition of the book – a chapter, a note and two appendices – in which he undertakes a point by point refutation of a book refuting his book, and this without adding anything new at all.

Several further articles were written against *Phases of Faith*, and Newman was surprised at the degree of hostility it aroused. His irreverence and his "vulgarity" alienated some who might have responded better to a more gracious and tolerant mode of expression. He did not receive the support he had expected from the Unitarians, nor from the intellectual theists, nor from the Broad Church disciples of Dr Arnold. He had evidently not done his homework as thoroughly as he thought and was, in places, misrepresenting the views he attacked. The novelist George Eliot, who had earlier praised his questioning mind, seemed now too busy composing her *Scenes of Clerical Life* to write anything in his defence. First published in 1850, *Phases of Faith* was reprinted ten times during the next thirty years, once more in 1907, and then sank into total oblivion until 1970 when it found a modest place in the "Victorian Library" of a minor university press. A volume written with the ambitious intention to "overthrow dogma" ended up as an obscure historical curiosity. Newman's other writings have disappeared almost without trace, and his career is now remembered – ultimate irony – by historians of the Brethren movement and almost no one else. After his death, no professional or academic biographer cared to document his varied and active life.

Throughout this time, Frank Newman's academic career continued to progress. Appointed Professor of Classics at Manchester New College in 1840, he moved six years later to London, where he became Professor of Latin at University College.[25] In 1852 he wrote a book entitled *The Soul, its Sorrows and its Aspirations*. By then he had become the archetypal eccentric professor – an unforgettable figure, wearing three coats, one on top of the other, with a large felt hat set far back on his head and counter-balanced by a thin goatee beard on the point of his chin. He was dark and thin, of middle height, always somewhat tense and shy, with a deliberate manner of speech and a formal, rather courtly manner of address. He was a vegetarian and he declared himself *against* a whole range of things: anti-alcohol, anti-smoking, anti-vaccination, anti-vivisection, anti-blood sports, anti-slavery. He wrote tracts on all these, and he also spoke publicly in favour of Indian independence, land reform and votes for women, at a time when these were all the views of an unpopular minority.[26]

There was certainly a streak of perversity in Frank Newman. "He was essentially one of those rare men who *prefer* to be on the weaker side, and whose sword is ever ready for its defence and championship."[27] It was probably this that attracted him in the first place to Darby, to Groves and to the Brethren – to throw in his lot with the idealists, the rebels, the radicals. And, naturally, the more his brother John was drawn towards the authority of the Establishment, the more he was repelled by it. There is little doubt that his brother's fame irritated Frank Newman, and especially the acclaim given to his influential *Apologia Pro Vita Sua* describing the spiritual odyssey that ultimately brought him to rest in the dogmatic securities of Rome. From the first, controversy soured their relationship. They exchanged critical views until they could no longer speak to each other; then they exchanged argumentative letters, until finally John died in 1890. Although Frank protested that in his latter years he enjoyed good relations with his elder brother, he could not resist the temptation, after his death, to "publish a little book designed to cast new doubts about the late Cardinal's consistency of conduct."[28] He was living in the past. "His intentions only underline a pathetic need to stir up the dust of battles that had been settled long, long ago."[29]

As time went on it was a real grief to Maria Newman to see her husband drifting further and further into scepticism and then agnosticism. Even at Oxford he had been warned of the dangers of thinking too much. "You will become a Socinian," he was told, "you will become an infidel." "What!" he replied. "Will you shrink from truth lest it lead to error?... Surely we do not love our doctrines *more than* the truth, but because they *are* the truth. Are we not exhorted to 'prove all things and hold fast that which is good'?"[30] Unconvinced, his friends still feared the outcome. Where would his uncontrolled free-thinking lead him? "The real saint," asserted Newman, "can never be afraid to let God teach him one lesson more, or unteach him one more error."[31] Very noble it might sound in theory; yet in making his own human logic, his own moral sensibilities and his own understanding of science and history the yardstick by which to measure the narrative details and moral judgments of scripture, Newman was asking a lot of any man. Human logic breaks down in the presence of a divine Creator able to work miracles. Moral sensitivities change from age to age. The historical knowledge of Newman's day now looks very limited, and its scientific knowledge even more so.

As it happened, Frank Newman lived in an age of transition, a time in which it seemed that the weight of scholarship was swinging irrevocably against traditional evangelical belief. He did not live to see the swing back to renewed confidence in the Christian scriptures resulting from archaeological discoveries proving the essential accuracy of the biblical accounts of ancient cultures, and from scientific discoveries revealing physical phenomena difficult to account for in the absence of a Creator. His obsessive concern for "truth" was sufficient to destroy a faith built, as it was, on inadequate intellectual foundations. And his sincere questions remained too long unanswered by anyone equipped to be an effective mentor. The easy way out would have been to carry on as a respectable orthodox church attender, keeping his doubts to himself. That would certainly have saved him a lot of trouble, and it would have pleased his devoted wife. "A little more stupidity," he said, "a little more worldliness, a little more mental dishonesty in me, or perhaps a little more kindness and management in others, would have kept me in my old state which was acknowledged and would still be acknowledged as Christian." Indeed, "if I had been slain at the age of twenty-seven when I was chased by a mob of infuriated Mussulmans for selling New Testaments, they would have trumpeted me as an eminent saint and martyr."[32]

Newman was an intelligent and well-meaning man. Would another fifty years of life, introducing him to fresh knowledge and better explanations, have restored his faith to him? Or had his heart become too hardened by time, and by bitter opposition, for him to retrace his steps? We cannot know. He was a child of his age, hampered by its restricted knowledge, wounded by its harsh prejudices, unaware of a living soul able to provide a satisfactory answer to his conscientious questions or his honest doubts. Many others in his generation followed the same path. Families were split, universities divided, churches rent by the ever-increasing onslaught on their biblical faith.

Some nineteenth-century readers may have experienced relief as they followed Newman through his "phases" of disintegration, discarding with him layer after layer of faith. Yet having reached the end of his book, with barely a vestige left of their former belief, they would find precious little to put in its place. No resounding call to action, no fine ethical principles, no vision of a brave new world, nothing but a faint "moral sentiment" for each to feel and to interpret as he would. To every man his own religion, his own experience of the divine, his own understanding of how, and what, and why. Newman proposes a faith without dogma, but he ends up with little more than vague feelings of right and wrong, of a divine presence, of conscience and nobility.

Long after he had left Baghdad, Newman spoke of the "noble-hearted Groves".[33] But the nobility of Groves was a fruit of Christian belief. How would the kindness, compassion, honesty, loyalty, faith, hope and love that Newman so admired survive in a society, or a man, severed from the spiritual roots from which these qualities grew? In the end Frank Newman resembles many who wistfully confess, "I wish I had your faith," as though such faith were impossible for them to obtain. The man hailed by George Eliot in 1850 as "blessed St Francis" finds mention again in her correspondence in 1874. "Poor Mr Francis Newman," she sighed, "must be aged now and rather weary of the world and explanations of the world... I have a sort of affectionate sadness in thinking of the interest I felt in his 'Soul' and 'Phases of Faith' and of the awe I had of him as a lecturer on mathematics at the Ladies' College. How much work he has done in the world, which has left no deep conspicuous mark, but has probably entered beneficently into many lives!"[34] Eliot graciously gives him the benefit of the doubt, something he would not do for Christ.

And towards the end of his life, it seems he came even to doubt his doubts. "It is a sad thing," he said, "to have printed erroneous fact. I have three or four times contradicted and renounced a passage... but I cannot reach those whom I have misled."[35] Loving him devotedly, his wife Maria's constant prayer was for a renewal of the faith he had held so strongly in his youth – that the "cloud", as she called it, might lift from his mind. She always believed he would return to true belief, though she died without seeing it. The epitaph he inscribed on her grave testifies to his respect for his wife's "Christian saintliness" and to her "constant sense of God's presence".[36]

In addition to his evangelical wife, Frank Newman's closest lifelong friends were professing Christians – the Anglican Dr John Nicholson, the Unitarian Dr James Martineau, and one of the earliest women intellectuals, Anna Swanwick. In his final year, aged ninety-two, he told Martineau that he wished it to be known he "died in the Christian faith". His last letter to Anna Swanwick expressed his wish "once again definitely to take the name of Christian". But how did he define "Christian"? A "Christian" is someone who holds the Lord's Prayer as "the highest and purest in any known national religion... The prayer of Jesus, older than any Gospel – this supplants all creeds." Not satisfactory, perhaps, as a statement of evangelical belief, yet by no means the words of an atheist. And, it must be said, the words of a man with a deeper longing for religious truth than many a conventional churchgoer.[37]

ENDNOTES

[1] M43

[2] Newman, *Phases*, 34. According to Darby (*The Irrationalism of Infidelity*), this letter was from John Bellett, who had heard from Hamilton about Newman's questioning of certain Trinitarian beliefs.

[3] *Phases*, 34

[4] Maria Giberne became an artist, making copies of religious pictures, and eventually a Roman Catholic nun and a close friend of his brother J H Newman.

[5] Sieveking, 56-57. Their marriage took place in 1835. Her father was Sir John Kennaway, a friend of Norris Groves, who lived near Exeter (M36). Her sister Frances married Edward Cronin in 1838 (Groves E K, *Successors*, 112; Stunt, *Awakening*, 287).

[6] His baptism probably took place at the Baptist chapel at Broadmead, although he was also known to the Brethren in Bristol.

[7] The diarist was John Hill, Vice-Principal of St Edmund's Hall, quoted by Stunt, *Awakening*, 298.

[8] *Phases*, 35

[9] *Phases*, 36

[10] *Phases*, 40

[11] The doctrine of Development is based on the idea that throughout biblical history God has gradually revealed higher and higher moral standards, thus educating and disciplining his people through the stages of spiritual infancy to ultimate maturity in Christ. Thus, for example, the Mosaic Law was a moral advance on the customs of the Patriarchs, as was the Sermon on the Mount on the Ten Commandments.

[12] *Phases*, 54

[13] *Phases*, 42

[14] *Phases*, 49

[15] Rom 5:12

[16] *Phases*, 60. The majority of early Brethren, including Groves himself, had a decidedly Calvinistic theology (though refusing to be labelled with the name of any man: 1 Cor 1:10-17; 3:3-9). John Wesley and others had, of course, by this time, proposed coherent scriptural grounds for rejecting Calvin's doctrines of predestination and irresistible grace.

[17] *Phases*, 60

[18] *Phases*, 64. In 1837 Groves's pamphlet *The New Testament in the Blood of Jesus* was prepared for the press by a certain "Mr Newman", almost certainly Frank (A Minister, *Perpetuity*, 32). In April 1838 the question was raised in Chittoor, and discussed by Groves and Gundert, "whether F Newman should join up with us" (Gundert, 29).

[19] *Phases*, 68

[20] *Phases*, 68-69

[21] The questions raised by Newman have been the subject of much thought and many books since his day. A recent and readable apologia is Lee Strobel, *The Case for Faith* (Zondervan, 2000). See also Henry M Morris, *Many Infallible Proofs* (Master Books, 1974, 1996), Gleason L Archer, *New International Encyclopedia of Bible Difficulties* (Zondervan, 1982) and Norman Geisler & Thomas Howe, *When Critics Ask* (Baker, 1992). Genealogies are considered in commentaries such as Hendricksen's *Matthew* and *Luke* (Banner of Truth). With regard to the land bought by Jacob and the identity of the martyred Zechariah see John Wenham, *Christ and the Bible* (Eagle, 1993, 84ff). On the moral difficulties in the Bible see John Wenham, *The Enigma of Evil* (IVP, 1985). Our generation has the benefit of more comprehensive answers to these questions than were available to Newman – which is not to say that we have final answers!

[22] *Phases*, 86

[23] *Phases*, 133

[24] *Phases*, 154

[25] In 1843 Newman was so excited about a new research project that he made himself ill; he was accumulating words for a Kabyle Berber dictionary (Sieveking, 133).

[26] He wrote and spoke much about political and social controversies – Ireland, India, European affairs, American slavery, and on one occasion, in a letter to his academic friend Dr Nicholson, on the evils of alcohol and tobacco: "I am reminded of it by

seeing today a statement made concerning *cricketers*, that no first-rate cricketer takes beer, ale or spirits which... 'jaundice the eye', nor tobacco in any form, which induces a kind of stupefaction... The recent celebrated victorious cricketer, a Mr Grace, it is said, will not even take *tea*, but prefers water." Having got that off his chest, he consults Nicholson about the exact dating of certain cuneiform inscriptions! (Sieveking, 186)

[27] Sieveking, 7

[28] Knoepflmacher, 8

[29] Knoepflmacher, 22. It is not generally known that in addition to J H and F W there was a third Newman brother, between them in age. Lacking their intellectual abilities, Charles Robert became a compulsive cynic, a caustic wit, a critic of everyone and everything, and a single-minded atheist.

[30] *Phases*, 70-71. Socinian: a person denying the deity of Jesus whilst respecting him as a good teacher and an example to be followed; after the teaching of the sixteenth-century Italian Protestant Faustus Socinus.

[31] *Phases*, 71

[32] *Phases*, 134. This happened at Aintab, as described in Chapter 15.

[33] *Phases*, 37

[34] Quoted by Knoepflmacher, 21

[35] Sieveking, 65-66

[36] Maria was a close friend of Harriet Groves. After Harriet's return to England they used to visit the poor together in Weston-super-Mare (Groves E K, *Successors*, 60).

[37] G H Lang offers further anecdotal evidence of Newman's final restoration to faith (*Groves*, 210).

Anthony Norris Groves
source: Groves H: Memoir

Northernhay House, Exeter, 1853
source: G Townsend, DALSS

John Gifford Bellett
source: Beattie

Edward Cronin
source: Sieveking

Frank Newman
source: Sieveking

John Nelson Darby
source: Neatby

Mary Müller (née Groves)
source: Müller, Autobiography (Bergin)

Henry Craik
source: Beattie

George Müller
source: Beattie

Bridge of Boats, Baghdad, 1882
source: Royal Geographical Readers no. 5, Alamy

Karl Gottlieb Pfander
source: Stock vol.2

John Kitto
source: Ryland

Harnie Thomas
source: Groves H: Faithful Hanie

Hermann Gundert
source: Frenz

Harriet Groves and Agnes
source: Groves E K: Successors

The four sons of A N Groves
Norris (George)   Edward
Frank   Henry
source: Groves E K: Successors

John Vesey Parnell (Lord Congleton)
source: Beattie

Edward Cronin in middle life
source: Beattie

A traditional Indian school (date uncertain)
source: Echoes archive

An Indian mission school (date uncertain)

source: *Echoes archive*

"Thirty years ago…
I put my mark upon this passage in Isaiah,
'I am the Lord:
they shall not be ashamed that wait on me.'
… I stand this day as one not ashamed."

John Kitto [1]

24

To Travel Usefully

"To travel usefully," said John Kitto, "one must carry information with him; and the information obtained will be in exact proportion to the weight of information carried."[2] In September 1832 a new phase of life was opening up for Kitto as he and Frank Newman left Baghdad on horseback, "accompanied into the open country by Mr Groves and the other dear friends, where we took leave of them with tears."[3] Useful travel was travel that one could write about afterwards, and Kitto now felt more ready than he had been to write about it. But with a history of repeated failures, his future was by no means certain. He confided, "I have equally weighed, I trust, the results of both success and disappointment, and have a mind prepared to look either quietly in the face."[4]

As travelling companions, Kitto and Newman made an unlikely pair. Kitto, sporting a moustache, "a dark cap of Persian lambskin, a Turkish gown and an Arabian black cloak," could pass for a traveller from almost any part of the Middle East, with his rather Oriental features, his "dwarfish stature", and his apparent inability to speak any recognisable language. This meant he could buy fruit along the road at a cheaper rate than his English companion. The two aroused great interest by their custom of talking together "on the fingers".[5] Kitto was constantly asking questions, and Newman patiently trying to explain what was happening. In Teheran Kitto was pleased to visit John McNeill, who added further to his stock of information about Eastern customs. Here both he and Newman were taken ill with "ague" and "bilious fever", and were bled by "an old barber with a red beard".

At Tabriz they were warmly welcomed by Nisbet and his wife.[6] From here Newman, keen to reach England as soon as possible, pressed on to Constantinople whilst Kitto (with no young lady in mind) was happy to linger in Armenia, enjoying the hospitality of missionaries in several places and accumulating information about the customs and culture of the people. Mount Ararat delighted him, as did the streets of Constantinople where he absorbed the exotic sights and smells and the feel of ancient history beneath his feet. The welcome he received from missionaries and other Christians throughout his time abroad had done much to renew in him a love for Christian people in general, which had taken heavy knocks during his earlier unhappy periods in England and Malta.

In Tabriz Kitto was introduced to a young diplomatic official by the name of Shepherd who was returning to England in the hope of recovering his health sufficiently to marry the young woman who was waiting for him. He and Kitto decided to travel together. Rejoining Newman in Constantinople, they boarded ship, and Kitto found himself once more "miserable and irritable, and with few prospects of happiness before me."[7] Time passed at sea in discussions with Newman, and Kitto's journal of the voyage to London is "filled with reports of Mr Newman's sayings and criticisms" which considerably perplexed him. The invalid's health continued to deteriorate however, and while the ship was anchored off the coast of England awaiting clearance from quarantine, Shepherd died, having entrusted to Kitto his last messages to his fiancée.

So it was, on 11th June 1833, that John Kitto set foot once more in England; he had been away exactly four years. Now nearly thirty years of age, he hoped to find some way of earning his living with his pen, perhaps by helping to edit a missionary magazine. But first things first: taking lodgings in Islington, he set out to fulfil the errand entrusted to him by the dying Shepherd. Calling on the young lady, he found her "a very interesting person", and decided to call again. Kitto, ever persistent in a cause of personal interest, proposed, was accepted, and three months later Annabella Fenwick became Annabella Kitto. He was unspeakably happy: "I have now a fireside of my own to sit down by, and on the other side is my wife darning stockings."[8] In the course of time, her skill as a darner of stockings was complemented by that of a willing secretary and indefatigable research assistant, daily visiting the British Museum with her husband and finding the information he needed for his writings.

And prolific indeed did those writings become! A London publisher, Charles Knight, asked Kitto to write up his travel journals for a series of articles in the *Penny Magazine*, a publication read at that time by a million people in Britain, reprinted in America and translated into French, German and Dutch. With this success behind him, he was appointed editor of the *Penny Cyclopaedia* and at the same time started work on a children's book called *Uncle Oliver's Travels in Persia*. Other projects followed as readers enquired about his experiences in the East amidst people living in such similar circumstances to the heroes and villains of sacred scripture. Granted, he had never actually travelled in Palestine, but he had seen an Eastern tax-collector, a meal shared at the tent of hospitable nomads, the slaughtering of a ram at a religious feast, the broaching of a wineskin, a night spent in a stable because there was no room in the inn, the sky darkened by a vast cloud of locusts, the varied salutations of the rich, the poor and the destitute, the fields of barley sown, reaped, threshed and winnowed. And having seen, he never forgot; deprived of the faculty of hearing, he had developed an almost photographic memory for things he had observed.

Towards the end of 1835 the great *Pictorial Bible* began to take shape. It was an exciting novelty and its readers eagerly awaited its monthly instalments. Previous commentators such as Matthew Henry had examined the theology and the history recorded in the sacred texts, and had drawn useful lessons from them, but never before had a writer looked so carefully at the physical detail – the hills, the valleys, the animals, architecture, agricultural methods, the manner of interaction between people. Kitto brought the Bible stories to life. What is more, he confirmed the accuracy of the ancient texts. He showed how the activities described by the prophets and apostles accorded with the realities of Eastern culture. This knowledge enabled the Bible reader to understand many things previously obscure or contradictory to the Western mind, and Kitto's careful research into the geography, biology and archaeology of Bible lands, far from undermining confidence in the accuracy of the Bible, served to support and encourage it. This provided a marvellous boost to the faith of a generation reeling from the first onslaughts of the Higher Critics.

Next came the *Pictorial History of Palestine and the Holy Land*, a work requiring a prodigious amount of library research. He laboured sixteen hours a day, and the longsuffering Annabella hardly less. Kitto, indeed, was blessed with a wife who would willingly spend her waking hours following him from study to parlour, and back again, with books, letters and the occasional meal. And this for a man so deaf that he always had to ask her what the children were saying. She spelt the words out on her fingers, he replied with his deep guttural voice, and in this fashion they seemed able to communicate quite happily.[9]

John Kitto was a devoted husband and father, and an equally devoted son to his aged mother, who came to live with them. As time went on Annabella was too busy with their four children to assist him as she had in earlier days. The *Pictorial History* was not a financial success, and another magazine, designed "to give sketches of the missionary enterprise in various parts of the world", had achieved only three issues when, in 1841, Mr Knight's publishing house ran into serious financial difficulties. Suddenly Kitto was out of work. Forced to sell his Islington house at a loss, he moved to the cheaper end of Woking. A little income still came in from book sales, but for a year he struggled to pay his debts. By now his name was quite well known, but a worthy name does not feed a growing family, and the market for biblical encyclopedias was limited. He proposed various projects to Christian publishers, some of which were accepted, and he set to work at once, turning out a succession of books on themes relating to biblical history and geography, with engravings showing typical scenes from the Holy Land.

Then in 1845 came the massive two-volume *Cyclopaedia of Biblical Literature*, a compendium of articles from a range of contemporary scholars, proudly bearing on the title page the editor's name – not John Kitto, shoemaker, pauper, workhouse boy, but John Kitto, DD, FSA.[10] His honorary doctorate had been granted the previous year by a German university in recognition of his services to biblical scholarship. The *Cyclopaedia of Biblical Literature* was an extraordinarily erudite production, hardly surpassed in modern times for the sheer bulk of information it contained, with copious line drawings of places, costumes and daily activities, and with linguistic references not just in Greek and Hebrew but also in Arabic, Coptic and other languages too, illustrating the usage of words and customs throughout the Middle East.

Further publications followed. Some made a little money, some none at all. It was during this period that Kitto saw Norris Groves for the last time, and found him, as always, a sympathetic friend. It is to Groves's credit that when asked to give details of his latter misfortunes Kitto confided, "There is no one in the world to whom I would make the statement I now make to you."[11] Finally, in 1849, Kitto returned to London and began his last and his most enduring work, the *Daily Bible Illustrations* in eight volumes. Labouring from 4 a.m. till 9 p.m., he was pleased to be writing about the practical spiritual lessons in the scriptural narrative rather than just the cultural and geographical context. For a while it supported his family, now increased to five sons and five daughters.

In 1850, the year of *David Copperfield*, he received a pension for life from Queen Victoria. But Kitto was suffering from severe headaches. He had never been one to take much exercise, and had become by now considerably obese. The day following the completion of the *Daily Bible Illustrations* he suffered a stroke, then during the next few days several fits and severe headaches. At this time his youngest child died. Physicians thought his health might improve overseas, but first he insisted on carrying a little wine and some cakes to the prison for "a poor invalid incarcerated for debt". This was the son of Mrs Barnicle, the Plymouth shopkeeper whose kindness he had never forgotten.[12] In August he left for Germany, in the hope of benefit from the local mineral waters, accompanied by Annabella and seven of the children. During this trip two more of his children died, before he too finally passed away at Cannstatt, in 1854, barely a year after Groves himself. He was fifty years old.

In his generation Dr Kitto was a most significant contributor to Christian scholarship, and he provided much help for Evangelicals defending the Bible against the attack of liberal critics. He eventually wrote a total of twenty-three books, of which Spurgeon considered the *Daily Bible Illustrations* to be "more interesting than any novel that was ever written, and as instructive as the heaviest theology."[13] One reason Kitto is so little known today lies in the fact that his writing, by its very nature, has dated more than most. His early essays dealt with social and philosophical themes that time has now passed by, and his later encyclopedic works have been superseded by the prodigious researches of a newer and more scientific generation of archaeologists, linguists and anthropologists. Yet his *Pictorial Bible* and *Cyclopaedia of Biblical Literature* held, for almost a century, a unique and valued place on the academic library shelf, and his *Daily Bible Illustrations* encouraged the faith of readers of all ages in many a humbler home and stimulated the imagination of many a Sunday school teacher.

Kitto's discussions at sea with the iconoclastic Frank Newman would have alerted him to the need for scholarly research. It is perhaps ironic that the stone-deaf child of a drunkard, schooled in the workhouse, would finally achieve more academic renown and sell many more books than the most brilliant son of a privileged family, holder of a double-first at Oxford. "All the fine stories we hear about natural ability are mere rigmarole," said Kitto. "Every man may, according to his opportunities and industry, render himself almost anything he wishes to become."[14] The secret of his success undoubtedly lay in his stubborn determination to make full use of what he had. "Talent is common," he said, "but the art of unfolding talent is not so common."[15] "I perhaps have as much right as any man that lives, to bear witness that there is no one so low but that he may rise, no condition so cast down as to be really hopeless, and no privation which need, of itself, shut out any man from the paths of honourable exertion or from the hope of usefulness in life. I have sometimes thought that it was possibly my mission to affirm and establish these great truths."[16]

Many of the world's great achievers have been disadvantaged in some respect, and it was probably the disadvantage, in many cases, that spurred them to achieve what they did. The poet John Clare was a contemporary of Kitto, also from a poor home, also jilted by the girl he loved, a labouring boy who loved books, painfully sensitive, lonely, and misunderstood by almost everyone. Clare's biographer observes, "The destruction of the man was the triumph of the poet. Whether the destruction was necessary is a matter for speculation. There is no reader who would not, on the score of compassion, sacrifice some at least of the poetry if it could have mitigated the tragedy. But out of Clare's unhappiness, as well as his happiness, sprang the poems. If we esteem the poems, we must accept the unhappiness."[17] Kitto himself in later years was always inclined to be positive, thankful that his fall, though depriving him of hearing, had not taken his reason or his life. He observed that deafness was a lighter affliction than many have to bear. Indeed, he could give thanks for a small catastrophe that perhaps kept him from a greater: "How do I know but that God permitted my deafness as an instrument through which I might be saved from some far worse evil?"[18] However we might account for it, his inability to hear was what impelled John Kitto to cultivate his habit of minute visual observation and focused all the intensity of his impressionable and affectionate nature into the writing that was his only way of expressing himself.

The relationship between Norris Groves and his young protégé was a crucial one for them both, and one of great interest to a biographer. Groves always spoke well of Kitto's efforts as a tutor and enjoyed seeing his happy relations with the boys. He was unfailingly patient and supportive, bearing kindly with Kitto's aberrations at times when other friends had given up hope of his improvement. Yet there remained certain tensions between them. Groves was by nature a talker, whilst Kitto was of necessity a writer, and Kitto's obsession with books might well seem a waste of time and effort to a man whose great interest was personal conversation about spiritual things. Groves was not a lover of literature; nor was he keen on the idea of overseas missionaries returning to a desk and a study in the homeland. The call to be a evangelist was a higher calling than that of a mere biblical scholar or compiler of encyclopedias! Groves expressed regret that the nine years he spent with Kitto seemed to have taught and influenced his young friend less than he had hoped.[19] Kitto himself, after attending Norris and Harriet's wedding in 1835, wrote to an Anglican friend, "I confess to you that there are many of his views in which I do not concur nearly so much as I seemed to myself to do while I was under that strong personal influence which I think he exerts over those who are in near connection with him, through the warmth and energy which, more than any man I ever knew, he throws into his opinions. Whether the difference between now and then... results from a more dispassionate and uninfluenced view of the same subjects or merely from the greater ascendancy of worldly influences in my mind, I cannot venture to determine. I fear Mr Groves might be disposed to consider the latter the most probable account; while you, perhaps, might be willing to allow the former."[20]

It was undoubtedly a disappointment to Groves that his earliest helper had declared his wish to leave Baghdad; it meant a weakening of the team just as it was relaunching its mission. Yet, to be fair, Kitto was given very little to do in Baghdad. His biographer tells us that even when freed from teaching duties by the coming of Newman and Parnell, "Kitto was not permitted to exercise any of the functions of a missionary."[21] He was not encouraged to make progress with the language; nor was he taken out on visits to interested neighbours. His deafness was naturally a handicap, but so too was his humble social origin. Groves could never quite bring himself to consider "poor little Kitto" as a friend and equal like Parnell, Cronin or Newman; and Kitto felt it keenly that Groves sometimes made arrangements "without thinking it necessary in the least to consult him."[22] Despite his impressive achievement in educating himself, Kitto would always be a workhouse boy raised by the kindness of others from a life of manual labour amidst the poor of England, and it is evident that Groves could neither understand nor approve of Kitto's obsessive desire to better himself – to become independent, self-sufficient, accepted as an equal by officers and gentlemen. Kitto's constant tendency to view his present occupation as a stepping stone to a future and higher one must have grated on Groves all the more in view of his own choice to give up a lucrative career, a large house and considerable social distinction in order to become a poor servant of Christ.

In fact the two men had backgrounds and abilities so contrasting that it is remarkable they got on so well together, especially as they could talk only by spelling out words with the fingers or by scribbling on a slate. Such communication requires constant effort and almost precludes the interchange of humour so essential to lighten and relieve moments of tension. "I have not had a soul to speak to," wrote Norris Groves from Baghdad, "in the midst of all my troubles and sorrows; for poor Kitto, though he would do what he could, when the heart is full the fingers will not let it out."[23] Comments, requests and opinions, when written, acquire a degree of terseness and dogmatism that would be tempered in speech by a smile, a kindly intonation or a further explanation. At times both men gave and took offence from this. And of course they could never pray aloud together.

The differences between Groves and Kitto are not hard to see, yet in other respects they were remarkably similar. Both were very strong willed, both were acutely introspective, and both were emotionally vulnerable. They felt things deeply, but rarely could they express their feelings, especially to one another, and especially in time of inner turmoil. In Baghdad Groves's tragic circumstances drove him into his shell. Immersed in his own griefs and disappointments, he had little to offer the tutor of his boys. It was typical of him that after Kitto had gone he condemned himself mercilessly for failing to show the affection and trust that might have enabled the younger man to comfort and support him in his sorrows, and perhaps to have avoided any separation between them.[24]

As a writer, of course, Kitto had to make his work acceptable to Christians of all persuasions. The majority of his potential publishers and readers were from the Church of England, and in certain Anglican circles the name of Groves was an unpopular one. This probably accounts for his reluctance, after his return, to mention his association with his former benefactor; he never, in any of his books, makes allusion to him. Groves was undoubtedly hurt by this, and found it hard to understand. But Groves, with his own unflinching commitment to speaking the truth in love, and supported by his circle of like-minded friends, would in the nature of things find it hard to understand the necessity for diplomatic manoeuvring on the part of one such as Kitto who remained dependent for his ministry and his livelihood on a fickle body of literary critics and a nation of prejudiced readers.[25] As far as his personal church connections went, Kitto regularly took Communion in the Church of England, where he was able to follow the order of service in the Prayer Book more easily than meetings of a more spontaneous nature, but he never hinted at the slightest antipathy to other denominations or to the Brethren. The welcome he had received overseas in the homes of Christians from many different backgrounds had confirmed the conviction learned from Norris Groves that denominational differences should count for nothing to a true disciple of Christ.

When asked to which church he belonged, he habitually replied "to the Church Universal",[26] and Groves would have said exactly the same.

In 1853, hearing that his old friend had returned to England in a state of ill health, Kitto was hoping to see him again, or at least to hear from him. It was a shock to learn of his death. He wrote immediately to Mary Müller, offering his sympathy and his appreciation of "one to whom I have owed so much and with whom my own lot has been so closely connected in many difficult and trying scenes." Kitto comforted her with the thought of the heavenly reward that would be her brother's "great gain... the realisation of all that he lived and longed for more entirely than anyone it has been my privilege to know."[27]

All things considered, it is probable that without the loving care of the man to whom, under God, he owed his conversion, John Kitto would have remained no more than a minor writer of topical essays in penny periodicals – as obscure in his day as in ours. Although his subsequent authority as an interpreter of Eastern ways stemmed in part from his voracious appetite for the travellers' tales of other men, he would have found little acceptance for what he wrote apart from his own four years' experience in the East. The credit for taking him eastwards must go to Norris Groves, along with much of the credit for constantly encouraging a most unlikely young man to ignore his disabilities, put behind him his previous failures and disappointments, and devote his curious abilities to the service of God.

ENDNOTES

[1] Eadie, 428
[2] Eadie, 241
[3] Eadie, 241
[4] Eadie, 248. Mail from infected areas was fumigated by the British authorities. Kitto remarked wryly that letters from Baghdad, "smoked and dried, like a neat's tongue, and stabbed through and through, as I suppose mine are," will have aroused greater interest than the same thoughts would do when written from the safety of a conventional English drawing room (Eadie, 226).
[5] Eadie, 245, 253
[6] Charlotte Nisbet (née Taylor) had travelled from England with Groves, Kitto and their party in 1829.
[7] Eadie, 269
[8] Eadie, 290
[9] Kitto never acquired the ability to lip-read. He calculated that two-thirds of his vocabulary consisted of words he had read but never heard, and his habit was to pronounce each word exactly as it was spelt.
[10] Doctor of Divinity, Fellow of the Society of Antiquaries.
[11] M460

[12] Eadie, 417

[13] Spurgeon, quoted in publisher's notice in endpages of Eadie.

[14] Eadie, 408

[15] Eadie, 400

[16] Eadie, 434

[17] Reeves, James, *Selected Poems of John Clare* (Heinemann, 1954), xxix

[18] Eadie, 110

[19] Eadie, 229

[20] Eadie, 315

[21] Eadie, 226. If encouraged, Kitto could surely have learned to read and write classical Arabic and Syriac, and fulfilled his early wish to compose tracts for the local people. He might also have found scope for designing decorated Bible texts for use as gifts to Jewish and Armenian friends.

[22] Eadie, 240. The problems associated with Kitto's strange appearance and manner would be compounded by Groves's knowledge of his lowly birth and upbringing. In nineteenth-century Britain, some were officers and some were men, and embarrassment was the certain result of anyone trying to cross that cultural divide. In the cricketing terms of the day, Mr Groves would always be the gentleman captain, J Kitto the professional bowler.

[23] M205

[24] Eadie, 239. Groves may have learned much from this experience. His later journals show him consistently treating his Indian co-workers and his missionary colleagues (some of them from very humble backgrounds) as friends and equals – an attitude contrasting sharply with that of contemporary British commercial and military officials.

[25] There was also, perhaps, an element of misunderstanding between them on this point. In the expectation of publishing his own journals, Groves may have asked Kitto not to write a formal account of the mission to Baghdad, which Kitto took as a request never to write about him at all (Eadie, 432).

[26] Eadie, 430

[27] M518

"How differently would the heathen look on our
endeavours…
if the hardy and suffering spirit of primitive times
were to descend again
on the silken age into which we are fallen,
and if they perceived in us that love
which led them to endure all things for the elect's sake."

Norris Groves [1]

25

That Burly Saxon Figure

O f all those who worked with Norris Groves, Karl Gottlieb Pfander was certainly the most colourful. It was just two weeks before the plague hit Baghdad in March 1831 that Pfander said farewell to the Groves household and set off with his *pastourma* sausages for the mountains of Persia. He joined convoys of travellers for each stage of his journey, cheerfully explaining the gospel to all who would listen and offering scriptures to all who could read. Trekking as far east as Isfahan, he then worked his way north, and eventually rejoined his former colleagues at Shushi in the Armenian foothills.

Here Pfander had already laboured for some years amidst a mixed population of Muslims and Armenian Christians. But talking with Muslims in public places had often led to hostile and angry exchanges. They "would not listen to any full and lengthened statement of Christian doctrine, nor to any explicit argument in favour of the gospel and in refutation of the Qur'an… Neither could such important subjects be brought forward without constant interruptions from the opponent."[2] The missionary team wondered whether written communication would be more effective. A letter or book could introduce facts and arguments without the emotional fluster of a face-to-face encounter.

In his early days at Shushi, Pfander had come upon a Muslim merchant, recently returned from a pilgrimage to a Shiite shrine in eastern Persia; this man was disputing in the marketplace with some local Armenian Christians. Concerned that the Armenians might suffer public humiliation, Pfander joined in the discussion. After some initial courtesies the merchant brought him twenty written questions, to which he replied with twenty written answers. They continued to correspond, but the exchanges became increasingly hostile, and eventually Pfander felt it wiser to desist. The exchange of letters, however, was to become a feature of Pfander's subsequent work, and it was in Shushi that he started to accumulate the ideas that eventually took shape in his remarkable book, the *Mizan ul-Haqq* (The Balance of Truth).

There are things a book can do that a missionary cannot. A book can find its way into the inner chambers of a mosque or palace or harem. It is available at any moment of leisure and can speak without a foreign accent. It can present facts without personal antagonism and develop a theme without interruption. It suffers no sickness or fatigue, and enjoys a lifespan much longer than its author's three-score years and ten. Pfander cast around in the extensive library of the Shushi mission house, searching for such a book – a volume demonstrating what Christians really believe, in contrast to the caricature of Christianity that all Muslims had been taught to despise; a book that would prove the Bible to be the inspired word of God, neither corrupted nor superseded; a book that would show how the Qur'an itself testifies to the reliability of the Christian scriptures and the supremacy of Christ; a book that would demonstrate from the Qur'an, the Traditions and the Commentators the fallibilities of Islam and its prophet; a book that would explain the triune nature of God and the redemption secured by Christ; a book that would contrast the violence of Islamic expansion with the peaceable spread of the gospel; a book that would, in short, help the Muslim reader to put his trust in Christ as Saviour and Lord. Eventually, realising that no such book existed, Pfander set out to write it. And once started on this formidable task, he remarked, "To my surprise, and contrary to all my expectation, my pen ran on with ease, and page after page was filled."³

Karl Pfander was optimistic that Christianity (carefully explained and proved from authenticated scriptures) would convince first of all the theologians, and then the worshippers, of the Islamic world. Many hours of discussion with Muslims had enabled him to enter into their manner of thought and to cast the gospel in a mould comprehensible to them. The style of the *Mizan ul-Haqq* is modelled on that of Islamic theological works. It has many expressions of respect for the reader, with appeals to his moderation, his understanding and his piety. At the same time, it is marked by a typically Germanic bluntness. There is much in the book which casts Islam in a bad light, and few modern apologists, though agreeing with many points Pfander makes, would attack their opponents as directly as he did. But his purpose was to shake the complacency of theologian and worshipper, and lead them to faith in Christ, and it must be said that no book has proved more effective to this end than the *Mizan ul-Haqq*.⁴

In 1837, six years after Pfander's sojourn in Baghdad, the Shushi team found their situation drastically altered. The whole region, including the territories of Georgia, Armenia and Azerbaijan, had just been annexed by the Russians, and the Tsar, impelled by the jealousies of the Russian Orthodox Church, issued a decree prohibiting all Protestant preaching of the gospel. Breaking up the Shushi mission, the CMS transferred Pfander to northern India. Here he married again and settled in Agra on the Ganges plain about 130 miles to the south of Delhi. In view of his particular interest in Muslims and his years spent in learning how to communicate with Persians, Turks and Arabs, it might seem strange that Karl Pfander should find himself in India, a nation peopled largely by Hindus, with an entirely different set of languages. Yet India had much to commend it as a strategic centre for reaching the Islamic world. In fact one-fifth of the world's Muslims lived there, many of them in the territories now recognised as Pakistan and Bangladesh. Under British authority, India enjoyed a degree of peace, prosperity and freedom from corruption unusual in the East, and with the approval of evangelical administrators, a Christian missionary could undertake direct evangelistic work with more confidence and safety than in territories under Turkish or Russian control.

Agra, the home of the Taj Mahal, was a city with a long history. From here the Mughal emperors Akbar (1556-1605) and Jahangir (1605-27) had ruled over a dazzling Islamic empire whilst the Tudors and Stuarts were still struggling in England to establish some political stability after the religious upheavals of the Reformation and Counter-Reformation. In the court of the emperor Akbar, Jesuit missionaries reported that "the wise men are wont every day to disputations on literary subjects before him."[5] The Jesuits themselves had engaged in public debate in Persian with the *'ulama*, the scholars of Islam, and enjoyed private conversation with Akbar on religious topics, both in his chambers and during the course of military or hunting expeditions. Three centuries later, Agra again witnessed a flowering of Christian eloquence with the public preaching of Henry Martyn's convert 'Abd ul-Masih prior to his sudden death in 1827.

Pfander himself arrived at a time of turmoil and resolved to take advantage of it. Severe drought and famine (with the death of 500,000 in Agra itself) had led to a breakdown in law and order and a general disillusionment with traditional customs and religions. Several upper-class Muslims had professed conversion to Christianity. Adding insult to injury, a Christian orphanage and printing press had been set up in a building housing a famous Mughal tomb, and several orphans – Hindus and Muslims – had been baptised. A stream of Persian and Urdu tracts now began to flow from the press, demonstrating the superiority of the gospel in a fashion that excited and enraged the religious leaders.[6] The writer of the tracts was Karl Gottlieb Pfander, and this was exactly his intention; he wanted to stimulate a public response to the gospel that would make it a talking point throughout the region.

Taking up his residence in 1841 at the heart of the city bazaar, Pfander had written letters to several leading Muslims. Hoping to engage them in written or verbal debate, he sent out copies of the *Mizan ul-Haqq*. They were reluctant to reply, thinking perhaps that open opposition to Christianity might jeopardise their standing with the British authorities or lead to reprisals of some sort. At this stage, in any case, they knew too little about Christianity to be able to debate the questions raised. Requests nevertheless came to Pfander for copies of the Bible in various languages, and his challenge had become a talking point, as intended, in the bazaars, colleges and mosques of Agra. His attempt to reproduce in his writings the idiom and even the outward appearance of scholarly Islamic works was successful enough to cause surprise and alarm. The *'ulama* began to fear the undermining of their influence, and a few months later their own letters and tracts began to circulate, countering Pfander's arguments. In response, he published a further book, *Hall ul-Ishkal* (The Solution to Difficulties), in 1847. The following year a friendly discussion took place between Pfander and some "respectable and learned Muslims" who came from Lucknow and Delhi. He was encouraged. For the first time his bait had been taken, and the outcome seemed productive, though far from conclusive. This was followed, however, by a lull in which nothing further was published on either side, although Pfander continued to talk with individuals and groups in public places and to revise his books. He enjoyed a brief furlough in Europe.

Karl Pfander, like Norris Groves, was a natural communicator. He had managed to retain the common touch, and his relaxed friendliness must have contrasted pleasingly with the stiff condescension of the British officials and also, perhaps, with the well-bred decorum of the army chaplains. "His rural origins, forthright manner and somewhat uncouth appearance... combined to lessen the distance and to remove some of the obstacles to communication with peasant audiences in India."[7] An evangelical East India Company officer wrote of him in glowing terms: "Who that ever met him can forget that burly Saxon figure and genial open face beaming with intellect, simplicity and benevolence? He had great natural gifts for a missionary – a large heart, a powerful mind, high courage and indomitable good humour... Pfander was the very man for a controversy. He not only was the essence of good nature, but *looked* it, and it was difficult for anyone to be angry with him for more than a passing moment."[8]

Returning to India in 1853, he was surprised to find a considerable stir among Muslims and Hindus in Delhi resulting from the conversion to Christ of a brilliant Hindu lecturer at the Delhi College. In the course of his work translating astronomy textbooks into Urdu, Ram Chandra had gradually come to doubt the assumptions and assertions of the traditional Indian religions. Initially, he slipped into agnosticism. Then, declaring himself a convinced Christian, he asked for baptism. Other conversions followed. Western science, it seemed, was about to destroy the great religions of India, and the *'ulama* decided it was time to take up the challenge repeatedly thrown at them by Pfander and the distributors of his books. In their eyes he had become "the fortress which must be taken".[9]

They commenced by publishing several scholarly works refuting his arguments, pointing out his grammatical errors and his "misunderstanding" of key Qur'anic texts. The recent publication of the Anglican *Book of Common Prayer* in Urdu had given them access to the Trinitarian complexities of the Athanasian Creed, which they set about demolishing with ruthless logic. The *Catholic Herald* in Calcutta proved a good source of anti-Protestant material, as did the proliferation of Bible translations, which manifested inconsistencies and disagreements amongst the Christians themselves.[10] But the real advance in the Muslim camp came with access to the English libraries attached to the major colleges and cathedrals in every city. Colonial officials (many of them Evangelicals) had stocked the shelves, often at their own expense, with encyclopedias, biblical commentaries, theological volumes, ecclesiastical and secular histories, works by agnostics, sceptics, deists and atheists and – most significantly – with the latest publications of the German pioneers of Higher Criticism. Muslim scholars now felt confident enough to play Pfander at his own game.

A public debate was arranged, to be conducted in the Urdu language. The two Muslim representatives complemented one another in personality and background. The self-styled "recluse" among Islamic scholars, Rahmat Allah Kairanawi, was supported by a well-travelled assistant surgeon from the government hospital in Agra who had profited from an English education, Muhammad Wazir Khan. Both were Sunnites with mystical Sufi connections.[11]

Pfander's "second" was a young man called Thomas French, associated like him with the CMS but in other respects quite dissimilar. French had arrived in India less than three years previously, to become (at the age of twenty-five) the founder and first principal of St John's College, a new Anglican missionary training school. He had enjoyed a liberal education under Thomas Arnold at Rugby, and had learned at Oxford University to temper his own evangelical convictions with an open-minded interest in current trends concerning the textual analysis of the Bible. Gentle and unassuming in character, he had doubts from the start about the value of Pfander's confrontational methods, preferring the quieter processes of education and personal friendship. This meant that the youthful French was, at best, a reluctant participant, one who was unused to dealing in dogmatic certainties, and one whose knowledge of Urdu was still rudimentary.

Letters were sent back and forth, attempting to fix the agenda, and eventually Pfander and French agreed to their opponents' proposal to debate five subjects in order. These were *naskh* (abrogation of Christian scripture), *tahrif* (corruption of Christian scripture), *tathlith* (the Trinity), *risalat-i Muhammad* (the prophethood of Muhammad), and finally the Qur'an. This was a serious tactical blunder on Pfander's part, born probably of over-confidence. It meant that he would be on the defensive from the start, trying to justify the two most difficult concepts in the Christian theological system.[12]

The debate was to be held in the missionary compound; it was April 1854. A number of high officials, both English and Indian, were present, with a strong representation of Muslim scholars and two local newspaper editors. An audience of several hundred Muslims and a scattering of Hindus were sitting cross-legged on the floor. On the second day, when news of the event had spread round the city, the number would rise to over a thousand, most of them crowded outside the hall and craning to hear what was being said. The East India Company was well represented, but few of the local Anglican or Baptist missionaries seemed to have turned up, perhaps sharing French's doubts about the wisdom of the whole procedure.

We have both Christian and Muslim reports of the unfolding stages of the contest. On one side sat Rahmat Allah and Wazir Khan, and behind them a company of Islamic students; opposite were Pfander and French and some Christian officials. As the debate opened, the Muslim camp immediately accused Pfander of misunderstanding the Qur'anic quotations used in the *Mizan ul-Haqq*, a thrust impossible for a foreigner to parry, however unjust it might be, especially as Islamic scholars cannot agree among themselves on the meaning of many such texts. Lengthy debate on passages from the Bible then secured the admission from Pfander that it was possible for scripture to be abrogated and for God's express commands to be superseded and replaced by different commands. So much for *naskh*.

The debate moved on to the second question. For nearly thirty years Pfander had steadfastly denied that the original scriptures, in the course of centuries of transmission, had been either deliberately falsified or unwittingly corrupted by Jews or by Christians. He admitted the existence of "insignificant copyists' errors" in some (though never all) of the hand-written copies but denied that there were "serious corruptions". Rahmat Allah and Wazir Khan reminded him of this, then fired volleys of quotations from the early Christian Fathers, from the latest Christian theologians, and from the New Testament itself, to support their assertion that there were discrepancies and interpolations in the Greek text that went beyond simple copyists' errors. A Christian eyewitness expressed his amazement at the amount of research they had done: "What piles of books are these on the table before them? Horne, Michaelis, Strauss and other authors of England and Germany."[13]

At this point French decided to intervene, somewhat unfortunately for his own cause, agreeing with Wazir Khan that some commentators identified many thousands of copyists' errors. Pfander's careful distinction between "copyists' errors" and "corruptions" began to seem a rather arbitrary and unfounded one. Pfander turned to the highest Muslim legal authority present, Mufti Riyaz ud-Din, asking him to corroborate his defence that the doctrinal purity of a revealed text need not be impaired by the presence of thousands of clerical errors. The Mufti, naturally, sided with Wazir Khan, ruling that if a single error is detected at any place in a document, the whole document can be considered invalid. The Mufti then turned to an English Judge seated near him, inviting him to add his own legal opinion. The Englishman, clearly embarrassed, chose to remain silent. Pfander was forced to concede the point, and with it, the question of *tahrif*. The Christian scriptures evidently *were* corrupted. And the audience, by now, was in uproar. The debate was adjourned, to be resumed after a day for rest and recuperation.

Pfander, hoping to force his opponents on to the defensive, reopened the discussion by attempting to show from the Qur'an that Muhammad himself had approved the authenticity of the Bible in circulation in his own day. Hardly had he commenced when a Muslim *qadi* (Qur'anic judge) objected to his Arabic pronunciation of the passages he was quoting; he was requested to read the Urdu translation instead. He kept a cool head and pressed his point, demanding that his opponents identify and exhibit the Bible which was in existence at the time of Muhammad. Wazir Khan astutely replied that it was disagreement amongst the early Christians themselves about the canon of scripture that made it impossible for Muslims to identify it with any certainty. Muslims would only accept as the true *Injil* (Gospel) those words actually spoken by Christ himself; everything else was a later interpolation.

Pfander then tried to initiate a discussion of textual problems in the Qur'an, the existence of variant readings and the attempt by the Caliph 'Othman to burn all but his own preferred version of the Qur'anic texts. It was too little and too late. French attempted to paper over the cracks by reading a prepared statement to the effect that his "thousands" of errors were not all in the same manuscript, that they had been identified and discounted by Christian scholars when issuing modern editions of the Bible, that they did not affect any matter of doctrine one way or the other, and that the contents of the gospel are the same now as they ever were. The Mufti attempted to further define the exact nature of *tahrif* (corruption), but the subtleties of dictionary definition held no interest for the excited audience, nor at this stage for the exhausted participants. They could do no more than restate their respective cases before it was time to close. Pfander refused to prolong the debate for another day unless his opponents could show him a copy of the *Injil* they considered to be the true Gospel. Rahmat Allah, for his part, would only continue on the condition that no evidence be drawn from those books he had now proved to be "corrupt". Each side was setting terms impossible for the other to accept, and the debate was over.

It was undoubtedly a setback for Pfander. He had been tactically outmanoeuvred. The arguments, so clear in his own mind, had proved far too subtle to compete with the simple propositions of his opponents, and even his "second" (presumably chosen as the best available Christian theologian to support his cause) had betrayed him in the most humiliating fashion conceivable to the Eastern mind. But perhaps Pfander's greatest mistake was to assume that his protagonists on this occasion would be as ignorant as his previous opponents, and to isolate himself complacently in his own Indian backwater from the intellectual currents flowing in the wider world.[14]

Muslim publications trumpeted the debate as a victory for Islam and published the proceedings verbatim with congratulations and endorsements from scholars, judges and religious councils in various languages. The missionary community distanced itself from what had happened, and all but Pfander seemed seriously embarrassed by the whole affair. He ordered a quantity of books from England and Switzerland, determined now to embark on a thorough study of Higher Criticism and of recent European apologetics. Rearmed and refortified, he would renew battle, and this time on his own terms. But it was not to be. The CMS ordered him to Peshawar on the far north-west frontier of India. He pleaded in vain for a reprieve; his opponents would think he was running away, he would have no chance to turn the tables, a whole generation would be left convinced that Christianity was comprehensively and permanently refuted. But the committee insisted, and as a servant of the committee Pfander had no choice but to obey. His thirteen years' labour in Agra were ended.[15]

But the story has a further twist. One of the Muslim scholars assembled to support Rahmat Allah at the debate was a young man by the name of Safdar 'Ali, the son of a Muslim *qadi*. Seven years later, Safdar 'Ali was arranging his books on the eve of his departure for the pilgrimage to Mecca when he happened to find among them a copy of Pfander's *Mizan ul-Haqq*, unread since his student days in Agra. So surprising and so challenging was the content of this book when he opened it, that Safdar decided he would be wise to consider and reject Christianity before proceeding with his pilgrimage. For the next three years his leisure time was devoted to reading the Bible, the Qur'an and controversial literature from both sides. His first year's study brought him to the conclusion that the Qur'an could not be from God and that Muhammad was not a prophet. A year later, distressed by a profound sense of man's alienation from his Creator, he confessed, "Neither Hindu nor Muslim nor Christian nor Jew am I. Sore perplexed is my soul to know what the issue will be!"[16] His third year was spent in long discussions with a scholarly Indian Christian from a Hindu Brahman background and a CMS missionary by the name of Champion. Gradually his questions were answered and his difficulties cleared away, and on Christmas Day 1864 Safdar 'Ali publicly and joyfully professed Christ in baptism.[17]

But there is still more to tell. A second young scholar sat among those supporting Rahmat Allah; his name was 'Imad ud-Din Lahiz. A short while after the debate, dissatisfied with the formal religiosity of his youth, he was drawn to the ascetic spiritual exercises of the Sufis: "I used to spend whole nights in reading the Qur'an... I retired into my private chamber and with many tears I prayed for the pardon of my sins... I left everybody and went out into the jungles and became a *fakir*, putting on clothes coloured with red ochre." For twelve days 'Imad ud-Din sat beside a stream "in a particular manner on one knee" reciting the prayer called Jugopar thirty times each day "with a loud voice". Fasting from sunrise to sunset, he wrote the name of

God on paper 125,000 times, cutting out each word separately with scissors, wrapping each one in a little ball of flour, and feeding them to the fishes of the river. Half the night was spent in sleep, the other in writing the name of God mentally on his heart. At the end of this time his emaciated frame and gaunt features proclaimed him a *fakir* of outstanding spirituality. Preaching in the streets and mosques, he acquired a company of disciples. "But still," he said, "my soul found no rest... I only felt daily in my mind a growing abhorrence of the law of Muhammad... During the next eight or ten years the examples of the Muhammadan elders and their holy men and *moulvis* and *fakirs* whom I used to meet, and my knowledge of their moral character and of the thoughts that dwelt in their hearts, and their bigotry and frauds and deceits and their ignorance which I used to observe, altogether combined to convince my mind that there was no true religion in the world at all."[18]

'Imad ud-Din then took a job as a lecturer at the teacher training college run by the government in Lahore. Here he heard about his old friend Safdar 'Ali: that he had abjured Islam and been baptised. 'Imad ud-Din was shocked. In order to win him back he decided he must become familiar with the errors taught by the Christians. He obtained a Bible and began to read Matthew's Gospel with the principal of the college who was himself a Christian. By the time he had completed the first seven chapters his entire outlook had changed. The Sermon on the Mount spoke to his heart as no other holy book had done. For a year he continued to compare the Bible with the Qur'an, Christ with Muhammad, discussing his questions with both Christians and Muslims, until in 1866 he was ready to declare his faith openly. His father, brother and brother's wife were all converted during the following year.[19]

Pfander, meanwhile, was making his presence felt in Peshawar on the Afghanistan frontier. This was a cosmopolitan town, full of traders, mountaineers, travellers, adventurers of many different races. Always at risk of his life, he spoke everywhere of Christ and was repeatedly told to stop. Warnings were sent to the British Commissioner; the CMS urged him not to take chances; but Pfander said he would let God be his guide, and went on preaching. "Scowling faces and muttered threats met him, and the mullahs loftily held aloof, seeing no reason why they should argue with an infidel. He sent copies of the *Mizan ul-Haqq* to them. Some thanked him; some returned the book without a word." But conversions followed. The first Afghan to accept Christ was Yahya Bakir. During a pilgrimage to Mecca and Medina he had a strange dream convincing him that *'Isa Masih* (Jesus Christ) was greater than Muhammad, and having heard that Pfander was in India, came directly in search of him. At last he tracked him down to Peshawar, plied him with questions, and was baptised in January 1856. A few days later, attacked by a fanatical Muslim, Yahya Bakir was found close to Pfander's house, unconscious and badly wounded. He recovered, with the loss of two fingers, and in subsequent years went "travelling all over Central Asia" with a box of medicines and a Bible. Such was Yahya Bakir's reputation that it was said he "prayed over his patients and they all got well."[20]

Another man converted at this time was Dilawar Khan, an Afghan robber, kidnapper and brigand chief with a price on his head. One day, during negotiations with the British border forces, he began discussing religion with the colonel, who gave him a copy of Pfander's book. Dilawar Khan sought out its author in Peshawar and questioned him about his beliefs. He then challenged the *moulvis* in his home town to refute the *Mizan*, and their refusal strengthened his conviction that Pfander had right on his side. In 1858 he was baptised as a Christian. Dilawar Khan gave a copy of the book to a Pushtu-speaking constable in the police force by the name of Fazl-i Haqq, and shortly afterwards he too was converted.

Pfander continued in Peshawar for three years. He was there at the outbreak of the Mutiny in 1857, and despite the fact that Indian Christians and missionaries were facing torture and death in many parts of India, he "went on preaching in the streets right through the most anxious time, when plots to murder all the Europeans were revealed by intercepted letters."[21] That same year he received the degree of Doctor of Divinity from Cambridge University in recognition of his scholarship.

In 1856 the British government had succeeded in persuading the Sublime Porte to guarantee religious freedom in the Ottoman Empire. Any Muslim in Ottoman territory could now declare himself converted to Christ without fear of legal reprisals. To profit from this, at the close of 1858, Pfander was asked by the CMS to launch a new evangelistic initiative in Constantinople (Istanbul). With a fresh team of young workers, Pfander started unobtrusively – personal conversations in the market, a little preaching in a room rented for the purpose, some distribution of Turkish scriptures. Soon the *Mizan ul-Haqq* itself was being sold within the precincts of the great mosque, formerly the church of St Sophia whose walls had echoed to the eloquence of John Chrysostom.

On Easter Day 1862 the first Turkish Muslim convert of the Constantinople mission was baptised, after twice being arrested and released by the authorities. Several others followed, until, in 1864, "without the slightest warning," the Turkish police attacked the premises of the CMS, SPG and Bible Society, seized all the Christian books, threw the Christians into prison and forcibly closed the buildings. Converts and enquirers disappeared. Enquiries later ascertained that at least forty-seven had been sent to the galleys. Of the missionaries, just one remained. He continued to talk with secret enquirers, but the days of public preaching and controversial books were over.

Or were they? The seed sown during the previous thirteen years continued to germinate in the most unexpected places. A Persian merchant from Teheran was baptised at Peshawar; a traveller from Central Asia in Agra itself; a *sharif*[22] at Farakabad; a government official in Sindh; a distinguished scholar at Amritsar – all these came to faith in Christ through Pfander's books. Shunned by other missionaries, and condemned by the British press, Pfander returned to Europe at the end of 1865 in ill health, and died shortly afterwards in London. But the debate went on. The Sultan invited the aged Rahmat Allah to Constantinople, where he published in 1867-8 a definitive refutation of Pfander in six thick volumes, an encyclopedic work called *Izhar ul-Haqq* (Demonstration of the Truth). In 1910 the *Mizan* itself was once more carefully edited "to remove all apparent ground for the attacks made upon the book" and republished.

The *Mizan ul-Haqq* continues to embarrass those advocating dialogue rather than evangelism, and to their surprise continues to lead Muslims to faith in Christ. It is both quoted and rebutted by Islamic apologists to the present day and is still banned in most Muslim countries – proof indeed of its undiminished potency. The book demonstrates Pfander's willingness to ask hard questions, to attack points of weakness, to discuss subjects of disagreement, to give reasons for the reader to change his mind. Samuel Zwemer defends Pfander's methods: "Those who at present deplore all 'controversy' so-called and are opposed apparently to the polemic and apologetic method of an earlier generation, would do well to consider that, after all, this method was on occasion used by our Lord himself and by his apostles... What was Christ's method of teaching the Pharisees and Sadducees? Even as a boy in the temple he began by both hearing and asking them questions. Nearly all the discourses recorded in the fourth Gospel were occasioned by controversy with those whose formal religion greatly resembled present-day Islam. Stephen's address is a masterpiece of apologetic, and ended in his martyrdom, but also in the conversion of Saul."[23] The same pattern is seen throughout the book of Acts. In Athens Paul reasoned in the synagogues with the Jews and God-fearing Greeks;[24] in Ephesus he argued persuasively and held daily discussions in the school of Tyrannus;[25] in Jerusalem he debated with the Greek-speaking Jews until they sought to kill him.[26] And Zwemer reminds us that the apostle's letters are "loving apologetic arguments addressed to the mind and heart to convince men of the truths of the gospel." To the Philippians he says, "I am put here [i.e. in prison] for the defence of the gospel."[27] To the Corinthians, "We demolish arguments and every pretension that sets itself up against the knowledge of God, and we take captive every thought to make it obedient to Christ."[28] The Christian is called both to proclaim a message and to "give an *answer* to everyone who asks you to give the reason for the hope that you have."[29] Karl Pfander was simply following the example of Christ and of his most effective missionary apostle.

Some years after his death, Thomas French wrote a generous tribute: "It was no small privilege I had in being the disciple of Pfander, a worthy successor of the heroic Henry Martyn."[30] And thirty years later Pfander was still considered by the CMS to be "the greatest of all missionaries to Mohammedans."[31] Temple Gairdner, himself an apologist of the first order, remarked that Pfander possessed the three great requisites for public controversy: absolute command of his subject; absolute command of the language, thought and manner of the people; and absolute command of himself.[32] Few have ever matched him. It was the privilege of Norris Groves to work with this man for two of their most formative years. In 1830 he said, "I cannot sufficiently thank God for sending my dear brother Pfander with me, for had it not been for him, I could not have attempted anything; so that all that has now been done must rather be considered his than mine."[33]

ENDNOTES

[1] D14

[2] Pfander to Venn, 4 Jan. 1856 (Powell, 138); *Church Mission Intelligencer* (1859), 47 (Stock II, 152).

[3] Powell, 139; Stock II, 152. The first German manuscript of the *Mizan ul-Haqq* was completed in 1829, and then (according to Powell) translated into Armenian and published in Moscow in 1831. Four years later a Persian translation was published in Shushi. The first Urdu edition appeared in 1843 (Schirrmacher makes it 1840), followed by Turkish (1862) and Arabic (1865). Zwemer gives the following dates: Armenian (1829), Persian (1835), Hindustani (1853), Marathi and Arabic (1865) and English (1867). These dating discrepancies probably stem from the existence of various official and unofficial versions, as Pfander himself continually reviewed and improved his work.

[4] Finding that the deity of Christ and the need for an atonement required more detailed treatment, Pfander amassed additional materials in two subsequent books, *Miftah ul-Asrar* (The Key to Mysteries) and *Tariq ul-Hayat* (The Way to Life). The first editions of these were all completed during his period in Shushi. A fourth work was later published in India, *Hall ul-Ishkal* (The Solution to Difficulties), followed by a short booklet in English on the *Hadith* (Traditions of the Prophet) intended for European readers.

[5] Powell, 18

[6] Powell, 160-163

[7] Powell, 137

[8] Stock II, 153. No trace has yet been found of correspondence between Groves and Pfander during the period 1840-52 when they were both in India. There is also no evidence of any contact between Groves and Robert Nesbit, the first tutor of his boys, who was also in India from 1827 until 1855. The reason may simply be that letters and journals proving such contact have not survived.

[9] Powell, 225

[10] At least thirteen variant editions of the Urdu New Testament had been issued between 1837 and 1845, ostensibly to simplify Henry Martyn's original translation but in fact perpetuating inter-denominational and inter-regional rivalries.

[11] Sufi: an adherent of any mystical Muslim sect. Powell (221, 228 etc) describes the Sunnite background of Rahmat Allah; Schirrmacher considers him a Shiite.

[12] Rahmat Allah and Wazir Khan headed unerringly for the weakest points in Pfander's "fortress", as do their successors to the present day. And Christian apologists still fall into the same trap. Rather than starting with a discussion of the plight of man in a fallen world facing a Day of Judgment, or the remarkable character, teachings and healing ministry of Jesus himself, they continue to open the debate on their opponents' terms, trying to prove the existence of an uncorrupted Bible and a Holy Trinity, followed by a search for historical evidence that Jesus died.

[13] T G Clark, quoted by Powell p.246

[14] The Basel seminary had declined to expose its students to the new methods of biblical criticism already beginning to influence Lutheran scholarship in the German-speaking parts of Europe. The debate, of course, took place before scholars had made much progress in their attempts to reconstruct the exact text of the original New Testament, and before other scholars had established a strong case for their acceptance of the Received or Byzantine as the authentic text.

[15] Thomas French continued in Agra to develop his successful college, and subsequently saw a number of his boys profess faith in Christ, along with friends from outside the college walls. Among them were some who became significant leaders in the Indian churches. Later, as principal of a theological college in Lahore, he taught a number of Indians who had been converted through reading Pfander's *Mizan ul-Haqq*. French subsequently became the first Bishop of Lahore (Vander Werff, 44-52).

Rahmat Allah resumed his own religious and educational activities in his hometown of Kairana and wrote a book, *I'jaz ul-'Iswi*, intended as a scholarly demolition of the Christian scriptures. Wazir Khan remained in Agra, making no further contacts with missionaries. Superficially he had seemed jubilant after the debate, but letters to his medical superiors indicate that he was actually very dejected in the aftermath, and on the ground of ill health he made repeated but unsuccessful attempts to be transferred away from Agra. There is evidence that Wazir became involved in subversive activities. Both he and Rahmat Allah took an active part with the rebels in the failed Mutiny of 1857-8, and both subsequently fled India, spending the remainder of their lives in exile (Powell, 262).

[16] Stock II, 557

[17] Baptised at the same time was a close friend, Kasim Khan, also converted out of Islam, and shortly afterwards another friend, Karim Bakhsh. Safdar 'Ali's family had been aware of his spiritual struggles but were quite unprepared for his astonishing conversion. His wife threw herself on the ground and remained lying there for three days, refusing to move or to take food. Then she walked out with their child, abandoning him to face alone the contempt of his Indian colleagues in the government offices. His life from then on was devoted to Christ – "wise, kind, earnest, ever about his Master's business, yet speaking and acting in the quietest

way, 'giving none offence', 'speaking the truth in love'" – until he died, as he had lived, "a consistent Christian" (Stock II, 559).

[18] Stock II, 562-563. Moulvi: a Muslim scholar, teacher or religious leader (especially in India). Fakir: a religious ascetic.

[19] Stock II, 563. 'Imad ud-Din later wrote several apologetic works, including the famous *Hidayat ul-Muslimin* (Guidance for Muslims) and *Tahqiq ul-Iman* (Inquiry into the Faith), along with an influential autobiography. In 1872 he was ordained as an Anglican clergyman.

[20] Stock II, 212-213

[21] Stock II, 220

[22] Sharif: a descendant of Muhammad.

[23] Zwemer, *Pfander*, 224-225

[24] Acts 17:17

[25] Acts 19:8-9

[26] Acts 9:29

[27] Phil 1:16. See 1:7.

[28] 2 Cor 10:5

[29] 1 Pet 3:15

[30] Stock II, 171

[31] Schirrmacher, 2 (quoting from *One Hundred Years, being the Short History of the Church Missionary Society*, London 1898)

[32] Gairdner, *The Reproach of Islam*, 247

[33] R2; M85. Pfander's influence in Baghdad might be seen in Groves's determination to learn the local language, in his willingness to establish a mission school, and perhaps also in the respect he habitually showed for other races and cultures. On the latter point, Bradley suggests that the typically condescending attitude of the British Empire towards native peoples under its paternal care, "contrasted sharply with the more cynical, and more respectful view of the African and Asiatic races taken by other European countries" (*The Call to Seriousness*, 89).

"Nature's love, in all the varied relations
of husband and wife, parents and children etc.
is the sweetest relic of the Fall."

Norris Groves [1]

26

Old Soldiers

Henry Groves was just ten years old when his parents took him by sailing ship through the storm-ridden Baltic, then by horse-carriage across Tsarist Russia and down the course of the Volga, by waggon through the bandit-infested passes of the Caucasian mountains and finally to an Arab house on the banks of the Tigris. Here he faced bullets and shells, floods, plague, famine and cholera, followed by the loss of his mother and his own close brush with death. Not surprisingly, it all made a lasting impression on young Henry. Like it or not, he was hustled into adult life and in later years pathetically observed that after leaving England he could not remember ever having been a boy. His father, in India, received letters from him and Frank: "My poor dear boys, in writing about the siege and their prospects in Baghdad, express themselves more like old soldiers than children, they have been so inured to trials and dangers."[2]

Throughout his life Norris Groves did everything he could for his family, and his children loved him as a father should be loved. The care he took in Exeter to find tutors of real quality for Henry and Frank shows the importance he attached to their education, and this makes his willingness to take them overseas, trusting God for their schooling, all the more impressive. Tutors came and went, but in each case God provided men of outstanding ability – Nesbit, Craik, Kitto, Newman and Parnell – and these young teachers were each in turn profoundly affected by their experience of the Groves household. In the end, the "home schooling" that Henry and Frank received amidst so many distractions equipped them remarkably well for adult life. They grew up knowledgeable and sensible, with a dedication to Christ that many parents today would long to see in their own offspring.

For some years after their father's death, Henry and Frank worked together in India. They complemented one another well. Whilst Henry dealt with contracts, sales and personnel, Frank's engineering skills enabled him to maintain and oversee the machinery of their sugar works at Palhully near Mysore. They opened a schoolroom and chapel in the village, appointed an Indian evangelist, and arranged meetings that were attended by both Hindus and Roman Catholics. In his free time, Henry in particular was doing the work of a missionary: "He visits from house to house among the people and encourages all to open their hearts to him, and preaches such plain beautiful gospel sermons that all can understand."[3] An Indian Roman Catholic (an overseer in the sugar works) and his wife were soon converted, along with a young man who had been a boy in the school at Chittoor. Others also came to faith in Christ. In 1851 and 1862 the brothers won medals at the Great Exhibitions in London for the quality of their sugar, and profits from the industry were used to support the work of God in many places.

Eventually the brothers were persuaded, under pressure from the government, to install a commercial rum distillery. They were never happy about producing spirits and in 1862 decided to sell the business. As Henry went to start a new life in England, Frank and his wife Harriet established a coffee plantation in the Nilgherry Hills. Frank, being a keen gardener, surrounded their home at Coonoor with flowers. They had three sons (Henry, Frank and Norris) and two daughters (Mary and Isabella), some of whom eventually settled in England, the others in India.[4]

Henry Groves had visited England more than once before his final return in 1857. He was now thirty-nine years of age and well qualified to take a leading role there in the growth and extension of the Brethren movement. He took the opportunity to visit assemblies throughout Britain and the United States, and was privileged to witness revival scenes on both sides of the Atlantic. It was a time of great encouragement and he saw many young Christians called to service at home and overseas.

As his younger brother Edward observed, Henry Groves was "a man born to command".[5] His first thought, after completing his travels, had been to settle in Bristol and help with the Bethesda assembly. Here, however, he found the respect accorded to George Müller so absolute that there seemed little he could contribute in terms of leadership. "Two cocks," he remarked, "cannot crow on the same dunghill."[6] He soon realised he would be happier pioneering unreached territory than building on another man's foundation, and in 1868 he moved to Kendal in the north of England, which became his base for the remaining twenty-three years of his life.

Henry Groves had learnt much from his father. He held the same beliefs and possessed the same gift of eloquence, but there was about him a certain toughness that Norris had lacked. He would never compromise with anything dubious or false, and he would fiercely defend what he believed to be the truth. "One of the saddest features of our time," he declared, "is the universal 'charity' which condones every form and degree of false doctrine... In both the church and the world, absoluteness and certainty in divine things are deprecated as presumption and pride, and to say 'we know', though God has plainly spoken, leads to hostility and opposition. Yet surely nothing is more humble than to say 'I know' when God *has* spoken." Henry saw many Christians quietly setting aside the teaching of the Bible in deference to human sensibilities and modern

science. "Thus the foundation truths of scripture are surrendered one by one…
In this, the worldly-minded Christian thinks to attract the worldling to Christ
by being like him. How vain a delusion! Not so did the Son of God seek to
lead sinners back to God. For him 'It is written' sufficed, whether speaking to
devil or to man, and he deigned not to argue when God had spoken."[7]

Henry had two great concerns. The first was to heal the breach caused by
John Nelson Darby. He travelled throughout the British Isles, attending and
addressing meetings attempting to restore unity, and until late in his life he
remained optimistic that the Brethren might be reunited. His second concern
was to develop the missionary vision of the assemblies. In 1872, with the
help of two friends, he launched *The Missionary Echo* (later renamed *Echoes
of Service*), in which letters from missionaries were published along with
items of news and matters for prayer.[8] He also edited a monthly devotional
magazine, *The Golden Lamp*, and eventually wrote at least twenty-two books
and booklets in addition to magazine articles. He was a welcome speaker at
conferences in many parts of the country. A contemporary summed up his
character with the words, "Mr Groves was of the stern 'Valiant for the Truth'
type, but mellowed much in his later years."[9] That seems a fair assessment.
Henry died childless in 1891.

Norris Groves's third son Edward was in some ways the most interesting.
Born in Chittoor, he was brought up almost single-handed by Harnie, who
adapted to the role of an Indian *ayah* as though born to it. But Edward's father
was preoccupied with problems in the farm and the school, and his mother,
busy preparing Bible studies, was very vague when it came to the needs and
interests of children. There was not the closeness that Henry and Frank had
enjoyed with their parents, and Edward later recalled, "I was always in the
way at home, and saw that my presence was an interference with the exalted
ideal of missionary life."[10] At the age of seven he was packed off to Harriet's
sister and her family in Devon. Four years later, in 1848, the family was split
by "the strife between Brethren". The Baynes clan sided with the Exclusives
and Harriet, returning to England, was compelled to remove her son from her
sister's care.

After a happy seaside vacation with his parents in north Devon, Edward
was enrolled in a boarding school at Bideford as his mother and father returned
to India. The school went by the name of Tusculum and suffered under the
tyranny of its headmaster William Hake. Here Edward was intensely miserable,
terrified most of the time by the threat of punishment and the violence of its
execution. Nothing he did was good enough, and Hake evidently could not
imagine the effect on a sensitive boy of being thrashed "not for any evil he
had done, but because he was *going on in a bad way!*"[11] Quiet despair gave
way to the dull ache of hopelessness. He had no family to go to, no visitors,
no treats, no outings, nothing to look forward to, and his school holidays

were spent at school because no one else had room for him. His mother wrote affectionate letters but seemed more interested in Indian children than in her own. It undoubtedly left a mark on Edward. Many years later he recalled, "We were deeply impressed with our misfortune in being children of missionaries, for it was clear nobody wanted us."[12]

When Norris Groves himself returned from India in the autumn of 1852, he was a stranger to his son. Hastening to Bideford he did three things for which Edward was profoundly grateful: "He took me at the age of sixteen from a hateful school and opened a new world of interest by sending me to a College of Chemistry in Oxford Street, London." And he bought the boy a pair of spectacles. This, Edward tells us, was "the greatest delight of my life". No one had noticed or cared that he was so short-sighted he could not recognise a face across the room. Now for the first time in his life he saw the stars in the night sky and the birds in the trees. His natural sense of humour began to reassert itself. Visiting his aunts and his cousin Lydia Müller in Bristol, he tells us how they "enjoyed hearing some of my experiences in school and in London. About a minute after we had done laughing, the joke began to dawn on my uncle's mind, and often his great amusement occasioned a second edition of merriment all the way round."[13]

Nine months later, a weeping Edward knelt beside his dying father. Receiving his blessing, "I dimly understood its value," Edward recalled fifty years afterwards, "but I resolved, boy as I was, that I would keep out of debt as long as I lived. The world would pronounce my father's career a failure, but apart from all the souls he was the means of turning from darkness to light, this very failure was a most valuable experience for missionaries in all time to come." It was a lesson not lost on the next generation. Indeed, Edward reckoned that "George Müller's education was in some respects finished at the dying bed of his brother-in-law, and he was confirmed in concluding that God has always the money to carry on his work, and if supplies fail it is not his will to *borrow*, even from those who urge the acceptance of a loan, but to *pray without ceasing* till deliverance comes."[14]

Harriet, knowing her husband to be dying, was hastening back to England with her daughters and Harnie, but Edward, after attending the funeral, was also at sea, travelling in the opposite direction. He joined Henry and Frank at their Palhully sugar works near Mysore. This suited him well, as he felt quite at home with mechanical gadgets of any kind. He was now nearly twenty – a Christian, but by his own account a confused and unhappy one – and here he fell in love with the adopted daughter of a widowed lady who lived there. It was an overwhelming experience for this sensitive and rather awkward young man to feel that somebody actually wanted him, and his joy was complete when her mother, who had known his parents, agreed to their engagement. To his surprise, Henry was greatly displeased and insisted on Edward breaking off all correspondence with the girl until Harriet had been asked and given her approval. "I had never in all my life resisted lawful authority," confessed Edward, "and I submitted to that of my brother." To send and receive letters would take three months, and Edward could not sleep for worrying about it. He attended to his work as before, but his mind was troubled and he suffered severe headaches. He tried to pray, he tried to trust God, but for a whole week he had not one wink of sleep. Then the hallucinations came; he started imagining things; he found himself talking nonsense. His letters to his mother and other people gave evidence of mental disorder. News of his strange behaviour reached the mother of the young lady, and the engagement was immediately cancelled. Three months later, distressed and confused, the girl was married to someone else. Edward was devastated; he had lost his only love and acquired a reputation for insanity.[15]

It was 1857, and because of the Mutiny the works at Palhully could obtain no raw sugar. The brothers sent Edward to supervise the extraction of sweet sap from palm trees, which would serve as a substitute. He was glad of something to occupy his mind, especially as there would be opportunity for mechanical inventiveness. He stayed with Colonel (now Sir Arthur) Cotton in Madras and decided at the same time to learn Hindustani. After an unsatisfactory attempt at Bible translation and a failed application to become a teacher of Hindustani, he returned for a year's leave in England in 1861. He had not seen his mother for twelve years and had never met his sister Agnes who was now eleven.

Harnie, of course, was overjoyed to see her boy again. Harriet introduced him to a suitable young lady, and their friendship blossomed. Edward plucked up courage: "I slipped a little note into her hand, asking if she could unite her life with mine and return with me to India. She showed it to her father, and the curt tone of his reply… went like an arrow into my soul."[16] News of Edward's mental problem six years earlier had evidently preceded him. For a second time he was overwhelmed with feelings of humiliation and disappointment. He could not sleep, and though he now kept a careful guard on his tongue, his behaviour became quite irrational. He was committed to an asylum where large doses of opium at last sent him to sleep.

On his recovery he was invited to stay with the Exclusive family of his childhood. Visiting them at that time were three orphan girls, distantly related by marriage. One of them played the harp. "I was just fascinated with the music and the musician," Edward recalled, "and found before long that my admiration was returned."[17] But before they could consider marriage, he had to "judge the question". The question was whether Bethesda had, or had not, acted wickedly in accepting some individuals excluded by John Nelson Darby. Edward, unable to face further disappointment, meekly accepted the conditions, and quarters were booked for the happy couple on a ship to India. Before the wedding could take place, however, the young lady contracted tuberculosis.

Edward was obliged to leave without her, and on arrival in Madras the first news to reach him was of her death.

As the sugar factory had been sold, he worked for some months on his own account, melting down old cannonballs for recasting as ploughshares. But having "judged the question", he could not find one Christian in India with whom he felt able to "break bread" – despite the fact that his brothers were there at the time! In 1864 Frank's mother-in-law came to visit, accompanied by her second daughter. Isabella had been a childhood friend of the family, and her mother hinted in a roundabout way that Isabella and Edward might be very happy together, especially if she – the mother – were invited to live with them. In the event, this arrangement worked well, and safely married at last, Edward decided he did not care at all what the Exclusives might think about it.

Having inherited his father's skill with his hands, he then set up a small engineering business in Coonoor, making and repairing machinery for the planters of the Nilgherry Hills. All went well until the price of iron suddenly doubled, and Edward, having contracted to supply ninety iron wheelbarrows at an agreed price, was faced with bankruptcy. Again he could not sleep. "How often had I misjudged my poor father for getting into debt," he said, "and how confidently I assured myself that it was possible to keep clear of it, and here I was overwhelmed."[18] His mind became confused with "absurd fancies" and a host of irrational fears. He was taken to the Madras Lunatic Asylum and "placed under medical care". Here he slowly regained his equilibrium. During his weeks away his younger brother Norris kept the company going, but as he convalesced Edward came to the conclusion that he must "relinquish business altogether".[19] He left everything to Norris.

So it was that in 1874 Edward Groves returned with his wife and two daughters to England; his son followed shortly afterwards. He was now thirty-eight years old. He stayed two or three months with Henry and his Irish wife in Kendal and then settled in Bristol, throwing in his lot with Bethesda where his uncle George Müller was still active. At that time the leaders at Bethesda oversaw four fellowships meeting in different parts of the city.[20] People would move from group to group quite freely, and this made it difficult to keep track of them. There were literally hundreds of people whose names were listed in the church records; some had died, some had changed address, some had moved away. Edward offered to visit them all and three years later had compiled an orderly list of nine hundred, including a hundred domestic servants.[21] Throughout this time he was supported largely by Müller's Scriptural Knowledge Institution.

As he visited people, Edward saw a need to explain the biblical principles of the church, and in 1885 he published a book, with the approval of the Bethesda leadership, under the title *Conversations on Bethesda Family Matters*. This was a helpful and balanced account of how the assembly was run. But Edward had become convinced that the people he was visiting needed something in addition to the devotional and prophetic teaching that formed the staple diet of the meetings at Bethesda. They needed clear guidance about practical Christian living. They needed exhortations and even rebukes, and some of his exhortations and rebukes did not meet with the approval of the church leadership.

There is no doubt that once the pattern at Bethesda had been set, there was a general reluctance to change it in any respect, and some of the changes were badly needed. Edward suggested making the seats more comfortable; he proposed establishing a children's Sunday school; he urged regular giving and practical missionary support. He wanted sermons to be written up and "cyclostyled" for the deaf; he suggested a wider variety of subjects for consideration at the Breaking of Bread, and he argued for the preparation of systematic teaching in advance. Edward describes himself as "intensely practical", "naturally straightforward", with a "thirst for improving all that was capable of improvement".[22] Such a person can be rather exhausting, and it is evident that both George Müller, and his successors, James Wright and G Fred Bergin, found him somewhat difficult.

But as time went by, some of his ideas bore fruit. One was the "Missionary Cheer Committee", which began to correspond with workers overseas and pray for them. "There is nothing that has been a greater cheer to me," he said, "than the distinct growth of interest in mission work among ourselves of late years. The demand for Echoes of Service is one indication; the amount of the collective gifts we have been able to distribute is another; the giving of their own selves on the part of some of our number, the best of all."[23] During his twenty-seven years at Bethesda, Edward saw the number of missionaries sent out and supported by the church rise from four to forty.

From his father, Edward had learned to *use* rather than accumulate wealth. In his book he suggested, "Every penny of your Lord's money is, you may say, a seed which it is his intention to return to you in a harvest of blessing, when scattered according to his will."[24] He continued to advocate systematic giving, pointing out that most of his readers, to their shame, were content to donate to the work of the gospel much less than the tithe required of God's people in an age of far less grace. He encouraged the Christian with a small income to set aside a little every week as an act of devotion to the Lord, and so to create a permanent store, always available to help a case of need.[25] He believed that each local church should, in principle, fully provide for its own missionaries. The drawback he saw in the system whereby contributions were sent to a central fund, such as Echoes of Service or the Scriptural Knowledge Institution, was that the missionaries themselves became vulnerable to the doctrinal disapproval or personal displeasure of the fund's trustees or directors, who at a stroke could cut off their entire means of support. He compiled a booklet with postal information and details of workers in many places to help individual supporters make contact with individual missionaries.[26] Having done so, he was bold enough to warn the assemblies that if they neglected to provide adequately for the Lord's servants, they would lose their most willing and gifted workers to other churches and missions.[27]

In the final chapter of his book about Bethesda he had to explain the controversy surrounding Darby's attack on the church. The process of researching events that happened thirty-six years previously, and the fear that he might unwittingly revive the controversy, so affected Edward's mind that he once more found he could not sleep. His head ached intolerably and he became obsessed with fears of insanity. He needed a complete change, a holiday, the opportunity to get away. Instead he was taken to a private asylum. That night he woke up with a pounding head and a raging thirst. He begged for a drink of water. The attendant refused. Edward declared he would give the attendant no rest until he had it. Help was summoned and resisting with all his strength he was forcibly wound up in a blanket. In the process he suffered two broken ribs. He finally received his drink of water, but at a price. Already certified insane, his records now showed him *violently* insane; he was described by the doctor as "a very dangerous lunatic".[28]

On his release he still felt an urgent need to travel. Isabella accompanied him to London, where he discovered it was she (following the advice of the Bethesda leaders) who had signed the paper admitting he had twice before been in an asylum, and which therefore justified his recent confinement. To be fair to Isabella, she was obviously very frightened by Edward's behaviour and believed he would benefit from being under medical supervision. But his trust in his wife was shattered. He found his way to Paris, where he ran out of money, and then returned to London. He declared he was leaving his wife and family, and after an unfortunate misunderstanding with someone else's housemaid, and a brief encounter with a sympathetic London prostitute, he was removed to the public Bethlehem Hospital, commonly known as Bedlam.[29] "My first waking thought after becoming an inmate was, 'Thank God my mother did not live to see this day!'" But as he began to relax, he started to study the other inmates with great interest, and conversed with them on many topics relating to their peculiar circumstances. Weeks went by and he wrote regularly to his children, but not his wife. Twelve months later, seeing no reason to detain him further, the authorities released him.

He returned to his family, full of remorse, convinced that Isabella had been blameless in the whole affair, and determined to make amends. They were on holiday at the seaside when he joined them. The children, Edward recalled, "were delighted to have their father back to teach them to swim and take them excursions in the neighbourhood; and the welcome I received in Bristol was like that accorded to one who had been all round the world and almost given up for lost."[30] He subsequently found great relief in a recently discovered drug, Sulphonal, that would induce sleep without the ill effects of opiates, and life resumed a degree of calm contentment. The following three years were occupied with perfecting an invention, the "Self-acting Sick Bed" which had a hole through the mattress, a removable bucket and a miniature flush, enabling the bedridden patient to do what was necessary without having to go to the bathroom. Unfortunately this made no money for Edward. He then invented and built a wheelbarrow in which two passengers could be conveyed by two attendants along paths no more than a foot wide. It was designed for the use of F S Arnot, the pioneer missionary in Central Africa, but Arnot showed little interest in the wheelbarrow and never used it.

All this is recorded in Edward's last book, *George Müller and his Successors*, and he justifies the inclusion of many personal sins, failings and disappointments by the fact that the Bible includes such things in its account of God's servants. Though not an example to follow, these misadventures help us to understand both God and man; they are worth knowing simply because they are the truth.

The truth mattered a great deal to Edward Groves. He had a keen eye for hypocrisy and humbug, and he was dismayed by the lack of Christian character he saw in some generally considered to be "deeply taught in the Word". He took issue in particular with a number who after some years with the Exclusive Brethren had decided to join Bethesda but in doing so brought with them the habit of judging and condemning inculcated by John Darby. It was a disappointment to him when his proposal to hold a sale of needlework for missionary support in church premises was refused on the grounds that the building was the house of God, which he considered quite unscriptural. He was upset when the church rebuked his daughter Constance for refusing to marry a young man who, after their engagement, acted in a manner obnoxious to her. But more serious was the reaction at Bethesda to his views on a different matter altogether. In 1870, when his mother and his sister Agnes were living in Bristol, a visiting evangelist had suggested that, according to the Bible, immortality is not an inherent property of the human soul but, on the contrary, a wonderful gift to the redeemed: those who die believing in Christ receive eternal life, those who die in a state of unbelief simply cease to exist. Agnes, then aged twenty-one, attended the evangelist's meetings with her friend, the eldest daughter of Henry Craik, and they were both comforted by a doctrine that eliminated the appalling prospect of endless and unrelieved pain for friends, relations and Sunday school children who had died unconverted. They started to tell others about it. The result was their exclusion from fellowship at Bethesda.

Harriet Groves felt this would be a good moment to leave Bristol, and she took her daughter to live in Weston-super-Mare.[31] Following Harriet's death two years later, Agnes went to India, where she kept house for her brother

Norris on the Nilgherry Hills. Edward attempted to effect a reconciliation by persuading Agnes to modify her views and Bethesda to accept her submission. But though Agnes died shortly afterwards of "brain fever", the doctrine would not go away. Perusing a tract at a bookstall and searching the scriptures for himself, Edward became convinced that eternal life is indeed a gift of God to the redeemed, that when the body dies the soul sleeps until the coming of Christ, and that after the Day of Judgment the unconverted will be annihilated in the Lake of Fire. He amassed texts and arguments in a book he proposed to publish under the title *The Key of Knowledge and How to Use it*, and he informed the Bethesda leadership of his intention. They were appalled. They urged him to resign from the church immediately. He refused, saying that though he believed the teaching of the church to be wrong on this point he remained a member of it. A public church business meeting was then held, at which Edward was present, and he was formally excluded from fellowship. He continued to attend, until he was requested never again to enter any of the buildings associated with Bethesda.

After his expulsion, his opposition to the doctrine of "eternal torment" became extreme, and he felt free to criticise many aspects of Bethesda, and of the Brethren movement in general. Some of his views are fair and have been borne out by time, others bear the marks of personal bitterness; hardly any are without some basis of fact. For a while he attended various Baptist chapels, before coming to rest in a Congregationalist church that concurred with his view of Conditional Immortality.[32]

Throughout this time, Edward enjoyed the support of his wife and family. He was very proud of his children, and in fact all of them grew up a great credit to him. In 1887 his elder daughter Constance was staying with her uncle Henry and his wife in Kendal. She was twenty years old. Here she met a couple from the China Inland Mission, about to return to China, who spoke of their need for a young lady to teach their three little boys. Although Uncle Henry did not approve of Hudson Taylor's willingness to combine Anglicans, Nonconformists and Brethren in missionary endeavour, Constance was convinced that this was God's call to her. A few months later she was on her way. Edward had long been an admirer of the China Inland Mission – especially of Hudson Taylor's ability to induce such happy co-operation and of the opportunities he encouraged for women evangelists and Bible teachers. Three years later, following a brief furlough, Constance returned to China with a party of ten young ladies and while at sea taught them Chinese. Shortly afterwards she married the widowed Dr Arthur Douthwaite, later responsible for the CIM medical centre at Chefoo.[33]

But Constance died young, leaving her husband with three little children. Plans for the twice widowed Douthwaite to marry her sister Irene were well advanced when he too died, and the little ones came to live with Edward,

Isabella and Irene in Bristol. To save expense they had only a part-time housemaid, and Edward himself took over the task of cooking. Irene supported them largely through her income as a private music tutor. She was a talented musician and a gifted evangelist, and Edward gave her every encouragement in this. He said, "If I cannot remember three people in all my life who testified to my having been the means of their conversion, there are more than three hundred who have been brought out of darkness into light through her ministry of the gospel." His youngest child, Ernest, won a scholarship to St Bartholomew's Hospital in London, and after qualifying, became Surgeon to the Bristol General Hospital, receiving further professional commendations in the course of his career.[34]

The leisure Edward enjoyed in his latter years enabled him to apply his questioning mind to many controversial issues, and to reach dogmatic conclusions about them all. He adopted a postmillennial view of the End Times, believing that Truth will gradually prevail over Falsehood. Allied to this belief was an abhorrence of the Victorian tendency to cover up awkward or indelicate facts, and he made a point of instructing young people on matters of procreation and hygiene about which they were profoundly ignorant. In admitting his own private sins so publicly, he wished others to be as honest as he was himself. He argued that the power of Satan (the father of lies and author of confusion) must yield ground as soon as God's people will make a love of Truth their all-consuming passion.

Edward was undoubtedly a difficult man, but his awkwardness was that of one who fears rejection, and his conflicts were always with those who possessed power to humiliate him. He had great compassion for anyone who had suffered misfortune, and he went to much trouble to visit and assist the humbler members of the church, especially those who had fallen on hard times. He could be prickly with strangers but he loved with a fierce loyalty anyone who genuinely loved him. In the end, whatever faults he might have found in others, he never had a hard word to say about his parents, his brothers, his children, or his longsuffering wife. And if every strength of character has a corresponding weakness, every weakness has its element of strength. Edward's strength was in telling the truth exactly as he understood it, whatever other people might think. "Brusque as I sometimes was in conversation," he admitted, "there was no one who felt his word to be his bond more than I."[35]

He too mellowed considerably in his old age, and lost much of his earlier bitterness, although he remained considerably eccentric to the end of his days. Much credit for the greater stability of his later years must be given to the patient understanding of his wife Isabella and to the respect given to him by his own children. He eventually found himself able to give thanks for all he had gone through, declaring that "the knowledge of the human mind in health and disease which I have gained could never have been acquired by one who had not seen and suffered what I have done."[36]

There remains one brother about whose later life we know little. According to Edward, his younger brother "was always an unfortunate man."[37] George, generally known by his middle name Norris, undertook an apprenticeship as a civil engineer. He suffered, however, from what we would now probably identify as dyslexia, which he tried to hide. Though highly intelligent and hard working, Norris found it very difficult to obtain a job, and having obtained one, invariably lost it through his inability to spell correctly. Edward thought he would be wise frankly to admit his infirmity to his business colleagues and clients, and so avoid the embarrassment of its inevitable discovery. "It is of no use," he advised, "to strive with our Maker if we find ourselves less favoured than our neighbours in mental or bodily endowments. If we give thanks for what blessings we enjoy, he is able to make our very infirmities a cause of praise."[38] Norris saw things differently, with the result that he was repeatedly dismissed as stupid and illiterate. According to his brother, this caused him to have "hard thoughts of God", and he "went through life as one who had been wronged."[39]

But along with this, like all the Groves children, Norris had a kind and sympathetic nature. He became a loving husband and father; his wife could not remember him ever saying an unkind word to anyone. Before leaving England he had withdrawn from Bethesda to worship with the Church of England "whenever its ministry was not distinctly ritualistic".[40] After an unsuccessful venture in New Zealand, he returned to help Edward establish a flour mill in India. He later took over his brother's concerns there, although they did not prosper in his hands, and he subsequently oversaw much of the engineering on the Coonoor railway. He had a daughter who settled in England and a son who emigrated to South Africa.

As we look back on the lives of the brothers, we might wonder how it was that Henry and Frank, who suffered all the physical horrors of Baghdad, grew up so sane, balanced and, we might almost say, conventional – whilst Edward, who had a commonplace private-school upbringing (like any other Victorian boy with parents overseas), should turn out so strangely. The reason may lie in the fact that Henry and Frank faced the horrors of Baghdad *with* their father and mother, secure in their parents' love and affection, whilst Edward, feeling uncared for and abandoned, suffered the horrors of Tusculum on his own. Experience shows that a child needs the love of his parents (or substitute parents) more than anything else. Assured of it, he can face almost any adversity; deprived of it, he may be left with scars that never heal. It is also a sobering thought that the unimaginative headmaster of an ordinary boarding-school could do more harm to a boy than war, flood, famine, plague and bereavement. Misery deliberately inflicted by a human being is far more crushing than distress from inanimate forces beyond man's control. Much more unhappiness in this world has been caused by human foolishness and cruelty than by physical sickness and natural disaster.

ENDNOTES

[1] M289

[2] M271

[3] M549

[4] Groves E K, *Successors*, 152-153

[5] *Successors*, 25

[6] *Successors*, 25. Henry Craik, who previously shared leadership with Müller at Bethesda, had died in 1866.

[7] Groves H, *The Battlefield of Faith*, 3,5,12-13

[8] *The Missionary Echo* and *Echoes of Service* are discussed more fully in Chapter 32.

[9] Beattie, 188

[10] *Successors*, 40

[11] *Successors*, 372

[12] *Successors*, 42. Hake had been a friend of Groves in Exeter. His first boarding school was established at Northernhay House in July 1828 after the Groves family had left. In the early 1860s he suffered "a severe breakdown in mental health" but later became a trusted co-worker of Robert Chapman in Barnstaple (Coad, 73).

[13] *Successors*, 43. The uncle was, of course, George Müller.

[14] *Successors*, 19. In fact, as early as 1834, Müller had recorded as one of the principles of his Scriptural Knowledge Institution, "We intend never to enlarge the field of labour by contracting debts… but in secret prayer, God helping us, we shall carry the wants of the Institution to the Lord, and act according to the means that God shall give" (Müller, *Narrative*, I, 111).

[15] It was the sleep deprivation that evidently caused Edward to have experiences like dreams or nightmares whilst wide awake. The "inflammation of the brain" which he describes "forces the thoughts which usually take an hour in their development to pass through the mind in a few minutes. By and by, the power to distinguish fact from fancy is withdrawn, and the tongue freely talks the wildest nonsense." He wrote it all down for his mother: "I told her I was going to be an apostle and should begin my career by casting Vesuvius and Etna into the sea etc. etc." (*Successors*, 48-49).

[16] *Successors*, 63

[17] *Successors*, 65

[18] *Successors*, 76

[19] *Successors*, 77

[20] *Successors*, 146

[21] *Successors*, 79-81

[22] *Successors*, 98, 55, 130

[23] *Conversations*, 109. "I began by taking thirty copies a month of *Echoes of Service*, and ended with circulating three hundred twice a month, mostly from house to house, with my own hands" (*Successors*, 89).

[24] *Conversations*, 106-109

[25] 1 Cor 16:2-3

[26] *Successors*, 146, 142-143

[27] *Successors*, 175

[28] *Successors*, 99. As a certified lunatic, no testimony he gave against the asylum would be accepted in a court of law. Being certified as such also meant he was not considered responsible for his behaviour, and so could be more easily excused.

[29] *Successors*, 96. The maid's thoughtful attention to "the poor gentleman" was misconstrued as interest of a more personal nature. The other lady appeared, at the time, as a fellow "unfortunate" with whom he could share his feelings of distress. Edward, in emotional turmoil, was by his own confession clutching at straws.

[30] *Successors*, 110

[31] *Successors*, 30. Harriet's closest friend here was Maria, the wife of Frank Newman. After Newman's death, it was Edward Groves who arranged for the sale of her husband's library (*Successors*, 353). In 1905 Edward wrote two short magazine articles under the title *An Apology for the Life of Prof F W Newman*.

[32] Proponents of Conditional Immortality point to scriptures indicating that God alone is *inherently* immortal (1 Tim 6:16), and that man *receives* immortality through the gospel (2 Tim 1:10; Rom 2:7; 1 Cor 15:53-54). They argue that the Greek word *aiōnios*, translated as "eternal" or "everlasting" in such verses as Mt 25:46 and 2 Thess 1:9, refers to "the *finality* of what happens when the advent of the New Age is consummated" rather than to a *continuity* of endless bliss or torment. Sodom and Gomorrah are given as examples, in Jude 7, of a people who suffered "the punishment of eternal fire", that is, of fire whose destructive effect is permanent and irrevocable rather than fire which continues to burn for ever (Wenham John W, *The Enigma of Evil*, Leicester, IVP, 1985, pp. 34-41; Fudge E W, *The Fire that Consumes*, Carlisle, Paternoster, 1994, pp. 11-20).

[33] *Successors*, 153

[34] *Successors*, 167-168

[35] *Successors*, 134

[36] *Successors*, 270

[37] *Successors*, 151

[38] *Successors*, 269-270

[39] *Successors*, 269

[40] *Successors*, 151

"I never ask my friends for money,
but leave it altogether in my Lord's hand."

John Arulappan [1]

27

An Indian Church

As Norris Groves, now a sick man, struggled back to England, the work at Chittoor went on. Harriet was teaching in the school, and Harnie oversaw the agricultural activity, whilst Henry and Frank were busy with their sugar refinery near Mysore. Early in 1853 word came from England that Norris was in decline, and the women hurriedly packed and found berths in a steamer from Madras, leaving the school and farm in the hands of the Indian evangelists Andrew and Yasadian. George Baynes met them at Southampton with the news of his death.

The following year Henry Groves handed over the Chittoor premises with its Indian workers to the American Dr Henry Scudder and his two brothers, and shortly afterwards William Scudder wrote from Chittoor, "Andrew is a great help to us in preaching, and his whole heart seems to be engaged in it... he has a very happy faculty of communicating the truth."[2] Yasadian, one of Arulappan's converts, also continued to make himself useful, teaching in the school when not out preaching the gospel. And bringing further encouragement, *The Missionary Reporter* for June that year recorded the happy conversion and baptism of a Brahman called Kistname who had been a pupil at Chittoor before continuing his education in Madras.[3] Kistname himself wrote to Harriet explaining how, ridiculed by his schoolmates, he had broken his caste, "given up" his mother, father and other relations, "forsaking all earthly prospects and advantages for our Redeemer's sake." He added for Harriet's encouragement, "I am indebted to you much more than to all other instruments under God for my conversion."[4]

The Barnstaple missionaries, William and Elizabeth Bowden and George and Elizabeth Beer, were pressing on in the Godavari Delta. Having made their first base with the help of John Parnell in the administrative centre of Masulipatam (Machilipatnam), they moved in April 1837 to the smaller town of Narsapur (Narasapur). Here there were no other Europeans to confuse matters in the minds of the Indians.[5]

Though disadvantaged, one might think, by a meagre education, the Beers and Bowdens made rapid progress with Telugu – not by memorizing word lists or by declining verbs or studying prepared texts, but simply by listening and

321

repeating what their friends and neighbours said. The two men gave out tracts in the bazaar and talked as best they could with anyone who seemed friendly. The women chatted with their female neighbours and with the girls who came to their house for reading, arithmetic, needlework and crochet. Such was the curiosity of the Indians in this town, still unfamiliar with Europeans, that they were never short of conversation practice. "In learning the colloquial use of a foreign language," said Bowden, "it is obviously best to follow in the track God has pointed out, and which is seen in the manner children learn their own or another language. A child only learns what it requires, and as it is called for, and almost always by the ear."[6]

Before long they had opened "a little school for a few boys". Here the children learned to write – not on paper but on a strip of palmyra leaf one or two feet long and about an inch and a half wide, using a stylus to scratch the letters and then blackening the marks with powdered charcoal. Living very simply, Bowden and Beer were soon itinerating widely and systematically, talking about Jesus boldly and earnestly in all the villages, and sleeping at night in a small tent. Whenever there was an idol festival or mass bathing in the sacred river they would be there with tracts, reading and preaching from dawn till dusk. Especially during the cholera epidemics that followed every season of heavy rain, the two couples were kept occupied for days on end prescribing medicine and nursing the sick. Many patients gave thanks to "the good God" who heard their prayers for healing.[7] But it was six years before they saw their first convert.

William and Elizabeth Bowden and George and Elizabeth Beer must stand among the most tenacious Christian workers of all time. Living absolutely on the bread line for their first ten years (before George Müller began to support them in 1846 and readers of *The Missionary Reporter* in 1853), they proved that God will not let his faithful servants starve. Subsisting on porridge made from "the commonest coarse black grain", they admitted that "the Lord has brought down our appetites to what he gives us to feed them on."[8] And with this basic diet they flourished; Bowden even found relief from his previous tendency to dyspepsia. Nevertheless, Norris Groves was distressed by the failure of their home church to support them adequately, and he expressed the hope that his silk farm would prosper sufficiently for him to contribute largely to their needs. In 1841 he noted, "The Bowdens have lost nearly all those who used to contribute to their support, but the Lord still provides. My desire is to pay all their expenses, should the Lord prosper me."[9] Inviting them for a holiday in Chittoor, Harriet enclosed a gift towards their travelling expenses; but the silk farm did not prosper, and the Lord alone would have to provide for them after that. And so he did, through unexpected gifts from here and there, often from Christians in India, which furnished them with a lifetime's testimony of remarkable coincidences and last minute provisions to match that of Müller himself.[10]

Initially the Bowdens and Beers had called themselves the Narsapur Baptist Mission. They later dropped the denominational label (following the example of their home church) and, having relocated, became known as the Godavari Delta mission.[11] Their policy of moving their home from town to town every few years enabled them to make friends over a wide area. Sometimes the two families lived close together, sometimes further apart. At one point, while the Beers moved back to Masulipatam, the Bowdens set up home in Palakol (Palakollu). It was hard going. Week after week, preaching in the Palakol market, William Bowden found the inhabitants utterly hardened against his message. Despairing of any progress, and ready to abandon the work, he fell to his knees in the public street and cried, "O Lord, let thy word take hold upon this people!" He and Elizabeth felt they should remain one more week, devoting that week to prayer. Then the first converts were given – a former concubine, a shoemaker and his wife, a travelling tradesman – and so it was, in Palakol in 1842, that the first group of Indian Christians in the Godavari Delta came together.

By 1850 George and Elizabeth Beer had gathered a similar group in Narsapur and felt led to establish a Christian village and farm colony on a hill.[12] After sixteen years' work there were eventually three congregations (at Palakol, Narsapur and Tirugudumetta), with forty baptised believers and many more who came to listen. A hundred children attended the various schools, where they heard Bible stories every day and learned verses of scripture.[13]

One of those who took great interest in all this was Arthur Cotton. He was the military engineer who had read *Christian Devotedness*, who owed his life to the careful nursing of Norris Groves, and who later introduced Groves to India. With civil engineering skills of the first order, Colonel Cotton was a godly man, concerned for the spiritual as well as the physical need of his workers. In 1844 he was appointed to oversee the construction of drainage and irrigation works in the Godavari Delta, and as the great camps were established to house the workforce, he invited William Bowden, tall and powerfully built, to come and preach the gospel to the thousands of Indians gathered there to dig and to shovel.[14]

George Beer also itinerated indefatigably throughout the region until, in 1853, he suffered a stroke after a long ride in the hot sun, and died at the age of forty-one.[15] Following the loss of his colleague, William Bowden continued to visit each of the centres in turn, trekking periodically into the highlands among the tribal people.[16]

He was not left for long without a missionary co-worker. In England there was a twenty-year-old seaman by the name of Thomas Heelis. On shore leave from a merchant ship in the London docks, he went to visit the assembly at Orchard Street in Marylebone, two years after Norris Groves had last spoken there. Heelis heard one of the elders (perhaps John Parnell) praying earnestly for a man to be raised up to fill the gap left in India by the death of Beer. The visitor recalled how he had himself been led to faith in Christ through the witness of an Indian sailor, and hearing the prayer, felt convinced he was the man. He sailed, as soon as he was free, to Godavari.

The number of conversions increased; sixteen were baptised just before Heelis arrived, more afterwards. Then came the conversion of the first Muslim, Alisahib, who became "one of the finest gospel workers the Godavari has ever had."[17] He was a physician and travelled widely healing the sick and preaching the Word.

The labour of the Bowdens and Beers was taken up by their children, and this gave it a stability and continuity often lacking in church planting initiatives. In 1861 the Beers' son John opened an English school for high caste students, with the help of his brother Charles. He also compiled a hymnbook and launched an Indian Christian magazine. The Bowdens' son William established a tanning works in Palakol, providing employment for Indian believers. His brother Fred was also active in India, and a third brother, Edwin Bowden, "a man of great gifts and personality," laboured for forty-eight years in the western part of the delta. In 1920 Edwin welcomed his grandson as his successor at the Chettipeta Girls' Boarding School – a fourth generation of Bowdens to serve in the Godavari Delta.

During this time hundreds of Indians came to faith in Christ. Many were pupils in the schools, others responded to the preaching, but most were drawn to faith through the testimony of someone in their own family. It was always the first in the family who had the greatest difficulty, and often it took many years for the momentous decision to be made. When newly arrived in India, the Beers and Bowdens had received a visit in Narsapur from some weavers enquiring about Christianity. Their guests stayed several days, but though they subsequently returned from time to time, nothing seemed to come of it. Eighteen years later William Bowden chanced to meet one of them in a village. Four years after this, three of the weavers visited Bowden and asked some further questions. It was not till 1885 (forty-eight years after the first encounter) that the son of the first William Bowden received and baptised a leading man from that weaving community. Two others, and later the wives of all three, subsequently came to faith in Christ, although the earliest Bowdens and Beers had long since passed away.[18] One sows, another reaps, but the work started by the Godavari pioneers continues to this day, with many daughter churches flourishing throughout the region.

Further south, the assemblies in Madurai province were making great progress under the leadership of that other disciple of Norris Groves, John

Christian Arulappan. The work here differed from the Godavari mission in speaking Tamil rather than Telugu, and perhaps more significantly, in being an Indian initiative led entirely by Indians. The village of Christianpettah, a little to the south of Trichinopoly (Tiruchchirappalli), had been founded in 1840 as the centre of a self-supporting farm settlement. From here, bands of Indian evangelists travelled continuously to preach throughout the region.[19]

Gospel preaching by Indians to Indians was remarkably successful, and families were converted in many villages round Christianpettah. By 1853, congregations had been established in 16 places, comprising nearly 200 believers. By 1856, there were 25 villages with 300 believers; and in 1859, 33 villages and 800 believers including children.[20] Arulappan himself regularly visited them all. He helped with baptisms, and he spent time teaching, comforting, exhorting, admonishing, reconciling and shepherding. "We enquire about their spiritual and temporal affairs," he reported, "and advise them and encourage them by the living words, comfort them in their afflictions, and ask for the lessons which they have heard and learned by heart, and make them learn a few verses for their future enjoyment."[21] From time to time the believers came in from these villages to conferences held at Christianpettah.

Arulappan was a humble man – not the kind of leader to dominate and overawe, but one with the rarer ability to bring out the best in others. His many absences from home meant that the church in Christianpettah could never become dependent on him for guidance or for ministry; they learned to seek these things from God. The groups he visited further afield understood this too. His was an apostolic role. He taught the Christians to break bread every week in remembrance of their Lord, to expect from God the gifts they would need for building up the body, to take part in meetings as the Holy Spirit led them, each in turn for the common good. He encouraged the emergence of suitable men as leaders in every place and he taught them how to exercise discipline where necessary. Arulappan was a mentor to many, but for almost twenty years Groves himself had been a mentor to the Indian apostle. "In writing to dear Arulappan," he said, "I tell him not to lay too much stress on the mere question of baptism, or the Lord's return, or unpaid ministry. They all have their place, but the important thing is Jesus Christ and him crucified: the grace, the fullness and freeness of the gospel."[22]

Despite their poverty these Indian fellowships erected their own buildings, paid their own schoolteachers and supported their widows and orphans. They expected men, women and children to learn the scriptures by heart, repeating verses to their leaders every Sunday.[23] All were encouraged to share with others what the Lord was teaching them, and this led to a practice of public testifying. Arulappan himself tells us about a typical Sunday in Christianpettah. "After 12 o'clock some of the church members will come from surrounding villages within ten miles distance. We have preaching with singing hymns and reading a chapter from the Bible. We divide a text into several heads and ask questions and they give answers as much as they can. After service is over we collect alms for the poor. The church breaks the bread every Sunday afternoon with prayer and exhortation and thanksgivings. There is liberty to feed the flock of Christ from the nourishing words of God, according to the ability of their gifts by the Holy Ghost... In the afternoon some of the congregation read with us one or two chapters in the Old Testament and repeat a verse by heart from the chapters read on the Sunday before."[24]

Arulappan was a gifted pastor and teacher, but he was also an evangelist with the ability to touch the heart and conscience of his hearers, whether they were Roman Catholics, Hindus or Muslims. He himself had relatives scattered widely over southern India, and his visits to preach and teach among them spread his influence over an area extending far beyond his base in Christianpettah and his original home in Tinnevelly. A typical trip took him twenty miles on foot, accompanied by a number of younger men, preaching along the road as they went, and pausing in the villages for a more leisurely explanation of their message whenever the opportunity presented itself. He took teams to preach and distribute tracts at the great Hindu festivals and he trekked high into the mountains among the tribal peoples. All this he did faithfully for twenty-six years.

Arulappan's diaries are filled with experiences familiar to those who "live by faith". He never knew when visitors might arrive hungry and thirsty, and yet the Lord always provided: "We receive strangers every day. Two or three, and sometimes more than ten, come to me from the far villages more than a hundred miles distant."[25] Once, when his family had nothing to eat, "not even a few measures of rice,"[26] a gift arrived from England, from Norris Groves himself. On another occasion, with nothing in hand for the coming week, he bought, in faith, an old wooden printing press and a simple Tamil font: "My plan is to make tracts according to the customs, and suitable to the truth itself, with some advice for Christians, Roman Catholics, Unitarians, Mahomedans and Idolaters. So everyone can read the tract and find the truth."[27] If it was God's work, God himself would provide. In 1847 Groves commented, "I think dear George Müller would be comforted in hearing an Indian speak that language of faith to which his own heart would so fully respond."[28] Thirteen years later, Arulappan's principles were unchanged. "I never ask my friends for money," he said, "but leave it altogether in my Lord's hand."[29]

The Indian evangelists associated with Arulappan had no contract or salary. They were not trained in a theological college or invested with authority by a church or mission agency. They simply looked to the Lord for their daily needs. A proportion of their support came from gifts sent for distribution at Arulappan's discretion but they were also expected to work with their hands for the benefit of the community. Some helped dig the fields and tend the irrigation channels; others manned the printing press; a couple of them saw to the medical needs of the villagers. Only the schoolteachers were given a modest wage for what was considered secular rather than spiritual work. Arulappan himself eventually agreed to receive a certain amount for translating Sunday school materials and other Christian literature from English into Tamil, but no one was ever paid for proclaiming good news to the lost or for teaching God's word to the church. "Every one of us," Arulappan affirmed, "should work according to their abilities, and in the mean time we preach the gospel to the people according to the gifts."[30]

This arrangement was not always popular. Arulappan himself admitted, "Some may not like to work with their own hands, because they see other mission servants live well without any hand's work and receive a monthly salary, but I advise them to see our fore-runner St Paul and other saints even in this time. May the Lord keep them steadfast in faith."[31] One who cheerfully supported himself as an evangelist was Aquillah. He had been offered a salaried post as a Church of England catechist, but Arulappan tells us "he had no mind to receive a salary for the preaching of the gospel." Aquillah trekked from village to village, selling sugar and salt fish. "When he entered a village he used to read the gospel and preach on the subject and distribute tracts, and sell his sugar and salt fish for a livelihood."[32]

Men like this were the legacy of Norris Groves to India and to the world. From him they had learned to "live by faith" and from him they had learned to love all who loved their Lord. Arulappan would enjoy fellowship with brothers and sisters in Christ, whatever their church or race or caste. He was always pleased to be invited as a simple Indian Christian (without ordination or membership in a foreign denomination) to address groups associated with a foreign church or mission. But it did not always happen. In some places the English chaplain or missionary refused him permission to preach in the chapel, and some prevented their own Indian employees from hearing him. A catechist cousin of Arulappan was actually "suspended" by a clergyman for the offence of "receiving" him.[33]

In 1860 news came to Arulappan of a great spiritual awakening in England and America. Knowing the needs of the Indian churches, he was filled with longing for a similar awakening in Christianpettah. Complacency and worldliness had crept into the lives of believers who should know better. Many were lukewarm and uninterested; some indulged in quarrels and even lawsuits with one another; some got drunk and some were habitual liars; many were not truly converted at all. Yet without the convicting power of the Holy Spirit, his exhortations seemed to fall on deaf ears. That year at the annual conference, he read out the text, "If you then, though you are evil, know how to give good gifts to your children, how much more will your Father in heaven give the Holy Spirit to those who ask him."[34] With great feeling he urged the company to unite in prayer for the Spirit of holiness. It made a deep impression, especially on one poor woman, the mother of five children. Though she and her husband had been baptised, "they were not earnest in their faith." She began to read her Bible, seeking the Lord. All that week she read, on and on. When Sunday came, Arulappan addressed the church again on the same subject. That night, in a vision, a man questioned her about her faith and about her sins. Leaving her bed, she hurried to the house of a younger woman, who to her surprise had seen a similar vision; they made their way to the early prayer meeting in the house of Arulappan. Here, convicted of sin, they broke down in tears. Drawn by the sobs and groans, other villagers came in, and were quickly affected in the same way.

For four days, Arulappan tells us, "the Holy Ghost was poured out openly and wonderfully. Some prophesied and rebuked the people. Some beat themselves on their breasts severely and trembled and fell down through the shaking of their bodies and souls. They wept bitterly and confessed their sins. I was obliged to pray without ceasing for the consolation of everyone. I thought it was strange to see them without their senses. They saw some signs in the air. They were much pleased to praise God... Some of those who were not baptised had no peace until we baptised them; so about twenty souls were baptised after they received the Holy Ghost. They were very anxious to enjoy the Lord's Supper – every day if they could have it. About one hundred souls, including children, all have rice in one place as one household." One by one they found peace and joy in trusting Christ to save. Many brought jewellery and silver articles to be sold for the use of the poor Christians. They continued like this for two weeks, meeting three times every day. "All the heathens marvelled, and came and saw and heard us with fearful minds."[35]

Throughout this time, Arulappan and his teams continued travelling and preaching, and the work at the printing press and in the fields went on. Then, three months after the first signs of revival, "some of our people praised the Lord by unknown tongues with their interpretations." The neighbouring villages were affected too, and the Holy Spirit came in power to convict and convert. In one place twenty-five were baptised in water; in another, "some prophesy, some speak by unknown tongues with their interpretations."[36] A number of people saw visions of heaven and hell, perceiving the awful consequences of disobedience to God. In the meetings there were many prayers and personal testimonies, with verses of scripture quoted from memory and applied to the circumstances of those present. Roman Catholics were born again; Hindus were drawn to Christ; half-hearted and worldly Christians were transformed. Those previously known for drunkenness, lying, quarrelling and lawsuits began to preach salvation. Women took a prominent part in many places, leading souls to faith in Jesus through personal testimony and exhortation. A class of boys, most of them no more than twelve years old, declared they were leaving school immediately to go and preach to the heathen.

It is significant that everywhere the first signs of spiritual awakening were marked not by praise and elation but rather by acute anxiety and a sense of guilt. The joy came later. As the Revival spread through the Tinnevelly district, it affected the Anglican CMS churches and schools in the surrounding regions. Individuals and groups were seized with trembling, falling to the ground under a deep conviction of sin and fear of judgment. Some lay there for hours pleading for mercy; others searched the scriptures desperately. When assurance of salvation finally came though the word of God and the witness of the Holy Spirit, they would jump up and cry out, joyfully praising their Saviour.

For five months things continued at this emotional level. There were mixed reactions in the English community. Arulappan noted, "Some missionaries admit the truth of the gifts of the Holy Ghost."[37] Others at first were sceptical, but as time went on the foreign workers could no longer doubt or deny that a remarkable work of God was taking place. The results proved it to be genuine. Congregations had doubled in size; the indifferent had been soundly converted, committed workers were brought to a deeper level of devotion and love for Christ. All had a fresh boldness in speaking about him. A CMS agent declared, "What a mighty change has come over this people for the better! Those who were at enmity before with each other have become reconciled of their own accord. They show great eagerness to learn the word of God. For these ten or twelve days I have not heard a single word of bad language, either from the new converts or from the heathen (the miracle of this is that the heathen know scarcely any other sort of language)."[38]

The Revival continued for five years in all. Then, from the end of 1865, the spiritual manifestations began to decline and five years later had become rare. Eventually the Revival became a thing of the past. Arulappan, for the rest of his life, continued preaching the gospel and teaching in the churches, but he did not dwell on the events of that period or attempt to recreate them. It was an exceptional work of God, meeting an exceptional need, and after it had passed the majority of Christians remained wholehearted in their witness and their commitment to the steady growth of the churches.

In later years Arulappan, like Groves, borrowed money in order to extend and maintain his agricultural projects. He frequently referred to the fields as a burden and a source of embarrassment. In fact these lands brought little benefit to his children "and had finally to be sold to pay off debts that he incurred towards the close of his life in legal disputes with Romanists [i.e. Roman Catholics]."[39] Debt was almost universal in India – but the word of God shows us how to be free from debt; more than that, it commands us to be free from it. Obedience to Romans 13:8 would have saved Arulappan (and

Groves) from untold anxieties and regrets.[40] As Hudson Taylor observed, "It is really just as easy for God to give *beforehand*; and he much prefers to do so. He is too wise to allow his purposes to be frustrated for lack of a little money; but money wrongly placed or obtained in unspiritual ways is sure to hinder blessing. And what does going into debt really mean? It means that God has not supplied your need. You trusted him, but he has not given you the money; so you supply yourself and borrow. If we can only wait *right up to the time*, God cannot lie, God cannot forget: he is *pledged* to supply all our need."[41]

In his old age Arulappan faithfully bore his share of sickness, disappointment and bereavement before falling asleep in 1867. But with their leader gone, the future of the churches looked uncertain. There was no one of his calibre to take his place, and from this time on, it all began to go wrong. Careful enquiry has failed to pinpoint the exact reasons. Perhaps the outstanding ability of Arulappan himself, like that of John Wesley, meant that no one could really take his place. Perhaps his spiritual children had learned to look too much to him for guidance, rather than to the Holy Spirit and the inspired word of God. Perhaps it was a neglect, as he grew older, to share the task of overall leadership with younger men. Perhaps it was his willingness to receive and distribute gifts for others that deprived his co-workers of personal contact with godly friends and supporters in Britain and India. Perhaps it was a failure to pass on to the next generation his purest vision for a biblical Indian church, or even a failure on their part to receive it. Or was it something more mundane: perhaps the care of houses and fields distracting him from spiritual concerns, or just the debilitation of illness, weariness and old age? We do not know.

John Arulappan had a son. "He had been educated under Church of England influence in the school some miles from his home," but "this son had not the shepherd heart. The widely-spread little flocks were not visited, and the sheep became sick and feeble." In 1875 he took the lead in placing the Indian churches, so carefully nurtured for twenty-five years by his father, under the authority of the English bishop. Only three, including that in Christianpettah itself, chose to remain independent, enjoying the ministry of another son by the name of Anthony.[42]

As a young man John Arulappan had learned from Groves that India needs no foreign denominations; her Christians require no foreign authorisation to preach, to baptise or to break bread in remembrance of their Saviour. As a boy he had seen Karl Rhenius rebuked by a committee, slandered by a bishop, condemned by a Mission and driven to an early grave.[43] Now he too was gone, and thirty years after the Tamil churches of Rhenius succumbed to Anglican control in Tinnevelly, so also did those of Arulappan in Madurai. No doubt the new Indian leaders saw some benefit in a salaried post with a foreign mission, and some comfort in relinquishing responsibility to a foreign committee. They took the easy way, and the consequences would soon be clear.[44]

Eighteen years after the death of John Arulappan, an English clergyman, the Reverend Thomas Walker, was appointed by the CMS to be "Superintendent of the Tamil Church". He was a godly man, but one sorely perplexed by what he found on arrival in Tinnevelly. During the intervening years, a famine had given the Christians an opportunity to feed and clothe the poor, and 30,000 grateful beneficiaries had flooded into the churches. Though warmly disposed towards Christianity, they had only the scantiest knowledge of its precepts and obligations. Caste prejudice, marriage with Hindus, and the old problems of drunkenness and litigation, soon compromised the newcomers; many names had to be removed from the church rolls, and church officers relieved of their responsibilities. "It is no light task to superintend fifty-five thousand Christians," admitted Walker, "specially when along with it you have to introduce and write a new set of rules."[45] Much of the Superintendent's time was taken up with requests by Indian Christians for money. He did not like it. "The power of the rupee in our Indian missions," he said, "has sometimes been more strongly felt than the power of the Holy Ghost. From personal experience I do not hesitate to say that our most living congregations are those which have received the least financial aid; and the converse is also true."[46] Then, writing up his journal, "I had close work today at the new regulations for Council. What a pity that such elaborate organisation is needed. One wonders how the Pastoral Department was managed in apostolic times."[47] On another occasion, "Conference of missionaries; much talk about Councils and Bodies, but oh, for a good apostolic prayer meeting!"[48] And again, "You often have to pay unspiritual people to do spiritual work – would the apostles have done that?"[49]

It was at this time that Thomas Walker began his earnest study of the Acts of the Apostles, which eventually bore fruit in his perceptive guide to apostolic methods under the title *Missionary Ideals*.[50] "Is it not a fact," he declared, "that multitudes of those who figure in the statistics of our Missionary Reports are Christians in name only? And is it not a fact that many of our congregations are stagnant, dead, lifeless? Nay, more, is it not true that there are those (and are they very few in number?) among our mission workers as to whose true conversion to God we entertain the greatest doubts?" Walker saw Anglican schools and colleges teaching a critical view of the Bible, turning out educated sceptics rather than convinced Christians: "We have been too much occupied with outward organisation and missionary routine. We have not sought for our Indian brethren, as we should, a Spirit of life from God. We have not loved them, wept over them, wrestled in prayer for them as we ought to have done." And then, "Have we not, all of us, deviated sadly from the lines laid down in the Acts of the Apostles?"[51]

Walker was not making himself popular: "His strong convictions concerning the growth of the Indian church were not shared by the home committee."[52] He set about trying to sift out the "unsuitable pastors, schoolmasters, catechists", and he challenged the pervasive influence of caste. Soon he faced a "torrent of remonstrances... much bitterness, finally furious anger." Appeals were made against him, authority was brought to bear, and eventually he was compelled to resign. "I feel that I have reached a point," he said, "when my obedience to the Committee is in danger of clashing with my obedience to God."[53]

Free at last to devote his energies to the itinerant evangelistic work he loved, Walker had returned to the path marked out by Rhenius, Groves and Arulappan. But even then he was grieved by the denominational rivalries that faced him day by day. "In India all the unhappy divisions of the home Church are being rapidly introduced, and thus the spread of the gospel is hindered... Satan's choicest weapon is the blade which cuts asunder the union of the Christian Church itself." Bishops still forbad Anglicans to take the Lord's Supper with fellow Christians unless the bread and wine could be administered by an ordained Church of England minister, and Walker would not accept this. Amy Carmichael tells us, "Letter after letter was written from a heart that dearly loved spiritual liberty and could not bear to be separated from fellow lovers by any laws of man. It was quite impossible for him to join his fellow servants in service and then to draw back from going to the Lord's Table with them. It is not the Table of any Church was his feeling. 'It's the *Lord's* Table.'"[54]

There is no evidence that Thomas Walker ever read *Christian Devotedness*, but he well knew the scriptures which inspired it. Attending a dinner on the advice of the bishop, he wrote, "On the whole spent a pleasant evening, though I cannot help feeling that the missionary ought to be more fully devoted to simplicity of life." Amy Carmichael recalls how he was "distressed at the inclination of some of our mission party to gaiety and pleasure." Indeed, for his insistence on a humble and spiritual lifestyle, he became "a very unpopular person in certain quarters".[55]

Norris Groves would have enjoyed happy fellowship with Thomas Walker, as indeed with Amy Carmichael, for they were all, at heart, servants of Christ rather than of a human organisation. But they could not swim forever against the tide. The more authority the foreign mission claimed, the more dependent the Indian churches became. In the end, the vision that Arulappan received from Groves, and Groves from the apostles, had been snuffed out by the determination of the Church of England to control the churches of India. Thomas Walker protested, but in vain. In our day, we can only wonder what might have been. If every missionary had followed Groves's example – discipling an Arulappan, encouraging him to plant biblical Indian churches – how wonderfully the gospel might have transformed the nation! What colossal building schemes would have been spared! What vast sums of money turned to better use! What numbers of poor people fed, and true servants of Christ provided for! How many children preserved from godless catechists! How many missionaries liberated from the office desk! How many young men sent out as evangelists, teachers, shepherds of souls!

But our story is not yet done. Arulappan had two great-grandsons. Their names were Rajamani and Dorairaj. In 1935 Rajamani returned to the village of Christianpettah to help bury a beloved younger sister, and here he and Dorairaj prayed at the grave of their great-grandfather John Christian Arulappan. Rajamani recalled, "It seemed that something of the influence of his remarkable life of faith clung to the place... On our return from the south Dorairaj and I felt a new awakening of our love for the Lord and we began to pray much together."[56] Soon the pair were preaching publicly, distributing tracts, marching with banners and musical instruments through the streets of Madras, and before long they had been joined by "an increasing number of young men from various denominations". This "Gospel League" possessed "no constitution, nor membership, nor subscription list, but found its unity and strength in our love for the Lord Jesus Christ and our free wholehearted committal to him."[57]

In 1938 there came to Madras a converted Sikh from the Punjab by the name of Bakht Singh. As he preached publicly, many bystanders came to faith in Christ and a number were miraculously healed. Rajamani and Dorairaj became two of his closest friends. The crunch came early in 1941 when Bakht Singh was refused permission to preach at a church compound in Madras. The reason given was simple: "We in the Indian Ministers' Conference have met and passed a resolution never again to make any place available to this Punjabi preacher. Our objection is that he is not an ordained minister and therefore has no right to baptise anyone."[58]

By this time, Lang's biography of John Arulappan had found its way to India, and the example of the Indian apostle was not lost on a new generation.[59] Many of those who responded to the preaching of Bakht Singh and his friends had no church background; others were disillusioned with existing churches and missions increasingly influenced by liberal theology. Bakht Singh's biographer describes what happened next. "By his side were godly and experienced men like Dorairaj and Rajamani. They felt the need of a new solution to India's pressing problem. With prophetic insight they could see the inevitable crumbling of the missionary system. If the Lord's interests were to be secured in the land there was need for a far stronger foundation."[60] After much prayer they were led to rent a large dilapidated house in Madras, and here they launched a new fellowship with the name Jehovah Shammah.[61]

Searching the scriptures for the apostolic principles of church life, they agreed that the first priority was to insist on the need for new birth. A true church, they observed, will consist of committed believers, not people "baptised" as infants or made "members" by signing a piece of paper. Secondly, their fellowship must be "free from foreign control and direction, and also from the slavish rule of foreign finance."⁶² And thirdly, the meetings should be like those described in the New Testament, where all who believed might freely participate, devoting themselves to the apostles' teaching, fellowship, breaking of bread and prayer.

A contemporary describes how, from this point on, Bakht Singh "founded churches based on New Testament principles."⁶³ In addition to being "scriptural" churches, they were thoroughly "Indian" churches. "He built simple bamboo sheds (as against the pretentious stone buildings of Western design); he sat his people on floor mats, native style (and not on Western-style benches); he had gifted fellow-workers compose their own hymns and psalms, and set them to native lyrics [*sic*]; he brought in Indian instruments of music to lead congregational singing; he kept meetings going for long hours, which Indians love (to debunk the infamous Western one-hour service); he taught believers to give and not to beg; he showed them how to seek guidance about every matter direct from the Lord instead of slavishly following the orders of the missionary. Bakht Singh ruthlessly brought the externals back to simplicity and placed the emphasis on 'life', the resurrection life of the Lord Jesus, lifting believers into a realm far above the cold dead things of religious formality."⁶⁴

Many people have longed for revival to come to the churches of India. Bakht Singh was bold enough to point out that revivals are not found in the New Testament. Revivals are only needed in sick churches, and if a church is healthy it will have no need for revival. His aim from the start was to establish healthy churches.⁶⁵ And here was the vision of Norris Groves, embraced and applied by the most influential Christian of his generation in India.

The assemblies associated with Bakht Singh quickly became the fastest growing Christian groups on the subcontinent. Within eighteen years, two hundred fellowships of this type had sprung up in many parts of India and Pakistan.⁶⁶ At the present day they number at least two thousand.⁶⁷

But what of Chittoor, Arcot and Vellore, the towns that consumed the energies of Groves himself and for which he prayed so earnestly? In 1951 Rajamani retired from his employment with the Indian railways in order to devote his time to the work of God. It was to this very district that he was led. "In Vellore," he said, "a new move of God was taking place in the town and in the district around. It was my privilege to give an extended period to building up this most encouraging work."⁶⁸ Prayers that may seem long unanswered have never gone unheard.

ENDNOTES

[1] M609

[2] M519. The Scudders have been called "the most distinguished medical missionary family in all history" (Tucker, 332). Dr John Scudder first commenced work in Ceylon in 1819. In the course of four generations a remarkable forty-two members of the Scudder family became missionaries. They developed a work in Arcot on the foundation laid by Groves before taking over at Chittoor. Dr Ida Scudder later established a highly respected Christian Medical College in Vellore.

[3] M520

[4] *The Missionary Reporter*, no. 11, June 1854, 141. Groves's influence can surely be seen in Kistname's resolve to follow Christ "without any reference to particular creed or sect".

[5] Bromley, 32-38. Most larger towns at this time were occupied by unconverted representatives of the East India Company, which still "required its officials to make public offerings with full military honours to the idols on occasions of important festivals." In fact many Europeans in India were prone to drunkenness, fighting and shady business deals; some were "maintaining harems", and many "were sunk into a state of moral turpitude akin to that of their heathen neighbours" (Bromley, 22).

[6] Bromley, 43-44

[7] Bromley, 100-103

[8] Bromley, 41-42, 60

[9] M398

[10] Bromley chronicles the Lord's provision over many years to these faithful workers. The Godavari Delta mission is the subject of a brief appendix in Harriet Groves's *Memoir* (641-652). Letters from the Bowdens and Beers were published in *The Missionary Reporter* and *The Indian Watchman*.

[11] The word "mission" was used loosely in the same way that Groves referred to "the Baghdad mission" and "the Chittoor mission". It did not imply the existence of a home committee, a structure of authority or an obligation to any denominational body (Bromley, 93, 96). In fact the Godavari workers were "not connected with any missionary society", as is stated plainly in *The Missionary Reporter*, no. 1 (July 1853), 2-3.

[12] Bromley, 122

[13] Bromley, 127. Influenced perhaps by Robert Chapman, the Godavari team were reluctant to indicate numbers of converts, and from this time on it becomes very difficult to quantify their results.

[14] Bromley, 78, 85-87. This canalisation of the Godavari Delta checked the endemic malaria of the swamps and the seasonal outbreaks of cholera. It brought large tracts of marginal land into cultivation and put an end to a dreadful sequence of famines that had afflicted the region.

[15] Bromley, 123

[16] When speaking to the tribal people, Bowden started with the story of Creation, then the Fall, leading gradually to the Redemption. The narrative was interspersed with appropriate songs from his Indian companions (Bromley, 129-130).

[17] Bromley, 140-141

[18] Bromley, 44-47

[19] Arulappan's letters were published in *The Missionary Reporter* (1853 and 1856-8) and *The Indian Watchman* (July 1860 to October 1861). Extracts from these and other sources appear in Harriet Groves's *Memoir* (571-640) and in Lang's *Histories and Diaries of an Indian Christian, J C Aroolappen.*

[20] Lang, *Aroolappen*, 90-91. These were villages with a sizeable Roman Catholic population, where converts were not subject to such severe social exclusion as in purely Hindu villages.

[21] *Aroolappen*, 97

[22] Letter dated Nov. 1852 (M481-482).

[23] *Aroolappen*, 62-63. Arulappan remarked, "One of the old men, who is more than 60 years of age, said to me that he once thought he was not able to learn the scriptures by heart, so he had put aside the books given him for his benefit, but lately he tried it with prayer and feels it is easy and pleasant to his soul. He now repeats more than ten verses of the scriptures every Sunday. He takes his Gospel wherever he goes, and converses with the people as much as he can, and speaks with his Lord and Saviour as he walks along, and feels very sorry on account of his spending precious time in vain on account of his doubtful mind" (*Aroolappen*, 96).

[24] *Aroolappen*, 96

[25] *Aroolappen*, 129

[26] *Aroolappen*, 128

[27] *Aroolappen*, 120-121

[28] M447

[29] M609

[30] *Aroolappen*, 132

[31] *Aroolappen*, 132

[32] *Aroolappen*, 107-108

[33] *Aroolappen*, 83; M589

[34] Lk 11:13

[35] *Aroolappen*, 144

[36] *Aroolappen*, 144-145

[37] *Aroolappen*, 145

[38] *Aroolappen*, 183. There was no claim to possess the gift of healing, and no healings were reported. The speaking in tongues commenced only after the Revival was already well under way, and there was no particular emphasis on tongues. The Revival spread as far as Godavari, where the Bowdens and Elizabeth Beer experienced similar scenes, though on a smaller scale (Bromley, 164-166).

[39] *Aroolappen*, 208

[40] "Owe no one anything" (RSV/NRSV). The New International Version strangely paraphrases this as "Let no debt remain outstanding". In fact the apostle's command in this verse is very emphatic, introduced by two negatives: *mēdeni mēden ofeilete*, literally: to no one / nothing / owe. J B Phillips correctly renders it, "Keep out of debt altogether." This means paying as quickly as possible whatever involuntary debts arise (rents, taxes, employees' wages etc), and it also means refusing to put

oneself under a financial obligation that cannot be immediately discharged. Freedom from debt is one of the many freedoms that Christ has brought to his disciples. If we follow the principles of his word, we have his promise of this freedom (Matt 6:25-33; 7:7-11; 2 Cor 9:8-11; Phil 4:12, 19 etc).

[41] Taylor, *Growth of a Work of God*, 54-55

[42] *Aroolappen*, 216-218. The children and grandchildren of Arulappan are listed by name in Rajamani, 140-142.

[43] *Aroolappen*, 16

[44] Lang writes of one CMS catechist whose reading of scripture convinced him he should ask for baptism as an adult believer. Knowing it would lose him his position and his salary, he hardened his heart on this point, and then on other matters, spending years in "sin and shame" before finally being baptised and restored. This illustrates well enough the tensions that could result from accepting a salaried post as a mission agent (Lang, *Groves*, 282-283).

[45] Amy Carmichael, *This One Thing*, 55

[46] *This One Thing*, 143

[47] *This One Thing*, 55

[48] *This One Thing*, 123

[49] *This One Thing*, 73

[50] first published in 1911

[51] *This One Thing*, 133-138

[52] Houghton, 96

[53] *This One Thing*, 73-74

[54] *This One Thing*, 123

[55] *This One Thing*, 126. Amy Carmichael joined Thomas Walker and his wife in Tinnevelly in 1896. Raised as a Presbyterian in Ireland, she learned from the Keswick Convention "to drop labels, and to think only of the one true invisible Church, to which all who truly love the Lord belong" (Houghton, 37).

[56] Rajamani, 45

[57] Rajamani, 47

[58] Rajamani, 76

[59] Rajamani himself refers directly to Lang, quoting his extracts from Arulappan's diaries (Rajamani, 107-108).

[60] Smith D, 45-46

[61] Jehovah Shammah, from Ezek 48:35, means "The Lord is there".

[62] Smith D, 48

[63] Koshy, *Brother Bakht Singh*

[64] Smith D, 52

[65] Smith D, 51. Questions relating to mission strategy in India and elsewhere are discussed in Chapters 31 and 32.

[66] Smith D, 53

[67] Koshy, *Brother Bakht Singh*

[68] Rajamani, 122

"I feel there is something in love so hallowing;
it kills that hateful selfishness
which twines round all that is human."

Norris Groves [1]

28

To Love as He Loved

A t first sight Anthony Norris Groves would have seemed a very ordinary
man. He had neither the sturdy self-confidence of Karl Pfander nor
the intense doggedness of John Kitto; neither the penetrating intellect of
Frank Newman nor the methodical composure of George Müller; neither the
cultured charm of John Parnell nor the scholarly acumen of Henry Craik;
neither the evangelistic skills of John Arulappan nor the administrative ability
of Alexander Duff. Amidst all these outstanding characters, he might pass
without notice. And yet, looking more closely, we would see it was Groves
himself who struck the spark that kindled the fire which made each of these
men in his own sphere a bright and shining light.

Someone asked John Kitto, settling in as a dental assistant at Exeter, what
sort of man his employer was. "Mr Groves," he replied, "is not a Methodist,
a Calvinist, a Lutheran or a Papist. What, then, is he? A Deist, a Unitarian,
an Antinomian? No, he is one of those rather singular characters – a Bible
Christian, and a disciple of the meek and lowly Jesus; not nominally, but
practically and really such. A man so devotedly, so fervently attached to the
scriptures I never knew before."[2] This it was that set Groves apart from the
respectable and religious people around him. "I have very little confidence
in man," he confessed. "My great desire has been to cast myself on the word
of God, that every judgment of my soul concerning all things may be right,
by being, in all, the mind of God. For exactly in proportion as this is the case
shall we be a blessing to others. Oh for a heart to love as he loved! Oh for
such meekness, gentleness and devotion as shone in everything he did, who
is our Great Exemplar."[3]

It was what Norris Groves saw of Christ in the scriptures that gave him the
desire to be like Christ in the home, in the surgery, in the streets of the city,
wherever he happened to be – to think as Jesus would think, to do what Jesus
would do, to be (as Jesus was) "a blessing to others". The four Gospels show
us a Saviour who, whenever he saw a person in need, stopped to help. "Oh,"
sighed Groves, "for more and more of that vital acquaintance with the love of
Christ to a perishing world which enables the soul in *truth* to say 'the love of
Christ constraineth me!'"[4] Throughout his life, wherever he was – England,

Ireland, Baghdad, Madras, Chittoor, on land or at sea – this was his greatest desire and motivation.

But how suited was Norris Groves for work overseas? He was not drawn to foreign cultures, he did not enjoy travel. He was not a gifted evangelist, nor a natural orator. He was not particularly sociable, and he often found relationships painful. He was never a great organiser or administrator; he was not physically or mentally tough. Frustrated, as he said, by "the natural badness of my memory", he bemoaned the difficulty he found with languages.[5] One might think he was not cut out to be a missionary at all. But he had one quality that more than made up for his deficiencies: he knew how to love. Love was the key to everything: "I feel there is something in love so *hallowing*; it kills that hateful selfishness which twines round all that is human."[6] It was love that drew people to Christ – not ceremonies or rules or customs, or even doctrines, but love. And it was love that drew people to Norris Groves. "He loved me sincerely as his dear child in Christ Jesus," said John Arulappan. "I never knew anyone who loved me so for the sake of the Lord Jesus."[7]

A lady wrote asking for some spiritual counsel. "How to lead a holy life?" was her great longing. The secret to a holy life, replied Groves, lies in a relationship of love. "When you really love, you soon find out what will please. And thus it is with Christ. If your love glows towards *him* you will have almost an *instinctive* sense of what will please *him*, and that will prove to be a holy life when followed on from day to day. Yet when you think to please one whom you truly love, till death, you do not plan a life of service. But the fruits of love... spring from the heart fresh and fresh as from an exhaustless spring. And so it is with Christ. Think not on a holy life but on a holy moment as it flies; the first overwhelms the heart by its immensity, the other sweetens and refreshes by its lightness... and yet a succession of holy moments constitutes a holy life. I know your anxious heart will say, how is the love to be obtained that makes the yoke so easy and the burden so light? I will endeavour to explain to you. During my first visit among you, neither to yourself nor to your dear daughter did I feel particularly drawn. I did not feel assured of your interest in the truth, nor of your kind feelings towards me; but at the conclusion of my second visit all was changed, and I feel now that to do you a service would not be merely a duty but a pleasure, bringing its own reward, as done to a sister and a daughter. Why? Because I have felt *your* kindness and its power. Thus it is with Christ; believe his love and all service is sweet. And that you may know him and how much he deserves all your love, pay him not hasty visits but *dwell* with him. The more we were together the more we loved each other; and thus it will be in heaven and should be always with the saints even here. But it may so happen (for so abounding is our natural weakness) that we fail to find love in one another;

but thus it cannot be with *him*; for whoever finds him finds love, for it is his *very nature* towards us."[8]

Whether Groves was speaking to groups or individuals, his words were always simple and practical. One who heard him in India described his message as "strengthening and refreshing; it spoke to the hearts of all, and all were edified... What I feel in his teaching is that it establishes the heart in grace; and there is something in it that touches the tender feelings of our nature, which he always seeks to have brought to his [i.e. Christ's] service."[9] Norris Groves had this unusual ability to awaken in others their own love for Jesus – their own desire to please their Master and Friend. He confided, "As a principle to guide the heart, I would say, seek such a deep acquaintance with Christ's mind, as revealed in his holy life and life-giving word, in order that when any little circumstance arises that requires instant decision, you may have himself, as it were, present to the memory of your heart to give you counsel. And that you may fully understand this mind, seek above all things the guidance of that Spirit that alone can guide you into all truth."[10]

A military man recalled, "On one occasion, when I was staying with Colonel Powney, a select committee of distinguished artillery officers was assembled at his house from all parts of India; and, as it happened, Mr. Groves, the missionary from Bagdad, came in for the night, on his journey from Persia to Calcutta. Never did I see the beauty of holiness so evidenced as in that servant of God. His whole conversation and his striking history, which he narrated to us, seemed to present the reality of religion to my mind, as though 'telling me all that was in my heart;' whilst his fascinating manner and intelligence so impressed this set of hardthinking, world-engrossed officials, that they sat till deep in the night, spell-bound... Before this I had experienced cravings in my spirit after a higher and more evangelic piety, which, like Nebuchadnezzar's vision, disappeared, 'and the thing was gone from me.' In Groves I saw the reality of such an attainment, and the interpretation of my vision. A new hope and object seemed to open on my soul."[11]

Norris Groves could speak spontaneously – to a small circle of friends or to a hall full of soldiers – and on such occasions he spoke well, but he also knew the value of preparing carefully and seeking the Spirit's guidance in preparation. He would draw his text from any part of the Bible, including the Old Testament. Before addressing any group, he prayed earnestly for those who would hear him: "O that the Lord would open my heart to feel for them, and so to realise the riches of his grace, that I may speak as one who tastes and knows how *precious* the truth is."[12] In preparing to speak, his concern was not for new ideas but for renewed fullness of the Spirit; he knew from experience that words will take wing when anointed by the Spirit of God. "My heart longs," he said, "for that fervency of spirit which is the strength of service. Oh for that spiritual *power* which led Paul to say, 'to me to live is Christ; to die is gain.'"[13]

When he taught, his style was informal and intimate. On his favourite themes, he could speak with energy and urgency. He delighted to show how much Christ has loved each of his hearers, then how worthy Christ is of our love in return, and finally how easily we can express our love by giving all we are and have to him. This was repeated many times in many places. "I believe the Holy Spirit has given me the gift of exhortation in the Church," he said, "and to this I principally confine my ministrations, first showing *what Christ is* in all his love manifested in all he has done and suffered for us, and in what he is now towards us, and therefore how worthy he is of all love from undivided hearts. I feel it is a blessed office to tell forth his praises among the saints, and I can often do it, with joyful lips, from the bottom of my heart."[14]

Norris Groves was a perceptive man, unusually sensitive to human frailty. "As I move among Christians," he said, "the thought often strikes me, how exceedingly they mar their own peace. Husbands and wives, brothers and sisters, are continually ruining each other's happiness about things that are not worth a second thought. And though you can *put your finger* upon the diseased spot in the soul from whence *the discord arises*, those whom you love and wish to make happy will not see it. Oh, how much must the whole Church grieve our dear and gracious and most long-suffering Lord!"[15] And again, "There is something particularly hateful in selfishness. Perhaps we do not see it in ourselves as in others; but sure I am, if my selfishness affects others as theirs does me, it must be worth every exertion to extirpate it, root and branch, and this I feel can only be by living in Jesus as the branch abides in the vine. I do pray I may so live in him."[16]

Those who heard him in Chittoor and Madras never forgot "the freshness and reality of his devotedness to and love of God... and there was a *geniality* in his religion as well as a catholicity that warmed those that were in his company." One who knew him there described how he brought a message of freedom and life: "I think the tone of many of us was, in some respects, very austere. We were exercised rather too exclusively, in a Levitical way, about clean and unclean things, separation from the world etc." To such a circle, Norris Groves came as a breath of fresh air. "If any united a deep realization of the vital points of Christianity with a smiling and sunny exterior and a happy mode of presenting them to others, it was he."[17] And as he spoke, it was his own example that showed the possibility of life on a higher plane – his faith in times of difficulty, his simple lifestyle amidst colonial extravagance, his kindness in the face of criticism, his hope when all seemed dark. He brought with him "so much life and energy and affection," it was a blessing just to behold "his happy face".[18]

John Wesley, in his journals, records chapter and verse for every sermon in every place. Groves did not do so, but like Wesley his basic themes were carried in his heart, whatever fresh Bible verses and illustrations he might use on each occasion to carry them home. The topics he chose were creative and imaginative, and yet he delighted to travel the old paths, feeling no compulsion to search constantly for fresh insights and scholarly clarifications. The great need, he thought, was for Christian people to take to heart and put into practice what they had already learned: "I feel what we really need, both to enable us to carry out and to suffer all God's will, is *realization* of the things we know. How searching is our Lord's word, 'If ye know these things, happy are ye if ye *do* them.'"[19] On his first trip to India Groves visited a district judge and his wife in Calicut. The judge confessed that their visitor had come "bringing before us truths which we had never heard of, and which, though contained in the scriptures, had been unknown. My precious wife and myself had long been Christians and readers of the Bible, but the certainty of God's love and faithfulness then began to dawn upon us as a new revelation from on high. It was not much that dear Groves taught us, but we saw in him a living Christian practising a life of self-denial, of devotedness to God, and of separation from the world, and one who was earnestly studying the word of our God... To me it seemed as if he had been taken up into the heavens, had there learned glorious facts which none had ever known, and which he had come down to reveal to us."[20]

His emphasis on a personal relationship with Christ, a personal calling, a personal ministry, made Norris Groves very much an individualist. To his mind the highest form of Christian service was always that of the wandering evangelist, free from worldly cares and family ties, at liberty to follow wherever the Spirit might lead, enduring hardship to carry the gospel to the ends of the earth. The itinerant life beckoned to the romantic in Norris Groves. Yet, paradoxically, Groves himself was a man who, perhaps more than most, needed the support of an affectionate wife and the stability of a happy home. Norris Groves – the individualist, the free spirit, the visionary – was at heart a family man, and he probably felt this tension throughout his life: the call to wider service, and the longing for home.

In reality his own gift lay not in preaching to Hindu or Muslim crowds. He could do this well enough, at least by interpretation, but he lacked the extravert self-confidence of the natural street preacher, and he lacked the restless urge, the unremitting passion for the lost, that drives the true evangelist always onward to the "regions beyond". His real work was personal work, pastoral work, the encouragement of Christians, and especially the drawing of nominal Christians to genuine faith in Christ and devotion to his service.[21]

He was never one to enjoy the limelight. Indeed, "Groves's unobtrusive but disciplined saintliness led him to shun the glare of publicity."[22] His best work was always in a small group, or with just one person, and the heady stimulus of public attention held no appeal for him. "Groves's disposition was naturally retiring, hesitant, and far more effective in quiet conversation and discussion."[23] If he was a spiritual leader, he was the kind of leader who brought out the best in others and was hardly noticed himself. "Be content," he advised, "to appear ignorant about many things which others think they know a great deal about, if you may but be permitted to exhibit *Jesus*, precious to all – *his* meekness, *his* tenderness, *his* forbearing pity in the midst of all our weakness and perverseness... And be always assured, the tree that is most loaded with God's fruit will bend its head most lowlily towards the ground. In spiritual things, humility and faithfulness always accompany each other. May you be rich in the love of the Church of God, for their profit as well as your own peace: but know nothing of Paul or Apollos."[24] Nothing, that is, of the knowledge that puffs up and makes for strife between Christian and Christian.

Unobtrusive he might wish to be, and yet, according to Kitto's biographer, Norris Groves "was one of those men who exercise an immediate and deep personal influence on others."[25] Long before Dale Carnegie introduced his bright idea to a world at odds with itself, Groves had learned how to win friends and influence people. There was no secret method – just the natural outworking of a genuine interest in other people, a mind fixed immovably on a few simple truths, and a resolve to talk about them with warmth and enthusiasm whenever anyone seemed inclined to listen.

It was often a quiet chat that people found most helpful. During his first trip to India Groves confided to his journal, "One missionary told me yesterday that he felt he had acquired new eyes since a little conversation we had together."[26] Many good things could be said at the meal table or round the fireside, as John Kitto recalled: "During the period of my abode with Mr Groves, I was enabled to imbibe a measure of those principles and opinions by which he is known... For this I have more cause to be thankful than for any other circumstance of my life. In the whole world, so far as I know it, there is not one man whose character I venerate so highly."[27] Henry Craik, describing his own time in the Groves household, agreed: "It was not at St Andrews, it was not at Plymouth; it was at Exeter that the Lord taught me those lessons of dependence on himself and of catholic fellowship which I have sought to carry out."[28] Alexander Duff in India remarked, "His warmth, his love, his zeal, his amazing energy, at once riveted and gained my heart... I could not help regarding him as one of the most loving and loveable of Christian men, while the singular fervency of his spirit made it quite contagious... O that a double portion of his spirit would descend upon all our drowsy and sleeping churches throughout Christendom!"[29] A youthful John Arulappan so enjoyed his company that he dropped what he was doing to join Groves on his travels. Many years later he paid tribute to "my beloved and affectionate father in Christ... that pious and faithful servant of Christ who brought us up in the true knowledge of Christ and loved us to the end as his own children."[30] Personal work of this nature brought Groves himself great pleasure, as he confided to his young friend William Caldecott, "by scattering God's heavenly seed on the rich soil of your heart; for it is indeed a higher honour than to be the medium of all earthly blessings."[31]

There was no guile to Norris Groves and nothing hidden. He was transparently honest, and would talk about faith, hope and love with unfeigned earnestness, and without the slightest embarrassment. In his day, as in ours, this was not common. "I do wonder," he remarked, "at the conversation of professing Christians when they meet together. With the world it may be different, but among themselves you would expect that out of the abundance of the heart the mouth would speak."[32] He did his best to lead conversations in more helpful directions. "So kind, tender and considerate to all," one friend described him, "except when the truth of his Master is concerned, and then he is *bold* and *earnest* in commending it."[33] Kitto too was impressed by "the warmth and energy which, more than any man I ever knew, he throws into his opinions."[34]

Not everyone took kindly to this. It was never Groves's behaviour that alienated them, always the views he expressed. He records, perhaps with a wry smile, "I was told I was the greatest enemy the Church of England ever had in India, because no one could help loving my spirit, and thus the evil sank tenfold deeper; but indeed I do not wish to injure but to help her by taking from her all her false confidences."[35]

What was it, we might wonder, that people found so offensive? The message of *Christian Devotedness* could certainly make some feel uncomfortable. The challenge to sell one's possessions, to go into all the world and preach the gospel, praying literally for one's daily bread, was never going to be a popular one with the average churchgoer. Groves continued to teach it throughout his life. But as he spoke to individuals and groups he went beyond this earliest idea of simple obedience to simple instructions, and set before his hearers the possibility of a personal *relationship* with God. There was more to being a Christian, he told them, than attending church: "The great point is to get each man to stand in his *individual* conscience before God, under the full assurance that aggregate religion is no religion at all. There must be a tasting and handling and knowing the truth for one's self; and this the mere formal unity which binds multitudes never can give."[36] Those who took comfort from the thought that they were doing all their church required of them found this extremely threatening. "I find daily that men would rather suffer any measure of bondage in the things of religion than dwell in individual responsibility before God for every action, thought and affection," he remarked.[37]

Others were startled by the thought that God might actually *do something*, perhaps even upset their plans and change their personality. Groves commented,

"I think there is far too little realization of the truth 'it is God which worketh in you both to will and *to do* of his good pleasure' and 'without me you can *do* nothing.'"[38] A God who dealt personally with individuals was not a very comfortable proposition to a generation whose religion consisted of chanting responses out of a little black book. "My only design in keeping a journal," said Groves, "was to record such circumstances of God's dealings with ourselves, or others, as might be useful to myself, or possibly to the Church of God."[39]

But beyond this, it was his concept of "Christian liberty" that aroused most resentment – his insistence on his freedom to preach, teach, baptise and break bread in remembrance of Christ, without any human authorisation. He was not a reverend, he had no clerical collar, he had no theological degree, he had no bishop or committee to keep him in line. Who on earth did he think he was? He was a servant of Christ – and a servant, moreover, who believed he should be faithful to his Master. He would state his principles without hesitation or equivocation, and he would expect others to be convinced. At times this caused difficulty with those who remained unconvinced, and it placed some, like John Kitto, in an embarrassing position. Leaving Baghdad Kitto confided, "I am persuaded no one can live happily with Mr Groves in a dependent situation."[40] There was too much pressure on Kitto to accept the views expressed by his employer.

Yet Norris Groves never liked being at odds with other Christians. Though willing at every opportunity to speak the truth in love, he would never enter into acrimonious debate with anyone. He did not like the strident dogmatism of men like Drummond or Wolff on prophetic subjects, any more than that of Darby on Christological or ecclesiastical themes, and it did no credit to a man, in his eyes, when that man criticised and denounced others. From India he wrote, "In all my ministry here, my great wish is to produce in the brethren, especially the poor, a distaste for questions that 'gender strife rather than godly edifying' which is in Christ Jesus."[41] "I wish you to understand distinctly that, whilst for myself I feel every ray of light given me of God to be a talent I dare not hide, yet I entirely disallow the right of judging and rejecting others, seeing the Lord has said, 'judge nothing before the time.'"[42]

In fact Groves made it a matter of principle to seek fellowship with those whose views he knew to differ from his own. In eastern Europe he sought out Congregationalists, Presbyterians, Moravians, Lutheran Pietists, a Quaker and, of course, the Anglicans who held chaplaincies in various places. In India he made a special point of visiting the Wesleyans in Jaffna, the Baptists at Serampore and the Lutherans in Tinnevelly. Some years later Frank Newman reminisced, "I remembered a saying of the noble-hearted Groves: 'Talk of loving me while I agree with them! Give me men that will love me when I differ from them and contradict them: those will be the men to build up a true Church.'"[43] In his travels Groves found his own human nature to be such that wherever he went something would grate on him a little and require the exercise of loving and patient tolerance: "But then, by becoming habituated to forego one's own will, it becomes at last easy, and we can rejoice and praise and love and intimately associate with the Lord's handiwork in his saints, though they may be associated with much that the heart longs to see away."[44]

This did not mean that he would hide his own convictions. On one occasion John Darby urged him to say nothing about baptism; his views, Darby thought, were divisive.[45] Groves replied that he must teach what he saw in the word of God, according to the light granted him, not looking to please men but to please God. Yet if everyone did this would there not be endless division? Certainly not, thought Groves, for it is impossible to divide the spiritual body of Christ. True unity does not consist in a uniformity of view on such matters as baptism but in our common faith in our common Saviour. This means that the Christian is free to say exactly what he believes (and to persuade others of its soundness) without fear of being divisive – for disagreement cannot separate what is intrinsically and irrevocably united.[46]

This "spiritual" view of Christian unity was difficult for some people to accept. They liked to be surrounded by Christians whose views on every point matched their own. Such people preferred to keep him at arm's length, and to Groves's sensitive nature this was painful: "I am so tried in acting towards those who are, I believe, really Christians yet with whom every word becomes, or is in danger of becoming, a subject of controversy. With the world [i.e. non-Christians] you know how to act, and with those you feel you can rely on as on brothers beloved, but it is most difficult to be kind without being more intimate than many minds can *bear*, and it is difficult to be in a measure distant without being unchristianly cold."[47] In reality there were few like him who could hold in balance a complete acceptance of a brother in Christ and an absolute denial of the views he held.

But if he wished to live in harmony with his fellow-men, he wished even more to live in harmony with his Lord. "I do so desire," he said, "to deal with my Father with that love and loyalty that hate rebellion against the *least* intimation of his will."[48] Endeavouring to do exactly what he believed to be the will of God, Groves sometimes felt he had said the wrong thing or done the wrong thing. He upset people, and though he was his own fiercest critic, the criticism that came from others cut him deeply. "Tell our dear friend Mr E," he wrote to Caldecott from India, "that I have not forgotten his deep reproof. I trust it only came to strengthen what the Lord had done, and in this I had the reason given me." The judgment passed upon him might seem harsh, and Mr E not the best person to make it, yet Groves continues, "I cannot think on all the Lord's gentleness towards me without almost tears of thankfulness... The Lord has not cast me out as I deserve, but gently drew me through the furnace, burnt away, I trust, a little of the dross and allowed many like you, unworthy as I am, still to love and comfort me."⁴⁹ It would be hard to hold grudges for long against such a man.

Groves himself had suffered much – both in Baghdad and in India – through mistakes of his own and through circumstances beyond his control. In these difficult times he learned of human frailty and of divine comfort. "I often feel deeply thankful for all I have passed through," he said. "It has taught me to pity and bear, from the remembrance of my own deep transgressions."⁵⁰ If anything, his sensitivity to any shadow cast between him and other Christians increased in his latter days. One who knew him well spoke of "the subdued and broken spirit which so especially marked the closing years of Mr Groves's life; indeed his willingness to *receive* reproof and to *confess* to *any defects* which persons of a contrary temperament thought they discovered in him."⁵¹

Norris Groves was never one who could hide his feelings. "How strange," he said, "that exposure to heat which others seem unable to bear has no effect on me, and yet a few thoughts strongly impressed on my mind quite unsettle both body and mind!"⁵² He admired the robust Germanic stoicism of men such as Karl Rhenius who could remain seemingly unmoved by circumstances. Rhenius could pick up a thought, a trial or a sorrow at will, said Groves, and then put it down to be picked up again the following day "as easily as I could a book. To this I feel perfectly unequal. The Lord enables me with patience, and even at times with much profit, to *bear* the *most painful* disappointments, yet as for getting rid of the weight I cannot." But despite the pain he suffered from his intensely emotional nature, he would not willingly change places with Rhenius: "I have the impression that I should lose more than I should gain if I could, for I think I have deep enjoyments that he does not know, and communion with hearts from which he would feel estranged by want of sympathy."⁵³

Whatever his personal weaknesses, Norris Groves's great strength lay in his sympathy and his kindness to others. We have seen how he befriended the Jewish converts of his early days, how he repeatedly came to the help of John Kitto, how he provided for Henry Craik, paid off the debts of his erring relatives, tended Harnie's dying brother, offered a home to the bereaved Serkies, cared for an orphan boy, adopted an orphan girl, and nursed both Cotton and Duff through times of almost fatal illness. In Malta John Kitto wrote, "The best thing in my room is a bookcase. The books are partly my own; for I was enabled, through the kindness of dear Mr Groves to repurchase many of the books I sold."⁵⁴ The following year when Kitto returned from the Mediterranean, dismissed by the CMS and out of favour with his other benefactors, Groves (in the midst of his own preparations for Baghdad) again took steps to ensure that this difficult young man would not be out of work. In fact a concern for the needs of those around him had long ago become an instinctive part of his nature: he did not even need to think about it. At sea he confessed, "I have, thank God, got over my seasickness and am therefore able to help others a little."[55]

His kindness and his awareness of his own frailties meant that Groves "had a love which could bear and endure all – an ability given him of God to sympathise with weakness to any extent." And Harriet tells us that God, who had given this grace, tested it many times. On occasion he was upset and disappointed by those whose good he sought, yet he would not become bitter towards any who failed him. "He never gave up anyone whom he had once befriended," she recalled. "He sought invariably to overcome evil with good."[56] Kitto himself admitted, "I find it really impossible to express half of that which his conduct towards me, on this and on other occasions, has made me feel. Mr Groves is the only representative of that which, before I had gone out into the world, I thought all men to be. Of all the blessings God ever gave me, and they are many, the chief and best have been the friendship of Mr Groves and the benefits which have flowed from it to me... He has been like a guardian angel, if there be such, appointed to watch over me for good, and to interfere between me and evil. In all my wanderings, stumblings, dangers, errors, mistakes and sins, he has not left me to myself – he has adhered to me still. And when I have fallen he did not, as others have done, say to me, 'Lie in the bed of your own making;' but, although himself the most aggrieved, has come forth repeatedly to my help, has spoken to me 'good and comfortable words,' and endeavoured to fix me again in the place from which I had fallen."[57]

How then does Norris Groves stand as a spiritual leader? The fact that Kitto, Newman, Cronin, Parnell, Gundert and George Baynes all chose to leave him, and that he never acquired a dedicated group of followers, might lead us to suppose that Groves lacked leadership qualities. That would be a serious misjudgment. His was essentially a leadership of influence rather than authority. He drew friends and fellow-workers to Christ rather than to himself, and he encouraged them to seek guidance from their Saviour, not from any man. This is the humblest form of leadership, and sometimes hardly recognised as such, but it is genuine spiritual leadership of the apostolic type in contrast to the officious administrative control that sometimes passes for it. In this respect Norris Groves resembles David Livingstone, Henry Grattan Guinness and C T Studd, men who powerfully inspired others but could never succeed in organising them.[58]

Yet Groves himself was far from impractical. His imaginative mind led him to take initiatives that, developed by others, proved wonderfully effective. It was Groves whose vision for informal Christian worship and fellowship took shape in the Brethren movement. It was Groves who encouraged John Arulappan to establish a network of indigenous churches throughout southern India. It was Groves, indeed, whose willingness to "trust and obey" inspired a generation of organised "faith missions". And seventy years before Amy

Carmichael launched her Dohnavur Fellowship, it was Norris Groves in 1834 who rescued "forty little orphan girls" (sold by their parents "for a rupee or two each") from a life of great unhappiness.[59] To care for these children he enlisted the help of two expatriate Christians in Calcutta who would support two workers if two workers could be found. Six months later he had located two willing workers in Switzerland. This orphanage and school in Sonamukhi flourished, and many of the girls became committed Christians. Some in due course became wives of Indian evangelists, and others joined the staff of the school. In all this we can no doubt see the hand of God, but the missionary couple responsible for the institution paid tribute to the man so remarkably used in its establishment. Mrs Weitbrecht declared she "had always considered Mr Groves as the father of her school."[60] This whole episode is typical of Norris Groves. He saw a need and he set about meeting it – without requiring that anyone submit to his authority or subscribe to his personal views. And having taken the initiative, he left others to fulfil the practical outworking of the vision.

Groves was a perfectionist; he had a clear view of how things ought to be. But even when things fell short of his ideal, and when other people let him down, he had learnt the secret of giving thanks in every circumstance and rejoicing in the Lord always.[61] This kept him from the sourness that afflicts many a perfectionist. Yet though he was always gentle with the failings of others, he demanded nothing less than perfection of himself. And though he knew his Master had forgiven him for his errors of judgment in Chittoor, he never really forgave himself: "Oh I have served him so wretchedly, so miserably. I know he has blotted it out, but I can never forget it. There is nothing but Jesus, nothing, nothing."[62] At times like this he could condemn himself mercilessly for the absence of that inner peace which he believed should be enjoyed by every child of God. In a period of discouragement in 1847, "I have had a sad, yet not an unblessed day. I feel as though God has been with me; yet I have been greatly tried with my constantly besetting burthen – the inability to feel the things of God have that power of giving peace to the soul, which they could not but do if I loved him as I ought."[63]

This rather morbid preoccupation with pious feelings was typical of nineteenth-century evangelical Christianity in the English-speaking world, and at times Groves railed against it: "Did you ever read with attention Jonathan Edwards 'On the Religious Affections'? I think it, with all books of its class, most truly calculated to deceive and distress the heart." Much perplexity comes from trying to test one's own feelings of devotion! "Surely, it is better to dwell continually on Christ. And if anybody, by contemplating Jesus in all his beauty and perfection of character, does not know whether he loves him or not, no examination of his affections will show him."[64]

The idea that a godly man should be burdened by a sense of inborn and hopeless depravity was a common one, a legacy no doubt of Calvinistic influence, and it oppressed Groves like many of his generation. He had a tendency, too, to worry about the future: "It is in this that Satan's power consists: that he casts into my mind the most strange unimaginable possibilities, and I am so foolish that whilst I feel they have not a shadow of truth, they trouble and perplex my mind and destroy its tranquillity and take up that spiritual power in subduing their inroads which I would spend in peaceful devotion to God."[65]

Prayer, at such times, seemed to bring more frustration than relief, and what he most needed in his darker moments was the presence of a loving wife or, failing that, a sympathetic friend. We have seen how, bereaved in Baghdad, he had longed for the arrival of his colleagues from Aleppo, and how quickly he wished to remarry after losing Mary. Facing uncertainty in Madras, "I should feel at times most desolate but for the fellowship of those in my own house. The sense of a happy home always cheers me."[66] When away from his loved ones, he wrote to them incessantly. Delayed in India for more than a year after Harriet had left for England, he spoke of "this most painful separation, unthought of when we parted."[67]

But though he liked and needed people, Norris Groves was one who also needed periods of time to himself. Loving everyone he met – perhaps *because* he loved to a higher degree than most of us – he could find people exhausting. On the one hand he could say, "Of brothers and sisters I can never have enough till my heart is filled with all the redeemed of the Lord."[68] On the other, he found the strain of constantly thinking how to encourage those he was with took its toll on his sensitive spirit. This was especially the case when travelling. He enjoyed the hospitality offered by Christian friends, but he snatched precious hours to himself at night, and it was a rare luxury when he could enjoy a whole day in "a quiet room in a quiet bungalow in the midst of the jungle."[69] On the coast of India he chose to sail in "a little French brig" rather than enjoy the comfort of the regular English passenger service – it was cheaper but it also allowed him some time on his own.[70] A few months later, on board ship for England, "In the evening, after dinner I go up into the mizzen top and there enjoy the sun's descending glory, the cool evening breeze, and that quiet which is to be enjoyed nowhere below. Even alone in the cabin, there are so many talking in the cuddy that the thoughts get perplexed and the ears full of strange sounds which harmonize not with the soul that would be alone with God."[71]

Of the four Hippocratic temperaments, the melancholic undoubtedly predominates in Norris Groves. He was a serious man, and humour is decidedly lacking in the pages of his journal. Even the self-conscious Kitto allowed himself an occasional witty comment or satirical pastiche; not so Groves. But to conclude that he lacked a sense of humour would be quite unjustified. In her *Memoir* of her husband, Harriet Groves would naturally include items she considered edifying rather than amusing, and just as a smile was not deemed suitable for a nineteenth-century portrait or photograph, so a joke would not easily find its way into a spiritual book. The writings of Müller, Craik, Darby and Newman are equally serious. Yet the affectionate nature of Norris Groves, along with his many friendships, must surely have given him lighter moments. Knowing that his sisters "had a keen sense of humour,"[72] we can be fairly sure he shared it. His letters written to his younger children might have revealed a more playful side to his character, but unfortunately none seem to have survived.[73]

There is no doubt that Groves was an exceptionally loving husband and father. He once remarked, "Nature's love, in all the varied relations of husband and wife, parents and children etc. is the sweetest relic of the Fall."[74] He had married young, at the age of only twenty-one, "after five years of trial," and despite their early differences Norris and Mary Groves were deeply in love. Whilst still in Exeter, he would not consider taking his family overseas until Mary was happy to go, and this meant a delay of ten years. By then she was as enthusiastic as he was himself, and her wholehearted support meant much to him as they travelled east and set up home in Baghdad. He shared with her, and later with Harriet, every aspect of his ministry. Each detail was prayed over, every decision discussed, every problem resolved together; nothing was done until there was agreement.

By all accounts Norris and Mary Groves were parents of great ability. Indeed, John Kitto considered the family circle at Northernhay quite idyllic. In addition to a daily Bible reading with family prayers, every opportunity was taken to discuss current affairs and personal happenings from a Christian perspective. The children were polite and helpful; husband and wife would speak to one another at all times with the utmost affection and respect.

It is a fallacy to suppose that the Victorian family was an oppressive institution, or that the *paterfamilias* was always feared and resented. The father was certainly head of the house, responsible for every aspect of its well-being – just as Christ takes responsibility for the church, loving her, providing for her and laying down his life for her. Such a husband would be worthy of his wife's warm appreciation and support. The typical middle-class household enjoyed many games and much fun – charades, musical performances, guessing games, hide and seek – especially when cousins or friends came to visit. Handcrafts and collections of flowers or insects would absorb the interest of children, alone or together. They would show one another what they had found, and demonstrate what they had done. Sometimes household or garden furniture would be transformed into a fort, a zoo or a sailing ship for an endless variety of imaginative adventures. Henry and Frank Groves grew up in just such a home.[75] Edward, too, tells us of a "happy vacation" with his parents by the sea, and another at Christmas time in Bristol.[76]

Norris and Mary knew their responsibility as parents to bring up their children "in the training and instruction of the Lord."[77] Their daughter Mary, at the age of four, was left one evening in the care of her two elder brothers and her cousin. She had a fit of bad temper, which led her cousin to remonstrate with her: "Mary, what would your *Mamma* say?" But it was not her Mamma that worried her; it was someone else: "What would *Jesus* say?" She then insisted that all the children kneel down with her and ask Jesus to forgive her. This done, they resumed their game. We might wonder how many four-year-olds today have such a desire to please Jesus. A year later, knowing her life was slipping away, little Mary asked to hear the twenty-third Psalm. Jesus, she assured her sorrowing parents, was *her* Shepherd and would guide *her* through the valley of death.[78] Was she unusual? No, she was acting exactly as a normal Christian child would act – a child who had been taught to love Jesus as a living person. Our modern age is accustomed to scoff at the Victorians, but we might do well to consider whether our children are as discerning, as happy and as well prepared for the trials of life and death as little Mary and young Henry and Frank. Whatever mistakes their father may have made, his children, throughout their childhood, teenage and adult years, all held him in the greatest love and admiration, and all grew up to become faithful, active servants of Christ.[79]

The only surviving picture we have of Norris Groves shows a man of great gentleness and sensitivity: "his countenance is radiant with love and sweetness."[80] Alexander Duff recalled, "No sooner did I meet with him than I felt drawn towards him with the cords of love. He was so warm, so earnest, so wrapt up in his Master's cause, so inflamed with zeal for the salvation of perishing souls, I regarded it as no ordinary privilege that he agreed to take up his abode in my house during his sojourn in Calcutta. I looked for incalculable benefit to my own soul from near and intimate and familiar contact with so fervent and glowing a spirit."[81] In the end, what made Norris Groves so special was not his achievement; it was his character – not what he did, but what he was. Perhaps, more nearly than anyone in his generation, he approached to "the whole measure of the fulness of Christ".[82] Look at him and you saw Jesus once more walking on earth in human form. In his humility he would deny it, but others saw it clearly enough.

ENDNOTES

1 M289
2 Eadie, 164
3 M43

[4] M43. Whereas some Christian circles are disposed to dwell on the heavenly glory of Christ, and others (including later generations of Brethren) on his sufferings, it is all the more striking that Groves focused so fully on the earthly life and character of Jesus. Neither the exalted Christ of heaven, nor the crucified Christ of Calvary, but the compassionate Christ of Galilee and Judea was what inspired him. Not mourning, or even worshipping, but *loving* Christ was Groves's great emphasis. Living with Jesus, having the mind of Christ, serving Christ: this was his inspiration and motivation.

[5] Whilst still in England, in the course of his preparation for missionary service, Groves had studied Latin, Greek and Hebrew, and he had also learned French and perhaps a little Italian at school. But he never found languages easy, and having laboured to learn colloquial Arabic in Baghdad, he was unable to make any significant progress with an Indian language (J47; R246, 257).

[6] M289

[7] M517

[8] M315-316

[9] M437-438

[10] M316

[11] Conran, 51. I am grateful to Neil Dickson for this reference.

[12] M396

[13] M447

[14] M320

[15] M264

[16] M340

[17] M515

[18] M516. One thing Groves could never be accused of was legalism. He was deliberately anti-legalistic and he constantly emphasized liberty. He taught that Christian behavior will follow naturally from love to Christ, never from conformity to rule or convention. He declared, "There is no truth more established in my own mind than this: that to occupy the position of maximum power, in witnessing to the consciences of others, you must stand before their unbiased judgment as evidently *wishing* to allow in them *more* than their own consciences allow, rather than less, proving that your heart of love is more alive to find a covering for faults than your eagle eye of light to discover them" (Letter to Darby, 10 Mar. 1836; M541-542). Neither church regulations nor the Mosaic Law (tithing, Sabbath observance etc), nor the scruples of other people, should be imposed upon a disciple of Christ. "I think there never will be an end to the confusion in the minds of professing Christians or in the true Church," said Groves, "until it be admitted that for us Christ is the *only* lawgiver and his message from heaven the *only* rule" ("Correspondence from the East", 198). Groves does not quote Augustine directly but would surely agree with his words, "Love and do as you will... Let the root of love be in your heart; from this root nothing can grow but what is good" (Augustine, *On the Epistle of John*, 7:8).

[19] M408

[20] Groves H, *Congleton*, 47

[21] Through experience Groves had acquired a fair knowledge of his own strengths and weaknesses, and had learned to do what he was best gifted to do. As Charlotte Paget observed, "God loves all his children with an infinite love, unchangeable in its nature and perfect in its power. Surely then, all the varieties of their existence and circumstances are the appointments of that love. And we are made to do good in different ways; therefore everyone's great wisdom lies in being able to determine correctly what he is made for, and to press towards the highest attainments in that precise way" (M569).

[22] Stunt, *Awakening*, 117

[23] *Awakening*, 128

[24] M439

[25] Eadie, 162

[26] M277

[27] M30

[28] Groves H, *Darbyism*, 25

[29] M536-538

[30] Lang, *Aroolappen*, 57

[31] M11. In September 1831 Caldecott resigned his curacy in the Church of England to become an evangelist in Devon. He first proposed joining Groves in Baghdad, then hoped to assist Start at Patna, but ill health interrupted his plans and led to his early death in 1840 at the age of thirty-eight. In 1835, when Henry Craik was ill, Caldecott temporarily took over Craik's duties alongside George Müller at Bethesda (M22; Coad, 48, 75).

[32] M341

[33] M437

[34] Eadie, 315

[35] M314

[36] M448

[37] M364

[38] M427

[39] J39; M57

[40] Eadie, 240

[41] M427 (paraphrasing 2 Tim 2:23 and 1 Tim 1:4 AV)

[42] M380 (1 Cor 4:5 AV)

[43] Newman, *Phases*, 37

[44] M433

[45] M231. Darby advocated infant baptism.

[46] The apostle in Ephesians 4:3-6 does not exhort Christians to *become* united but rather to "keep" or "maintain" the unity which already exists. He does not say "there should be one body" but "there *is* one body". On this subject Robert Chapman observed, "The titles given to the Church in scripture bespeak heavenly unity, such as the body, the vine, the temple of God, a holy nation, a chosen generation, a royal priesthood. Such words set forth the Church of God as a witness for him in the world; but the names which have been invented by men are names of sects, and declare our shame."

47 M341

48 M333

49 M251. Mr E was a leading minister who found Groves too willing to question traditional views and practices, accusing him of "ungodly tempers" and excessive "self-confidence". Groves was devastated. He had spent only "three or four hours" with Mr E, but months afterwards he wept before the Lord at the remembrance. If he had so injured this one man in such a short time, how much harm had he done to hundreds of others who had heard him speak about the same things? It did not seem to occur to Groves that the fault might lie in Mr E rather than himself (M221-222).

50 M352

51 M220

52 M307

53 M258

54 M7

55 M328

56 M6

57 Written in April 1827 (Ryland, 231; M6).

58 A number of younger workers accompanied Livingstone to Africa in 1857, attracted by his heroic vision and his unflinching toughness. Before long "most... were complaining bitterly about his autocratic rule and difficult personality" (Tucker, 152). "Grattan Guinness was a man of vision and had become a man of learning. He could inspire and teach, he could move men, but he had little understanding of the labour that makes the vision possible" (Guinness, Joy, quoted by Broomhall, *Refiner's Fire*, 344). On C T Studd, see Anderson D, 59-60, Tucker, 316-8.

59 M319, M321

60 M312

61 1 Thess 5:18; Phil 4:4

62 M498

63 M436

64 M346

65 M334

66 M365

67 M453

68 M258

69 M261

70 M283

71 M341

72 Groves E K, *Successors*, 43

73 As executor for his brother, Edward Groves felt obliged to destroy all but "a handful" of Henry's personal papers and letters on his death in 1891 (*Successors*, 145). This was the usual fate of such documents.

74 M289

75 In fact their childhood took place during the reigns of Victoria's predecessors George IV and William IV.

76 *Successors*, 42

[77] Eph 6:4

[78] M528-529

[79] Norris and Mary Groves did not require Henry and Frank to memorise and recite large amounts of scripture. Edward Groves, who was compelled to do so by his mother Harriet and by his Baynes relatives and his school (often as a punishment for minor misdemeanours), remarked that although his knowledge of the Bible was greater than Henry's, many years passed before he could read it with pleasure. Norris Groves, always sensitive to the feelings of others, may well have appreciated that the word of God loved and obeyed would do more good to a child than the same word memorised and resented, but he was much less involved in the upbringing of his later children than he had been in that of Henry and Frank (*Successors*, 25, 41, 43).

[80] Lang, *Groves*, 118

[81] M536

[82] Eph 4:13

"Faith is a thing that we are to
have to ourselves before God,
but love is to be poured on the Church
in rivers and seas."

Norris Groves [1]

29

Enthusiastic or Mad

Christian Devotedness

During the weeks of his final illness Norris Groves visited some old friends from India, now retired in Devonshire. A member of the family told Harriet, "That verse often comes to my mind in thinking of him: 'They that be wise shall *shine as the firmament*, and they that turn many to righteousness, as the stars for ever and ever.'"[2] The words were well chosen. Norris Groves was unquestionably a man who *shone*, and never more so than during his last days on earth. He left no debts – all had been paid off in full – but he left a radiant vision to hundreds who knew him personally, to thousands who heard him speak, and to many more who read his journals, tracts and letters.

It was, of course, the message of *Christian Devotedness* – written, spoken, and lived out – that initially made the greatest impact. As we have seen, there was nothing novel in its content. Everyone knew what Jesus had said about selling one's possessions, providing for brothers in need, going into all the world to preach the gospel, confident in the care of a heavenly Father. But what was really radical was the determination actually to believe it and do it. The publication of Groves's booklet in 1825, and its widespread circulation during the following decade, meant that the groups drawn into the Brethren movement embraced and taught these principles from the start. Then, especially in the universities, and during the Revival of 1858-9, these ideals found their way beyond the confines of the Brethren and were taken up by the Keswick Convention, the "faith missions", the "Christian unions", and their supporters in every denomination. At the same time, many people who had known Groves in India returned to Britain, having completed their military service or their term of office. The majority were drawn into the Brethren movement,[3] but some carried his principles directly into the other churches. Before long the vision for wholehearted, trusting, self-sacrificing, obedient devotion to Christ had entered the mainstream of evangelical life in Britain.[4]

But how did these principles work in practice? What did it mean to devote all to Christ? Firstly, it went far beyond *tithing*. Groves, in his booklet, never mentions tithing. Not one tenth, but *all*, is to be given to Christ. The heavy burden of tithes laid by the Church of England on poor parishioners for the support of the clergy had left Britain permanently resistant to the concept of tithing. In 1836, after years of agitation, and at times violent protest, the tithe was reduced by law to a less onerous level, and was eventually abolished altogether. Neither Groves nor other evangelical leaders found good reason to retain an unpopular custom or to apply an Old Testament rule to a New Testament church. Jesus himself declared, "Any of you who does not give up *everything he has* cannot be my disciple."[5] For a man to divide his goods or his income into one tenth for the Lord and nine tenths for himself would fall far short of this principle; it could never satisfy a true disciple. As Isaac Watts declared, "Love so amazing, so divine, demands my soul, my life, my all." Whilst drawing a professional income in Exeter, Norris and Mary Groves had wondered whether they should continue to support other missionaries or whether they should go to the East themselves. In fact, whichever course they followed, their entire income and capital were already dedicated to Christ for use in the work of the Gospel. Following their example, the wise stewardship and prayerful distribution of personal resources became a major emphasis in British evangelical Christianity for a century or more.[6]

Secondly, we should note that the idea of Christian devotedness was a challenge given to committed Christians alone. Groves never asked unconverted people to contribute money for anything. On this point, as always, the New Testament was his guide. The apostle Paul, in his missionary outreach, was determined that no one should question his motives. "We do not peddle the word of God for profit," he said.[7] Though happy to receive some help from the established Christians of Philippi, he would accept nothing from the pagans or Jews who heard him in Corinth or Thessalonica.[8] Committed to "preaching the gospel… free of charge," he would rather support himself, working with his own hands if necessary, "in order not to be a burden to anyone."[9] The apostle John, too, commended evangelists who "have set out for [God's] sake and have accepted nothing from the heathen." And John advised his Christian friends, "We ought to support such men."[10] God's work is clearly the responsibility of God's people.

Thirdly, the outworking of Christian devotedness brought every Christian family into a practical and personal relationship with the poor around them and with evangelists and missionaries trusting God to provide for their daily needs. After a conversation with Groves in India, two Christian men offered each to finance the passage out and ongoing support of a missionary for the new orphanage at Sonamukhi; others provided food and clothing for the forty little girls in their care.[11] Such friends would follow with great interest the progress of these girls as many grew up to become loyal Christian workers and wives of Indian evangelists. A little later, as the Bowdens and Beers set off for India, a young woman sold her gold watch to help with the cost of their passage. To one like her, news of conversions in the Godavari Delta would bring special joy.[12] This, indeed, was the vision that thrilled a generation – the thought that the sacrifice made by the clerk or engineer or housewife might correspond with that made by the missionary, enabling them to be partners in reaching the world for Christ. From his earliest days in India, Groves shared this idea with the expatriate families who welcomed him into their homes. Some, to his delight, responded wholeheartedly; they "adopted the simple manner of living I approve." A number cheerfully "began to alter their expensive style of living." One couple "parted with their superfluities in a very sweet spirit."

In reality it was a happy way to live, and all who tried it recommended it, whether they were missionaries or commercial or military families. Amidst spiritual darkness and material destitution, exposed day and night to the sights and sounds of a great multitude without God and without hope in the world, they felt at last they were living as true disciples of Christ, loving their neighbours as themselves. And as their savings dwindled and their luxuries disappeared, they could testify to a warmer sense of his presence, to the reality of his daily provision, to the appreciation of those they were able to help, and to the confidence that when they spoke of the love of Jesus their words carried conviction. Groves remarked, "I think the principle laid down for the guidance of the saints in 2 Cor 8:14 is most beautiful. As it was with Israel and the manna so it should be with us. No man should look on his abundance otherwise than as given that he might have the joy of contributing to a brother's need, so that the care of the body for all its members may be fully seen."[13]

As time went on, many missionaries and many Indian evangelists were fully supported by expatriate Christians who had dedicated to Christ their entire salary or the proceeds of their business. A government official and an itinerant preacher could live quite comfortably off a single income shared between them. As the apostle observed, "God is able to make *all* grace abound to you, so that in *all* things at *all* times, having *all* that you need, you will abound in every good work."[14] "This has been *my experience*," Groves commented. "Never had I so much in my hands to give as at this moment, when I have not a shilling in the world of my own."[15]

This degree of "devotedness" made many feel uneasy, but Norris Groves did not let politeness or "a desire for unity" tie his tongue when it came to the teachings of Christ. And however kindly he might express it, he did not shrink from raising sensitive issues: "When I ask them what is the difference between their principles and those of the merest worldling they cannot tell... I do think many begin to feel ashamed to keep back anything from Christ who kept back nothing from them."[16] And again, "On the whole I think the Christians here feel the truth of these and other principles that I hold, but they dread them and their consequences. However they are all discussing them: some holding with, some opposing. This discussion is at all events good... I can truly say: If it be not of God, let it come to nought; but if it be, it shall stand."[17]

It was the calm and gracious demeanour of Groves himself that some people found so threatening; he could not be waved away as an inconsequential idiot. "It is astonishing," he remarked, "what the world will endure from a child of God whose manner gives them excuse for calling him an interesting eccentric madman, because then all he says they feel at liberty to laugh at, whereas if the same truths were declared to them in the calm seriousness of our Lord's manner it would make them gnash on him with their teeth."[18] Quite frequently he was branded, like Wesley, with the stigma of "enthusiasm", something that no well-bred Englishman would admit to. "Enthusiasm," observed Kitto, "is a charge to which men acting as Mr Groves does lay themselves peculiarly open. And if they are husbands and fathers, to this the charge of being unmindful of the interests of their wives and children will most probably be superadded... I have generally found that, from the time when the Redeemer walked visibly among men to the present day – nay, I might even go farther back and say that from the creation of the world to this moment – the best of men, the wisest of men, the men to whom we are the most indebted, the men who were lights shining in a dark world, and in these latter days the men who have most implicitly and unreservedly acted on the principles of Jesus Christ, have seldom if ever escaped the stigma of being enthusiastic or mad." If the world said Jesus was out of his mind, would it say less, wondered Kitto, of his true disciple? "The Spirit of Christ is the same now as it was in former times, and the spirit of the world is radically the same as it ever was."[19]

There were occasions when living economically actually made it more difficult to serve Christ. Once, travelling by sea, Groves admitted, "I miss very much the retirement of a closet [i.e. small room] which I enjoyed on shore. To avoid expense I allowed a Christian brother to have a third of my cabin, and I have up to this time slept on the floor of the cuddy. Sometimes I have felt the spiritual loss to be greater than the value of a few hundred rupees, yet I think again it is right."[20] Yes, it was *right*, he thought – as a way to save money for the benefit of others, as an example for any who might doubt his sincerity, and as a sacrifice offered in love to Christ who gave everything.

The Rules of the Apostles

Norris Groves made it a principle to seek his guidance directly from God. Much of his personal direction he received, in fact, from providential circumstances, and throughout his life he was remarkably adaptable, ready to respond immediately to what he believed to be the divine ordering of events. It was *en route* to Persia, hearing of Major Taylor's removal to Baghdad, that he resolved to make his first base in that city rather than Shushi or Basra. It was on board ship for India, perhaps even after landing, that he found good reason to settle in Madras rather than Calcutta. Seeing providential opportunities at particular times and places, he felt led to establish a clinic or a school or a farm. He welcomed guests when they happened to call; he took up invitations when they were offered. He accepted the departure of old missionary colleagues and the arrival of new. It all meant that his plans could change at any time. A chance meeting, a letter, a verse of scripture, any of these might prove to be God's way of showing him what to do. It meant he was always available, always ready to respond to a need or give his attention to a particular problem.

We see the same in Scripture. Peter and John made the most of some quite unexpected encounters. Stephen and Philip took the unforeseen opportunities presented to them. Paul preached wherever he found an open door, moving on when he saw it close. In the Gospel records almost everything Jesus said and did came in response to an interruption. Some would find this degree of flexibility frustrating, others inspiring, but to a greater or lesser degree it was an attitude adopted by those who aspired to live and walk by faith in the generations that followed Norris Groves. Once, at least, in his own experience, it led to disaster. The offer of a loan for the extension of the silk farm had seemed providential, but on this occasion, as Harriet freely admits, he misread the circumstances.[21] It went to show that divine guidance can only be assured when divine providences accord with biblical principles, perhaps the only time he forgot it.

The Bible was never, for Norris Groves, merely a source of good sermons or a textbook of doctrine. It was food and drink to satisfy his own spiritual hunger and a source of clear direction in his personal decisions. Working as a dentist in Exeter, "What little leisure I have for reading is confined to God's word, the book of our Father's wisdom."[22] Contemplating missionary service, "My firm purpose is, by the grace of God, to follow simply the word of God."[23] And on board ship somewhere off the coast of India, "I feel that there is no time more usefully employed than in searching God's word, unless it be by living it... I cannot tell you the interest I feel in my analysis of the New Testament. This is something that steadily occupies my mind many hours a day."[24] In fact he had just embarked on a major research project: he was working out how to start and run a church according to the method of the apostles.[25]

The best thing, Groves believed, in every circumstance, in every doubt, in every controversy, will be to discover what God has caused to be written on the subject, and then simply follow his instructions. "I love the *spirit of obedience*," he declared "The loveliest part of a *child's* character, and the most marred by the Fall, is simple unquestioning obedience and willing dependence... May we be willing to sit at our dear Lord's feet and learn of him, for he is meek and lowly in heart. Then, and not *till then*, we shall find *rest to our souls*."[26] Our obedience may lead us in paths little approved by the people around us, but that should cause no surprise: "I do feel so sure that we have lost our true power by decking ourselves out and prosecuting our plans according to the spirit and principles of the world, whereas I am sure we ought to stand in *contrast* with it at *every point*. Wherever I can literally follow scripture, I feel easy as to the act. Where I cannot, or fancy I cannot, I feel weak in proportion to my distance from it."[27] And he reminded his friend William Caldecott, "Remember our old rule, to judge according to God's word. Let us be neither frightened nor allured from it… Therefore now learn to *trust* your sword, for it will cut deep if well wielded under the power of the Spirit."[28]

On questions of business, politics and the arts, every man might form his own views, but in spiritual matters, Groves insisted, there is only one option – we must defer to the mind of the Lord: "As to the opinions of men, I feel they have their place and value in the things of the world, but in the things of Christ they are of no value but in proportion to their accordance with that word, and to that they must be brought as to the scales in which they are to be weighed… For myself, I wish no man living to show the least regard for my opinion for any other reason than its being the same as the mind of God."[29] In India he had found expatriate Christians reluctant "simply and fully to follow the word of the living God. Most persons you meet will hardly look at even the picture of it; and if we will not, how can God fully bless us? for it must be his *own* ways, his *own* plans, his *own* principles that he will honour, and not ours."[30] Here is the reason why so many make a mess of their professional lives, their church activities and their family happiness. How very easy it is to make plans and then look for a verse to justify them. "There is but one remedy," said Groves: "to read the word of God with a single view to know his will… I believe the delusions of Satan in this matter are more numerous and subtle than in any other; because he knows if he can but poison the fountain of life, so that those who drink with the appetite of the sick, seeking to be healed, find that which should have been an instrument of their health turned into a means of destruction, he has gained a momentous victory – and so much the more as it is over those he always dreads, the Bible readers."[31]

It was the issue of pacifism that first brought Norris Groves into conflict with the principles of the Established Church. In particular he had to consider whether he could reconcile the teaching of Jesus with the Article of Religion stating, "It is lawful for Christian men, at the commandment of the Magistrate, to wear weapons and serve in the wars." Could a Christian allow himself to maim and kill a friend, or an enemy, or a brother in Christ? "I never would sign it," he declared.[32] And then the doctrine of Baptismal Regeneration, which had troubled the young Frank Newman, troubled Groves too. Was infant baptism the God-given sign of the New Covenant in the same way that circumcision had been for the Old? The Anglicans, Methodists, Presbyterians and Congregationalists thought so. But "I see not in the New Testament the slightest allusion to a covenant in connection with baptism." Indeed, "if baptism be a sign of the covenant, of what covenant was John's baptism a sign?" And "if they argue that our infants should be baptised because the Jewish infants were to be circumcised, why should not our infants partake of the Lord's Supper as theirs did of the Passover?... If you allow baptism to the unbelieving, then follows communion with the same, worldly Christianity and every other evil."[33] Other questions also arose. What could be said about the *liturgy*, so prominent in every service of worship? "However valuable it may be, no one will pretend today the apostles used one." And what of the wealth and splendour of the churches and cathedrals? They were "equally unlike the places of meeting of the apostles, who were happy to assemble in an upper loft!"[34]

But it was the issue of episcopal ordination that led Groves to his final break with the Church of England, and in his mind this remained the biggest problem. "The miserable substitute of man's ordination for the Holy Ghost's," he said, "has destroyed the true unison and order of the Church of Christ by substituting that which is artificial for that which is of God."[35] Where did the idea of a "priest" and an "altar" come from? Not from the New Testament but from the Old: "The more I trace the existing evils of the Church of Christ, the more I believe, in my inmost heart, they have originated in the natural worldliness of man seizing on that in the Jewish dispensation which suited his carnal nature, and grafting it into the spiritual dispensation of the Lord of glory."[36]

Early in Baghdad, Groves had written about "that awful distinction between clergy and laity," "that yoke of mere human ordination, the necessity of a title from man to preach and administer, as it is called, the sacraments, of which not so much as a hint is contained in the New Testament."[37] Scripture makes sound doctrine and a godly life the only qualifications needed for a man to preach, to baptise, to remember the Lord in bread and wine: "We should learn to judge of men's fitness for their work, not by their being ordained or unordained by this or that denomination, but according to the rules of the apostles." The apostle Paul, indeed, made a point of insisting that he was not "ordained" by any man, but had been set apart from his birth *by God* to preach among the Gentiles.[38] "Perhaps you may think I am proud in not submitting to human authority," said Groves, "but of this, indeed, my heart does not accuse me. In all civil matters I will *willingly* be subject, but the *liberty* of the church is not mine to yield."[39]

Throughout his life he considered the division between clergy and laity a great hindrance to the gospel; the clergy were too busy with church services, and the laity felt they could do nothing: "And as I desire to break down caste among the Hindus, to pave the way for the reception of truth, so do I desire to break down caste in the Christian Church, to prepare the way for publishing it."[40] "Daily my desire is strengthening," he said, "to see the Church free in the use of God's word and in his modes of ministry, every one being free to exercise the gift the Spirit has given."[41]

Groves himself was torn between his love for his many Anglican friends and the sadness he felt as he watched them justifying and defending an institution they admitted to be in many respects degenerate: "The effects of centuries of traditionary thought are visible everywhere, and hardly anyone seems able, on certain subjects, to trust himself simply with God's word."[42] Political bishops and dissolute clergymen shamed the name of Christ: "I do not feel a doubt that the union of church and state, and ecclesiastical Establishments on carnal principles, are the hot-bed of all those corruptions into which many are plunged at this day; yet the very persons who condemn the fruit nourish the root and water it with every care."[43] "Oh, if this principle of the apostles were set up, in proving all things and holding fast that which is good, we should not hear so good a man and one so much beloved as Mr Bickersteth misleading his readers by telling them to adhere to an unsound *authorised* teacher (By whom authorised, of God or man?), rather than go to a sound and unauthorised one (to one who is authorised by the Head of the Church though not by the head of the state)."[44]

But even as he reflected on these things, Groves's deep dissatisfaction with the institution could not affect the genuine affection and esteem he felt for many of its members: "Has not your heart deep sympathy with that character of piety one meets with in spiritual members of the Church of England? I acknowledge the system to be wrong, very wrong, yet my heart finds great repose in those fair pearls which lie within what seems to me so naughty a shell."[45] After a visit to Madras in 1834 he confided, "Dear Mr Tucker, who has the charge of the Church Missions, asked me before we parted to join him in prayer, and we spent a holy parting moment near our uniting Lord, the savour of which so remains on my heart that I feel how impossible it is for anything to divide when love reigns and rules."[46]

Liberty of Ministry

In his journals and letters Norris Groves says much less about the Nonconformist denominations, perhaps because he had less personal experience of them. It is evident that he did not like to see Dissenters collaborating with irreligious political agitators, and he had never been impressed with the type of dissenting minister who bound people under his own authority, exercising "that sectarian zeal that magnifies every weakness and infirmity into a mortal sin and which delights in evil surmisings and evil speakings."[47] Such negative perceptions, however, never in the least prejudiced him against the Nonconformists he met or knew personally. Sarah Kilham in St Petersburg, John Scudder in Ceylon, William Start in Patna, Carey and his colleagues in Serampore, Henry Craik and the Paget sisters in England: he loved and respected them all.

It is hard for us now to appreciate just how radical was Groves's determination to belong to no denomination. He had seen too much of contention between

Churchman and Dissenter, and would not be silenced on this point: "Does Paul set up the principle that men are to be received... according to the sect to which they belong or the mode or circumstance of their ordination? Never." They are received "according to the truth or error of their doctrine... With the apostle it is always the truth – the truth – the truth; let those judge who wish to see."[48] This he wrote three years after resigning from the CMS, resolving to preach the gospel wherever the Spirit might lead and to "break bread" with any who loved Christ. It was not an easy path to follow. It meant launching out in faith, without salary or stipend, trusting God to provide. But in addition to that, it meant becoming a nobody – without connections, without a title, without authority – and it meant doing what almost everyone considered he was not fit to do. A modern parallel would be a man who presents himself as a lecturer in some academic field without possessing a single university qualification in his subject. To our generation the concept of an "unordained" Bible teacher is commonplace; to religious people of the early nineteenth century it was distinctly odd, if not positively subversive.

In fact, as we have seen, Norris Groves was happiest when he could simply ignore the existence of church denominations. This he could do when speaking, as he often did, to groups of Indian Christians. The pioneer among an unreached people has this wonderful privilege: he can teach what the apostles taught, and do what the apostles did, without reference to any ecclesiastical institution or tradition. Groves saw Arulappan and his friends establishing indigenous churches, and he supported their efforts in every possible way. A first generation of Christians received the scriptures at face value, pure and strong. "When the truth is impressed upon a person's mind in India," he remarked, "it seems to seize it with a more powerful and tenacious grasp than generally in England." And how vital it was to protect these biblical Indian churches from the dead hand of foreign denominational control. This he saw from his earliest visit in 1833: "Never was there a time when it was more important than now to make every effort that they do not rivet on this land the evils of ecclesiastical dominion, viz. the pride and earthliness under which the Established Churches in Europe have groaned... Let us stand up for the Church's liberty and not be again brought under the yoke of bondage."[49]

Groves himself made no attempt to establish or organise Indian churches. With the New Testament as their guide, the Indian believers themselves had that responsibility. Following the example of the apostles, they would learn to "exhort" or "encourage" one another every day.[50] They would find that "to each one the manifestation of the Spirit is given for the common good."[51] They would see that, meeting together, "every one has a hymn, or a word of instruction, a revelation etc."[52] They would discover that "we have different gifts, according to the grace given us."[53] Groves offered no additional advice on these matters. He believed, of course, that any group of Christians might "break bread" in remembrance of Christ, and that any individuals – that is, any men – might expound the word of God, and he would encourage the appointment of elders in each fellowship.

All this was clearly described in the New Testament. But beyond the simple meetings of an individual congregation, Groves himself seems to have given no further thought to the question of organisation. He offers no wider strategy for the planting and leadership of new fellowships in pioneer situations – no practical definition of a local church, no description of how it might be run, no hint of how a number of congregations might relate to one another. Indeed, some might think his emphasis on "liberty of ministry" a recipe for spiritual anarchy.

The balance lay in his emphasis on the devotion of every disciple to his Master and the submission of every fellowship to his word, inspiring a love and an understanding that must unite all in a common faith. And although "liberty of ministry" would allow everyone the opportunity to participate, the scriptures showed that in the church Christ has given "some to be apostles, some to be prophets, some to be evangelists, and some to be pastors and teachers."[54] Groves believed that people with manifest gifts should take the largest part in the ministry of the local fellowship: "I quite feel that it would be desirable that those brethren who speak to the church's edification should have opportunity to speak. But of this I think I can now feel practically convinced (as I ever have in theory) that recognised pastors and teachers are *essential* to the good order of all assemblies and, as such, required and commanded of God."[55]

He would willingly take on such a role himself. In 1847, looking back with regret on years occupied with contracts and consignments, "it is much my desire," he said, "if the Lord clears away difficulties, to give the rest of my short space to an uninterrupted ministry some where or in some form."[56] To teach the Bible effectively, he now believed, a suitably gifted man must commit his full attention to his task. Christ, addressing the crowds and training his disciples, had no more time for the carpenter's bench; the apostles, devoting themselves to prayer and ministry of the Word, had laid aside their nets and their tax records; and even Paul, determined to take nothing from the heathen, resorted only in special circumstances to making tents. "I have no question but that those whom God has called to minister should wait on their ministry," concluded Groves, "and give themselves *wholly to it* if their profiting is to appear in all things."[57] They must "give themselves not only to the study of the Word but to the collective and individual state of those among whom they minister."[58]

But how might such a teacher be "recognised" in the church? Before being asked to instruct others, a man should certainly prove he has a sound knowledge of the Word and a gift for teaching – but it is not a council or an archbishop who should decide this. "It is before the Church at large that the minister of God stands to be judged," said Groves. "The flock of Christ, in whom the Spirit dwells, is as competent now to know whom the Holy Spirit has qualified to be a minister of the Word as in the days of the apostles, both by comparing the Word ministered with the Word written and by the edification they experience in their own souls. Nay, if they are spiritual, they are *bound* to recognise such."[59]

Then what name should such a man bear? Groves himself was happy to be known as a missionary, a teacher, or even as a "minister of the Word", but he never accepted for himself the title Reverend or Pastor or Minister. Such honorifics pointed to a distinction between clergy and laity that he considered quite unscriptural and saw to be a cause of sorry weakness in the Church. He was simply a brother in Christ and he would not, by exercising his gift, stifle the gifts of others. "I greatly approve and value a fixed ministry," he said, "but will ever protest against an *exclusive one*, and especially that hypocritical freedom which in words grants liberty but in fact denies it."[60]

In this way Groves advocates a careful blend of formal teaching prepared by gifted men and informal contributions from any whom the Spirit might lead. He was not impressed by the totally "impulsive" form of ministry advocated by John Nelson Darby. "For myself," he said, "I would join no church permanently that had not some constituted rule. I have seen enough of that plan, of everyone doing what is right in his own eyes and then calling it the Spirit's order, to feel assured it is a delusion."[61] For teaching the church, for preaching to outsiders, even for ministering to the family circle, it was necessary to spend time beforehand in prayerful meditation on the scriptures, identifying lessons of practical value and preparing suitable illustrations: "We have no more reason to expect the bread of life to be miraculously supplied to us for feeding others than we have the natural bread."[62] Those who speak should study to show themselves approved by God, workmen that need not be ashamed, rightly dividing the Word of Truth,[63] and "instead of waiting for particular impulses from without, they ought to stir up the gift within."[64]

In India Norris Groves often found himself the only experienced Bible teacher in companies of Christians he had been invited to address. In Britain and Europe, on the other hand, there were many in the prayer groups, the drawing room meetings and the assemblies who were quite capable of expounding the Word, and here George Müller went perhaps further than his brother-in-law towards encouraging spontaneous ministry. But this did not mean that those present should presume to say whatever came into their head. Nor should they request one another to comment or to pray. They should allow the Spirit to move each of them in contributing what would build up the body as a whole. Müller spent several weeks instructing a new group in Stuttgart, Germany, about the principles of body-life, demonstrating how to let the Holy Spirit lead an open meeting. They were slow learners; they still tended to read out a scripture and then ask Müller to comment on it. "I... reminded them," he said, "that all these matters ought to be left to the ordering of the Holy Ghost, and that if it had been truly good for them, the Lord would have not only led me to speak *at that time* but also on *the very subject* on which they desired that I should speak to them."[65]

Where there is free participation, of course, every meeting is an adventure. No one knows exactly what will happen. Informal gatherings of this nature, where the majority of contributions are spontaneous, depend for their success on the creative gift of the participants, their knowledge of scripture, their sensitivity to the needs of others, and on a genuine awareness of the leading of the Spirit. As we have seen, Groves, Müller and others took the trouble to prepare beforehand – a scripture to read and explain, some thoughts on a devotional theme, a testimony, an exhortation, a hymn appropriate to their particular circumstances. But along with this went freedom for a spontaneous response from any who found themselves uplifted by what they heard. Groves made it his aim "to try and impress upon every member of Christ's body that he has some ministry given him for the body's edification – and instead of depressing, encouraging each one to come forward and serve the Lord."[66] In New Testament times, he noted, "there was positively no limitation whatever on the right of every individual brother teaching, preaching and administering the sacraments, without asking leave either of the apostles or anyone else... Every man's duty is to minister according to the ability that God giveth."[67] This emphasis on "liberty of ministry" was one of Norris Groves's greatest legacies to the church of Christ.

The Coming of the Lord

On all the basic evangelical doctrines, Norris Groves was considered, in his day, quite orthodox. He held to a Calvinistic view of grace; he believed that the unconverted will suffer unending punishment, and he was convinced of the need for adult baptism. The only doctrinal area in which he was considered somewhat unusual was his view of the Second Coming of Christ.[68]

The imminent return of the Saviour was, for Groves, a great incentive to mission. In 1833 he wrote, "I consider the *testimony* of Jesus is to be published through every land before the Bridegroom comes. This makes my heart feel an interest in heathens, that we may hasten the coming of the Lord."[69] He was particularly drawn to the Middle East, where he believed, according to prophecy, the final drama would be enacted. From his house in Baghdad he reflected, "Oh how happy shall we be to await the Lord's coming on the banks of those rivers which have been the scene of all the sacred history of the old church of God [i.e. the Israelites], and are destined still, I believe, to be the scene of doings of yet deeper interest at the coming of the Lord."[70]

The majority of Anglicans gave no thought to the return of Christ, assuming such an expression to be simply a euphemism for death. Nonconformists, in general, took the scriptural promise of his return literally, but held a postmillennial view of the End Times, in which the kingdom of God would gradually extend throughout the whole world. The remarkable spread of British influence by means of trade and military occupation had encouraged the thought that soon the entire globe would be civilised and Christianised in readiness for a golden age lasting a thousand years, to be followed by the coming of the King in glory. Yet as the wealth of the Indies flowed to London, there was still little sign of heathen peoples turning to Christ. The few workers who had gone overseas as missionaries did not find the world becoming more Christian. Indeed, remarked Groves, "This view seems to me very discouraging, for surely after labouring for years and so little having been done, we may all naturally be led to doubt if we are in our places."[71]

Prophetic study at Powerscourt and elsewhere had shifted the thinking of the early Brethren (and the early "pentecostals" associated with Edward Irving) away from the idea that the world was getting better. According to scripture, things would become not better but worse before the return of the Lord. Jesus himself had spoken of a Great Tribulation, and Groves saw it as "the cloudy and dark day that is coming on Christendom."[72] After the wars and famines and earthquakes and bitter persecution, after the rise of Antichrist and the battle of Armageddon, Christ would be seen coming on the clouds to rescue a faithful remnant. The role of the missionary, therefore, was not to Christianise the world but rather to gather out of it a band of survivors – lights shining in the darkness, a sweet savour of Christ amongst those who are perishing, a people for the Lord called out from among the nations. Groves declared, "While I feel assured of there being some choice fruit from here and there a fruitful bough, I feel no less assured that the great harvest will be of wickedness, and that the pestilence of infidelity is the great spreading evil to be expected, not the spreading of millennial blessedness. As it was in the days of Noah, so do I believe it will be at the coming of the Son of Man; and as it was in the days of Lot, the great mass of mankind will be taunting the Church with, 'Where is the sign of his coming?'"[73]

This view was far from triumphalistic, and yet it inspired feelings of great optimism. Norris and Mary Groves were sustained in Baghdad by their assurance that the terrible signs of the times all around them meant they would soon see their Saviour. "This spread a gilded halo round every trial," said Groves.[74] Christ, coming on the clouds, would stand once more on the Mount of Olives, bind the Evil One and reign on earth for a thousand years: "Oh, then, how happy it is to be among those who love his appearing, who long for the termination of that dispensation which witnessed the humiliation of the church under the world, and the rise of that glorious kingdom which shall not be dissolved and into which no sorrow or sighing can enter."[75] This perspective was one of the distinctives of the early Brethren. They taught it, and they discussed its finer points at great length. And it has become increasingly influential. It was with this doctrine in mind that J Edwin Orr declared, "Conservative Evangelicals have been more and more influenced by the Brethren interpretations of scripture."[76]

Norris Groves did not shrink from making his premillennial views known to individuals he met and groups he addressed. Some who heard him were considerably startled. But he never made prophetic interpretation his chief emphasis. It was the joyful anticipation of meeting his Lord that occupied his mind, not the identity of nations and angels and battles yet to come. He was always a very practical man, and he lived very much in the present.

ENDNOTES

[1] M288

[2] M484 (Dan 12:3 AV)

[3] M385; M480

[4] The impact of Groves's ideas on wider Christian circles will be discussed in Chapter 33 and Appendix ii of this book.

[5] Lk 14:33. Groves dismissed the tithe as "a mere badge of judaism, yet since adopted by the state" (*Remarks on a Pamphlet*, 4). For arguments against the idea that Christians should tithe, see <http://cnview.com/on_line_resources/christians_and_the_tithe.htm>.

[6] Frank Newman heard from a mutual friend in Ireland of one occasion that well illustrates Groves's generous view of Christian stewardship: "Someone asked him [i.e. Groves] to take charge of a package of goods to Liverpool for a Mrs X, and to pay the carriage, for which he should be reimbursed. 'Mrs X?' said he: 'does she not spend all her money in Christ's cause? I think I know the name.' On learning that he was right, 'Oh then,' he said, 'I may as well pay it as she; it comes to the same end'" (F W Newman to C P Golightly, 25 Oct. 1827). (I am grateful to Timothy Stunt for this reference.)

[7] 2 Cor 2:17

[8] Phil 4:15-18

[9] 2 Cor 11:7-9; 1 Thess 2:9

[10] 3 Jn 7-8 RSV

[11] M312

[12] Bromley, 14

[13] M244

[14] 2 Cor 9:8

[15] M244

[16] M321
[17] M321
[18] R229
[19] Ryland, 204
[20] M328
[21] M397
[22] M43
[23] M46
[24] M334
[25] On 13th September 1834 Groves noted, "I am now thinking of arranging my extracts from the Word of God and entitling them 'The Rule of Life for the Gentile Church'" (M338). Although his Bible and notes were lost at sea two weeks later, he set to work a second time, hoping "to have a great deal ready again" before arriving in England (M342).

Eighteen months later an anonymous article appeared in *The Christian Witness* (April 1836) under the title "Church Canons". It comprised a forty-page compilation of New Testament texts, grouped according to subject and introduced with the words, "In bringing forward the following collection of Scripture Rules for the ordering of the Lord's Church, it may not be amiss to state that the immediate object in collecting them together was that they should form in themselves an answer to the commonly received opinion that the scripture did not adequately provide in detail for the *outward* order and discipline of the Church of God so that it is commonly believed that if the Church were to lose the aid of human laws and human systems it would become all confusion and be 'without law'... And it is hoped likewise that the children of God may be led to see that the secret of *true* order and *true* unity... is to be found in forsaking the tradition of men and cleaving only to the commandments of God."

The article was reprinted in the form of a tract, whose author was believed to be Groves by more than one reader, including "A Minister of the Established Church" who took strong exception to it (*Perpetuity*, 77, 82). Groves himself denied responsibility: "I would simply say I had nothing to do either with the compiling or printing of the tract". He claimed he had not circulated it, or even read it, until his attention was drawn to it by the "Minister". He nevertheless defended it and expressed his hope for certain additions to be made to a second edition which he had heard was shortly to be published (Groves, *Remarks on a Pamphlet*, 24, 25). It seems likely that Groves's work had been adapted, without acknowledgement or permission, in order to produce the "Church Canons". No copy of his original compilation appears to have survived.

[26] M233
[27] M229
[28] M249
[29] M47
[30] M280
[31] M11
[32] M41

[33] M320

[34] R269

[35] R300

[36] M330. In 1834 Groves published a small book entitled *On the Liberty of Ministry in the Church of Christ*. It is chiefly remarkable for showing how the Established Church mimics the Jewish Temple, "entangled again," he observes, "in the yoke of bondage" (Gal 5:1 AV). He lists the similarities:

temple consecrated as House of God	=	*church building consecrated as House of God*
most holy place	=	*sanctuary*
altar in temple	=	*altar in church*
high priest	=	*bishop*
priests	=	*priests*
Levites	=	*deacons*
distinctive robes	=	*handsome vestments*
high priest's mitre	=	*bishop's mitre*
laity excluded from ministry	=	*laity excluded from ministry*
admission of infants by circumcision	=	*admission of infants by baptism*
tithes paid to priests	=	*tithes paid to clergy*

Groves concludes, "I think we can without any difficulty trace every stone to its place in the Temple" (p.58).

[37] R261

[38] Gal 1:15-16; 2:9

[39] M245

[40] M242

[41] M256

[42] M363

[43] M248

[44] R262. Edward Bickersteth was a leading evangelical clergyman in the Church of England. He was Secretary of the CMS between 1824 and 1830, and had visited Groves to discuss his missionary prospects during this period. Bickersteth was a strong supporter of the movement to abolish slavery, and would be a prime mover in the subsequent creation of the Evangelical Alliance, but he still considered ordination an essential requirement for a Christian minister who would administer the "sacraments" (Hylson-Smith, 144; Bebbington, 97). The religious condition of Britain at this period is discussed in Appendices i and ii of this book.

[45] M297

[46] M332

[47] R268

[48] R266

[49] M252-253

[50] Heb 3:13 NRSV & NIV. See Heb 10:24-25.

[51] 1 Cor 12:7

[52] 1 Cor 14:26

[53] Rom 12:6. See 1 Pet 4:10-11.

[54] Eph 4:11. See Acts 13:1; 1 Cor 12:28-30.

[55] M421

[56] M421

[57] M421

[58] M443. Groves was not implying that these men would be paid a regular salary. Like Müller, Craik, Chapman and himself, they would receive gifts (often anonymous) from churches and individual Christians in answer to prayer.

[59] M441

[60] M455

[61] M420

[62] M423

[63] Referring to 2 Tim 2:15 AV.

[64] M424

[65] Müller, *Narrative*, I, 523ff; Neatby, 99. The opportunity for free participation naturally means that such freedom can be abused. In many early assemblies it was the custom of the elders tactfully to restrain verbose or unprofitable discourse. On this subject, however, Edward Groves advised, "I do not think anything would surprise you more than to hear the difference of judgment expressed by those whose opinion you might ask concerning ministry you found it hard to listen to with patience. Some admire and profit by that which others lightly esteem… I have been told by brethren of large experience of a more excellent way of dealing with unedifying ministry than that of raising a protest against it. It is for those who feel tried by the frequency or quality of any brother's ministry to meet regularly to pray about it; and the Lord has either increased his gift or shut his mouth. It seems to me that if we were fitly joined together as a spiritual family we ought to be able to tell a brother that we do not understand the drift of his remarks, or suggest to him something that would improve his ministry" (*Conversations*, 131).

[66] M285

[67] Groves, *On the Liberty of Ministry*, 27, 30

[68] See especially Groves, *Remarks on a Pamphlet*, 11-24.

[69] M258

[70] M105

[71] Written in July 1830 (R20; M88). Timothy Stunt suggests that emendations to the second edition of *Christian Devotedness* indicate a change in Groves's thinking from postmillennialism to premillennialism between 1825 and 1829 (*Awakening*, 126-127).

[72] M287

[73] M109 (R68)

[74] R170

[75] R69. It should be noted that Darby's premillennialism differed from that of Groves, Müller and B W Newton. Darby (like Irving) taught that Christ might come at any moment to snatch away those who are his. This so-called "Secret Rapture of the Saints" Darby placed prior to the Great Tribulation. He developed a detailed framework of dispensations, dividing biblical history into successive ages, the last of which will see Christ on the throne of a restored nation of Israel in which the

church has no part at all. This scheme was later popularised by the so-called *Scofield Reference Bible*.

Groves did not hold this view; nor have the majority of Bible teachers among the Open Brethren in Britain. They have taught that the Church must endure the Great Tribulation described in Matthew 24 before Christ comes to raise the believing dead, bind Satan, and inaugurate the Millennium on earth. After a literal thousand years, the rest of the dead will then be raised, and the final judgment will introduce Eternity.

We might add that more recent generations of Open Brethren have tended to favour an amillennial view of the Last Days, in which the thousand years of Revelation 20 are symbolic of the "church age" in which we now live, to be followed by the Great Tribulation, the return of Christ, the raising of both sheep and goats for the Day of Judgment, and then the creation of a new heaven and a new earth which will last forever. (See Coad, 129-137.)

[76] Orr, 253. This is more largely true of the USA than the UK.

"In God we find that which all men seek…
the maximum of present peace and happiness,
with the certainty of future blessing."

Norris Groves [1]

30

A Mystery in God's Dealings

A Very Simple Faith

Norris and Mary Groves would not look out of place among the heroes of faith in the eleventh chapter of Hebrews. "By faith," they gave up everything in order to carry the gospel to the heart of the Muslim world. And they did it gladly, knowing it to be the toughest assignment of all. "Whilst I should not hesitate," said Groves, "to go to the farthest corner of the habitable earth, were my dear Lord to send me, yet I feel much pleasure in having my post appointed here, though perhaps the most unsettled and insecure country beneath the sun. Without, are lawless robbers, and within, unprincipled extortioners; but it is in the midst of these that the almighty arm of our Father delights to display his preserving mercy. And while the flesh would shrink, the spirit desires to wing its way to the very foremost ranks of danger in the battles of the Lord."[2]

Here was a faith that dealt directly with God. Cut off from the outside world by flood, plague and insurrection, with no mission board or home committee to raise support, there seemed every human likelihood that the Baghdad mission would sink without trace. But it was in such a setting that Norris and Mary Groves would prove the faithfulness of God who answers prayer: "The Lord gives us great peace and quietness of mind in resting under his most gracious and loving care, and *as the great object of our lives is to illustrate his love to us*, we believe that in the midst of these awful circumstances he will fill our tongues with praise, as he now fills our hearts with peace."[3]

For a husband and wife to trust God to provide and protect in such conditions would seem hardly sensible. But to take two small boys with them might be considered positively irresponsible. Some might feel that looking literally to God for food in a place of famine, and for safety in a place of danger, would be to display "presumptuous confidence". Indeed, was it not "tempting God"? And was it not written, "Thou shalt not tempt the Lord thy God"?[4] Groves could not agree: "Many are affrighted and made sad in the ways of the Lord by the erroneous application of this scripture... If they hear of a man selling his property and becoming poor like Barnabas, according to the exhortation of the apostles and the example of our Lord, he is considered as *tempting God...* Again, if he exposes himself to dangers he might avoid, troubles he might escape, for what he believes the Lord's service, far from receiving any comfort or encouragement he is again accused of *tempting God.*"[5] But that is to misunderstand the scriptures: "Tempting God is the deadly sin of an unregenerate mind and is never charged on any saint, either in the Old or New Testament." When the unfaithful Jews in the wilderness *tempted* the Lord, it was not by depending on his provision, but by doubting it.[6] When the Pharisees and Sadducees *tempted* Christ, their demand sprang not from faith but from disbelief.[7] When Jesus from the pinnacle of the Temple said, "Do not put the Lord your God to the test," he was rebuking not bold faith but craven incredulity.[8] We tempt God by unbelief, by defiance and by sin; never by depending on him to do what he has promised. The Groves family, so very vulnerable, went to Baghdad not tempting God but *trusting* him.

Launching a mission to the Muslim world was a step which inspired that great exemplar of faith, George Müller, and was, in certain respects, a bolder step of faith than his. By the end of his life, Müller had provided through prayer for more than a hundred thousand orphans without asking a soul for a penny. Yet many Christians visited the orphan houses, and many heard Müller preach. His work of faith took place very visibly in the midst of what was still a Christian country with wealthy generous donors among its evangelical aristocrats and industrialists. Norris and Mary Groves proposed to place the same absolute trust in the faithfulness of God where there were no open-days for interested visitors, no supportive churches, no guaranteed communications – where there was no safety net, no lifebelt, no one to turn to if things went wrong except God himself. This, indeed, was part of the attraction. Though his primary reason for going to Baghdad was certainly to proclaim the gospel, Groves wished no less keenly to demonstrate the fact that the life of faith, as taught by Christ, was the most practical and the most joyous way for any Christian to live. "The great object of our lives," he declared, "is to illustrate his love to us." And where better to illustrate it than the hardest place of all?

Though cut off from financial support, and from any place of human safety, the little family was not forgotten. They were borne up by the prayers of friends at home, as proved by the few letters that did get through. And though their friends could do little but pray for them, it was evidently no vain thing to pray to the living God. "I think it not only a great loss of present comfort but a great sin not to trust God's promises," Groves affirmed,[9] and he found his trust well justified. Though he did not, like Müller, compile a detailed account of specific gifts received and needs met, he could testify no less clearly of God's perfect provision. In October 1831, "He has supplied me, I know not how, in the midst of famine, pestilence and war. And though I have heard from none in England for more than a year, especially from those that supply my wants, the Lord has not suffered me to want, or to be in debt. And though the necessities of life have amounted to almost twenty times their value during our late trials, he has not suffered me personally to be much affected by it. His loving-kindness and care have been wonderful."[10]

Throughout that year, amidst the turmoil of Baghdad's afflictions, the family were kept fit and well. In famine they had bread; in flood their house stood firm; in warfare they suffered no injury; amidst cholera and typhoid they enjoyed perfect health. With almost the entire city wiped out by the plague, they remained unharmed. Their faith held firm, and Providence, it would seem, had guarded them from every form of evil. Yet at the very moment when their testimony to God's miraculous providence seemed brightest – as the plague abated, as the waters subsided, as food returned to the markets – mother and baby were carried off. Eventually five out of thirteen of the household died. It was hard to understand then, and it seems hard to understand now.

Contemplating the closure of his school earlier that year, Groves had written, "Missionaries in these countries have need of a very simple faith, which can glory in God's will being done though all their plans come to nothing."[11] But now his faith faced a sterner challenge. Both he and Mary had firmly believed the angel of death would pass over their home. They trusted that as they called upon the Lord in the day of trouble, so he would deliver them and they would glorify him.[12] To find their confidence misplaced brought feelings that could hardly be analysed. "Her strongest assurance," Groves tells us, "was certainly that the Lord would not allow the plague to enter our dwelling; but when she saw that the Lord mysteriously accepted not this confidence, but let it rest even on her, it never disturbed her peace... She said to me, 'I know not which is to me most mysterious, that the Lord should have laid his hand upon me, or, having laid it, that I should enjoy such peace as I do.'"[13]

Their assurance was based, Groves tells us, on a literal understanding of Psalm 91: "He who dwells in the shelter of the Most High will rest in the shadow of the Almighty... Surely he will save you from the fowler's snare and from the deadly pestilence... His faithfulness will be your shield and rampart. You will not fear the terror of the night, nor the arrow that flies by day, nor the pestilence that stalks in the darkness, nor the plague that destroys at midday... If you make the Most High your dwelling... then no harm will befall you, no disaster will come near your tent." Norris and Mary Groves believed that these were promises a Christian could claim in faith. But were they? Or were they promises only to the Israelites under the Old Covenant? Or were they just for a specific time of trouble in the life of the Psalmist himself? Or were they merely the expression of a pious wish, or a prayer, rather than a divine promise to anyone? In short, we might wonder, what value is there for a Christian today in such passages of Old Testament scripture?

The death of Mary was a tragedy, and Groves, as we have seen, took it hard. Weeping with those who weep, it is not hard for us to feel the pain of such a loss whilst trying to make some sense of it. In his bereavement, of course, Groves shared an experience common to many of his generation. Childbirth, in particular, was a perilous undertaking for women before the use of sterile instruments and antibiotics. In the relative safety of Britain, Henry Craik and Edward Cronin lost their young wives shortly after marriage, as did John Parnell at Latakia, Karl Pfander in Shushi and Henry Groves in Chittoor. Every pregnancy brought with it the prospect of death. But men, on average, lived hardly longer than women. In 1837 the expectation of life in Manchester was seventeen years for a labourer, twenty years for a tradesman, and thirty-eight for professional men and landowners.[14] To people of the nineteenth century, prolonged sickness and sudden death were a normal part of human existence: life was never to be taken for granted. Indeed, throughout most of human history our wiser ancestors held that "death is not an injury, but rather life a privilege."[15] In our own day, medical technology may shield us from physical pains so well that a comfortable existence can appear a basic human right, which means that death may take us by surprise. Unjust, unfair, it seems an affront to human freedom and dignity. And we are, perhaps, more prone than our forebears to find ourselves racked with doubt and distress, and in the face of bereavement to question the ways of God.

But even in 1831 John Kitto struggled to come to terms with what had happened. Why should a loving missionary wife, mother of three young children, be taken at a time when she was most needed by her family and by the people to whom she was called? To see God rebuff the faith of one who had trusted him as a Father: this was hard to comprehend. Recalling her husband's belief that Mary was being prepared for great usefulness among the women of Baghdad, Kitto mused, "How short sighted are the best of men when they leave the proper sphere of faith in forming definite expectations for the future beyond the general persuasion that all things shall 'work together for good' to the children of God. I know many other instances of similar miscalculation. When we see the children of God become more strongly built up in Christ and more visibly grown and strengthened and fructified in him, we have concluded them to be ripening for great usefulness in the Church, while in fact (as in this case) they were all the while ripening for the garner of Heaven."[16]

All from the Lord

We may well share Kitto's perplexity. Such sad events raise many questions. Does God himself bring upon us the hardships, the frustrations, the illnesses, the bereavements we face? Or are they the random blows of blind chance, permitted but unplanned – perhaps even unforeseen – by the Creator? Or, worse still, is the world so far fallen that evil defies the will of God, so that we are forced to say in every hour of distress, "An enemy has done this,"[17] hoping merely that God can bring out of it some good?

Norris Groves firmly believed in the detailed providence of God, guiding and directing every circumstance of life. "I am struck," he said, "with the whole current of prophetic scripture which asserts the great truth that there is no evil affecting the nation, the city, the family or the individual that God does not challenge [i.e. claim] himself as the author of, either in discipline or in judgment."[18] Our trials do not take God by surprise. Nor are they blows inflicted by powers of darkness beyond his control. "Is it not from the mouth of the Most High that both calamities and good things come?"[19] So the prophet affirms, and elsewhere the Lord himself declares, "I am the Lord, and there is no other. I form the light and create darkness, I bring prosperity and create disaster; I the Lord do all these things."[20]

In view of such scriptures Groves had always accepted adversity as the work of God, giving little or no thought to the malicious presence of an active spiritual Enemy opposing the will of the Creator. But was it, after all, the devil who had afflicted their home rather than God himself? Pondering these things Groves remarked, "Christians generally have little other notion of Satan than of evil personified, instead of his being an intelligent and active foe, ever on the watch to wound and enfeeble the church. I believe the real power of the Enemy will be increased in proportion to the careless security of his opponent. We have felt again and again his effort to drive us away from our work."[21] But further study made it clear that the Evil One possesses no power of his own. Though he may tempt us to throw ourselves down, like Jesus from the pinnacle of the Temple, he cannot cast us down himself. He may indeed sift the poor disciples like wheat, but he must first beg permission (and when he does, their Master already knows the outcome).[22] He may afflict Paul with a thorn in the flesh, "a messenger of Satan," but the thorn is "given" for a divine purpose.[23] He may put some Smyrnan Christians in jail, but their Lord knows it long beforehand and promises them the crown of life.[24] And though permitted to afflict the health of Job, the Accuser cannot shorten his life by a single day.[25] In every case (for the disciples, for Paul, for the Smyrnans, for Job, and indeed for us) there is a heavenly purpose directing the earthly adversity, a purpose hidden from the sufferer but known to God. It is all part of his perfect plan. "So then," the apostle affirms, "those who suffer *according to God's will* should commit themselves to their faithful Creator and continue to do good."[26] As a *cause* of suffering, the devil can be discounted: he may tempt but he cannot destroy, and he does only what God allows. Yet the question remains: Why *does* God allow such things? Why would he not wish, like any human parent, to protect his children from all harm?

Throughout his life, the difficulties he faced caused Groves to ponder questions such as these. Where is God when the fare for a long-awaited trip to Dublin is stolen? "We had not a doubt it was of the Lord... thinking on the Lord's goodness in so caring for us as to stop our way up when he does not wish us to go."[27] Where is God when the notes and jottings of many weeks are knocked overboard? "I know the Lord is good, even in this, and would have me dig and dig again, for more and still richer treasures than I have yet found."[28] Where is God when a spar falls on a sleeping man? "Amidst many trials, I trust I can say 'It is all from the Lord,' and I will praise him for all, only praying that I may receive every impression, whether of joy or sorrow, as from a *Father's* hand, that it may promote my transformation into his image and the sanctification of my affections and tempers till I have learned obedience like my Head [i.e. Christ]."[29] But where is God when lies and rumours are spread concerning a man of integrity? "If we could but see, in every hand raised up to wound us, God's permissive sanction, what peace we should enjoy!"[30] Then where is God when friends fail to bring much-needed help? "I, however, receive this last trying providence at my loving Father's hands... The Lord allows me to feel assured he will yet do something for me."[31] Where is God when a boy tumbles from a rooftop, when a young woman is crushed by a waggon in a Devonshire lane, when silkworms perish, when sugar prices crash? Where is God when a young missionary wife and mother dies? "How easy it is to kiss our dear and loving Father's hand when he turns bright providences towards us! How easy then it is to praise! But I feel my dearest Teacher is teaching me the hardest lesson – to kiss the hand that wounds, to bless the hand that pours out sorrow, and to submit with all my soul, though I see not a ray of light. O, thou holy and blessed Spirit, come and help thy poor wayward scholar."[32]

Hudson Taylor, in similar circumstances, held the same faith. On the death of his wife Maria, he could say, "From my inmost soul I delight in the knowledge that God does, or deliberately permits, *all* things, and causes all things to work together for good to those who love him... *He* and he only knew what my dear wife was to me. He knew how the light of my eyes and the joy of my heart were in her... But he saw that it was good to take her; good indeed for her... and not less good for me who must henceforth toil and suffer alone – yet not alone, for God is nearer to me than ever."[33] And again, "Love gave the blow that for a little while makes the desert more dreary, but heaven more home-like. 'I go to prepare a place for you', and is not our part of the preparation the peopling it with those we love? And the same loving Hand that makes heaven more home-like is the while loosening the ties that bind us to this world." And again, "I feel like a little child... But with the weakness of a child, I have *the rest of a child*. I know my Father reigns: this meets all questions of every kind." Though "utterly crushed", "I would not have it otherwise... My Father has ordered it so – therefore I know it *is*, it must be best, and I thank him for so ordering it."[34]

It was while travelling that Norris Groves had most time to ponder the mysteries of Providence. At sea in 1834 a heavy gale had driven the ship well off course: "Yet, I feel most happy in the thought that the Lord knows all his holy reasons for our delays and troubles, so that I can happily commit all my earthly and heavenly interests to him."[35] Eighteen years later, at sea again, "Quiet waiting is the thing in all such journeys. You cannot hasten matters by impatience, and it adds much to the discomfort not seeing the Father at the helm of all one's affairs."[36] Delayed in Palamcottah by officialdom: "Here I am a prisoner for want of a passport; this is the Lord's pleasure, and it may be at least twelve days before I can go on my way. However, it is all well; I have much to hear and see that is truly interesting."[37] Norris Groves had discovered, in calm acceptance of the will of God, the secret of freedom from all that frustrates and irritates in the smaller circumstances of life – and the secret, too, of victory over the harder blows that come more rarely but strike more deeply.

And yet a question remained to trouble him. Might we, by our own failure, step out of the will of God and bring adversity upon ourselves? Might we, by our own sin, even place ourselves under the judgment of God? In his desolation Groves could not help dwelling on Mary's final days. It seemed likely that he himself had brought the infection into the house. As an act of kindness he had gone to help salvage some of Major Taylor's property from the ruins of the Residency. He had gone because he wanted to help and because he trusted in the Lord's protection. "The Lord therefore leaves me nothing to regret," he thought, "unless it be that I ought perhaps to have kept myself quite apart from the rest of the family after I had been obliged by a sense of duty to go out during the time the plague was raging."[38] But the doubt remained. By not taking care to quarantine himself, had he acted contrary to the will of God; and had he thus brought sorrow on them all? Yet if his faith had been too childlike, and if he had been careless, was God such a god as to punish his innocent wife on account of her husband's carelessness? Such a thing was unthinkable for a God of justice, let alone a God of love. In the end their heavenly Father must have had some good purpose in view. "He designed by it," said Groves, "her speedy glory and my final good."[39]

Her speedy glory was not in doubt, but how could it work for her husband's final good? And what about the needs of her motherless children? As Groves mused further on these "dark providences" he found in the Bible many occasions when suffering proved to be God's appointed means of blessing. Joseph, sent into slavery, could say to his brothers, "You intended to harm me, but God intended it for good."[40] "In the history of God's dealings with man," Groves observed, "there is nothing more striking than his way of overruling the most *ruinous events* for the blessing and prosperity of his children. We see it in Job, and in Naomi, but above all in looking at *Jesus* cast out and suffering on the cross we see the *darkest* of Satan's deeds made to accomplish his *own* overthrow… In the case of Moses, how were the ways of God the very opposite of all that man could expect! How much more likely it would seem that by remaining at the pharaoh's court he could work out the deliverance of his people. And to look at him, cast out for forty years, feeding a stranger's sheep, all would think him lost to his people; yet in all this God was working in him that discipline of heart which fitted him for another forty years' probation in the wilderness… What misinterpreters are we of God's gracious dealings! How many, like Naomi, misjudge God and say, 'He hath dealt very bitterly with me'… We might learn from Naomi's history not to complain as she did but to believe the Lord is 'very pitiful' [i.e. full of compassion] and to feel satisfied with his ways, not judging by present appearances, but waiting to see the *end*, and resting ourselves on his word and the revelation of himself therein."[41]

Waiting to see the end! In time of loss we become aware how darkly the shadows of earth hide things visible in the light of heaven. "You do not realise now what I am doing," said Jesus to Peter, "but later you will understand."[42] "I have been much struck of late," remarked Groves some years afterwards, "with the pilgrim character stamped on all those who have left Egypt, and on whom the blood of the Paschal lamb has been sprinkled: staff in hand, loins girt, shoes on the feet, and all in haste for the promised land. Surely, if we were always thus equipped, we should think little of the trials by the way. The land of promise beaming brightly before us, we should think much of the end and little of the road."[43] Similar thoughts came to John Kitto in old age, weak and ill, grieving for the death of his daughter and knowing he would shortly follow: "I have no ground to expect – I never have expected – that the Lord should establish on my behalf an exemption from all trouble; but I believe and know that all must be for *eventual* good, though it may be by ways I should not prefer, or by ways that I might even wish to avoid."[44]

This Disjointed World

But what of their testimony to God's faithfulness? For more than a year Norris and Mary Groves had trusted that the protection of their household from cholera and plague would prove to the people of Baghdad that God was with them and that their gospel was the truth. Their testimony to a visible and tangible salvation would win Muslims and nominal Christians to faith in their Saviour. Such was their hope. And yet, strange as it may seem, experience from an early stage showed the opposite. For as long as the family remained immune they were resented and even blamed. At the height of the troubles Groves marvelled, "I have been struck two or three times lately, in going out, with the intense hatred that lurks at the bottom of the hearts of this people against Christians… Some Arabs I met, particularly the women, cursed me with the most savage ferocity as I passed, two or three calling out at me as though I were the cause of all their calamities. And the people who are come to live next door to us are bitter against us, especially one man among them who seems to have his heart quite corroded because they are dying and we are preserved by our Lord's love. He sits and talks under our window saying, 'These Christians and Jews alone remain but in the whole of Baghdad you will hardly find one hundred Mohammedans.'"[45] The protection of the Groves household did not open Muslim hearts and minds to their faith as they had thought it would. On the contrary, it seemed to bring an increased hardening. God's blessing upon their family did not open doors for the gospel at all.

Experiences such as this led Norris Groves to think long and hard about the nature of the world and the place of God's people in it. He saw a city afflicted with many troubles, and he realised how fully he and his household must share in them. John Kitto, too, reflected on all they had been through: "I know not what stronger evidence we could have of the misery of man and the ruined state of the world than what we have seen and heard in Baghdad in the course of the year 1831. In Europe, particularly in England, the world is presented under so many disguises and in features so externally attractive that it requires no ordinary discernment to perceive the utter worthlessness, vanity and hopelessness of all it can offer. She is here naked, and the heart sickens at the deformity which sin has made in her once excellent form of character, and in the depth of its abhorrence and disgust at all it looks on is tempted to cry, perhaps too impatiently, 'Oh that I had wings like a dove, for then I would fly away and be at rest.'"[46] Musing further Kitto confided, "We have known and seen what can never be forgotten and which, while we remember, we cannot easily fall into the error, which most do, of mistaking earth for heaven."[47] All around them were signs of the Fall: the "oppression and cruelty" (the bitter fruit of man's first disobedience to God) and the groaning in travail of the whole world "connected with that event... And thus, not only the earth, which was cursed for his sake, but the whole animate creation may be considered as lifting up its voice against the father of mankind and exclaiming, 'O Adam, what hast thou done?'"[48] Never again would mankind know the peace and security of Eden.

From its earliest pages the Bible shows the Creator exercising justice in the affairs of men. He judges individuals;[49] he judges families;[50] he judges churches;[51] he judges cities;[52] he judges nations.[53] He is the Judge of all the earth.[54] It is a mistake, Groves now realised, to think that because we are saved individually God views us just as individuals. Each of us is tied into a bundle. We belong to a family, a church, a city, a nation and ultimately to a fallen humanity, and God deals in justice and in mercy with the totality of which we are a part. As members of the community we take our share in the blessing or curse that falls upon the whole. And when Adam fell, the whole of creation under his authority – tied up in his bundle – fell with him.

The Fall changed everything. "Cursed is the *ground* because of you!" was the sentence pronounced, and this was no mere spiritual change; it was a physical change. It affected the physical earth. It brought "painful toil", "thorns and thistles", "pains in childbearing", and it set a limit to the biological lifespan: "dust you are and to dust you will return."[55] From that moment the world started to disintegrate, to break down, to die. All around us we can see the effect of that terrible judgment. It brought a change in the biology and geology, perhaps even in the chemistry and physics, of the earth. "For the creation was subjected to frustration, not by its own choice, but by the will of the One who subjected it."[56] We see plants and animals afflicted with horrible diseases; we see "nature red in tooth and claw"; we see natural disasters that maim and destroy. Desperately the earth longs to be "liberated from its bondage to decay," and yet, year after year, "we know that the whole creation has been groaning as in the pains of childbirth right up to the present time. Not only so, but we ourselves, who have the firstfruits of the Spirit, groan inwardly as we wait eagerly for... the redemption of our bodies."[57] And this is why, so long as this old earth remains, "through many tribulations we must enter the kingdom of God."[58]

The heated furnace of Baghdad brought the Groves household face to face with realities that could be more easily overlooked in the beautiful gardens at Northernhay. The effects of the Fall here were stark indeed. Groves looked out upon a "dispensation of suffering",[59] a scene of universal devastation that could only be described as "this disjointed world".[60] Before leaving England he had remarked to a companion, "O my dear friend! this is a wicked and foolish world, and the only good thing that can be said of it, since God has ceased to bless it, is that it is the thorny way by which his servants approach his presence."[61] Six years later he had discovered that even the most basic blessings – of health and life itself – could not be guaranteed to the child of God.

It is not immunity from trouble in this world that God promises his people. "In this world," said Jesus, "you will have trouble. But take heart! I have overcome the world."[62] At first sight this may seem a paradox. How, we might wonder, has Jesus overcome, conquered, mastered the world, whilst leaving it full of trouble? And how can we take heart in such circumstances? All too evidently, the incarnation of Christ did not immediately restore the entire corrupted creation to the idyllic state of Eden; that was clearly not his purpose. But we find he did something rather remarkable in one small part of it. For a few brief years, among a poor despised people, he overthrew the laws of nature, annulled the Curse, reversed the Fall. He forgave sins, healed the sick and raised the dead; he calmed the storm, walked on water, fed five thousand in a lonely place. His miracles would not remove evil from the earth or restore a perfect harmony to the natural world. His miracles were simply "signs"[63] – tokens of what will be in the age to come – a foretaste of a work to be completed and fulfilled in the new heaven and new earth.[64] Here lay the secret, Groves believed, to understanding God's purpose for his people in this world. "I can only look forward for comfort to that day," he declared, "when the Lord himself will come to put an end to this dispensation of desolation and introduce his own peace. Yea, come Lord Jesus, come quickly!"[65]

From the vision of a guilty world at odds with its Maker, Groves turned his thoughts to those lesser judgments that fall periodically on nations, families and individuals. At first both he and Mary had thought that the child of God would be shielded from the specific acts of judgment laid on the ungodly. "We did feel assured," he said, "that the Lord would spare our dear little united happy family."[66] Surely the Psalmist had promised, "A thousand may fall at your side, ten thousand at your right hand, but it will not come near you. You will only observe with your eyes and see the punishment of the wicked."[67] At length the realisation came. "A missionary in these countries," Groves reflected, must "really cast himself upon his Lord and share in its revolutions and national judgments."[68] Carrying the gospel of Christ into all the world, the servant of Christ must settle among peoples who are guilty before God. It is a brave step for him to take, for he deliberately ties himself into their bundle. And then, "Oh! what wrath there must be against these lands, if not only the inhabitants are swept away, but the Lord transplants also his own, who would teach them, to his own garden of peace."[69]

Looking back on it all Groves admitted, "I feel now that I had been led to expect a greater measure of freedom from the troubles which fall on the people in the midst of which I find myself than the dispensation under which I live warranted. I do not mean from those which spring directly out of the Lord's service, but those natural and national evils which God sends as judgments on the ungodly. This error arose from considering the temporal promises of the 91st Psalm, and other similar ones in multitudes of places, as the legitimate objects of faith, whereas I have been now led to see that they... are but 'typical' representations of that kingdom in which the saints of the Lord shall rejoice and be safe when his enemies are swept away as the chaff of the summer threshing floor."[70] The promise in question may be seen as proof of the Creator's power to save, and his willingness to save, and as a description of the salvation that will be ours in a future age, but it is not a promise of permanent immunity for all Christians from sickness, sorrow and death in this present time. Only when Christ returns – when the old earth is burnt up, when all things are made new, when the dead are raised incorruptible, when there is no more curse, no more death, when the dwelling of God is with men – only then will we be free from the afflictions described in the psalm, and not till then will it become applicable literally to us.

Groves found, as have many others, that prolonged and severe doubts ultimately brought him to a deeper understanding and a stronger faith: "Had I seen years ago, as the Lord has given me now to see, I think I should, by his grace, have suffered in many cases much more patiently than I did. I might have pursued courses I did not, and avoided some which I chose, and I should not have given advice in all cases as I have done. I feel my Lord has passed it over, but this only makes me more than ever desirous to enter into the true nature of his kingdom at present in the world. How much do I owe to the light imparted to me in that one truth, that this is a dispensation of *suffering* and *sorrow* and will remain such till the Lord come. It leads me to look on the thousand trials incident to my path and possibly, yea certainly, to my future course as *no strange* things, but as fiery trials appointed to try and purify."[71] There is much to be done and much to be endured, but the coming of the Lord will heal all ills – on "that bright morning when the Lord shall wipe away all tears from our eyes."[72]

Then if this offers a key to the mystery of suffering, perhaps it can also show us the nature of our message to the world. The gospel of Christ offers not an easier life in this age but eternal life in the age to come, not preservation in a fallen world but preparation for a perfect world. And so long as we live on a sick and dying planet, we are called, like our Master, to support and comfort our fellow-wanderers, helping them find the narrow gate that leads to eternal life.

To Strengthen and Bless

All this, however, raised in the mind of Norris Groves a further question. If promises given to Old Testament saints, and promises relating to a future age, cannot be applied to the present circumstances of the Christian, are we then left without assurance of protection from harm in this world? With no immunity from tragedy, is the child of God left anxiously to fear the worst? Such a conclusion, thought Groves, would require us to ignore much that God *has* revealed to us. "Not a hair of our head," he recalled, "shall fall to the ground without our heavenly Father's permission. Therefore I feel these thoughts ought neither to trouble us, nor any *more* prevent our hand undertaking for Christ any service than if a greater exemption was promised. For we know that whatever is allowed to befall us, whether natural or spiritual, if Christ is ours and we are his, they shall only so operate as to work out for us a far more exceeding and eternal weight of glory. For these sufferings and trials must be among the 'all things' that work together for good to those who love Christ."[73]

"Do not be afraid!" is a command Jesus gave his disciples more often than any other, and always accompanied by the assurance of his Father's loving care in time of trouble. Watching the silkworms die, and with them all his hopes for the Chittoor mission, Groves could say, "Be the cloud never so dense, the way never so perplexed, there will always be something in the midst of it which will reveal a Father's love, a *Father's* care; there will be ever a *bow* [i.e. a rainbow] in the cloud. In the midst of midnight darkness, the believer knows that 'light *is* sown for the righteous'. Therefore he occupies himself, not with forebodings as to how things will turn out, but rests on the promise of God, and above all on his *purpose* in afflicting us, even to make us 'partakers of his holiness'." If we are faithfully serving our Lord, we may be sure our troubles are sent not in judgment but in love. Then we may "seek to extract out of the trial the spiritual blessing for which it is sent, namely, conformity to Jesus and partaking of his holiness. Be it perplexity of circumstances or other trials, God has in all but one intent: *deliverance*, not death, is his aim. If he made Israel hunger, it was not to starve, but to *feed* them."[74]

In the course of his life Groves often saw good come out of circumstances that initially seemed adverse or even ruinous. "It is the characteristic of our walking in Christ not to be *moved* by evil tidings," he declared.[75] On board ship for England, unsure what awaited him in London and Plymouth, he could face delays and setbacks with equanimity. His journey, if shortened by a day, might lead to a chance meeting with someone at the docks or on the coach. Arriving a day later he might encounter someone else – but it was all in the Lord's hands. "We have now a calm, and know not how our next wind is to blow. If it were fair we should be thankful, yet how many unknown reasons there may be why we should be detained a day longer. It may lead to events, even though we know them not, that would modify all our future history."[76] Impatience at such times paralyses the soul and separates us from our Lord. "I do so deeply realise the importance, to those whom God calls to pass through trials, of setting their hearts with all diligence to make a sanctified use of *all* the *little* events that happen; for if this be neglected, the heart by imperceptible yet sure degrees departs farther and farther from God. It is the setting the heart to crucify self in every form that makes all events subservient to blessing instead of grief. And I feel sure, where this is really undertaken in the fear of God, and simply to please him, and because he would have us so live, we shall find a peace of soul in nearness to him which... abundantly compensates for every sorrow and self-denial."[77]

In Baghdad Groves found that, possessing little, he had little to worry about, and little to lose. Property, income, reputation, honour: these can be a blessing when we have them, but to lose them may be a greater blessing still. "What a mercy it is to us," he remarked, "to have the world, with its honours, its pleasures and its hopes, crucified with Christ; how it takes away the edge from the Enemy's weapons. When he thinks to make a deadly thrust at us he finds he can only touch that which we have ceased to value, because we have a better inheritance: one incorruptible, undefiled and that fadeth not away."[78] To walk with God, to live by faith: this comes most easily to a person who claims little of this world's goods. "Those to whom it is given to know this is not their rest, and that having food and raiment they must be content, are made to feel the reason why so many of the family of God are in trial is that as a *state* it most leads to dependence on God. The moment a man feels adequate to his own wants, his tendency is always to self-reliance, and in order to destroy this, the Lord comes in and breaks his pleasant vessels."[79] At such times, though he mourns his loss, he has good reason to value his gain. "I have had much to try me," confessed Groves, "yet I know it is to strengthen and bless me. Why then should I regret it?"[80]

Groves himself often struggled with a sense of personal failure, and, strange as it may seem, this may be one reason why he had so many friends. Such is human nature that whilst success can arouse both admiration and jealousy, failure will cause a brave man to be both pitied and loved. After the death of her sister Charlotte in 1832, Bessie Paget found among her possessions some writings composed during the last year of her life – a year during which she had prayed constantly for Norris and Mary Groves and their children in Baghdad. "My sympathies are hardly ever called forth by any gladness," admitted Charlotte, "but in sorrow I can embrace every human being as a sister and a brother. Sorrow is a sacred thing. It is, as it were, an atmosphere prepared by the Holy Ghost for himself. The sanctuary of grief in the sorrowful heart *is* a sanctuary, because the messenger of the Lord has been there to prepare the way of the Most High. And the stillness, the solemn impression of emptiness, which pervades the soul of the desolate, is but the sacred silence which succeeds that fearful shaking of the earth – that removing of the things that may be shaken, so that those things which cannot be shaken may remain in the Temple of the Holy One."[81] Many, like Charlotte Paget, have found sympathy to be one of the sweetest fruits of adversity.

But Norris Groves was not merely one who suffered; he was pre-eminently one who ministered to the suffering. A deaf youth jilted and misunderstood, a Chaldean girl homeless and alone, a civil engineer at death's door, a missionary perplexed with problems, a teacher too ill to move, a little boy orphaned at sea – all these stirred in the heart of a man of God the love which Christ had planted there. Alexander Duff recalled, "Truly his visit to us was like an angel's visit, a visit of surpassing kindness and brotherly love."[82] The darker the sky, the brighter the stars will shine, for it was, of course, the sickness of Duff that brought out the best in his friend. Trials there will always be, but also blessing, and as Bessie Paget said, "Though we have had our share of trials, we have had more than our share of blessing."[83] And may not the blessings justify at least some of the trials?

Scripture tells us that it was through suffering that Christ himself learned obedience; through suffering that he was made perfect.[84] Sometimes we hear a gifted speaker – sound, eloquent, brilliant, a master of his art – yet to our surprise his words leave our heart and soul untouched; we receive little help from him. It will take a comprehensive failure, a profound tragedy, a devastating loss, before a clever man becomes a minister of life. Only then will he have power to speak the words of God into the hearts of men. This is no natural ability; it is a divine gift; and it almost always comes through suffering. Norris Groves, after his months in Baghdad, was never the same again. A facet was added to his already beautiful character, and from then on, wherever he went, he did more than teach the scriptures; he "ministered life". What is more, the trials of the Baghdad mission opened hearts and doors in India, which meant that for the first time Christian people heard a preacher and teacher from beyond the confines of their own denomination. Without his sufferings he would never have had his ministry. Looking back on all he had been through, he did not regret the disappointments, the frustrations and the heartache. "I often think I would not have gone through one trial less than I have," he said, "for I feel they were all necessary to make me able to minister at all to his Church's edification."[85]

Prepared for the Inheritance

The death of Mary Groves on 14th May 1831 was, in one sense, just a small personal loss touching a few people in a particular house for a short time. But as such it forms part of a universal tragedy affecting the whole people of God. In every generation young evangelists and missionaries are cut off in their prime, and their anguished friends and loved-ones wonder why. Does God *not* want his kingdom to come? Does he have no desire for the gospel to reach the ends of the earth? Stephen, his sermon half finished, is stoned to death; James, a faithful apostle, is slain with the sword; Abel, who pleased God, is violently murdered, righteous Zechariah struck down between the altar and the sanctuary. William Tyndale, translating the Old Testament, is burnt at the stake; Matthew Henry, labouring at his commentary, breaks down in health; Henry Martyn, preaching in Persia, expires of a fever; Jim Elliot, befriending the Aucas, is speared and left for dead. Not an efficient way to get a job done, we might think! Paul's thorn in the flesh is a hindrance; a traitor amidst the disciples is a hindrance; forty years in the wilderness are a hindrance; shipwrecks and imprisonments are all a hindrance – they hold back the ministry of God's servants. The apostles must wait forty days, then ten days more, before the Spirit comes. Abraham must wait many years for the birth of his son, the children of Abraham many generations for the birth of their Saviour. Centuries pass between the Old Testament and the New; more centuries till the Reformation restores the Bible to the church; then more before the gospel is taken into all the world!

We have to conclude that God is in no hurry; efficiency is not his great concern. His purpose is not to save the largest number of people in the shortest possible time. In fact the Bible shows us God at work not simply for time, but for eternity. Pondering on these things, Groves had learned to take a long-term view of adversity. "Affliction," he said, "is the discipline for heaven's school.

In it we are prepared for the inheritance and nowhere else."[86] Scripture never leads us to suppose the Creator's objective is a successful church in a corrupted world; his objective is a holy church in a sinless world, "to *purify* for himself a people of his own", to make for himself "a *radiant* church, without stain or wrinkle or any other blemish."[87] If our Lord considers that failure or pain or loss will best prepare us for the radiant life ahead of us, then we may have sufficient reason given for every difficulty we face. Norris Groves, through his tears, could yet confess, "Truly, whatever makes Jesus precious, and eternity a reality, is most blessed, though it cuts up all earthly things by the roots."[88]

There were many who considered the Baghdad mission a failure, and wondered if God was in it at all. Yet the deepest work of God is rarely marked by what we would call success. In the eleventh chapter of Hebrews we read of some who by faith *achieved* great things, others who by faith *endured* great things. "These were *all* commended for their faith, yet *none* of them received what had been promised." For "God had planned something better" – that these faithful ones might share in the greater blessing of a greater promise in the age to come.[89] Norris Groves endured, perhaps, more than he achieved, but he was content. "Elijah," he observed, "fully fulfilled God's purpose, yet he does not appear to have made more than one convert (Elisha)... Nor did Noah make one convert, yet he fulfilled the Lord's purpose in his preaching. So before the Lord comes again, 'as in the days of Noah', we shall, I expect, have to stretch forth our hands without many regarding; but let it be our concern that we do as individuals, and as a mission, preach Christ faithfully and love him truly."[90] To some who suggested he had accomplished little Groves replied, "It may be said 'you have not succeeded'; I say that is begging the question. If we have *done the Lord's will* we have succeeded. The angels that went to Sodom succeeded as well as Jonah who went to Nineveh, though the former destroyed, the latter preserved the city."[91]

If his labour sometimes seemed in vain, we should remember that Norris Groves was in every respect a pioneer. The rocks must be cleared from a mountainside before the seed is sown, and the first tough evangelists in virgin territory will often toil many years before their children gather a harvest. "These are deeply interesting countries," said Groves from Baghdad, "to those who can be happy in bestowing all their strength in planting under the prospect that others will reap the fruits."[92] The pioneer may face, as he did, the challenge of both indifference and violent opposition. Indeed it would seem that the powers of darkness rise up with all their fury when the servants of Christ first dare to trespass on forbidden ground. Was it a coincidence that just when the gospel reached Baghdad war broke out and the city was besieged, two-thirds of its inhabitants swept away by plague, two-thirds of its houses by floods? And that the missionaries were blamed? Yet Groves saw the turmoil not as the work of Satan, but rather the work of God – a work of judgment preparing the people for a more gracious work of salvation. "Amidst all these trials to the servants of God," he said, "my heart does not despair for the work of the Lord, for no ordinary judgments seem necessary to break the pride and hatred of this most proud and contemptuous people."[93] To live amidst such chaos is a price that must be paid by those who would fulfil the Great Commission. But when the harvest is finally gathered in, sower and reaper will surely share the reward.[94]

The reward was something Norris Groves looked forward to with great hope and anticipation, even if its character was obscure and its time far distant. After months of hardship, anxiety and bereavement he wistfully confessed, "I feel Christ my Lord has in store for me in himself some great and special good in exchange for all this."[95]

It perplexed him to hear some say that a Christian should serve God simply as an act of obedience with no thought of personal benefit. In a popular biography, the *Life of Brainerd*, Groves saw Jonathan Edwards recommending a "*disinterested* and *unmercenary*" love of God, by which he means the love of him for his abstract perfections apart from the consideration of any personal interest or happiness arising out of his especial love to his chosen."[96] "This," thought Groves, "was all very fine and very philosophical, but in my humble apprehension, most unscriptural." Christian service should spring not from a mental appreciation of God's "abstract perfections" but from a personal experience of his love and an earnest desire for his blessing. And if our Lord sees fit to encourage us in our labours with the promise of his smile and his "Well done!", why should we spurn that happy prospect?[97] In the eleventh of Hebrews we are shown a host of witnesses who "by faith" drew strength to endure present hardships from the thought of future blessings. Paul, too, looked forward to receiving his crown, and Christ himself "for the joy set before him endured the cross, scorning its shame."[98] To be insulted, said Jesus, is to be blessed: "rejoice and be glad, because great is your reward in heaven."[99] A heavenly recompense is promised for a cup of cold water, for prayer, for fasting, for help to the poor, for kindness to a righteous man, for willingness to leave family and home for the sake of the gospel.[100] "In fact," concluded Groves, "the doctrine of Rewards, as an incentive to the saints, prevails from one end to the other of the sacred volume."[101]

But an eager desire for blessing need not be at all selfish. Here again Norris Groves saw with great clarity the significance of our corporate identity, our membership in a community. The servant of Christ (like Christ himself) is tied into the bundle of God's people; he shares their reward and they share his. He will gladly suffer so that others may be blessed. He will cheerfully bear the burden and the heat of the day so that the lost may be found, the guilty brought to repentance, the weak made strong, the ignorant led to faith. "I am happy about my sufferings for you," said the apostle, "for by means of my physical sufferings I am helping to complete what still remains of Christ's sufferings on behalf of his body, the church."[102] Serving our Christian brothers and sisters, and those who are seeking the truth, we are happy to see *them* receive the reward of our labour, in this world or the next. "A natural mind," said Groves, "seeks natural rewards, which are *selfish*; a spiritual mind seeks spiritual rewards which are *unselfish* and spring from being allowed to contribute to the glory and blessing of others." "This view," he said, "has eased my heart of many a sad thought and enabled me to feel reconciled, nay, *encouraged*, to a life of labour and suffering and sacrifice with the full expectation of the *sweetest rewards*. Before the Spirit taught me this from the word of God, all was darkness. I always thought on rewards as something *directly personal*, instead of *corporate* and coming through that sweet consideration that all my brother's glories and blessings and happinesses are my own, as all his humiliations and sorrows are, so that we seem to live only as our brethren stand fast in the faith."[103]

A long-term view – an anticipation of blessings to come – will often refresh a jaded spirit. Yet even as our thoughts are drawn to the golden age ahead, our bodily strength is tested and sometimes exhausted in our endeavour to achieve something worthwhile in *this* world. For an idealist like Norris Groves, faith must always struggle to accept present realities that fall far short of the ideal. A man who has great visions will suffer many disappointments. The failure of the farm at Chittoor profoundly coloured his final years in India. It was meant to be a blessing to Indian believers and missionary teachers and evangelists. It was all taken on with the best of intentions, but it all went wrong. After his death, when Harriet was compiling her *Memoir*, Henry wrote to her, enclosing some of his father's papers. "I see great difficulties," he said, "in explaining to *others* the last few years of my dear father's life: the *uprightness* of the *intention*, the complete failure of the object pursued."[104] In financial terms perhaps Henry was right, but Harriet had no doubt that her husband's pure intentions were not forgotten. "His desires to benefit both the natives of India and the European residents are recorded on high," she said.[105] David the king, who earnestly desired to build a house for the Lord, must leave that task for his son. And yet the Lord still has a word for David: "Whereas it was in your heart to build a house for my name, you did well that it was in your heart."[106]

Writing to Harriet during Norris Groves's final weeks, a lady friend confided, "I dare say you hear of his state from himself – the blank, as he calls it, of his ten years at Chittoor. Indeed, I do not like to hear him speak of it, he feels it so acutely; and I do not think it *right*, because he was the means of bringing many to Jesus, and a witness for the Lord in his consistent walk."[107] Indians and Europeans had come to faith in Christ at Chittoor, and the schools, the gospel outreach and the Christian community continued long after he had gone. Those who saw nothing but failure were too short-sighted. "There is a mystery in God's dealings with each individual," suggested Henry, "which eternity alone will unravel, and then the purpose of the heart and not the success of the undertaking will be taken into account. There is a natural shrinking from disappointed expectations; we like to see the garden flourish. But the beloved Jonathan, the faithful self-renouncing friend of David's sorrows, must fall on Mount Gilboa. We do not like to think of it; it seems so mysterious. But *God* ordered it, and Jonathan who falls on Gilboa and David who is crowned in Bethlehem both stand before us equally men of faith, and we must be content to judge of them not by the accidents [i.e. the incidental events] of their career but by the light of that Day which shall bring to light the hidden things of darkness."[108]

In the light of that day we shall see clearly. Meanwhile, we know that fretting in the night will not hasten the dawn. As age creeps upon us, or sickness saps our strength, we may feel we can do less good than in times past, and far less than we would wish. In the midst of pain and disability, some may find they can only trust and pray; and some can only trust. Job, in his day, was one who appeared to achieve very little. He was neither a prophet nor priest nor king; he performed no great exploits for God. Yet by holding true to his faith in his hour of darkness, he fulfilled all the will of his Lord and was honoured with the title "my servant Job".[109] Henry Groves tells us of John Parnell, now an old man, incapacitated and discomforted with rheumatism of hands and feet: "God only knows the heavenly fragrance that breathes its sweetness before him as it rises from the subject heart that has learnt to bow to a will that in infinite love appoints its daily measure of suffering, and that is content to say, 'Even so Father, for so it seemed good in thy sight.'"[110] While fit and young we advance boldly with "the sword of the Spirit which is the word of God"; old and weary it can be an achievement just as great to stand firm with the "shield of faith".[111] Seven times Jesus says, "To him who overcomes, I will give...,"[112] and we can overcome as well through stout defence as bold attack. The invalid, unable to preach or even speak, may have no service to offer his Master beyond faith, hope and love – but there is nothing greater than these.[113] Charlotte Paget said, "Faith takes up the cross; love binds it to the soul; patience bears it to the end."[114] It is the *bearing* to the end that wins the victory.

The bearing, the waiting may seem long. Lazarus is dying and Jesus tarries two days more. And then among the mourners Jesus weeps. Mary and Martha must wait – the hour has not yet come for the dead to rise. The sickness, the death, the weeping and the raising are all in God's perfect plan, and each has its appointed time. The story unfolds, and faith will read to the final page. Adversities and adventures may challenge and change us, but we should never forget that all God's stories have a happy ending. "How slow we are," said Groves, "to learn that all the discipline of life is to prepare us for eternity; that nothing that has not God in it is either worth caring for or desiring."[115]

So here it is – the final piece in the puzzle that once seemed so muddled and confused. In a small boat off the coast of India, Norris Groves recorded their progress in his journal: "Still slowly pursuing our way, in a stormy sea. How like the Christian course!"[116] And stormy it will be, until we reach our "longed-for haven".[117] In 1837, receiving letters from England, he mused, "I find dear Lady Powerscourt has gone to her sweet rest. The thought greatly refreshes me; for it is an evil world, and now the Lord is sure to keep her till the day of glory – Ah how blessed a day!"[118]

On that day, reunited with our loved ones, we will honour Henry, Frank and Norris Groves for their many years of Christian service – but we will honour Mary too, for her faith in an hour of great darkness! Indeed, of all the people moving through these pages, Mary Groves is the one we may be most glad to see; for she, more clearly than any, will show how death is swallowed up in victory.[119] "Therefore, my dear brothers, stand firm. Let nothing move you. Always give yourselves fully to the work of the Lord, *because you know that your labour in the Lord is not in vain.*"[120]

But the final word must be her husband's. Suffering intensely, pitifully weak, knowing he would soon be gone, Norris Groves saw everything once more bathed in a fresh light. "How precious it is," he whispered, "to feel that all these human ills are, to the redeemed of the Lord, what the chariots of fire were to Elijah – alarming to look at, but the Father's way of bringing his own home."[121]

ENDNOTES

[1] M403

[2] M105

[3] M120 (R97)

[4] Mt 4:7 AV

[5] R217-221

[6] Deut 6:16; Exod 17:1-7; 1 Cor 10:9

[7] Matt 16:1

[8] The fact that Christ subsequently walked on water was proof to Groves that if he *had* thrown himself down from the Temple he would certainly have been borne up by angels. It was the devil who doubted this, not Christ. Indeed, "the object of Satan was to get our Lord's mind into a condition of doubting God" (R218).

[9] M17

[10] M207 (R298). See chapter 15.

[11] R128; M136

[12] Ps 50:15; 91:15 AV

[13] R171

[14] Wood, 97

[15] Viscount [Herbert] Samuel, *Memoirs* (London, Cresset Press, 1945), 297

[16] Eadie, 205

[17] Mt 13:28 NRSV

[18] M417-418. Groves had in mind such scriptures as Is 10:5-7,12, 22-23; 14:24-27; 45:7; Ezek 24:16,18; Dan 4:35; Amos 3:6. Elsewhere in the Bible we see the same testimony to Providence: Gen 6:17; 45:5-8; 1 Sam 2:25; 2 Sam 24:15-16; 1 Ki 11:11-14; 12:15; 22:19-23; Ezra 6:22; Prov 16:9; 21:1; Hab 3:1-18; Acts 4:28; Heb 5:8; 12:4-13.

[19] Lam 3:38. See 3:32.

[20] Is 45:6-7

[21] M223

[22] Lk 22:31-32

[23] 2 Cor 12:7

[24] Rev 2:10

[25] Job 2:6

[26] 1 Pet 4:19

[27] M42

[28] M342

[29] M332 (Heb 5:8)

[30] M390-391

[31] R200

[32] R161; M159

[33] Taylor, *Growth of a Work of God*, 199

[34] *Growth of a Work of God*, 201-202

[35] M327-328

[36] M477

[37] M254

[38] R174

[39] R207

[40] Gen 50:19

[41] M404 (Jas 5:11 AV)

[42] Jn 13:7. See 2 Cor 5:7.

[43] M438

[44] Eadie, 378

[45] R137-138

[46] Eadie, 218

[47] Eadie, 219

[48] Ryland, 172-173

[49] Acts 12:23; Num 21:6; Ps 75:6-7; 1 Cor 11:29-32

[50] Ex 20:5; Num 14:18; Josh 7:24-25; 1 Ki 21:29 (2 Ki 10:10-11) etc.

[51] Rev 2:5

[52] Lk 21:20-22; Gen 19:13, 29; Rev 18:10

[53] Ex 12:29; Deut 23:3-4; Josh 22:20; Ezek 25:12-14; Amos 4:6-12 etc.

[54] Gen 6:11-13; 18:25; Rev 16:1-21

[55] Gen 3:16-19. See also Rom 5:12-14.

[56] Rom 8:20

[57] Rom 8:21-23

[58] Acts 14:22 RSV. Like most Christians of his generation, Norris Groves accepted the biblical account of origins as a straightforward factual narrative of events. With the completion of the six days of creation, the book of Genesis describes a world absolutely perfect in design and function: "God saw everything that he had made, and behold, it was very good" (Gen 1:31 ESV). A perfect creation could not possibly include such terrible evils as plagues, cancers, crippling injuries and death. We may thus picture a planet with no animals or insects harmful to man, no poisons, and no infectious or degenerative diseases. There would be no earthquakes, volcanoes, floods or avalanches, and perhaps no dangerous oceans, mountains or ravines. Providential and angelic intervention may also have kept our earliest ancestors safe from accident and injury, along with a more rapid and complete regeneration of any damaged tissue. This idyllic state was brought to an abrupt end with the Fall, which transformed the whole created order.

In our own day there is a tendency to view the Fall as a spiritual rather than a physical catastrophe. But many evangelical scholars and scientists now advocate a return to the older view, contending that belief in an act of divine judgment (allowing satanic powers to corrupt a previously perfect creation) is essential for a sound biblical understanding of suffering, evil, and the character of God. See, for example, the scientific and exegetical evidence offered at <https://creation.com/> and <https://answersingenesis.org/>.

[59] M289

[60] M350

[61] M8 (letter to Caldecott, 26 April 1825)

[62] Jn 16:33

[63] Jn 2:11; 3:2; 4:54; 20:30

[64] Scripture describes in some detail the new heaven and new earth: 2 Pet 3:10-13; Rev 20:11-22:5.

[65] R134. Theologians, ancient and modern, have had great difficulty persuading the sceptical that we currently live in "the best of all possible worlds". The Bible would advise them that "the best of all possible worlds" is yet to come. On this question and others relating to the subject of suffering see Joni Eareckson Tada and Steve Estes, *When God Weeps* (Grand Rapids, Zondervan, 1997) and Edith Schaeffer, *Affliction* (London, Hodder, 1978, 1993).

[66] R143

[67] Ps 91:7-8

[68] R252

[69] R142

[70] R220

[71] M289-290 (referring to 1 Pet 1:6-7; 4:12)

[72] M291. Groves felt he had finally understood "the true nature of his kingdom at present in the world". But we might still wonder why the redeemed children of God are not better protected in this "dispensation of suffering and sorrow". It may be helpful to imagine the alternative – a fallen world in which all Christians are shielded

from all harm. Here in a corrupted creation where dangers abound and powers of darkness roam, no sickness or pain or accident can touch them. It must, of course, be a world of miracles, repeatedly overturning the physical laws of nature that govern all life on earth. Fire fails to scorch, ice ceases to chill, poison does no harm, gravity is suspended, water cannot drown. Knives become blunt, bullets swerve aside, falling rocks are checked, lava flows diverted. Speeding vehicles are halted, gunpowder fails to explode, avalanches change direction; earthquakes, floods and pestilence are seen but hardly felt. Undoubtedly such things happen – a token, perhaps, of what will be in the age to come – but at present only on rare occasions.

In fact a world of suffering in which Christians are exempt would be a strange world, a world where science and technology could predict and guarantee nothing. And if this were the case, then the accusation of Satan concerning Job would stand – that God buys for himself worshippers by giving them an easy life (Job 1:9-11). What is more, if sickness and death could not touch us we would live for ever amidst corruption and temptation, and would probably have no wish for a new heaven and earth at all. In our weakness we are not wrong to pray for miracles, and sometimes God in his grace does suspend the laws of nature, but our normal course is to bear our share of adversity, to experience our measure of fallenness, to weep with those who weep before finally and thankfully entering the unfallen realm which will be our eternal home.

[73] R220-221 (cf. Mt 10:29-31; Lk 21:18; Rom 8:28). Many have found comfort and assurance in time of trial through such New Testament scriptures as Jn 17:15; Rom 5:3-5; 8:31-39; 2 Cor 1:3-11; 4:6-18; 2 Thess 3:3; Heb 12:1-11; Jas 1:12; 1 Pet 4:12-13; Jude 24.

[74] M401 (Ps 97:11 AV; Heb 12:10 AV)

[75] M401

[76] M354

[77] M418

[78] M9 (1 Pet 1:4 AV)

[79] M469

[80] M340

[81] M566-567

[82] M537

[83] M565

[84] Heb 5:8-9; 2:10

[85] M258

[86] M403

[87] Tit 2:14 RSV; Eph 5:27

[88] M445

[89] Heb 11:39-40

[90] M53

[91] M225

[92] R202

[93] R127

[94] 1 Cor 3:6, 8; Jn 4:37-38

[95] R163
[96] R282
[97] Mt 25:21
[98] 2 Tim 4:7-8; Heb 12:2
[99] Mt 5:11-12
[100] Mt 10:42; 6:6; 6:18; 6:3-4; 10:41; 19:29. On treasures in heaven see Lk 12:33; 18:22.
[101] R283
[102] Col 1:24 GNB
[103] M233 (referring to 1 Thess 3:8). See also Groves, *Christian Influence*, 63. An understanding of our corporate standing in Christ may shed light on that famous assurance which has comforted so many in time of trial: "All things work together for good to *them* that love God, to *them* who are *the called* according to his purpose" (Rom 8:28 AV). This verse does not claim that sickness and death are "good" for the individual. On the contrary, they are a great evil, evidence of a judgment and a curse; death indeed is the last and greatest enemy (1 Cor 15:26). But it shows that God works individual suffering for communal good, i.e. to the collectivity of "those who love him", those who are in their totality described as "the Called". An individual may endure pain with no personal benefit in this world. Stephen battered by stones, John confined on Patmos, Jeremiah thrown down a well, John the Baptist imprisoned, Jesus himself crucified – none of these saw an earthly reward. But each of them, through suffering, brought everlasting blessing to the people of God, and from an eternal perspective the blessing of the whole will never fail to bring joy to the one.
[104] M413
[105] M400
[106] 1 Ki 8:18 RSV
[107] M437
[108] M414
[109] Job 42:7-8
[110] Groves H, *Congleton*, 109, quoting Luke 10:21
[111] Eph 6:16-17
[112] Rev 2:7 etc.
[113] 1 Cor 13:13
[114] M567
[115] M478
[116] M329
[117] Ps 107:30
[118] M368
[119] 1 Cor 15:54
[120] 1 Cor 15:58
[121] M489. Theologians generally identify three elements that must find a place in any Christian view of suffering. We have seen the profound insight that Norris Groves had into all three: 1. punitive (*this disjointed world*) 2. educative (*to strengthen and bless*) 3. eschatological (*prepared for the inheritance*).

"My earnest desire is
to re-model the whole plan of missionary operations
so as to bring them
to the simple standard of God's word."

Norris Groves [1]

31

This Plan of Missions

The Whole Circle

When Norris Groves first left England there were many things on his mind, and one of these was a desire to put into practice his conception of the Church – to demonstrate his willingness to enjoy fellowship with all disciples of Christ, whatever their doctrinal peculiarities and institutional labels. Travelling east he wrote of the freedom he enjoyed in not having to represent any religious denomination or organisation: "I feel I am happy in having no system to support in moving among either professing Christians or Mahomedans. To the one, a person so situated can truly say, 'I do not desire to bring you over to any church, but to the simple truth of God's word.' And to the others, 'We wish you to read the New Testament that you may learn to judge of God's truth, not by what you see in the churches around you, but by the word of God itself.'"[2] Groves could relate to every Christian he met simply as a brother or sister in Christ, equally loved, equally precious, and equally worthy to be honoured and served. And he could offer Christ to the Muslim or Hindu without having to defend or justify the transgressions of churches ancient or modern.

On his journey to Baghdad, wherever he found Anglican chaplains, Moravian colonists, Lutheran evangelists, or the occasional Congregationalist, Presbyterian or Quaker, Groves invariably introduced himself, and he always received a friendly welcome. Despite the lack of a common language, and contrasting views of doctrine and practice, his vision was everywhere confirmed by the sense of oneness in Christ he experienced with these hardy pioneers.

Four years later, one of his stated aims on his first visit to India was "to become united more truly in heart with all the missionary band there, and show that notwithstanding all differences we are one in Christ, sympathising in their sorrows and rejoicing in their prosperity."[3] Groves, indeed, was pleased with what he found on the subcontinent, especially in Ceylon where missionaries from various societies were meeting regularly for prayer. John Kitto was similarly impressed with the happier sense of Christian unity he found beyond the shores of England. In Malta everyone was pulling together – English,

Germans and Americans; Anglicans, Methodists and Congregationalists. "Christians in all places," he said, "are known to each other and sympathise with each other."[4] Experience everywhere showed a much warmer sense of Christian love and co-operation on the mission field than in the comfort of the so-called Christian homeland.

Although Norris Groves, in 1828, had severed his formal connection with the Church Missionary Society, he was pleased to maintain friendly relations with its home committee. Indeed, as he left for Baghdad, Edward Bickersteth arranged to send out "by the first ship" any personal letters his friends might wish to send him addressed to the CMS office in London. "I take this most kindly at their hands," said Groves.[5] He also kept in close touch with the Lutherans of the Basel Mission, and in due course was happy to be equally yoked with one of their most promising young workers, Karl Pfander. In India he went out of his way to help the CMS agent Karl Rhenius, sent assistance to William Start's Baptist mission in Patna, asked the Lutheran Gundert to join him at Chittoor, welcomed the Congregationalist Scudder brothers to Arcot and Vellore, and ministered for twenty years to groups of Anglicans wherever he was invited. It delighted him to hear of clergy and laymen of the Church of England supporting Bowden and Beer, identified at that time as "poor unordained Baptist missionaries".[6] Norris Groves was a fisher of men, not a stealer of sheep, and he would never wish to compete with other Christian workers or missionary agencies. Indeed, the twelve young workers he recruited for India, during his fourteen months in Europe (1835-6), went on to five different centres and served with four different denominations. His desire was to be a servant to all who served Christ, and in his own words, "to show them the beauty and glory of being contented with Christ as a *Head* and his word as a *guide*."[7]

To Groves's mind Christian unity, both overseas and at home, was a very simple matter. "The unity of God," he said, "is found in the union of all who possess the common life from Jesus."[8] And this, as he described it, meant "union with the whole circle of God's redeemed family, without exclusive attachment to any section of it."[9] It was a spiritual unity embracing all who had personal faith in Jesus: "Loyalty to Christ is what I seek in every Christian, not zeal for his own particular views, or the views of any sect, however designated."[10]

One might have thought this would compel him, when settled in Madras, to participate as a regular member in one of the existing congregations, or perhaps to visit and minister to them all. But he was too much of a free spirit to conform to the expectations of any traditional church, and those that existed would not, in any case, allow him to minister. His own regular fellowship in Madras was with "the little church in our house" where "thirteen of us generally break bread together."[11] In Chittoor too, the Anglicans and Nonconformists who met with him developed under his leadership into an informal fellowship of a type familiar to the Brethren in England and elsewhere. He encouraged similar groups to develop in neighbouring towns, and over the years he continued to visit and prepare teaching for them. But attendance at such meetings required no one to sever other church connections, and these fellowships were given no formal name or identity. He would not see them as the start of a new denomination – simply as an expression of the freedom that Christians possess to meet together wherever and whenever they feel led to do so. Norris Groves saw himself as a servant of Christ and of the Church of Christ, not of any small part of it. "He was an incurable individualist and yet his sympathies were so large that it can rightly be claimed that he belonged to the Christian community at large."[12]

Groves was sensitive to the dilemma faced by a Christian unhappy with the church he attended. Without denying the importance of unity, he believed it equally important for a disciple of Christ to act according to his conscience and his personal reading of God's word. And the two desires – for unity and for obedience – might sometimes pull a believer in two different directions. What was to be done in such a case? "In *theory* nothing can be more simple and apparently true than that if you are all 'baptised into one body' by one Spirit you ought to speak the same thing and be of the same judgment. But in *fact*, nothing is more certain than that, notwithstanding the unity of the body and the unity of the baptism, this is not and never has been the case. We must therefore in a multitude of cases leave every man to be 'fully persuaded in his own mind'. In smaller matters, this will be easy; in graver, it will be better to form small separate households of faith, in love, each preserving their conscience inviolate, than that either party should coerce others into their views and opinions."[13]

This meant that if a Christian could not reconcile it with his conscience to participate in one congregation, he should find another where he saw the doctrine and practice to be more scriptural. As a last resort, he would be free to form his own group. Unity would not be broken by his doing so, for he would still be part of the spiritual body of Christ that included the brothers and sisters he had left. Indeed, it would be better to separate in love than to remain bound to those whose teachings and practices forced him to act against the leading of the Lord and the principles of his word.

The unity that Groves envisaged was a mystical unity, not an organisational unity. It was a unity of individuals, each individual walking with God, and each individual free to follow the guidance of his conscience. But far from absolving the individual of responsibility for others, it increased his responsibility, extending it beyond the limits of his own church or mission or denomination to embrace all true Christians everywhere. The believer was part of the spiritual body of Christ comprising all who belonged to Christ, wherever and however they might worship, and he must play his part for the well-being of the body as a whole. "Jesus meant his church to be a body," Groves observed, "not isolated members. We have each a little ministry essential to the happiness and building up of the mystical body – that there should be no schism, but that all the members might love and care one for the other."[14]

In practice, Norris Groves never attempted to draw Christians away from other groups to a circle of his own, and he was never accused of causing actual divisions.[15] Introducing himself first to clergy or missionary leaders in every town he came to, he was careful never to undermine existing authority. He taught, when invited, in churches and fellowships of whatever denomination, and when this privilege was withdrawn (as it was in his home town of Chittoor), he resisted the temptation to split the congregation and take away from it a body of his own supporters. "To have a ring of churches looking up to him as their founder does not seem to have had any attraction for him; else he might surely have had it."[16]

Even less attractive was the idea of founding his own missionary society. Had he wished to do so – perhaps an India Inland Mission – there was ample opportunity, but his journals and letters show no trace of such an idea. He knew how to recruit workers, but as we have seen, he sent almost all to assist Anglican and Nonconformist pioneers in other places. Perhaps he lacked the toughness, the thick skin, the air of authority required for a successful church or mission director. Perhaps he remembered that those who joined him in Baghdad and Madras did not long follow his lead. Perhaps he sensed a personal lack of administrative ability (although a capable assistant could have met that deficiency). But over and above all these personal considerations stood his belief that the fulfilment of the Great Commission required not the establishment of a new denomination or organisation but a simple obedience of individual Christians to the word of Christ.

In modern terms Groves was what we might call a "facilitator". He would be an advocate of "partnership", drawing together workers from existing agencies rather than creating a new agency of his own. Arriving in Jaffna, Ceylon, in 1834, he looked forward to attending "a meeting of all the missionaries of all denominations for prayer and general communication which takes place every month." He was not disappointed; it was "a very delightful meeting… The subjects of discussion were most interesting."[17] As early as 1806, William Carey had made his worthy proposal for a missionary conference "of all denominations of Christians from the four corners of the world."[18] But Groves would go further than this. "I have every reason," he said, "to hope that the elements of union, which the Lord allows to exist among us, will lead to a missionary combination and service that, to some extent at least, will resemble what there was in the days of the apostles."[19]

In the mid-nineteenth century the idea of actually working together was regarded as unrealistic by most, and vigorously opposed by some. Despite his desire for consultation and prayer with "all denominations", Carey himself would take the Lord's Supper only with believers baptised as adults; many

Anglicans in their turn would refuse to take it with him. Andrew Fuller for the Baptist Missionary Society discouraged Carey's "pleasing dream", believing it could do more harm than good.[20] Likewise for the Church of England, although Henry Venn could say, "God grant that unity of spirit may ever exist," he warned that "unity of operations we are not prepared for, except where the object is so definite as in the Bible Society."[21] As General Secretary of the Church Missionary Society, Venn would not even contemplate combining CMS activity with the other Church of England agencies such as the SPG and SPCK, far less with denominations outside the Established Church. "In the constitution and management of missionary societies," he declared, "each section of the Church must conduct its operations upon its own distinctive denominational principles."[22]

The closest that the societies of the nineteenth century would approach to "missionary combination" was a system they termed "comity". A given area would be parcelled out between two or more missions or denominations so that each took responsibility for a defined district or language group. Where a mission agency had already occupied a territory, other agencies agreed not to intrude unless invited. The aim was to avoid unnecessary competition and duplication of effort, but the system caused serious difficulties, especially when a mission was thought to be failing to fulfil its commitment or when agencies not party to the original agreement subsequently arrived on the scene. In 1900 Edward Groves attended a joint mission conference in Madras where he found Anglicans, Nonconformists and Open Brethren, each working in distinct districts of southern India. He called it "a considerable advance in the way of 'comity' from the condition of former years."[23] But it fell far short of his father's ideal. Carey's successors were setting up Baptist churches in one district, Venn's establishing Anglican congregations in another, Methodists and Congregationalists elsewhere, but Groves had hoped for missionaries everywhere to work in partnership for the creation of local Christian fellowships quite independent of the foreign denominations.[24]

Subsequent years saw a measure of formal and informal missionary co-operation in many parts of the world, but the development of "partnerships" and "consultations" to support the growth of independent indigenous churches only became a major emphasis towards the very end of the twentieth century, through the influence of non-denominational agencies such as Interdev and the Billy Graham Organisation. But the idea goes back a long way. It may, in fact, be considered one of the greatest contributions of Norris Groves to the missiological scheme of things.

Messengers of the Churches

We could see this emphasis on missionary co-operation as the first facet of a threefold vision of Norris Groves for the kingdom of God in India. The second was for teams of Indian evangelists to take the gospel throughout their nation, and the third was for the establishment of genuinely biblical Indian churches.

Always sceptical of received wisdom and traditional assumptions, Groves looked directly to the Bible for guidance in developing these ideas. He was never so ill-mannered as to find fault with other missionaries, and he happily gave honour where honour was due, yet he believed there was a place – and a very significant place too – for some like himself who would simply follow the apostolic pattern. "I do not desire for one moment," he said, "to set myself in opposition to those blessed institutions whose labours roused us from our lethargy." On the contrary, "I desire to bless God for them and to co-operate with them whenever I can... I should rejoice to see them multiplied a hundredfold, for whosoever brings a stone to the temple of our Lord and King, by whatever different means they may have laboured with from ourselves, shall be our father, mother, sister, brother." And yet, he added, "I must say that I do not think their plan is the best, or the only good one."[25] As we look more closely at his approach to mission, we shall see why.

The most important single source for Norris Groves's missiological thought is "A Letter on Missions to the Heathen" reproduced in *The Christian Witness* of April 1840.[26] Here Groves sets out what he calls his "plan for carrying out missions". He starts by quoting extensively from a recent article in a periodical called *The Friend of India* which was highly critical of the missionary societies currently at work on the subcontinent. "In consequence of the monopoly of all power and influence in London," said the article, "a vast machinery has gradually been constructed, in the management of which the spirit of the missionary cause is deteriorated and runs every risk of becoming eventually extinct." The writer noted that "the affairs of these bodies are managed by an oligarchy, endowed with the dispensation of large sums... Through their affiliated societies they have acquired a paramount influence in the country, and by means of their salaried agents they wield that influence at will." Even the Indian newspapers must toe the Establishment line "so that nothing can reach the public ear but with their permission." The cost of religious buildings and salaries required such an enormous income that "they are obliged to use the most strenuous efforts to maintain their pecuniary position, and these efforts are not always in scrupulous accordance with the sacredness of the object." The tendency was all too clear: "The support of the *Society* becomes the primary object; that of the *cause* one of secondary importance."

So what is to be done? "The important question," Groves suggests, "is not so much to know what is *wrong* as to learn from the Lord what is *right*."[27] And as always he asks, "What does scripture teach?" Groves observed that the earliest Christians, meeting as "households of the faithful", were concerned for two things: firstly for the progress of their own family in the faith, and then, secondly, for the "spiritual welfare of others... For exactly in the same proportion in which any church realizes [i.e. fulfils] what it has found in Jesus will its *desire* be that others may be similarly enriched." How, then, did the early Christians set about sharing their spiritual riches with others? "I believe the offspring of this sympathy and love were the 'messengers of the churches'."[28] These "messengers of the churches" went sometimes to help other churches, but more often to preach the gospel to the unconverted. Taking nothing from the heathen, "they were entitled to the support of that church from whence they came out, to the extent of their reasonable wants, as also to the hospitality and love of those to whom they might come on their way."[29]

This is a plan easily adapted to any age. Some churches might be able to provide for several "messengers"; some might need to pool their resources together to support just one. But the missionary must always be considered the "messenger" of his or her own home fellowship. "Should it happen, as is very possible, that among the *poorest* churches there may be many whom the Lord had fitted and made free, it should be the *glory* of the richer churches to give them help, but never attempt on *that account* to transfer the *church* connection of the poorer church to themselves, because that would be breaking a spiritual connection which God has formed."

In practice, just as the Lord will guide the missionary in his service, so the Lord will guide the churches in their support of him – through a sense of the Spirit's leading and in answer to prayer. Nevertheless, "whatever support was given to help on any brother should be without any pledge of continuance or amount [*sic*]." There would be no arrangement that might put the missionary under obligation to those who supply his needs, or compel him to conform to their wishes. He must be free to obey God without desire for man's approval or fear of man's displeasure.

In the book of Acts Groves saw how the earliest missionaries were appointed. The local leaders at Antioch, through fasting and prayer, were led by the Spirit to set apart Barnabas and Saul for the work to which God had called them. With the blessing of the church, they were "sent on their way by the Holy Spirit."[30] This simple scheme bore no resemblance to the current custom of missionaries obtaining salaried appointments from official committees meeting in city offices, and financed through public appeals, subscriptions and the gracious patronage of prominent figures and men of the world. Groves took pains to emphasize that the missionary should be *sent* from the local church and *supported* by the local church, and he concluded, "The grand point therefore to be ever kept in view, in the union between the church and the evangelist going forth, is that it should be *as close as possible*, and this beyond all doubt will be when the messenger is sent by those who know him."[31]

In fact, as Groves pointed out, the apostolic method has a number of significant advantages. Firstly, it is "calculated to draw out the strongest and best affections as well as the sympathies of the church from which the missionary proceeds." He himself has been an active participant in the fellowship; they all know and love him. His friends and family will thus "seek for themselves a spirit to care for and sympathise with those who do thus go, and of whom they are the divinely appointed guardians on earth."

Secondly, it ensures that suitable people will be sent. "Christians in the midst of whom an individual has been walking would, as a general principle, be far better able to estimate both his excellencies and weaknesses, appreciating the one and making allowances for the other." The mischief caused by worldly men taking missionary appointments for the sake of salary and status would be ended, for the church would refuse to send or support them, and "few such, without the expectation of sympathy or support would be induced to undertake so profitless a service."

Thirdly, it will encourage cheerful giving. A church that has confidence in its "messenger" will be glad to support him generously, without any need for appeals, publicity or other forms of fund-raising. Once overseas, the missionary will write regularly with news of his progress, and the church will reply with encouragement, assurance of prayer and with whatever financial help they can send. "There would therefore be no need of that ensnaring evil, the publication of reports to excite the liberality of the public, as it is called."

Fourthly, it will allow the missionary complete freedom to do what he believes to be God's will. He will not be restricted by the resolutions of a committee, the decrees of a superintendent, or by a book of "principles and practice" that might take no account of the complex circumstances facing him. Although a home church will willingly offer counsel or advice to its "messenger", it will trust his own judgment concerning what he should do, without seeking either to direct or to obstruct his service to his Lord.

Fifthly, it will enable every fresh opportunity to be taken without deliberation or delay. If a need arises, the missionary can go immediately to meet it, without waiting for approval from a finance committee or a board of control.

Sixthly and lastly, it will greatly reduce the cost of taking the gospel into all the world. Indeed, Groves estimated, "it would enable us to carry out missions at one third the expense." The "messenger", without the social standing of an ordained clergyman, would have no need of a fine house, a carriage, servants, banquets and entertainments. He will choose to live as cheaply as he can, so that funds may provide for additional workers to join him or to pioneer in other places. And unlike a clergyman, he will quickly look for ways to provide for himself and for his co-workers. If he can become self-supporting, he may soon need no financial help at all.

This was what Groves called his "plan of missions", at least with regard to the sending and support of the missionaries themselves. What made it so radical was its focus on the local church. On biblical grounds Groves argued that a missionary should be sent by a church to plant churches, not appointed by a committee to promote a society. In his judgment, the greatest problem with missionary societies was that in practice their salaried agents felt more loyalty to the society than to the Church. "Very many of us," he remarked, "have felt the utter want of Church character and authority in all existing societies." Though he was glad for everything that the denominational missions had accomplished, the time had come, he believed, to look for a better way of working: "The grand point to be arrived at is that the Church act so as to prove that the work societies endeavour to accomplish with the world's help can be done better, because more scripturally, *by the Church herself.*"[32] And what is more, if the local church feels itself responsible to set apart and send "messengers", there will soon be "a real deep missionary spirit" in the church – a desire to send out more workers and as many workers as possible.[33]

The Native Churches

Anthony Norris Groves has been called "a neglected missiologist",[34] and there are reasons for the neglect. Among them we might recognise the fact that he was a great individualist (never the leader of an organisation wishing to immortalize his name), that his ideas lie scattered throughout his journals and letters (never collected into a systematically reasoned monograph), that the Brethren always regarded the New Testament itself as their manual of missionary principles (never feeling the need to supplement it with another), and that his own missionary efforts ended with some embarrassment. Seen in this light, the neglect was almost inevitable, and yet many ideas attributed to later writers find their first expression in the letters and journals of Norris Groves. And unlike some more recent missiologists, he actually learned a foreign language, spent most of his adult life in an alien culture, recruited missionaries, established them in pioneer situations and personally led people from other races to faith and to maturity in Christ.[35]

The nineteenth-century is often said to have produced three great mission thinkers: the British Anglican Henry Venn, the American Congregationalist Rufus Anderson and the American Presbyterian John Nevius. Of the three, only Nevius was a career missionary, and his experience was limited to China. Venn and Anderson have been described as "armchair missiologists" although both accumulated a great deal of information from the work of others.[36] The fact is that Norris Groves had a far wider personal knowledge of missionary problems and opportunities than any of them. He was concerned with the same issues that they raised, and his conclusions, scattered throughout his journals and letters, are as clear and coherent as anything to be found in the better-known writings of his three celebrated contemporaries.[37]

The fact that his thoughts are presented in letters and journals is typical of Groves himself. Although he was by nature an idealist, accused at times of being far too idealistic, his missiology was intensely practical. It grew out of personal experience and was tested in real situations. Though not by aptitude or inclination a scholar, he was a sensitive and perceptive man, and he had qualities that ideally equipped him to examine missionary strategy. To start with, he spent many hours in personal study of the scriptures, prayerfully waiting on God for fresh light on matters of difficulty. This indeed was his daily habit, and with his mind full of what Christ and the apostles had said and done, the life of the early church was fully as real to him in imagination as that of the churches in which he ministered. He was, of course, an experienced missionary and could speak colloquial Arabic with fluency. He had discussed the gospel with innumerable individuals from Muslim, Jewish, Catholic, Orthodox, Nestorian, Mar Thomist, Zoroastrian, and Hindu backgrounds. He had personal knowledge of Christian schools, villages and industries in many different places. He had debated missionary methods with scores of workers in western and eastern Europe, Russia, the Caucasus, Mesopotamia and most parts of India. For a period of fifteen years he had watched the growth of indigenous Indian churches under the leadership of John Arulappan. But in addition to this, there was one quality that made Norris Groves almost unique in his generation. It was his habit of seeking fellowship with Christians from backgrounds quite different to his own. His ecumenical spirit, and his freedom from obligation to any particular missionary agency or denomination, meant that he was open to influences from every direction, without being required to toe any party line, or feign a diplomatic neutrality on any issue, or patch up systems inherited from others.

The question that exercised Venn, Anderson, Nevius, and Groves himself, was simply this: How might an English or American missionary establish churches in a foreign country – churches that would be thoroughly indigenous, flourishing under the leadership of people native to that country?

In 1854 Venn proposed his "three-self" vision for an emerging national church. Established initially by the missionary society, the church would gradually acquire a capability for self-government, self-support and self-propagation. Though started by Church of England missionary agencies such as the CMS or the SPCK, it would become a Church of India, for example, administered by Indians, or a Church of Nigeria led by Nigerians. Along with this went Venn's concept of the foreign mission as a *scaffolding* which must remain until the national church has been firmly built, and then *removed* once it is able to stand alone. Venn saw the missionary society as a temporary necessity. It would buy land, construct buildings, and train and ordain local ministers to lead services and administer the sacraments, and then "once the mission has brought a church into being, it may die out in that area."[38] Venn summarised his proposal: "It is important ever to keep in view what has been happily termed 'the euthanasia of a mission', where the missionary is surrounded by well-trained native congregations under native pastors, when he gradually and wisely abridges his own labours and relaxes his superintendence over the pastors till they are able to sustain their own Christian ordinances, and the district ceases to be a missionary field and passes into Christian parishes under the constituted ecclesiastical authorities."[39] Simultaneously, and perhaps coincidentally, Rufus Anderson in America proposed a similar scheme, whereby his Congregationalist *mission* would establish Indian or African Congregationalist *churches*.

Fourteen years earlier, Norris Groves had suggested a very different approach. He would make no distinction between *church* and *mission*. Indeed, the mission was the church, and the church was the mission. "The work societies endeavour to accomplish," he said, "can be done better, because more scripturally, *by the Church herself*."[40] There was no question in his mind of a foreign scaffolding to be erected and then dismantled, no extension and then "euthanasia" of a Western organisation.

Missionaries and ministers whose institutions have ceased to follow the apostolic example are taught to see nothing of particular ecclesiological significance in the New Testament, or at best to discern in it vague parallels to systems that developed several centuries later. Venn's biographer characteristically claims that "the Acts account is silent concerning the form of ecclesiastical order and discipline."[41] But Norris Groves, from the Acts account, learned a great deal about ecclesiastical order and discipline, and he saw no reason to reject the apostolic method in favour of one developed by a later generation. In the New Testament Groves saw churches sending messengers to establish churches. The process could not be more clear and simple – the preaching of the gospel, the gathering of converts, the growth of an active local fellowship, the spontaneous emergence of gifted local leaders, the sending of new messengers to preach the gospel further afield. Here was a dynamic vision for the spontaneous growth of indigenous churches bearing the word of God to the ends of the earth.

In order to appreciate the radical nature of Groves's thought, we must give some attention to the assumptions and objectives of his contemporaries. A belief in the White Man's Burden was deeply rooted in the missionary psyche of the day – the benevolent responsibility of the favoured nations to labour for the improvement of native peoples in less fortunate parts of the globe. Rufus Anderson, as Secretary of the American Board of Commissioners for Foreign Missions, rejoiced that "the civilisation which the gospel has conferred upon our New England is the highest and best, in a religious point of view, the world has yet seen."[42] In his generation the contrast between the developed West and the primitive societies found elsewhere was too obvious to need any emphasis, and his biographer simply observes that he "had no respect for Oriental, Pacific and African cultures and religions."[43] Anderson's ambition was to introduce Christian principles to foreign lands and thus raise them gradually to the spiritual level of New England. The more that native peoples became Christianised and civilised the more closely they would naturally come to resemble the cultured citizens of Boston or London. Henry Venn likewise believed that undeveloped nations particularly needed the "European mind and intelligence to regulate, mature and discipline the congregations of native converts." "Let it be remembered," he said, "that the great principle of Protestant missions is *native agency under European superintendence*. Hence our large and expensive educational establishments to raise up an educated class."[44]

To mission secretaries with this background, the "scaffolding" was absolutely essential, for as yet only the Americans and Europeans really knew how a proper church or community or civilisation might be established and maintained! To his credit Venn believed "that the new church ought to be left as free as possible to adapt ecclesiastical forms inherited from the missions."[45] This was certainly an improvement on the view that the national church should *retain* the ecclesiastical forms inherited from the missions, but it assumed that the mission must introduce "ecclesiastical forms" in the first place.

The year 1851, however, marked a turning point for Venn. For twenty years he had approved the extensive education of native peoples by missionary teachers, but financial pressures meant that the CMS could no longer afford to pay the salaries of the vast body of workers associated with the Mission. He now suggested turning over all the schools in India to the secular government so that missionaries would be set free from the classroom to rediscover the joys of itinerant evangelism. The CMS would still guarantee the salaries of the missionaries and their "native assistants", but the local congregations must start to pay their own ministers and schoolteachers. The wages of the Indian catechists – previously paid by the Mission – must become the responsibility of the local churches too. Venn's proposals met with resistance everywhere. The missionaries protested that they would be deprived of a valuable teaching role and would be separated from the congregations that required their oversight. The Indian Christians complained that they could not afford to maintain the large buildings and the multitude of employees associated with the Church of England in India. As for handing over the mission schools to the government, this would cause the whole nation to identify the Christian religion with the British Empire, which would be disastrous for the cause of the gospel. Ten years later, to Venn's frustration, little had changed. The CMS was still paying the salaries; the missionaries were still looking after the churches; and a "mission station" mentality was still stifling *mission*.[46]

Venn bemoaned the fact that Anglican agencies were less successful in producing indigenous churches than the Baptists in Burma, the Congregationalists in Armenia and the native Christians (after the expulsion of the foreign missionaries) in Madagascar. The need was simply for better organisation. In England, he noted, "the clergy find everything relating to elementary organisation settled by the Law of the Land – as in the provision of tithes, of church rates, of other customary payments, in the constitution of parishes, and in parish officers. Our clergy are not prepared for the question of Church organisation, and therefore in the Missions they exercise the ministry of the word without reference to the non-existence of the organisation by which it is supported at home." Venn then proposed a method to remedy "this imperfection in Church Missions". He would start by "introducing into the Native Church that elementary organisation which may give it 'corporate life' and prepare it for its full development under a native ministry and an indigenous episcopate."[47] "It will be seen," he said, "that the proposed scheme or organisation will prepare the Native Church for ultimately exhibiting in its Congregational and District Conferences, the counterpart of the Parish, and the Archdeaconry, under the Diocesan Episcopacy of our own Church system."[48] This, Venn hoped, would enable Anglicanism to become Indian.

Across the Atlantic, Rufus Anderson was following the same line of reasoning. His biographer asserts that by the end of his life he had been "acclaimed as the restorer of the apostolic model for mission, and all North American overseas missionary agencies professed to follow his teaching and to act on his principles."[49] Impressive as this eulogy may sound, its warrant is simply his insistence on establishing churches rather than educational or medical institutions.[50] But Anderson himself argued that the Congregationalist missions under his control differed substantially from those of apostolic times, and were, he believed, in most respects superior! Firstly, the missionaries themselves were sent out by "churches of long standing and experience", from a land of "freedom and high religious intelligence", which gave them "a great advantage over the primitive missions". Secondly, modern missionaries, though lacking the apostles' miraculous powers, possessed the entire New Testament in printed form. But thirdly, and most significantly, Anderson observed that "the pastorate in modern missions differs from that of the apostolic age, in that it ordinarily has but one pastor for each church, whereas the New Testament always uses the plural in speaking of the pastorate in the churches planted by the apostle Paul." He quotes appropriately from the Acts of the Apostles, "They appointed elders for them in each church."[51] But then he comments, "This practice seems to have been lost, with the very idea of the apostolic church, in the great decline of the Early and Middle Ages; and when that idea was recovered, as it was at the Reformation, and put in practice, the usage of having but one pastor in each church was adopted by all evangelical denominations as being more conformed to the demands of the age. And this is now the general usage in all the evangelical churches; and it has thence been transferred to the mission churches among the heathen. The apostolic principle is retained, but the form is changed."[52] The change is undeniable, but we might wonder whether Anderson's justification of it as "more conformed to the demands of the age" would make it something to be imposed automatically on every culture in every age. In reality, the "apostolic principle" had been lost, and the "form" he advocated was, by his own admission, that of the Middle Ages.

The implication was very clear. For Anderson, the ordination of a "native pastor" was the key to creating a local church. "I now enquire," he said, "what should be the nature of the mission church? It should be composed only of hopeful converts, and should have, as soon as possible, a native pastor, and of the same race, who has been trained cheerfully to take the oversight of what will generally be a small, poor, ignorant people, and mingle with them familiarly and sympathetically. And by a native pastor I mean one recognised as having the pastoral care of a local church, with the right to administer the ordinances of baptism and the Lord's Supper." In short, the foreign missionary (paid by the mission) should hand over his responsibilities as soon as possible to a native pastor (paid by the church): "As soon as the mission church has a native pastor, the responsibilities of self-government should be devolved upon it...The salary of the native pastor should be based on the Christianised ideas of living acquired by his people, and the church should become self-supporting at the very earliest possible day."[53]

But where were these pastors to come from? Anderson urged the establishment of a seminary at each major mission station, where suitable young men could, in his own words, "pursue their theological studies" before being "set apart for the sacred ministry". He elaborates his scheme: "It is an essential feature of the plan that the pupils be taken young, board in the mission, be kept separate from heathenism, under Christian superintendence night and day. In general, the course of study should embrace a period of from eight to ten or twelve years, and an even longer time in special cases... In due time they may be licensed to preach, and after proper trial, receive ordination as evangelists or pastors."[54]

Anderson admitted that the education of such pastors was a difficult process, especially as they must be "trained to system and order".[55] He advised against "requiring too much of the native converts before we are willing to entrust them with the ministry of the word." "Generations," he judged, "must pass before a community emerging from the depths of heathenism can be expected to furnish a body of ministers equal to that in our country."[56] Indeed, there were inevitable dangers to forestall, one of them being the ordination ceremony itself, which could "inflame the self-conceit and ambition remaining in the heart of the heathen convert." He warned that "the native pastors themselves are, for a season, but 'babes in Christ', children in experience, knowledge and character. And hence missionaries who entertain the idea that ordination must have the effect to place the native pastors at once on a perfect equality with themselves are often backward in intrusting the responsibilities of the pastoral office to natives. They fear, and justly, the effects of this sudden comparative exaltation."[57] But he reassured his apprehensive missionary colleagues that they would still retain a powerful means of control over the churches, since "a wise disbursement of funds will provide all the checks which are necessary or proper."[58]

Here then was Anderson's implementation of his vision for self-governing, self-supporting and self-propagating churches. It was well-intentioned, benevolent and optimistic, but the exact opposite of what we see in the New Testament. He cheerfully pointed out that in India native pastors should cost a lot less to support than American missionaries. They might be expected to "travel on foot", to "live... upon rice alone, with a piece of cotton cloth wrapped about their bodies for clothing, and a mud-walled grass covered cottage without furniture for a dwelling."[59] But Anderson evidently failed to foresee, until it was too late, that an Indian pastor, ordained after ten years' theological study, might consider himself entitled to the same living standards as an American missionary. Such a pastor would need a large wealthy church to assure his salary. Failing that (heaven forbid!), he must be added to the payroll of the American Board! And having been "kept separate from heathenism" for ten years, would such a pastor still remember how to communicate anything useful to the Hindus and Muslims outside?[60]

By 1850 Anderson had become thoroughly disillusioned with these English-speaking schools and seminaries. He attempted to close them, and he encouraged his colleagues on the field to direct their energies to itinerant evangelism, and, if they really felt it necessary, to small schools taught in the local dialects. But his proposed changes, like Venn's, met with vehement opposition from members of his own mission. He was continually frustrated by colleagues on the field who wanted to pastor churches, teach in boarding schools and oversee mission stations. Like Venn he became increasingly desperate to dismantle the mission scaffolding, but the missionaries knew better than he did that without the scaffolding the building would simply collapse.[61]

John Nevius added a number of useful and perceptive refinements to the "three-self" formula. He proposed that a Mission should only introduce programmes and institutions which the national churches desired and could support, that native evangelists should be given intensive Bible training, and that local Christians should choose their own pastors and erect their own buildings using local materials.[62] But though Nevius wished to simplify things, and to make it as easy as possible for local Christians to take responsibility, he too, like Venn and Anderson, was the salaried agent of a Western denomination, in his case the American Presbyterian Mission Board. Even as he wrote, a *Presbyterian* synod existed in China to oversee the *Presbyterian* churches that he and his colleagues hoped to establish. Rufus Anderson, for his part, confidently declared that *Congregationalism* was the system "best adapted to our day". Henry Venn fully expected his CMS missionaries to translate the *Anglican* Prayer Book into every language so that the Native Churches could follow the order of service with its designated Lessons and Collects, morning and evening, every Sunday of the Church calendar. Venn's biographer remarks, "Few men have done more to promote episcopacy as a form of church government all over the world."[63]

For Venn, Anderson and Nevius, "indigenisation" simply meant appointing native Christians to do what foreign missionaries had previously done, according to the requirements of their particular denomination. But it is clear that for each of them the real key to indigenisation lay in the management of money. Of the "three-selfs" which they advocated, it was "self-support" that really concerned them. Anderson frankly admitted that among the missionaries themselves, "most of the questions that arise have more or less connection with finance."[64] For Venn the priority was the establishment in each locality of a "Native Church Fund" to which the local believers would contribute. Indeed, as soon as there were a few converts, they must be instructed about "making the weekly collections".[65] "The first step in the organization of the Native Church," he said, "will be taken when any company, or one or more neighbouring companies unitedly, shall be formed into a congregation having a *Schoolmaster*, or Native Teacher, located among them, whose salary is paid out of the Native Church Fund." The missionary in charge would judge when enough money had been contributed. Then, "the second step in the organisation of the Native Church will be taken when one or more congregations are formed into a *Native Pastorate*, under an ordained native, paid by the Native Church Fund... This step may be taken as soon as the congregations are sufficiently advanced and the payments to the Native Church Fund shall be sufficient to authorise the same."[66] The third step involved the establishment of a District Conference consisting of clergy and laymen, nationals and missionaries. Then when the Native Church Funds were finally able to afford an episcopal stipend, a bishop would be enthroned for them, with mitre and crosier and coloured robes brought out from England. What it meant was that the church could progress through the stages of increasing organisational complexity just as far as the congregations paid money into the Native Church Fund. This was the meaning of "self-support". On the same basis, "self-propagation" meant the congregations paying the wages of the evangelists; "self-government" meant the congregations paying for the upkeep of the properties.

This was Venn's ideal. In practice the local catechists, teachers and pastors were already receiving salaries from the CMS and were reluctant to lose them. They naturally raised the question: If the wealthy patrons of the CMS are able to finance the church, why should the poor Indian believers be asked to do so? Venn was forced to concede, "In older missions the change of system should be very gradual. For when a mission has grown up in dependence upon

European missionaries and upon native agency salaried by European funds, the attempt to curtail summarily its pecuniary aid, before the introduction of a proper organisation, will be like casting a person overboard before he has been taught to swim."[67]

Despite Venn's optimism it is all too evident that indigenous churches cannot be created by well-meaning London secretaries imposing "a proper organisation". There is a basic problem underlying his whole scheme. If a mission has put up the organisational scaffolding then the mission has already designed the building. But the New Testament does not show us wealthy missions establishing complex organisations and then charging others with their maintenance; it shows us poor apostles preaching the gospel, teaching those who respond, and letting them develop their own fellowships in their own premises. Groves saw clearly enough the dire consequences of foreign denominations making everything far too complicated, far too static, and far too expensive. Rather than projecting an eventual shift from foreign government, support and propagation to self-government, support and propagation, Groves would start with no organised government, support or propagation at all, expecting these to develop naturally as local believers considered the needs and possibilities before them in the light of the New Testament. "My earnest desire," he said, "is to re-model the whole plan of missionary operations so as to bring them to the simple standard of God's word."[68] As an administrator, Norris Groves cannot compare with Henry Venn or Rufus Anderson, but as a practical missiologist he is arguably their superior. "It must be obvious to all," he declared: "If the native churches be not strengthened by learning to lean on the Lord instead of man, the political changes of an hour may sweep away the present form of things, so far as it depends on Europeans, and leave not a trace behind."[69]

To be fair to both Venn and Anderson, we must recognise that they were responsible for the administration of things as they were, having inherited a system not of their making. They were never free to imagine the ideal and pursue it. Indeed, they were forced to compromise in almost every situation, and often had great difficulty persuading missionaries to allow native converts any responsibility at all. In fact, after Venn's death, the CMS abandoned his policies altogether and built up an ever more elaborate, expensive and intimidating organisational structure under European control. Subsequent missionary leaders have added a multiplicity of suggestions and propositions in their attempts to put the "three-self" scheme into effect. But almost all are starting from a position of weakness. Their first assumption is that one institution (a mission board) must create a separate institution (an indigenous church). Their second is that both must be staffed and supervised by salaried employees. Their third is that denominational identities and authority structures, hallowed by long usage in the homeland, should be imposed on the rest of the world. These assumptions we might think seriously flawed.

Indigenous Movements

Missionaries and missiologists have almost always paid lip service to what they perceive as apostolic principles, but few have been able to step outside their denominational framework sufficiently to admit that the church denominations born in one country have no right at all to exist in another. In his day, as in ours, Norris Groves stands out as a most unusual kind of missionary. He belonged to no denomination; he was subject to no mission board. No one could claim the right to oversee his work or to discipline his converts. There was no reason for Arabs or Indians to think he might provide them with status or a salary, or a church building, for he was obviously as poor as they were themselves. All he could offer was spiritual, and it was the spiritual that drew people to him, and through him to Christ. By helping local Christians *spiritually* he enabled *them* to take the initiatives that would give rise to a genuinely indigenous church.

This is surely the most exciting aspect of Norris Groves's vision – the ease with which it stimulates vigorous indigenous initiatives. Church of England missionaries were astonished to see Indian believers setting out from Christianpettah and preaching to their own people. The *Church Missionary Intelligencer* for August 1860 declared, "It is indeed a new era in Indian missions – that of lay converts going forth, without purse or scrip, to preach the gospel of Christ to their fellow-countrymen, and that with a zeal and life we had hardly thought them capable of." Here, the writer believed, was "the first entirely indigenous effort of the native church at self-extension."[70] Perhaps he was led to wonder why he had never seen such things among his own converts.

What he saw was, in fact, the fulfilment of Norris Groves's vision. In 1840 Groves had encouraged John Arulappan and his Indian friends to establish a completely Indian fellowship at Christianpettah. Eighty-five years later a British visitor to Christianpettah wrote, "The meeting continues to grow with no European control, presence or money. It is this fact, almost unique in India, that brought me down for their three-day annual meetings... Two trained lads are supported to teach their two primary schools, and for their support, and the repairs to the buildings, the church has one yearly offering... when they bring sacks (or handfuls) of grain, an egg or a basket of eggs, vegetables, fowls by the score, calves etc. and the girls bring babies' garments, fancy bags etc. Much is sold at once to the village merchants. It was... carried through with a good deal of heart exercise on the part of many of these very poor folk."[71] This assembly was an Indian initiative from first to last, and the building in which three hundred regularly met had been erected by them at their own expense. Arulappan's biographer asks why it is that other churches – those connected with foreign denominations – seem unable to provide for themselves like this, and he remarks, "The fact is that they can and will... if Arulappan's plan, that is the apostolic plan, be followed, of first building the spiritual house, the company of really converted people, and then training and leaving them to build the material things needed."[72]

After the death of Venn and Anderson, most of their ideas were forgotten amidst the scramble of competing denominations. In 1910 a controversial International Missionary Conference in Edinburgh gave a fresh airing to the concept of the indigenous church as the offspring of the foreign mission. Two years later, largely as a reaction to what was said there, a book appeared with the title *Missionary Methods, St Paul's or Ours?* Its author, Roland Allen, was acclaimed as "prophetic", "one of the most seminal missiological and ecclesiological minds of this century".[73] He was reckoned to be fifty years ahead of his time. Allen advised a return to the methods of Christ and the apostles. He warned that national church leaders would not long tolerate the dominion of foreign church leaders, that technological progress and social justice should not be confused with faith in Christ, that truly indigenous churches cannot be established by foreign mission boards, that Christian institutions cannot turn people into Christians. He argued that evangelism must be the task of ordinary people rather than paid professionals, that the best way to train disciples is by living with them, that unordained native Christians must be trusted to preach and teach and celebrate the Lord's Supper, that Christian unity is unity of life rather than organisational control. All this had been said by Norris Groves eighty years before.

Allen suggested that the reason missionary societies have struggled to plant churches is because they have started with a society rather than a church. Groves, as we have seen, had his mind focused from the very beginning on the church, and on the missionary calling of the church, as did the friends who caught his vision (Bowden, Beer, Arulappan and his circle of Indian evangelists). "My object in India," said Groves, "is two-fold: to try to check the operation of these exclusive systems by showing in the Christian Church they are not necessary for all that is holy and moral; and to try and impress upon every member of Christ's body that he has some ministry given him for the body's edification – and instead of depressing, encouraging each one to come forward and serve the Lord. I have it much at heart, should the Lord spare me, to form a church on these principles."[74]

Many recent thinkers have come round to this point of view. Among Anglican historians, Stephen Neill, writing in 1964, considered Venn's distinction between "church" and "mission" ill-advised, favouring the methods of Bishop Tucker who, from 1897 onwards, encouraged missionaries in Uganda to identify with the "Native Anglican Church" rather than with the CMS.[75] Likewise in Cairo, Temple Gairdner emphasized the partnership of foreign missionaries and local Anglican clergy working together as brothers and equals in the ongoing life of the church, and he himself set an outstanding example in this.[76] Similarly in Lahore, Thomas French endeavoured to draw together the divergent Indian and English wings of the Anglican Church and pressed for the creation of Indian synods to oversee church activities.[77]

But these men, though enlightened to a large degree, still took for granted the idea that their foreign denomination (considered catholic or universal) should be exported to other continents and then directed by foreigners until such time as leadership could be passed to local men. Gairdner himself, though strongly committed to inter-mission and inter-denominational co-operation, deliberately directed his energies to the establishment of an "Egyptian Anglican Church". In 1921 he wrote, "We decided to have one real shot at getting *on*: to take stock of our members, quasi-members, adherents, see who was who, have a campaign of explaining what the Anglican Church is, what it stands for in Egypt, what is its order, liturgy, aim, spirit: regularize, take hold, take stock, rekindle, and finally ordain the first Egyptian pastor, as a first step towards building up a really indigenous non-foreign church."[78] As Canon of St Mary's (and subsequently The Church of the Saviour), he habitually walked through the streets of Cairo in clerical collar, cassock and mortar-board, and he would expect ordained Egyptians to do the same.[79] Thomas French in Lahore, though wary of high-church rituals likely to stifle the growth of Indian forms of worship, still held firmly to the idea of apostolic succession, whereby episcopal authority had been handed down from the apostles to each successive generation of Catholic and then Anglican bishops, who must in turn pass on this mystic authority to Indians ordained at their own hands.[80] Mission strategy for these men was defined by the nature of the Church to which they belonged, and there was no escaping from it.

In 1938 Watchman Nee observed missionaries in his native China promoting Venn's "three-self" values in their frustrated attempts to hand over leadership of their congregations to the Chinese, and he commented, "Such problems would never have come up for consideration if the principles shown us in God's word had been adhered to from the very beginning…Wherein lies the failure of missions today? They keep the results of their work in their own hand. In other words they have reckoned *their* converts as members of *their* mission, or of *their* mission church."[81]

Nee gave honour to the sacrificial work of many missionaries in China, but he observed what kind of Christianity they had brought with them. "According to the present-day conception," he remarked, "three things are regarded as essential to the existence of a church… These three are a 'minister', a church building and 'church services'… But what is considered essential to a church these days was considered totally unnecessary in the early days of the church's history."[82] His proposal was, "Let us see what the word of God has to say on the matter,"[83] and he observed, "The apostolic procedure was quite simple. The apostles visited a place, founded a church, left that church for a while, then returned to establish it. In the interval, certain developments would naturally take place. When the apostles left, some of the professing believers would leave too. Others… would make no appreciable progress. Others again would eagerly press on… Those who had more spiritual life than others would spontaneously come to the front and take responsibility for their weaker brethren. It was because they had proved themselves to be elders that the apostles appointed them to hold office as elders, and it was *their* business to shepherd and instruct the other believers."[84]

Nee's study of the New Testament convinced him that churches should be led by a group of unpaid elders, that these should be "local brothers" rather than men trained elsewhere, that full-time workers should be evangelists rather than pastors, and that these evangelists should look directly to God for guidance and support without salary or obligation to man. He observed that all who are born of the Spirit are automatically members of the church, that every member has a vital function in the body, that meetings will be informal with much spontaneous participation, and that they will generally take place in the homes of the believers. Although a hall or public place may be rented or borrowed for occasional conferences, "we must remember," he said, "that the ideal meeting places of the saints are their own private homes."[85]

For Watchman Nee this was not just abstract missiological theory; it was the practical basis of an indigenous movement that grew rapidly from small beginnings in the early 1920s. It evidently satisfied a widely felt need, for within a short time the loose network of house fellowships associated with Nee had more adherents than any other Christian group in China. Though some undoubtedly transferred to his "Little Flock" from other churches, most were conversions. He described how he and his co-workers would take the gospel to an unreached town and start a church. "Suppose we go to Kweiyang to work, what should be our procedure? On arrival in Kweiyang, we either live in an inn or rent a room, and we begin to preach the gospel. When men are saved, what shall we do? We must encourage them to read the word, to pray, to give, to witness and to assemble for fellowship and ministry… We should teach them to have *their own* meetings in *their own* meeting place."[86]

This approach differed fundamentally from that of the missionary societies known to Nee. He commented, "One of the tragic mistakes of the past hundred years of foreign missions in China (God be merciful to me if I say anything amiss!) is that after a worker led men to Christ, he prepared a place and invited them to come there for meetings, instead of encouraging them to assemble by themselves." Nee expected his own converts to take responsibility from the very moment of their conversion. "The worker [i.e. evangelist] must leave the believers to initiate and conduct their own meetings in their own meeting place, and then he must go to *them* and take part in *their* meetings, not ask them to come to *him* and take part in *his* meetings."[87] The beauty of this plan is that, hearing and responding to the gospel, converts identify immediately with the body of Christians in their locality, rather than with any national or international organisation. For as Nee concludes, "there is no such thing in scripture as the building up of denominations; we only find local churches there."[88]

Influenced by Watchman Nee, an equally impressive indigenous movement sprang up at much the same time in India under the leadership of Bakht Singh. This gifted Indian evangelist was convinced that by paying local believers to serve their Lord, the denominational missions had started out on the wrong foot. He suggested, moreover, that the appointment of Indians to positions previously held by foreigners was no proof of "indigenisation": a church led by Indians could still be thoroughly alien to the Indian mentality if established on a foreign plan and led by men trained in foreign ways. In fact Bakht Singh disliked the term "indigenous", believing it to have unhappy racial connotations. The real problem, he argued, was not racial but spiritual; the need was not for "indigenous churches" but "scriptural churches".[89]

Like Arulappan and Nee, Bakht Singh insisted on using the New Testament as his manual of missions and, like them, he would commence a work with an evangelistic thrust, teaching those who responded, letting them grow as a body, then recognising those who had become leaders. The first of his assemblies was launched in Madras in 1941. Over the next eighteen years, more than two hundred sprang up in places he visited, and these rapidly became the fastest growing churches in India.[90] Most were the result of a gospel campaign conducted by a team of several dozen volunteers. Arriving in a town they would first of all rent a house. Then, with literature distribution and open-air processions during the day, and a major evangelistic meeting every evening, the whole population was soon introduced to the gospel. When the team left, after a week or a month, a few workers would remain to answer questions and advise those who had responded until local leaders had emerged from among them.[91] Once established with recognised elders, the new assembly, meeting in a home or a rented house, would only rarely receive a visit from Bakht Singh himself or from a leader associated with him. Two or three thousand believers from these assemblies in many parts of India would gather periodically in Madras for a "Holy Convocation" of worship, teaching and fellowship, but he never created an organisation to oversee or direct them. Financial needs were never mentioned, and the cost of the campaigns and conferences, and the support of the evangelists, were covered by unsolicited freewill offerings. Visiting Hyderabad in the 1950s, Norman Grubb of the Worldwide Evangelisation Crusade remarked, "In all my ministry experience I think these churches on their New Testament foundations are the nearest I have seen to a replica of the early church, and a pattern for the birth and growth of the young churches in all the countries which we used to talk about as the mission fields."[92]

Although Bible teachers were active in all these indigenous assemblies, neither Bakht Singh nor Watchman Nee established a Bible school or seminary for their training. The local church, they believed, was the place to study the word of God and develop the skills to teach it. Taking away the most gifted young people for training elsewhere would simply weaken the assembly, cutting off a vital part of the body and depriving it of the joy of seeing its own members serving Christ and growing in him.[93]

Only a small proportion of missiological writing is devoted to the subject of indigenous church movements. Mission administrators at the time of Watchman Nee and Bakht Singh tended to consider them a threat rather than a fulfilment to their own work, and some probably still do. Independent indigenous leaders of this calibre cannot be appointed and directed by boards and committees; their teachings and their churches cannot be manipulated through "a wise disbursement" of dollars or pounds. But it is surely time, as Watchman Nee suggested, to "see what the word of God has to say on the matter."

The apostle Paul launched his work in each city by preaching publicly and teaching from house to house. Those who accepted his message he then instructed thoroughly for a period of several weeks. At this point he would move on, leaving them to mature, returning some months later to be greeted by a body of local men already worthy to be recognised as elders.[94] If this method was effective then, why should it not be so now? In any culture we find leadership qualities emerging naturally within an informal group of friends and neighbours. Pastoral gifts develop as men and women deal with real situations. Teaching abilities grow as small groups discuss the New Testament together. Poets, apologists and theologians, faced with real questions, find real answers. Genuine spiritual leadership develops through genuine spiritual fellowship, the fruit of a tree growing in its own native earth.[95]

ENDNOTES

[1] M285-286
[2] M69 (J95-96)
[3] M226
[4] Ryland, 365
[5] M53
[6] M426
[7] M307
[8] M427
[9] M433
[10] M380
[11] M368

[12] Stunt, *Awakening*, 142

[13] M441

[14] M206. Whilst Groves defended the right of every Christian, or group of Christians, to act according to their own convictions, he denied that any would have the right to insist on others doing as they did. "Uprightness of conscience is essential to all spiritual prosperity," he said, "but coercion into some judgment is not. Infinitely better is it for each household of faith to seek to walk in all things well-pleasing to the Lord than to undertake the management and direction of other households" (M441-442). He took strong exception to Darby's practice of offering fellowship to some Christian assemblies and refusing it to others. "I do not object to anyone's enjoying the forms he holds to be most scriptural," said Groves, "but I do absolutely object to his imposing his yoke on the neck of his fellows" (M321).

[15] Although the CMS leaders blamed him for Rhenius's resignation from their society, they credited Groves with good intentions, believing that his desire was not for division but rather for a change in CMS policy. In this he was considered naïve, as indeed are most idealists (Coates to Blumhardt, 17 Feb. 1835; Strachan, 37).

[16] Neatby, 66

[17] M277-278

[18] George, 163. It was not until 1888 that the first major inter-mission conference actually took place, followed by the celebrated International Missionary Conference in Edinburgh in 1910.

[19] Journal entry for 13 Jan. 1834 (M270).

[20] Carey himself had earlier advised, "In the present divided state of Christendom it would be more likely for good to be done by each denomination engaging separately in the work than if they were to embark in it together... If all were intermingled, it is likely their private discords might throw a damp on their spirits and much retard their public usefulness" (Carey, *Enquiry*, in George, Appendix E.56).

[21] Letter dated 1845, quoted by Shenk, 32. Groves came across a biography of Venn's grandfather (who bore the same name): "In reading H Venn's life, I was struck with the sweet savour of Christ which seemed to rest on his heart, and his dependence on the Spirit of God in ministry, mixed though it was with sectarian feeling about the system to which he belonged. Our place is to imitate his grace and avoid his narrowness" (M450).

[22] Statement dated 1867, quoted by Shenk, 57.

[23] Groves E K, *Successors*, 194; Newton, *Brethren Missionary Work in Mysore State*, 12-15

[24] Groves quotes with approval an article criticising "the large societies" which "have made a territorial division of the heathen world among themselves... consolidating and perpetuating their power by making it the common interest to keep out interlopers" (Groves, "A Letter on Missions", 128).

[25] R95-96; M118

[26] The editorial policy of *The Christian Witness* was to publish all contributions anonymously, but this particular article is attributed to A N Groves by a contemporary who carefully noted the identities of the contributors in his copy (now held in the John Rylands University Library of Manchester). The attributions made by this

reader were based on information derived from the editor, J L Harris, and show every indication of being accurate. The style and content are typical of Groves.

[27] Groves, "A Letter on Missions", 130

[28] In 2 Cor 8:23, the word "messengers" (AV) or "representatives" (NIV) translates Gk. *apostoloi* (apostles). Epaphroditus was one such "messenger" (*apostolos*), sent from the church in Philippi to help Paul (Phil 2:25). Groves later, in 1840, expressed a preference for the term "messengers of Christ" (1 Thess 2:6; Jude 17) as representing more clearly the source of their authority and nature of their work (*Remarks on a Pamphlet*, 32).

[29] Groves, "A Letter on Missions", 130 (3 Jn 5-8; 2 Cor 11:7-9)

[30] Acts 13:4

[31] Groves, "A Letter on Missions", 132

[32] Groves, "A Letter on Missions", 141

[33] As always, Groves was propounding an ideal, and he would never turn an ideal into a law. He himself was not formally commended or sent by any local church in Britain, and neither, so far as we know, were Baynes, MacCarthy, Walhouse or Henry and Frank Groves in India. Like the evangelists in the New Testament (Barnabas, Silas, Timothy, Mark and many others) such workers belonged to the whole Church of Christ without claiming a special *permanent* relationship to a "sending church".

Although Groves considered the support of a home church to be of great benefit, especially in the early stages of missionary service, it was by no means an essential requirement for a servant of God willing to live by faith. In fact he was particularly aware of the problem faced by potential missionaries in churches that, in consequence of extreme Calvinistic or dispensational teaching, disapproved in principle of overseas missionary work. He advised that, in such a case, if called by God, the missionary should simply trust and obey, "going forth where he feels the Spirit leading him, without any prospect of sympathy or support from man." This condition, "whilst on the one hand it is the most deeply trying to which the soul which is faithful can be subjected, yet it is one which in a peculiar degree fits the missionary to direct the eyes of those to whom he preaches to the living God as their only object of trust, while he is to them a living witness of the faithfulness of God... a God who never fails, never disappoints those who put their trust in him" ("A Letter on Missions", 131).

[34] The title of Ken J Newton's paper is *Anthony Norris Groves: A Neglected Missiologist* (1985). In it he notes that neither Neill in his *History of Christian Missions* nor Latourette in his volume on *The Nineteenth Century Outside Europe* saw fit to make any mention of Groves at all. One may search in vain for any reference to him in the standard missiological texts.

[35] Professor Andrew Walls has recently observed that "a new generation of mission scholars is arising with all the necessary skills and equipment but without the opportunity for overseas service" (*The Missionary Movement in Christian History*, 156). The uninitiated might wonder how "all the necessary skills and equipment" for the analysis of missionary matters could be acquired by anyone who lacked the opportunity for overseas service. Here may be seen one reason why missionaries

and missiologists, though labouring with the best of intentions, sometimes find each other completely incomprehensible.

[36] Shenk, 59; Beaver, 26.

[37] The CMS historian Eugene Stock speaks of Venn as the first person to propose a strategy for "the development of native churches". Stock asserts, "Before he gave his mind to the subject no one had done so. It was an untrodden field. We may search the missionary papers during the first half of the nineteenth century, and search in vain, for any signs that the matter was even thought of" (Stock, II, 83). This simply shows how little Stock had read outside the archives of the CMS.

Venn himself never visited any CMS mission overseas; Anderson undertook four brief trips: to Malta and Greece (1828), to Turkey, Syria and Palestine (1843), to India (1854) and to Hawaii (1863).

[38] Neill, *History*, 260

[39] CMS Minute 71, [1853/4?] (Warren, 63)

[40] Groves, "A Letter on Missions", 141

[41] Shenk, 29

[42] *The Theory of Missions to the Heathen*, sermon dated 1845 (Beaver, 73). Anderson urged each mission station to see itself as "a self-governing republic where every man has an equal vote and where the majority rules" – not because this was an apostolic practice, but because it was the way things were done in New England. To Anderson's chagrin, European workers had proved awkward in this respect, and he suggested that all missionaries should be "trained to feel fully the moral responsibility of a majority vote (as it has been found that Europeans, from a deficiency in their early education, seldom are)" (Anderson, *Foreign Missions* ch. 9; Beaver, 203).

[43] Beaver, 35-36, 73-74

[44] Letter dated 1846, quoted by Shenk, 81.

[45] Shenk, 54

[46] Shenk, 43-45, 110. In 1840 Groves observed, "The native naturally loves a provision and ease, and thereby he is kept in dependence on the creature [i.e. rather than the Creator]. The European, on the other hand, loves to keep the native in subjection and himself in the place of rule" (M393).

[47] CMS Minute 116, 9 July 1861 (Warren, 67-68)

[48] CMS Minute 116, 9 July 1861 (Warren, 70)

[49] Beaver, 11

[50] Anderson, *Foreign Missions* ch. 7 (Beaver, 97)

[51] Acts 14:23

[52] Anderson, *Foreign Missions* ch. 7 (Beaver, 100-101)

[53] Anderson, *Foreign Missions* ch. 7 (Beaver, 98)

[54] ABCFM, *Annual Report*, 1841, 44-47 (Beaver, 103-104)

[55] ABCFM, *Annual Report*, 1848, 62-80 (Beaver, 124)

[56] ABCFM, *Annual Report*, 1841, 44-47 (Beaver, 104-105). In 1843 the Congregationalist seminary in Jaffna was rocked by the discovery in its dormitory that "the teacher and many of the students were practising sodomites," including "almost the entire select class of students who were being specially trained as native preachers." Fifty-seven were then dismissed. As one might expect, the blame was

placed on the primitive culture of the trainee pastors rather than the method chosen for their training (Harris, 71).

[57] ABCFM, *Annual Report*, 1848, 62-80 (Beaver, 123-124)

[58] ABCFM, *Outline of Missionary Policy*, 1856, 15-16

[59] ABCFM, *Annual Report*, 1841, 15-16 (Beaver, 105)

[60] Anderson's biographer remarks, "From his point of view, the chief obstacle to self-support came from native pastors who expected higher salaries than their congregations could afford – pastors, in other words, who expected to live more like the missionaries than like their own impoverished flocks. He therefore urged missionaries to maintain a clear hierarchical division between themselves and their native assistants to guard against the danger that the natives might come to see themselves as the missionaries' equals" (Harris, 114).

[61] In 1847 Daniel Poor bemoaned the fact that, after more than thirty years of Congregationalist activity in Jaffna, their only congregations were composed of the mission's own "beneficiaries and dependants", who preferred services to be led by the missionary – especially if the appointment of an ordained "native preacher" would mean they must pay him (Harris, 136).

[62] Nevius could not persuade his colleagues in China to accept his scheme. He discussed his ideas with Hudson Taylor and had some influence on CIM pioneers in certain parts of South-East Asia. In 1890 his advice was sought by the American Presbyterian Mission in Korea, but it is probable that the remarkable growth of the South Korean churches in the middle years of the twentieth century should be attributed to factors other than "the Nevius Plan" – perhaps, in particular, to the nationalistic stance of the Christians against Japanese aggression, to the well-organised Bible class system, and above all to the substantial Western investment in Christian hospitals, schools and industries that contributed to South Korea's rapid transformation into a modern capitalist state. Material prosperity also enabled Korean Christians to finance their own building schemes and social programmes to an extent that would be quite impossible in poorer countries. How far this numerical growth and vigorous church activity represents genuine spiritual life remains a matter of debate.

[63] Warren, 29. It was Venn who secured the ordination of the first African bishop in 1864, although the role of Bishop Samuel Crowther was to lead a mission in another part of Africa rather than govern a circle of churches in his own. Crowther was, by this time, an old man who had lived away from Africa for many years and considered himself a "black Englishman". He was a gifted and godly man, but as he depended on interpreters for communication with those under his charge he could hardly be considered an indigenous church leader. His successor was an Englishman (Shenk, 107-109; Neill, *History*, 377; Warren, 30).

Anderson, Venn and Nevius all took it for granted that in their "native churches" infants should be baptised, despite the obvious problems this caused. On this point, Venn himself admitted, "As the generation baptised in infancy rise up under this system, the Society has found itself in the false position of ministering to a population of nominal Christians, who in many instances give no assistance to the progress of the gospel" (CMS Minute 116, 9 July 1861; Warren, 67).

[64] Anderson, *Foreign Missions* ch. 9 (Beaver, 204)

[65] CMS Minute 116, 9 July 1861 (Warren, 71). In the Punjab, Robert Clark of the CMS also regarded finance as the key to creation of an indigenous church. "The first condition of any independence that was not a sham," he said, "must lie in financial self-support." In 1877 a Punjab Native Church Council was established under his chairmanship with the purpose of collecting money from Indian believers. This Council, however, met with "suspicion, jealousy and opposition" from among the CMS missionaries themselves and their converts, who preferred the local churches to be governed and financed by the Church of England. Clark endeavoured, without success in his own lifetime, to free the Indian Church from its official subjection to the authority of the Church of England and of the bishops and archbishops appointed by the British government. In fact, freedom from such subjection came only with the political independence of India (Clark, 305-310; Vander Werff, 52-54).

[66] CMS Minute 116, 9 July 1861 (Warren, 69-70)

[67] CMS Minute 116, 9 July 1861 (Warren, 70). To Venn's pleasure, the Anglican missionary Thomas G Ragland proposed that the Indian congregations in each district of North Tinnevelly "should bear the expense of one native catechist to labour for a month." Ragland reckoned this was a financial burden even they could bear (Warren, 64). It appeared to work, at least for a while, but local Christians in such circumstances are always prone to ask, "Why should we, in our poverty, be expected to foot the bill when you with your pounds and dollars can do so much more comfortably?"

[68] M285

[69] M393

[70] M622. The writer admitted that "Church of England clergy are backward in accepting such movements as these".

[71] Letter dated 1925 from Handley Bird, quoted by Lang, *Aroolappen*, 218

[72] *Aroolappen*, 219. Lang adds, "The New Testament knows nothing of money being sent from land to land, save for the relief of the poor in special circumstances such as famine (Acts 11:27-30; Rom 15:25-26; 1 Cor 16:1-4) or for the help of one labouring in the gospel (2 Cor 11:9; Phil 4:10-20)."

[73] Kenneth G Grubb in foreword to Allen, *The Spontaneous Expansion of the Church*; review by William J Danker, quoted on back cover of Allen, *Missionary Methods* (1962 edn). Roland Allen was a high-church Anglican and served with the SPG in northern China from 1895 to 1903. Among his childhood influences were an aunt and other relatives active in the Brethren assemblies (Allen, Hubert J B, 12).

[74] M285

[75] Tucker met with vehement opposition among his missionary colleagues and was not able to carry his point (Neill, *History*, 260, 387; Shenk, 113-115).

[76] W H T Gairdner was an ordained clergyman and CMS missionary in Cairo between 1899 and 1928. He was a gifted Arabist, an outstanding church leader and a key figure in the Edinburgh Conference of 1910. Such was his brilliance that Egyptian Christian leaders must have found him a hard act to follow.

[77] Vander Werff, 51

[78] Padwick, *Temple Gairdner*, 263

[79] Vander Werff, 204; Padwick, *Temple Gairdner*, 282

[80] French found the responsibilites of the Lahore bishopric exhausting. He "persisted in his effort to shape a truly indigenous yet catholic young church in spite of the organizational machinery, fund-raising, cathedral building and party in-fighting for ten years before passing the reins to another and returning to his first love, evangelism" (Vander Werff, 51). Similarly, in Chapter 27 we saw Thomas Walker in Tinnevelly frustrated by the failure of a "new set of rules" and "new regulations for Council" to create churches of the apostolic type. He resigned his post as "Superintendent of the Tamil Church", advised the CMS to return to the methods of the apostles, and turned his own energies to itinerant evangelism.

[81] Nee, *The Normal Christian Church Life*, 1980 edn., 109-110

[82] Nee, *TNCCL*, 163-164

[83] Nee, *TNCCL*, 164

[84] Nee, *TNCCL*, 40

[85] Nee, *TNCCL*, 171

[86] Nee, *TNCCL*, 107. The title "Little Flock" was given to the movement by those outside it. Nee himself argued that no distinguishing title should be used for any group of Christians, other than the name of their locality.

[87] Nee, *TNCCL*, 107-108. It was evidently possible to follow this ideal at this time in China. In a Muslim or Hindu context, however, and especially where converts have neither a home of their own nor a sufficient income to rent property, one might think they would benefit from discreet help towards the provision of a temporary room for meetings.

[88] Nee, *TNCCL*, 135. This might lead us to suppose that Nee had been influenced by Groves. We shall consider the evidence in Chapter 33.

[89] Smith D, 48-50. Bakht Singh liked to see Indians and foreigners working together without distinction of race or thought of payment. Like Watchman Nee he insisted that in Christ there is neither Greek nor Jew; there is no such thing as Eastern money or Western money, only the Lord's money. He saw no reason for Indian Christians to expect payment from foreigners, pointing out that the New Testament shows us no case of a younger church financially dependent on an older church, no case of an evangelist receiving money in order to preach to his own people. In fact we see the opposite: the young Gentile churches of Syria and Macedonia offered help to the older Jewish church in Jerusalem (Acts 11:29; 2 Cor 8).

[90] Smith D, 53

[91] Smith D, 56-57

[92] Grubb, *Once Caught No Escape*, 152. Some observers might judge that with the passage of time the assemblies associated with Bakht Singh have lost some of their earliest ideals. The reality may be that every wave of reform or revival will rise and then sink, to be replaced in due course by another. As John Bellett observed more than 130 years ago, "In man there is ever a tendency to the mere ways of nature and to the course of the world, and in order to sustain a thing spiritual and living like the Church, the natural way, yea, necessary way (save that God is sovereign), is by a fresh putting forth of light and power to revive it again and again" (*Interesting Reminiscences*, 12).

[93] The problem is still with us today. We see mission agencies recruiting potential Nees and Singhs for enrolment in theological seminaries. After semesters of lectures and examinations in an alien language, sometimes in a different country, they return with foreign clothes, a foreign accent, sometimes a foreign spouse, and with a dignity that sets them apart from their brothers and sisters. With a diploma on the wall, they are no longer qualified to lead their own people.

[94] This sequence is evident in Acts 14:1-3 and 21-23. Then in Acts 19 and 20 we see the same method followed at Ephesus, which, for the space of two years, became Paul's base for outreach to the entire region (19:10). A little later he sent Timothy to help and advise the elders at Ephesus, showing how a missionary may continue to offer pastoral support to the local leaders for some time after his departure (1 Tim 1:3). I have discussed the mission methods used by Jesus and his earliest apostles in Robin Daniel, *Mission Strategies Then and Now* (Tamarisk, 2012).

[95] In some cultures a leader, in order to be accepted, must have been born into a certain social class, or have attained a certain age of maturity, or have a wife and children. Appointments that ignore such expectations have often failed.

"The work societies endeavour to accomplish
with the world's help can be done better,
because more scripturally,
by the Church herself."

Norris Groves [1]

32

As Free As Our Hearts Could Wish

Our Dear Lord's Plan

" **A**s a missionary thinker, Groves was a man 'born out of due time.'"[2] He identified problems, and he proposed what might seem imaginative solutions. But they were not imaginative; they were simply the methods described in the New Testament. In 1830, during his early days in Baghdad, he remarked, "I am sometimes led, in contemplating the gentlemanly and imposing aspect which our present missionary institutions bear, and contrasting them with the early days of the church, when apostolic fishermen and tent-makers published the testimony, to think that much will not be done till we go back again to primitive principles and let the nameless poor and their unrecorded and unsung labours be those on which our hopes, under God, are fixed."[3]

Four years later in India he was saddened to see how British Christians felt they must maintain the respect of the local people by a display of gracious affluence demonstrating the supremacy of Western ways. He was always disappointed if his hostess, in his honour, brought out the best china or put one or two extra dainties on the table, assuming that despite his words he remained as much a lover of luxury as anyone else.[4] And he was dismayed to hear one missionary declare that he himself would never live *among* the people, for "nothing was to be done with [them], without keeping them at a distance and not making yourself too cheap, and keeping a certain degree of external respectability."[5] Groves himself was suggesting a radical new approach to indigenisation. Rather than encouraging the Indians to model their behaviour on that of English ladies and gentlemen, he aspired to become himself like an Indian. "We purpose that our domestic arrangements should all be very simple and *very inexpensive* and our plan strictly evangelical. One great object will be to break down the odious barriers that pride has raised between natives and Europeans."[6]

Groves proposed that the house, food and furnishings of the missionary be as similar as possible to those of the people he is called to serve – and not just when he runs short of money but permanently, as a matter of principle. "The farther I go," he said, "the more I am convinced that the missionary labour of India, as carried on by Europeans, is altogether above the natives; nor do I see how any abiding impression can possibly be made till they mix with them in a way that is not now attempted."[7] This was confirmed in his mind when he received a letter from a lady missionary in Burma who had spoken to some "native sisters" about "the importance of modesty, cleanliness etc." and they replied "that they should very much like to live as we did if they had money enough to do so."[8] The need was to demonstrate a Christian lifestyle with an income no greater than theirs. Living like the Indians at the level of bare subsistence, giving away any surplus, trusting God to supply one's *daily* bread; this was something that no reputable missionary society would allow. "It must be some who, like us, are free to act thus," he concluded. "Those who act under societies are in so many ways fettered."[9] And it would not be easy. "I feel assured, without inconceivable crucifixion of self the work that is to be done in these lands cannot be accomplished; for the material you have to work on is so very low that close and real contact, so as to leave a lively impression, involves an abasement so great that none have yet had the heart to attempt it."[10]

"However the Lord may dispose of you," Groves urged, "let this be your firm abiding purpose: to share in the humiliations of the gospel."[11] Far from requiring the local people to accept foreign ways, the missionary should adapt to theirs: far from taking offence, he must avoid causing it. "The time spent in the learning of a language among a people, every thought and purpose and habit of whose lives are diverse from your own, has this advantage," said Groves, "that you become in some measure acquainted with their peculiarities before you are in a situation to offend against them."[12] Realising that it would displease the Muslims of Baghdad for Christians to occupy an upper room, the family left it unused.[13] Yet as he travelled Groves saw no inconsistency in taking with him an Indian to assist as "tailor, cook and every thing by turns". Local culture would expect an educated traveller to have a servant, and by treating his servant with courtesy Groves would show how Christian principles might be lived out within that culture. Indeed, during their days together on board ship, the man was more of a disciple than a servant. Groves taught him to read and led him to faith in Christ.[14] He was determined to become an Indian in order to win Indians.[15]

Norris Groves arrived in India at a time when there was still plenty of room for everyone. But he saw the danger ahead as existing missions opened additional stations, and newer agencies began to move in and compete for influence. Where two societies are working in the same place, the result is predictable: converts will flit from one to another as soon as they encounter difficulties here or anticipate rewards there. Groves observed, "Never was there a more important moment than the present for India. Up to this time everything in the Church has been as free as our hearts could wish. Persons have been converted, either by reading God's word or through one another, and have drank [*sic*] the living waters, wherever they could find them, full and clear. But now the Church of England is seeking to extend its power, and the Independents and Methodists are seeking to enclose their little flocks."[16] The Baptists, too, were acquiring "members".[17] Indians were rapidly absorbing all the prejudices that divided Christian from Christian in Europe and America.

In addition to this, Groves could see the difficulties caused by mission boards and committees, especially when their members were secular men who misunderstood the issues. The high-handed decision of the CMS to dismiss Rhenius was a striking example. Another was the extraordinary demand by the home committee of the Baptist Missionary Society that William Carey submit to their direct control from England.[18] There were many other tensions. Missionaries obliged to follow instructions sent by a committee would be compelled at times to stifle their own sense of calling, and such men could not easily teach their converts to be guided by the word of God or the leading of the Holy Spirit. Legal conflicts arose periodically over property and work contracts, and there were racial tensions too, as foreign clergymen enjoyed homes and incomes appropriate for British colonials whilst their Indian assistants had hardly enough to eat. The committees no doubt meant well, but their efficiency and authority, and their ability to pull strings with the government, overawed the poor Indians. Opening a new "station", the land would be acquired by the committee. A massive stone or brick "church" would be designed by a foreign architect appointed by the committee. The steeple, altar and bells would be paid for by the committee; the salaries of the Indian staff and the clergy would be assured by the committee. No one had the slightest doubt that the church belonged to the committee.[19]

On his first visit to India in 1834 Groves observed, "From my arrival in Bombay to the day I reached Jaffna, I had been continually hoping to find missionary institutions carried on with that simplicity which I think so highly becomes us, but I have been deeply disappointed. Wherever I have been, the system of the world and its character of influence have been adopted instead of the moral power of the self-denial of the gospel."[20] Though Groves might wish with all his heart to work in harmony with existing agencies, he could see great benefit in starting from scratch wherever possible, not building on another man's foundation. "I do hope the Lord will allow us," he said, "to gather a holy little band who will unite in defending the liberty of the Church of God from the supremacy, pride and control of man."[21]

Above all, it was Indian evangelists he longed to see at work: "My heart has particularly brought before it today the importance of the office of an evangelist. I long to see immense additions to the blessed little band. I shall be very thankful to be the servant of such the remainder of my worthless life."[22] He wondered what would be the best way to train such national believers. Rufus Anderson hoped that eight or ten years in a seminary might make a man suitable for ordination (though still by no means the equal of a regular New England "minister"). Henry Venn proposed theological training for suitable natives, but all too rarely could a candidate be found with the required moral and intellectual stature.[23] In 1834 Groves wrote home, "I have been greatly exercised relative to the best way of bringing forward the native ministers of Christ in these countries, and I have finally rested on our dear Lord's plan: that is, to get from two to twelve, and to go about constantly with them, eating what they eat and sleeping where they sleep and labouring, whether in a *choultry* at night or by the way, to impress on their souls a living exhibition of Jesus."[24]

But was this not too difficult, too much to ask of a Western missionary? The simple fact is that Groves himself by this method trained two highly effective Christian leaders, Andrew and Arulappan (three if we include Mokayel; four if we add Serkies). And they in turn trained dozens. "It would be desirable," he said, "for every evangelist [i.e. missionary] to take with him wherever he went from two to six native catechists, with whom he might eat, drink and sleep on his journeys, and to whom he might speak of the things of the kingdom as he sat down and as he rose up, that they might be, in short, prepared for ministry in the way that our dear Master prepared his disciples, by line upon line, precept upon precept, here a little and there a little, as they could bear it, feeling from beginning to end that our place is not to set others to do what we cannot do ourselves... but that we are rather to be ensamples of every thing we wish to see in our dear brethren. And I do not yet despair of seeing in India a church arise that shall be a little sanctuary in the cloudy and dark day that is coming on Christendom."[25]

Before setting out for the East in 1829, Norris Groves had held a rather heroic view of the pioneer missionary – a tough, self-sufficient ambassador for the gospel, preaching the Word in season and out of season, doing the work of an evangelist, able to accomplish all things through Christ who strengthens him.[26] He never lost this vision, but his chastening experiences in Baghdad, and his discovery that his own gifts lay more in the area of teaching and pastoral care, brought him a deeper awareness of the spiritual body of which the evangelist is a part. In fact his conception of the missionary evangelist expanded to embrace that of the missionary church. And though the work of an itinerant preacher was always, to Groves, the highest of all callings, he recognised the need of the evangelist for the support, the prayer, the teaching, and the encouragement of other mature Christians – and the necessity for the evangelist's gifts to be complemented by the gifts of others.[27]

It was, of course, in the New Testament that he sought guidance about evangelistic methods. An evangelist, as we have seen, should be sent out by his local church and prayerfully supported by its members.[28] But once the evangelist, labouring in some distant place, has led a number to Christ and gathered a small group together, he faces a dilemma. Should he remain in that place and feed the new flock? Or should he press on to further unreached fields? The apostles generally stayed only a matter of weeks or, at most, a few months before leaving their converts to fend for themselves. For this reason, Groves thought, "missionaries ought to go from place to place, preaching the gospel, and only become stationary when they have gathered a church. And rather than remain so, if called to the office of an evangelist, they should do as the apostle did: set some over the church and go on."[29] The temptation to settle and become the permanent pastor of the fellowship was hard to resist, but "I think that missionaries would not only be more useful but in much better health if they were to move about more."[30]

Subsequent experience in India confirmed this. At Allissic, near Quilon, he found an excellent Church of England missionary, overwhelmed by the amount of work required to keep his station going. "He is here alone, and what with translating, schools, and a hundred other things, his hands are so full that though he seems most anxious to go about preaching among the people, he is not able to do it. I do think the plan of locating missionaries singly is most pernicious. The American plan of sending three or four together is far, far better."[31] It was, indeed, more scriptural. Christ sent out his disciples two by two; Paul worked with Barnabas and then Silas, and he established missionary teams with the help of Mark, Luke, Timothy, Aristarchus and others mentioned in his letters. If that was the best plan then, why not now? The presence of co-workers will not only provide fellowship and encouragement for the missionary; it will also enable him to leave church, school and clinic in the hands of capable colleagues whilst absent for days or weeks on preaching tours. It was with this in mind that Groves himself established a team in Madras and Chittoor, and recruited help for solitary missionaries in several locations.

But the greatest practical contribution of Norris Groves to the work of God in India was undoubtedly the encouragement he gave to Arulappan and others in taking initiatives of their own. He enjoyed close fellowship with these Indian Christians. To him they were friends and equals, and he respected the skills they brought to the work of the gospel in their own culture.[32] He would never expect greater frugality or stronger faith from an Indian than he would require of himself and his English colleagues. In 1840 he wrote of the British ex-soldier MacCarthy and a newly converted Indian bookbinder called James. Both, on their evangelistic itinerations, were trusting the Lord to provide by means of casual labour, or through things they might sell, or in other unexpected ways.[33] Groves commented, "Those who know the natives will, I am sure, feel with me that this plan of missions, whereby the native himself is thrown on God, is calculated to develop that individuality of character, the absence of which has been so deeply deplored, and the remedy for which has so seldom been sought."[34]

Norris Groves was a humble man, and humility marked his dealings with people of other races. He had learnt from wide experience that a missionary will achieve far more by friendly persuasion than by displays of authority. "The office [i.e. role] of a missionary in these countries," he said, "is to *live* the gospel before them in the power of the Holy Ghost, and to drop like the dew, line upon line, and precept upon precept, here a little and there a little, till God give the increase of his labours. But it must be by patient continuance in well-doing against every discouraging circumstance, from the remembrance of what we ourselves once were."[35] Groves himself had no official position, no title, no authority over anyone. He could influence others only through qualities of personal character – a godly example, wise advice, sound teaching, and of course through effective prayer. Like the apostle Paul he could say "I appeal to you" or "I urge you", but never "I command you". This attitude would seem distinctly odd to the average colonial official, accustomed to exploit and humiliate his Indian underlings as a matter of course; it would be completely incomprehensible to a contemporary army officer, taught to maintain discipline over the natives with a confident lordly manner, never admitting to any weakness.

Not surprisingly, there was considerable agitation when Groves expressed his view that Indians were perfectly capable of creating and leading their own churches, and even more when he encouraged them actually to do so. In a letter home, dated 1840, he confided, "The fact that our position here puts pastoral work and fellowship on a simple Christian footing among the natives is by no means the least important feature of our work. Until we came, no one but an *ordained* native was allowed to celebrate the Lord's Supper or to baptise; and when our Christian brethren Arulappan and Andrew partook of the Lord's Supper with the native Christians it caused more stir and enquiry than you can imagine. The constant reference to God's word has brought and is bringing the questions connected with ministry and church government into a perfectly new position in the minds of many."[36] The method Groves advocated was remarkably successful. As Arulappan and others travelled round southern India, preaching, baptising, teaching, and breaking bread in remembrance of Christ, assemblies came together in many places, and local leaders began to emerge among them. Before long the Indian churches were writing their own hymns, their own tracts and teaching materials.

Norris Groves was not the only active evangelist to have thought out a strategy of missions in the years before Venn and Anderson put pen to paper on the subject. One other was Charles Gützlaff. Eight years younger than

Groves, he was a German who had become thoroughly English. Ordained as a Lutheran pastor, Gützlaff had been trained at the Moravian Missionary Institute in Berlin, although he then served in China as a translator for the British governor of Hong Kong. In 1844 he drew together a number of Chinese evangelists in what he called the Chinese Christian Union with the daring ambition to reach the whole of inland China by means of itinerant preaching. By 1849 reports spoke of a hundred and thirty evangelists proclaiming the gospel, selling books over a wide area and leading hundreds of Chinese to faith in Christ.[37]

Gützlaff was no fool. He urged great care in selecting the evangelists to be supported with the funds at his disposal, and he expected them to bring some of their converts to meet him personally. He placed complete trust in the judgment of several relatively experienced Chinese Christians and he left the management of the enterprise entirely in their hands, regarding himself simply as an advisor and provider of finance. He was devastated to discover in 1850 that all but thirty of the "evangelists" were confidence tricksters from the Hong Kong underworld, who had never itinerated anywhere. Gützlaff judged his earnest efforts a ruinous and humiliating failure, and he died barely a year later. Those of his evangelists who were genuine, however, continued to preach the gospel. Through their witness, groups of Chinese Christians came together in various places, and one of these groups gained as many as eighty-seven members within the space of five years.[38]

Gützlaff has been "a man much maligned".[39] Like Groves he was a person of outstanding spirituality, energy and vision, and like Groves he made one error of judgment which undermined the influence he might otherwise have exerted on his and subsequent generations. In a number of respects the missiological visions of the two men coincide. Gützlaff, like Groves, had little interest in management; he would not take on any formal post as secretary of a committee or director of a mission, nor would he even agree to be the official administrator for a company of evangelists. Like Groves, he could speak with eloquence and power about the missionary cause, and although he too declined to solicit funds, he went further than Groves in communicating with Christians in Britain and Europe concerning needs and opportunities overseas. He could pull strings and make suggestions; he could propose tasks to be accomplished and places to go; he could offer advice to missionaries newly arrived on the field, and like Groves he believed that single women could achieve much for the kingdom of God abroad. He too encouraged national believers to meet together without waiting for a foreigner to lead them. He argued that the task of reaching a people would be most effectively accomplished by their own compatriots, and he believed that the role of the foreigner was simply to encourage and facilitate their efforts. "Gützlaff recognised the missionary's task as tuition short of tutelage, the helping but not the controlling hand – *autonomy from the very start of the relationship*, yet with close spiritual and pastoral oversight of the emerging church."[40]

But the most striking point that Groves and Gützlaff had in common was their view of the personal relationship between foreign Christian and national Christian. Gützlaff proposed that the young missionary don Chinese clothes and devote himself to the task of discipling twenty or thirty Chinese believers: "It is necessary that he should entirely live with the natives, identify himself with them... penetrate further and further in the country and give up all foreign society and connections... Local opposition will always be experienced wherever the gospel of salvation is announced... His pay therefore will be small, his troubles many and unless he be a heavenly minded man, he will soon sink under them." But Gützlaff was confident that the Lord would provide. "No real workman," he said, "will ever be left to starve, no great enterprise for the glory of God be allowed to stand still for want of means, for God who is rich above all that call upon him never abandons his own... How little is required when one can live with contentment among the natives; what happy hours can be passed in sharing a meal with them."[41] From what he said, we might wonder whether Charles Gützlaff had read *Christian Devotedness* or corresponded personally with Norris Groves.[42]

Groves himself had been only four months in India when he begged, "Pray for *all* who love the Lord in India, and for me especially, that I may be the instrument in the Lord's hand to promote the *liberty and love of the church*."[43] The prayer was abundantly answered; he saw teams of Indian evangelists freely at work creating a wide network of Indian fellowships. And yet, within twenty-five years of his departure, the area of his labours, and those of John Arulappan, had fallen once more under the control of foreign bishops and committees, and in the words of Thomas Walker, "the power of the rupee". The conclusion was all too clear. "In India, as in the missionary world of the day, it was the denominational polity of Venn and not the ecumenical dream of Groves which prevailed. Groves's vision was too idealistic, too impracticable in a protestant world still marking out its denominational missionary boundaries."[44]

In the final analysis, however, it was not the Church that mattered most for Norris Groves – it was the Saviour. "We preach not ourselves, but Christ" – hardly a new idea in any age, but one which each generation seems to rediscover as though no one had noticed it before. The early twentieth century saw a radical reappraisal of evangelistic methods by an American missionary, E Stanley Jones. His desire was to reach the intellectuals of India, and to do this he shifted his focus from "the ministry of the church" to "the person of Jesus". His public meetings held in public halls, convened and chaired by friendly Hindu and Muslim leaders, were attended by hundreds who listened with the greatest respect to his courteous expositions of the life and teachings of Christ. Abandoning church buildings and church services, he engaged his Indian converts in a more indigenous style of fellowship with lengthy spells of informal interaction. Jones was criticised, as was Groves, for having a "broad concept of Christian unity".[45] It was not the Church, or a church, and certainly not a denomination, that either of them wished to offer to India. It was Jesus Christ himself.

Stirring up their Minds

As it happened, a large part of Norris Groves's missionary life was spent teaching children in the schools he had established in Baghdad and Chittoor. This might seem surprising in view of the early doubts he expressed about the value of education for missionary purposes. In 1829, on his way through eastern Europe, he declared, "Education is one thing, which may or may not be a blessing; the knowledge of God's word is another. To forward the one, separated from the other, I would not put forth my little finger; to the latter, all my strength."[46]

Groves was influenced by the fact that the New Testament gives no instance of apostles or evangelists acquiring properties or setting up educational or medical institutions of any kind. Although Paul held discussions in the School of Tyrannus for more than a year, he did not own the school, nor did he teach children in it.[47] And though there are many miraculous healings recorded in the New Testament, they were viewed as "signs" authenticating the spoken message rather than as the inauguration of a systematic medical ministry.[48] Granted that the gospel has inspired Christian compassion and many forms of Christian service throughout the centuries, its earliest pioneers were preachers pure and simple, devoting themselves to prayer and ministry of the Word. Missionaries in more recent times have often been torn between the call to follow the apostolic method and the opportunities presented for a more sedentary ministry. The fact is that itinerant preaching requires arduous travel; it causes offence and at times danger, and it brings no financial reward, whilst schools, clinics and orphanages offer congenial surroundings, with the appreciation of rulers and people, and sometimes a significant income.

Among Norris Groves's contemporaries, Alexander Duff advocated education at all levels, including English-speaking secondary schools, as a serious missionary method. Many others had invested heavily in local schools with lessons taught in local languages. By 1817 William Carey and his colleagues had opened 103 Bengali schools, with an average attendance of 6703 boys and girls.[49] Venn and Anderson both saw a need for elementary schools in the vernacular, especially for the children of Christian families, although Venn (holding to the concept of an Established Church) eventually came to believe that the provision of a Christian education was the responsibility of the Christian government rather than that of the Mission or the Church.[50] John Nevius and Hudson Taylor were altogether less optimistic about the spiritual benefit of education.

Groves's views on the matter changed with time. His own frustrating experiences in Baghdad led him to suggest that when it was impossible to preach openly (in an Islamic context for example), and when the people seem hardened against the gospel, the pioneer missionary should not be "discouraged from attempting schools, for although they may not stand above a year or two, you may by the Lord's blessing be the instrument of stirring up their minds to think and examine for themselves, and without violence lead them to question the truth of some of their dogmas. And when you have once dislodged the principle of implicit faith you have at last opened the door for truth."[51]

The value of educational institutions for the kingdom of God was confirmed in his mind when he saw Duff's far more ambitious work in Calcutta. "My interest in boarding schools is very much increasing," he said, "not because I think it was the way in which the apostles propagated Christianity, but because I see the Lord now blessing it." The apostles, in their day, had the advantage that their preaching was confirmed by signs and wonders, but their message and their aim were the same as that of the modern Christian educator. "I think direct preaching to the natives a much higher and more noble work," said Groves, but the spiritual work which, "in the days of the Spirit's energy, was done by a single sentence brought home and sealed," may even now be accomplished through the slower process of teaching children the truths of the gospel.[52]

Duff went on to recommend the establishment of English high schools and colleges throughout the world in order to create an enlightened and educated elite in every nation, capable of promoting Christian values among their own people. Anderson and Venn became increasingly uneasy about the vast amount of missionary money, time and effort poured into secondary schools, where the lessons merely prepared pupils for careers in law or commerce and led relatively few to profess faith in Christ. The experience of a century and a half since then has still failed to answer the question whether the finance, time and effort invested in educational institutions have brought a commensurate spiritual benefit. Direct evangelistic work has undoubtedly brought larger numbers to faith in Christ, and yet the fact remains that many significant Christian leaders in each generation have good reason to thank the founders and teachers of the Christian schools they attended. One such was Watchman Nee; another was Bakht Singh.

Groves spoke warmly of other types of Christian institution, although he never established any of his own. In offering dental care in India and ophthalmic care in Baghdad his intention was both to relieve physical suffering and to open hearts to the message of eternal salvation; but once he had moved on, he left behind him no permanent medical work in either place. He valued the literature produced by the CMS printshop in Malta, and he even arranged for a small portable press to be sent to Baghdad with a view to producing Sunday school materials and scriptures in the spoken dialects of Mesopotamia.

But Groves himself was a talker rather than a writer, and though he composed several articles and booklets in English, he gave no thought to establishing a publishing house, and he never undertook major writing or translation projects for India or the Arab world.

Of greater concern to him was the plight of abandoned and endangered children. Orphans never failed to find him a protector and provider, and he went to great lengths to help with the creation of the orphanage at Sonamukhi. He valued Müller's foundation in Bristol as much for its practical provision for the physical needs of destitute children as for its effectiveness in leading them to faith in Christ. On at least one occasion he urged his fellow Christians to establish hospitals and hostels where believers and others who had fallen on hard times could find healing for body and soul and enjoy wholesome Christian fellowship.[53] In fact wherever Groves himself established a home for his wife and children it became a place of refuge for people in need. In Baghdad he welcomed both Serkies and Harnie into the family when they had nowhere else to go, and as members of the Groves household both came to personal faith in Christ. Throughout his life Norris Groves simply cared for people. This was not a matter of missiological theory; it was the natural response of a loving heart to human need.

Making Tents

It has been suggested that the most novel contribution of Norris Groves to mission thinking lies in the sphere of what is now called "tent-making".[54] In fact he always felt a certain ambivalence towards this subject. At Sarepta, pausing on his journey to Baghdad, he enjoyed fellowship with a Moravian pastor caring for a Christian community of four hundred men and women. But government intervention had prohibited them from preaching the gospel or teaching the Bible to the Russians, Tartars and Calmucs who inhabited the region. Having invested in extensive fields, houses and workshops, the Moravians could not simply move away to proclaim the good news elsewhere. They continued their agricultural and artisanal activities and maintained their religious rules and exercises in their own community. But Groves sadly observed, "all missionary character is now lost here; they are a simple colony of artificers who, for the sake of the preservation of *this* character, have relinquished that of missionary." And what was to be learned from this? "I see here the great evil of having anything mercantile connected with missionaries, unless as a simple accident [i.e. accessory] of support and not as an essential part of the constitution."[55] The missionary, he believed, was called to be an evangelist, not a farmer or an artisan.[56]

During his subsequent missionary career Norris Groves gave much thought to the "tent-making" idea, experimented with it, and later abandoned it. For a while in Madras he supported the missionary team through his earnings as a dentist, although they also received gifts from friends in Europe and India. By 1837 the subject of "a self-supporting mission" was occupying the minds of Groves and his colleagues, and they had "much correspondence on the subject".[57] It was not only the missionaries who needed to earn their living. One of their main reasons for moving to Chittoor was to buy farmland which could provide work for the Indian converts, "who by embracing Christianity lost their means of support."[58]

Having settled there, Groves outlined his ideal "plan of missions". A missionary, supported at first by his home church, will endeavour as soon possible to become self-supporting. This will enable the church to direct its available funds to other workers. It will also demonstrate to the missionary's converts the value of honest toil providing for personal needs and for generous help to those less fortunate.[59] "I think we all feel an increasing interest," Groves said, "in that plan of missions which we are now pursuing: either labouring ourselves, or being associated with those who profess some 'honest trade', that we may have 'lack of no man' and also set an example to others, that by so doing they may support the weak."[60]

The farm settlement in Chittoor was intended to provide food and other necessities for the support of full-time evangelists engaged in itinerant outreach. Families with agricultural or craft skills would do the bulk of the physical work whilst Arulappan, Groves and others went out preaching the gospel. But this too brought problems. Groves saw the young Indian's motives questioned at every turn; his hearers reckoned he was only promoting Christianity because he was paid to do so. Groves thought of the apostle Paul, who had worked with his own hands during the week and then reasoned with Jews and Greeks in the synagogue every Sabbath.[61] He thought too of a Muslim moolah in Baghdad who said, "I know you are devoted men, and give much away, but I know not what your motives are, or what the extent of your riches. If I saw persons labouring from day to day and giving the fruit of their labour to the poor or to missions, I should then see they were making sacrifices for God."[62] It all pointed to the need for the evangelist himself to be a working man, preaching in his spare time at his own expense, and Groves began to feel there was much to be said for an evangelist (whatever his nationality) to be seen working with his own hands and earning his own living from a craft or trade.

These ideas were not original to Norris Groves. Since the 1820s the Moravians had made it a basic principle that "every Christian is a missionary and should witness through his daily vocation."[63] William Carey, arriving in Calcutta in 1793, supported himself at first by overseeing a number of small indigo plantations. He had already proposed a policy of sending with each full-time missionary "two or more other persons, with their wives and families... who should be wholly employed in providing for them."[64] Karl Pfander's experience among Muslims had led him to favour the concept of the "missionary craftsman". An itinerant watchmaker, he believed, would be more likely to gain the confidence of the local people than would a self-proclaimed propagandist.[65] In Baghdad Groves himself had received a letter from Dr Robert Morrison, the first Protestant missionary to China, "in which he expresses his conviction of the importance of missionaries learning to earn their subsistence by some occupation, however humble, rather than be dependent as they are now on societies." Groves found this persuasive: "I confess my mind so far entirely agrees with him, that if I had to prepare for a missionary course I would not go to a college or an institution but learn medicine or go to a blacksmith's, watchmaker's or carpenter's shop, and there pursue my preparatory studies."[66]

The farms and industries that Groves set up at this time were designed to provide an honest income for missionaries and local believers. The fact that these projects proved generally unsuccessful was due partly to Groves's lack of commercial expertise, partly to some unwise decisions, and partly to economic circumstances beyond his control. In his early days, still feeling his way in an alien culture, he had been reluctant to rush into new ventures. In 1831, when the British and Foreign School Society offered to provide means for establishing schools in Mesopotamia, he replied cautiously that he would need to find out more about the local conditions, "for nothing is so discouraging as failures from precipitate attempts. But so variable is the state of affairs in these countries that previous to your judgment being matured by experience you may be led, with the best intentions possible, to undertake on a bright day plans which, before they can be executed, prove as baseless as a vision and which will leave nothing behind but the remembrance of useless expense and unproductive labour."[67] In the light of future events this looks distinctly prophetic.

Groves was not alone in these failures. It might be thought that *indigenous* commercial initiatives would be more sure of success, but Arulappan and others were hardly more successful than Groves himself. The skills needed to start a new business were in some cases lacking; in others the business plan was not commercially viable. Drought at times withered the crops in the fields, and the level of government taxation was far too high to enable the settlement at Christianpettah, for example, to be self-supporting. Elsewhere things were no better. The entrepreneur for whom Carey worked "found his private indigo enterprise to be disastrous"; he abandoned it and returned to England.[68] In the Punjab, Robert Clark's "Christian agricultural settlement" under Indian leadership was "a melancholy failure".[69] The Basel Mission likewise attempted and abandoned agricultural projects in India: sugar, food crops, a coffee plantation, small-scale weaving, carpentry, clock-making – all were tried, and all failed. A printing and bookbinding business proved a little more successful, providing employment for a number of Indians. Real commercial success came to the Basel Mission only with a large weaving factory in Mangalore and with the growth of major tile manufacturing industries in the south.[70] Frank Groves, a man of "mechanical genius", eventually did well with his substantial sugar refinery near Mysore.[71] These many and varied experiences showed that small-scale projects (cottage industries and food crops) could not compete with existing suppliers or create and adequately protect new markets, but that large industries with the latest technology and a dedicated professional management could sometimes do so.

One particular difficulty the "tent-maker" faced in India was the caste system. As a dentist in Madras, Groves had a large European clientele, and his profession placed him in what had become a respected expatriate caste within Hindu society. But Bowden was a stonemason, and Beer a shoemaker. In India both these occupations were the preserve of low caste families. A man was born into a family of builders or cobblers; there was no mechanism for a foreigner to enter the caste. Indeed, if he attempted to do so he would exclude himself from social contact with all higher castes.[72] This meant that "tent-making" was not an option for Bowden and Beer; they never exercised their crafts in India.

Another problem encountered by "tent-makers" almost everywhere is that of commercial and professional jealousy. This may account for the fact that Groves never established a dental practice in Baghdad. He had carried with him his dentist's implements, evidently with some thought of supporting himself through exercise of his professional skills. But the local people, for generations, had taken their rotten teeth to native dentists who, in return for a few coppers, simply pulled them out. These traditional practitioners would certainly not welcome the encroachment of a foreigner on their domain.[73] As we have seen, Groves did offer medical care in Baghdad, especially for diseases of the eye, which no local physician could cure, and he performed a number of cataract operations; but he rarely, if ever, asked for a fee. Whatever the reason, he did not establish himself in Baghdad as a "tent-maker". Perhaps this is what he meant when he wrote, "Surely the Lord has most graciously seen fit to dry up those sources from whence we anticipated supply, that we might know we depend on him alone and see how he can supply even here."[74] With the arrival of the doctor Edward Cronin, and the establishment of a proper clinic, the medical work in Baghdad expanded for a while, but it was seen as a way of winning the trust and respect of the people rather than as a serious source of income.

Other hard questions have been asked concerning the advisability in general of establishing industries for the support of Christian converts. The plight of those driven out of their families because of their faith weighed heavily on the first generation of missionaries in India, and where land was available with government approval, Christian villages were established in many parts of the country. Settlements tended to grow up around a mission station, and the missionary often became a well-loved father-figure to the Christian community. But what was originally an emergency solution, providing refuge and sustenance for converts with nowhere else to go, became in the course of time an approved institution – the mission compound. Homes were provided for believers and for interested friends and relations; farms, workshops and schools were built with foreign money. The inhabitants found no further need for contact with their Muslim and Hindu compatriots, and before long Indian Christians had become aliens in their own homeland, separated from all the normal relationships of family, community and caste. The modern tendency is to criticise the early missionaries for this policy, but it is difficult to know what else they could have done in the circumstances.

Groves eventually found from experience just how much time and energy (and capital) can be sunk in commercial ventures, to the detriment of spiritual ministry. He saw John Arulappan distracted with fields and finances, and he began to feel that faithful gifted men like him should be set free to devote their time to the work they did best – the work of the gospel which would endure not for a few years but for eternity. It was through the influence of Groves that *The Missionary Reporter* recommended Arulappan to its British readers as one worthy of support: "Mr Groves considered it would be failure to allow him to spend his strength in ordinary occupations when there is such abundant need for the entire services of men capable of performing the work of an evangelist."[75] The example of the apostle Paul was clear enough. His work as a tent-maker (or leather worker) never tied him to one place; he could pick up his tools or put them down as the Spirit might lead. In case of need, wherever he happened to be, there was work he could do with his hands, but his freedom to preach the gospel was never compromised.[76]

Norris Groves himself, at the age of fifty-two, felt a considerable degree of relief in the anticipation of being free at last from commercial responsibilities. "It is much my desire," he said, "if the Lord clears away difficulties, to give the rest of my short space to an uninterrupted ministry some where or in some form."[77] Perhaps for this reason the following generation of Brethren missionaries did not follow his earlier "tent-making" example. Those known to *The Missionary Reporter*, *The Missionary Echo* and *Echoes of Service* were (and still are) supported for full-time Christian work, although many continue to offer medical or educational services free of charge or at rates below the market level. But the "tent-making" idea refuses to go away. An Indian evangelist is still likely to find his message ignored when his hearers discover he is paid to deliver it. And in some countries where Christian missionaries are not welcome the necessity remains for the evangelist or church planter to establish himself in some secular capacity. The ideal solution is often a part-time job that earns a small amount yet leaves abundant time for Christian service. There are not many such jobs, and not many people willing to take them. And even fewer able to provide them.

This is where the Christian businessman or industrialist can play his part. Colonel Cotton (later General Sir Arthur Cotton) offers an admirable example. He never considered himself a missionary, yet it was his standing as a civil engineer that enabled him to invite William Bowden to speak of Christ to the labourers on his irrigation schemes. It also equipped him to provide financial support for Bowden and his family. In later life Frank Groves too was an industrialist rather than an evangelist, and it was through his successful sugar and coffee industries that he was able to provide for others to devote their energies to the work of the gospel. Writing of the sugar refinery which he and Henry had set up in Palhully, Harriet Groves remarked, "Thus, in the providence of God, they illustrate the principle their father so desired to see carried out in India, of uniting spiritual and manual labour, and while availing themselves of the facilities the country affords for their support, they not only seek the blessing of the people among whom they dwell, but strengthen the hands of other missionaries."[78]

In the mind of Norris Groves this partnership between Christian industry and Christian mission was one aspect of a complete strategy for the creation of indigenous fellowships in a land such as India. Associated with it we have seen three simple principles: the sending of missionaries by local churches to plant local churches; the training of disciples in the course of active Christian service; and the liberty of local Christians to take responsibility without reference to foreign organisations. Even in our day these might be considered radical ideas. In his they were revolutionary.

ENDNOTES

[1] Groves, "A Letter on Missions", 141
[2] Rowdon, *Origins*, 199 (quoting 1 Cor 15:8 AV).
[3] R22
[4] M275
[5] M282
[6] M287
[7] M271. "Andrew Murray pointed out that the Lord and his apostles could not have accomplished the work *they* had to do had they not been actually poor. He who would lift up another must descend, like the Samaritan, to where he lies, and the infinite majority of mankind always have been, and still are, poor" (Lang, *Groves*, 54).
[8] M278
[9] M280

[10] M279. Venn argued that if a local Christian progressed so far as to receive ordination, he should be given a settled pastorate and no longer preach in public. The reason given is strange indeed: "If Native Ministers were associated in the work of evangelisation they must necessarily assume too much of the European status. As Clergymen of the Church of England they would appear before their countrymen as belonging to a different class and as the well-paid agents of a foreign Society" (Warren, 65). Indeed, one Brahman catechist, to Venn's knowledge, had refused ordination because it would compromise his position as an evangelist. Here was an ecclesiastical system that prevented church leaders from preaching the gospel to their own people.

[11] M275

[12] R69; M110

[13] M80

[14] M284, 288

[15] See 1 Cor 9:19-23.

[16] M285

[17] Having baptised an Englishman a year after his arrival, William Carey cheerfully reported, "A Baptist church is formed in this distant quarter of the globe." A charter had just been drawn up, with four "members", and Carey, for the first time in India, presided at a celebration of the Lord's Supper (Letter dated 1795, quoted by George, 113-114).

[18] After the death of Andrew Fuller in 1815, a younger generation of committee men sided with a younger generation of missionaries, who expressed harsh and unjust criticism of the Baptist pioneers, especially of Dr Marshman. The controversy lasted sixteen years, and the main issue under dispute was the claim of the home committee to own the property in Serampore because they had raised a large proportion of the funds which paid for it (George, 164-165; Smith G, *Carey*, 359-376; Tucker, 120-121). Hudson Taylor, too, had great difficulty throughout 1891-2 in persuading the London council of the CIM to agree that control of the mission should be retained by the leadership in China once he himself had retired (Taylor, *Growth of a Work of God*, 506-507).

[19] Rhenius had to concede to the CMS that "the property is theirs," but stoutly disputed their claim to the Indian believers: "You maintain that the whole Mission is yours because in the first instance you sent me to Tinnevelly, gave me the temporal support which I needed, and defrayed other expenses of the Mission... You say that *we* have no right whatever – what monstrous doctrine is this!.. Henceforth money is to be deemed the principle consideration... The sweat of the missionary's brow, his anxious labours, are nothing to be accounted of in the matter!" (Rhenius to Tucker, 30 May 1835, in Rhenius, 482; Rhenius to Jowett, 18 July 1835, in Groves, *Tinnevelly Mission*, 33; Rhenius, 513).

[20] M274

[21] M331

[22] M280

[23] From 1880 onwards, Keswick holiness teaching raised standards and expectations in the missionary community even higher; it became ever more difficult to find men

sufficiently spiritual and knowledgeable for ordination. This led to serious tensions between local Christians and missionaries, and hindered the indigenisation of the churches in certain places, notably in west Africa (Shenk, 112; Stanley, 166). The fact is that the pioneer missionary must often turn a blind eye to lapses and shortcomings in those who first emerge as leaders among a previously unreached people. He has this choice: either he remains in place until he sees perfection in his converts, or else he encourages them to take responsibility while still imperfect. Unlike many of his contemporaries, Groves would always do the latter. He "had a love which could bear and endure all – an ability given him of God to sympathise with weakness to any extent" (M6). In a different context Groves himself urged, "What we want is spirituality of mind, subduedness of spirit... and power to manifest our spiritual strength by our ability to bear with weakness in others rather than by our skill in finding out faults and failings" (M461). And on another occasion, "Really when I see how many weaknesses and prejudices the apostles had to bear with in their early converts, I am quite reconciled to bear the same in the converts of India" (M350).

On this issue Watchman Nee argued the necessity to recognise every local group of Christians as a church, and the most spiritually mature among them as elders, despite the faults and failings that might still be evident in them. The qualifications listed in 1 Timothy 3 and Titus 1 he believed applicable to a mature church, such as that in Ephesus at the time Timothy was sent there, but should not be imposed on every group of new converts (*TNCCL*, 42-43).

[24] M280. Choultry: a caravanserai or inn where animals occupy a central courtyard (from Telugu: *chawadi*).

[25] M287

[26] R301. After the plague in Baghdad, though longing for spiritual fellowship amongst a settled group of co-workers, he wrote, "I therefore now purpose, the Lord enabling me, after nearly six months interruption, to return to the studies preparatory to my future duties as an itinerating missionary. To this service I ever thought the Lord had called me" (R240).

[27] R303.

[28] See section above entitled *Messengers of the Churches*.

[29] M308-309

[30] M254. It was in North Africa that Groves's ideas seem to have been most fully adopted by his contemporaries, largely through the influence of Edward Glenny and other Brethren associated with the North Africa Mission and with groups that later merged with it. These have been described collectively as missionary "bands", whose watchword "dispersal and distribution" demonstrated their commitment to itinerant evangelism rather than church planting. The historian of NAM suggests, "It may well have been the view of the Bands that the local church should be developed by converted North Africans, rather than be superimposed upon them as was the program of [the Methodist Episcopal Mission]." In North Africa, however, the particular difficulties of work amongst Muslims and Jews meant that neither strategy was notably successful (Steele, 142).

[31] M247

[32] By way of comparison, Henry Venn only ever met an indigenous leader when one sufficiently educated to speak English, and sufficiently wealthy to book a sea passage, happened to come to London and make an appointment with him. In theory, of course, Venn advocated indigenous leadership, but his efforts to ordain the African bishop, Samuel Crowther, and his subsequent failure to support him against missionary opposition, contributed to the years of conflict that ensued between local West African leaders and the CMS. The evidence suggests that Venn simply failed to comprehend the difficulties faced by indigenous church leaders (Warren, 30).

[33] M392

[34] M393

[35] R19; M88

[36] Letter dated 1840 (M393).

[37] Gützlaff's acceptance for missionary training was the result of a personal letter from Karl Rhenius to the King of Prussia. Gützlaff and Rhenius corresponded regularly after that (Rhenius, 258-259, 440). An account of Gützlaff's life appears in Broomhall A J, *Barbarians at the Gates*, 180-187, 315-361, and an assessment of his Chinese Union in Lutz & Lutz, 269-291.

[38] Fifteen years earlier, some of the catechists (evangelists) associated with Rhenius were likewise found to be of dubious spiritual quality. Rhenius defended them, saying that individually they might be far from perfect but collectively were nevertheless accomplishing a highly significant work, establishing local schools and congregations over a wide area. He met regularly with the catechists as a group for teaching, discussion and prayer, and he sometimes found it necessary to discipline or dismiss those who proved unsatisfactory (Rhenius, 549-555, 561).

[39] Broomhall, *Barbarians*, 9

[40] *Barbarians*, 330. Broomhall suggests that "the principle was rediscovered and clearly demonstrated by J O Fraser in the Lisu church, since when it has been widely applied."

[41] Gützlaff, quoted by Broomhall, *Barbarians*, 333

[42] We will consider the evidence in Chapter 33.

[43] M243

[44] Newton, *Anthony Norris Groves*, 13

[45] Tucker, 285-286. Jones looked at the content of previous missionary preaching and identified three traditional approaches: 1. Demolishing the other religions and then establishing your own on the ruins; 2. Showing how Christianity fulfils the vision of the ancient faiths; 3. Starting with a subject of general interest, then leading into a gospel appeal. He proposed a fourth which he believed superior: to speak frankly of Christ – his character, teaching and purpose.

Jones spoke in English, sometimes with interpretation. He once confided to Mahatma Gandhi his longing "to see Christianity naturalised in India, so that it shall be no longer a foreign thing identified with foreign people and a foreign government, but part of the national life of India and contributing its power to India's uplift and redemption." Gandhi offered some advice: "I would suggest, first, that all of you Christians, missionaries and all, must begin to live more like Jesus Christ... If you will come to us in the spirit of your Master we cannot resist you... Second, I would suggest that you must practise your religion without adulterating or toning it down... Third, I would suggest that you must put your emphasis upon love, for love is the centre and soul of Christianity" (Jones, 146-148). On such terms, Gandhi would surely have found Groves a man to his liking.

[46] J44-45; M59

[47] Acts 19:9. The Greek *scholē* (school) is now often translated "lecture hall" (NIV, NRSV, GNB etc).

[48] Jn 2:11; 3:2; 4:54; 20:30

[49] George, 145

[50] Shenk, 87-88

[51] R192

[52] M326-327

[53] *Christian Influence*, 52

[54] Newton, *Anthony Norris Groves*, 13

[55] J49-50; M59 (see chapter 10)

[56] At this time it was common for Nonconformist ministers in Britain to earn their living through secular employment. As a young man, William Carey served as Baptist pastor in Moulton whilst teaching an elementary school by day and selling shoes by night. But such an arrangement would not normally require him to invest in property or remain permanently in one place.

[57] M370-371

[58] M371

[59] Groves, "A Letter on Missions", 136, 140 (2 Thess 3:6-13)

[60] M391

[61] Acts 18:1-4; 1 Thess 2:9; 2 Thess 3:7-8

[62] M371

[63] Tucker, 69

[64] Carey, *Enquiry*, in George, Appendix E.50. His employment in this work for three months of the year, by an official of the East India Company, enabled Carey to live in British India at a time when Christian missionaries were still prohibited by law. Carey later acquired a more secure and independent income as a teacher of Bengali, as a professor of Sanskrit and Marathi, and as a government translator. He gave away at least a quarter of what he earned, to further the work of God (George, 105-106).

[65] Powell, 136

[66] R261. Morrison was a Congregationalist, working with the London Missionary Society, whose energies were divided between translation of Christian literature, discreet personal evangelism, and his duties as an official interpreter for the East India Company.

[67] R214-215

[68] Smith G, *Carey*, 109

[69] Clark, 264-267

[70] "The Basel Mission" at <http://www.geocitiessites.com/Athens/2960/basel.htm>. For primary sources see <http://www.bmarchives.org/>.

[71] Groves E K, *Successors*, 45

[72] Newton, *Anthony Norris Groves*, 13 (citing his Theol M Thesis, *The Plymouth Brethren in India from 1833 to 1970*, Melbourne, 1978)

[73] In China the young Hudson Taylor found local doctors and druggists resentful of the fact that he was taking away their customers, which almost caused a riot on at least one occasion (Taylor, *Growth of a Work of God*, 111n.; Broomhall, *Survivors' Pact*, 299). Sabotage has never, to my knowledge, been proposed as a reason for the repeated infection of the silkworms at Chittoor but perhaps it should not be ruled out. Christian commercial projects are always vulnerable to the jealousy of commercial as well as religious rivals.

[74] R78

[75] *The Missionary Reporter*, no. 1 (July 1853), 3

[76] Paul's tent-making in Corinth was evidently a temporary arrangement. Once Silas and Timothy had arrived (probably bringing financial support from Philippi), he "devoted himself exclusively to preaching" (Acts 18:5). He appears quite flexible in all but his determination to accept nothing from the unconverted (1 Cor 9:18). Groves develops this theme in *On the Liberty of Ministry*, 50ff, and more briefly in "A Letter on Missions", 138. For a discussion of missionary support in the New Testament, see Robin Daniel, *Mission Strategies*, 145-50; 165-6.

[77] M421

[78] M549

"For myself,
I wish no man living
to show the least regard for my opinion
for any other reason than its being
the same as the mind of God."

Norris Groves [1]

33

So Few Pretensions

Almost Forgetting

Reviewing a missionary career that had started so brightly, Norris Groves was not merely modest about his achievements; he was positively despondent. "So poor and wretched a cumberer of the ground," he called himself, whilst "looking back on a worse than useless life".[2] He had failed, he thought, in Baghdad, and failed again in India: "I am at times very, very low when I think what I am, after all the Lord's loving culture. I feel I ought to have rendered to him such different fruit."[3] But there was one, at least, who had much to thank him for.

George Müller, four years after becoming a Christian, could look back on the summer of 1829 as an experience "like a second conversion".[4] How did this come about? He had read *Christian Devotedness*, and it was then, he tells us, that "I gave myself fully to the Lord. Honour, pleasure, money, my physical powers, my mental powers, all was laid down at the feet of Jesus, and I became a great lover of the word of God."[5] Groves's decision literally to forsake all and follow Christ "made such an impression on me," said Müller, "and delighted me so, that I not only marked it down in my journal but also wrote about it to my German friends."[6]

A year later Müller had resigned from the London Society for Promoting Christianity amongst the Jews. "I… had a conscientious objection against being led and directed by *men* in my missionary labours," he said. "As a servant of Christ, it appeared to me I ought to be guided by the Spirit, and not by men, as to time and place."[7] After lengthy deliberation he decided, in this also, to follow the example of Groves, looking to God alone for guidance and for financial provision. But could he really depend on what the Bible said about these things? "The Lord most mercifully enabled me to take the promises of his word and rest upon them, and such as Matthew 7:7-8, John 14:13-14, Matthew 6:25-34 were the stay of my soul concerning this point. In addition to this, the example of brother Groves, the dentist… who gave up his profession and went out as a missionary, was a great encouragement to me. For the news which by this time had arrived of how the Lord had aided him on his way to Petersburg, and at Petersburg, strengthened my faith."[8]

In 1832 George Müller moved to Bristol, having married Groves's sister Mary, and for the next sixty-six years he applied the simple New Testament principles of fellowship and faith to the life of the local church and to the famous orphan houses on Ashley Down. The influence of Groves is seen in every stone, every window and every loaf of bread. "My wife and I," recalled Müller, "had grace given to us to take the Lord's commandment 'Sell that ye have and give alms' (Luke 12:33) literally and to carry it out. Our staff and support in this matter were Matthew 6:19-34, John 14:13-14. We leaned on the arm of the Lord Jesus. It is now sixty-four years since we set out on this way, and *we do not in the least regret the step we then took*... It has, in particular, made the Lord known to us more fully than we knew him before *as a prayer-hearing God*."[9]

After a long and eventful life, Müller died in 1898, at the age of ninety-three. He had provided a home for exactly 122,683 orphans, of whom almost two thousand made a clear profession of faith in Christ. He sent out 250,000 Bibles and 1,500,000 New Testaments to many parts of the world in many different languages, and he channelled a quarter of a million pounds (a vast sum at nineteenth-century values) to missionaries overseas – and all this without asking a penny from any human source. The influence of Norris Groves on George Müller alone would be sufficient to earn him an honoured place in the annals of evangelical Christianity, but his significance extends far further than that.

For was he not, in some sense, a founder of the Brethren? Influential as he was, this would be to misunderstand both him and his part in the events of those days. W Blair Neatby, the earliest major historian of the Brethren movement, claims, "It seems fair to say of Groves that he had a larger share in its foundation than anyone else."[10] But as with almost everything Groves did, his contribution was spontaneous, artless and idealistic, and produced results rather different from his hope and expectation. He obviously had no grand design in mind. In December 1833 he wrote in his Indian journal, "I was almost forgetting, till a letter from Mr Bellett of Dublin reminded me, that I was the first to propose that simple principle of union, the love of Jesus, instead of oneness of judgment in minor things... Little did I then think to see that dear brother and many others united in a holy loving fellowship on these blessed principles, and to see that they are extending. Here the Lord allows me blessed encouragement."[11]

It fell to Bellett, to Parnell, to Percy Hall, and especially to George Müller, to work out in practice the impromptu idea that Groves had tossed out before disappearing to the other side of the world. None of these men proposed to institute a new church denomination, and none but John Darby attempted to co-ordinate Brethren activities on a national or international scale. No man, or men, could take the place of Christ as head of the Church, or of his word as its guide and inspiration. Yet the fact remains that within fifty years the "little churches" had acquired a denominational label. In 1883 the local newspaper reporting Lord Congleton's funeral referred to those present as "Plymouth Brethren".[12] They were not Anglicans or Baptists or Quakers; they had become a distinct group with a recognisable identity. To the newspaper reporter, as to all interested observers, the Brethren had become a denomination among the other denominations of the Christian Church, and an important one at that.

The friends in Dublin may not have foreseen this, but the fact that in May 1830 they started to worship together at Aungier Street, and ceased to do so elsewhere, meant that in the nature of things they constituted a group in competition with the Established and Nonconformist churches of the city, and able to attract adherents from them. Despite this, there was no great effort to make Aungier Street the headquarters of a wider movement or to institute similar groups elsewhere. On the contrary, "To follow Groves to Baghdad on a mission that must be deemed singularly unpromising was the prevailing passion in Dublin."[13] Whereas the formative years of other church denominations and renewal movements have invariably been marked by a desire to consolidate the home base before moving overseas, Groves and his companions were setting out for the uttermost parts before any thought was given to a stable home base. Of the early leaders in England and Ireland, he not only took with him Parnell, Cronin and Newman, but urged others such as Wigram, Müller and Craik to join him as soon as possible. "That we thus get a list of almost all the names of men who had taken a leading part in the movement before 1830 is a striking proof, not only of the fervour of the zeal of the first Brethren and of their readiness to stake everything on principles of action that may now appear to us rather visionary, but also of their superiority to any ambition to found a new sect."[14]

In fact the whole organisation in the early days seems to have been distinctly haphazard. "It was, at the first, far less a theory than a sentiment that lay at the root of the new separation."[15] What is more, the feeling (in Cronin's circle at least) was as much negative as positive. "Special membership, as it is called among Dissenters," he recalled, "was the primary and most offensive condition of things to all our minds, so that our first assembling was really marked as a small company of evangelical malcontents."[16] The earliest leaders in Dublin were young and inexperienced. Bellett later recalled, "It was poor material we had... There was but little spiritual energy, and much that was poor treasure for a living Temple, but we held together in the Lord's mercy and care, I believe advancing in the knowledge of his mind."[17] Cronin confirms this rather sorry state: "We were also, from ignorance or indifference, careless as to conscience and godly care one for another."[18] Nothing could be more unlike the methodical programme instituted by John Wesley a century earlier, and nothing could contrast more completely with the dynamic sense of purpose and bold evangelistic enterprise of the Brethren as the movement gained momentum during the second half of the century.

Once Groves had left for the East in 1829, events in Dublin and southern England continued to develop without him, and in ways of which he could not wholeheartedly approve. He tried to keep in touch by mail, although few letters actually got through to Baghdad. The booklet *Christian Devotedness*, circulating widely, continued to play its part, and the heroic aspect of the Baghdad mission contributed to the visionary challenge of the new spiritual movement, but beyond this, its author played no active part in the somewhat erratic growth of the independent congregations throughout the British Isles.

The accounts that survive show that many sprang up as a spontaneous response to local circumstances. This is not surprising in view of the general dissatisfaction with both the Established and Nonconformist churches of the day, for a universally felt need can lead to a similar response in places far apart. But as these independent fellowships began to make contact with one another, they were drawn into a common stream that received much inspiration from accounts they heard of a certain Exeter dentist and a certain Bristol orphanage. And although Groves had not planned or foreseen these developments, he followed the news of events from afar with much interest. "Sometimes," he said, "my heart overflows with the thought of visiting the little churches."[19]

Little churches they might be, but certainly not, in Groves's mind, a Church! He referred to the informal gatherings as "little flocks", "households of the faithful" and "the various congregations of the Lord's people", but never as "the Assemblies" or "the Plymouth Brethren" or even "the Brethren" in a corporate sense. From the start, his idealistic mind allowed no room for a new denomination in competition with those already in existence. He believed it possible to meet with others for breaking of bread and still remain an Anglican or a Baptist or a Wesleyan. Into the equation, however, we must throw John Nelson Darby, a man whose extraordinary energies were now directed towards uniting all these groups under his own authority. Many that had started well became hard, judgmental, quarrelsome. It was a tragic turn of events. "Groves... with his singularly pure, lofty and tender spirit, had no more interest in a sect than he had capacity to form one. He was essentially catholic, and he had to endure the grief – which to a man less pure from the taint of self-seeking would have been the bitter mortification – of seeing another man enter into his labours and convert them to purposes that he abhorred."[20] Committed to his work overseas, there was little he could do but watch and pray.

Neatby charts subsequent events: "As time went on, Groves grew to hope less and less from the movement that he had done so much to inaugurate. From the time that Darby's principles of fellowship gained the ascendancy in England, Groves considered that the downfall of the Brethren was decreed. Though he personally adhered through life to their communion, he evidently ceased to expect them 'to work any deliverance in the earth'. The disease he had grappled with so hopefully at the first seemed now beyond remedy."[21] He remained loyal to groups with an open character, and he continued to speak of the principles he had always held, but he never had any sympathy with Darby's idea that other Christians and churches should be shunned as apostate, and it grieved him to see how seriously the movement had shifted in this direction.

Norris Groves lived only five years after Darby's final rejection of the open assemblies in 1848 and his departure to lead the Exclusive Brethren into what many would consider the wilderness. The bitterness of that process took the shine off what had started as a gloriously idealistic movement, and it would require a further decade, and the conversion of a fresh generation through the great Revival of 1858-9, before it could regain its equilibrium and its lost momentum. Indeed, it was not until 1940 that a book about *Brethren* could be given the subtitle *The Story of a Great Recovery*, with reports of 80,000 adherents in England and more than 120 open congregations in the greater London area alone.[22] By then the assemblies had rid themselves of many harsh and unbiblical prejudices inculcated by John Darby. They are still, in some places, trying to rid themselves of the remainder.

Some Evangelical Alliances

After the departure of Darby it was the strong vision for Christian unity proposed by Norris Groves that prevailed among the Open Brethren. His vision, moreover, had soon extended well beyond the confines of groups identified with the movement. The unifying influence of the Brethren assemblies, and especially of their travelling evangelists, has been warmly commended by many outside their number. A recent independent commentator describes the Open Brethren in simple and somewhat heroic terms: "In the 1830s and later they were an innovative revival movement whose influences reached far beyond their own ranks."[23] Even more striking is the assessment of J Edwin Orr: "The early Brethren view of Christian unity gradually permeated the thinking of the evangelical denominations via the Evangelical Alliance and the Evangelical Awakening of 1859."[24] If this is true, it means that in hardly more than a single generation Groves's idea of free fellowship between all disciples of Christ had advanced from the outrageous to the questionable... to the desirable... to the commonplace... and this throughout the evangelical community of England.

It was largely through the Revival itself that the Brethren came to the notice of the wider Christian public. All Protestant denominations were involved in the city-wide campaigns of 1858-9, and all grew dramatically through conversions. Many of the most effective evangelists were not clergymen; many admitted to no denominational identity; many others declared themselves openly as "Brethren". The Revival stirred up a spirit of fervent prayer, a sensitivity to sin and holiness, and a renewed emphasis on two great doctrines – the spiritual unity of believers in Christ and the authority of the scriptures. These were the great principles of the early Brethren, and their adoption brought credit to the Brethren movement as a whole. But these very principles, now so widely accepted, were to be severely tested as the nineteenth century drew towards its close. Christians from every denomination were brought face to face with theories of biological evolution and geological succession, and with critical reappraisals of the Greek and Hebrew manuscripts, that challenged the very basis of their biblical beliefs. Fresh lines of demarcation were driven among Christians. And these divisions, for the first time, took place *within* the denominations. Anglican was now at loggerheads with Anglican, Baptist with Baptist, Methodist with Methodist. As time went by, Evangelicals from every denomination found common ground in their determination to defend the scriptures as the authority for their faith. In the end, the vision of Norris Groves for Christian unity came to fruition in the form of evangelical solidarity, and it was the challenge of liberal criticism that brought it about.

The Evangelical Alliance, founded in 1846, gave Christian leaders the opportunity to express their agreement on the basic doctrines of the faith whilst agreeing to differ on secondary matters. In that year, as the constitution of the Evangelical Alliance was being discussed, an Irish participant declared, "When I heard of this alliance, my whole heart went out; and when I see the Basis, I see, permit me to say, (I hope I do not offend), that the grand principle of this Alliance is the principle of the Plymouth Brethren.'"[25] Eighteen years later, in 1864, came the first of the Mildmay Conferences in London which, along with similar inter-denominational gatherings in Oxford and Brighton, prepared the way for the first "Convention for the Deepening of the Spiritual Life" at Keswick in 1875. The famous motto "All One in Christ Jesus" was borrowed directly from the 1858-9 Revival, and for a considerable period the majority of Keswick leaders and speakers were either evangelists or converts of the Revival. The distinctive Keswick teaching on "holiness", "full surrender", "the rest of faith" and "unbroken communion with the Lord" would seem to echo the Brethren emphasis on separation from the world, devotion to Christ and willing response to divine guidance. In tracing the progress of these ideas a historian of the period draws our attention to "the wider Brethren role in fostering expectations of higher attainments in practical holiness." Indeed, he suggests, "Brethren influence helped cultivate the belief that entire consecration is possible."[26] In all these developments we might see an enthusiastic acceptance of the vision for Christian unity and for personal devotion to Christ proposed so many years earlier by Norris Groves.

Closer investigation, however, reveals that Brethren were conspicuously absent from the earliest committees of both the Evangelical Alliance and the Keswick Convention. Why was this? The early leaders of the Brethren were men of intellectual power, social standing and moral influence; many had been trained as clergymen, barristers, solicitors, military and naval officers and physicians; among them were prosperous businessmen, manufacturers and landowners. Were none asked to participate? Or did they decline to do so? Their absence testifies to a certain tension between the Brethren and the Anglicans and Nonconformists who took the lead in the Evangelical Alliance and the Keswick Convention. Just as Groves met with prejudice, misunderstanding and opposition in India, so did his friends in Britain. The assemblies were young, fresh and energetic; they had attracted people from the older and more conventional churches, and the loss created no little alarm. The existing denominations, in fact, were very worried about the Brethren movement. "It seemed at first to be a movement great enough to threaten the whole organisation of the Christian Church." So said an article entitled "Plymouth Brethren" in a *Popular Encyclopaedia* published in the mid-twentieth century.[27] The Brethren indeed! Who were these people? What were their beliefs? And what heresy did they hold that required them to go off and start something new? On investigation, no heresy was found – simply a desire for more freedom in worship, more holiness of life, more active engagement of lay people in preaching and teaching the word of God. So the thought came that if the older churches could combine to provide these things, perhaps there would be no call for their members to desert to the Brethren.

It is possible, therefore, to see the Evangelical Alliance as a kind of "Counter-Reformation" in response to the Brethren "Reformation". And in that sense, the Evangelical Alliance, far from being a fruit of Brethren influence, was rather a reaction to it. This, indeed, was expressed quite clearly at the time by John Angell James when calling for a union of Evangelicals to combat "infidelity and Popery, Puseyism and Plymouth Brethrenism".[28] The Scottish churchman Dr Robert Candlish declared, "The unity of the church is greatly promoted by a resistance to the common enemy," and for many Anglicans and Nonconformists, the Brethren would undoubtedly count among the "enemy".[29]

So we have a paradoxical situation of "Brethren principles" adopted in the hope of competing with and eclipsing the Brethren. Had he lived to see it, Norris Groves would have been quite content; the principles mattered to him more than the Brethren. And yet the kind of unity instituted by the Evangelical Alliance was different in nature from that envisaged by Groves himself. It represented a co-operative unity of Christian denominations (retaining their denominational identities) over against his emphasis on the inherent unity of Christian individuals (obliterating their denominational identities). It was not quite what he had in mind, but he would have been happy enough to see evangelical unity of any sort. In fact, a century and a half later, it is the original and most radical vision of Groves that shows signs of fulfilment in modern Britain. For if the nineteenth century was marked by denominational rivalry, and the twentieth by inter-denominational co-operation, the twenty-first looks set to be one where denominational loyalties fade and disappear altogether.[30]

Every Church a Missionary Society

In the immediate aftermath of the 1858-9 Revival, the energies of the older churches were taken up with teaching the tens of thousands of new believers and trying to maintain the momentum of evangelistic activity in the towns and villages of the British Isles. Little thought was given to the foreign field. In many Anglican and Nonconformist churches there was still indifference, if not outright hostility, to the idea of overseas missionary work. William Carey was not the only one to find difficulty in persuading church leaders to consider the need of the heathen. In 1787 a colonial administrator had written to Charles Simeon and William Wilberforce begging for eight Anglican missionaries to be sent to India, but not one Church of England clergyman could be found to go.[31] Henry Venn bewailed the fact that in 1865 only one in four or five clergymen of the Church of England would allow a Church Missionary Society representative to speak to their congregation.[32] The other Anglican societies, the SPG and SPCK, fared no better. Funds were scarce, suitable missionary recruits even scarcer.[33] At the same period in the United States, Rufus Anderson reckoned that only half the evangelical Christians in America gave any financial support to foreign or home missions, and those who did rarely gave more than half a dollar a year.[34]

This contrasts strikingly with the healthy vision for overseas mission that inspired the early Brethren in Dublin. The Baghdad venture had all the vigour and optimism of youth. When he set out in 1829, Groves himself was only 34 years old, Kitto 25 and Pfander 26. Of those who went to join them, Cronin was just 28, Parnell and Newman 24. The imagination of a generation was stirred by the prospect of a successful dentist, a qualified medical doctor, a member of the landed aristocracy and a first-class Oxford graduate all abandoning wealth, comfort and career in order to live by faith and proclaim the gospel to Persians and Arabs. Nothing like it had been seen before. And it all took place a full twenty-six years before David Livingstone, returning from his early explorations, made his famous appeal to the students of Cambridge: "I go back to Africa, to try to make an open path for commerce and Christianity. Do you carry out the work which I have begun. I leave it with you!"[35] Indeed, not till the departure of the Cambridge Seven in 1885 was there a similar event among the cultured elite of British evangelicalism.

And yet the missionary enterprise initiated by Norris Groves so nearly came to nothing. Just eight years later, having failed in Baghdad and in Madras, it almost seemed that Groves was finished. Abandoned by his co-workers, rejected by the English community, bereaved, depressed, and unable to communicate in any Indian language, what could he hope to achieve? Letters came advising him to come home. Some counselled that preaching to the heathen was not the will of God for the present age. Groves must have wondered if it was all a terrible mistake. But there were five who stood with him. "It was left to the humble Godavari workers to prove the others wrong, and the noble Groves right! A singularly high honour was appointed them of God."[36] The Bowdens and Beers were straightforward people, bred from generations of Devon farmers; they knew how to press on doggedly with the job in hand until it was thoroughly done. Lacking the emotional intensity of Norris Groves, they were not prey to the turbulent feelings that afflict a man who considers himself responsible for everyone he meets, and their simple tenacity enabled them to be more effective church-planting missionaries than he could ever be. The other who "proved him right" was, of course, his Indian disciple John Arulappan. And Groves watched, humbled and delighted, as these younger folk surpassed him, laying foundations that remain to this day.

But Norris Groves did more than set an example for missionaries and national workers. It was actually he who envisaged the method of their support – a method that would provide for their needs without seeking to control their activities. In July 1853, just two months after his death, the first issue of *The Missionary Reporter* came off the press. It continued to appear month by month, and the fifth issue described its origins: "This little periodical may be said to have resulted from a few faithful words spoken by Mr Groves this time last year. It was on the 31st Oct. 1852 when Mr Groves, having lately returned to this country on account of his health, gave to one of the churches a statement concerning the work of the Lord in India. With a feeling heart he also spoke of the necessities of some of the Lord's servants there whom he knew to need and to be worthy of help. He stated his views that care for missionaries was one of the duties of a church, and he urged the necessity for activity in its discharge."[37]

Individual members of this congregation in Tottenham had long been interested in overseas mission, but only now did the church as a body begin to organise missionary support. Hearing that "some Christians in another locality" (Hackney) were being led in the same direction, they joined forces to publish the eight pages that made up the first magazine.[38] From the beginning its purpose was clear. The first editorial was headed "Every Church a Missionary Society", and the opening article affirmed that "the wide world is in truth the mission field, and the one church of Christ on earth is, or should be, the Missionary Society."[39] The editor and his associates disclaimed any intention of organising missions or appointing missionaries, but they encouraged local churches to take initiatives both in outreach to their own neighbourhood and in sending workers overseas. The editor soon became a channel for gifts sent by individuals and assemblies to missionaries whose letters appeared in its pages.[40]

The *Missionary Reporter* nowhere claimed to be a "Brethren" publication, and it included reports of missionary meetings and activities conducted by Anglicans and Baptists as well as those without a formal denominational identity. The majority of letters from the field were sent by missionaries who had gone out, like Groves, simply trusting the Lord to guide and provide. Most had no connection with a missionary society – in some cases because there was no society operating in the land to which they were called, others because they could not subscribe to the doctrinal or practical requirements of a society, or were unable to fulfil the academic requirements for ordination. Bowden and Beer sent regular letters. Issue number four contained a long report from Arulappan and another from Marian, a young man working with him. There was a notice of an inter-denominational missionary conference convened by the Evangelical Alliance, an extract from George Müller's current *Narrative*, and a request for prayer concerning a young man named James Hudson Taylor, about to sail for the first time to China. Subsequent issues included further accounts of the work in India, and number thirteen in 1854 contained a long letter from Hudson Taylor with news of his arrival in Shanghai and initial impressions of China. By the time it lapsed in 1858, *The Missionary Reporter* had carried news from forty different countries and more than a hundred missionaries.[41]

It is not clear why the periodical ceased at this point, but the year 1872 saw the first issue of its successor, *The Missionary Echo*.[42] By this time, with the influx of Revival converts, the Brethren assemblies had become the most active of all British denominations in sending and supporting missionaries overseas.[43] In 1885 the name of the magazine was changed to *Echoes of Service*, and since then, for well over a hundred years, its editors have published letters and forwarded gifts to workers throughout the world. Similar magazines were launched in America, Australia and a number of other countries. A worldwide total of 1760 Christian Brethren missionaries working in at least 74 different nations are currently noted in the prayer digest *Operation World*.[44] Over and above this are thousands of national workers sent out by indigenous assemblies in many parts of the developing world. All these might look to Norris Groves as their forerunner, and some were led to their field of labour directly through his example.[45]

Father of Faith Missions

But the influence of Norris Groves extends far beyond the limits of what is now generally identified as the Brethren movement. His emphasis on seeking guidance from God rather than man has led many others to undertake God-given initiatives that have flourished and assumed an identity in their own right. And his determination to trust God for his daily needs, without a salary or appeals or pledges of support, has inspired thousands to live, as he did, "by faith".

When Rowland Bingham was led to found his Sudan Interior Mission in 1893, his determination to live by faith, with no denominational restrictions or financial appeals, owed much to Hudson Taylor, founder of the China Inland Mission, and thus, we might say, to Groves.[46] "For Hudson Taylor was greatly influenced by the faith and example of George Müller, and as we have seen George Müller had been guided and stimulated by A N Groves."[47] Bingham was not alone in this. In fact a whole generation of mission leaders and innovators were influenced and inspired by the CIM, which grew quite clearly from Brethren roots.

It may be of interest to trace the connection. The newly converted Hudson Taylor, aged nineteen, was away from home gaining medical experience. His biographers suggest, "It was no small mercy that led him during this sojourn in Hull into fellowship with a company of Christians exceptionally fitted to meet his need." Disturbed by divisions among the Methodists, he "had begun to feel himself something more than a Wesleyan, bound by more important ties to all who love the Lord Jesus Christ in sincerity and truth. While still in Barnsley he had enjoyed the meetings of the so-called Plymouth Brethren... and now in Hull was glad to renew associations that had already proved helpful." Here he heard about George Müller – how by faith Müller provided for hundreds of orphans and supported many missionaries in other parts of the world – and all this, without appeals or any guarantee of a stated income, simply through "effectual fervent prayer". "It made a profound impression upon Hudson Taylor, and encouraged him more than anything else could have in the pathway he was about to enter."[48] It was in this "company of Christians", in 1852, that he was baptised, just a few months before the death of Norris Groves.

Moving to London for medical training, Hudson Taylor frequently visited Groves's friends in Tottenham. A few years later from China he wrote, "I love Tottenham. I love those I know there dearly. Of no other place can I say that my every recollection is sweet and profitable, marred by no painful thought or circumstance, save that I see it no more."[49] Taylor enjoyed fellowship with Christians of every denomination, but "if it was prevailing prayer about urgent matters that he needed... he turned to the saints [i.e. the Brethren] at Tottenham, Hackney and Clevedon... This was the measure of their attitude to him as much as of his appreciation of them."[50]

We have seen how these same friends in Tottenham and Hackney, responding to Groves's appeal, had joined forces to produce *The Missionary Reporter*. And as we trace the influence of Norris Groves on his contemporaries, it is in these two London suburbs that we see his missionary vision most strongly supported. In Hackney, for example, there was a stockbroker by the name of George Pearse. In 1850 Pearse founded the Chinese Evangelisation Society, and three years later it was this society that sent Hudson Taylor on his first voyage to China. It was Pearse, moreover, who introduced the young Yorkshireman to another member of the assembly, William Berger, who in due course became Home Secretary of the China Inland Mission.[51]

Retiring from business at the early age of fifty-five, Pearse himself then served as a missionary for some years in Paris and Algeria. In 1881 he became one of three founder members of the North Africa Mission. Associated with him in this new venture was Edward Glenny, who as a Bristol schoolboy had been "converted under the preaching of George Müller".[52] Glenny, serving for forty years as General Secretary of NAM, was identified throughout his life with the Brethren. The third of the trio was Henry Grattan Guinness, who had worked as an itinerant evangelist during the 1858-9 Revival and enjoyed fellowship with assemblies of Brethren in many places. In 1866, as an elder at Merrion Hall in Dublin, he invited Hudson Taylor to visit the assembly.[53] In 1873 Guinness founded the East London Missionary Training Institute at Harley House, where in the course of his life he prepared a total of 1330 missionaries for forty societies of thirty denominations. In 1898 he launched his Regions Beyond Missionary Union.[54]

From this point onwards the "faith mission" network continues to expand. Through Grattan Guinness, the young A B Simpson was converted in Canada, and he became the founder of the Christian and Missionary Alliance.[55] Among those trained by Simpson was Peter Scott, who launched the Africa Inland Mission.[56] One Guinness daughter, Geraldine, joined the CIM, married the son of Hudson Taylor, and with him wrote the most famous of all missionary biographies.[57] The other daughter, Lucy, married Karl Kumm, who had received his missionary call through Edward Glenny, and then in 1904 helped him launch the Sudan United Mission.[58]

Four years later Kumm addressed a meeting in Liverpool. One of those present was a middle-aged C T Studd, who in his youth had mixed freely with Brethren at Cambridge University and learned much about "faith mission" from his years with Hudson Taylor in China. From that moment Studd's path was directed to central Africa where his vision would take shape in the Worldwide Evangelisation Crusade.[59] From these same roots grew the Christian Literature Crusade, with its bookshops and supply depots in many parts of the world.[60] As a modern mission historian affirms, the links in the chain are all there, stretching back to Norris Groves: "To sum up: the initiative for starting a faith mission usually came from men and women who belonged to the Brethren, who were influenced by them, or who belonged to independent congregations… The role of the Brethren is conspicuous."[61]

We have looked briefly at the story of Charles Gützlaff and his remarkable vision for a Chinese Christian Union, sending evangelists throughout China in the late 1840s. Gützlaff had personal links with the Brethren, and his Chinese workers were largely supported by Brethren in England, especially Richard Ball of Taunton and George Pearse. Gützlaff's emphasis on living frugally amongst the local people raised the question whether he had been influenced by Norris Groves, perhaps through correspondence. In April 1834 Groves was greatly encouraged by a letter from Gützlaff, sent either to himself or to someone else in Calcutta, which spoke of "extensive openings for publishing the gospel" in China.[62] Had Gützlaff read *Christian Devotedness*? It seems probable, for we know that among his close friends in China another influential government translator, Robert Morrison, had studied the booklet carefully and had been moved to commend its message. In his private journal for 20th November 1827 Morrison wrote, "A tract entitled 'Christian Devotedness' has appeared a little in my way with views as some deem them fanatical, of devoting all to God and not laying up treasures in the earth." A current periodical, the *Eclectic*, "opposed it fiercely," but Morrison defended Groves's position: "Christ's precepts, high spun impracticable dogmas? Oh no; let it not be said! I think them the words of truth and soberness."[63] Although Gützlaff's own efforts ended in some confusion, the historian of the China Inland Mission considers that no less than eleven missions were founded through his influence.[64] Hudson Taylor later called him the grandfather of the CIM, and though Gützlaff himself never knew it, his vision for reaching inland China through Chinese evangelists was finally fulfilled through the hundreds subsequently associated with the CIM and the thousands who have been active since the Communist takeover.

It would be impossible to document every initiative inspired by the faith of the early Brethren and by Hudson Taylor. A few must suffice. In 1883 an Indian lady, Pandita Ramabai, was converted to Christ. Shortly afterwards she read the biographies of George Müller, Hudson Taylor and John Paton.[65] Moved by the plight of unwanted children, she prayed for guidance, and in her own words, "I wondered, after reading their lives, if it were not possible to trust the Lord in India as in other countries."[66] By faith she opened a Christian school and orphanage in Bombay, and then in Pune, and subsequently developed a wide range of ministries now known as the Ramabai Mukti Mission. Through this work, hundreds of Indians, especially girls, have come to faith in Christ.

Another such initiative is linked with the name of Florence Young. Norris Groves himself, on his first visit to India in 1833, had enjoyed warm fellowship with her father, Henry Young, an official with the East India Company.[67] "After twelve years in India," Florence recalled, "my father returned to England, and spent some years in preaching the gospel. I have often heard him speak of the joy of this ministry and of the blessedness of entire dependence upon God for the supply of daily needs."[68] The family then emigrated, becoming active supporters of the Brethren movement in New Zealand and Australia. In 1886, when Florence felt led to start an evangelistic work among Pacific island labourers in Queensland, the first donation towards her Queensland Kanaka Mission came from George Müller, who visited Australia that year.

She subsequently joined the CIM, and then in 1904 founded the South Sea Evangelical Mission.[69]

Better known than either of these is Amy Carmichael, who in 1892 offered herself to the CIM and was refused on medical grounds. She went on to adopt the familiar principles of seeking guidance and provision from God alone, ignoring denominational identities and living like the local people in her much loved Dohnavur Fellowship in the Tinnevelly district of southern India. Here "no one received a salary, but the needs of all… were met in answer to prayer. No money was ever borrowed, no debt ever incurred."[70] Hundreds of endangered children were rescued through her efforts, and thousands of Christians blessed through her writings.[71]

Many early leaders in more recently established agencies such as Youth For Christ and Operation Mobilisation will cheerfully admit to having been "brought up in the Brethren". Evangelistic teams led by the young George Verwer so impressed the Brethren commentator William MacDonald that he wrote, for their encouragement, his modern classic *True Discipleship* in which he restated the message of Christian Devotedness, quoting several times from the words of Groves himself.[72] At that point *True Discipleship* became required reading for OM recruits and Verwer himself recently observed, "The booklet Christian Devotedness greatly influenced us in the early days."[73] In addition to the thousands of Europeans and Americans called to overseas service through George Verwer's speaking and writing are many, especially in India, who have been encouraged, through their experience with Operation Mobilisation, to undertake significant indigenous mission initiatives.[74]

Roger Forster, founder of the Ichthus Fellowship, with its circle of churches in Britain and further afield, was a young friend of George H Lang, biographer of Groves and Arulappan. He recently recalled, "As for myself, I've sought to live as it's popularly called 'by faith', and anticipated that God would always supply my needs. So I think it could be said that Norris Groves, through Lang, has certainly had a great part to play in my lifestyle in that way."[75]

Edith Schaeffer was the child of CIM missionaries in China, and her background is evident in the financial basis of L'Abri Christian Fellowship which she and her husband Francis established in Switzerland in the middle years of the twentieth century.[76]

Elsewhere, Brethren have had a leading role in societies such as Missionary Aviation Fellowship, New Tribes Mission and Wycliffe Bible Translators, and have played a part in other agencies too many to mention.

Throughout the twentieth century the "faith missions" were pleased to recruit young workers from the Brethren assemblies. Among their strengths was the fact that, almost uniquely among European and American churches, the Brethren stoutly resisted the influence of liberal theology. Perhaps more than others they also encouraged the development of personal gifts and abilities, and taught the "faith principles" that would enable young people to cope effectively with the rigours of overseas service.

Europeans and Americans, however, were not alone in learning to "live by faith". In China a youthful Watchman Nee "was greatly influenced by accounts of the faith of George Müller of Bristol and Hudson Taylor of the China Inland Mission."[77] Nee resolved to commit himself fully to the work of God and never to ask for money from anyone or to accept gifts for Christian work from the unconverted. Visiting London in 1938, he met G H Lang, who was then working on his biographies of Groves and Arulappan.[78] Immediately afterwards Nee wrote his influential book *Concerning our Missions*, in which he advocated mission strategies very much akin to those envisaged by Groves.

In a subsequent commentary on the book of Revelation, Nee suggested that the seven letters of Christ to the churches of Asia prophetically describe seven successive epochs in the history of the Christian Church, extending from the apostolic age to the second coming of Christ. He identified the Brethren movement as the sixth (Philadelphian) epoch, describing it as "the church which returns to the orthodoxy of the apostles."[79] He then claimed, "This movement was greater than the movement of the Reformation... Philadelphia gives us the things which the Reformation did not give us."[80] Referring to Bellett's account of Brethren origins in Dublin, Nee quoted the words of Groves in the drawing room meeting of 1827 and the following year in Lower Pembroke Street.[81] Although Nee found fault with both the Exclusive Brethren (for creating a centrally controlled denomination) and the Open Brethren (for multiplying local assemblies rather than maintaining, as he did, a single assembly in each "locality"), he concluded his analysis with the words, "In any situation, no matter what happens, we must choose the way of Philadelphia."[82]

By 1949 Nee's "Little Flock" had over 70,000 members in five hundred fellowships, and by 1956 it was believed to outnumber any other Christian group in China.[83] Following New Testament principles, these groups closely resemble the early Brethren assemblies in Britain and elsewhere, and they continue to flourish in most difficult circumstances, without a paid ministry, recognised buildings or set times of worship.

As we have seen, news of Watchman Nee reached a converted Sikh in India by the name of Bakht Singh. He commenced a series of open-air campaigns in the 1930s, through which he became "the spiritual father of tens of thousands".[84] When Bakht Singh established his first assembly in Madras, two of its three elders were the brothers Rajamani and Dorairaj. It can be no coincidence that on their mother's side they were great-grandsons of John Arulappan and that their father was "an evangelist associated with the Christian Brethren".[85] Together these men established hundreds of simple assemblies after the New Testament pattern, which are now said to number at least two thousand in India, Pakistan, Sri Lanka and other parts of the world.[86]

In addition to the fellowships associated with Bakht Singh, recent reports speak of more than two thousand indigenous assemblies in India identifying themselves simply as Christian Brethren and tracing their origins, in some cases, back to the personal influence of Norris Groves himself.[87] A recent article from India describes how "the movement of Brethren churches in Kerala" was launched in early 1872 by an evangelist called Mathai from Tamil Nadu. The writer then notes that "Mathai was a disciple of John Arulappan, who himself was attached to Anthony Norris Groves."[88]

Besides the six hundred Kerala assemblies, five hundred are found in Andhra Pradesh, the state in which Groves spent twenty years of his life, four hundred in Tamil Nadu, where Arulappan had his base, and three hundred in the Godavari Delta, pioneered by Bowden and Beer.[89] These Indian assemblies currently support at least 1300 missionaries and evangelists sent out to other parts of the country and further afield.[90] These fellowships see themselves not as the creation of foreigners, nor as Indian branches of a foreign denomination, but as the fruit of Indian initiatives. As such, they fulfil Groves's vision for the spontaneous growth of biblical Indian churches.

More than Enough

With all this evidence before us, it is no surprise to find Anthony Norris Groves described as "the father of faith missions".[91] But what was it, we might wonder, that made Brethren influence, and particularly Groves's influence, so significant to the missionary task of the Church?

Firstly, we have seen how revolutionary it was for a missionary to abandon the security of a salaried position with an established denomination and entrust himself and his family simply to the care of God. The experience of Groves himself would be echoed by that of countless others. Travelling overland from St Petersburg in 1829, the missionary party soon found their expenses exceeding the amount brought with them from England. To their delight, however, unexpected gifts along the way met all their needs. "I cannot help being overwhelmed with the Lord's goodness in this respect," said Groves. "Instead of being in want, we have always had more than enough."[92] Stranded in Baghdad, the family was then deprived for more than a year of all support from home. "I often think my dear friends in England will be sadly discouraged at the Lord's dealings with our mission," confessed Groves. "However, should their faith and hope fail, the Lord will either raise up others or find me some little occupation by which I may live. His goodness in the way of provision has been so wonderfully manifested that my heart feels quite easy that he will find a way for the support of his servant."[93] This testimony to God's provision was continued throughout his life. From India in 1834 he confided, "One dear brother offers me 1000 rupees a year, and I have just received from another an offer of 500 or more annually, and yet I never hinted that I wanted. On the contrary, I assured them we had more than enough."[94] No doubt Norris Groves's willingness to "live by faith" seems less strange in our day than it was in his, and this may, in itself, be a token of his profound influence upon us.

Secondly, we should not underestimate the direct and indirect impact of the booklet *Christian Devotedness* demonstrating the scriptural basis for missionary support. Groves argued that if a missionary is called to *trust God to provide*, then his friends at home are called to *obey God and provide*. For the system to work well, both missionary and supporter must play their part. In fact Groves's booklet led thousands of ordinary Christians to look earnestly and prayerfully for ways to use their wealth for the kingdom of God, and they found in missionaries living "by faith" a body of men and women well deserving of their interest. Congregations committed to the principles taught by Groves needed no financial appeals to persuade them to give, for they considered careful stewardship to be a natural expression of their devotion to Christ. In the earliest years of the CIM its financial support came almost entirely from personal friends of Norris Groves (Berger, Müller and the Howards of Tottenham), and it could be argued that the "faith missions" in general owed their creation and survival to home churches strongly committed to the principles he taught. We might wonder whether the more recent tendency for some of these missions to abandon their "faith principles" represents not so much a weakening in their own faith as a culpable failure in their supporting churches to teach and practice Christian devotedness.

Thirdly, we have in Groves himself the first mission leader in the English-speaking world to ignore the idea that a missionary, in order to establish churches, must be an educated gentleman. He was willing to take working class men and women (including single women) to the East, confident they could learn languages, lead souls to Christ and gather their converts into Christian congregations. He had seen Swiss and German craftsmen preaching and teaching in eastern Europe, and he saw no reason why the British working class should not make an equally significant contribution to the worldwide mission of the Church. The only qualification he saw in scripture for a Christian missionary or minister was a wholehearted response to the call of Christ. Indeed, personal experience of soul-winning in revival meetings and "ragged schools" might prove a much better preparation for work overseas than long years of theological study. Missionaries drawn from families with limited means would know how to live simply. In fact the hardship and squalor following on the heels of the Industrial Revolution in Britain and America had given the working class a toughness that the more privileged might lack, along with a degree of compassion wrought from personal familiarity with disease, poverty and crime. Through visiting gypsy encampments, Jewish ghettos and the slums of Irish immigrants, they had first-hand experience of gospel work among people very different from themselves, and in the face of human need they had learned to co-operate humbly and happily with Christians from other backgrounds. Groves's two most effective recruits were the stonemason Bowden and the shoemaker Beer, and following this pattern, the first CIM party with Hudson Taylor on the *Lammermuir* included a blacksmith, a mechanic, an agricultural engineer, two carpenters and a mason.[95]

Norris Groves and Hudson Taylor had this much in common. In fact neither was an ordained minister, neither claimed a denominational identity, and neither could promise a penny to his co-workers. But in other respects their paths diverge. From its inception the CIM enjoyed the help of outstanding home directors: William Berger, and then Benjamin Broomhall and Richard Hill. A CIM missionary could feel assured that a dedicated home staff were taking every opportunity to awaken interest in his work; he could feel reasonably confident that, so long as the society and its home committee existed, funds, even if inadequate, would be sent; he knew that the field and home directors would take personal steps to ensure everything humanly possible was done to prevent him starving to death. In the same way Carey and his Baptist colleagues had the gifted Andrew Fuller speaking on their behalf from many pulpits, and even asking for money. The Anglicans and Congregationalists had Henry Venn and Rufus Anderson working full-time to promote their interests. Groves had no one like them to advise candidates, organise prayer meetings, write articles, distribute magazines, or speak about the work in churches and conferences. Once committed to the missionary life, Groves himself spent only a few months in Britain. And when he did return, preoccupied with business matters, he addressed no conferences and spoke but rarely to the assemblies in Devon and London. Although his letters and journals found their way to his personal friends, they were not widely circulated: few in the homeland could say they had ever met him. Humanly speaking, Groves and his co-workers were on their own, forced by their circumstances to put their trust entirely in God. It was to facilitate support for such workers that he later urged the creation of a magazine to report on progress and to stimulate prayer, but the fact remains that Brethren work overseas remains far less publicised than that of the great missionary societies, and is far more dependent on prayer for God's provision of both workers and finance than on human efforts to obtain them.

Secondly, although "faith missions" in general owed much to Groves in breaking the old denominational mould with its entrenched hierarchy of command, they still followed the traditional course in establishing a structured organisation of their own. Significant to this was the question of authority. Groves might be respected as the unofficial leader of the team in Baghdad, Madras and Chittoor, but Hudson Taylor went one stage further in compiling a list of principles to be accepted and obeyed, and requiring formal recognition of his overall control.

Thirdly, although Groves and Taylor shared the ideal that missionaries from diverse denominations could work happily side by side, there was a significant difference in the way they put this into practice. Groves had drawn together the Nonconformist Cronin, the Anglican Parnell and the radically independent Newman. But these three had each, before leaving Britain, abandoned their previous denominational loyalties in favour of a consciously non-denominational stance. Hudson Taylor had the harder task of uniting workers who still retained their original denominational identities and who saw no need to abandon them. A "faith mission", such as the CIM, represented a divergence from Groves's scheme. In Groves's mind, a missionary was called overseas to establish a church (and a group of missionaries to establish a number of churches), but no organisation beyond this was found in scripture or required in practice. It was the simplest possible plan, and missionaries following Groves would encourage each indigenous group to read the New Testament and then just do as the earliest Christians did. Hudson Taylor, on the other hand, faced the more complicated task of superintending missionaries with denominational loyalties who would want to see churches established according to the pattern of their denomination. He eventually decided to group his workers on the basis of their affiliation, allocating them to specific areas and allowing them to establish there the kind of churches to which they were accustomed (in many cases under the ministry of ordained clergymen). And here is a fundamental difference. Groves brought unity through ignoring denominational identities, Hudson Taylor through respecting them; but there is no doubt that Groves's method would make it easier for indigenous fellowships to develop under local leadership.[96]

Throughout his life Norris Groves longed to be an example worthy to be followed. This meant he would never dare teach what he had not attained in his own experience, and he would never expect of his friends more than he required of himself. "I must first act myself," he said, "for I could not desire any brother to live more simply than I did. In all these cases I feel it infinitely better to say, 'Let us' than 'Do you.'"[97] He accepted the challenge of Persia precisely because it was the hardest place of all. "While the flesh would shrink," he said, "the spirit desires to wing its way to the very foremost ranks of danger in the battles of the Lord."[98] It was only his own complete dedication to Christ that entitled and enabled him to ask of others a similar sacrifice.

Judged in one way, the Baghdad mission might appear a barren exercise; yet in another it has proved astonishingly fruitful. Receiving a first bundle of letters in the great Muslim capital, Groves confided, "Surely no missionaries with so few pretensions to the love and confidence of the Church of God ever received more solid proofs of deep and hearty interest than we have during these ten months. This is no small point gained, and I think we may go further and add that many may be led, by this weak effort of faith in us, to take steps they might not otherwise have ventured upon."⁹⁹

Thousands did. Following the example of Norris and Mary Groves they have set out in simple dependence on the living God to proclaim the story of a Saviour's love to the ends of the earth. They have gone cheerfully, without appeals for money, without contract or salary, without the protection of weapons or law, without the support of trustees, patrons or governments. They are sons, daughters, heirs of Norris Groves, and like him they have proof of the faithfulness of God. They too can say, "We have always had more than enough."¹⁰⁰

ENDNOTES

[1] M47

[2] M442, 448

[3] M449

[4] Müller, *Narrative*, I, 48

[5] Müller, Letter to J G Logan dated 17th July 1895 (referring to July 1829) reproduced in Lang, *Groves*, 39.

[6] *Narrative*, I, 52

[7] *Narrative*, I, 50-51

[8] *Narrative*, I, 52

[9] *Narrative*, I, 69-70

[10] Neatby, 65

[11] M259. In 1879 Alexander Duff's biographer hailed Groves as "the first and best of the Plymouth Brethren" (Smith G, *Duff*, I, 266). But nineteenth-century writers who described him as the founder of the Brethren were all outside the movement and in most cases hostile to it (Rowdon, *Origins*, 38).

[12] Groves H, *Congleton*, 132

[13] Neatby, 67

[14] Neatby, 67. Wigram's interest in Baghdad is noted by Bellett, *Interesting Reminiscences*, 17. In 1829 Benjamin Newton, too, was keen to accept a senior teaching post in Calcutta or Bombay and was held back only by his mother's refusal to countenance it (Rowdon, *Origins*, 200).

[15] Neatby, 29

[16] *Interesting Reminiscences*, 17-18

[17] *Interesting Reminiscences*, 7

[18] *Interesting Reminiscences*, 18. At the time of writing, both Bellett and Cronin were concerned to emphasize Darby's positive role in the Brethren movement, and this may have led them to exaggerate its weaknesses prior to his arrival on the scene.

[19] M333. This he wrote in August 1834. By that time assemblies had been meeting at Aungier Street (Dublin) for four years, in Plymouth for two and a half years, and at Barnstaple and Bethesda (Bristol) for two years.

[20] Neatby, 65

[21] Neatby, 73-74

[22] Beattie, vi, 117

[23] Fiedler, 169

[24] Orr, 253

[25] Quoted by Stunt, *Awakening*, 292. Since 1804 the British and Foreign Bible Society, with both Anglican and Nonconformist representatives on its committee, had attempted to serve every denomination without enquiring too closely into their doctrinal stance. But this indiscriminate desire to facilitate Bible translation and distribution was not without its problems. Some considered the BFBS far too ecumenical in its willingness to co-operate on terms of equality with Unitarians and Roman Catholics, and this was sufficient ground for the establishment of several alternative agencies, such as the Trinitarian Bible Society in 1831.

Another early attempt at inter-denominational co-operation was the London Missionary Society. In 1837-8 David Livingstone was attracted to the LMS by the catholicity of its principles. It existed "to send neither Episcopacy, nor Presbyterianism, nor Independency to the heathen, but the gospel of Christ." "This," said Livingstone, "exactly agreed with my ideas" (Horne, 15-16). But though the LMS, like the BFBS, attempted to attract support from Churchman and Nonconformist alike, it still required its missionaries to be ordained in one or the other. In the course of time, it became impossible for ministers from diverse communions to agree on church organisation, and the LMS was obliged to become a conventional denominational mission, connected simply with the Congregational Church.

[26] Bebbington, 159

[27] Quoted by Lang, *Groves*, 16

[28] Brady and Rowdon, 153; Randall and Hilborn, 30

[29] Brady and Rowdon, 153

[30] A recent study of church trends in the UK makes this very point: "Old tribal labels (Anglican, Baptist, House Church, Methodist, Pentecostal), and loyalties which once hindered ecumenical progress, seem increasingly irrelevant. Christians moving home generally choose a new church not by its label, but for such factors as its style of worship, quality of teaching, sense of community, concern for justice, commitment to mission. Weaker denominational ties might be considered advantageous in working towards unity but, in a post-modern context, institutions, hierarchies, bureaucratic structures and grand schemes are all suspect. Grass-roots action, small groups and networking are preferred ways of relating and operating." The question is then raised, "Will we need to find new ways of working with this tension, celebrating diversity more wholeheartedly and pursuing a messier form of unity, which goes beyond the currently accepted denominational bodies and ecumenical processes? Will the ecumenism of the future be local rather than national, grass-roots rather than structural, rooted in mission partnership rather than doctrinal agreement?" (Murray and Wilkinson-Hayes, 15). Norris Groves would certainly hope so!

[31] Smith G, *Carey*, 54

[32] Warren, 128

[33] In 1849 Henry Venn estimated that only one in ten of the sixty or seventy who offered themselves to the CMS every year could be considered suitable candidates for missionary service. Many were refused on grounds of health, age, character, moral standing or mental ability (Shenk, 50).

[34] *The Religious Magazine* 1837-38 (quoted by Beaver, 69-70)

[35] Horne, 110

[36] Bromley, 41, 98

[37] *The Missionary Reporter*, no. 5 (Nov. 1853), 63. A missionary periodical had previously appeared in 1850, with the title *The Gleaner in the Missionary Field*. In 1853, with the interest of this publication directed more particularly to China, it was renamed *The Missionary Gleaner*. The need thus arose for a magazine that would include news from other parts of the world.

[38] The second issue, dated August 1853, included a long letter to the editor from William Bowden in which he wrote, "The scripture of the New Testament indicates clearly, both by precept and example, that God requires not merely believers in their individual capacity but requires the congregations of the saints as such to take the care of the temporal concerns of its own members who are from any cause incapacitated for caring for themselves, as well as to care for the spread of the gospel and the temporal supply of those who are engaged therein. But it appears to me, dear brother, that most of the churches with which we are connected do not see these matters in this light" (p. 21). It was exactly this failing which *The Missionary Reporter* sought to rectify.

[39] *The Missionary Reporter*, no. 1 (July 1853), 8, 2

[40] This system contrasts strikingly with that of the CMS, for example, which under the guidance of Henry Venn forbade its missionaries to receive support directly from a local church or prayer group, or to supplement their income with secular employment. Venn's biographer suggests that the CMS adopted this policy in order to retain complete authority over its agents (Shenk, 52).

[41] Like the missionaries themselves, the editor, James Van Sommer of Tottenham (previously of Hackney), was a young man, aged only thirty-one at the time when the magazine was started. His sister was the wife of William Berger, the first home secretary of Hudson Taylor's CIM (Stunt, *James Van Sommer*, 3, 5). Questions relating to contributors, quantities, finances and circulation are discussed by Forrest (1971).

[42] The editors were Henry Groves, Henry Dyer and Dr John Lindsay MacLean. Mrs MacLean ran a training school in Bath for young lady missionaries, one of whom was Constance Groves.

From 1872 onwards, increasing numbers of workers went abroad in connection with *The Missionary Echo* (and then *Echoes of Service*) and with magazines established for the same purpose in the USA, Canada, Australia and New Zealand. During the ten years from 1885 to 1895 the number of such missionaries trebled. From 1895 to 1925 the numbers trebled again. By 1945 there were a thousand Brethren missionaries associated with these magazines, quite apart from those who had joined the "faith missions" and other societies (Tatford, *That the World May Know*, vol. 4, 309). It is estimated that these workers have now planted churches in more than a hundred countries (Rowdon, "The Brethren Contribution to World Mission", 45).

[43] This could not be said of the Darbyites (Exclusive Brethren), who after 1848 confined their attentions overseas to fomenting the same kind of bitter and critical divisions that they had at home.

[44] Mandryk, 941

[45] Missionaries with a Brethren identity now work in association with magazines and support groups in at least twenty different sending countries. In addition to Echoes International in the UK, there is The Lord's Work Trust in Scotland, Christian Missions in Many Lands in the USA, Global Connections in Mission in New Zealand, Missionary Services Canada, Australian Missionary Tidings, and the more recently established Gospel Literature Outreach and International Teams, both originating in Australia. International Teams, now based in the USA, has sent more than 5000 workers overseas. In India there are major Christian publishing houses such as Gospel Literature Service in Bombay and MSS in New Delhi, both started by workers associated with the Brethren. The Emmaus Bible Correspondence Courses are administered by Brethren in many parts of the world. Among Brethren publishers in America are Walterick and Loizeaux Brothers, and others are based in Germany, France, Spain, Switzerland and Brazil, producing literature in many different languages.

Some well-known Brethren missionaries from the past are Jim Elliot, Pete Fleming and Ed McCully (martyrs to the Auca Indians in Ecuador), F S Arnot, Dan Crawford and J R Olley (pioneers in central Africa), Geoffrey Bull (Tibet) and Charles Marsh (Algeria). Drawing on her childhood experience of the Brethren in the early twentieth century, Anne Arnott remarked, "They were undoubtedly seen at their best on the mission field. Determined, intrepid, dedicated, they ventured into many lands, often pioneering where none had been before... The large number who went overseas was higher than that of almost any other Christian group or denomination in proportion to their membership" (*The Brethren*, 182).

[46] The SIM is now known as Serving In Mission or SIM International.

[47] Lang, *Groves*, 19. Rufus Anderson questioned whether Müller's method of "living by faith" was any different from that already practised by the denominational missions. It certainly was. Neither Müller nor the "faith missions" who followed his example appealed for funds. Nor did they take out subscriptions or pass round collecting bags. They accepted nothing from the unconverted and they refused to contract debts. They offered no stated salary to their missionaries and conferred no ordained status or guarantee of future security. These were significant differences (Anderson, *Foreign Missions*, ch. 9; Beaver, 201-202).

In recent years the application of the term "living by faith" to a policy of asking God alone for financial support has suffered some criticism. Perhaps the expression "walking by faith" should be preferred (2 Cor 5:7, compare NIV and NRSV), as it dissociates the idea from the biblical context of Justification (Rom 1:17 etc). To "walk by faith" simply means to trust and obey God. In Hebrews 11 many examples are given of people who lived in this way, not seeking direction or provision from man but from the Lord. In 2 Corinthians chapter 5 there is a direct link between "walking by faith" (v.7) and making it one's aim "to please him" (v.9). In this regard, both Groves and Müller withdrew from missionary societies whose requirements conflicted with what they believed to be the will of God for them; they found it impossible both to please the society and "to please him". To "live by faith" in such circumstances would mean regarding oneself simply as a servant of God, directly accountable to him, free at all times to follow his direction, seeking first his kingdom and his righteousness, and trusting him to provide for one's daily needs (Matt 6:25-33). This was Groves's meaning when he said, "I can with my whole heart pray for myself and all who are nearest and dearest to me that we be so circumstanced in life as to be compelled to live by faith on the divine promises day by day" (D22). For a fuller discussion of "living by faith", see Dann, *Primitivist Missiology*, 131-169.

[48] Taylor, *Growth of a Soul*, 111-113

[49] *Growth of a Soul*, 116

[50] Broomhall, *If I had a Thousand Lives*, 389-390. During his five years in London before departing for China, Hudson Taylor enjoyed membership at the Baptist Church in Bayswater whilst attending a Congregational Church in Stepney and breaking bread with the Brethren in Hackney, Tottenham, Bristol, Clevedon and East Grinstead. He would preach wherever invited – Anglican, Baptist, Methodist, Presbyterian and Brethren and some other churches beside – in the same catholic spirit with which he spoke in support of all the existing missionary societies. Broomhall's Appendix 2 considers Hudson Taylor's links with the Brethren. Elsewhere Broomhall comments, "The early Brethren particularly approved of his conciliatory, supra-sectarian attitude toward 'all who loved the Lord Jesus in sincerity and truth.'" (Broomhall, *Survivors' Pact*, 131) Hudson Taylor's successor as General Director of CIM, Dixon Hoste, was baptised in a Brethren assembly on the Isle Of Wight (Beattie, 134).

[51] Broomhall, *If I had a Thousand Lives*, 448. Two early letters from Pearse were published in *The Missionary Reporter* (Feb. 1854; Nov. 1855). In 1856 he wrote to Harriet Groves, "I cannot help expressing the great gratification I have in reading the 'Memoir' and how much the large-hearted catholic noble christian principles of Mr Groves's Brethrenism commend themselves to me, in contrast with that which is *called* Brethrenism in the present day" (Preface to *Memoir* 2nd edn). The CIM is now known as the Overseas Missionary Fellowship.

[52] Steele, xii, 15-19. The NAM has been renamed Arab World Ministries.

[53] Broomhall, *Survivors' Pact*, 115; Fiedler, 173

[54] Beattie, 84; Broomhall, *If I had a Thousand Lives*, 494; Fiedler, 34-40

[55] Fiedler, 41

[56] Anderson D, 18-19

[57] Dr and Mrs Howard Taylor, *Hudson Taylor in Early Years, the Growth of a Soul* and *Hudson Taylor and the China Inland Mission, the Growth of a Work of God*.

[58] Tett, 8. The SUM has been renamed Action Partners.

[59] Grubb, *C T Studd*, 126. The society founded by Studd is now known as Worldwide Evangelisation for Christ or WEC International. The outworking of "faith in God alone" during the first fifty years of WEC is described by Grubb, *The Four Pillars of WEC*, 21-50.

[60] The CLC operates "on the same total faith basis, with home-workers unsalaried, as in WEC" (Grubb, *Once Caught, No Escape*, 127).

[61] Fiedler, 177

[62] M294

[63] M16

[64] Broomhall, *Barbarians*, app. 6. It was through an appeal by Gützlaff in 1834 that David Livingstone received his initial call to become a missionary (Fiedler, 66).

[65] Paton was a pioneer missionary in the New Hebrides (Vanuatu), a group of islands off the east coast of Australia.

[66] Ramabai, 37; Dyer, 45

[67] M227

[68] Young, 12-13

[69] Newton, "Christian Brethren, World Mission and an Australian Contribution", 6

[70] Houghton, 144

[71] Houghton, 143-145, 255-258. The Dohnavur Fellowship developed gradually from small beginnings in 1901. Though not formally constituted until 1926, it had been independent of the Zenana Missionary Society in all practical respects for many years prior to this.

[72] *True Discipleship* (STL 1963). MacDonald's best known work is the *Believer's Bible Commentary*.

[73] Verwer, personal communication with the author.

[74] One such is K P Yohannan (founder of Gospel for Asia) who dedicates his book *Revolution in World Missions* to George Verwer, "whose life and example have influenced me more than any other single individual's."

[75] Forster, personal communication with the author.

[76] Schaeffer, Edith, *L'Abri* (London, Crossway, 1993)

[77] Kinnear, 69

[78] Lyell, 75

[79] Nee, *The Orthodoxy of the Church*, 1994 edn., 61

[80] *Orthodoxy*, 70

[81] *Orthodoxy*, 66

[82] *Orthodoxy*, 102

[83] McCallum, 14; Adeney, 146-148

[84] Koshy, *Brother Bakht Singh*

[85] Rajamani, 13

[86] Koshy, *Brother Bakht Singh*

[87] Daniel, xiv

[88] Kerala Brethren History, <http://www.brethrentoday.com/keralahistory.htm> accessed January 2004.

[89] Rowdon, *International Partnership Perspectives*, no. 3, 40. From Kerala province Dr Johnson C Philip, Dean of the Brethren Bible Institute, writes with reference to the Brethren, "The church in India is a vibrant one, having a large number of outreaches with scores of new churches established every year." Growth has been particularly pronounced during the last 30 years of the twentieth century. Writing in 2001, Dr Philip calculates, "If the growth continues at this rate, then the present

assembly strength would become double by 2025" (Philip, *The Brethren Movement in India*).

[90] Daniel, 375

[91] Stunt W T, *Turning the World Upside Down*, 20

[92] J98

[93] R299; M207

[94] M311

[95] Shortly before the foundation of the CMS in 1799, John Venn, father of Henry Venn, proposed that a class of unordained missionaries be created for the Church of England, with the title of catechist. This would enable "a person of inferior station" to serve overseas despite his lack of such "talents, manners or learning as are necessary in an officiating minister in England". Most of the earliest British CMS agents were unordained and from a relatively modest social background. They were commissioned simply to preach to the unconverted under the authority of local superintendents and committees, not being entitled to officiate in church services or to administer the sacraments (Walls, 164-165).

To an even greater degree the Pietist artisans of the Basel Mission were formally required to follow the instructions and disciplines imposed by "duly constituted authority" – an "inspector", a home committee, and field leaders drawn from higher social ranks (Miller, 32, 84, 95). In the Nonconformist sphere, the LMS had sent artisan-missionaries overseas as early as 1796, but only under the strict supervision of ordained and educated "ministers" (Walls, 166).

Groves, in contrast to all these, considered men such as Bowden, Beer and Arulappan to be church-planters and church leaders in no lesser sense than the aristocratic Parnell and the theologically trained Gundert. They were accountable not to any human organisation or superintendent but directly to God.

[96] Watchman Nee's biographer comments, "The CIM Editorial Secretary, Norman Baker, had kindly shown Nee the current edition of the Mission's *Principles and Practice*, and Nee had had to point out that under the heading of 'church government' the document gave little or no room for Chinese opinion concerning the pattern of worship to be followed in any given case" (Kinnear, 256 n.3).

[97] M279

[98] M105

[99] R95; M117-118

[100] J98

"Mr Groves does not care a fig
about fame or distinction or anything of that sort."

John Kitto[1]

34

A Most Unprofitable Life?

Anthony Norris Groves launched a grand experiment in real Christianity. As a young man, disillusioned with the moribund religiosity of his day, he resolved to get back to basics – to believe what Christ told us to believe, and to do what he told us to do. Though some people in every age might dispute his understanding of the normal Christian lifestyle, none could question his sincerity. He was totally committed to his vision of Christian devotedness, and for the remainder of his days he practised exactly what he preached.

Having looked in detail at the course of his life and the growth of his character, we are now in a position to assess the results of his experiment. Did the authentic article, as conceived by Norris Groves, prove better than what had gone before? Did it work? It might seem that he himself concluded his experiment a failure. Yet as he reviewed "a most unprofitable life",[2] he never had cause to question his basic ideal of Christian devotedness, for it was clearly taught by Christ. The failure, if failure there were, lay elsewhere.

The miseries of Baghdad had so affected him that, much as he wished to return and resume his work there, Groves was never able to summon up the emotional strength to do so. This he felt to be his first failure. Then when his longed-for reinforcements, John Parnell and Edward Cronin, joined him in India, they, like Kitto and Newman, declined to follow his leadership. This he took as a second failure. The persistent opposition of the Church of England to his friendly overtures hurt him deeply and eventually separated him from his flock in Chittoor, and this must have seemed a third failure. But the biggest failure, to his mind, was his decision, against his earlier principles, to finance agricultural projects with borrowed money, consuming the best years of his life with commercial obligations and leaving him with crippling debts.

But these all represent personal failures rather than a failure of his grand experiment. In fact his early resolution to sell his possessions and trust God to provide was abundantly vindicated. Throughout his life he consistently gave away everything surplus to immediate requirements, but he never lacked food, clothing and a home. What is more, he never lacked friends. There have been few men more loved than Norris Groves. And through all his ups and downs, he enjoyed the unfailing respect and loyalty of his own children. They had seen, more closely than anyone, the reality of Christian devotedness. It was lived out before their eyes, and they were convinced it worked.

We should not forget that Groves was a pioneer in both Iraq and India, doing what had not been done before. The man who digs the well may not be the one who draws the water, but in fact he achieved as much, if not more than other missionary pioneers. Four years' labour in Baghdad yielded three known converts (Serkies, Harnie and Mrs Taylor's Armenian sister), which was more than could be said for some famous contemporaries. William Carey, after nearly seven years in Bengal, could not identify a single Indian converted to Christ through his efforts. Robert Morrison after seven years in China finally baptised his first.[3] In Baghdad Groves's purpose was to show what *could* be done; he expected others to follow and help fulfil the vision. In Madras and Chittoor he was again breaking fresh ground, assessing the situation, proposing new ways of working. The ideas of one man rarely find acceptance until his peers have tested them and proved him right.

Norris Groves was a motivator, an inspirer, a visionary. He was a prophet rather than a priest, and as we have seen, his strength lay in stimulating others rather than organising them. Such a man needs colleagues capable of transforming the vision into a methodical programme of action. The lack of a capable assistant we may feel to be the greatest weakness of his own efforts in Baghdad, Madras and Chittoor, yet there were many who caught his vision and applied it to spheres of their own.

The nineteenth century produced three outstanding evangelical books – books that Christians bought in bulk and sent to their friends, books that transformed lives and changed priorities. They were *China's Spiritual Needs and Claims* by Hudson Taylor (published in 1865), *A Narrative of Some of the Lord's Dealings with George Müller* (1837) and, of course, *Christian Devotedness* (1825).[4] In point of time, Groves's work came first, and it laid the foundation on which the other two were built. In some ways the printing of this little tract, barely a year after he came to full assurance of salvation, was the most significant thing he ever did.

Yet, even as he wrote, still pulling teeth in Exeter, his greatest desire was to be a missionary of the gospel. So what, in the end, did Anthony Norris Groves achieve as a Christian missionary? He gave refuge and fellowship to Solomon Alexander, who became the first Bishop of Jerusalem; he led John Kitto to faith in Christ and introduced him to the cultures of the East; he inspired a "second conversion" for George Müller, who supported hundreds of missionaries and sent gospel literature to many different countries; he personally distributed scriptures in eastern Europe, Russia and the Caucasus; he gave Karl Pfander his first base in the Muslim world; he set up a school in Baghdad and taught Iraqi children the word of God; he explained the gospel to Armenian priests and Catholic merchants; he sent Bibles to many parts of Mesopotamia and

Persia; he offered a home to Serkies and to Harnie, who both found Christ there; he taught Erasmus Calman and many others how to live by faith; he discipled Mokayel, who preached throughout the Middle East; he kept Rhenius of Tinnevelly "in his work"; he preached to Hindu and Muslim crowds; he established schools in Chittoor and taught Indian children the scriptures; he trained Indian evangelists and Bible teachers; he brought religious expatriates to faith in Christ; he led worldly believers to Christian devotedness; he inspired a vision for Christian unity; he set the example for a generation of "faith missions"; he encouraged inter-denominational "missionary partnership"; he recruited workers in England, Scotland and Ireland; he recruited more in Switzerland and Germany; he sent them to the north, south, east and west of India; he saved forty little girls from a life of misery; he provided funds and workers for an orphanage in Sonamukhi; he was a mentor to John Arulappan, who was a mentor to thousands; he encouraged Indian evangelists to live by faith; he stimulated a growing network of biblical Indian churches; he established the Bowdens and Beers in Godavari; he launched the Gunderts on their life-work in Kerala; he opened Vellore, Arcot and Chittoor for the ministry of the Scudders; he probably saved the life of Alexander Duff, who influenced thousands through Christian education; he certainly saved the life of Colonel Cotton, who halted the famines of the Godavari Delta; he cared for an orphan boy, adopted an orphan girl and raised four sons and a daughter, who became devoted servants of Christ; he was the most innovative missiologist of his day; and he was (we almost forgot it) "one of the founders of the Brethren".

ENDNOTES

[1] M5

[2] M456

[3] Tucker, 118, 167, 170

[4] This implies no disrespect for William Carey's remarkable tract, *An Enquiry into the Obligations of Christians to use Means for the Conversion of the Heathens*, published the previous century in 1792.

APPENDICES

"The important question is not so much
to know what is *wrong*,
as to learn from the Lord what is *right*."

Norris Groves [1]

i

Troubled Times

Anthony Norris Groves studied both the teachings of Christ and the needs of the age. Indeed, it was the desperate plight of a world in distress that, to his mind, made the rediscovery of New Testament Christianity a matter of such urgent concern.

Poised between the old order and the new, the early years of the nineteenth century were anxious ones for the people of Great Britain. For a whole generation the shadow of the French Revolution had lain darkly across Europe, foreboding the probable eruption of corresponding tumults nearer home – nightmare visions of fanatics baying for the blood of monarchy, aristocracy and church; the mob at the gates with farm cart and guillotine, intent on wiping out a whole social order.

The Napoleonic wars had then followed, with a real possibility of military invasion – the prospect of cities thrown down, looting, rape and murder; the small islands of the United Kingdom swallowed up in subjection to a vast continental empire tyrannized by the monstrous power of Bonaparte. Thousands of young ploughmen, fishermen and shopkeepers, knowing nothing of the world beyond the next market town, had been seized by the press-gang from their taverns and their beds, and marched off to be starved, beaten and shot at in Spain, Egypt and the West Indies. Many returned maimed and disabled; many did not return at all – their grieving wives and children must find ways to make ends meet without them. These terrors were subdued and these miseries ended only in 1815 with the decisive Battle of Waterloo. A short distance from the naval dockyards of Plymouth, Norris Groves, aged twenty, had just opened his first dental practice.

Soldiers coming back from the wars found an exhausted homeland where work was scarce and money scarcer. The year 1830 marked the accession of a new king, William IV, and elections that threatened to snatch political power from the aristocracy. Further revolutionary upheavals rocked France and Belgium, and the following year cholera swept through Europe. Harvests in Britain failed repeatedly, and a number of peasants' revolts were savagely suppressed. In 1832, "after fifty years of proposals, disappointments and agitation" culminating in scenes of protest and riotous anarchy at public rallies in several parts of England, the old parliamentary system was swept away.² Another election followed, but the outcome was inconclusive. Enough had been done to undermine the old order, but no one knew what shape the new would take.

The contrast remained between the gentleman (rich, cultured, clean) and the labouring man (poor, rough, dirty), but a new element of fear, suspicion and resentment had entered into the relations between them. The old rural England, peopled by sturdy farm workers and independent craftsmen, was set on a course which would make it the "workshop of the world". Gone for ever was the stable society of the pre-industrial era. The labouring poor were sucked into the furnace of the industrial age, where the factory, the mine and the mill must employ thousands on never-ending shifts. In twenty years, major cities such as Manchester and Birmingham almost doubled in size. The change was traumatic in the extreme. "It is hard to escape the impression that very large numbers of people in the 1840s were completely bewildered by the environment in which they found themselves."³

In 1829 Roman Catholics had been given the right to hold public office and to stand for election to Parliament – and this at a time when many Protestants believed the Pope to be the Antichrist. There was talk of evicting the bishops of the Establishment from the House of Lords, of making the Church of England just one among the competing religious denominations of the land. For many people all these unsettling developments – social, political and religious – brought a feeling that the last days were upon them, that their generation would see the stars fall and the Saviour coming on the clouds. Norris Groves, in 1831, quite expected Christ to return in his lifetime and catch him up from beside the Euphrates river.⁴

Yet before the coming of the Saviour to separate Sheep and Goats, the word of salvation must surely be sent out to the uttermost parts of the earth. "This gospel of the kingdom will be preached to the whole world," Christ had said, "as a testimony to all nations, and then the end will come."⁵ Many people believed that the remarkable spread of British influence – the *pax britannica* bringing law and order, efficient transport, modern medicine, scientific technology and every other benefit of civilisation – would prove to be the means prepared by Providence to carry the gospel to every corner of the globe. The universal waning of Muhammadan power, accelerated with the rout of "Muslim" Turkey by "Christian" Russia in 1828, along with ambitious new plans to translate the Bible and establish missions in distant parts, led many optimists to suppose that the Christianisation of the world was imminent. The kingdom of God would soon come on earth, with the full flowering of the millennial age and Christ gloriously enthroned as King in Jerusalem. Prophetic portions of the Bible acquired a fresh fascination, and conferences were arranged for the exposition of Daniel, Revelation and Zechariah in the light of current political events. And if the Holy Spirit were to be poured out as promised in the book of Joel, and if the gift of speaking unknown foreign languages were to be restored to a revived church, was it not a realistic hope that every nation should be converted in their generation?

But first the Church must be revived, and as yet there seemed small sign of revival. In theory, Britain was divided into parishes, and each parish had its parish church. Here every villager was baptised, married and buried, and here every villager attended worship at least occasionally, making his contribution to the upkeep of stonework, organ, graveyard and priest. This orderly scheme was born in an age when few travelled beyond the boundaries of their parish and when a working man was content to be illiterate, deferring out of long habit to the views of his superiors. But soldiers and seamen returning from the wars had chatted round mess fires with Irishmen, Negroes, Scots, Americans, Poles, Swedes and Lascars.[6] The experience of sailing and marching under tropical skies had widened their mental as well as their physical horizons.

In the homeland too, farm workers moving to the industrial towns encountered fresh ideas. In the shadow of the mills and mines the Nonconformist chapels gained converts – Methodists, Presbyterians, Congregationalists,[7] Baptists, Quakers, Unitarians and smaller sects with their own distinctive views and practices. These had in common their belief that the Church of England remained too tied to traditions derived from medieval Roman Catholicism. As Dissenters they "dissented"; as Nonconformists they would not "conform"; and they claimed to draw their beliefs and practices not from tradition but from the Bible or in the case of the Quakers from the inner "witness of the Spirit". Many looked back on the days of Cromwell and William III with affection and considered themselves heirs to the Puritans. Some, especially the Methodists, drew their inspiration from John Wesley; others had a strong Calvinistic emphasis. All were inclined to radical politics and concern for the poor.

Radical politics worried the Church of England, as did the prospect of its parishioners defecting to chapels of Dissent. The Established Church had for its supreme governor the king or queen of England; the clergy in their convocation were obligated to ensure that church ordinances and constitutions conformed to the laws and customs of the land.[8] The bishops and archbishops voted on major political issues in Parliament, and rarely was one in doubt which way they would vote; the Church of England was said with some justice to be "the Tory party at prayer".

The Church had been "established" under King Henry VIII when the bishops cut themselves loose from papal authority and defined the nature of their newly independent ecclesiastical body. The hierarchy of its clergy, the thirty-nine Articles of Religion describing its beliefs and practices, and the Book of Common Prayer detailing the content of its public services, had all been carefully put in place. The intention was to provide a degree of stability in an age of religious passions, and to allow the Church a significant role in the government and administration of the country at every level, from the royal court to the parish council. Three centuries later, the Established Church stood for sensible, unemotional religion of the type preferred by all who would consider themselves pillars of society, to whatever social class they might belong. Indeed, by the early nineteenth century, "Christianity was often valued primarily as a bulwark against revolution, and in consequence the content of its message was liable to be reduced to a sort of moral cement whose main function was to maintain the fabric of society."[9] The downside of this was that those who disliked its politics resented its authority. And their problem was that they remained by law subject to that authority.

Indifference marked the attitude, in general, of the labouring people towards the Established Church, though occasionally this erupted into outright hostility. Every citizen, unless very poor, was obliged to pay local "rates", some of which were spent on maintenance and repair of the parish church. Tithes were also demanded, for the support of the local clergyman, even if he never set foot in his parish, and at times the demand for tithes brought real hardship. The rector himself would be somewhat better off than his parishioners. His social standing placed him above all except the squire and his lady, and he would establish his own circle of friends in the more cultured domains of "the county". "Socially the gulf between a vicar with an income of as much as £1000 a year and a handloom weaver with twelve shillings a week, if he were lucky, was felt to be too great to allow of any common interests."[10] Well-meaning intellectuals such as Thomas Arnold aimed to educate promising young men for clerical service. The idea was to place "a Christian scholar and gentleman in every parish," a parson or priest who would set the tone for the community. In reality his education and his social graces kept him at a respectable distance from his parishioners. "No one ever suggested that a labouring man might become a vicar; the ideal of a scholar and gentleman in every parish made such an idea preposterous."[11]

There were, of course, godly men among the clergy of the Established Church and some, such as the evangelical Bishop J C Ryle, were outstanding. But others had "taken the cloth" simply because they were born the third son of a well-to-do family. The eldest inherited the land, the second went to the army, the third to the church. A "living" would be procured for him by means of a well-placed gift or other interest in high places. Most such men probably had a faith of sorts but few were sufficiently interested to study it, cultivate it or teach it effectively to their parishioners. A rector commonly preferred to pay a poorer clergyman to care for his flock whilst he engaged in pursuits more to his taste elsewhere. In 1807 (the first year for which we have any figures), out of some 10,000 benefices nearly two-thirds were held by men who lived outside their parish. Some received an income from several parishes, appointing a curate or vicar to deputize in each. Paid a pittance, these were rarely well-instructed or spiritual men. The curate at Grasmere, for instance, was frequently drunk, and "Wordsworth declared to a rather startled Dorothy in 1812 that he would gladly shed his blood for the Church of England but confessed he did not know when he had last been inside his local church."[12] Many like him were moved by religious feelings but disenchanted with religious practitioners. "All our ministers are such vile creatures," concluded the poet.

Perhaps the greatest evil in the religious Establishment of nineteenth century Britain was the fact that the Church could furnish an extremely lucrative career for any man of breeding who was willing to display the outward trappings of religion and curry the favour of his superiors. The political appointment and political activity of bishops and other ecclesiastical dignitaries had two dire effects: it raised worldly men to power in the Church, and it distracted godly men from their spiritual duties. Anglicans spoke of "our apostolic church", but Norris Groves wondered what the apostles would have thought of it. What would they say to "the state and pomp of the episcopacy, the titles 'Your Grace' and 'Your Lordship', your palaces, your carriages, and fame, and hosts of idle livery [i.e. uniformed] servants?" What would they think of "the mode of appointment to the cure of souls… publicly sold like cattle in the market to the highest bidder, and a large proportion of the remainder may be in the hands of an infidel Lord Chancellor, to give as he pleases"?[13]

There were many who felt that the Church of England had not just failed the Faith; it had also failed England. Frank Newman was one such. "In the last century and a half," he noted, "the nation was often afflicted with sensual royalty, bloody wars, venal statesmen, corrupt constituencies, bribery and violence at elections, flagitious drunkenness pervading all ranks and insinuating itself into Colleges and Rectories. The prisons of the country had been in a most disgraceful state; the fairs and waits were scenes of rude debauchery,[14] and the theatres were – still, in this nineteenth century – whispered to be haunts of the most debasing immorality. I could not learn that any bishop had ever taken the lead in denouncing these iniquities." And when any man or class of men did rise to denounce them, the bishops invariably joined ranks "to defend corruption by, at least, passive resistance." None of the great reformers had been bishops; indeed the bishops had opposed those of their own church who met to establish the Church Missionary Society and the Bible Society. "Their policy seemed to be to do nothing until somebody else was likely to do it; upon which they at last joined the movement in order to damp its energy and get some credit from it."[15] Bishop Ryle himself was frustrated by the general attitude to baptism. "Why is it," he asked in 1858, "that the sacrament of baptism appears to bear so little fruit? How is it that thousands are every year baptised, and never give the slightest proof of having received benefit from it?... Parents bring their children to the font, without the slightest sense of what they are doing. Sponsors stand up and answer for the child, in evident ignorance of the nature of the ordinance they are attending... Such baptisms may well be barren of results. They are not baptisms according to the mind of Christ."[16]

But it was by no means easy to leave the Established Church. Acts of Parliament in Tudor times had compelled every person "above the age of sixteen years... to hear divine service established by her majesty's laws and statutes." All who offended would be "committed to prison, there to remain without bail or mainprize until they conform."[17] In 1660 John Bunyan had been tried and sentenced for failing to attend his parish church and for preaching without the authorisation of a bishop; he spent the next twelve years in Bedford jail.

In 1672 the Nonconformists, to their great relief, had received the freedom to meet publicly and to ordain their own licensed ministers. But the stigma of Nonconformity remained well into the nineteenth century, as did many of its inconveniences. For one thing, births could only be legally registered in the baptismal records of the parish church, and a child with no legal record of its birth might find great difficulty in proving its inheritance or other rights. A man and woman could only be legally married (unless they were Quakers or Jews) by a clergyman of the Establishment. Graveyards were the property, in almost all cases, of a parish church, and few families, if refused a place in the village churchyard, could afford to buy themselves a private burial plot. In 1719 Parliament passed a bill forbidding anyone who attended a dissenting meeting from accepting a post as a schoolteacher, and a century later the leading English universities (Oxford, Cambridge and Durham) still issued academic degrees only to men who would publicly subscribe to the Thirty-nine Articles of the Church of England.[18]

It was, even at this time, a relatively novel idea that a person should be free to decide his own beliefs and shape his own religious identity. For more than two thousand years, since the earliest days of the Roman Empire, most Europeans had taken it for granted that their rulers decided the nature of their religion and decreed how and where it should be practised and propagated. Parishioners might grumble at alterations in the Prayer Book, and would at times be willing to fight for king or for parliament in order to preserve or to change the national religion, but the basic concept of a national religion remained deeply rooted in the common culture of the day.

The Great Awakening of the eighteenth century had taken place largely within the Church of England. The Wesleys and Whitefield had remained members of the Established Church (although they found more response outside it), and never wished to be known as Dissenters. Their popular success had roused Anglican leaders for a while from their lethargy, bringing some attempts at reform. Local priests, in particular, were encouraged to make their preaching more interesting and their worship less formal. But a general suspicion of "enthusiasm", in the best social circles, had made it difficult to introduce such innovations as extempore prayer, evangelistic appeals, or lively hymns sung vigorously by the whole congregation. Anglicans also suspected the political agenda of the Dissenters, and many genuinely disliked the divisive tendency of unauthorised, and sometimes illiterate, field preaching. Though many Methodists had left the Church of England after John Wesley's death, many others remained within it. And though they were at first a small and despised minority, these Anglican Evangelicals gained strength during the first decades of the nineteenth century. Most had Calvinistic leanings, and they wielded an influence beyond their numbers through such leaders as William Wilberforce and Charles Simeon.

By the 1830s, however, Anglican evangelicalism was starting to decline. The urgent call for individual conversion and personal holiness instigated by Wesley and Whitefield had given way to a more pragmatic desire for unity – an emphasis on loyalty to the Church in the face of Nonconformist competition. Evangelical Anglicans might go occasionally to hear a gifted Baptist or Congregationalist preacher, but few would forsake the family circle on a Sunday to become permanent members of a dissenting chapel. The dilemma faced by many is well illustrated by the case of John Bellett's cousin in Chigwell, London. Raised in a respectable Anglican family, she could find spiritual nourishment only in the chapel of a Nonconformist pastor. "Charlotte has certainly in heart become a Dissenter," wrote Bellett. "Can it be wondered at, when all the spiritual consolation she receives is from members of Mr West's congregation, having continually before her the worldly life and worldly conversation of their own parish clergyman?"[19] Mr West, though no doubt a worthy man, would be less educated, less cultured and less well-connected than the priest of Charlotte's parish; he probably spoke with a vulgar local accent too. But if the Anglicans looked askance at Dissenters, the majority of Dissenters themselves were so prejudiced against the abuses and corruptions they saw in the Church of England that they made strict separation from the Established Church a condition for membership in their own communion. Becoming a "member" in a Baptist Chapel required a solemn promise to take the Lord's Supper only with believers who had been baptised as adults, and never with those baptised as infants. This meant that a Baptist, on pain of expulsion from his church, could never partake with an Anglican of the Supper instituted by their common Lord.[20]

Times, however, were changing. The first decades of the nineteenth century marked, in literature and music, the beginning of the Romantic Movement. The Scottish Presbyterian minister Edward Irving was a great Romantic preacher. His sermons aimed to create an effect as much as to impart information, and it is no coincidence that he was a close friend of the poet Samuel Taylor Coleridge. Where the genteel Augustan age had looked to "reason" as the key to progress and to civilisation, the more rugged Romantics preferred the beauties of primitive simplicity, aspiring to get back to nature and to recapture an idealised past. Where the "eighteenth century wanted a simple word to be acted on, the nineteenth century wanted a word to be enjoyed, to light up not simply the path of duty but the whole world of life."[21] The emphasis was shifting from "reason" to "sentiment", from "thinking" to "feeling", from the head to the heart, from the real to the ideal. In this respect, the yearnings of radical Evangelicals for a more "apostolic" vision and a more "personal" religious experience owed much to the spirit of the age inspired by the Romantic Movement. But other currents were also beginning to flow.

For generations, the wealthy had organised extravagant house-parties and excursions, financed by almost unlimited family fortunes. Friends and relations could visit for days and weeks without putting undue strain on the household budget. But for poorer people it was different. The Sunday school outing was the only leisure trip of the year, and chapel was the one place where they could meet old friends, make new friends, and enjoy – if still young and unattached – a little decorous courting. They had no great interest in the burning doctrinal issues that led national bodies and representatives in London to combine and to divide in the heat of acrimonious debate; their loyalty was to their local congregation. At chapel the talents of working men and women could be appreciated, their wisdom affirmed, their sorrows shared, their needs met. Here they felt part of something special, something blessed by God, a circle unsullied by worldly values and coarse language; here they enjoyed the confidence of shared beliefs and common experience. And it was in the dissenting chapels that ordinary working people learnt to follow Christ. They acquired a simple faith, a concern for others, an assurance of personal salvation and a hope of a better age to come; and they invited their friends and neighbours to join them.

In the growing industrial towns the Nonconformists flourished. "The real fact is that the established religion in Leeds is Methodism." So wrote a Yorkshire vicar in 1837, eighty-five years after Methodism had been introduced to the city by a stonemason who had heard John Wesley preach at Moorfields.[22] This perceptive clergyman confided that the best and most committed of his own Anglican congregation were those who had learned from the Methodists about salvation through personal faith in Christ. But Methodism was no longer what it had been. John Wesley himself had died in 1791, and from then on Methodism was rent by successive schisms, each new faction claiming to return to the original ideals and spirit of the movement. Some, such as the Primitive Methodists, retained a distinctly working class flavour, and many Methodist meetings were conducted by lay preachers and class leaders. Nevertheless, among the Methodists, as in almost all the Nonconformist chapels, the old distinction between clergy and laity persisted. Only the Society of Friends (Quakers) had dispensed with an ordained ministry, but their willingness to give more authority to the inner voice than the written scriptures furthered among them a general tendency for every man to do what was right in his own eyes.

There was some truth in the assertion that the dissenting chapels were divisive and anarchic. In some places they certainly did draw away from the parish churches many of the most devoted Christians, and in some places free interpretations of scripture did result in beliefs and practices very different from those hallowed by centuries of use in the Church of England. And the Nonconformist denominations tended to be as suspicious of one another as the Anglicans were of them all. In 1837 one observer wrote, "We question whether there is one dissenting body which would permit *their* members *occasionally* to break bread with another body of believers in the same place."[23] Staunch Irish Presbyterians considered it sheer presumption that anyone could be sure of being saved, whilst others made Assurance of Salvation the keystone of their doctrinal system.[24] A later writer describes "the narrowness, alienation, bitterness and bigotry that then characterised Nonconformity... An extreme example was that of two small Irish sects who nearly arranged to unite, but at last did not, because one party could not accept a declaration upon which the other party insisted, that John Wesley is in hell."[25]

The dissenting minister was often a figure of great authority, accountable only to his own deacons, a body of men he could overawe and overrule at will. In fact he could act as a little pope in a way quite impossible to an Establishment clergyman, who knew himself liable to be held to account by his bishop or archbishop. Current prejudice assumed that all Dissenters were narrow, vulgar and joyless, and experience sometimes seemed to bear this out. The young Frank Newman was unimpressed by his limited contact with Nonconformists. One he had heard speak at a meeting of the Bible Society: "I remember that one of them talked in pompous measured tones of voice, and with much stereotyped phraseology about 'the Bible only, the religion of Protestants.' Altogether it did not seem to me that there was at all so much of nature and simple truth in them as in Church clergymen."[26] In 1828, or thereabouts, John Bellett had similar experiences: "We went occasionally to the dissenting chapels together, but we had not much sympathy with the tone prevalent. The sermons we heard had generally, perhaps, less of the sympathy of Christ in them than what we had in the pulpits of the Established Church, and the things of God were dealt with more for the intellect and by the intellect than, as we judged, suited the proper cravings of the renewed and spiritual mind... So we held on (loosely though it was) by the Established Church still."[27]

Some Nonconformist ministers, like the great Matthew Henry of the previous century, were marvellous Bible teachers, and many were serious students of the scriptures. Though critics might consider their sermons "little more than a unique form of entertainment,"[28] some acquired a considerable following, especially in the major cities, their skills of oratory attracting a fashionable class of professional and literary people. But pastors with an eye for popularity hesitated to preach a gospel that might cause offence, and when they did their admirers went elsewhere.

For the most part, religious loyalties followed social and economic divides. Although exceptions undoubtedly occurred, contemporary sources paint a fairly consistent picture. "The aristocracy and gentry remained solidly Church of England, or Roman Catholic, and the high Anglicans catered for those with ritualistic tastes; the middle classes were mainly Congregationalist, Unitarian or Methodist; and the lower classes Baptist or Primitive Methodist. In the country the lazy old ways of the eighteenth century lingered on much longer, under the paternal eye of the local squire and village parson."[29]

As yet, little thought had been given to the spiritual needs of lands beyond the shores of Britain. Responsibility for such things was traditionally reserved to the bishops, and if the bishops did nothing, nothing was done. Throughout the Middle Ages, Roman Catholic missions had been established in many parts of the world, but the Reformation had not immediately led to a similar Protestant advance. "Martin Luther was so certain of the imminent return of Christ that he overlooked the necessity of foreign missions. He further justified his position by claiming the Great Commission was binding only on the New Testament apostles, who had fulfilled their obligation by spreading the gospel throughout the known world, thus exempting succeeding generations from responsibility."[30] This was the view of most eighteenth-century churchmen. "The Great Commission was given only to the apostles, and therefore converting the heathen was no concern of theirs."[31] Indeed, the failure of the world to accept the apostolic preaching meant that its many and varied peoples now lay under judgment. To offer them salvation or attempt to alleviate their woes would be to oppose the will of the Almighty.

Along with this went the general assumption that in every nation the monarch or parliament, instituted by God, bore ultimate responsibility for the religious beliefs and observances of its citizens and subjects. "The Reformers could not conceive of a missionary outreach into countries in which there was no Protestant government."[32] Indeed, "the 'wandering' of the Anabaptist evangelists was widely condemned by the Reformers."[33] Although Calvin himself supported some evangelistic initiatives, most of his followers considered that the doctrine of election rendered any extravagant missionary effort unnecessary. "The hyper-Calvinism of the day had convinced many that the conversion of the heathen would be the Lord's own work in his own time, and that nothing could be done by men to hasten it."[34] A case in point was the Baptist minister who famously instructed the youthful William Carey,

"Young man, sit down. When God pleases to convert the heathen, he will do it without your aid or mine."[35]

The religious condition of mid-nineteenth-century England corresponds, in many respects, to the condition of Europe, and especially German-speaking Europe. Indeed, many of the changes to be seen in Britain followed similar changes already observable in Switzerland and Germany. In the 1820s a number of independent assemblies were found in Geneva and the Swiss cantons of Vaud and Berne, prefiguring in certain respects the Brethren movement of the following decades in Ireland and England.[36] But especially significant for our story is the growth of German Pietism from the late seventeenth century onwards. The Lutheran pastor Philipp Spener, "troubled that German Protestantism seemed to have been reduced from a living faith to a body of orthodox dogmas," invited his parishioners, many of whom were barely educated, to midweek meetings for prayer, Bible study and mutual encouragement.[37] At about the same period Professor Auguste Franke introduced devotional studies to his university theology courses and established a poor-school and orphanage in Halle, eastern Germany.[38] Franke's doings and writings influenced John Wesley, George Whitefield, and in due course, George Müller. One of Franke's pupils was Count Nicholas von Zinzendorf, who in 1722 gave up his inherited wealth and established a number of small working communities of Christians known as Moravians. It was the Moravian Peter Böhler whose influence played a significant part in Wesley's conversion in 1738. The Moravians and other Pietists were drawn largely from the artisan and labouring classes. They set little store by education or intellect but emphasized holy living, practical Christian service and daily communion with the Saviour – a disciplined and somewhat mystical form of devotion with strong eschatological expectations. Their growth and influence gained momentum in the 1820s. Inspired by early Danish settlements on the south-east coast of India, they set up missionary colonies in several parts of the world.

In Britain too, as faith became more personal, interest in other peoples and places grew. The Napoleonic Wars had taken many Englishmen halfway round the world. Explorers such as Captain James Cook had brought back accounts of exotic wonders in foreign lands. Trading companies had taken adventurous young men to the Spice Islands, the Gold Coast and the icy wastes of Hudson Bay – and brought them back with money in their pockets and many a tale to tell. Across the oceans lived black people, red people and yellow people, and had not Christ died for them too? The Protestant churches were waking up to the reality of the big wide world and its vast spiritual need.

But many obstacles stood in the way! William Carey faced opposition not only from his fellow-Baptists but also from the East India Company, which refused him access to the territory under British influence, fearful that religious controversies would jeopardise mercantile interests. Undaunted, in 1793, he left for India, accompanied by his rather reluctant family, and "the day of the English-speaking peoples in overseas missions had begun."[39] The Church of England was not far behind. The earliest Anglican missionaries were chaplains, inspired by the great Charles Simeon of Cambridge, sent ostensibly to care for the spiritual needs of British administrators and merchants but free to learn local languages and share the gospel discreetly with the people around them. From these tentative beginnings commenced the era of the great missionary societies. To support William Carey in 1792 the Baptist Missionary Society was formed. Three years later came the London Missionary Society, sponsored largely, and soon entirely, by Congregationalists. The Church Missionary Society of the Anglican communion followed in 1799, and the Wesleyan Missionary Society in 1818. From this point onward, missions were rapidly established by almost every denomination and sent to work in almost every European country. By 1810, evangelistic work had spread to India, South-East Asia, North and Central America and the West African coast. It was then that thoughts turned slowly and with some trepidation to the Muslim lands of the Middle East.

This was the world in which Anthony Norris Groves lived, a world of almost unprecedented political, social and religious instability. This is the context in which he urged practical means to fulfil a threefold vision: to meet the needs of the poor, to restore the pattern of New Testament church life, and to take the gospel to the ends of the earth. It was in the face of these needs and opportunities that he offered radical solutions: the principles taught by Jesus himself.

ENDNOTES

[1] "A Letter on Missions to the Heathen", *The Christian Witness*, April 1840.
[2] Harrison, 180. The Reform Bill of 1831, pushed through by the party in power (the Whigs) against the impassioned resistance of the opposition (the Tories), gave a vote to the larger tenant farmers in the country and to men owning their own homes in the new industrial centres, but it still left the real political power in the hands of the landed aristocracy.
[3] Harrison, 35. Trades unions were still illegal, and throughout the period 1804-46 the infamous Corn Laws imposed high duties on imported foreign grain, thereby protecting British agriculture at the expense of the poorer people for whom the cost of bread was crucial.
[4] M105. Roman Catholic bishops and archbishops were reinstated in England in 1850, and the great influx of poor Irish quickly added a large working class membership to the Roman Catholic Church in England.

[5] Mt 24:14

[6] Lascars: sailors of Indian origin.

[7] The Congregationalists at this time were generally called Independents.

[8] This was stipulated in "His Majesty's Declaration" of 1562 (preface to the Articles of Religion), "reprinted by command of his majesty King Charles I" in the Book of Common Prayer.

[9] Stunt, *Awakening*, 92

[10] Harrison, 152

[11] Harrison, 154

[12] Prickett, 117

[13] R268-269. Norris Groves himself on one occasion sat opposite a man in a mail coach who "began a most obscene conversation with a gentleman who came to see him at the door of the mail while it was changing horses." From the coarseness of his manner, Groves assumed him to be an officer in the army but was shocked, on enquiry, to discover he was a clergyman, and even more shocked to read shortly afterwards that this clergyman had risen to become a "dignitary of the Church of England". "Am I to remain under the ministry of such a teacher?" asked Groves. "What example does a man give to his children or neighbourhood, when he continues to sit under the ministry of one whom he believes to be not a preacher but a perverter of the truth?" (R266-267)

[14] Waits: bands of itinerant musicians usually performing in the open air.

[15] Newman, *Phases of Faith*, 12

[16] Ryle, 102

[17] Act of Parliament under Queen Elizabeth I, 1593; in Bettenson, 242-243

[18] Watts, 266; Chadwick vol. 1, 80ff, 142ff. Nonconformist students were accepted at St Andrews (Scotland) and at University College London. The late 1830s saw changes in England favourable to Dissenters. The Marriage Act of 1836, for example, legalised Nonconformist marriages.

[19] Bellett, *Recollections*, 16

[20] The same was true on the continent. In Stuttgart two friends of George Müller applied for baptism in a Baptist church. This was refused unless they would "promise never to take the Lord's Supper any more with unbaptised believers or with those who belonged to any State Church." The friends could not accept this condition and were subsequently baptised by Müller himself in Bristol (Neatby, 96).

[21] Willmer H, quoted by Stunt, *Awakening*, 95

[22] Harrison, 154-155

[23] *The Christian Witness* 1837: 1, 306, quoted by Lang, *Groves*, 15

[24] Beattie, 292

[25] Lang, *Groves*, 15

[26] Newman, *Phases of Faith*, 23-24. Henry Craik, identified as a Baptist before throwing in his lot with the Brethren, would have agreed: "We have no sympathy with the levelling spirit of Political Dissent and have frequently found more union of spirit to those connected with our national Establishment" (Letter dated 30 June 1833, quoted by Stunt, *Awakening*, 295-296n).

[27] Bellett, *Interesting Reminiscences*, 3-4

[28] Dallimore, 60

[29] Wood, 92

[30] Tucker, 67. Among the Brethren, the editor of *The Christian Witness* in Plymouth also held this view (Groves, "A Letter on Missions", 129n.).

[31] Tucker, 115

[32] Bosch, 246

[33] Tennent, 4

[34] Neill, *History*, 26. See also Smith G, *Carey*, 47.

[35] George, 53

[36] Stunt describes these developments in detail (*Awakening*, 25-89).

[37] Stunt, *Awakening*, 3. See Neill, *History*, 227ff.

[38] See Franke, *Faith's Work Perfected.*

[39] Neill, *History*, 262

"We wish you to read the New Testament
that you may learn to judge of God's truth,
not by what you see in the churches around you,
but by the word of God itself."

Norris Groves [1]

ii

The Brethren Movement

I n 1854 there was issued a *Census of Great Britain* categorising all the places of worship to be found at that time throughout the country. A total of 132 worshipping groups identified themselves as "Brethren", in addition to 96 who were simply "Christians" and a remarkable 539 under the general heading of "isolated congregations".[2] How many of these groups were related to what we have called "the Brethren movement" it is impossible to tell, but the presence of such a number is proof enough that many Christians (approximately 25,000 according to the Census) were seeking a simpler and more biblical form of fellowship than could be found in the older denominations. And this was before the Revival of 1858-9, and before the great campaigns of Moody and Sankey in the 1870s, which added many thousands more. By 1906 a total of 800 assemblies were recognised as Open Brethren in England and Wales, with 300 more in Scotland, and 150 in Ireland.[3]

Historians have sometimes conveyed the impression that the Brethren movement simply spread through Britain from its original bases in Dublin and Plymouth. The true picture is far more complex. In fact it drew together dozens, if not hundreds, of independent groups, many of which started quite spontaneously. Professor F F Bruce, for example, tells us, "In my own part of the British Isles (North-East Scotland) many of these independent churches, including that in which I was brought up, came into existence as a result of the 1859 Revival and its aftermath, without any prior knowledge of the independent churches formed earlier in Dublin, Plymouth and Bristol… The Christians with whom I first enjoyed local church fellowship, when hearing about movements between 1825 and 1848, did not feel that this was where *they* came in, and appeals to them to conform their ways to those of 'the early brethren' would meet with the response 'Why should we?'" They saw their origins not in Dublin or Plymouth but in the New Testament. And yet Bruce affirms, "Many of us who belong to independent churches of this general pattern find membership in them specially congenial because of the exhilarating atmosphere of spiritual freedom which we breathe in them: long may it be so!"[4]

In 1940 a book of reminiscences was published, recording for posterity the verbal recollections of some who had been present at the start of these earliest independent fellowships in many parts of Britain. Quaint and fascinating reading they make, and some are worth quoting in full.

"Had a passer-by stopped outside a certain joiner's workshop in a Lanarkshire village one Saturday night in the early 'sixties, and peered through the half-closed window shutters, the glimmering light of an oil lamp burning within would have revealed a scene reminiscent of what is recorded of the first public meeting of Brethren in Dublin thirty years earlier. Charles Millar, the owner of the little workshop, with his wife, had removed some of the stock-in-trade to one side and swept the place, for in the morning a little company would meet together in that humble apartment to remember the Lord for the first time. Those who sat round the table on that occasion were: James Anderson, draper; Gavin Cooper, weaver; and Charles Millar with his wife. They began breaking bread, not knowing of any other meeting of the kind but taking the word of God as their guide, carrying out what they believed to be the will of the Lord." Soon this little group in Lesmahagow discovered others who had been led to meet in a similar way. In due course they rented an old schoolroom and started open-air work in the public square and the streets of the town. Crowds of several hundred regularly gathered to listen, and they stayed until nightfall. Millar recalled, "Many, under deep conviction of sin, refused to go home. Anxious ones were led into the hall and pointed to the Saviour." Before long, four hundred children were attending a Sunday school staffed by thirty-six teachers. Preachers walked out from Lesmahagow to take the gospel to all the towns and villages of the region – often insulted, sometimes stoned, but almost always leading some to Christ. Before long, similar groups of believers had been established in a number of places nearby.[5]

In 1864, in a village on the edge of Dartmoor, a young man bought a volume of printed sermons and started to read them to the mill workers and other villagers assembled in the schoolroom. As his confidence grew he began to preach sermons of his own, and a number who heard him were converted. Not knowing what to do next, he sent for the creeds, articles and confessions of the various church denominations in order to decide which of them to adopt.[6] But the more he compared them with each other, the more difficult it became to choose between them. He then heard of a group in a neighbouring village that had dispensed with all denominational confessions and simply followed the New Testament. This example he and his friends decided to follow. The whole village turned out to watch the first baptisms in the millstream. Among the onlookers was the owner of a small tool factory. "I came to laugh," he said, "but went home to cry, and the next time was baptised myself."[7]

Several fellowships started similarly in South Wales from 1852 onwards, including one comprised largely of seamen converted through meetings held in an old wooden sailing ship moored in Cardiff docks. These "Christians of the seafaring class" later moved to a large room above some stables. "Oft-times the horses in the stables underneath disturbed us," reminisced one of them, "but we look back with joy to those happy days... We recollect how the tears of joy would fill our eyes as we remembered our Lord around the table."[8] Other assemblies in Wales were established by relatively prosperous business and commercial men. In 1861 a group came together in Abergavenny. One of their number was the railway engineer Richard Hill who ten years later became the London Secretary of the China Inland Mission.

There was often a price to be paid for attending such meetings. At Grove Common, for example, near Ross-on-Wye, "So long as the people went nowhere, the vicar did not appear to mind, but directly he heard they were attending this meeting room the offenders were visited and warned that unless they returned to church they would lose the right to derive benefit from certain charities left for the poor who attended that church."[9] In the 1880s there were four men in Inverness perplexed that on the few occasions Communion was offered in their Nonconformist chapel they had to take it alongside unconverted people. Knowing nothing of the Brethren movement, they decided to rent a room where they could share bread and wine together on the first day of every week in remembrance of their Lord. One lost his job as a result; the others were "slighted by former friends and threatened in many ways".[10] But they continued to meet to express their worship in their own words, looking to the leading of the Holy Spirit and the guidance of the scriptures. Others joined them, and before long they had become a "large and active assembly".

Evangelists associated with these scattered fellowships would ride or walk to neighbouring villages to preach in the open air. In fact many local groups started with a tent campaign in a vacant field, where the gospel was preached sometimes every night for two months. Elsewhere, when the weather was fine, open-air meetings would be arranged on Sunday afternoons beside a public footpath or in a place where families gathered to take the air. Many would stop to listen; frequently there would be conversions and baptisms, and local people would come back week after week to hear more. Sometimes, in wet weather, preachers followed John Wesley's example, transforming the dim recesses of an empty hay-barn into a cheerful meeting place, courtesy of a kindly farmer and "a score and a half of tallow candles".

In 1865 a godly woman was moved to pray that the crowds attending the fair at Kingston-upon-Thames might have the chance to hear the gospel. Two or three young men went to preach in response to her request. One stayed on afterwards to visit the homes of those who had shown interest, and a gospel meeting was arranged in one of the cottages. At the appointed time so many turned up that some stood and listened outside the open door. Soon afterwards a large room was hired and regular meetings arranged.[11]

The rural assemblies often lacked hymn books, and sang from memory; few people of the labouring classes could read in any case. A correspondent from Woolwich remembers, "The outstanding features of the work in those early days seem to have been intense love to the Lord and a longing desire for the salvation of souls; and these traits were common to all members of the assembly, which was composed for the greater part of young believers."[12]

The preaching was simple, practical and down to earth. Those like Henry Craik and John Parnell who were university men made a point of speaking plainly to their uneducated congregations, but many of the preachers themselves were craftsmen and labourers. Some listeners would scoff at the presumption of the unordained preacher, but the novelty of a large tent in the corner of a field and the earnest sincerity of the young men speaking in it, invariably set the whole village buzzing. Above all, the preaching was biblical, commencing with a text and ending with a practical application. Those who had Bibles were asked to bring them and consult them. So different was this biblical preaching that it seemed, to many, a "new kind of doctrine"[13] – not the customary lecture on "the duty of regular churchgoing" or "the supreme rightness of the social order as it then existed,"[14] but good news of eternal life through personal faith in Jesus Christ.

Men and women brought to faith in Christ by exposition of the Bible were naturally keen to read it for themselves and discover what it said about such matters as baptism, worship and Christian ministry. Converted in a barn or tent, they had no connection with any particular church and felt no obligation to any existing denomination. Many of the evangelists decided simply to follow the example of the New Testament, meeting informally with their converts for the apostles' teaching, fellowship, breaking of bread and prayer. In such a gathering there was freedom for all to participate. Edward Groves in 1885 describes his early experience of these open meetings: "It is in such a meeting as we have been considering that these labourers got their first lessons in testimony for the Lord. First it may be there is only courage and ability to give out a hymn, then to read a suitable portion of the Word; afterwards as the heart becomes enlarged there is power and utterance given to engage in prayer, and so on for a few words of exhortation. And this progress is wonderfully quickened if, instead of coldly criticising, the silent worshippers bear him who takes part on their hearts in prayer."[15]

Worship would often commence in the kitchen or workshop of a local convert, but as numbers outgrew even the drawing rooms of moderately prosperous doctors, manufacturers and store owners, they began to look for a suitable public room where larger numbers could be welcomed to the Lord's Supper. A room of this sort could also be used for regular gospel preaching, and perhaps for a children's Sunday school and women's meetings too. Some bought land and built a hall; others rented a storeroom or a cottage; some, by agreement, took over the schoolroom or Town Hall at times when other activities were not in progress. Some erected a prefabricated wooden building or a portable "iron room" on the land of a sympathetic farmer; others adapted a dance-hall, a grain-store, a workshop or a public alehouse. In one town, part of a corn exchange was hired; elsewhere, a Temperance Hall, a music academy, a lecture room and even a law-court. It is surprising how many groups first met in rooms above stables. One writer recalled climbing, as a very small boy, "up a rickety old wooden stair which led to a long narrow room over a stable, where during the service the ceaseless crunching of the bit and the erratic movements of restless horses below could be distinctly heard... The walls were coloured pink and the ceiling whitewashed, the only attempt at decoration being a few modest-looking card texts displayed here and there, as if to break the wearisome monotony of this bare, uninviting meeting room. Those were the days of what is now regarded as old-fashioned gospel preaching – but preaching which drew many a lost one to the Saviour, and where at those hallowed meetings even the most lukewarm soul could not fail to perceive a truly spiritual atmosphere."[16]

In Manchester, four Presbyterians discovered, as they read the New Testament, that many things done in their church were not found in the word of God. Reluctant to rush into any new departure, and unaware that others were following a similar path, they agreed to search the scriptures at home and meet once a week to discuss their findings. In due course they were led to hire a room above a coal-shed in a poor part of the city, where they could enjoy simple fellowship and "break bread" on the Lord's Day in obedience to his command. Conversions and baptisms followed, and then the happy discovery of another group nearby that had been led along the same lines. One of its members recalled that to reach this second assembly you had to penetrate a "small dark street", then climb "a long spiral sort of staircase" to a room above the premises of a candy manufacturer who sold cough syrup in the market on Saturday nights. "Often the smell of horehound and other ingredients became almost suffocating as we met in the upper hall on Sunday mornings."[17]

Some saw a certain incongruity in the choice of poor quarters by men and women who obviously possessed the means to pay for something better. One observer wrote, "I could not help inwardly contrasting the apparent affluence of our brother who owned the big store in the town with the cold and uninviting room above the stable."[18] But the choice of such modest premises reflected a deliberate concern for the poor and unfortunate, and was influenced by the desire to establish a witness in places and among people unreached by the established denominations. It also owed something to the genuinely frugal lifestyle of Brethren who gave away a large proportion of their income.[19]

In some cases, of course, they could afford nothing better. One group met in an old ferry waiting room. "At times the tide could be seen surging through the floor, but it was the only available place within the limited means of those faithful workers."[20] Elsewhere, gospel meetings were arranged "in a large fish-curing shed, dimly lighted with two crude oil-lamps, and having rough planks of timber for seats." It was in such mean surroundings that labouring people were converted to Christ, and "strong men were broken down in tears of repentance."[21]

In 1880, near the railway works entrance at Swindon, dinner hour meetings were held in the open air. Such was the interest, and also opposition, that on one occasion the leaders were summoned by the police for obstruction. News of this naturally drew even larger crowds, and it became necessary to hire a hall. Conversions followed and an assembly was established there.

An Eastbourne newspaper reported on some meetings in "a plain building in Church Street", noting that "the congregations nearly fill the building and are made up chiefly of the working-class with a sprinkling of the persons in the middle walk of life." There followed an interview with "an intelligent farm labourer who attends the meeting regularly" and who spoke warmly of efforts made for the well-being of poorer people. "It seems," concluded the newspaper, "that the services are greatly appreciated by the people of his class, and are preferred to the more formal services of the Church of England."[22]

There was often opposition from the mainline denominations, which tested the courage of both evangelists and converts. A public baptism was arranged at a village in County Down. "Where the river crosses the road it was dammed at the bridge and the volume of water allowed to increase till of a sufficient depth to suit the purpose of baptism… and people gathered in large numbers to witness the ceremony… A large crowd (mostly Roman Catholics) gathered and threw stones and sticks at the converts. Mr Campbell, who was baptising the believers, was cut in the face while several others received injury from missiles thrown during the ceremony. The house was then attacked and most of the windows were broken."[23] In another place an evangelist recalled, "A man threatened to shoot me if I dared to immerse anyone in this locality, and while the baptism was taking place, he came armed with a gun and concealed himself adjacent to the river bank."[24] In the event, both evangelist and converts survived this experience unscathed.

In Lanarkshire and Aberdeenshire a number of women were among the most effective open air preachers associated with the Brethren during the Scottish revivals of the 1860s. Isabella Armstrong of Wishaw travelled throughout the region and addressed many hundreds every week. Mary Paterson of East Kilbride and Mary Hamilton of Larkhall, both converted in 1859, frequently spoke alongside male preachers in the open air. There were a number of others, and their emergence as "prophetesses" was seen as a fulfilment of Joel 2:28-29, a sign that the Second Coming was imminent. The majority of these women were young and unmarried, and they preached eloquently and at times with fierce emotion. Some had opportunity to instruct groups of young Christians too, and the fact that the Brethren generally met in cottages, workshops and hired rooms meant that women could take a far more active part than would be allowed from the pulpit of a parish church or Chapel, where ministry would be restricted to ordained men.[25]

In other parts of the British Isles, women exerted a quieter though no less effective influence through personal initiatives and individual conversations. It was Lady Powerscourt who drew together companies of Christian leaders in Ireland for prophetic study in her home, and it was Bessie Paget in Devonshire who challenged and inspired a number of younger men (Groves, Müller, Hake, Chapman and Craik), inviting them to address her cottage meetings in Poltimore. The Society of Friends had long encouraged women to "pray and prophesy",[26] and those coming from such a background would expect to do so. In his reminiscences Benjamin Newton speaks of a colleague's wife as "a gifted person in meetings"; he urged her to participate, and even rebuked her for neglecting her gift.[27] Edward Groves remarked that in the early days of the Brethren "the sisters too were fully as zealous, many of them deep students of the Word."[28] His own mother was quite capable of leading family prayers, and after the death of her husband generally did so.

Although there is no evidence that these women aspired, in a formal sense, "to teach or to have authority over a man,"[29] it was quite common for educated ladies to advise and encourage men from humbler backgrounds in their efforts to establish and lead local congregations. We have the example of a certain Christian lady who visited Peterhead in north-east Scotland in 1868, where she met a well-known evangelist, William McLean. When McLean declared himself a Baptist, she politely asked him, "Do you not think that the names given us in the word of God should be sufficient for a believer?" McLean was quick to agree that believers are "all one in Christ Jesus" and was before long persuaded that "what therefore God hath joined together" no man should "put asunder". The immediate result was an advertisement in the local newspaper announcing that "the Church of Christ in Peterhead will meet in a room at No.1 Rose Street." More than a dozen were seated in the best room of McLean's house, when the lady herself entered with a female friend. He rose to welcome them and she, familiar with similar meetings in London, whispered to him, "We saw your advertisement." Her keen eye, we are told, "ran over the room as if taking in its dimensions." Then she said, "Was it not rather a big claim to make – the Church of Christ in Peterhead – to meet in this room? I believe you really meant, 'Where two or three are gathered together in my name, there am I in the midst of them.'" "Yes, yes," replied the obliging McLean, "that's exactly what we meant." The narrative concludes by observing, "This lady afterwards gave Mr McLean many helpful suggestions from the scriptures and the assembly was launched."[30] It is clear that women could do much in these informal fellowships that would be quite impossible in the older churches, and they undoubtedly appreciated the opportunities newly available to them.[31]

The Brethren had attracted members from all the major British denominations during the middle decades of the nineteenth century, but it was the Revival of 1858-9 that made the movement a real force to be reckoned with. The great Revival, sometimes called the Second Evangelical Awakening, started in America two years before the election of Abraham Lincoln.[32] During the decade 1845-55 spiritual life in the USA and Canada was at a low ebb. The land was by then largely settled, commerce booming, and the populace engrossed in the business of making money. All who might be sensitive to higher ideals were preoccupied with the issue of slavery. Then came the crash. The banks failed, thousands of merchants were bankrupted, businesses closed, and despair fell upon the whole nation. There were 30,000 unemployed in New York alone. Brash confidence gave place to sullen resentment, then gloom and desperation. In 1857 a noonday prayer meeting was announced in Hamilton, Ontario. Anyone could attend; all denominations were welcome. Those who came were encouraged to pray freely and spontaneously. Within a few days, more than three hundred conventional religious people had discovered the reality of personal faith in a living Saviour. The idea of the "noonday prayer meeting" then took off throughout Canada and the USA, and within two years, a million converts had been added to the North American churches.[33]

Early in 1857 a young man newly converted in Northern Ireland was reading the *Narrative of Some of the Lord's Dealings with George Müller*. The simple account of how God led Müller to open his orphan house convinced James McQuilkin that the Lord hears and answers prayer. He shared his discovery with three friends and suggested that they meet to pray. Before long they saw the first results of their prayers: a farm servant and another friend were converted. At this point news came of the American awakening and they asked one another, "Why may we not have such a blessed work here, seeing that God did such things for Mr Müller simply in answer to prayer?"[34] Their prayer became more ambitious. At Christmas one of the young men converted through this group went home to Ballymena. He read the scriptures to his family and prayed aloud for them with great feeling. Later that night his mother woke the household, crying to God for mercy. There and then his mother and sister found peace in Christ, and "after three weeks of fearful conviction" so did his brother.[35] A second family heard about it, and they too came to personal faith in Christ. McQuilkin and his friends were now thoroughly convinced that God hears and answers prayer. Public prayer meetings were arranged, and before long crowds of three thousand were assembling to hear the young men preach the gospel. Undeterred by wind and rain, Irish Presbyterians and Roman Catholics, under intense conviction of sin, fell to their knees in the mud. "Drunkards, blasphemers, harlots, thieves on the one hand, and the respectable, the moral, the educated and the intelligent on the other, were instantaneously converted to a new way of life."[36] From this point on, the Revival spread rapidly throughout the whole of Ireland.

Soon there were public meetings in Scotland and Wales too, where Christians from all denominations met together to pray, and with similar results. Many of the evangelists were young unmarried men who with cheerful faith could face almost insuperable difficulties and hardships, and many new fellowships were formed of converts who had responded to the simple message of the three Rs – Ruin, Redemption and Regeneration. In Aberdeen, a hundred conversions were reported every night. In Wales, as Wesleyans and Calvinists prayed together, a rough old preacher raised his voice: "There's only a barrier of straw between us. Let's put a match to it!"[37] Immense crowds filled seven theatres in London, where Anglican and Nonconformist ministers together proclaimed the gospel. When a bishop rebuked one of his clergymen for preaching in an unconsecrated place, he replied, "My Lord, I do not preach in unconsecrated places. When our Lord Jesus Christ descended from heaven, he consecrated to himself every space!"[38] The historian of the Revival concludes, "The effect of united prayer upon Christians of all denominations is always the same. Towards God their hearts are stirred with love which must find expression in worship; towards other Christians their hearts are filled with love which finds expression in a Christian unity transcending the artificial boundaries of race, people, class and creed; towards the outsiders their hearts are filled with love which sets out immediately, like the Good Shepherd, to bring the lost sheep into the fold."[39]

In total, the Revival added more than a million souls to the churches in Britain – a greater number than those converted through Wesley, Whitefield and their contemporaries in the Great Awakening of the eighteenth century. All denominations gained substantially, but it was the Brethren who gained most, especially in Lancashire, Yorkshire and Northern Ireland.[40] In fact the evangelical revival and the Brethren movement had much in common. Both marked a response to a general sense of frustration, a disillusionment with conventional religion, and both encouraged ordinary people to be active participants in Christian life and witness. Men and women freshly inspired by revival scenes could not sit passively following a formal "order of service". Having seen the power of God at work, they knew how to win souls and they had faith to attempt great things. They found in the assemblies of Brethren the freedom they needed to exercise their spiritual gifts and to engage in active Christian service.

Revival scenes were repeated twenty years later with the preaching tours of the great evangelists Harry Moorhouse and Dwight L Moody. Moorhouse, plain and simple with a noticeable Manchester accent, was one of many itinerant preachers associated with the Brethren, and Moody himself "drank deeply of Brethren teaching."[41] Visiting Chicago, Moorhouse preached from Moody's pulpit six successive nights on John 3:16 while its normal occupant was away. Returning from his trip, Moody was curious to hear the "boy preacher". It was the seventh night, and Moody himself describes the scene as Moorhouse rose to speak. "He went to the pulpit. Every eye was upon him. 'Beloved friends,' he said, 'I have been hunting all day for a new text but I cannot find anything so good as the old one; so we will go back to the third chapter of John and the sixteenth verse', and he preached the seventh sermon from those wonderful words 'God so loved the world.'"

It was from this multitude of Revival converts that the assemblies sent missionaries all over the world, with the result that 2,500,000 Christians worldwide, including children, now identify themselves as "Brethren".[42] What started life as an English-speaking movement has become thoroughly international. In fact the Brethren of the industrialised West are now outnumbered six to one by those in other countries; the centre of gravity has shifted very decidedly to the developing world. And as church life in the West decays, the future of the movement lies largely in the hands of men and women for whom English is a foreign language.[43]

Although the earliest Brethren in Dublin and Plymouth were drawn from the educated and aristocratic sections of society, the Revival generation that followed was considerably more mixed, including many whose origins were distinctly humble. Since then the movement has attracted people from all walks of life and equipped them for a wide range of ministries. A number of early Brethren established schools and orphanages in Britain. One was J W C Fegan who opened his first "boys' home" in 1872 and whose success in reforming alcoholics considerably impressed Charles Darwin.[44] In 1866 a young medical student, Thomas Barnardo from the assembly in Stepney, was about to join Hudson Taylor in China when he came upon the street children of London's East End. It was from the assemblies that he recruited many of his early workers in Barnardo's Homes.

The Brethren emphasis on Bible study, and especially on the need to ascertain the exact meaning of the original text, gave them an early reputation for scholarship that was enhanced by published works such as *The Englishman's Greek Concordance of the New Testament*, edited by G V Wigram, and the *Hebrew and Chaldee Lexicon* of S P Tregelles. Henry Craik and Tregelles, among others, were outstanding writers on academic issues relating to the biblical texts. More recent Brethren biblical scholars of international repute are W E Vine, H L Ellison, F F Bruce, D J Wiseman and A R Millard.

We have seen how Newman, Newton and others at Oxford University in the early 1830s were caught up with enthusiasm for simple apostolic Christianity. Once they had left the Established Church, these men and others like them would be excluded from Britain's oldest and best universities.[45] In 1871, however, the former rule requiring acceptance of the Thirty-nine Articles of the Church of England was abolished, and the doors were opened to students with a more radical approach to the Christian faith. "In Cambridge the influx of men of Brethren background was strong by 1880... Some of these men injected a fresh and perhaps more reckless concern for evangelism into the more stolid Church of England majority. They must have strengthened the insistence on the need for new birth rather than just baptism."[46]

But these were days of transition, in which churches of almost every denomination had been intimidated by scholarly assertions that "old-fashioned evangelicalism had no future." Many Christian leaders "had accepted the liberal (rationalist) principle that human reason was as valid a source of our knowledge of God as the Bible and 'Tradition'. This meant, of course, that they accepted only as much of the Bible and of Tradition as 'the modern mind' could find acceptable; and that proved to be less and less as time went on."[47] Only a few had sufficient independence of mind to resist the trend. Apart from the Brethren, there were "some old-fashioned Church of England parishes" and "a few students in Cambridge".[48]

The students in question were a group who had resigned in 1910 from the Student Christian Movement, unable to accept its liberal theology. They had formed their own Cambridge Inter-Collegiate Christian Union (CICCU). Observers did not expect this evangelical minority to survive very long. The First World War then intervened, but in 1928 CICCU widened its horizons with the launching of the Inter-Varsity Fellowship (IVF), whose aim was to encourage the establishment of evangelical Christian Unions in universities throughout the British Isles, and to foster links between them.

At this time in Bristol there was a surgeon by the name of Arthur Rendle Short. With his keen intellect and wide general knowledge he could engage in discussion with critics of the Bible and of Christian belief, and give convincing reasons for faith. He welcomed students to his home, and before long was invited to universities in many parts of the country. A historian of the evangelical student movement observes, "Professor Rendle Short belonged to the 'Open Brethren' and was an indefatigable visitor to tiny groups of students to help CUs to get going. He was a constant visitor and speaker at Cambridge and did much to inspire the vision of a nation-wide network of Christian Unions, and to give a sense of responsibility for helping other universities in other countries."[49] Rendle Short later wrote a number of carefully reasoned books for students, justifying and advocating Christian belief.

Evangelicals, however, were still a very small minority in the British universities, and many students found their faith under attack from contemporaries studying science, history and theology. The Brethren did much to keep the evangelical flag flying. In the 1930s, "CICCU was mainly Church of England or Brethren with a mere handful of others."[50] North of the border, "most of the early leaders in Scotland... were from a Brethren background."[51]

In the universities everywhere, Brethren speakers were especially welcome. "A number of the most articulate CICCU members came from that background. They seemed to keep to an orthodox faith in this difficult period better than many of the Anglican majority." Their strength lay in the fact that they knew and firmly believed the Bible. They avoided the university theology courses offered to trainee ministers and clergy of the older denominations. "They were also helped by the fact that their tradition was, in any case, staunchly independent of prevailing religious opinions."[52]

During the following decades Professor F F Bruce and Dr W J Martin were two of the leading intellectuals who helped the Christian Unions in their resistance to liberal theology. The stability that these Brethren brought to the intellectual standing of the IVF was matched by that given by Sir John Laing to its financial basis. The profits from his substantial civil engineering company were directed both to the missionary outreach of the assemblies and to the university Christian Unions (and also to the inter-denominational London Bible College established in 1943).[53]

Although the IVF (now UCCF) has always discouraged student fellowships from seeing themselves as churches, such groups do, in many respects, resemble Brethren assemblies. The free participation in open meetings, the strong commitment to evangelism, the emphasis on personal Bible study and prayer, the informal discussion of Bible passages in small groups, the determination to be separate from the world, the belief that scripture is to be believed and obeyed, the sense of spiritual unity overriding denominational identities: these were all emphases dear to the Brethren. It is through these university groups, perhaps more than the "conventions", "alliances" and "faith missions", that Brethren ideals have found their way into the wider evangelical circles of the British Isles.

The lines dividing Brethren from other Evangelicals became increasingly blurred as the twentieth century progressed. The 1970s and 80s saw a sharp decline in the morale of many assemblies as the cream of their young leaders and preachers left to join para-church organisations or other churches that would employ them as "pastors" or "youth leaders". But whilst they were a loss to the assemblies they had left, they carried with them the biblical convictions acquired in the Sunday school and Young People's Fellowship. By the end of the twentieth century many Evangelicals in the United Kingdom had accepted biblical principles identified by the early Brethren, and during these decades a number of influential books by Anglicans and Baptists were written advocating them – plural leadership, active body-life, spontaneous worship and free fellowship with other Christians.[54] Led by trained professionals, the evangelical Baptist and Anglican churches could now offer excellent teaching, dynamic youth programmes, lively music played on a range of instruments, opportunities for women to participate, and in some cases an impressive range of charismatic "gifts".

The final two decades of the twentieth century saw a rapid and seemingly irreversible decline in the Brethren movement in England and Wales. Many assemblies lost so many members that, amidst great discouragement, they were forced to close. Others, desperate to avoid this fate, re-created themselves as conventional evangelical churches after the Baptist or Pentecostal model with a full-time "pastor", pre-arranged "services" and a music group to inspire "worship". A few conservative assemblies are still soldiering on, following what they believe to be Brethren tradition or New Testament principles, largely ignorant of their true origins and fearful for their future. Most independent observers in Britain would conclude that the Brethren movement is now a thing of the past. The cycle of birth, life and death has turned full circle.

Yet strange to say, our generation is facing many of the very same ills, in church and country, that challenged Norris Groves and his contemporaries: dissolute and unbelieving clergy, apathetic and frustrated laity, a society racked by misery and fear, moral chaos, personal loss, family breakdown, and a longing in many hearts for spiritual peace and comfort. It is said that the fastest growing denomination in the UK is that of Evangelicals who "used to go to church". For some, the ongoing hassle of personality clashes, administrative complexities, conflicting expectations and doctrinal tensions has made "church" a place of stress rather than a place of refreshment. For others, the passive entertainment, the dumbing down, the forced emotion, the tedious repetition and the political correctness have left them spiritually hungry and confused. At the same time, thousands of ordinary people languish outside who want nothing to do with "church", although they have no difficulty believing in God. We might wonder if the time has come to relaunch the Brethren movement, or something very like it – to get back once again to the simple New Testament pattern of welcoming one another in our homes for the apostles' teaching, for fellowship, for the breaking of bread, and prayer.

ENDNOTES

[1] J96; M69
[2] *The Missionary Reporter*, no. 8 (Feb 1854), 101; Forrest, 35-36
[3] Groves E K, *Successors*, 6
[4] Foreword to Coad, 13
[5] Beattie, 210-213
[6] The thirty-nine *Articles of Religion* of the Church of England were first published by authority of Queen Elizabeth I in 1562. The Presbyterian *Westminster Confession of Faith* was drawn up in 1643 by the Scottish "Assembly of Divines" and became

the official basis of the Church of Scotland in 1689. (The Church of Scotland chose to be governed by councils known as presbyteries rather than by bishops.) The Congregationalists (Independents) adopted *The Savoy Declaration of Faith and Order* in 1658. The Society of Friends had their *Chief Principles* drawn up in 1678, and the Methodists their *Deed of Declaration* composed by John Wesley in 1784, with a further *Plan of Pacification* issued after his death. Extracts from all these are found in Bettenson, *Documents.*

[7] Beattie, 69-70

[8] Beattie, 163

[9] Beattie, 45

[10] Beattie, 269-270

[11] Beattie, 136-137

[12] Beattie, 104

[13] Beattie, 138

[14] Quoted from Flora Thompson, *Lark Rise to Candleford*, 211-212. Flora Thompson describes the rector of the parish church at "Lark Rise". His surplice billowing, he would "hammer away… for forty-five minutes" chiding those present for the sins of the absent. His gospel amounted to "eternal punishment for sin" and "the bliss reserved for those who worked hard, were contented with their lot and showed proper respect for their superiors." She adds that "the holy Name was seldom mentioned, nor were human griefs or joys, or the kindly human feelings which bind a man to man. It was not religion he preached, but a narrow code of ethics, imposed from above upon the lower orders." The novel effect of vigorous gospel preaching on congregations unaccustomed to it is entertainingly described by W Haslam, *From Death into Life.*

[15] Groves E K, *Conversations*, 52, 130-131

[16] Beattie, 105-106. Some might regard the hiring, and certainly the purchase, of a hall to be a mistake, believing that the natural and scriptural place for Christian fellowship and worship is the home. The difficulty faced by a group becoming too large to meet in one house will be resolved by dividing in two, thus extending the activity of the Christian community over an ever-increasing area. (Nee, *TNCCL*, 168-171; Simson, *Houses that Change the World*). Groves, in 1829, observed that church buildings gave him no pleasure. He saw in their magnificence a "carnal, external and visible sign" opposed to "the spiritual essence of the thing they are meant to represent". He believed that money would be much better spent in "sending out the written word or the living teacher," and he saw no difficulty at all with "worshipping in houses" (J45-46).

[17] Beattie, 178

[18] Beattie, 107

[19] Hence the old saying, "Down an alley, up a stair; you're sure to find the Brethren there" (anon., courtesy of David Brady).

[20] Beattie, 183

[21] Beattie, 274-275

[22] Beattie, 131

[23] Beattie, 289-290

[24] Beattie, 293

[25] Dickson, 96-98; Beattie 213. Twenty years later, with the acquisition of more formal buildings and a more structured leadership and ministry, considerably less scope would be allowed for the spontaneous and unconventional. An increasingly self-conscious identity as "Brethren" tended to curb local practices disapproved by the wider movement, and by the late 1880s the era of women preachers among the Brethren of Scotland was over (Dickson, 110-111).

[26] See 1 Cor 11:5.

[27] Coad, 67. The Society of Friends (Quakers) suffered a division in 1835, with the loss to the Brethren of some influential families in London and large numbers further north, especially in Cumbria. Benjamin Newton, William Hake, Richard Ball, Samuel P Tregelles, the Howards of Tottenham and the Paget sisters had personal and family connections with the Quakers (Stunt, *Early Brethren*, 8-11; Groves E K, *Successors*, 370).

[28] Groves E K, *Conversations*, 145

[29] 1 Tim 2:12

[30] Beattie, 275-276

[31] One observer recalled that in the mid-nineteenth century, "their ladies were modest and retiring, accepting without question the teaching of the scriptures by S. Paul. They never spoke in public, although some had a remarkable flow of language which was listened to with delight at the home or house meetings" (Harris A N, *BHR* 5).

[32] The movement inspired by Wesley and Whitefield in the eighteenth century is considered to be the first Evangelical Awakening.

[33] Orr, 17

[34] Orr, 39

[35] Orr, 40

[36] Orr, 40

[37] Orr, 82

[38] Orr, 99

[39] Orr, 97

[40] Orr, 202. Among those who professed faith at this time were some two hundred children in Müller's orphanage.

[41] Orr, 202

[42] Fellowships with an Open Brethren identity are found in 130 nations. Recent reports indicate about 2230 in India, 2050 in Guatemala, 2017 in Angola, 1300 in Argentina, 1255 in Zambia, 1198 in Britain, 1125 in Honduras, 1107 in Chad, 1060 in Congo DR, 780 in the USA, 727 in Romania, 580 in Brazil, 510 in Papua New Guinea, 500 in Nigeria, 482 in Canada, 459 in Germany, 280 in Australia, 275 in Dominican Republic, 270 in Italy, 240 in New Zealand, 230 in Peru, 225 in Mexico, 215 in the Philippines, 212 in Bolivia, 210 in Spain, 200 in South Korea, 174 in Laos, 168 in Malaysia, 160 in Rwanda, 145 in Tanzania, 145 in Chile, 145 in Japan, 140 in Malawi, 140 in South Africa, 122 in Paraguay, 108 in France, 106 in Burundi, 100 in Pakistan, 100 in Portugal, 95 in the Netherlands, 80 in Ethiopia, 70 in Myanmar (Newton and Chan).

[43] Report by Don Fleming in Rowdon (ed.), *International Partnership Perspectives*, no. 3, 17.

[44] Darwin wrote to compliment him: "Your services have done more for the village in a few months than all our efforts for many years. We have never been able to reclaim a drunkard, but through your services I do not know that there is a drunkard left in the village!" (Short, 74-75)

[45] Although Oxford, Cambridge and Durham would not accept them, they could apply to University College London or to the Scottish or continental universities.

[46] Barclay, 16-17

[47] Barclay, 72

[48] Barclay, 72

[49] Barclay, 97

[50] Barclay, 107

[51] Fielder, 82, 85, 29

[52] Barclay, 106

[53] Bebbington, 260

[54] Among them were David Watson, *I Believe in the Church*; Michael Harper, *Let My People Grow*; Michael Griffiths, *Cinderella With Amnesia*.

iii

Glossary

Aramaic: the ancient language of the Aramaeans, a semi-nomadic Semitic people who settled in many parts of the Middle East, adopted as a common or trade language with the expansion of the Persian Empire from the sixth century BC. It was largely, but not entirely, replaced by Arabic from the thirteenth century onwards.

Armenian Church: a monophysite body founded in the early fourth century as the national church of the first officially Christian nation, Armenia. The Armenian Church severed its connection with the Greek Orthodox Church in AD 552, and its patriarch resides in the holy city of Etschmiezin (Edschmiadsin) in the foothills of Mount Ararat. The traditional Armenian Bible contains some books found in no other Bible. In the fifteenth century many Armenians joined the Roman Catholic Church and became known as Armenian Catholics.

Arrack: a coarse colourless spirit distilled from grain, rice, sugar etc., milky white when mixed with water (from Arabic *'araq* = sweat, perspiration).

Assyrian Christians – see **Nestorian Christians**

Brahman (or Brahmin): a member of the highest or priestly caste of Hinduism in India.

Caliphate: the spiritual and temporal authority governing the Islamic faithful, inherited in line of succession from Muhammad himself and assumed at this period by the Sultan of the Ottoman Empire with the personal title of "Caliph".

Calmucs: pagan tribes inhabiting parts of Russia.

Catechist: a person who teaches others how to answer the basic questions concerning Christian faith and practice contained in a catechism. In nineteenth century India the catechist often did the work of an evangelist, preaching the gospel and instructing new believers.

Chaldean: the colloquial spoken form of the Aramaic language used in the Baghdad region.

Chaldean Church: a body of Nestorians of Assyrian descent who from the sixteenth century onwards accepted the authority of the Pope in Rome whilst retaining their own Patriarch. They generally speak Aramaic or Arabic.

Choultry: a caravanserai or inn where animals occupy a central courtyard (from Telugu: *chawadi*).

Dervish: a Muslim ascetic, often a member of a fraternity known for particular rites and trance-like states.

Druses (or **Druzes**): a group which split from orthodox Islam in the eleventh century AD, named after their founder Ad-Darazi.

Effendi: a scholar or man of social standing in the Ottoman Empire.

Fakir: a Muslim or Hindu ascetic (especially in India).

Jacobites: a Christian faction named after Jacob (a mid-sixth century monk) which formed a separate monophysite church in AD 451. Their patriarch has his official seat in Antioch but normally resides in a monastery at Diarbekr (now usually spelt Diyarbakir) in eastern Turkey. Jacobite monks were noted for their rigorous asceticism and extravagant superstition.

Maronite Christians: a monophysite body, deriving its name from St. Maron, who founded a monastery in Syria in AD 400. They speak Arabic but use ancient Syriac as a liturgical language. Whilst submitting to the authority of the Pope in Rome, they maintain their own patriarch on Mount Lebanon. They are traditional enemies of the Druses.

Mesopotamia: the wide plain occupied by the Tigris and Euphrates rivers, leading down to the Persian Gulf (from the Greek, meaning "between rivers").

Monophysite Christians: sects teaching that there is only one nature in the person of Christ, which is primarily divine with human attributes. Included among them are the Egyptian Copts and the Syrian Jacobites and Maronites.

Mullah (or **Moolah, Moulah, Mollah**): a Muslim scholar, teacher or religious leader (especially in Persia, Mesopotamia and Turkey).

Moulvi (or **Moolvi**): a Muslim scholar, teacher or religious leader (especially in India).

Mughal (or **Mogul**) **Empire**: a powerful Muslim state established in northern India by peoples of Mongolian origin in the sixteenth and early seventeenth centuries.

Nestorian Christians: a body led since the fifth century by its own patriarch, who after AD 762 resided for several centuries in Baghdad. Of Assyrian descent and preferring the title "Assyrian Christians", they traditionally maintained that Christ possessed two natures, and that the divine *Logos* clothed itself with humanity but did not truly become man. Renowned for scholarship and for the founding of schools and hospitals, the Nestorian Church flourished for several centuries and spread with great missionary zeal from Persia to India, Arabia, and even to China and Tartary. They generally speak a form of Aramaic (Syriac) or Arabic. A Nestorian community, known as the Mar Thoma Church, still survives in south-western India.

Ottoman Empire: a powerful Muslim state with its capital in Constantinople (Istanbul) controlling territories in eastern Europe, North Africa and Asia from the late thirteenth century until the end of the First World War.

Pasha: a provincial governor.

Persia: in the mid-nineteenth century, a term loosely used for the area between Turkey and India, comprising the Persian Empire (modern Iran) and the wide fertile valley of the Tigris and Euphrates rivers (modern Iraq).

Qadi: a Qur'anic judge.

Sepoys: Indian soldiers trained in European fashion.

Sufi: an adherent of any mystical Muslim sect.

Syriac: a dialect of Aramaic spoken in the Middle East until about the thirteenth century AD, and still in use as a formal liturgical language in some Eastern churches. The term Syriac is also used of the modern colloquial Aramaic spoken by people with a Christian identity in certain areas.

Tartars (or **Tatars**): a people of Mongolian origin settled in many parts of the Russian and Persian Empires and speaking their own language of a Turkic type – a residue of invasions under Genghis Khan in the thirteenth century. In the mid-nineteenth century most were nominal Muslims, converted from Buddhism, still adhering to ancient shamanistic and animistic practices.

'Ulama: a body of Islamic scholars, guardians of Islamic religion.

Uniate Churches: Eastern churches that chose to submit to the authority of Rome but retained their own liturgy – Greek Catholic, Coptic Catholic, Syrian Catholic, Chaldean Catholic and Armenian Catholic, and in Lebanon the Maronite Church.

Wartabiet: an Armenian priest.

Yazidis (or **Yezidis)**: a sect based in the area round Mosul (Nineveh), combining elements of Islam and Christianity and incorporating belief in the devil as an agent of God. (Yazid is the local name for the devil.)

iv

Dates

Anthony Norris Groves *and his contemporaries*

1793 (16ᵗʰ July) *birth of Mary Bethia Thompson* in London
1795 (1ˢᵗ Feb) born at Newton Valence, Hampshire
c.1808 hears John Owen speak at Fulham about missionary work in India
1814 (Feb) commences dental practice in Plymouth
1816 influenced by evangelical clergymen Joseph Richards and Thomas Hitchins;
conversion as a disciple of Christ; has thoughts of missionary work in India and
enquires with CMS; (22ⁿᵈ Oct) marries Mary Bethia Thompson in Fulham Parish
Church; moves to Northernhay House, Exeter
1818 (Nov) birth of Henry Groves
1820 birth of Francis (Frank) Anthony Groves
1822 birth of daughter Mary; starts visiting poor in Exeter
1823 (July) death of Mrs Lydia Groves, mother of ANG; meets Bessie and Charlotte
Paget, also John Marriott and William Caldecott
1824 adopts Calvinistic views and gains assurance of salvation; conversion of Mary
Bethia Groves; visit of Bishop Chase and thoughts of missionary work in Ohio;
(May) John Kitto joins Groves household at Northernhay
1825 (spring?) publishes "Christian Devotedness"; (July) visit of Edward Bickersteth;
helps Jewish converts Alexander, Belsom and Abrahams; *Kitto moves to Islington*;
(Aug) accepted by CMS with idea of working in Malta; (Nov) Robert Nesbit
joins Groves household; *conversion of George Müller in Halle*; *John Parnell and
friends start "breaking bread" in Dublin*
1826 (Aug) Henry Craik joins Groves household; (autumn) first trip to Dublin
1827 (Mar) CMS propose Persia as destination; decision taken for Persia; receives
legacy on death of Mr Thompson; (spring) takes Bessie Paget to Dublin and
suggests to Bellett that believers may break bread together; (June) *Kitto to Malta*;
(early summer) starts preaching at Poltimore; (21ˢᵗ Oct) theft of passage money
for Dublin; abandons plans for ordination and withdraws from Trinity College,
Dublin; (autumn) *F W Newman visits Dublin*; *Edward Cronin and friends start
meeting to "break bread"*
1828 (Jan) vacates Northernhay House and takes his family to live with the Paget sisters;
(spring) severs connection with CMS; (summer) *Craik leaves for Teignmouth*;
(?Nov) comment to Bellett in Lower Pembroke Street on freedom of ministry;
baptised in Exeter; (Dec) death of little Mary

1829 (Jan) final visit to Dublin to explain missionary plans; *Kitto returns from Malta*; *Craik preaching at Shaldon*; (May) agrees to escort Mrs Taylor and party to Baghdad; (12ᵗʰ June) missionary party embark in "Osprey" for St Petersburg; (Sep) joined by K G Pfander at Shushi; (Nov) *Bellett, Cronin, Darby & Hutchinson meet in Hutchinson's house for "breaking of bread"*; *Müller visits Devon and meets friends of Groves*; (Dec) arrives in Baghdad

1830 (Jan) *Müller appointed pastor in Teignmouth*; (May) *room in Aungier Street opened*; *Darby visits Oxford University*; *reports of tongues and miraculous healing in Scotland*; *Strong starts independent meetings in Georgetown*; (Sep) Parnell, Cronin, Newman and party set off to join Groves; (Oct) birth of baby girl; *Müller marries Groves's sister Mary*; (Nov) Harnie Thomas joins Groves household

1831 (Jan) Parnell and party arrive in Aleppo; (Feb) *Bulteel's sermon at Oxford*; (March) *Pfander leaves Baghdad*; plague in Baghdad; (April) *first tongues and prophesyings in London*; (14ᵗʰ May) death of Mary Groves; (spring?) publication of "Journal during a Journey from London to Baghdad"; (24ᵗʰ Aug) death of baby; (Oct) *first Powerscourt conference*; (Dec) *start of Plymouth assembly*;

1832 (Apr) Parnell and party leave Aleppo for Baghdad; *Chapman to Barnstaple*; (May) *Müller and Craik to Bristol*; (Aug) *launch of Bethesda assembly*; (Sep) Kitto & Newman leave Baghdad; (autumn?) publication of "Journal of a Residence at Baghdad"

1833 (May) to India with Cotton, touring mission stations from Bombay via Ceylon to Calcutta; publishes "On the Nature of Christian Influence"; *Wigram starts assembly in London*

1834 (Jan) *first issue of "The Christian Witness" published in Plymouth*; *J N Darby secedes from Established Church*; (Apr) letter to Darby about union and communion; article entitled "Correspondence from the East" appears in The Christian Witness; publishes "On the Liberty of Ministry in the Church of Christ"; (July) leaves India with Alexander Duff; (autumn) Parnell & Cronin abandon Baghdad; *Torquay assembly started*

1835 (1ˢᵗ Jan) arrives with Duff in Scotland; (early spring) to Basel and Geneva with Müller recruiting workers; (Mar) visits Kitto; (25ᵗʰ Apr) marries Harriet Baynes in Church of St Mary, Great Malvern; (June) death of Mr Anthony Groves, father of ANG, in Bristol

1836 (Mar) letter to Darby from Milford Haven; leaves for India with Gundert, Julie Dubois, Marie Monnard, Emma Groves, Bowdens, Beers, Kälberer and Brice; publishes enlarged edition of "The Present State of the Tinnevelly Mission"; *Müller opens first orphan house in Bristol*; (July) missionary party lands at Madras; reunited with Parnell, Cronin, Henry, Frank & Harnie; (Aug) *Bowden & Beer to Godavari*; (11ᵗʰ Aug) Edward Kennaway Groves born; *assemblies launched in Bath and Salcombe*

1837 (June) Parnell, Cronin & Serkies return to Britain; (July) moves to Chittoor and establishes small farm; "Remarks on the Typical Import of the Kingly History of Israel" appears in The Christian Witness; publishes "The New Testament in the Blood of Jesus"; *assemblies started in Hereford, Kendal and Stafford*; *first issue of Müller's Narrative*

1838 travels 800 miles visiting expatriate communities; (July) *Gunderts move to south-west coast of India; assembly started in Tottenham*

1840 (April) "A Letter on Missions to the Heathen" appears in The Christian Witness; (spring?) *Arulappan leaves to start independent work*; publishes "Remarks on a Pamphlet"; (6th Dec) George Norris Groves born

1841 silk farm established at Chittoor

1842 loan contracted and silk farm extended; Mary Leslie adopted; *Christianpettah established by Arulappan; assembly started in Hull*

1843 *Müller assists creation of assembly in Stuttgart*

1845 silk farm abandoned; *Darby splits Plymouth assembly*

1846 *Müller starts to support workers in India; foundation of Evangelical Alliance*

1847 (Feb) Harriet to England; final collapse of commercial projects in Chittoor

1848 (Feb) leaves India for second visit to England; (20th Mar) lands in England and joins Harriet in Bristol; (Aug) *Darby announces breach with Bethesda, leading to permanent split between Exclusive and Open assemblies*

1849 publishes "The Tottenham Case"; (20th June) leaves England with Harriet and Mary Leslie for final trip to India

1850 (Feb) Agnes Groves born

1851 (Sep) death of Judge Lovell and rejection of ministry in Chittoor

1852 (14th Aug) leaves India for England; (25th Sep) arrives at Southampton; (Oct) removes Edward from school in Bideford; speaks to Tottenham assembly about missionary support

1853 (Feb) death of Mrs Baynes; debts paid off; (20th May) dies in home of George Müller; (July) *"The Missionary Reporter" launched*; (Aug) Harriet lands at Southampton; (Sep) *Hudson Taylor to China*

1857 Henry Groves returns to England

1858-9 *Revival (Second Evangelical Awakening)*

1864 *first Mildmay Conference*

1865 *Hudson Taylor founds China Inland Mission*

1867 *death of Arulappan*

1872 *first issue of "The Missionary Echo"*

1874 Edward Groves returns to England

1875 *first Keswick Convention*

1887 Constance Groves to China with CIM

V

Genealogy of

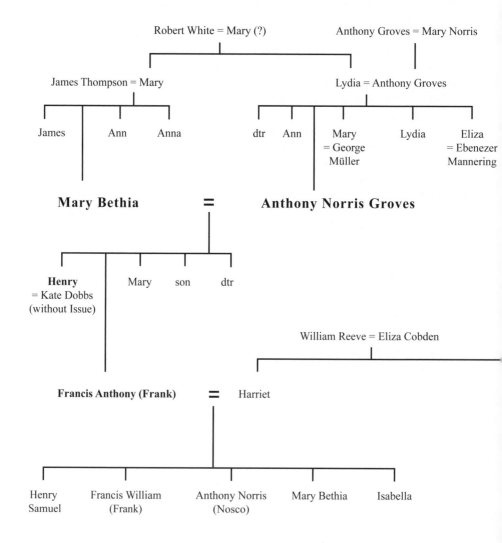

Robert White = Mary (?)   Anthony Groves = Mary Norris

James Thompson = Mary   Lydia = Anthony Groves

James   Ann   Anna   dtr   Ann   Mary   Lydia   Eliza
                                                = George   = Ebenezer
                                                Müller   Mannering

Mary Bethia   **=**   **Anthony Norris Groves**

Henry   Mary   son   dtr
= Kate Dobbs
(without Issue)

William Reeve = Eliza Cobden

Francis Anthony (Frank)   **=**   Harriet

Henry   Francis William   Anthony Norris   Mary Bethia   Isabella
Samuel   (Frank)   (Nosco)

Anthony Norris Groves

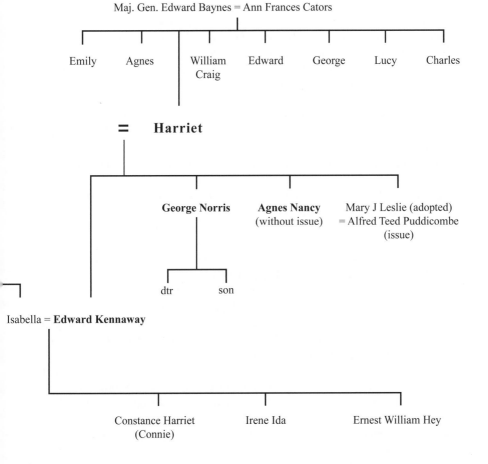

Maj. Gen. Edward Baynes = Ann Frances Cators

Emily   Agnes   William   Edward   George   Lucy   Charles
Craig

=   **Harriet**

George Norris   **Agnes Nancy**   Mary J Leslie (adopted)
(without issue)   = Alfred Teed Puddicombe
(issue)

dtr   son

Isabella = **Edward Kennaway**

Constance Harriet   Irene Ida   Ernest William Hey
(Connie)

vi

Bibliography

[Anon], "Church Canons", *The Christian Witness*, vol. 3 (April 1836), 105-146

Adeney, David H, *China: The Church's Long March* (Ventura, CA, Regal Books, 1985)

Allen, Hubert J B, *Roland Allen: Pioneer, Priest and Prophet* (Grand Rapids, Eerdmans, 1995)

Allen, Roland, *Missionary Methods: St Paul's or Ours?* (London, World Dominion Press, 1912; 2nd edn. 1927) (reissued, Grand Rapids, Eerdmans, 1962)

——————, *The Spontaneous Expansion of the Church* (London, World Dominion Press, 1927; 2nd edn. 1960) (reissued, Grand Rapids, Eerdmans, 1962)

Anderson, Allan, "Signs and Blunders: Pentecostal Mission Issues at 'Home and Abroad' in the Twentieth Century" (JAM 2/2, 2000)

Anderson, Courtney, *To the Golden Shore: The Life of Adoniram Judson* (Grand Rapids, Zondervan, 1956, 1972)

Anderson, Dick, *We Felt Like Grasshoppers: the story of Africa Inland Mission* (Crossway, Nottingham, 1994)

Arnott, Anne, *The Brethren, an Autobiography of a Plymouth Brethren Childhood* (London and Oxford, Mowbray, 1969, 1982)

Barclay, Oliver R, *Whatever Happened to the Jesus Lane Lot?* (Leicester, Inter-Varsity Press, 1977)

Bat Ye'or, *The Dhimmi: Jews & Christians under Islam* (London & Toronto, Associated University Presses, 1985)

Beattie, David J, *Brethren, the Story of a Great Recovery* (Kilmarnock, John Ritchie Ltd, 1940)

Beaver, R Pierce, *To Advance the Gospel: Selections from the Writings of Rufus Anderson* (Grand Rapids, Eerdmans, 1967)

Bebbington, D W, *Evangelicalism in Modern Britain: A History from the 1730s to the 1980s* (London, Unwin Hyman, 1989; reprint, London, Routledge, 2002)

Bellett, J G, *Early Days: A Series of Letters Showing How the Spirit of God Led in the Recovery of Various Great Truths Relating to the Church, Some Ninety Years Ago* (New York, Loizeaux Brothers, 1920)

——————, *Interesting Reminiscences of the Early History of "Brethren", with Letter from J G Bellett to J N Darby* (Weston-Super-Mare, Walter Scott, c.1871)

Bellett, L M, *Recollections of the Late J. G. Bellett by his Daughter* (London, Rouse, 1895)

Bettenson, Henry (ed.), *Documents of the Christian Church* (Oxford, OUP, 2nd edn., 1963)

Bonar, Andrew A & McCheyne, Robert Murray, *Narrative of a Mission of Enquiry to the Jews*, Vol.1, 2nd. edn (Edinburgh, William White & Co, 1842)

Bonk, Jonathan J, *Missions and Money: Affluence as a Western Missionary Problem* (Maryknoll, Orbis, 1991)

Bosch, David J, *Transforming Mission: Paradigm Shifts in Theology of Mission* (New York, Orbis, 1991)

Bowen, Desmond, *The Protestant Crusade in Ireland, 1800-70* (Dublin, Gill & Macmillan, 1978)

Bradley, Ian, *The Call to Seriousness: The Evangelical Impact on the Victorians* (London, Jonathan Cape, 1976)

Brady, Steve & Rowdon, Harold (eds.), *For Such a Time as This* (Milton Keynes, Scripture Union / London, Evangelical Alliance, 1996)

Brecht, Martin (trans. Meldrum, David), "The Relationship Between Established Protestant Church and Free Church: Hermann Gundert and Britain," in Robbins, Keith (ed.), *Protestant Evangelicalism: Britain, Ireland, Germany and America, c.1750 - c.1950* (Oxford, Basil Blackwell, 1990)

Broadbent, E H, *The Pilgrim Church* (London, Marshall Pickering, 1931, 1989)

Bromley, E B, *They were Men sent from God: A Centenary Record (1836-1936) of Gospel Work in India amongst Telugus in the Godavari Delta and Neighbouring Parts* (Bangalore, Scripture Literature Press, 1937)

Broomhall, A J, *Hudson Taylor and China's Open Century*, Book 1, *Barbarians at the Gates* (London, Hodder, 1981)

—————, Book 2, *Over the Treaty Wall* (London, Hodder, 1982)

—————, Book 3, *If I had a Thousand Lives* (London, Hodder, 1982)

—————, Book 4, *Survivors' Pact* (London, Hodder, 1984)

—————, Book 5, *Refiner's Fire* (London, Hodder, 1985)

—————, Book 6, *Assault on the Nine* (London, Hodder, 1988)

Brown, Stewart J, *Thomas Chalmers and the Godly Commonwealth in Scotland* (Oxford, Oxford University Press, 1982)

Bynum, W F, *Science and the Practice of Medicine in the Nineteenth Century* (Cambridge, CUP, 1994)

C. [Congleton], *The Open Meeting*, 2nd edn. (London, J E Hawkins, 1877)

Carey, William, *An Enquiry into the Obligations of Christians to use Means for the Conversion of the Heathens* (reproduced in George, Timothy, *Faithful Witness*; Leicester, Inter-Varsity Press, 1991)

Carmichael, Amy, *This One Thing: The Story of Walker of Tinnevelly* (London, Oliphants, 1950)

Chadwick, Owen, *The Victorian Church*, 2 vols. (London, A & C Black, 1966, 1970)

Chilcraft, Stephen J, *Anthony Norris Groves' Theory and Practice of Mission* (Birmingham Christian College, MA dissertation, 2003)

Clark, Henry Martyn, *Robert Clark of the Panjab: Pioneer and Missionary Statesman* (London, Andrew Melrose, 1907)

Coad, F Roy, *A History of the Brethren Movement* (Exeter, Paternoster, 1968); reprint (Vancouver, Regent College Publishing, 2001)

Collingwood, William, *The "Brethren": A Historical Sketch* (Glasgow, Pickering & Inglis, 1899)

Conran, Henry Mascall, *Autobiography of an Indian Army Officer* (Morgan and Chase, London, 1870)

Cornforth, David, "Exeter Memories", http://www.exetermemories.co.uk/em/_ buildings/northernhay-house.php

Cragg, Kenneth, *The Arab Christian: A History in the Middle East* (London, Mowbray, 1991)

Dallimore, Arnold, *The Life of Edward Irving* (Edinburgh, Banner of Truth, 1983)

Daniel, Robin, *Mission Strategies Then and Now* (Chester, Tamarisk, 2012)

Daniel, Roy T (ed.), *Prayer Handbook: Indian Commended Workers Working in India and Abroad* (Bangalore, Operation Barnabas, 2002)

Dann, Robert Bernard, "The Legacy of Anthony Norris Groves", *International Bulletin of Missionary Research*, Vol. 29, No. 4 (Oct. 2005), pp. 198-202

──────────, *The Primitivist Ecclesiology of Anthony Norris Groves: Church as it was meant to be* (Chester, Tamarisk, 2006, 2015)

──────────, *The Primitivist Missiology of Anthony Norris Groves: Mission as it was meant to be* (Chester, Tamarisk, 2006, 2015)

Darby, John Nelson, *Collected Writings of J N Darby*, ed. *W Kelly* (Kingston-on-Thames, Stow Hill Bible and Tract Depot, c.1960) 34 vols; <http://www.stempublishing.com/authors/darby/>

──────────, The Apostasy of the Successive Dispensations (*Collected Writings*, vol. 1)

──────────, The Bethesda Circular (*Collected Writings*, vol. 15)

──────────, Considerations on the Nature and Unity of the Church of Christ (*Collected Writings*, vol. 1)

──────────, Evidence from Scripture of the Passing Away of the Present Dispensation (*Collected Writings*, vol. 2)

──────────, The Hopes of the Church of God, in Connection with the Destiny of the Jews and the Nations, as Revealed in Prophecy: Eleven Lectures delivered in Geneva, 1840 (*Collected Writings*, vol. 2)

──────────, The Irrationalism of Infidelity: Being a Reply to "Phases of Faith" (*Collected Writings*, vol. 6)

──────────, The Notion of a Clergyman Dispensationally the Sin against the Holy Ghost (*Collected Writings*, vol. 1)

──────────, The Rapture of the Saints and the Character of the Jewish Remnant (*Collected Writings*, vol. 11)

──────────, Remarks on the State of the Church, in Answer to the Pamphlet of Mr. Rochat (*Collected Writings*, vol. 1)

──────────, Separation from Evil God's Principle of Unity (*Collected Writings*, vol. 1)

──────────, What the Christian has Amid the Ruin of the Church, being a Reply to Certain Articles in the "Jamaica Magazine" (*Collected Writings*, vol. 14)

Dickson, Neil, *Modern Prophetesses* (Records of the Scottish Church History Society, vol. 25, 1, 1993); reissued (London, Partnership Publications, n.d.)

Drummond, Andrew Landale, *Edward Irving and his Circle* (London, James Clarke, 1935)

Drury, Elizabeth & Lewis, Philippa, *The Victorian Household Album* (London, Collins & Brown, 1995)

Dyer, Helen S, *Pandita Ramabai* (Glasgow, Pickering & Inglis, n.d.)

Eadie, John, *Life of John Kitto, DD, FSA* (Edinburgh, Oliphant, Anderson & Ferrier, 1886)

Edwards, David L, *Christian England*, vol. 3, *From the 18ᵗʰ Century to the First World War* (Glasgow, Collins, 1984)

Elliot-Binns, L E, *Religion in the Victorian Era* (London, Lutterworth, 1936)

Ex-Member of the Society of Friends, An, *Open Communion with Liberty of Ministry, the Only Practicable Ground for Real Union amongst Christians*, 4ᵗʰ edn. (London, Central Tract Depot, 1840)

Fiedler, Klaus, *The Story of Faith Missions* (Oxford, Regnum, 1994)

Fielder, Geraint, *Lord of the Years* (Leicester, Inter-Varsity Press, 1988)

Firth, Cyril Bruce, *An Introduction to Indian Church History*, revised edn. (Delhi, ISPCK, 1976)

Forrest J W, "The Missionary Reporter", *Journal of the Christian Brethren Research Fellowship*, no. 21 (1971), 24-42

Franke A H, *Faith's Work Perfected, or Franke's Orphan House at Halle* (ed. Wm L Gage, Anson D F Randolph, New York, 1867; Univ. Michigan, Historical Reprint)

Gairdner, W H T, *The Reproach of Islam* (London, Student Volunteer Missionary Union, 1909)

George, Timothy, *Faithful Witness: The Life and Mission of William Carey* (Leicester, Inter-Varsity Press, 1991)

Green, Michael, *Evangelism in the Early Church* (London, Hodder & Stoughton, 1970, 1978)

Groves, Anthony Norris, *Christian Devotedness* (Piccadilly, J Hatchard & Son, 1825); 2ⁿᵈ edn. (London, James Nisbet, 1829); reprint, N Ireland, Raven Publishing Company, n.d.; reprint, Kansas, Walterick, n.d.; Midwest Christian Publishers, n.d.; <http://www.gutenberg.org/ebooks/24293>

——————, "Correspondence from the East", *The Christian Witness*, vol. 1 (April 1834), 196-201

——————, *Journal of a Residence at Bagdad during the years 1830 and 1831, by Mr Anthony N Groves, Missionary*, ed. A J Scott (London, James Nisbet, 1832)

——————, *Journal of Mr Anthony N Groves, Missionary, during a Journey from London to Bagdad through Russia, Georgia and Persia. Also a Journal of Some Months' Residence in Bagdad* [ed. A J Scott?] (London, James Nisbet, 1831)

——————, *Last Will And Testament of Mr Anthony Norris Groves*, with two codicils, London, 8ᵗʰ Feb. 1854 (held in The National Archives, Kew, ref. PROB 11/2186/104), <http://discovery.nationalarchives.gov.uk/details/r/D31022>)

——————, "A Letter on Missions to the Heathen", *The Christian Witness*, vol. 7 (April 1840), 127-141

——————, *On the Liberty of Ministry in the Church of Christ* (Neyoor/Madras, 1834; Sidmouth, J Harvey, 1835)

——————, *On the Nature of Christian Influence* (Bombay, American Mission Press, 1833)

——————, *Remarks on a Pamphlet Entitled "The Perpetuity of the Moral Law"* (Madras, J B Pharaoh, 1840)

——————, "Remarks on the Typical Import of the Kingly History of Israel", *The Christian Witness*, vol. 4 (April 1837), 123-136

——————, *The New Testament in the Blood of Jesus, the Sole Rule of Morals and Discipline to the Christian Church* (Madras, J B Pharaoh, 1837)

——————, *The Present State of the Tinnevelly Mission, Second Edition enlarged with an Historical Preface and Reply to Mr Strachan's Criticism; and Mr Rhenius's Letter to the Church Missionary Society* (London, James Nisbet, 1836)

——————, *The Tottenham Case* (Brighton, printed for private circulation, 1849)

Groves, Edward K, "An Apology for the Life of Professor F W Newman" (*The Faith*, Feb. 1905, Mar. 1905)

——————, *Conversations on "Bethesda" Family Matters* (London, W B Horner, 1885)

——————, *George Müller and his Successors* (Bristol, privately printed, 1906)

[Groves, Harriet], *Memoir of the Late Anthony Norris Groves, containing extracts from his Letters and Journals, compiled by his Widow* (1st edn., London, James Nisbet, 1856; reprint, ed. Kulp, Sumneytown, PA, Sentinel Publications, 2002) (3rd edn. with supplement, London, James Nisbet, 1869)

Groves, Henry, *The Battlefield of Faith: A Warning for the Times* (London, H A Raymond, n.d.)

——————, *Darbyism: Its Rise and Development*, 3rd edn. (London, J E Hawkins, c.1880)

——————, *Echoes: A Memorial of the Late Henry Groves, consisting of Brief Expositions from "Echoes of Service"* (Bath, Echoes of Service, 1891)

——————, *Faithful Hanie, or Disinterested Service* (London, J Nisbet, 1866)

——————, *Living by Faith* (London, J F Shaw, n.d.)

——————, *Not of the World: Memoir of Lord Congleton* (London, J F Shaw, 1884)

Grubb, Norman P, *C T Studd, Cricketer and Pioneer* (London, 1933); paperback edn. (Fort Washington, CLC, 1972)

——————, *The Four Pillars of WEC* (London, Worldwide Evangelisation Crusade, 1963)

——————, *Once Caught No Escape* (London, Lutterworth, 1969)

Gundert, Hermann, *Tagebuch aus Malabar 1837-1859, herausgegeben von Albrecht Frenz* (Stuttgart, Kommissionsverlag J F Steinkopf Verlag, 1983)

Harris A N, "The Plymouth Brethren: Reminiscences Of Over Fifty Years Ago, By A. N. Harris F.R.A.S., November 1911" (*Brethren Historical Review* 5:88-101)

Harris, Paul William, *Nothing but Christ: Rufus Anderson and the Ideology of Protestant Foreign Missions* (New York, Oxford University Press, 1999)

Harrison, J F C, *Early Victorian Britain 1832-51* (Weidenfeld & Nicolson, 1971); (Glasgow, Fontana, 1979)

Haslam, W, *From Death into Life* (London, Morgan & Scott, c.1880); reissued (St Austell, Good News Crusade, 1976)

Hay, Alex Rattray, *The New Testament Order for Church and Missionary* (Temperley, Argentina, New Testament Missionary Union, 1947); 4th edn. reprint (NTMU, n.d., distributed by Searching Together, 366 Bench St. Box 377, Taylors Falls, MN 55084, USA)

Horne, C Silvester, *David Livingstone* (London, Macmillan, 1912)

Houghton, Frank, *Amy Carmichael of Dohnavur* (Fort Washington, Christian Literature Crusade, 1953, 1979)

Hutton, J E, *A History of Moravian Missions* (Moravian Publication Office, London, 1922)

Hyland, K G, "Roland Allen: The Man who Understood New Testament Missionary Principles", *Journal of the Christian Brethren Research Fellowship*, no. 13, Christian Missions Today (Oct. 1966), 28-34

Hylson-Smith, Kenneth, *Evangelicals in the Church of England 1734-1984* (Edinburgh, T & T Clark, 1989)

Jones, E Stanley, *The Christ of the Indian Road* (London, Hodder & Stoughton, 1925)

Kerr-Jarrett, Andrew, *Life in the Victorian Age* (London, Reader's Digest, 1993, 1994)

Kinnear, Angus I, *Against the Tide: The Story of Watchman Nee* (Fort Washington, Christian Literature Crusade, 1973)

Kirk, J Andrew, *What is Mission? Theological Explorations* (London, Dartman, Longman & Todd, 1999)

Kitto, John, *A Cyclopaedia of Biblical Literature*, 2 vols. (Edinburgh, Black, 1845)

——————, *Daily Bible Illustrations,* 8 vols. (Edinburgh, Oliphant, 1854, 1881)

——————, *Scripture Lands* (c.1850); (London, Bell & Daldy, 1866)

Knoepflmacher, U C, Introduction to Newman, F W: *Phases of Faith*, 6th edn. (Leicester University Press, 1970)

Koshy, T E, *Brother Bakht Singh: A Saint of God*, <http://www.BrotherBakhtSingh.org>

Lang, George H, *Anthony Norris Groves, Saint and Pioneer* (1939); 2nd edn. (London, Paternoster, 1949); reprint (Haysville, NC, Schoettle Publishing, 2001)

——————, *The History and Diaries of an Indian Christian, J C Aroolappen* (London, Thynne & Co. Ltd, 1939); reprint (Haysville, NC, Schoettle Publishing, 2001)

Latourette, Kenneth Scott, *Christianity in a Revolutionary Age*, vol. 3, *The Nineteenth Century Outside Europe* (New York, Harper & Row, 1970)

——————, *A History of the Expansion of Christianity*, vol. 6, *Northern Africa and Asia 1800-1914*, (New York, Harper & Brothers, 1944); reissued (New York, Harper & Row / Exeter, Paternoster, 1971)

Lewis, Donald M (ed.), *The Blackwell Dictionary of Evangelical Biography 1730-1860*, 2 vols. (Oxford, Blackwell, 1995)

Lutz, Jessie G & Lutz, R Ray, "Karl Gützlaff's Approach to Indigenization: The Chinese Union," in Bays, Daniel H (ed.), *Christianity in China, From the Eighteenth Century to the Present* (Stanford, CA, Stanford University Press, 1996), 269-291

Lyell, Leslie, *Three of China's Mighty Men* (London, OMF, 1973); new edn. (Tain, Ross, Christian Focus, 2000)

MacDonald, William, *True Discipleship* (STL, 1963; OM/Walterick, 1975; reprint, Gospel Literature Service, Bombay)

Mandryk J, *Operation World* (7th edn., Carlisle, Paternoster, 2010)

Marsden, Gordon (ed.), *Victorian Values: Personalities and Perspectives in Nineteenth Century Society* (London, Longman, 1990)

Marshman, John Clark, *The Life and Times of Carey, Marshman and Ward, Embracing the History of the Serampore Mission*, 2 vols. (London, Longman, Brown, Green, Longmans and Roberts, 1859)

Martin, Roger H, *Evangelicals United: Ecumenical Stirrings in Pre-Victorian Britain, 1795-1830* (Metuchen, NJ and London, Scarecrow Press, 1983)

McCallum, Dennis H, *Watchman Nee and the House Church Movement in China* (1986), <http://www.xenos.org/essays/neeframe.htm>

McGavran, Donald A, *Understanding Church Growth* (Grand Rapids, Eerdmans, 1980)

Miller, Jon, *The Social Control of Religious Zeal: A Study of Organizational Contradictions* (New Brunswick, Rutgers University Press, 1994)

Minister of the Established Church, A, *The Perpetuity of the Moral Law; being a Reply to Mr Groves's Book Entitled, The New Testament in the Blood of Jesus, the Sole Rule of Morals and Discipline to the Christian Church* (Madras, J B Pharaoh, 1838)

Mitchell, J M, *Memoir of the Rev. Robert Nesbit* (London, Nisbet, 1858)

Müller, George, *A Narrative of Some of the Lord's Dealings with George Müller* (1837); 9th edn, 4 vols. (London, J Nisbet & Co, 1895);
<http://www.gutenberg.org/ebooks/search/?query=narrative+george+muller+>
Autobiography of George Müller (ed. Bergin, G Fred, 3rd edn., London, 1914)

Murray, Stuart & Wilkinson-Hayes, Anne, *Hope from the Margins: New Ways of Being Church* (Cambridge, Grove Books, 2000)

Neatby, William Blair, *A History of the Plymouth Brethren*, 2nd edn. (London, Hodder & Stoughton, 1902); reprint (Stoke-on-Trent, Tentmaker Publications, 2001);
<https://archive.org/details/ahistoryoftheply00neatuoft>

Nee, Watchman, *Concerning Our Missions* (1939); reissued as *The Normal Christian Church Life* (Anaheim, CA, Living Stream Ministry, 1980)

———, *The Orthodoxy of the Church* (1945); reissued (Anaheim, CA, Living Stream Ministry, 1994)

Neill, Stephen, *A History of Christian Missions* (Harmondsworth, Penguin, 1964)

———, *A History of Christianity in India, 1707-1858* (Cambridge, Cambridge University Press, 1985)

———, *The Story of the Christian Church in India and Pakistan* (Grand Rapids, Eerdmans, 1970)

Newell, J P, *A J Scott and his Circle* (Edinburgh University, PhD thesis, 1981)

Newman, Francis William, *Personal Narrative in Letters, principally from Turkey in the Years 1830-3* (London, 1856)

———, *Phases of Faith* (1850); 6th edn. reprint with introduction by U C Knoepflmacher (Leicester University Press, 1970)

Newton, Ken J, "Anthony Norris Groves (1795-1853): A Neglected Missiologist", *Journal of the Christian Brethren Research Fellowship* (Brisbane, Australia), no. 60 (1985)

———, *Brethren Missionary Work in Mysore State* (Scripture Literature Press, Malvalli, 1971; Christian Brethren Research Fellowship Occasional Paper no. 6, Pinner, 1975)

———, "Christian Brethren, World Mission and an Australian Contribution", *Brethren Archivists and Historians Network Review*, vol. 1, no. 1 (Autumn 1997), 3-9

Newton, Ken & Chan, Andrew eds., *The Brethren Movement Worldwide: Key Information*, 3rd Edition, Opal Trust, 2011

Oliphant, M O W, *The Life of Edward Irving*, 2nd edn., 2 vols. (London, Hurst & Blackett, 1862)

Orr, J Edwin, *The Second Evangelical Awakening in Britain* (London & Edinburgh, Marshall Morgan & Scott, 1949)

Padwick, Constance E, *Henry Martyn, Confessor of the Faith* (London, Inter-Varsity Press, 1922, 1953)

——————, *Temple Gairdner of Cairo* (London, Society for Promoting Christian Knowledge, 1930)

Pfander, C G, Letter dated 20 Oct. 1829 in *Gazette des Missions Evangéliques*, 19, 1 Feb. 1830 (Basel, Basel Mission).

Philip, Johnson C, *The Brethren Movement in India*, <www.biblebeliever.co.za/.../Brethren%20Movement%20in%20Indiar.htm>

Pickering, Henry, *Chief Men among the Brethren* (London, 1918); reissued (Neptune, NJ, Loizeaux Bros, 1961)

Pierson, A T, *George Müller of Bristol* (London, Pickering & Inglis, 1899, 1972)

Powell, Avril Ann, *Muslims and Missionaries in Pre-Mutiny India* (Richmond, Curzon Press, 1993)

Prickett, Stephen (ed.), *The Context of English Literature: The Romantics* (London, Methuen, 1981)

Railton, Nicholas M, *Transnational Evangelicalism: The Case of Friedrich Bialloblotzky* (1799-1869), (Göttingen, Vandenhoek & Ruprecht, 2002)

Rajamani, R R (with Kinnear, Angus I), *Monsoon Daybreak* (London & Eastbourne, Open Books, Associated Christian Publishers, 1971)

Ramabai, Pandita, *A Testimony of Our Inexhaustible Treasure* (1907); 10th edn. (Kedgaon, Mukti Mission, 1977)

Randall, Ian & Hilborn, David, *One Body in Christ: The History and Significance of the Evangelical Alliance* (Carlisle, Paternoster, 2001)

Rhenius, Josiah, *Memoir of the Rev C T E Rhenius, Comprising Extracts from His Journal and Correspondence, with details of Missionary Proceedings in South India* (London, Nisbet, 1841)

Richter, Julius, *A History of Protestant Missions in the Near East* (Edinburgh, Oliphant, Anderson & Ferrier, 1910)

Robbins, Keith (ed.), *Protestant Evangelicalism: Britain, Ireland, Germany and America, c.1750 - c.1950* (Oxford, Basil Blackwell, 1990)

Robbins, William, *The Newman Brothers* (London, Heinemann, 1966)

Rosslyn W & Tosi A, eds, *Women in Russian Culture and Society, 1700-1825* (Palgrave Macmillan, 2007)

Rowdon, Harold H, "The Brethren Contribution to World Mission", in Rowdon (ed.), *The Brethren Contribution to the Worldwide Mission of the Church* (Carlisle, Paternoster, 1994), 37-46

——————, (ed.) *International Partnership Perspectives* nos. 3, 4 (Carlisle, Paternoster, 2001, 2002)

——————, *The Origins of the Brethren 1825-1850* (London, Pickering & Inglis, 1967)

Ryland, J E, *Memoirs of John Kitto DD, FSA* (Edinburgh, Oliphant, 1856)

Ryle J C, *Expository Thoughts on the Gospels: Luke* (Cambridge & London, James Clark & Co, 1858, 1969)

Schaff, Philip, *History of the Christian Church*, vol. 3 (Grand Rapids, Eerdmans, 1910, 1989)

Shenk, Wilbert R, *Henry Venn: Missionary Statesman* (New York, Orbis, 1983)

Schirrmacher, Christine, *The Influence of German Biblical Criticism on Muslim Apologetics in the 19th Century,* <https://www.contra-mundum.org/schirrmacher/rationalism.html>

Short, A Rendle, *Why Believe?* London, IVP, 6th edn. 1955

Sieveking, I Giberne, *Memoir and Letters of Francis W Newman* (London, Kegan Paul, Trench, Trübner & Co. Ltd, 1909)

Simson, Wolfgang, *Houses that Change the World* (Carlisle, OM/Paternoster, 1998)

Smiles, Samuel, *Self-Help, with Illustrations of Character and Conduct* (London, Ward, Lock & Co. Ltd, 1859)

Smith, Daniel, *Bakht Singh of India, a Prophet of God* (Washington, International Students Press, 1959)

Smith, George, *The Life of Alexander Duff,* 2 vols. (London, Hodder & Stoughton, 1879)

———, *The Life of William Carey, Shoemaker and Missionary* (London, Murray, 1885); <http://www.biblebelievers.com/carey>

Stanes, Robin, *Stanes History 1771-1964, City of London and South India* (UK, privately printed, 2001)

Stanley, Brian, *The Bible and the Flag: Protestant Missions and British Imperialism in the Nineteenth and Twentieth Centuries* (Leicester, Apollos IVP, 1990)

Steele, Francis R, *Not in Vain: The Story of North Africa Mission* (Pasadena, William Carey Library, 1981)

Steer, Roger, *George Müller, Delighted in God* (Wheaton, Harold Shaw / Sevenoaks, Hodder, 1981)

Stern, Henry A, *Dawnings of Light in the East; with Biblical, Historical and Statistical Notices of Persons and Places Visited During a Mission to the Jews in Persia, Coordistan and Mesopotamia* (London, Charles H Purday, 1854)

Stock, Eugene, *The History of the Church Missionary Society,* 3 vols. (London, Church Missionary Society, 1899)

Strachan, J M, *Mr Groves' Brief Account of the Tinnevelly Mission Examined, in a Letter to a Provincial Member of the Church Missionary Society* (London, Hatchard & Son, 1835)

Stunt, Timothy C F, *A N Groves in a European Context: A re-assessment of his early development* (forthcoming)

———, *Early Brethren and the Society of Friends* (Pinner, Christian Brethren Research Fellowship, Occasional Paper no. 3, 1970)

———, *From Awakening to Secession: Radical Evangelicals in Switzerland and Britain 1815-35* (Edinburgh, T & T Clark, 2000)

———, "James Van Sommer, an Undenominational Christian and Man of Prayer", *Journal of the Christian Brethren Research Fellowship,* no. 16 (Aug. 1967), 2-8

Stunt, W T, *Family Adventure* (Bath, Echoes of Service, n.d.)

———, "James Van Sommer, Missionary Enthusiast", *Echoes Quarterly Review,* vol. 9, no. 4 (Oct.-Dec. 1957), 18-23

———, *Turning the World Upside Down: A Century of Missionary Endeavour,* 2nd edn. (Bath, Echoes of Service, 1973)

Tatford, Frederick A, *A N Groves, the Father of Faith Missions* (Bath, Echoes of Service, 1979)

——————, *That the World May Know*, 10 vols. (Bath, Echoes of Service, 1982-6)

Tayler, W Elfe, *Passages from the Diary and Letters of Henry Craik of Bristol* (J F Shaw & Co, 1866)

Taylor, Dr & Mrs Howard, *Hudson Taylor and the China Inland Mission, the Growth of a Work of God* (London, Morgan & Scott, 1918)

——————, *Hudson Taylor in Early Years, the Growth of a Soul* (London, Morgan & Scott, 1911)

Tennent, Timothy C, "William Carey as a Missiologist: An Assessment", *American Baptist Evangelicals Journal*, vol. 7, no. 1 (Mar. 1999), 3-10

Tett, Mollie E, *The Road to Freedom: Sudan United Mission 1904-1968* (Sidcup, Sudan United Mission, 1968)

Thompson, Flora, *Lark Rise to Candleford* (Harmondsworth, Penguin, 1973)

Tippet, Alan, *Introduction to Missiology* (Pasadena, William Carey Library, 1987)

Tuck, Patrick J N, *Britain and the China Trade 1635-1842* (London, Routledge, 2004)

Tucker, Ruth A, *From Jerusalem to Irian Jaya: A Biographical History of Christian Missions* (Grand Rapids, Zondervan, 1983)

Turner, W G, *John Nelson Darby* (London, 1944)

Van Sommer, James (ed.), *The Missionary Reporter*, vol. 1 (July 1853 to Dec. 1854); vol. 2 (Jan. 1855 to Sep. 1856); nos. 40-54 (Oct. 1856 to Jan. 1858)

Vander Werff, Lyle L, *Christian Missions to Muslims, the Record: Anglican and Reformed Approaches in India and the Near East, 1800-1938* (Pasadena, William Carey Library, 1977)

Vine, W E, *The Divine Plan of Missions* (London, Pickering & Inglis, c.1940)

Walker, Thomas, *Missionary Ideals* (London, CMS, 1911); 2nd edn. (London, IVP, 1969)

Walls, Andrew F, *The Missionary Movement in Christian History: Studies in the Transmission of Faith* (New York, Orbis / Edinburgh, T & T Clark, 1996)

Walsh, J D, "Origins of the Evangelical Revival", in Bennett G V and Walsh J D (eds.), *Essays in Modern English Church History* (London, A & C Black, 1966)

Warren, Max, *To Apply the Gospel: Selections from the Writings of Henry Venn* (Grand Rapids, Eerdmans, 1971)

Watts, Michael R, *The Dissenters Vol. 2: The Expansion of Evangelical Nonconformity* (Clarendon, 1995)

[Weitbrecht, M], *A Memoir of the Rev John James Weitbrecht, by his widow* (London, Nisbet, 1854)

Willey, Basil, *More Nineteenth Century Studies: A Group of Honest Doubters* (London, 1956)

Winter, Ralph, *Perspectives on the World Christian Movement*, 3rd edn. (Pasadena, William Carey Library, 1999)

Wolff, Joseph, *Travels and Adventures of the Rev. Joseph Wolff*, 2nd edn, 2 vols, (London, Saunders, Otley & Co, 1860, 1861)

Wood, Christopher, *Victorian Panorama: Paintings of Victorian Life* (London, Faber & Faber, 1976)

Wright, Denis, *The English among the Persians* (I B Taurus, 2001)

Yohannan, K P, *Revolution in World Missions* (Carrollton, USA, Gospel For Asia, 1986, 1998)

Young, Florence S H, *Pearls from the Pacific* (London, Marshall Brothers Ltd, 1925)

Zwemer, Samuel, "Karl Gottlieb Pfander", *The Moslem World*, vol. 21, no. 3 (July 1941), 217-226

——————, *Raymund Lull: First Missionary to the Moslems* (New York, Funk and Wagnalls, 1902)

Zwick, Henry Augustus, *Calmuc Tartary, or a Journey from Sarepta to Several Calmuc Hordes... from May 26 to August 21, 1823... on behalf of the Russian Bible Society* (Holdsworth & Ball, London, 1831)

(Note: websites accessed December 2017 and correct at that date.)

****

Unpublished sources mentioned in this book are located as follows:

Alnwick: Northumberland Archives, Alnwick Castle, Alnwick
Drummond Papers
    Two undated letters, A N Groves to H Drummond [?Apr. 1829].

Basel: Basel Mission Archives, Missionstrasse 21, 4003 Basel
General Correspondence
    Letter, A N Groves to R Pearson, 14 Oct. 1829.
    Letter, C G Pfander to C G Blumhardt, 1 Nov. 1829.
Gundert papers
    Letter, D Coates to G C Blumhardt, 17 Feb. 1835.
    Letter, A N Groves to C F Spittler, 7 Apr. 1835.
    Letter, A N Groves to W Büchelen, 30 Nov. 1835.
    Letter, A N Groves to C F Spittler, [received] 24 Dec. 1835.
Letter, A N Groves to W Büchelen, 22 Mar. 1836.

Birmingham: University Library, Edgbaston, Birmingham
Church Mission Society Archives (Formerly in CMS House, London)
    Minutes of the Corresponding Committee of the CMS, London, 9 Aug. 1825.
    Letter, A N Groves to E H Bickersteth, 15 Sep 1825.
    Letter, A N Groves to E H Bickersteth, 14 Mar. [1826].
    Minutes of the Corresponding Committee of the CMS, London, 20 Feb. 1827.

Cambridge: University Library, Cambridge
British and Foreign Bible Society Archives (formerly in Bible House, London)
    Letter, A N Groves to Rev. Dr [Robert] Pinkerton, 23 May 1829.

London: Lambeth Palace Library, Lambeth Palace Road, London SE1 7JU
Golightly Papers
    Letter, F W Newman to C P Golightly, 25 Oct 1827.

Index

a second volume in the author's Groves trilogy:

The Primitivist Ecclesiology of Anthony Norris Groves
CHURCH AS IT WAS MEANT TO BE

The decade in which Anthony Norris Groves offered a new approach to church and mission coincided, between 1825-35, with a turning-point in the religious history of the Western world. The eighteenth-century belief in order, design and gradual development was yielding to the free, dynamic, iconoclastic spirit of the nineteenth century.

While Norris Groves had many friends in the Anglican and Nonconformist denominations of his day, he was troubled by the evident contrast between the churches he knew and those of New Testament times. He resolved to search the scriptures with one purpose in mind – to find out exactly what Jesus and his apostles taught and did, and then, if possible, to do the same.

His first tract *Christian Devotedness*, written in 1825, proposed literal obedience to the teaching of Christ concerning faith, possessions and world mission. This was followed in 1828 by his suggestion that the Lord's Supper might be freely shared in the homes of believers without the sacramental blessing of an ordained minister. He argued that if ministry were no longer restricted to one man in each church, the gifts of every believer would be released for the benefit of all. In 1829 he and his wife set out as missionaries to the Muslim world. They went "by faith" with no authorisation or support from any recognised church or missionary society.

All this came at a time when the "romantic" and the "primitive" were newly fashionable. While some of his contemporaries were shocked, others agreed with him, and some of his early circle in Ireland and Devonshire became leading figures in the Brethren movement (sometimes known as Plymouth Brethren).

Moving to India, Norris Groves continued to write controversial tracts and to correspond with friends and former colleagues such as John Parnell, Henry Craik, Robert Chapman, John and Robert Howard, and especially his brother-in-law George Müller. His correspondence with J N Darby addressed issues that would eventually divide the Brethren into "open" and "exclusive" streams.

Norris Groves's primitivist ecclesiology became characteristic of the open Brethren, and through Brethren influence in university Christian unions and "faith missions", entered the mainstream of British evangelical life. For a century and a half, "the early church" was offered as a model for the emulation of evangelical congregations. Anthony Norris Groves played a key role in formulating and popularising these elements of evangelical primitivism.

> *"Dann's examination of Groves as a radical is thorough and will establish itself*
> *as the standard treatment for those interested in either Brethren or primitivist*
> *ecclesiology, nineteenth-century Anglican seceders and restorationism."*
>
> **Neil Dickson**, *Ecclesiology* 8 (2012) 241–281

Tamarisk Publications, distributed by John Ritchie Ltd (UK), Lewis and Roth (USA).

a third volume in the author's Groves trilogy:

The Primitivist Missiology of Anthony Norris Groves
MISSION AS IT WAS MEANT TO BE

In every age missionaries are pulled in three directions. They are influenced by the Christian customs of their homeland, by the need to adapt to foreign cultures, and by the example of Jesus and his apostles.

Anthony Norris Groves challenged the consensus of his day by attaching little importance to the customs of his homeland, or indeed to other cultures of the world. It was the example of Jesus and his apostles that inspired and motivated him. He took the New Testament as a practical manual for church and mission, applicable to every age and culture.

As the Gospel reaches new places, the men and women who respond to it will learn from the scriptures what to do next. With this approach, Norris Groves expected fellowships to start and grow spontaneously. They would not resemble anything in his homeland or in the local culture of the people – they would be like those described in the New Testament.

This stands in sharp contrast to the attempts at indigenisation advocated twenty years later by Henry Venn and Rufus Anderson. Rather than projecting an eventual shift from foreign government, support and propagation to self-government, support and propagation, Groves would start with no government, support or propagation at all, expecting these to develop naturally as local believers help one another cultivate their own spiritual abilities and ministries. These ideas were revived eighty years later by Roland Allen.

The missionary career of Norris Groves himself illustrates the varied consequences of his strategy. In 1829 he and his wife launched the first evangelical mission to Muslims in the Arab world. He spent the remainder of his life in India.

To him we can trace back ideas that inspired a new generation of missions following what have been called "faith principles". These include worldwide pioneering initiatives by Brethren (sometimes called Plymouth Brethren), in addition to many interdenominational "faith missions" following the example of Hudson Taylor, whose earliest supporters were friends of Norris Groves.

But his ideas were taken up with greatest effect by the leaders of some remarkable indigenous movements, notably his own Indian disciple John Christian Arulappan, and at a later date Bakht Singh and Watchman Nee.

> "*a work of impressive scholarship, founded on wide reading in both primary and secondary sources... Dann's case is more subversive of missiological orthodoxy than he admits, but it deserves careful evaluation.*"
>
> **Brian Stanley**, *International Bulletin of Missionary Research*, July 2008

Tamarisk Publications, distributed by John Ritchie Ltd (UK), Lewis and Roth (USA).

by the same author, writing as Robin Daniel

Mission Strategies Then and Now
an introduction to biblical missiology

Many of our missionary methods and institutions were inherited from the days of the British Empire, when foreigners were welcomed for the technology and commerce that came with them. But Jesus and his apostles faced a more difficult task in a Roman world more like that of today, where ordinary people travelled widely, entered new cultures and learned new languages while facing many uncertainties and dangers. What cross-cultural strategies can we see in the New Testament itself? And might they help us to be more effective in the modern world?

"brings together sound biblical scholarship and refreshing insights into global mission... the cross cultural sensitivity is outstanding."

Jacob Thomas,
Tutor in Missions and Ethics,
Belfast Bible College

Biblical Missiology
a university course in cross-cultural mission

All the resources you need to embark on a study of Christian mission, or to teach this subject in a field conference, training school or theological institution.

Covering the biblical basis of mission, the methods of Jesus and Paul, the essence of the gospel, biblical perspectives on culture, the process of conversion, the lessons of history, cross-cultural communication, current issues and controversies, rapid mass movements, opening new fields, surviving culture shock, caring for missionaries, and much more.

Comprising teachers' book and students' notes, with questions for discussion, exam papers and research topics, accompanied by a CD-Rom containing all the required and recommended reading.

Tamarisk Publications, distributed by John Ritchie Ltd (UK), Lewis and Roth (USA).